The Resurrection of Ireland

The Sinn Féin Party, 1916–1923

Between 1916 and 1923 Ireland experienced a political as well as a military revolution. This book examines how, after the Easter rising of 1916, radical revolutionaries formed a precarious coalition with (relatively) moderate politicians, and analyses the political organization of Irish republicanism during a crucial period.

The new Sinn Féin party routed its enemies, co-operated uneasily with the underground Irish government which it had helped to create, and achieved most of its objectives before disintegrating in 1922. Its rapid collapse should not distract from its achievements – in particular its role in 'democratizing' the Irish revolution. Its successors have dominated the political life of independent Ireland. The book studies in some detail the party's membership and ideology, and also its often tense relationship with the Irish Republican Army. A final chapter examines the fluctuating careers of the later Sinn Féin parties throughout the rest of the twentieth century.

MICHAEL LAFFAN is Lecturer in Modern Irish History, University College, Dublin. His previous publications include *The Partition of Ireland, 1911–1925* (1983).

THE RESURRECTION OF IRELAND

The Sinn Féin Party, 1916–1923

MICHAEL LAFFAN

CAMBRIDGE
UNIVERSITY PRESS

PUBLISHED BY THE PRESS SYNDICATE OF THE UNIVERSITY OF CAMBRIDGE
The Pitt Building, Trumpington Street, Cambridge, United Kingdom

CAMBRIDGE UNIVERSITY PRESS
The Edinburgh Building, Cambridge CB2 2RU, UK   http://www.cup.cam.ac.uk
40 West 20th Street, New York, NY 10011–4211, USA   http://www.cup.org
10 Stamford Road, Oakleigh, Melbourne 3166, Australia
Ruiz de Alarcón 13, 28014 Madrid, Spain

First published 1999
Reprinted 2000

Printed in the United Kingdom at the University Press, Cambridge

Typeset in 10/13 Adobe Minion in QuarkXPress™ [SE]

A catalogue record for this book is available from the British Library

Library of Congress Cataloguing in Publication data
Laffan, Michael.
The resurrection of Ireland: the Sinn Féin Party, 1916–1923 /
Michael Laffan.
p. cm.
Includes bibliographical references and index.
ISBN 0 521 65073 9 (hb)
1. Sinn Féin.   2. Political parties – Ireland – History – 20th
century.   3. Revolutionaries – Ireland.   4. Irish Republican Army.
5. Nationalism – Ireland – History.   6. Ireland – Politics and
government – 20th century.
JN1571.5.S56L34   1999
324.2415′083′09–dc21   99-11331 CIP

ISBN 0 521 65073 9 hardback

To my nephews,
ROBERT, JACK AND BILL

Contents

List of illustrations	*page*	viii
List of figures and tables		x
Preface		xi
Note on the text		xiv
List of abbreviations		xv

PROLOGUE: BEFORE THE EASTER RISING

1.	Irish nationalists: politicians and rebels	3

THE IRISH REVOLUTION, 1916–1923

2.	Rebellion and hibernation, 1916	43
3.	Organizers and converts, 1917	77
4.	Reverses and victory, 1918	122
5.	The party: structures and members	169
6.	Policy: beliefs and attitudes	214
7.	War and repression, 1919–1921	266
8.	Ministers and bureaucrats, 1919–1921	304
9.	The treaty and the split, 1921–1922	346
10.	The Pact election and the Civil War, 1922–1923	386

EPILOGUE: AFTER THE CIVIL WAR

11.	Irish republicans: fundamentalists and compromisers	433

Select bibliography		466
Index		491

ILLUSTRATIONS

1.1 Sinn Féin propaganda. 'Sinn Féin – a modern Samson'. Poster, National Museum of Ireland   22

1.2 Sinn Féin propaganda. 'Vote for Dolan & Sinn Féin'. Leaflet, National Library of Ireland   28

2.1 Retrospective popularity, the Rising, as seen in 1924. 'Don't worry about accommodation'. *Dublin Opinion*, August 1924   45

3.1 An image of N. Roscommon. 'The old men were carried upon the backs of the young'. *Catholic Bulletin*, March 1917   82

3.2 Stepping-stones. 'Ireland, freedom/subserviency'. Leaflet, National Library of Ireland   114

4.1 Sinn Féin propaganda. 'Separation women'. 'The Irish Party's props in Longford'. Leaflet, National Library of Ireland   127

4.2 Anti-recruitment propaganda. 'Join an Irish regiment to-day'. Poster, National Museum of Ireland   131

4.3 Anti-conscription postcard. 'First Irish conscript'. Postcard, National Library of Ireland   143

4.4 Griffith and Dillon. 'The East Cavan handicap'. *Irish Fun*, July 1918   148

6.1 The new broom. 'Some work before us'. *The Leader*, 7 January 1922   219

6.2 An Irish view of Britain. 'The conscripts' chorus'. Leaflet, National Library of Ireland   225

7.1 'Peace offering to Ireland'. *The Star*, reprinted in the *Irish Independent*, 16 December 1920   293

9.1a Rival images of the Treaty. 'St Michael driving bad angel out of
      Paradise', *Dublin Opinion*, April 1922

9.1b 'The butchery of Ireland', *Dublin Opinion*, April 1922   352

9.2   Republican propaganda. 'The free will of the people', *Irish Fun*,
      May 1922   364

9.3   A British view of Collins's dilemma. 'The evil genie', *Punch*,
      12 April 1922   377

10.1 'Count Plunkett insures his beard', *Dublin Opinion*, July 1922   393

10.2a The pact: an Irish view. 'The coming elections', *The Leader*, 3 June
      1922   396

10.2b The pact: a British view. 'A son of Liberty', *Punch*, 21 May 1922 397

10.3 Cartoon images of de Valera, Griffith, Collins, Figgis and
      Cosgrave. *Irish Fun*, May 1922   405

10.4 Free state propaganda. 'This is where he was in 1921'. Leaflet,
      National Library of Ireland   415

11.1 'Midnight assassins raid on Mrs Eamon de Valera'. Watercolour by
      Countess Markievicz. National Library of Ireland   435

11.2 Cumann na nGaedheal propaganda. 'The hen that took 5 years to
      lay an egg'. Poster, National Library of Ireland   445

FIGURES AND TABLES

Figures

4.1   The 1918 election   *page* 167

5.1   Party structure, December 1917   171

5.2   Ratio of inhabitants to each Sinn Féin club, December 1917   186

10.1 The 1922 election   402

Tables

5.1   Ratio of inhabitants per county to each Sinn Féin club,
      December 1917   187

5.2   Emigration figures for the years spanning the First World War   189

10.1 Percentages of votes in contested seats, 1922, by constituency   401

PREFACE

It was as a research student in University College, Dublin that I first became fascinated by the history of the Sinn Féin party. Desmond Williams supervised my MA dissertation, portions of which were to be cannibalised and absorbed into chapters 3 and 5 of this book. He was kindly, supportive, insightful, stimulating and frequently absent. From time to time during his legendary disappearances his place was taken by his learned and terrifying colleague, Robin Dudley Edwards. Dudley scrutinized all that I wrote with great care, fretted about my work and even dreamt about it. They were a colourful combination, and I cherish their memory.

After years abroad I returned to Dublin and to the subject of Sinn Féin. I researched intermittently on what ultimately became this book, deflected by work on two other books, by various articles, and by an infinite number of other less productive distractions. It grew; the time span to be covered doubled; new sources became available; and I developed different ways of looking at the period and its problems. The book has been many years in the making, and if its appearance is long overdue it can at least benefit from the vast literature which has appeared in the course of recent years.

It is a lengthy work, and unapologetically so. The subject of the Irish revolution has provoked numerous books, articles and dissertations, but its political aspects have remained underexplored. *The resurrection of Ireland* is an attempt to right this imbalance, to examine in some depth the complex and often difficult interaction between military and civilian manifestations of a moderate and almost 'accidental revolution'; a revolution which depended on freak circumstances for its initial impetus and which was reined in, at least in part, by an organized expression of mass civilian opinion. Political developments are also examined in their own right, independently of their links with soldiers and warfare. One of my aims has been to understand, describe and explain what it was *like* to be a supporter of Sinn Féin in the years after the Easter Rising.

The Sinn Féin party navigated the Irish democratic tradition through the squalls and storms of a military revolution. It helped ensure that, at the end of the day, the army was subordinated to civilian authority. This democratic triumph was one of Sinn Féin's greatest achievements. The party helped win over and marginalize the radicals, the 'real' (and unrepresentative) revolutionaries. It was often ignored and disparaged, but it was always present, either in the foreground or as a background influence. It could always be exploited or annexed by the more moderate or realistic of the revolutionaries. At the most basic and negative level, Sinn Féin provided an important element of continuity between the Irish Parliamentary Party, which it supplanted, and its own successor parties of Fianna Fáil and Fine Gael. Above all else this is a *story* of a party, a movement, a mood, a group of often fascinating individuals, and a complex series of relationships.

It is a pleasure to acknowledge at least some of the many debts which I incurred in writing the book. The first and most basic of all, to my mother and father, goes back long before my present preoccupation with the political aspects of the Irish revolution. They encouraged my interest in history, which began in my early childhood and which was stimulated by dedicated reading of comics with titles such as *To sweep the Spanish Main* and *In the reign of terror* – works which left me impatient to begin studying the past as one of my subjects in school. Later my parents supported my wish to pursue historical research, even though they worried about where it would lead and what would become of me.

More recently, as this book was nearing its close, friends and colleagues have read and commented on one of the later drafts. I am most grateful to Ciaran Brady, Tom Garvin, Patrick Lynch, Agnès Maillot and Cormac Ó Gráda for their generosity with their time, for the advice they offered and for the corrections which they made. In some cases, doubtless unwisely, I did not follow their suggestions, so they cannot be blamed for the errors or infelicities which remain. I am also indebted to Sheila Kane, who in copy-editing this book has displayed both a meticulous attention to detail and an exemplary patience with my failings.

Others have assisted me in different ways. As always, Ruth Dudley Edwards provided lively and generous hospitality. Many people have made helpful comments or have drawn my attention to useful sources, among them Gary Agnew, Cathal Brugha, John Coakley (who suggested the book's title), Marie Coleman, Seán Collins, Mary E. Daly, Pauric Dempsey, Tom Dunne, Colm Gallagher, Keiko Inoue, Lar Joye, Jim McGuinness, Patrick Maume, Risteárd Mulcahy, Brian S. Murphy, the late Thomas P. O'Neill, Timothy P. O'Neill, Paul Rouse, Mary Ruane, Richard Sinnott and Pauric Travers. Like all historians I have depended on the efficiency and goodwill of archivists, and I am indebted to Aideen Ireland of the National Archives, Peter Young and Victor Laing of the

Military Archives, David Sheehy of the Dublin Diocesan Archive, Fr John Gates of the Armagh Diocesan Archive, Breandán MacGiolla Choille and Fr Ignatius of the Franciscan Archive (for access to the de Valera papers when they were in Killiney), Colette O'Daly of the National Library, Philip Hannon of Fianna Fáil; and, in particular, to Seamus Helferty of the UCD Archives Department and Patricia McCarthy of the Cork Archives Institute.

I am also grateful to the many students in University College, Dublin who, over the years, have attended my lecture courses on the history of the Irish Revolution. I have been stimulated by some of the questions which they raised in tutorial discussions, and (although they might be surprised to learn of it) also by some of the arguments in essays which they wrote. None the less I needed to escape from them, and the publication of *The resurrection of Ireland* would have been delayed even further had I not been able to exploit periods of study leave. Parts of these were spent with my file cards and computer in the distraction-free environments of Rasteau (Vaucluse) and Pontaubert (Yonne).

The book is dedicated, with great affection, to my nephews – and not merely because, years ago, they demanded that it should be.

Note on the text

Contemporary custom is followed in referring occasionally to the Irish Parliamentary Party as 'the Irish Party' or even simply as 'the party'. The words 'Nationalist' and 'Unionist', beginning with capital letters, refer to the two political parties; in lower case 'nationalists' and 'unionists' refer more generally to communities, movements or traditions. Unless the context clearly indicates otherwise, 'treaty' refers to the Anglo-Irish Treaty. The term 'treatyite' is used as a synonym for a supporter of this agreement, but sparingly because it is awkward and ugly. The words 'club' and 'branch' are used interchangeably. The English rather than the Irish form of names is normally used, as was the pattern at the time covered by this book, and a few short passages have been translated into English from Irish and French.

Errors of spelling and grammar within quotations have been corrected silently, and the text has not been spattered with condescending *(sic)*s. It is impossible to be consistent in using the acute accent (or 'síne fada') when citing the name 'Sinn Féin' in direct quotations; in general the accent has been used when quoting friendly but not hostile sources. This conforms to normal usage and intention (supporters being generally anxious to spell it correctly, and opponents being less concerned about the matter), but exceptions are inevitable.

The de Valera papers (UCDA, P150) are being re-classified as this book goes to press. 'Old' notations have been removed, and the least unsatisfactory form of citation is probably to give a brief description of the document (e.g., 'de Valera to Collins'), and the date.

Abbreviations

ADA	Armagh diocesan archives
AOH	Ancient Order of Hibernians
AW	Archbishop Walsh MSS, Dublin diocesan archives
BL	Andrew Bonar Law MSS, House of Lords Record Office
Cab.	Cabinet papers, Public Record Office, London
CAI	Cork Archives Institute
CI	County inspector, Royal Irish Constabulary
CO	Colonial Office files, Public Record Office, London
CP	Count Plunkett MSS, National Library of Ireland
DE	Dáil Éireann
DE, 1919–21	*Dail Éireann. Minutes of proceedings of the first parliament of the Republic of Ireland 1919–1921*
DE, 1921–22	*Dáil Éireann. Tuairisg oifigiúil* [official report] *for periods 16th August, 1921, to 26th August, 1921, and 28th February, 1922, to 8th June, 1922*
DE, official report	Dáil debates, September 1922 –
DE, private sessions	*Dáil Éireann. private sessions of second Dáil: minutes of proceedings 18 August 1921 to 14 September 1921 and report of debates 14 December 1921 to 6 January 1922*
DE, treaty debate	*Iris Dháil Éireann: Official report. Debate on the Treaty between Great Britain and Ireland signed in London on the 6th December, 1921*

DELG   Dáil Éireann Local Government Department files, National Archives of Ireland

EdeV   Eamon de Valera MSS, University College, Dublin, Archives Department

EO'M   Ernie O'Malley MSS, University College, Dublin, Archives Department

FG   Fine Gael MSS, University College, Dublin, Archives Department, P/39/Min/1

FJ   *Freeman's Journal*

FO'D   Florence O'Donoghue MSS, National Library of Ireland

GAA   Gaelic Athletic Association

GD   George Gavan Duffy MSS, National Library of Ireland

GHQ   General headquarters

GPO   General Post Office, Dublin

Hansard   Parliamentary Debates, House of Commons, 5th series

HC:DD   *High Court of Justice, 1942: documents discovered by plaintiff and briefed to counsel on behalf of defendant Charles Stewart Wyse Power* (Dublin, 1944)

HHA   H. H. Asquith MSS, Bodleian Library, Oxford

HSS   Hanna Sheehy-Skeffington MSS, National Library of Ireland

IG   Inspector general, Royal Irish Constabulary

IHS   *Irish Historical Studies*

II   *Irish Independent*

IMA   Irish Military Archives

IO's report (M. and C./N./S.)   [British Army] Intelligence officer's report, Midland and Connaught/Northern/Southern district, Public Record Office, London, CO.904/157/1

IRA   Irish Republican Army

IRB	Irish Republican Brotherhood
IT	*Irish Times*
JD	John Dillon MSS, Trinity College Dublin Library
JR	John Redmond MSS, National Library of Ireland
JO'M	James O'Mara MSS, National Library of Ireland
LG	David Lloyd George MSS, House of Lords Record Office
MacN	Eoin MacNeill MSS, University College, Dublin, Archives Department
MacS	Mary MacSwiney MSS, University College, Dublin, Archives Department
McG	Joe McGarrity MSS, National Library of Ireland
NAI	National Archives of Ireland
NLI	National Library of Ireland
PG	Provisional government
PR	Proportional representation
PRO	Public Record Office, London
RB	Robert Barton MSS, National Library of Ireland
RIC	Royal Irish Constabulary
RM	Richard Mulcahy MSS, University College, Dublin, Archives Department
SCM	Sinn Féin standing committee minutes, National Library of Ireland, P3269
SDLP	Social Democratic and Labour Party
SFFC	Sinn Féin funds case, National Archives of Ireland
STO'K	Seán T. O'Kelly MSS, National Library of Ireland
TCDL	Trinity College, Dublin, Library
UCDA	University College, Dublin, Archives Department
UIL	United Irish League

PROLOGUE:
BEFORE THE EASTER RISING

1

IRISH NATIONALISTS: POLITICIANS AND REBELS

On 16 June 1904, as Leopold Bloom walked the streets of Dublin, he paused to browse in a bookshop at Merchant's Arch. Nearby, in a small cluttered room at the back of a house on Fownes Street, the author of a bizarre political tract was nearing the end of his labours. Between 2 January and 2 July, Arthur Griffith's *The resurrection of Hungary* made its first appearance as a series of articles in the columns of his weekly newspaper, the *United Irishman*. It was a strange manifesto.[1] By Bloomsday twenty-four of its twenty-seven instalments had already been published, but although Griffith had provided a massively detailed treatment of Austro-Hungarian relations in the mid-nineteenth century he had, so far, barely mentioned Ireland. Nonetheless *The resurrection* became for many years the bible of the Sinn Féin party which Griffith dominated for over a decade, and with which he remained closely associated for the rest of his life. Not only did its final chapter lay down a blueprint for a political programme, part of which would be implemented many years later, but its very title hints at images that inspired radical Irish nationalism.

By the early twentieth century most Irish people were prepared to exploit the opportunities provided by their citizenship of the United Kingdom. Many grievances and injustices had already been remedied. In the course of the preceding decades Ireland had already experienced a social revolution, and most of the land which had been conquered and confiscated in the sixteenth and seventeenth centuries was by now restored to the Catholic, Gaelic-Norman majority of the population – or at least to the dominant section of that majority. The Wyndham Act of 1903 accelerated the transfer of land ownership by providing

---

[1] In November 1904 the articles were published as a booklet consisting of ninety-nine pages of text and costing one penny. This was the same price as an issue of *The United Irishman*, and one-third the price of a pint of Guinness. Its mixture of lively journalism and pedantic detail is illustrated by the chapter headings, which ranged from 'And how the emperor of Austria lost his temper' to 'The meeting of the Hungarian diet of 1865'. The contents will be examined in more detail in pp. 17–18.

generous state loans to tenant farmers. But a small minority of nationalists deprecated all such reforms and insisted on regarding the country as oppressed, deracinated and moribund. These radicals believed that the Irish people should be jolted out of their trust in British measures, their bland acquiescence in an improved version of the status quo; only as a fully separate state could the nation be regenerated. Some members of this faction planned to fight for a republic on the French or American model, while Griffith argued that Ireland should follow the peaceful example provided by Hungary in the mid-nineteenth century.

For many decades their cause had seemed hopeless, but they revealed an almost religious faith as they awaited and prepared for a national resurrection. It was appropriate that a symbol often associated with them was that of the phoenix rising from its own ashes; failure, however often repeated, was no more than a prelude to ultimate triumph. Eventually the most daring of these revolutionaries seized the unexpected opportunities which became available to them. On Easter Monday 1916 they staged a rebellion, and although it failed their action brought their cause the mass support which the Irish people had always denied it. Soldiers soon joined forces with politicians, and for the next few years virtually all those who sought a fully independent Ireland were able to work together within the Sinn Féin party. (Some also worked through another body, the Irish Republican Army.) By now, however, Sinn Féin had been transformed into a movement vastly different from anything which Griffith could have imagined as he wrote *The resurrection of Hungary* in the weeks before and after Bloomsday.

In February 1922 Joyce's *Ulysses* was published in Paris. A month earlier Griffith had been elected president of an independent Irish parliament remarkably similar to that which he had advocated in 1904. Only his opponents recognized him as the president of an Irish republic which he had not sought and which he now disowned. This paradox illustrates the complex history of the ideas which he propagated, the party which he led, and the conflicts in which he became embroiled.

Sinn Féin, the political manifestation of the Irish revolution, was born in the aftermath of a doomed rebellion and died in the bitterness of a civil war. In most respects it was a new organization, although it retained the name of Griffith's party, together with some of its predecessor's structures and policies. It represented a synthesis of different beliefs, traditions and methods. It was a coalition between two forms of Irish nationalism, one committed to the establishment of an Irish republic by revolutionary measures, the other aiming at a more limited degree of independence which would be achieved through political organization and passive resistance. Although dominated by soldiers, the party became a triumphant political force; although committed to a goal which necessitated violence, it helped lay the foundations of a democratic state; although success-ful and massively popular, it was soon repudiated and abandoned by almost all its members; and although its ultimate enemy was the British government, many of its heroic struggles were fought against fellow nationalists. Its first opponent (and also its first victim) was the moderate home rule movement, or the Irish Parliamentary Party.

Home rulers and their enemies

The home rule party had dominated Irish public life for decades. Inaugurated in a diffident manner by Isaac Butt in the early 1870s, re-established in an imperious style by Charles Stewart Parnell some years later, it had succeeded by 1885 in crushing or marginalizing all rival forms of Irish nationalism. It was faction-ridden, and at local level its organization remained weak, but outside the unionist stronghold of the north-east it faced no serious competition. The party was able to disengage itself from its involvement in the Land War and from its tactical co-operation with Irish republicans. It replaced this short-lived 'new departure' by a strategic alliance with the British Liberals which lasted until the First World War. In social terms the home rule movement became increasingly conservative, and it prospered through its close links with those tenant farmers who benefited from the land acts of the late nineteenth and early twentieth cen-turies. However the fact that so much of its programme on the land question was implemented by British governments made the party appear irrelevant to many who had supported it as an agent of social change;[2] home rule became its only significant remaining objective, and its survival became ever more depen-dent on achieving this one aim.

The Parliamentary Party was an inclusive, 'catch-all' movement which thrived on imprecision. Its ranks included mutually suspicious and even mutually hostile groups which could be expected to quarrel among themselves once home rule had been achieved. Its members were encouraged 'to restrict discussion to generalities about the "national cause" to which no interest group could take exception. Vague slogans could win acceptance from a far more diverse army than any well-formed, and therefore controversial, pro-gramme of future action could have done.'[3] For over thirty years nationalist

---

[2] Paul Bew, 'Sinn Fein, agrarian radicalism and the War of Independence, 1919–1921', in D. G. Boyce (ed.), *The revolution in Ireland, 1879–1923* (London, 1988), p. 224.

[3] David Fitzpatrick, *Politics and Irish life, 1913–1921: provincial experience of war and revolution* (Dublin, 1977), pp. 92–3.

Ireland was overshadowed by this one party, either in its original united and disciplined form or else in the changing shapes of its different factions. From 1900 until his death eighteen years later its leader was John Redmond, who was accompanied (often unhappily) by his deputy, John Dillon, and it was supported by all but a small minority of Irish nationalists.

To maintain this mass democratic following was in itself a triumph, since the party failed to translate its popularity into the achievement of its main objective. For decade after decade Westminster consistently ignored or rebuffed the demand made by the vast majority of Irish electors, and yet their faith in parliamentary methods remained largely intact. The habit of seeking British support became ingrained, and one radical nationalist lamented long afterwards that the people were preoccupied by performances in the House of Commons. 'To all appearance Ireland had abandoned Physical Force and thrown its all on the political spell-binders at Westminster.'[4]

The process of democratization proceeded slowly, despite the changes in land ownership, and the Protestant ascendancy retained much of its old dominance. By the outbreak of the First World War many intelligent and ambitious young people felt frustrated and resentful. In 1911 Catholics comprised 74 per cent of the population, but they accounted for only 46 per cent of those who worked in insurance companies, 44 per cent of barristers and solicitors, 42 per cent of commercial travellers, 39 per cent of auctioneers, 36 per cent of civil engineers, and 35 per cent of bankers and bank officials;[5] 78 per cent of policemen were Catholics, but five years later thirty-three of the thirty-seven RIC county inspectors were Protestants.[6] The mass of the population might reasonably feel that it was excluded from many of the country's better-paid or more prestigious occupations, and a sense of victimization was one of the driving forces behind Irish nationalism. Yet despite the remaining injustices, and despite latent (at times, blatant) anti-British sentiment, those radicals who demanded drastic social or political changes could attract only a few followers. In most respects the 'wild Irishman' was no more than a British caricature, and a large majority of the population sought moderate aims by political means.

Redmond varied his tactics in the course of the long struggle for home rule, and having attempted to conciliate unionists between 1893 and 1903 he sought to overcome them in the years after 1909.[7] But his basic strategy remained unal-

---

[4] J. J. Walsh, *Recollections of a rebel* (Tralee, 1944), p. 16.

[5] *Census of Ireland, 1911. General report, with tables and appendix* (London, 1913), pp. 9–10.

[6] Henry Duke, *Hansard*, 87, col. 414 (9 Nov. 1916).

[7] Paul Bew, *Conflict and conciliation in Ireland, 1890–1910: Parnellites and radical agrarians* (Oxford, 1987), pp. 193–4, 199.

tered. He depended on his alliance with the Liberal party – even though in some respects the Conservatives proved to be more thoroughgoing reformers, and even though the Liberals' return to office in 1905 seemed to bring home rule no closer. Irish unionists grew uneasy as their British protecters relaxed their vigilance, and their most energetic Conservative champion, Walter Long, found it difficult to defend a union which did not seem to be endangered.[8] But after the deadlocked 1910 elections it seemed as if the Nationalists' long years in the wilderness had come to an end. Asquith's Liberal government now depended on Irish support for its survival, and it introduced a new home rule bill soon after the House of Lords' power of veto had been abolished. Under the protective umbrella of the 1911 Parliament Act a devolved legislature would be elected in Dublin within three or four years. It appeared that the Nationalists' faith in the Liberals and in British democracy had been vindicated, and that their patience would be rewarded at last.

The Conservative opposition and its unionist allies realized that they could no longer block home rule by constitutional means. They resorted to treason. Inspired by Sir Edward Carson they formed a paramilitary force, smuggled German arms into unionist Ulster, and threatened rebellion against the government. Andrew Bonar Law and his Conservatives were able to combine principle with cynicism as they incited their unionist protégés to defy the Liberal cabinet and a majority of MPs. Irish moderates were embarrassed and discredited. In the words of one republican observer, 'it seemed to the Irish people that the English desired to have it both ways. When they [the Irish] sought to enforce their national rights by the methods of Fenianism they were told to agitate constitutionally, and when they acted constitutionally they were met by the methods of Fenianism.'[9] In the Curragh Incident of April 1914 a group of army officers made it clear that they would resign their commissions rather than obey any orders which involved suppression of the Ulster Volunteers; they claimed the right to pick and choose between the various instructions which they received from their superiors, a liberty which (as Labour spokesmen and others pointed out) they would not tolerate among the soldiers under their command. For virtually the only time in recent British history a government felt it could not rely on its army, and there were widespread fears of civil war in both Britain and Ireland.

At least part of the reason why home rule perished was that the Tories refused to regard it as anything less than revolutionary and destructive;[10] thereby they precipitated a more full-blooded upheaval which destroyed far more of the

---

[8] John Kendle, *Walter Long, Ireland, and the union, 1905–1920* (Dun Laoghaire, 1992), p. 53.

[9] Bulmer Hobson, *A short history of the Irish Volunteers* (Dublin, 1918), p. 92.

[10] Patrick O'Farrell, *Ireland's English question* (London, 1971), p. 175.

system which they wished to preserve. They began the process of radicalizing Irish nationalists, of pushing them into support for drastic measures which would have been unthinkable in the early years of the century. On the Conservative and Unionist leaders lies the ultimate responsibility for redirecting the course of Irish politics. Bonar Law and Carson were to be deeply shocked and repelled by much that happened in Ireland during the decade which followed their defiance of parliamentary government, but without their example the Irish revolution would not have come about. General Maxwell, who suppressed the Easter Rising, appreciated this influence when he remarked that the Ulster Volunteers were responsible for Ireland's inflammable situation: 'from this date the troubles. The law was broken, and others broke the law with more or less success.'[11]

Already before the outbreak of the First World War Redmond's Parliamentary Party had been gravely weakened by the unionists' armed challenge. After September 1914, when the Home Rule Bill was simultaneously enacted and suspended for the duration of the war, the party did little more than follow Asquith's earlier advice to his opponents that they should 'wait and see'. Its members watched in dismay when the Conservatives returned to office in May 1915 as the junior partners in a wartime coalition. Nationalists could only hope that this shift in the political balance of power would not be followed by any dilution of the concessions which Redmond had earlier squeezed from the Liberal government. As disillusionment spread among home rule supporters their fervour and optimism seeped away.

Police records provide one indication of this weakening support for the Parliamentary Party. Every month the RIC prepared sets of figures relating to the United Irish League (UIL), the party's national organization. The statistics are unlikely to be accurate in detail, but they nonetheless provide a revealing general impression of its drift after the Redmondites had been blown off course by the unionist wind. Every year between 1913 and 1918 there was a drop in the police estimates of party membership, from 132,000 at the beginning of the period to 105,000 at the end. The number of branches fluctuated, but here too there was an overall decline, from 1,244 to 1,077.[12] In July 1915 it proved impossible to hold a convention in North Tipperary to choose a successor to the deceased MP because, in Redmond's words, 'the branches of the organisation have been allowed to die out'.[13] Subventions from the United Irish League of

---

[11] Maxwell, 'Report on the state of Ireland since the rebellion', 24 June 1916, Cab.37/150/18.

[12] 'United Irish League meetings', CO.904/20/2.

[13] Paul Bew, *Ideology and the Irish question: Ulster unionism and Irish nationalism 1912–1916* (Oxford, 1994), p. 145.

America virtually dried up when Redmond urged Irish Volunteers to join the British army after the outbreak of the First World War; by 1915 he was obliged to reverse the normal direction of the flow of money sent across the Atlantic, and he supported the American organization with funds from Ireland.[14] Even though Irish revolutionaries did not seize the initiative until the Easter Rising and its aftermath, the Nationalists had lost their momentum before the outbreak of the war. Carson had already knocked Redmond off his pedestal before Clarke or Pearse, de Valera or Griffith were able to do so.

The unionists were only one of several forces whose combined efforts formed a broad (if often unconscious) coalition of interests opposed to the cause of home rule. Another was the 'Irish-Ireland' movement which, despite its commitment to cultural and non-political objectives, nonetheless helped undermine the bases of the party's support and beliefs. In the late eighteenth century and throughout the nineteenth, the Irish people had changed their vernacular from Irish to English, and in contrast to many of its European counterparts Irish nationalism expressed itself in the language of the occupying power.[15] A small minority took a different path; working mainly through the Gaelic League, its members hoped to create an Irish-speaking Ireland which would throw off British cultural (rather than political) domination. For centuries Catholicism had been the traditional badge and shield of Irish identity, differentiating the majority of the island's population from Protestant Britain. But both political and cultural nationalists rejected this equation; many of their early leaders were Protestants, and they all wished (at least in theory) to appeal to the million Protestants who lived in Ulster. In some quarters it was hoped, improbably, that the propagation of a separate language would smooth over Irish sectarian divisions. The more radical among the cultural nationalists planned not merely to reform and regenerate the Irish people; they also hoped to achieve a separate state in which the people's distinctive identity could be fostered by a sympathetic government. They saw this as a natural and logical progression.

Early in the twentieth century a new intolerant mood emerged, a determination that Irish would be made 'essential' or compulsory for educational

---

[14] Francis M. Carroll, *American opinion and the Irish question, 1910–23* (Dublin, 1978), p. 42; Alan J. Ward, *Ireland and Anglo-American relations, 1899–1921* (London, 1969), p. 80.

[15] On the Irish experience see Garret FitzGerald, 'Estimates for baronies of minimum level of Irish-speaking amongst successive decennial cohorts: 1771–1781 to 1861–1871', in *Proceedings of the Royal Irish Academy*, 84, C (Dublin, 1984), pp. 117–55 (summarized in *IT*, 10 June 1985); on parallel developments elsewhere see Benedict Anderson, *Imagined communities: reflections on the origins and spread of nationalism* (2nd edn, London, 1991), pp. 73–5.

advancement; it would become what English had been in the past, the language of opportunity.[16] The Gaelic revival movement achieved some success in ensuring that knowledge of Irish became a prerequisite of higher education, but the British authorities blocked its attempts to 'nationalize' both the educational system and public appointments in the Gaeltacht (the remaining Irish-speaking districts which were concentrated on the Atlantic coast). Its members tended increasingly to think in terms of capturing the state machine as a first step towards implementing their programme.[17]

Nationalism rescued the Irish language revival from what many people dismissed as mere scholarly antiquarianism, and the Gaelic League's political neutrality became harder to maintain. Douglas Hyde prided himself on being a 'non-political' president throughout the first twenty-two years of its existence, but even he singled out the Parliamentary Party for attack.[18] Eoin MacNeill – who with perfect symbolism was the main inspiration both for the Gaelic League in 1893 and the Irish Volunteers twenty years later – was able to write in 1908 that 'while I believe in working the language movement honestly for its own ends, I cannot hide from myself the conviction that this movement is also steadily building up the foundations of political freedom'.[19] Some years later the MP for West Kerry referred to 'the poison of the Gaelic League', and complained that Irish language students were nearly all anti-party men.[20]

Long before the First World War the failure of a purely cultural movement had become apparent, and some of those who were committed to a linguistic revolution came to believe also in the necessity of a military struggle. Patrick Pearse and Eamon de Valera were merely the most prominent among those idealists who concluded that their aims could be achieved only by rebellion. And a growing number of radicals saw cultural nationalism simply as one of many weapons which could be used to fight the British; for them 'the Irish language was valued not for itself but as a symbol of national distinctiveness. Beyond that, it was fit only for children and for others who needed protection against English civilization.'[21] Many cultural revolutionaries rejected the constitutional

---

[16] See R. V. Comerford, 'Nationalism and the Irish language', in Thomas E. Hachey and Lawrence J. McCaffrey (eds.), *Perspectives on Irish nationalism* (Lexington, 1989), pp. 33–5. Also see below, pp. 236–9.

[17] John Hutchinson, *The dynamics of cultural nationalism: the Gaelic revival and the creation of the Irish nation state* (London, 1987), p. 293.

[18] D. George Boyce, *Nationalism in Ireland* (3rd edn, Dublin, 1995), p. 239.

[19] Michael Tierney, *Eoin MacNeill, scholar and man of action, 1867–1945* (Oxford, 1980), pp. 104–5.

[20] Thomas O'Donnell to Dillon, 14 Oct. 1914, cited in J. Anthony Gaughan, *A political odyssey: Thomas O'Donnell, M.P. for West Kerry, 1900–1918* (Dublin, 1983), p. 97.

[21] Tom Garvin, *Nationalist revolutionaries in Ireland, 1858–1928* (Oxford, 1987), p. 102.

methods of the Parliamentary Party, along with what they believed to be its complacency and corruption. MacNeill loathed the way in which 'Ireland's representatives wheedled, fawned, begged, bargained and truckled for a provincial legislature.'[22]

Every setback experienced by Redmond and his followers in their battles with the Conservatives and Ulster unionists made them more vulnerable to the attacks of enemies within their own camp. They were assailed and undermined by the 'separatists', those nationalists who sought a far more thorough degree of separation or independence than was provided by the Home Rule Bill. Over time the party became increasingly exposed to critics who demanded more assertive tactics than negotiation and compromise with British ministers.

The IRB and the Volunteers

Among the fiercest opponents of moderate nationalism was the Irish Republican Brotherhood, or IRB, whose aim was the achievement of a fully independent Irish republic. It was the successor of the Fenians, the more flexible of whom had engaged in electoral politics and had co-operated briefly with Parnell in the 'new departure' of 1879, but most of whose members repudiated even a tentative flirtation with constitutional methods. Wariness of political activity was an enduring characteristic of Irish republicanism. The brotherhood was dedicated to achieving its aims by conspiracy and rebellion, and its members were always a small minority, unrepresentative of most Irish nationalists; it was a secret society like the Italian Carbonari, a revolutionary underground like the Russian Bolsheviks.

The IRB infiltrated the various bodies which flourished in the late nineteenth and early twentieth centuries, and in particular it concentrated on the two main expressions of 'Irish Ireland', the Gaelic League and the Gaelic Athletic Association. Long before the 1916 Rising the brotherhood had begun to appropriate the Irish language and Gaelic games.[23] In turn it was observed closely by the British authorities, and its activities were reported to Dublin Castle by spies and informers.[24] This surveillance was eased after 1905 when the Liberals returned to power, largely because of an over-confident belief that (in the words of one senior Castle official) 'there is no evidence that the IRB is anything but

---

[22] Eoin MacNeill, *Daniel O'Connell and Sinn Féin* (Dublin, 1915), p. 15.

[23] Garvin, *Nationalist revolutionaries*, p. 98.

[24] Leon Ó Broin, *Revolutionary underground; the story of the Irish Republican Brotherhood, 1858–1924* (Dublin, 1976), pp. 117–20.

the shadow of a once terrifying name.' Such views were reinforced by a similar impression that the usual result of its meetings was no more than the 'liquidation' of its American funds through an increased consumption of porter and whiskey.[25]

For decades the brotherhood followed Mr Micawber's practice and waited for something to turn up, hoping that it would be able to exploit some favourable opportunity; in the words of the old Fenian John O'Leary 'we cannot say when the time will come – only that it will, and that we must be ready.'[26] Like most revolutionary movements it survived on a meagre diet of faith and hope, and the struggle was never so 'pure' as when it was not actually taking place.[27] But while there was much rejoicing at Britain's embarrassments, such as its military defeats and diplomatic isolation during the Boer War, the IRB remained unable to exploit the openings which these might have offered. In 1902 John MacBride discussed the prospects of a war involving Britain and concluded 'we are disgraced forever if we miss another opportunity'.[28] When Britain's ally Japan attacked Russia two years later a London-based IRB member remarked that 'this war is not, so far, as satisfactory as I could wish. I want Russia to win, of course. Still, I'm getting great hopes of a big European fight wherein England shall get her deserts.'[29] At least for the time being, he was disappointed. One policy recommended by the IRB was 'to attract the attention of England's enemies by acts of disloyalty', but this, too, seemed to produce no results.[30]

Denis McCullough, a future president of the IRB supreme council, had been told by his father 'you can't do much son, but you must carry on the tradition'.[31] For many in the brotherhood this aim sufficed, although by the second decade of the twentieth century direct links with previous rebellions were becoming ever more tenuous. Nonetheless a precarious line of succession was maintained, and James Stritch, who had participated in the rescue of Fenian prisoners in Manchester in 1867, was among those interned after the Easter Rising.[32]

Shortly before the First World War the IRB was purged and revived by Tom

[25] James Dougherty (assistant under secretary), Dec. 1903, cited in W. F. Mandle, *The Gaelic Athletic Association and Irish nationalist politics, 1884–1924* (Dublin, 1987), p. 137; Ó Broin, *Revolutionary underground*, p. 134.   [26] Cited in *Irish Freedom*, Oct. 1914, editorial.

[27] Maurice Goldring, *Pleasant the scholar's life: Irish intellectuals and the construction of the nation state* (London, 1993), p. 41.

[28] MacBride to John Devoy, n.d. [1902], William O'Brien and Desmond Ryan (eds.), *Devoy's post bag* (Dublin, 1948), II, p. 349.

[29] P. S. O'Hegarty to Terence MacSwiney, 15 Feb. 1904, MacSwiney MSS, UCDA, P48b/375.

[30] *Irish Freedom*, June 1911, editorial.

[31] McCullough, interview with Richard Mulcahy, 1961, RM, P7/D/14.

[32] Sean O'Mahony, *Frongoch: university of revolution* (Dublin, 1987), p. 137.

Clarke and his group of young followers, and only then could it be taken seriously as a revolutionary force. Denis McCullough represented the earnest new mood; as he reminisced long afterwards, 'I cleared out most of the older men (including my father) most of whom I considered of no further use to us.'[33] Despite such zeal the IRB's numbers remained tiny, its influence slight and its prospects negligible. Bulmer Hobson remarked later that until 1913 it was no more than 'a little secret movement meeting in back rooms'.[34] Its members continued to look to the past for example and inspiration, and they hoped to imitate or even transcend the record of earlier generations. Yet it was not inspiration which Irish revolutionaries needed, but practical instruction, example and opportunity. These were provided by Edward Carson, James Craig and the Ulster Volunteers.

Unionists were able to achieve in a matter of months what IRB members had dreamed of doing for many decades, but what they could not even attempt because of public indifference, police surveillance and their own fear of British repression. Even though the cabinet in London and the chief secretary in Dublin Castle were broadly sympathetic to Irish nationalists, Britain's ability to avert rebellion in Ireland was displayed against only one section of the population. Judges and generals, peers and policemen were all prepared to turn a blind eye to the formation of the Ulster Volunteers, and in many cases the 'establishment' offered encouragement and support to these potential rebels against the crown. The unionists organized a mass movement, and they trained and supplied their own army. They committed themselves to staging a rebellion if they could not achieve their objectives by peaceful means; they would take arms against the government unless it abandoned a policy which had been approved by a large majority in the House of Commons. They undermined Irish nationalists' faith in British politicians and in democratic methods.

Along with other, more moderate observers the IRB envied and emulated the unionists. Many nationalists reasoned that if the Conservative Party, reinforced by elements in the House of Lords, the British army, the judiciary and the worlds of business and finance, were all ready to support or incite one section of the Irish population in its plans for rebellion, the authorities would be unable to restrain others (who supported the government's home rule policy) from imitating this example. But the initiative came from outside the brotherhood, from Michael O'Rahilly, who was a supporter of Griffith and a member of the Gaelic League. He persuaded Eoin MacNeill, a distinguished historian of medieval Ireland, to write an article in the League's journal *An Claidheamh Soluis* proposing that nationalists should follow where the unionists had led. O'Rahilly,

[33] McCullough, statement, 14 Oct. 1957, McCullough MSS, UCDA, P120/29(1).

[34] Ruth Dudley Edwards, *Patrick Pearse: the triumph of failure* (London, 1977), p. 212.

MacNeill, Bulmer Hobson and a small group of others then decided to convene a public meeting in the Rotunda, the largest hall in Dublin;[35] 7,000 people attended, an Irish Volunteer Force was founded, and its numbers increased rapidly; by the end of 1913 a paramilitary body had been established in nationalist Ireland as a mirror image of the Ulster Volunteers. The unionists' example was contagious, and their parading of emotion, their posturing and their oratory all helped eradicate the national fear of looking ridiculous.[36] Although Hobson was the only member of the IRB who was involved in the preliminary steps which led to the founding of the Volunteers (and he would soon be purged by his more radical and impatient colleagues) the brotherhood promptly infiltrated the new army and occupied many of its key positions. For the first time since the days of the Land League extreme republicans were in association, if under cover, with a large body of Irish public opinion.[37] But the IRB was anxious to avoid alarming the moderate majority. It was content that the president of the new force should be MacNeill, a widely respected supporter of the home rule cause.

The formation of the Irish Volunteers was a direct response to the combination of excitement and anger which Carson's actions had provoked, to the feeling that he had stolen a march on Redmond, and to the widespread hope that the advantage which the unionists had gained would be nullified if nationalists followed their example. In his speech at the meeting which launched the Volunteers, MacNeill declared that the Ulster Volunteer movement had established the principle of Irishmen's right to decide and govern their own national affairs.[38] Many nationalists shared his respect for the Ulstermen's defiance of the British government. The IRB newspaper *Irish Freedom* rejoiced that 'the sheen of arms in Ulster was always the signal for the manhood of the rest of Ireland . . . By the Lord, it is good to be alive in these days.'[39] Pearse had 'boldly preach[ed] the antique faith that fighting is the only noble thing, and that he only is at peace with God who is at war with the powers of evil';[40] after the unionists' initiative such righteous combat now seemed less remote. The more moderate Arthur Griffith saw Ulster unionism as marching to national salvation in the spirit of Sinn Féin and political nationalism.[41]

Within a few months of their formation the Irish Volunteers numbered

---

[35] Aodagán O'Rahilly, *Winding the clock: O'Rahilly and the 1916 Rising* (Dublin, 1991), pp. 93–9.

[36] Maureen Wall, 'The background to the rising: from 1914 until the issue of the countermanding order on Easter Saturday 1916', in Kevin B. Nowlan (ed.), *The making of 1916* (Dublin, 1969), p. 161.   [37] Robert Kee, *The green flag: a history of Irish nationalism* (London, 1972), pp. 501–2.

[38] Hobson, *History of the Irish Volunteers*, p. 30.   [39] *Irish Freedom*, Jan. 1914, editorial.

[40] Pádraic H. Pearse, 'The murder machine', *Political writings and speeches* (Dublin, n.d.), p. 14.

[41] *Sinn Féin*, 24 Aug. 1912, editorial. For Griffith's Sinn Féin movement, see below, pp. 21–33.

about 150,000. They could be seen as an Irish manifestation of Europe's 'generation of 1914', young men who were dissatisfied with what they saw as a dull or decadent world, idealists who (in at least some cases) revelled in the excitement of militarism and the prospect of heroic conflict.[42] The Parliamentary Party was deeply suspicious of these developments and it adopted its traditional methods of dealing with potential threats; it tried to infiltrate and neutralize the new body, first at local level and then in the form of an ultimatum by Redmond to MacNeill and his colleagues. In turn the Volunteer leaders were wary of politicians, indoctrinating their troops with a belief in the nobility of the soldier's calling and warning them against the snares of constitutionalism. MacNeill later instructed them 'on no account to divert their own attention from their own work to the work of political elections . . . Party management and Volunteer organisation go badly together.'[43] The revolutionaries' cult of violence and their scorn of politics are illustrated by the declaration in *Irish Freedom* that 'under existing conditions war is the final court of appeal . . . the battle is to the strong rather than to the glib of tongue, to the tall talker, to the election agent, to the adroit manipulator of ballot papers'. The writer (probably Hobson) continued: 'we do not care, fellow-countrymen, what you arm for. We only care that you arm.'[44] In the course of the next decade this distaste for the compromises of civilian and political life would flourish and fester. In the short run, however, the secret society had little to show for its efforts. The only serious attempt to arm the Irish Volunteers was the Howth gun-running of July 1914, and it was planned by a group which included Roger Casement, Erskine Childers, Darrell Figgis and Alice Stopford Green. None of them was a member of the IRB.

The Irish Volunteers' popularity did not mean that Irish nationalists had been converted *en masse* to the idea of revolution. The limited appeal of the radicals is illustrated by the split within the force which took place a month after the outbreak of the First World War, after Redmond had urged its members to join the British army and to fight 'in defence of the highest principles of religion and morality and right . . . wherever the firing line extends'.[45] As many as 150,000 may have followed Redmond, while only a small number remained with MacNeill and the IRB men who manoeuvred in his shadow; estimates range from a minimum figure of 2,000 to a maximum of 12,300.[46]

---

[42] See Robert Wohl, *The generation of 1914* (London, 1980), pp. 215–17.

[43] *Irish Volunteer*, 4 Sept. 1915.   [44] *Irish Freedom*, Dec. 1913, editorial.

[45] Denis Gwynn, *John Redmond* (London, 1932), pp. 391–2.

[46] Tierney, *Eoin MacNeill*, p. 154; O'Rahilly, *Winding the clock*, p. 109. The RIC inspector general put the figures at 9,700 out of a total membership of 156,000 (report, Dec. 1914, CO.904/95).

This re-emergence of the tradition of armed defiance of a London government, first by the Ulster Volunteers and then by their IRB-influenced nationalist counterpart, represented a grave threat to the Parliamentary Party and to the methods which it followed. Ultimately the consequences would prove fatal. The resort to military measures by both unionists and nationalists also transformed a third group whose actions and fortunes already intertwined with those of the republican revolutionaries, and which would in future years become even more closely linked with them: Sinn Féin.

Arthur Griffith

The Sinn Féin party was the most important of several new political movements which emerged in the first decade of the twentieth century. Its dominant figure was Arthur Griffith, 'an extraordinarily clever journalist' according to the chief secretary, Augustine Birrell, who was one among many victims of his pen.[47] He was a gifted writer and a cantankerous politician, an obsessive compiler and manipulator of statistics, a theorist who revelled in improbable past and present models for a future Irish state. Unlike most other radical Irish nationalists he was hard-headed and down-to-earth in his concern with economic questions, and he showed little sympathy for the clichéd shamrocks, wolfhounds and round towers which were cherished by so many of his contemporaries. He hoped to build an 'ascetic, sober and industrious urban middle-class nation', and he has been described, harshly, as wanting the Irish to be free so that they could make their own pots and pans.[48] He hated British rule but did not simply reject British wealth and power; Ireland, too, should have its place in the sun. Some years later one admirer described his newspaper as being urgently of the present, and as escaping the musty odour of ransacked files; 'it looked forward gladly to hope of the future, rather than sadly backward to the defeat of the past'.[49]

Griffith was often narrow-minded. One famous example of his intolerance was his opposition to Synge's *Playboy of the Western World,* which he regarded as 'a story of unnatural murder and unnatural lust, told in foul language'. He

---

[47] Leon Ó Broin, *The chief secretary: Augustine Birrell in Ireland* (London, 1969), p. 120.

[48] Hutchinson, *Dynamics of cultural nationalism,* p. 169; William Irwin Thompson, *The imagination of an insurrection: Dublin, Easter 1916* (New York, 1967), pp. 171–2.

[49] Brinsley MacNamara, *The clanking of chains* (Dublin, 1920), p. 16.

even suggested that it was the production of a moral degenerate.[50] Yeats was denounced in the columns of *Sinn Féin* (probably by Griffith himself) for his disparagement of 'Paudeen' and 'Biddy' in his 'To a wealthy man'. The poem was attacked as 'drivel' and Yeats himself, although praised for his earlier work, was accused of setting an example of immorality to the young men of his country.[51]

But Griffith was also honest and courageous, he mellowed with the years, and at times he could be supple and imaginative. Long afterwards it was claimed that 'all the journalists of Dublin spoke well of him in private, which is the greatest tribute to any man'.[52] He was on good terms with the socialist James Connolly who disagreed profoundly with him on many issues, and with James Joyce who entertained him in the Martello Tower in Sandycove. Joyce might later describe Griffith as an 'indignant little chap', but he nonetheless praised Griffith's writing for its intelligence and directness.[53] He paid an indirect and improbable tribute in the Cyclops episode of *Ulysses*: John Wyse informed the inhabitants of Barney Kiernan's pub that the person who gave Griffith the idea for Sinn Féin was none other than Leopold Bloom.[54]

Griffith constructed an idealized image of Grattan's Parliament in the late eighteenth century, and he recommended it as a model for the Irish future. He took his stand on the Renunciation Act of 1783, by which the British parliament abandoned all future right to legislate for Ireland, and he preferred to forget that this act had been superseded by the Act of Union less than two decades later.[55] He paid no attention to the most fundamental principle of the British political system: that every parliament could repeal any previous legislation, including all restrictions on its own powers. Like Montesquieu, he based his theory on a misreading of the British constitution.

The resurrection of Hungary was a variation on the same theme; an argument in favour of reforming Ireland's relations with Britain along the lines of the

---

[50] *Sinn Féin*, 2 Feb. 1907. Other nationalists shared these views. Pearse also attacked Synge as a kind of evil spirit and believed that 'it is not Ireland he libels so much as mankind in general, it is not against a nation he blasphemes so much as against the moral order of the universe' (cited in Edwards, *Patrick Pearse*, pp. 102–3).

[51] *Sinn Féin*, 18, 25 Jan. 1913. For details of Griffith's *Kulturkampf* and his quarrel with Yeats, see R. F. Foster, *W. B. Yeats: A life. I. The apprentice mage, 1865–1914* (Oxford, 1997), pp. 360, 399, 458.

[52] Desmond Ryan, *Remembering Sion: a chronicle of storm and quiet* (London, 1934), p. 279.

[53] James Joyce to Stanislaus Joyce, 15 Mar. 1905, 6 Nov. 1906, Richard Ellmann (ed.), *Selected letters of James Joyce* (London, 1975), pp. 57, 125.

[54] James Joyce, *Ulysses* (London, 1937), pp. 319–20.

[55] The Renunciation Act was so central to Griffith's thinking that its text formed an appendix to the booklet version of *The resurrection of Hungary*.

Austro-Hungarian dual monarchy. (Ironically, in introducing his first Home Rule Bill in 1886, Gladstone too had alluded to the Habsburg model.[56]) Griffith argued that the Act of Union of 1800, which joined Ireland and Britain in the United Kingdom, was illegal and should be ignored; that a separate Irish legislature should follow 'the Hungarian policy – the policy of Passive Resistance – with occasional excursions into the domain of Active Resistance at strategic points'; and that Ireland and Britain, like Hungary and Austria, might agree to share a monarch – provided that the two nations should be equal and independent.[57]

He proposed that Irish nationalists should launch a campaign of passive resistance against British rule and that their MPs should abstain from Westminster, thereby following the example of the Hungarian deputies who withdrew from the imperial parliament in Vienna. Griffith had read many writings by Hungarian and other historians, but in some respects the booklet was less a work of history than a myth or a parable.[58] His beliefs were unaffected by the collapse shortly afterwards of a similar dual monarchy linking Sweden and Norway, and he was able to dismiss its failure as the consequence of Swedish folly and selfishness.[59] Later he argued that the General Council of County Councils provided 'the nucleus of a National authority' and that it should extend its range of responsibilities until it would become a *de facto* parliament.[60] He denied legitimacy to a sovereign parliament while assigning it to a subordinate tier of government.[61]

Abstention from Westminster was a basic principle of the Sinn Féin movement. O'Connell had toyed with the idea of a 'council of three hundred' which would meet in Dublin, repeal the Act of Union, and re-establish the Irish House of Commons. The policy of abstention had been floated by the *Nation* in 1842, and Davitt had proposed it to Parnell in 1878.[62] Some years later Gladstone was informed 'on reliable authority . . . that Parnell is going to move a definite resolution in favour of a separate parliament for Ireland and when this is refused

---

[56] Nicholas Mansergh, *The unresolved question: the Anglo-Irish settlement and its undoing, 1912–72* (New Haven and London, 1991), p. 25.

[57] *The resurrection of Hungary: a parallel for Ireland* (Dublin, 1904), pp. 91, 95.

[58] Brian Maye, *Arthur Griffith* (Dublin, 1997), pp. 98–9; Padraic Colum, *Arthur Griffith* (Dublin, 1959), p. 78.   [59] *United Irishman*, 17 June 1905.

[60] *The Sinn Féin policy* (Dublin, 1907), p. 35.

[61] Peter Murray, 'Citizenship, colonialism and self-determination: Dublin in the United Kingdom, 1885–1918' (Ph.D. dissertation, Trinity College, Dublin, 1987), p. 203.

[62] Oliver MacDonagh, *The emancipist: Daniel O'Connell, 1830–47* (London, 1989), p. 221; Michael Davitt, *The fall of feudalism in Ireland: the story of the Land League revolution* (London and New York, 1904), p. 112.

to withdraw all his men *en bloc*. He was alarmed by this report, and felt that such a step would be 'by far the most formidable thing that can happen. It will be followed by an assembly in Dublin, which brings into view very violent aberrations.'[63] But there was no evidence of such a dangerous plan being taken seriously by the Parnellites, and it remained dormant until Griffith revived the idea nearly twenty years later; after his death it would develop a new life of its own, and it would be a disruptive influence in Irish republicanism until the end of the twentieth century.

Early in his career Griffith had proclaimed himself a separatist and had demanded 'an Ireland with its own sovereign government and its own free flag'.[64] But he realized that most Irish people did not share these radical objectives and that he would have to compromise his own beliefs in order to win a mass following. The public might be more easily persuaded to support a less ambitious programme, and he believed that an Irish statesman who attempted to introduce a dual monarchy would have won the same widespread support as his hero Ferenc Deák had gained in Hungary.[65] In propounding such arguments he neglected the fact that, for many nationalists, the monarchy was tainted by folk memories of the anti-Catholic bigotry of kings such as George III and George IV, by Victoria's prejudices against the Irish, and by the cloying adulation which unionists lavished on the royal family. In similar fashion Grattan's Parliament was disliked by many nationalists who associated it with the Protestant Anglo-Irish ascendancy.

Griffith was an economic nationalist whose gospel, Friedrich List's *National system of political economy*, argued that nationalism was central to the fostering of economic growth. He was dishonest in his omissions, and he ignored the awkward fact that in the book's 435 pages the only two references to Ireland were at odds with his own beliefs. List remarked that 'territorial deficiencies of the nation can be remedied . . . by conquests, as in the case of Great Britain and Ireland'; and – even worse – he saw the union of Britain and Ireland as an example of 'the immeasurable efficacy of free trade between united nations'.[66] But like any sensible propagandist Griffith selected only what suited his cause.

He wished to convert the Irish Parliamentary Party to his views, rather than supplant it, and he hoped that his theories might bridge the gap which divided the separatist minority from the majority of nationalists who still adhered to parliamentary methods. But he failed in his efforts to win over a significant

[63] Conor Cruise O'Brien, *Parnell and his party, 1880–90* (Oxford, 1957), p. 162.

[64] *United Irishman*, 28 June 1902, cited in Seán Ó Lúing, *Art Ó Gríofa* (Dublin, 1953), p. 81.

[65] Griffith, *Resurrection of Hungary*, p. 95.

[66] Friedrich List, *The national system of political economy* (London, 1885), pp. 176, 123.

number of home rulers, while his moderation alienated many of the more radical separatists who sought an Irish republic freed from all British influences. Yet he clung to the idea of a dual monarchy, even though his most active supporters were full-blooded separatists and he claimed to be one himself.[67] Many of his early admirers soon drifted away, and in preaching the compromise doctrine of a dual monarchy he became his own most fervent convert.

The first Sinn Féin

The origins of the Sinn Féin party were confused and incongruous. The name 'Sinn Féin', meaning 'we ourselves', was already in wide circulation, and as early as 1882 Thomas Stanislaus Cleary wrote a play entitled *Shin Fain; or Ourselves Alone*. Among the characters were 'Erin', 'the Spirit of Irish Fun' and the 'Spirit of Self-Reliance'. One stanza of the chorus, 'Shin Fain', went as follows:

> We craved for bread, they gave us stones;
> We looked for drink, they gave us gall;
> Our calendar was marked by groans,
> Their rise was measured by our fall.
> No more we bow to kiss the rod,
> But to this health a cup we drain,
> Our native sod, our trust in God,
> And under Him, Shin Fain! Shin Fain![68]

A decade later the parliamentarian T. M. Healy referred to 'the good old watchword of old Ireland – Shin Fain – ourselves alone', and at the turn of the century the term was used by members of the Gaelic League.[69] Soon afterwards in Meath a short-lived newspaper was published with the title *Sinn Féin – the Oldcastle Monthly Review*; its principal concerns were the Gaelic League, teetotalism and the misguided 'national' views of some local priests. Griffith claimed afterwards that the idea of describing his policy of national self-reliance as one of 'Sinn

---

[67] Donal McCartney, 'The Sinn Féin movement', in Nowlan, *Making of 1916*, p. 40. See Maye, *Arthur Griffith*, pp. 109–10.

[68] Tom Telephone [Thomas Stanislaus Cleary], *Shin Fain; or ourselves alone: a drama of the exhibition* (Dublin, 1882), p. 11; see John Eglinton, *Irish Statesman*, 17 Jan. 1920, p. 61.

[69] Frank Callanan, *T. M. Healy* (Cork, 1996), p. 351; J. J. O'Kelly ('Sceilg'), evidence, 27 Apr. 1948, SFFC, 2B/82/118(39), p. 28; Brian P. Murphy, *Patrick Pearse and the lost republican ideal* (Dublin, 1991), p. 20.

Féin' had been given to him one evening in late 1904 by his friend Mary Butler when she and her sister called to his office in Fownes Street.[70]

Above all else Griffith was a journalist, a man of ink and print, of headlines and deadlines, and from 1899 onwards he edited (and in large part he also wrote) a formidable series of newspapers. But in the early years of the twentieth century he was also involved in a number of committees, lobbies and factions, many of which had the same overlapping membership. It was at his suggestion that Cumann na nGaedheal was formed in 1900 to serve as a loose federation of several of these groups, but the new society soon became little more than a front for the IRB. Two years later Griffith secured the defeat of a motion by the more radical Maud Gonne that the society should transcend its objective of Irish 'sovereign independence' and adhere to the republican tradition.[71] Already he was engaged in seeking a compromise or consensus which would include moderate nationalists.

Griffith's own organization, the National Council, was formed in 1903 as an *ad hoc* body which mounted a protest against Edward VII's visit to Dublin. Its initial aim was 'the stamping out of toadyism and flunkeyism in this land', but it acquired a permanent character of its own and developed into an intellectual pressure-group. It was a movement or a club rather than a political party, and those who wished to join had to be proposed and seconded by existing members before their applications could be vetted by a committee.[72] The Council's literary or propagandistic nature is illustrated by its ability to raise more money in 1906–7 from the sale of pamphlets than from affiliation fees.[73] It was soon pledged to Griffith's idea of a dual monarchy, and for the next few years it became (second only to his journalism) the main channel of his influence.

In March 1905 a group of Ulster nationalists led by Bulmer Hobson formed yet another body, the Dungannon clubs. The fact that their initial aims had included the restoration of Grattan's Parliament could be seen as a tribute to Griffith's theories, but this early moderation was soon abandoned. The clubs were earnest and exacting. All their young members were obliged 'to attend the Gaelic League and to be absolute teetotalers', although those aged above twenty-five were by now clearly beyond redemption and less was demanded of them; it was merely expected that they 'must never be seen drunk'.[74] The

---

[70] Griffith to Mère Columba Butler, 12 May 1921, NLI, MS 4577; Mary Ellen Butler, 'When the Sinn Fein policy was launched', in William Fitz-Gerald (ed.), *The voice of Ireland* (Dublin and London, n.d. [1924]), p. 106.

[71] Richard Davis, *Arthur Griffith and non-violent Sinn Fein* (Dublin, 1974), p. 18.

[72] *United Irishman*, 9 Dec. 1905.   [73] *Sinn Féin*, 7 Sept. 1907.

[74] Patrick McCartan to Joe McGarrity, 23 Oct. 1906, McG, 17,617(1).

1.1 Sinn Féin propaganda, *c.* 1911

opening sentences in the first issue of Hobson's newspaper *The Republic* made it clear that both it and the Dungannon clubs belonged to 'the Sinn Féin movement', and it went on to reject compromise, repeal of the Union, home rule or devolution: 'an Irish Republic is our aim. We do not ask it as a concession from England – we will take it as our right.'[75] Few nationalists followed this lead, and the paper survived for less than six months. In a letter partly written in code (according to which 'wgeobwgt qbnwqot' meant 'National Council') Hobson explained to the Irish-American leader Joe McGarrity that 'advertisements won't come in no matter what we do'. However he was able to negotiate a merger with W. P. Ryan's *The Peasant*, and ensured that his writers would be able to contribute to the new paper.[76]

Griffith's National Council contested the elections for the Dublin poor law boards in June 1905 and thirteen of its twenty candidates were returned.[77] At its annual convention some months later it transcended local politics and, following the example of the Dungannon clubs, remodelled itself as a full political party. Griffith and his supporters were unenthusiastic about the change. In response to a suggestion that the National Council should become the political arm of the Sinn Féin movement, one of his colleagues argued that 'if we had one central body it was all that was possible at present. The rule in its present form was designed for Dublin simply, and if they decided on forming branches that rule would have to be considerably altered.' The delegates rejected this metropolitan view, those from outside Dublin being particularly anxious that the party should spread, and there was a large majority in favour of establishing branches throughout the country.[78] P. S. O'Hegarty remarked later that Griffith and his allies wished 'to keep merely the central body in Dublin and educate by press and pamphlet rather than by anything else; and they opposed organisation at the first Convention'.[79] In his reluctance to form a national party Griffith followed the example of Butt's Home Government Association in the early 1870s.

The National Council enjoyed a modest success at local level; in 1907 four of its seven candidates were elected to Dublin Corporation, and two years later it won five seats out of the nine which it contested.[80] But elsewhere its fortunes seemed to vindicate Griffith's pessimism. A sarcastic observer of the party's efforts to spread to Cork city described some of the arguments used to woo the audience: it was 'taken away to Hungary and told of the stock market there',

[75] *Republic,* 13 Dec. 1906.   [76] Hobson to McGarrity, 30 Apr. 1907, McG, 17,453.

[77] *United Irishman,* 3 June 1905.   [78] *Ibid.,* 9 Dec. 1905.

[79] O'Hegarty to George Gavan Duffy, 11 Apr. 1907, GD, 5581.

[80] *Sinn Féin,* 12 Jan. 1907, 23 Jan. 1909.

informed of a newly established press agency which would acquaint European countries with Irish affairs, and exhorted to sobriety in order to lessen British tax revenues.[81] The following year an attempt by Hobson and others to explain Sinn Féin policy in Newry was howled down by Redmondites, and the *Freeman's Journal* account of the incident concluded in satisfied tones that 'the entire proceedings were a regular fiasco'.[82]

The National Council and the Dungannon clubs soon became rivals, and Hobson commented later on the differences in style and emphasis between the two bodies: 'Griffith looked to local and parliamentary elections, to economic exposition of a logical and hard-headed character, and used satire with great skill and effect. We, in the Club, while advancing much the same arguments, sought to give them an emotional content and force and an intensity of conviction.'[83] However, their manoeuvrings took place on a modest, insignificant scale, and most Irish nationalists remained unaware of these sectarian squabbles between rival leaders who had few followers. Griffith continued to devote most of his efforts to writing. The party's congress was informed that in 1906–7 the National Council had published eight pamphlets (with a claimed distribution of over 40,000 copies) as well as producing its weekly newspaper.[84]

An incident which took place in Cork illustrates the overlapping of these different interests, and also the tensions which might ensue. In January 1906 one of Griffith's followers, Liam de Róiste, tried to spread the influence of the Celtic Literary Society outside what he described as 'the four walls of a room in 13 Great Georges Street, Cork', but some members were suspicious when a meeting was summoned to expound 'a New Policy for Ireland'. They feared a conspiracy to change the Literary Society's objective from that of seeking an Irish republic to acceptance of Griffith's 'king, lords and commons of Ireland' and, as de Róiste put it, 'some do not like Sinn Féin. They consider it the lowering of an ideal.'[85] Here, in miniature, can be seen the divisions which were to tear nationalist Ireland apart sixteen years later.

Towards the end of that year discussions were held with the aim of combining the different groups, and 'it was agreed that the new body should include men who believe in the Constitution of 82 as a final settlement and men who believe in separation and that the demand should be *independence*'.[86] Some

---

[81] *Leader*, 3 Feb. 1906, p. 399, cited in Patrick Maume, '"This life that is exile": Daniel Corkery (1878–1964) and the search for Irish-Ireland' (MA dissertation, University College, Cork, 1990), pp. 61–2.   [82] *FJ*, 19 Aug. 1907.

[83] Bulmer Hobson, *Ireland yesterday and tomorrow* (Tralee, 1968), p. 22.

[84] *Sinn Féin*, 7 Sept. 1907.   [85] De Róiste, revised diary entry, 18 Jan. 1906, CAI, U271/A/9.

[86] McCartan to McGarrity, 19 Oct. 1906, McG, 17,617(1). '82' refers to Grattan's Parliament of 1782.

months later Joe McGarrity took up the idea, proposed an amalgamation of the 'different Sinn Féin Clubs', and urged that if at all possible this should be achieved without provoking a quarrel with Griffith or any of the other leaders.[87] The process began in April 1907 when the Dungannon clubs merged with Cumann na nGaedheal and the new party adopted the name 'the Sinn Féin League'. One of these organizations had been based in Dublin and the other in Belfast, so the negotiations were held half-way between the two cities, in Dundalk.[88] Hobson was able to report to McGarrity that 'the temperance rule' had been forced through, despite objections from Cumann na nGaedheal; the young zealots had won another battle against the demon drink. The new party's president was P. T. Daly, a member of the IRB, and the first of its declared aims was to regain Irish sovereign independence. However it hoped to extend its appeal beyond the small number of radical nationalists, and the list of its five objectives and its twenty rules made no mention of the divisive 'republic'.[89]

Almost a year earlier Griffith had appropriated the term 'Sinn Féin' by using it as the title for his own newspaper, and a feeling of affronted proprietorship may have been part of the reason for his hostility towards the new party. He virtually ignored it in the columns of *Sinn Féin*. He and his National Council still held out against a merger, but Hobson was confident that they would soon give way.[90] P. S. O'Hegarty described Griffith as small-minded and bitter, complained that he was not prepared to discuss or explain anything, and felt that his platform was one which excluded the separatists; 'he doesn't want any of us in the N.C. [National Council] lest we'd scare away the priests or the mythical commercial '82 men'.[91] The new Sinn Féin League was committed to sovereign independence, but since it did not specify any particular form of government it was the sort of group which Griffith could easily have joined without sacrificing his principles. He preferred to keep his distance, even though the formation of the new party weakened him by isolating his National Council.

North Leitrim

With fortuitous timing Griffith's hand was strengthened in mid-June 1907 when one of the Parliamentary Party MPs was converted to his views. C. J. Dolan of North Leitrim announced his belief in the methods which had been

---

[87] McGarrity to Hobson, 22 Mar. 1907, McG, 17,612.

[88] Denis McCullough, statement, *c*. 1950, STO'K, 27,729, p. 5.   [89] *Republic*, 11 Apr., 2 May 1907.

[90] Hobson to McGarrity (partly in code), 30 Apr. 1907, McG, 17,453.

[91] O'Hegarty to Gavan Duffy, 9, 11 Apr. 1907, GD, 5581.

outlined in *The resurrection of Hungary,* and he declared that, after resigning his Westminster seat, he would campaign for re-election as an abstentionist candidate. In Cork one activist rejoiced that 'Sinn Féin has become a battlecry! It is news, important news . . . [Dolan's] action has "advertised" Sinn Féin.'[92] Yet Griffith displayed only limited enthusiasm as he rallied to his new champion, and although he called for support from every Sinn Féiner in the country he also grumbled that 'Sinn Féin did not seek the contest in North Leitrim, but it accepts it.'[93] He acted as if he, rather than Hobson and his League, represented 'Sinn Féin'. The fact that other vacant parliamentary seats were left uncontested indicates the extent to which his involvement in electoral politics had been forced by circumstances (or by an individual) beyond his control.

Griffith's critics had earlier accused him of avoiding any amalgamation of forces, but Dolan's conversion, combined with the failure of Hobson's newspaper *The Republic,* enabled him to impose favourable terms when his National Council merged with the Sinn Féin League soon afterwards. In effect he took over his rival and forced it to adopt his policy. His newspaper described the union with obvious approval:

> both bodies united under the title of the National Council for the common purpose of achieving by Sinn Féin methods the re-establishment of the Independence of Ireland and declaring that no voluntary agreement would be entered into with England until the British Government recognised the compact made in 1783 between the Parliament of Ireland and Britain.[94]

The new party was also described in this account as 'the Sinn Féin Organisation'. O'Hegarty had complained some months earlier that Griffith 'wants us to follow him blindly and sink our own minds; that all other organizations should dissolve and come into the N.C. [National Council] meekly and humbly'.[95] At least to outward appearances, it now seemed as if he had succeeded in imposing his 'moderate' views on his republican colleagues.

Griffith regarded the united party of 1907 as no more than an extension of the National Council (which had been re-structured as a political organization two years earlier) and its origins were ante-dated accordingly. In 1908 it changed its name to Sinn Féin. It was soon forgotten that Griffith had not been a member of the first party which called itself 'Sinn Féin', and that during the few months of its existence, from April to September 1907, his attitude towards it had been both suspicious and resentful. The title became permanently associated with him.

---

[92] De Róiste, revised diary entry, 18 July 1907, CAI, U271/A/14.   [93] *Sinn Féin,* 29 June 1907.
[94] *Ibid.,* 7 Sept. 1907.   [95] O'Hegarty to Gavan Duffy, 11 Apr. 1907, GD, 5581.

Even before this union had been completed on Griffith's terms, Dolan's decision to run for re-election had forced the leaders of both the National Council and Hobson's Sinn Féin League to offer him their support. The most recent challenge to the Parliamentary Party by radical nationalists, John MacBride's South Mayo campaign in 1900, had resulted in defeat by a margin of almost six to one, and both the National Council and the Dungannon clubs had refrained from contesting any seats in the 1906 general election. Griffith still viewed elections and political activity as distractions from his true vocation. He would have preferred to confine his energies to journalism and propaganda, yet he was caught off guard in summer 1907 and his *Resurrection of Hungary* was out of print. Almost all the available copies of the Sinn Féin programme were dispatched to Leitrim.[96]

Hobson's feelings were mixed; by now he and his colleagues disapproved thoroughly of the 'Hungarian' policy to which the new recruit had been converted in such a spectacular manner, but they also believed that the Irish Party was breaking up, that 'if a good fight is made in Leitrim other M.P.s will resign and once we win a seat the fight will be on and we will rouse the whole country'.[97] Dolan's allies might have had reservations about his action, but they all realized that they had no alternative to helping him seek re-election.

The Redmondites wanted to rush the contest, but Dolan needed time if he were to have any chance of converting the voters to his new beliefs and he delayed resigning his seat in parliament for another eight months. The campaign was protracted, and polling did not take place until February 1908. Griffith and Dolan worked hard to win support, and by the time of the election eleven Sinn Féin clubs had been formed in the constituency and £625 had been raised to help meet the campaign expenses.[98] Griffith addressed 'the men of Leitrim' every week in his *Sinn Féin*, and Dolan's weekly paper, *The Leitrim Guardian*, survived for thirty-one issues. Its losses were defrayed from his election funds.[99] Hobson (a Quaker) described how, on one of his visits to the constituency, he was denounced from the altar by a priest and was described in the local press as a Salvation Army preacher from Belfast.[100] Crowds were addressed by Redmond and many other MPs, and the language used by both sides was

---

[96] Patrick McCartan to McGarrity, 8 July 1907, McG, 17,617.

[97] Hobson to McGarrity, 29 June 1907, McG, 17,612.

[98] Ciarán Ó Duibhir, *Sinn Féin: the first election, 1908* (Manorhamilton, 1993), p. 53; *Sinn Féin*, 22 Feb. 1908.

[99] Dolan to O'Mara, 18 Jan. 1908, and *Leitrim Guardian*, 29 Feb. 1908, JO'M, 21,545(1).

[100] Hobson to McGarrity, 24 July 1907, McG, 17,612.

Vote for Dolan & Sinn Fein.

A THING OF THE PAST.

JOHN REDMOND—"Bad luck to that infernal machine with the foreign name. Ever since it come on the road I have lost any fares I had. I can't afford to give the poor baste a feed of oats. I'm to blame meself. Me ould yoke is a bit slow, and it's out of date. I was wan time in comfortable circumstances."

1.2 Sinn Féin propaganda

often robust; at one meeting, for example, Dolan was attacked as a turncoat, a factionist, a tool, a puppet and a catspaw who had depraved his constituency; his policy was dismissed as foreign-made, and he was described as being supported by Orangemen, Castle clerks and Kildare Street club-men; and, perhaps worst of all, he 'had the audacity to preach Sinn Fein from the windows of a pub'.[101] In turn the electors were urged that

Ireland looks to Leitrim, and waits with throbbing heart
In hope that every man of you will act a manly part.
The God of Nations gives to you a noble weighty trust
To raise aloft your country or to strike her in the dust . . .
If, in short, you'd have your country a nation once again
In God's name men of Leitrim vote for DOLAN and SINN FEIN.[102]

Election meetings were turbulent, following an old Irish tradition, and the Redmondites' Belfast supporters were aggressive campaigners.[103] But Leitrim's home rulers were also willing to fight for their cause, and the disruption of one of Dolan's meetings in Manorhamilton was described in the following terms: 'the local football team . . . were waiting in the inner hall to hold a club meeting, but, growing impatient, they started kicking football and finished by kicking Sinn Feiners'.[104] In the polling station on election day Dolan was involved in a brawl with one of the Redmondites.[105]

As in South Mayo the Parliamentary Party won the seat comfortably, and it secured 72.8 per cent of the vote. Its supporters rejoiced in what was seen as the failure of Dolan's attempt 'to plunge his native constituency into senseless warfare, and to sow amongst its peaceful and kindly inhabitants the seeds of enduring rancour and strife'.[106] But because Leitrim had been regarded as one of the party's strongholds, optimistic radicals could regard the result as a moral victory for Dolan and the Sinn Féin cause. Griffith boasted that it marked a political revolution greater than that which followed O'Connell's triumph in Clare in 1828: 'Ireland's resurrection would be dated from the day when 1,200 Irishmen in the poorest and most remote county in Ireland voted for Sinn Féin.'[107] Characteristically he played with the idea of exploiting the support which had been generated during the campaign by reviving Dolan's *Leitrim Guardian*.[108] His own *Sinn Féin* became, briefly, a daily newspaper.

---

[101] *FJ*, 13 Feb. 1908.   [102] *Dolan and Sinn Féin* (pamphlet), JO'M, 21,546(1).

[103] Ó Duibhir, *Sinn Féin*, pp. 73–5.   [104] *Sligo Champion*, 1 Feb. 1908.   [105] *FJ*, 22 Feb. 1908.

[106] *Sligo Champion*, 29 Feb. 1908, 'The rout of faction' (editorial).

[107] *Sinn Féin*, 29 Feb. 1908, editorial.   [108] *Ibid.*, 28 Mar. 1908.

Decline

At least in relative terms the new Sinn Féin party flourished during and after the extended by-election campaign. It tried to establish a nation-wide system of branches, and according to a witness before the royal commission on the rebellion, 'the worst disposed individuals in the country joined the organisation'.[109] But it also encountered apathy and opposition. Even while the Leitrim election generated publicity and enthusiasm, Hobson lamented that 'sometimes the people make one despair all-together but we have just got to stick at it and make them national in spite of themselves';[110] in the course of later decades radicals would continue to find this an elusive aim. The party's growth was uneven. While one of its members, Tom Kelly, topped the poll in the Dublin municipal elections, Co. Sligo had only two Sinn Féiners, a student and a shop assistant. They met on the few occasions when the student could borrow a neighbour's bicycle.[111]

The party's fortunes soon changed, and its slow early growth was followed by a rapid decline. During its first four years the number of its branches increased at a modest rate: the figures were 1906, 21; 1907, 57; 1908, 115; and 1909, 128.[112] But even this sluggish advance exaggerates Sinn Féin's real strength. The secretary's annual report in August 1909 revealed the party's weakness with blunt honesty. He admitted that in the course of the previous year no less than 45 of the 106 clubs in Ireland had fulfilled none of their obligations (such as paying levies and affiliation fees); the number of party members who had paid their annual subscription of one shilling was a mere 581, 215 of whom lived in Dublin; and total income for the year had been only £700, of which the branches contributed an unimpressive £120.[113]

Sinn Féin soon slid downwards from this low peak. After less than six months the attempt to publish a daily paper was abandoned in January 1910. The weekly sales in early September 1909 were 64,515, while little more than two months later they had fallen to 35,176 and by January they stood at 29,961.[114] The weekly *Sinn Féin* was kept afloat only with a subsidy from James O'Mara, Michael O'Rahilly and other wealthy sympathizers, and debenture holders had

---

[109] CI, E. Galway, evidence, 27 May 1916, *Royal commission on the rebellion in Ireland. Minutes of evidence and appendix of documents* (London, 1916), p. 78.

[110] Hobson to McGarrity, 17 Feb. 1908, McG, 17,453.

[111] Alasdair MacCaba, 'Cradling a revolution', *An tÓglách*, Christmas 1962, p. 7.

[112] Davis, *Arthur Griffith*, pp. 81–2.   [113] *Sinn Féin*, 28 Aug. 1909.

[114] Minute-book, Sinn Féin printing and publishing co., 1909–10, NLI, MS 2139 (figures for 3 Sept. 1909, 7 Nov. 1909, 16 Jan. 1910).

to provide further assistance to prevent the debts of the daily newspaper from driving its weekly successor into bankruptcy.[115] The Sinn Féin party stood aside from both the general elections of 1910. Even at the humble level of local politics its fortunes were mixed, and while it won seats in the municipal elections in Galway, Kilkenny and Limerick, these were balanced by losses in its Dublin stronghold.[116]

The party's internal tensions grew more acute, and critics showed it little sympathy. In Cork the radical Terence MacSwiney came to regard it as 'a kind of compromise on the national question', while O'Hegarty complained about Griffith's autocratic habits and his concern with 'minor points, materialistic bread and butter points . . . Patents Acts, and so on'. He feared that Sinn Féin was becoming a 'party faith' rather than a national faith.[117] Romantic republicans had little interest in activities such as asking branches to 'forward specimens of the mineral products of their districts with a view to a permanent exhibition in America of the resources of the country'.[118]

George Gavan Duffy (then a London-based separatist) was disgusted by what he saw as the incompetence of the Sinn Féin executive, but although he was resigned to the party's continuing ineffectiveness under its present leadership he believed nonetheless that it would collapse without Griffith. The dissidents should wait until an alternative leader appeared.[119] Another critic accused Griffith of wishing to keep Sinn Féin exclusive and unappealing.[120] The IRB had infiltrated the party, as it infiltrated so many other groups, but it began to lose interest. There was no formal split within Sinn Féin, but IRB members such as Hobson, O'Hegarty and Seán T. O'Kelly did not seek re-election to the national executive after they had failed to weaken Griffith's hold on the organization. They chose instead to devote their energies to *Irish Freedom*, the new IRB-run newspaper which was edited by Hobson and Patrick McCartan.

By 1912 the IRB was able to claim that the Sinn Féin movement 'is temporarily suspended, because some of its leaders directed it into an '82 movement, thinking that they could collar the middle classes and drop the separatists; but when the separatists were dropped there was no movement left'.[121] By 1913 the

---

[115] O'Rahilly to James O'Mara, 10, 18 Jan. 1910, JO'M, 21,545(1); Griffith, circular, 5 May 1910, Sighle Humphries MSS, UCDA, P106/211(1).   [116] *Sinn Féin*, 21 Jan. 1911.

[117] O'Hegarty to MacSwiney, 28 Oct. 1908, MacSwiney MSS, UCDA, P48b/378.

[118] *Sinn Féin*, 7 Sept. 1907.

[119] Gavan Duffy to O'Hegarty, 6, 10 Aug. 1908, O'Hegarty to Gavan Duffy 8 Aug. 1908, GD, 5581.

[120] W. P. Ryan, *Irish nation and peasant*, 2 Jan. 1909, cited in Virginia E. Glandon, *Arthur Griffith and the advanced-nationalist press, Ireland, 1900–1922* (New York, 1985), p. 61.

[121] *Irish Freedom*, Jan. 1912, editorial.

main topic of discussion at its national council meetings was how to block enlistment in the British army. One decision reached was that Patrick Pearse might use the council's ass and cart for a period of about ten days to help advertise a fête at his school, St Enda's, provided that he undertook 'to see that the ass was cared for during that time'.[122] When Douglas Hyde responded to Sinn Féin criticism of the Gaelic League he alluded in passing to the party's own problems, 'as if the Sinn Féin organisation itself were in so flourishing a state as to need little or no attention'.[123] No convention was held in that year.

The party survived, at least in theory, but not much activity took place outside its headquarters at 6 Harcourt Street. In the aftermath of the by-election campaign Leitrim was one of the areas where Sinn Féin was strongest, but by mid-1912 the RIC noted that all seven branches in the county were dormant.[124] Shortly after the outbreak of the Great War a Cork member observed that 'there is no Sinn Féin political party at present. The National Council of Sinn Féin in Dublin still meets occasionally, I believe, for lectures, debates, etc. There is no organised party.'[125] In effect Sinn Féin had returned to the role of a Dublin-based pressure group which Griffith had originally desired, and he was faced with fewer distractions as he continued to write with manic industry.

Many supporters of the Parliamentary Party had grown disillusioned after the Liberal victory of 1906, during the years when home rule seemed to be as far away as ever despite the government's nominal commitment to its cause. Sinn Féin and other more radical groups used this weakness to increase their own following. But after the 1910 elections Redmond held the balance of power in Westminster, and soon the Liberals committed themselves to the prompt enactment of home rule. As the Parliamentary Party regained its lost aura of power and patronage, the revival in its fortunes coincided with and hastened the decline of more militant alternatives.

This process continued until 1912–13. But Carson's successful defiance of the government brought about a new mood of uncertainty among Irish nationalists, and many of them began to fear that home rule might be blocked yet again. Redmond's followers became more dubious about his strategy and tactics, and once more the pendulum swung back in favour of extreme measures. However, as the Parliamentary Party suffered a loss of confidence and authority even more drastic than that which Sinn Féin had been able to exploit

---

[122] Minutes, 22 May 1913, UCDA, P163/1.   [123] *Sinn Féin*, 26 July 1913.

[124] CI's report, Leitrim, May 1912, CO.904/87.

[125] De Róiste, diary, 30 Dec. 1914, CAI, U271/A/16.

in 1907–9, nationalist opinion now turned to a military and not to a political group, to the IRB-influenced Volunteers (often, wrongly, called the 'Sinn Féin Volunteers') rather than to Griffith and his party. The IRB activist Ernest Blythe remarked loftily that 'those of us who were somewhat carried away by the "Sinn Féin policy" when it was first expounded have had time to realise that it must be valueless except as the complement of military organisation'.[126] Even Sinn Féin was caught up in the militarization of Irish society which had been inspired by the Ulster unionists. In early 1913 its national council passed a resolution, proposed by Eamonn Ceannt and Michael O'Rahilly (both of whom would be killed in 1916), that 'it is the duty of all Irishmen to possess a knowledge of arms'. Soon afterwards Ceannt reported that he had secured a suitable rifle range.[127]

Griffith was unperturbed by these developments, he continued to pour out propaganda, and over the years he educated or indoctrinated large numbers of young separatists. Many of these converts had little interest in the details of his policies, and they viewed Grattan's Parliament and the Habsburg monarchy with equal indifference, but they were entranced by his uncompromising nationalism and his vigorous prose. He himself remained an influential figure, and his newspaper *Sinn Féin* appeared weekly, even though his party had virtually disappeared. After the 1916 Rising, Major Ivor Price, the director of military intelligence in Dublin Castle (and, according to John Dillon, 'the head spy') remarked that his wartime paper *Nationality* was supposed to have a circulation of 4,500, but that the actual figure was 8,000, and that copies passed from hand to hand.[128] Griffith welcomed the formation of the Volunteers,[129] joined their ranks, and participated in the Howth gun-running in July 1914, but it seemed as if events had passed him by and that he was out of tune with the new mood of the times. Yet among the many consequences of the rising was the prospect of a second chance for both him and his party.

A new Sinn Féin movement emerged after Easter Week, different in many respects from that which had seemed to be in terminal decline by 1914. This revived party would be able to blend creatively the experience of the politicians with the energies of soldiers who, before 1916, had never envisaged a political career for themselves. Their insurrection would help bring about a short-lived but dramatically effective combination of the different elements within the advanced nationalist movement.

---

[126] *Irish Freedom*, Dec. 1913. [127] Minutes, 20 Jan., 6 Feb. 1913, UCDA, P163/1.

[128] Dillon to Lloyd George, 11 June 1916, LG, D/14/2/25; Price, evidence, 25 May 1916, *Commission on the rebellion . . . evidence and appendix*, p. 57.

[129] See, for example, *Sinn Féin*, 20 Dec. 1913, editorial.

Conspirators

The Easter Rising was long prepared. After Tom Clarke's return to Ireland from America in 1907 he was determined to launch a rebellion within his own lifetime, but this became a serious possibility only when the IRB managed to infiltrate the Irish Volunteers. Even then he and his colleagues faced an awesome range of obstacles. The IRB was not a monolith, and although all its members shared a commitment to the principle of armed rebellion, many of them wished to avoid following the precedents of 1848 and 1867; there would be no more doomed and unpopular revolts. The constitution of 1873 declared that 'the I.R.B. shall await the decision of the Irish nation, as expressed by a majority of the Irish people, as to the fit hour of inaugurating a war against England' – a self-denying and self-defeating ordinance which would deprive future rebels of one of the key ingredients of success: surprise.[130]

Those who felt a greater sense of urgency knew that they would have to deceive many of their colleagues in order to achieve their aims. As treasurer and secretary, Clarke and Seán MacDermott formed a majority of the three-man executive, and they had a simple means of ensuring that they would not be troubled by their associate, the president: they secured the election of Denis McCullough, who lived in Belfast and therefore could not monitor their activities. They and other conspirators manipulated the constitution and by-passed the supreme council; they were determined to use and exploit the IRB for their own revolutionary ends, in a similar manner to that in which the IRB in turn used and exploited the Volunteers.[131] They formed a military council which was outside the control of the supreme council, and eventually this body comprised the seven signatories of the Easter Week proclamation. The brotherhood was divided between a minority of its members who were determined on an insurrection, and their more numerous colleagues who either were opposed to such a step or were uninformed about the conspirators' plans. Only in early 1916 did the supreme council commit itself to a rebellion, but it did so in a vague manner and without deciding a date.[132]

The First World War provided the rebels with a deadline, since their doctrine that England's difficulty was Ireland's opportunity demanded an attack on Britain before these 'difficulties' with Germany would come to an end. They

---

[130] T. W. Moody and Leon Ó Broin, 'The I.R.B. supreme council, 1868–78', *IHS*, 19, 75 (1975), p. 314.   [131] Wall, 'Plans and countermand', in Nowlan, *Making of 1916*, pp. 169–71.

[132] Patrick McCartan, 'Extracts from the papers of the late Dr. Patrick McCartan', *Clogher Record*, 5, 2 (1965), pp. 193–5; McCartan to Denis McCullough, 9 Jan. 1932, McCullough MSS, UCDA, P120/11; McCullough, statement, *c.* 1950, STO'K, 27,729, p. 12.

took more literally than did many of their comrades the *Irish Volunteer*'s declaration in August 1914 that

> Tone in his brightest dreams never imagined a more glorious opportunity for the land he loved than now opens for Ireland if her sons are only loyal enough and brave enough . . . Everything is possible for people of courage and determination . . . The name of Ireland must now or never be written on the scroll of nations.[133]

They would strike their blow while Britain still faced Germany and its back was turned to Ireland. The war also provided them with an ally who might supply guns and even troops in the fight against their common British enemy. But their preparations were leisurely, and 'had the war finished as quickly as expected, the ineffectuality of the IRB would have been even more ignominiously exposed than during the Boer War'.[134]

Few of the conspirators actually sought martyrdom, and they hoped and planned for a successful revolt. Nonetheless their main concern was to make a heroic and principled gesture, to salvage what they viewed as the remnants of Ireland's tarnished honour, to end the country's passivity and its tame acceptance of British rule. In at least some cases the most important of their aims was to renew the tradition of insurrection; to achieve an independent republic would be a bonus, a welcome but secondary consideration. There is some truth in the view that the insurgents were more concerned with enhancing the dramatic impact of their revolt than with maximizing their (slight) chances of victory. Their failure to make serious plans for distributing the arms shipment from Germany reveals a lack of professionalism in military terms.[135]

They had no illusions about the state of Irish public opinion. Even though the country contained many frustrated and discontented people, in terms of its social and class grievances Ireland as a whole was less disturbed or discontented than it had been for centuries. Rebels could appeal to a tradition of romantic nationalism, to Anglophobia, and to a historically justified suspicion of London governments, but no longer could they exploit the injustice and misery which had helped fuel unrest in the eighteenth and nineteenth centuries. Many people prospered as a result of the First World War, and the RIC inspector general noted that farmers all over Ireland appeared to take no interest in the conflict except as a means of making money.[136] At the beginning of the war large

---

[133] *Irish Volunteer*, 8 Aug. 1914. Wolfe Tone was an eighteenth-century Irish revolutionary leader.

[134] J. J. Lee, *Ireland 1912–1985: politics and society* (Cambridge, 1989), p. 24.

[135] Charles Townshend, *Political violence in Ireland: government and resistance since 1848* (Oxford, 1983), pp. 298–300.   [136] IG's report, Jan. 1916, CO.904/99.

numbers of young men joined the British army; Ireland's total male contribution to the wartime forces has been estimated at 210,000, and the families of these men formed a powerful lobby opposed to any disloyal or subversive activities.[137] Long afterwards, Bulmer Hobson recalled a conversation in which James Connolly had described Ireland as a powder magazine and claimed that what was necessary was for someone to apply a match. Hobson replied that Ireland was a wet bog and that the match would fall into a puddle.[138]

Apart from this absence of widespread support, Tom Clarke and his colleagues had other grounds for secretiveness. Almost all previous rebellions had been betrayed in advance, and their leaders had been arrested before they could give the signal for a co-ordinated insurrection. The 1916 conspirators made determined efforts to confine knowledge of their plans to as few people as possible. One result of their caution was that key figures in the Volunteers, whose positions made them crucial to the success of any rising, were informed of the rebels' plans only days before these were due to be put into effect. On the other hand, IRB men carried MacNeill's countermanding order to Volunteer units throughout the country, and some of those who later fought in the rising had unwittingly done their best to prevent it. According to one critical verdict, secrecy was pushed to such extremes that ultimately it defeated its purpose.[139]

The rebels worked out a seemingly ingenious solution to the intractable problem of how to stage a mass uprising while retaining the advantage of surprise. All Volunteers in the country were to be called out for manoeuvres on Easter Sunday, and only when they were gathered together, carrying whatever arms they possessed, would they be informed that an insurrection was in progress. Many would disobey their orders and slink home, but it was assumed that others would join in the fight – even though some of them would resent having being excluded from the conspiracy.

In one respect all these efforts at concealment were futile. British naval intelligence had succeeded in breaking German radio codes, and it was well aware of the plans to stage a rebellion in Dublin, to supply the insurgents with German

---

[137] See David Fitzpatrick, 'Militarism in Ireland, 1900–1922', in Thomas Bartlett and Keith Jeffery (eds.), *A military history of Ireland* (Cambridge, 1996), p. 388; Joost Augusteijn, *From public defiance to guerrilla warfare: the experience of ordinary Volunteers in the Irish War of Independence 1916–1921* (Dublin, 1996), pp. 49, 255–6.

[138] Hobson, 'The rising' (statement to bureau of military history, 1947), p. 7, Hobson MSS, NLI, MS 13,170.

[139] Leon Ó Broin, *Dublin Castle and the 1916 Rising* (2nd edn, London, 1970) p. 143. For the countermanding order, see below, p. 39.

arms, and to send Roger Casement to Ireland by submarine.[140] But the Admiralty was resolved never to give the Germans any reason for guessing that their codes had been broken; information gathered in this way was used with the greatest care and its source was concealed whenever possible. The navy felt, justifiably, that Dublin Castle was too leaky to be trusted. In December 1914, Matthew Nathan, the under-secretary, remarked that 'for some reason which I am unable to fathom, a large proportion of the people treasonable to England (patriotic to Ireland, they would put it) are to be found in the lower ranks of the government service'.[141] Within a few years, Michael Collins's rival intelligence network would exploit the Castle's unreliability. Even 10 Downing Street itself was viewed warily, and once more with good cause. The prime minister posted details of British strategy and tactics to his friend Venetia Stanley, and Lord Kitchener complained of him that while most cabinet ministers repeated military secrets to their wives, Asquith told them to other men's wives.[142]

The Admiralty did not simply hoard its knowledge in silence, and it provided the British authorities in Ireland with discreet warnings of trouble ahead. One secret dispatch, citing an 'absolutely reliable source', reported, a month in advance of the rising, the consensus among the Irish rebel leaders: further delay would be dangerous, and an insurrection should be launched by 22 April at the very latest.[143] But at a time of frequent false alarms Dublin Castle remained sceptical. Everyone knew that any pre-emptive move, such as disarming the Volunteers, would provoke a violent response. Only a revelation of the source of this new warning would have jolted the authorities into taking the drastic measures which would have been necessary to forestall a rising. The navy was unwilling to run such a risk; it would prefer to allow a rebellion break out in Dublin than take any steps which might jeopardize its ability to decipher the German codes. The director of naval intelligence may even have preferred that an insurrection *should* take place, knowing that it would be crushed and that the government would be obliged to follow a policy of repression in its wake.[144] The rebels were able to continue with their plans.

They outwitted and manipulated many of their associates, and in particular

---

[140] Casement had been in Germany, seeking assistance for the rising and trying to recruit prisoners of war who would form an 'Irish brigade' to fight the British.

[141] Ó Broin, *Dublin Castle*, p. 33.

[142] Philip Magnus, *Kitchener: portrait of an imperialist* (London, 1958), p. 289.

[143] Dispatch to D.M.O. and others, 22 Mar. 1916, EdeV.

[144] Eunan O'Halpin, 'British intelligence in Ireland, 1914–1921', in Christopher Andrew and David Dilks (eds.), *The missing dimension: governments and intelligence communities in the twentieth century* (London, 1984), p. 60. See also O'Rahilly, *Winding the clock*, pp. 181–2, 186.

they deceived the Volunteers' president, Eoin MacNeill. He did not exclude all possibility of a rising, but the conditions he laid down were very different from those of the group which was centred on Clarke and MacDermott. For him any rebellion by the Volunteers should be a defensive reaction to a British act of aggression (such as the suppression of the Volunteers, or the enforcement of conscription in Ireland); otherwise, it could be justified if there were a reasonably calculated prospect of success. He displayed an insight into the mentality of his revolutionary colleagues when he went on to explain that this must be 'success in the operation itself, not merely some future moral or political advantage which may be hoped for as the result of non-success'.[145]

As things turned out the rebels were extraordinarily lucky. They had tempted fate by staging military manoeuvres in Dublin, and a few years later one observer asked 'how could any one believe in the seriousness of a conspiracy that so flaunted itself?'[146] But the Castle administration displayed a quite exceptional tolerance and refrained from any retaliatory measures. (Redmond encouraged this mild response and warned the British that they should avoid creating martyrs.) MacNeill was told that the project of an immediate rising 'was being rather loosely talked about' in America, but still he did nothing to prevent it.[147] Thomas MacDonagh's remark that 'we are going out on Sunday. Boys, some of us may never come back' was noted by the police, but they took no action.[148] The collapse of their plans prevented the rebel leaders from organizing the nation-wide insurrection which they had envisaged, but their ability to stage even a localized rising was partly the result of chance and good fortune.

When Bulmer Hobson was warned on Holy Thursday that a rebellion was scheduled for the following Sunday he informed MacNeill at once, and at 2 a.m. on Friday the two men confronted Pearse, the Volunteers' director of military organization. He admitted that a rising was imminent, and made it clear that he and his colleagues intended to persevere with their plans. MacNeill decided to do all he could to stop them – short of informing the British authorities; the quarrel would be kept within the family. Later that day, however, MacDermott told him that the German supply ship, the *Aud*, was due to land its arms consignment; this would fulfil his condition of a rebellion having a reasonable chance of success. A forged 'Castle document', which detailed plans for sup-

---

[145] MacNeill, memo, Feb. 1916, F. X. Martin (ed.), 'Eoin MacNeill on the 1916 Rising', *IHS*, 12, 47 (1961), p. 234; For a different interpretation of MacNeill's actions see O'Rahilly, *Winding the clock*, pp. 184–5, 194–9, 238–9.

[146] Katharine Tynan, *The years of the shadow* (London, 1919), p. 189.

[147] MacNeill, memo, 1917, Martin, 'MacNeill on the 1916 Rising', p. 247.

[148] Superintendent (G. division), memo, 22 Apr. 1916, 'Sinn Fein activities 1916', CO.904/23/3.

pressing the Volunteers and other bodies, and for the arrest or detention of hundreds of nationalists (including the archbishop of Dublin), had already satisfied the other condition: British provocation. Any action taken by the Volunteers would therefore be defensive rather than offensive. The Easter Sunday manoeuvres would serve as a distraction from the arms landing in Munster, and this in turn would enable the Volunteers to deter or resist any attempts at suppression by the British authorities.[149] MacNeill decided to let things take their course; he would not interfere with the mobilization.

Then the rebels' plans collapsed. The *Aud* waited for two days off the Kerry coast, but due to misfortune, confusion and incompetence, no Volunteers arrived to unload its supply of arms. The ship was then intercepted by the British navy and was scuttled by its crew. On the same day, Good Friday, Casement was captured after landing near where the arms should have been delivered, while in Dublin Bulmer Hobson was kidnapped by the rebels. When MacNeill was informed that the 'Castle document' was a forgery, and when he learned that the *Aud* had been intercepted – thereby depriving the rebels of both secrecy and weapons – he countermanded the Easter Sunday manoeuvres. By so doing he denied them their cover for a nationwide rising.

On Sunday Dillon warned Redmond that Dublin was full of the most extraordinary rumours, and that he should not be surprised if something very unpleasant and mischievous happened during the week.[150] Other people shared his apprehensions, and that night an old man who had heard that there was to be a rebellion called to Tom Clarke's house and shouted abuse at him, 'asking was he mad, what was going to happen to his wife and family, hadn't he suffered enough for Ireland?'[151]

Once Dublin Castle was alerted to the fact that an insurrection had been intended, its leading officials drew all the obvious and wrong conclusions: that Casement had arrived to take command of the rising (rather than to prevent it because he believed that the scale of German assistance would be inadequate); that his arrest deprived the rebels of their leader; that without the arms shipment they would have no weapons with which to fight; and that with the cancellation of the manoeuvres the whole plan had been abandoned. In the course of lengthy deliberations the viceroy sought the arrest of the principal rebels, and he warned, accurately, that they 'are probably sitting in conclave conspiring against us'.[152] Eventually it was decided to compile a list of those separatists who were to be rounded up. This was done without excessive haste, partly because

---

[149] Tierney, *Eoin MacNeill*, p. 214.   [150] Dillon to Redmond, 23 Apr. 1916, JR, 15,182(22).

[151] Kathleen Clarke, *Revolutionary woman: Kathleen Clarke, 1878–1972: an autobiography*, Helen Litton (ed.) (Dublin, 1991), p. 77.   [152] Ó Broin, *Dublin Castle*, p. 84.

Birrell was on holiday in England and could not be contacted easily. (He received the crucial telegrams from Dublin only on the morning of the rising.) It was also felt that Easter Monday would be an unsuitable day for carrying out the arrests, since it was a public holiday and the streets of Dublin would be crowded with visitors from the country. Action would be postponed until Tuesday. Of all the many mistakes made on both sides in the days preceding the outbreak of the Easter Rising, this was to be the most important.

The rebel leaders were dismayed by the turn of events which had removed any chance of military success, but when they met on Sunday they decided to persevere. They knew that at the very least they would be arrested and imprisoned for years to come, so their choice lay between the certainty of pathetic failure if they did nothing and the possibility of heroic failure if they went ahead and staged their insurrection. They felt that they might as well be hanged for a sheep as for a lamb. In some cases such views may have been reinforced by personal reasons for martyrdom. Joseph Plunkett was dying, Pearse was virtually bankrupt, and Countess Markievicz too was in financial difficulties; she was reported to have remarked that 'if this bally revolution doesn't take place soon I don't know how I'm going to live'.[153] Tom Clarke had waited for decades and was now unwilling to accept a further delay of even twenty-four hours, but his colleagues overruled him and decided to implement their plans a day later than they had intended. Thereby they would lose the symbolic satisfaction of launching their revolt on Easter Sunday, Resurrection Day, when Ireland was to have risen from the dead.

---

[153] Frank Robbins, *Under the starry plough: recollections of the Irish Citizen Army* (Dublin, 1977), p. 65.

The Irish revolution,
1916–1923

2

REBELLION AND HIBERNATION, 1916

The Easter Rising revived the use of political violence and transferred it from the margins to the centre of Irish nationalism. It restored continuity with past insurrections, it maintained and enhanced the revolutionary tradition, and it provided a model for later generations of Irish republicans who would take arms to achieve their objectives. In all these ways it fulfilled the hopes of the rebel leaders. Its immediate effect was to transform Irish public life, and it did so in ways which were often unexpected and sometimes paradoxical.

Insurrection

The rebellion was a Dublin affair. A few incidents took place outside the capital: a skirmish in Galway, shooting incidents in Cork and Wexford, and a guerrilla campaign in Meath and north Co. Dublin which foreshadowed the war of 1919–21. But with these exceptions the rising was confined to the capital. The separatist newspaper *The Spark* had recently prophesied a Volunteer revolt during 1916 which would involve a landing by the Germans, the liberation of most of Ireland, and Dublin remaining in British hands. It was wrong in every detail.[1] (Curiously H. G. Wells's recent novel *The new Machiavelli* anticipated indirectly one aspect of the Easter Rising; its hero imagined a revolutionary provisional government in London 'which occupied, of all inconvenient places! the General Post Office at St. Martin's le Grand'. Similarly in 1913, when Eamonn Ceannt wrote about nationalists' appeal to physical force, he remarked that 'no political body could afford to march its forces up the hill to the G.P.O. and down again'.[2])

The rebels implemented a scaled-down version of their original plans, seized a number of prominent buildings in the city centre and waited to be attacked by

---

[1] *Spark*, 19 Mar. 1916.

[2] H. G. Wells, *The new Machiavelli* (London, 1911), p. 116; *Sinn Féin*, 15 Feb. 1913.

the British forces. Their action conformed to the nineteenth-century romantic tradition of manning the revolutionary barricades. Joseph Plunkett was an armchair strategist, and he and his colleagues attempted in an amateur fashion to employ modern techniques of warfare. Not all of their efforts were successful. Some rebels acted as if they were on the Western Front and began digging trenches in St Stephen's Green – although when British troops fired down at them from the surrounding buildings they retreated to the shelter of the nearby College of Surgeons. The capture of the General Post Office represented a serious attempt at interrupting their enemy's communications, but the central telephone exchange was left untouched. Dublin Castle was feebly guarded and the revolvers in its armoury had no cartridges, but the insurgents made only a half-hearted bid to seize the centre of British rule. Judged by their own theatrical standards this was a failure in revolutionary choreography; the fall of the Castle would have had a symbolic appeal to even the most unliterary and unromantic of Irish nationalists. Inside, in his office, the under-secretary was planning the arrest of known conspirators when he heard shooting outside and realized that his response to the events of recent days had been delayed too long.[3]

About 700 rebels took arms on Easter Monday, although the number increased in the course of the six days of fighting. Near-contemporary and later accounts concur in an estimate of about 1,500,[4] less than 1 per cent of the total number of Irishmen who served in the British army during the war. Most of the insurgents were Irish Volunteers, though a minority belonged to the women's ancillary force Cumann na mBan and to James Connolly's Citizen Army, which had been formed to protect the workers in the lock-out of 1913–14. Of those who were arrested in Dublin after the rising, 55 per cent were labourers, shop-assistants, salesmen and clerks; another 30 per cent were tradesmen. (Outside Dublin, about 28 per cent were farmers and 23 per cent agricultural labourers).[5] The rebels who fought in the General Post Office and elsewhere were no more than a fraction of the multitudes who later claimed a patriotic record in 1916; once the rising was safely over, and once it had begun to acquire a posthumous popularity, there was a dramatic increase in the number who felt able to boast of their revolutionary zeal. Within a decade this tendency had become a subject of jokes and cartoons.

---

[3] Eunan O'Halpin, *The decline of the union: British government in Ireland, 1892–1920* (Dublin, 1987), p. 115.

[4] E.g., de Róiste, diary, 14 Aug. 1916, CAI, U271/A/19A; Desmond Ryan, *The rising: the complete story of Easter Week* (4th edn, Dublin, 1966), p. 265.

[5] John O'Beirne-Ranelagh, 'The Irish Republican Brotherhood in the revolutionary period, 1879–1923', in Boyce, *Revolution in Ireland*, p. 144.

ABOUT ACCOMMODATION

THIS BUILDING HELD 30,000 PATRIOTS IN 1916

2.1 Retrospective popularity: the Rising, as seen in 1924

The fighting was characterized by heroism and chivalry, as well as by the suffering and tragedy inseparable from all warfare. In many respects its conduct was engagingly casual. Joseph Sweeney went to the rendezvous at Pearse's school, St Enda's, to find that he had arrived too late; his comrades 'had taken a tram from Rathfarnham and gone to war'.[6] Pearse's authority as commander-in-chief and president of the republic must have been shaken when his sister arrived in the rebel headquarters and told him to 'come home, Pat, and leave all this foolishness!'[7] On Tuesday, Dick Humphries's mother made her way to the GPO and persuaded him to go home, but after a night of comfort and safety he returned the next day and remained with the garrison until the end of the week.[8] Seán MacEntee drove and walked to Dublin from Louth, made his way through

---

[6] Kenneth Griffith and Timothy E. O'Grady, *Curious journey: an oral history of Ireland's unfinished revolution* (London, 1982), p. 54.   [7] Edwards, *Patrick Pearse*, p. 277.

[8] O'Rahilly, *Winding the clock*, pp. 211–13.

the British lines, and joined the rebels in O'Connell Street for the final three days of the rebellion.[9] Desmond FitzGerald's experience was even more remarkable. After fighting with the GPO garrison throughout the week he was able to bluff his way through the besieging British troops, and then, after wandering through the suburbs and the hills of south Dublin, he made his way home to Bray.[10] He was soon arrested.

Many Dublin citizens were fascinated by the rising, and the end of O'Connell Street was 'crowded by people watching the fight at the Post Office as if it were a Cinema show'.[11] Most people confined their participation to the serious business of plunder, although at least one observer commented on the restraint which many slum dwellers had shown, and their failure to exploit opportunities for looting.[12] Some of the more acquisitive even tried to dismantle and take home the objects forming the barricades which the rebels had erected across O'Connell Street. The crowds were watched by Bulmer Hobson, who had been released by his kidnappers once the rebellion began. He vanished so completely from public life that a few months later Maxwell was able to report 'an unconfirmed rumour' that he had been shot as a traitor by the rebels during Easter Week.[13] (He died in 1969.)

Their inability to forestall the rising was an indictment of the British authorities' judgement and competence, but once fighting began they used drastic measures in bringing it to an end. The rebel positions were besieged, the GPO was destroyed, and after six days' resistance a majority of the leaders decided to surrender. Clarke remained intransigent, but Pearse decided to abandon any further resistance when he saw civilians shot down while carrying a white flag.[14] In his earlier role of a revolutionary theorist he had sat safely at his desk, like so many of his counterparts, while he exulted in the joy of combat and the 'red wine of the battlefields'.[15] As a rebel commander he was more humane. In terms of killing British soldiers the most successful garrison had been that commanded by de Valera at Boland's Mills. Over 450 people lost their lives during Easter Week, and more than 2,500 were wounded.

The 1916 Rising was the most serious and sustained rebellion in Ireland for more than a century, and even if it failed to achieve Irish independence it was

---

[9] Seán MacEntee, *Episode at Easter* (Dublin, 1966), pp. 113–44.

[10] *Memoirs of Desmond FitzGerald, 1913–1916* (London, 1968), pp. 162–80.

[11] J. R. Clark, diary, 26 Apr. 1916, UCDA, P169.

[12] J. R. Clegg, 'The Sinn Fein Rising . . . a citizen's diary', *IT*, 2 May 1916.

[13] Maxwell to Asquith, 3 Aug. 1916, HHA, 37(116).

[14] Ryan, *Rising*, p. 253; Edwards, *Patrick Pearse*, p. 304.

[15] Pearse, 'Peace and the Gael', *Political writings*, p. 216.

triumphantly successful as a protest in arms. Pearse exulted that 'they will talk of Dublin in future as one of the splendid cities like they speak to-day of Paris', while towards the end of Easter Week the novelist James Stephens wrote that there was almost a feeling of gratitude to the rebels for holding out; had they been beaten on the first or second day, Dublin 'would have been humiliated to the soul'.[16] One member of the GPO garrison dated his messages '1st Day' or '2nd Day of the Republic' in the style of the French revolutionary calendar, depressing Desmond FitzGerald who knew that these days were numbered.[17] But by the time of the rebels' surrender their republic had already reached a respectable age.

Many inhabitants of Dublin were indignant at the bloodshed and at the devastation of the city centre, as well as at the accompanying inconvenience and financial loss. Some of the rebel prisoners could feel grateful that they were guarded by British soldiers while they marched through the streets on their way to detention; at least they were protected from angry Dubliners who showered them with abuse and rotten vegetables. But the overall public reaction is impossible to calculate with any accuracy.[18] Undoubtedly there was widespread bewilderment and even dismay, and a common response seems to have been 'the British will never grant home rule now'. The element of German involvement was exaggerated by the Redmondite press, and some newspapers were inspired to extravagant flights of rhetoric. The *Galway Express,* for example, began its commentary as follows: 'Easter Monday, 1916, has made history in Ireland. But, oh, what rank nauseating stains will besmear its pages! – how generations yet unborn will burn with shame when, in the calm light of detailed and exalted impartiality they scan its humiliating chapters!'[19] Critics continued to express their opposition in melodramatic terms. Even a year later a member of the Roscommon board of guardians remarked that

> the people were just after celebrating the anniversary of the suffering of our Lord Jesus Christ; they [the rebels] went out on the streets of Dublin and shot down the people representing the Government, and tried to liberate the German prisoners who were in the internment camp. They wanted to set more Cromwellians adrift on our Irish girls.[20]

---

[16] Ryan, *Remembering Sion,* p. 201; James Stephens, *The insurrection in Dublin* (Dublin, 1916), p. 39.   [17] FitzGerald, *Memoirs,* p. 143.

[18] For an examination of the information (or lack of information) available to the public as it reacted to the rising, see Lee, *Ireland 1912–1985,* pp. 29–36.

[19] *Galway Express,* 29 Apr. 1916, editorial.   [20] *Roscommon Journal,* 14 Apr. 1917.

Some of the Catholic hierarchy's initial pronouncements were highly critical. The bishop of Ross (who had close links with the Parliamentary Party) denounced the 'senseless, meaningless debauchery of blood', while his colleague in Kerry warned against 'evil-minded men afflicted by Socialistic and Revolutionary doctrines'.[21] According to Dr Hoare of Ardagh and Clonmacnoise, the Catholic Church taught that there was no excuse for revolution, and that it was never lawful to take up arms to depose the ruling sovereign. The rebellion itself was 'a mad and sinful venture'.[22] Other bishops were more cautious and discreet.[23] RIC county inspectors commented frequently on the silence of the priests, and they were disappointed by this unwillingness to condemn the rising. Worst of all was Co. Clare, where 'practically all the R.C. clergy showed open sympathy with, and approval of, the action taken by the rebels'.[24]

Respect and support for the insurrection seem to have become more widespread as the fighting continued, day after day, and as it became clear that it was far more than a shameful fiasco. Even in Dublin the defeated rebels encountered some sympathy, and shortly afterwards one prisoner described how, as he and his comrades were dispatched to jail or to internment camps in Britain, they 'got a great send off – all the girls were down to wave us a good-bye and blow kisses after us'.[25] The RIC county inspectors' monthly reports, which in many cases were written about ten days after the rebels' surrender, referred predictably to shock, outrage, anger and confusion. But they also recorded mixed feelings, and, in some cases, even disappointment. In Clare more sympathy than expected had been shown to the rebels; in Co. Dublin 'at first the attitude of the people was sullen'; in East Cork, 'only that the plans miscarried for the landing of arms on the Kerry coast, the whole country would have been in a blaze'; while in Longford the county inspector believed that, if the rebellion had been successful, 'a great many more, who have not as yet disclosed their Sinn Fein sympathies would then have done so openly'.[26] A change of attitude had already begun, if only on a very small scale, while the insurrection was still in progress. Its aftermath saw a process of wholesale conversion, along with a pattern of retrospective endorsement of the defeated rebels and of their objectives.

---

[21] *FJ*, 9, 8 May 1916.   [22] *II*, 16 May 1916.

[23] See John H. Whyte, '1916 – revolution and religion', in F. X. Martin (ed.), *Leaders and men of the Easter Rising: Dublin 1916* (London, 1967), pp. 222–3.

[24] 'Intelligence notes, 1916', Breandán MacGiolla Choille (ed.), *Intelligence notes, 1913–16* (Dublin, 1966), p. 212.

[25] Denis McCullough to James Ryan, n.d. [June/July 1916], Ryan MSS, UCDA, P88/4(1).

[26] CIs' reports, Clare, E. Cork, Dublin, Longford, Apr. 1916, CO.904/99.

Executions and arrests

General John Maxwell was given full civil and military powers in Ireland, and he was determined to display a soldier's common sense in dealing with the insurgents. Under the circumstances nothing could have been more natural than a firm response which would both punish and intimidate. Dublin Castle had already shown quite extraordinary tolerance and patience under Birrell's easy-going regime, and the results had been catastrophic; a reversal of policy was only to be expected. However unwise the British reaction might have been, not only in the distorting light of hindsight but even as seen by a few discerning observers at the time, it was in no way disproportionate to such a grave provocation. Hobson wrote later:

> I fully expected that after the suppression of the insurrection England would dragoon the country, bring in conscription, and drive a whole generation of young Irishmen to slaughter in the European war. If England had done so, Ireland could have offered no resistance . . . That England would bungle and throw away her opportunity to finally smash the national movement in the way she afterwards did could not then have been foreseen.[27]

Within days of their surrender, prisoners were being court-martialled and executed. Fifteen of them were shot, their deaths spread out over a period of ten days; Pearse, Clarke, Connolly, MacDermott and other less well-known or less important figures all died facing British firing-squads. Three months later, as a brutal postscript, Casement was hanged in London. Far more men were killed than was necessary to remove dangerous revolutionary leaders, and too few to deter future rebellions. Maxwell's policies provoked immediate and widespread outrage, and moderate nationalists joined with republicans in protest.

John Dillon had spent Easter Week trapped in his house near O'Connell Street, but once he could move about freely he was able to gauge the nature of public opinion in Dublin. He advised Redmond, who remained in London, that no-one should be killed for the present and that 'if there were shootings of prisoners on a large scale, the effect on public opinion throughout the Country might be disastrous in the extreme'. He had no doubt that the leaders would be court-martialled and executed, but he believed that others should not suffer the death penalty. A week later he warned that the Dublin working class

---

[27] Hobson, 'Statement given to Joseph McGarrity', 1934, p. 9, Hobson MSS, NLI, 13,171. After the rising Carson repeated his earlier suggestion that conscription should be extended to Ireland (*Hansard*, 82, cols. 490–4 (9 May 1916)).

was becoming extremely bitter, and that there was strong resentment even among those who had no sympathy with the rebels or the rising.[28]

Redmond met the prime minister after the first three prisoners had been shot, and he protested when he was told that a 'very few' more executions would be necessary.[29] At this stage Asquith seems to have confined himself to expressing surprise at the speed of the trials and sentences, and to asking that Lord French (the commander-in-chief of the home forces) should warn Maxwell 'not to give the impression that *all* the Sinn Feiners would suffer death'. French reassured him that it would be better to leave matters to the general's discretion.[30] In the House of Commons, Redmond begged the government not to show any undue severity to 'the great masses of those who are implicated, on whose shoulders there lies a guilt far different from that which lies upon the instigators and promoters of the outbreak'.[31] The next day he threatened implausibly that he would probably retire if any more shootings took place, but five days and six deaths later he was still party leader when Asquith told him of his hope that the executions would cease, 'unless in some quite exceptional case'.[32] Three days afterwards Connolly and MacDermott became the last victims of the firing squads.

Until then the pattern of what was later described as 'a dribble of executions'[33] had continued remorselessly, provoking rumour and dread throughout the country. One newspaper referred to the sickening thud which went through the heart of Ireland at the announcement of each new victim.[34] There were plans for even more thoroughgoing punishment. On 3 May Lord French wrote to Maxwell about Countess Markievicz that 'personally I agree with you – she ought to be shot',[35] and it is probable that her life was saved only by Asquith's express instruction that no women should be killed. (British propaganda had recently exploited the Germans' execution of Nurse Edith Cavell, thereby making it an embarrassing example to follow.) Ninety death sentences were imposed, although the great majority of them were reduced to terms of imprisonment.

The British response in May 1916 was relatively mild when compared with

---

[28] Dillon to Redmond, 30 Apr., 7 May 1916, JR, 15,182(22).

[29] Redmond, memo, 3 May 1916, JR, 15,165(6).

[30] French to Maxwell, 3 May 1916, describing his conversation with Asquith, EdeV.

[31] *Hansard*, 82, col. 137 (3 May 1916).

[32] Redmond, memo, 4 May 1916, JR, 15,165(6); Asquith to Redmond, 9 May 1916, *ibid.*

[33] J. A. Bryce, *Hansard*, 91, col. 496 (7 Mar. 1917).

[34] *Sligo Champion*, 20 May 1916, editorial.

[35] French to Maxwell, 3 May 1916, EdeV.

the repressive measures taken after the crushing of revolts in other major European cities. For example, after the defeat of the Paris Commune in 1871 (a far bloodier and more destructive rebellion than the Easter Rising) probably as many as 20,000 prisoners were shot.[36] After the Soviet Union suppressed the Hungarian revolt in 1956, 350 of the rebels were executed and 13,000 were sent to prison or labour camps; the prime minister and other leaders were imprisoned for nearly two years and were then hanged.[37] But such comparisons are cold statistics, and in 1916 people responded with warm emotions; rightly or wrongly, Irish nationalist opinion *perceived* British measures to be harsh and disproportionate.

Many people felt that the rebels were prisoners of war and should not have been executed after their surrender. Parallels were drawn with an insurrection in South Africa two years earlier, after which only one insurgent had been shot. Everyone remembered that Carson had planned armed defiance of the government, and had threatened to stage a rising comparable in some respects to that which the Easter rebels actually carried out. Yet until recently he had been attorney-general in the British cabinet. The rising was an undemocratic act carried out in defiance of the people's wishes, but (thanks largely to the Conservative party and the Ulster Volunteers) Irish trust in British democracy had been eroded long before Easter Week. Many people did not perceive themselves as belonging to a self-governing unit.[38]

Newspapers, police reports and private letters all convey an impression of anger and revulsion. In the course of his powerful speech in the House of Commons Dillon deplored the rebels' action but praised their courage; thereby he outraged Conservative backbenchers, and also General Maxwell who referred to 'that fiend Dillon'.[39] The bishop of Limerick became a national hero soon afterwards when he rejected Maxwell's request that he should discipline two politically outspoken priests in his diocese. In a letter which was circulated widely he denounced the general's actions as wantonly cruel and oppressive, declaring that 'personally I regard your action with horror, and I believe that it has outraged the conscience of the country'.[40] Possibly only interference in the bishop's control over the clergy of his diocese could have provoked such a

---

[36] Robert Tombs, *The war against Paris, 1871* (Cambridge, 1981), p. 191.

[37] György Litván, *The Hungarian revolution of 1956: reform, revolt and repression, 1953–1963* (London, 1996), pp. 141–3.

[38] Guy Chauvin, 'The Parliamentary Party and the revolutionary movement in Ireland, 1912–1918' (Ph.D. dissertation, Trinity College, Dublin, 1976), p. 451.

[39] Maxwell to John Mahaffy, 16 May 1916, Mahaffy MSS, TCDL, 2074.

[40] *Letters of the late Bishop O'Dwyer* (pamphlet, n.d.).

furious response. Some time later, in another letter, he referred to 'that brute Maxwell'.[41]

James Stephens wrote that Ireland 'was not with the revolution, but in a few months she will be, and her heart which was withering will be warmed by the knowledge that men have thought her worth dying for'.[42] In Cork a group of prominent home rulers issued an appeal for leniency, and soon even the Redmondite *Freeman's Journal* protested against a policy which seemed to be merely vindictive; its effect on public opinion was seen as disastrous, and 'sympathy is being aroused with the victims where nothing but indignant condemnation of their criminal enterprise previously existed'.[43] George Gavan Duffy reported that hundreds of Redmondites had veered around completely 'since the military atrocities began'.[44]

One obvious image recurred in comments and speeches: blood. The reaction to the executions was compared to watching a stream of blood coming from beneath a closed door, while Dillon warned the House of Commons that a river of blood was being let loose between Britain and Ireland, and that 'you are washing out our whole life work in a sea of blood'.[45] The Irish Party, which was later to be attacked by separatists because of its hostility to the rising, was criticized in some British circles on opposite grounds; one writer complained that it 'has constantly shown a greater anxiety to save the rebels from punishment than to condemn the rebellion', and he cited Anatole France's jibe that 'moderates always oppose violence moderately'.[46]

Some months later, Maurice Moore, commander of the Redmondite National Volunteers, wrote to Asquith and drew his attention to Machiavelli's advice to the Prince 'regarding the wise and unwise use of severities . . . as it applies so nearly to the present case'. The recommendation was that 'in the laying hold of a state, the Usurper ought to run over and execute all his cruelties at once so that he be not forced often to return to them . . . for his injuries should be done altogether, that being seldomer tasted, they might less offend.'[47] The prime minister did not follow this shrewd counsel, and shortly afterwards the government's earlier errors were compounded when Casement was hanged in London.

The Nationalist MP T. P. O'Connor warned Lloyd George that the executed

---

[41] O'Dwyer to Tipperary board of guardians, 23 June 1916, NLI, ILB. 300.P.3(72).

[42] Stephens, *Insurrection*, p. ix.   [43] *FJ*, 9 May 1916, editorial.

[44] Gavan Duffy to M. J. FitzGerald, 10 May 1916, GD, 5581.

[45] Elizabeth Countess of Fingall, *Seventy years young* (London, 1937), p. 375; *Hansard*, 82, col. 940 (11 May 1916).   [46] *Edinburgh Review*, July 1916, p. 116.

[47] Moore and Agnes O'Farrelly to Asquith, 21 July 1916, Moore MSS, NLI, 10,564(2) and (6).

leaders were already passing into legend as sober and pious martyrs, and that already the rebellion's legacy had taken on a semi-religious aspect in the form of requiem masses for the dead. One little girl was overheard in the street praying to 'St Pearse'.[48] Lloyd George informed Asquith that 'Sinn Feinism is for the moment right on top' and murmured about the need for more tact and restraint.[49] A few days later even Maxwell recognized that a change of feeling had set in. There was a new mood of sympathy with the rebels, many people wore the 'Sinn Féin mourning badge' of green and black ribbon, or photographs of the dead leaders, and 'they now think that Sinn Feinism and Irish patriotism are synonymous terms'.[50] The Irish taste for martyrolatry had been satisfied. A student in University College, Dublin, wrote enthusiastically to one of the prisoners in Stafford Jail 'you have all become great heroes now . . . You never saw such wholesale conversion. There are not half a dozen people in the College now who are not Sinn Féiners . . . You should see us all now sporting republican flags down Grafton Street.'[51] A few weeks later the RIC county inspector for West Cork warned that if the Irish Volunteers revived they would be four times as numerous as they had been before the rising, and Maurice Moore summed up neatly the change in opinion: 'a few unknown men shot in a barrack yard has embittered a whole nation'.[52]

The executions were accompanied by widespread arrests. Griffith and MacNeill were imprisoned, even though neither had joined in the rising and MacNeill had tried to stop it. It is said that when Griffith arrived at Wandsworth Jail he was greeted as the man who 'ad been a h-inciting of 'em', and this was not an unfair verdict.[53] Throughout May the authorities detained more than 3,400 suspects, and since a majority of them were released within a month their internment can have had little effect other than to provoke nation-wide resentment. Because these arrests impinged directly on many people's lives they may have been almost as important in alienating public opinion as were the firing squads in Kilmainham. In Dromcolliher a man who shouted 'up the Sinn Féiners' was arrested and conveyed to Limerick under military escort, while a Tipperary parish priest wrote to the *Irish Independent* complaining that

---

[48] T. P. O'Connor to Lloyd George, 13 June 1916, cited in F. S. L. Lyons, *John Dillon: a biography* (London, 1968), p. 394.   [49] Lloyd George to Asquith, 10 June 1916, LG, D/14/2/22.

[50] Maxwell, 'Report on the state of Ireland since the rebellion', 24 June 1916, Cab.37/150/18.

[51] Madge Callanan to James Ryan, 8 June 1916, Ryan MSS, UCDA, P88/19/1–2 (envelope addressed to 'James Ryan Esq, Irish patriot, Stafford').

[52] CI's report, W. Cork, June 1916, CO.904/100; *New Ireland*, 24 June 1916, p. 310.

[53] Darrell Figgis, *A chronicle of jails* (Dublin, 1917), p. 104.

another batch of worthy young citizens was arrested this morning, and they are being hurried off to prison as I write. If the authorities want to exasperate our peaceful and law-abiding people and leave wounds in their hearts that will take long to heal, they are going just the right way about it.[54]

Many of those who were rounded up had no sympathy with the rising, and in some cases they featured on out-of-date RIC lists because of a youthful radicalism which they had long outgrown. Asquith conceded that in some cases the police had acted with excessive zeal and without careful discrimination.[55] One detainee wrote to his mother that 'it is especially distressing to see a lot of those who were fighting escaping scot free and innocent men being kept a great deal longer in prison'.[56] Dillon complained that Mayo had been totally calm, yet after troops arrived in the county supporters of the Irish Party were arrested – thereby turning them into enemies of the government. He concluded that 'if Ireland were governed by men out of Bedlam you could not pursue a more insane policy'.[57] In October an indignant detainee (the brother of a Redmondite MP) wrote to the governor of Reading Jail claiming that no charge of law-breaking had been made against him since his arrest five months earlier, and that the authorities had never complained about his newspaper, the *Mayo News,* during his twenty-three years as proprietor.[58] The Easter Rising had been an explosion of urban violence; it was the British reaction which spread discontent into the countryside.[59]

The prisoners were soon regarded as folk heroes, and already within weeks of the rising sympathizers distributed petitions seeking a general amnesty for all the deportees; public opinion followed the precedents which had already been established after the insurrections of 1848 and 1867. At least some of the female students in University College, Dublin professed a romantic interest only in those male colleagues who had been imprisoned after the rising; 'the very least of us wouldn't be bothered with those that are left. An ordinary "beardless boy" has no attractions for us now.'[60] Within six weeks of the executions Maxwell complained of a demonstration in Dublin which had followed requiem masses for the rebel leaders. Congregations joined up spontaneously until eventually they formed 'a procession of perhaps 2,000 people marching

---

[54] *Limerick Leader,* 15 May 1916; *II,* 18 May 1916.

[55] Asquith, memo, 19 May 1916, Cab.37/148/13.

[56] Seamus Fitzgerald to Alice Fitzgerald, 10 June 1916, Fitzgerald MSS, CAI, PR6/11.

[57] *Hansard,* 82, col. 939 (11 May 1916).

[58] P. J. Doris to governor, Reading Jail, 17 Oct. 1916, Christina Doyle MSS, NLI, 5816.

[59] Chauvin, 'Parliamentary Party', p. 160.

[60] 'Margaret' to James Ryan, n.d. [summer 1916], Ryan MSS, UCDA, P88/23.

along the Quays and streets waving Sinn Fein flags, booing at officers, and sol-diers'.[61] At the same time James Campbell (the Unionist Irish attorney general) reported that when some of the released men had landed in Dublin, dressed in the rebel uniforms which they had worn in Easter Week, they were received by cheering and exulting crowds.[62] In South Tipperary a group of returning pris-oners was welcomed by a band and a crowd of between three and four hundred.[63] In Clare it was soon noted that disloyalty increased after the prison-ers were freed, and the RIC inspector general observed that

> the release of so many of the interned rebels instead of exciting gratitude appears to stimulate resentment. These men generally appear unsubdued by internment, and their release is by ignorant country folk regarded as a proof that they were interned without any just cause, and that the police who arrested them in pursuance of orders acted vindictively.[64]

Similar reports were made from other counties. A Cork Sinn Féiner noted in his diary that, at a time of martial law, censorship and the prohibition of public meetings, 'it is remarkable how much is being said despite all efforts at sup-pression'.[65] From June onwards the Jesuit journal *Studies* published a series of articles on 'Poets of the Insurrection'. A month later the *Catholic Bulletin* began printing monthly profiles of the dead rebels under the heading 'Events of Easter Week'; these accompanied features such as 'Notes from Rome' and a series (by Fr Tom Burbage, a Republican priest soon to be prominent in Sinn Féin) on 'Ritual Murder among the Jews'. Leaflets, ballads, and photographs of the rebel leaders were distributed widely, and police reports from various parts of the country revealed an increasing tendency to wear 'mourning badges'. These became talismans, and they were central to the iconography of the Irish revolu-tion.

The people were provided with constant reminders of the rebellion and of those connected with it. Like the executions, the arrests took place over an extended time-span; the inquest on civilians killed in North King Street drew attention to the actions of undisciplined British soldiers; Eoin MacNeill was not sentenced to life imprisonment until a month after the end of the rising; the Hardinge commission's report on the rebellion, which was heavily critical of the Dublin Castle administration, was published on 3 July; Casement was executed a month later; and the investigation into the murder of the pacifist Francis

---

[61] Maxwell to Asquith, 17 June 1916, HHA, 37(52); also Maxwell to Archbishop Walsh, 19 June 1916, AW, 385/5.   [62] Campbell, memo, 19 June 1916, Cab.37/150/4.

[63] CI's report, S. Tipperary, July 1916, CO.904/100.   [64] IG's report, Sept. 1916, CO.904/101.

[65] De Róiste, diary, 25 June 1916, CAI, U271/A/19A.

Sheehy-Skeffington by a deranged British officer began only at the end of August. Martial law was ineffective and even inoperative, but it was maintained (at least in theory) until the end of the year.[66] Dillon wrote to Lloyd George that the government's policy in Ireland was 'irritating the people to such a state of madness that our influence over them will be wiped out', while T. M. Healy remarked that British measures had aroused a contempt and dislike for which there was no recent parallel. Already small boys were singing 'Who fears to speak of Easter Week'.[67] W. B. Yeats, protesting at Casement's impending execution, warned that 'the evil has been done, it cannot be undone, but it need not be aggravated weeks afterwards with every circumstance of deliberation'.[68] Casement was hanged, and nationalist impressions of British vindictiveness seemed to be confirmed.

The death of home rule

The government's one positive and constructive move after the rising was its renewed effort to bring about a home rule settlement, but the negotiations which followed soon collapsed in bitterness and disillusionment. Not only did they ruin what little remained of British credibility in nationalist Ireland, but they also undermined the reputation of the Irish Parliamentary Party. At one stage it seemed as if they might even bring about the collapse of the Liberal–Conservative coalition.

On 25 May Asquith admitted to the House of Commons that the system under which the country had been governed had broken down, and he expressed the hope that the rebellion would provide a unique opportunity to solve the Irish question.[69] The resulting home rule conversations of summer 1916 were an attempt to exploit these supposedly favourable circumstances, and to provide the country with an alternative system of government which would be acceptable to all sides. Lloyd George was given the task of mediating between Nationalists and Unionists.

The negotiations were also an effort to bolster the Redmondites against the appeal of revolutionary republicanism before it was too late, and before the

---

[66] Townshend, *Political violence in Ireland*, pp. 309–13; D. G. Boyce and Cameron Hazelhurst, 'The unknown chief secretary: H. E. Duke and Ireland, 1916–18', *IHS*, 20, 79 (1977), pp. 296–7.

[67] Dillon to Lloyd George, 11 June 1916, LG, D/14/2/25; Healy to Maurice Healy, 10 June 1916, Callanan, *T. M. Healy*, p. 518.

[68] Yeats to Asquith, 14 July 1916, NLI, MS 10,564(1). This letter is not to be found in the Asquith papers.   [69] *Hansard*, 82, cols. 2,309–10 (25 May 1916).

moderates' position had been weakened irreparably. While he watched the fighting on Easter Monday the Irish solicitor general remarked that 'the man I am sorry for is John Redmond',[70] and it was widely recognized that the principal victim of the rising was constitutional nationalism. An army officer writing from the Kildare Street Club towards the end of May observed that Maxwell had succeeded where the Ulster unionists had failed: he had 'shaken the foundations of all Mr. Redmond's loyal work in Ireland and made potential rebels of a whole population, 75% of whom were as loyal as himself as lately as last Easter Sunday'.[71]

Lloyd George took advantage of the Nationalists' weakness. He pressurized the Irish Party, telling Dillon that 'unless the settlement goes through quickly, nothing can be accomplished until the war is over. Heaven knows what will happen then! . . . Great opportunities once lost are rarely recovered, either by men or nations.'[72] One of their colleagues reported the opinion of Redmond, Joe Devlin and others that 'without reaching an arrangement now the Irish Party is dead',[73] but Dillon was rightly sceptical and he did not believe that any workable arrangement was possible. A Conservative critic remarked scathingly that the Nationalists were 'to be imposed on Ireland by the British Parliament and every one knows that one of the reasons for that course is that they would have little hope of being returned to power by the Irish electorate'.[74]

The Redmondites hoped that agreement might now be reached on a speedy implementation of home rule, which had been on the statute book since September 1914. It had been postponed for the duration of the war, at a time when almost everyone assumed that the fighting would end within a few months. All sides agreed to Asquith's request that they should preserve a discreet silence and refrain from the use of any language which might lessen the chances of a settlement.[75] The result was that the Nationalists were muzzled for the crucial two months between 25 May and 24 July, unable to protest against government measures in ways which would have been in tune with Irish nationalist sentiment. By remaining mute at a time of fluid and malleable public opinion the party deprived itself of opportunities which would never recur.

Redmond and his colleagues committed themselves whole-heartedly to this venture, seeing in it their last chance of gaining home rule, of redeeming their tattered reputations, and of redirecting Irish politics along a constitutional

---

[70] Ó Broin, *Dublin Castle*, p. 94.   [71] Gerald Dease to T. P. Gill, 26 May 1916, NLI, MS 13,488(10).

[72] Lloyd George to Dillon, 10 June 1916, JD, 6796.

[73] T. P. O'Connor to Dillon, 18 May 1916, JD, 6741.

[74] Lord Hugh Cecil, memo, 26 June 1916, Cab.37/150/21.

[75] *Hansard*, 82, col. 2,311 (25 May 1916).

path. They were so anxious to ensure the prompt implementation of home rule that they were prepared to accept the exclusion of Fermanagh and Tyrone from the area which would be administered by a Dublin government. The nationalist majorities in these counties were now forgotten, along with the battles which had been fought to save them from minority unionist control during the negotiations of 1914.

Asquith wished to minimize the risk of new face-to-face confrontations such as those which had taken place two years earlier, and he told the cabinet that a home rule act would not come into effect until after the war. Lloyd George went beyond his brief and commenced discussions on the basis that it would be implemented in the near future.[76] He held separate meetings with Nationalists and Unionists, in the course of which he made apparently contradictory statements to both sides. The Parliamentary Party was convinced that the exclusion of six counties would be merely temporary, while the Unionists believed they were promised that 'at the end of the provisional period Ulster does not, whether she will it or not, merge in the rest of Ireland'.[77] Lloyd George's assurances to Redmond were verbal, while Carson was given a written undertaking.

A. J. Balfour, a former chief secretary and prime minister (and also a resolute opponent of Irish nationalism), recommended acceptance of the proposals on the grounds that they could be seen as a triumph for the unionists. The exclusion of six counties had been their maximum demand at the Buckingham Palace conference in July 1914, and he doubted whether, if a settlement were to be postponed until the end of the war, 'terms equally good could be obtained without a dangerous struggle'.[78] On the other hand, the UIL national directory accepted 'the proposals of Mr. Lloyd George for the temporary and provisional settlement of the Irish difficulty'.[79] James Campbell warned that 'one side or the other is going to be deceived in this matter, with the inevitable consequence of bitter recrimination and renewed agitation'.[80]

Even the temporary exclusion of most of Ulster, an element of the package deal which the Parliamentary Party believed it had been offered, was resented deeply by nationalists in the province. There was widespread unease throughout the country, while in Derry, Tyrone and Fermanagh, the three counties

---

[76] David Savage, 'The attempted home rule settlement of 1916', *Éire-Ireland*, 2, 3 (1967), p. 136; Kendle, *Walter Long*, pp. 96–9.

[77] Ian Colvin, *The life of Lord Carson*, III (London, 1936), p. 166. Years later Carson embarrassed Lloyd George by publishing the letter in which he had made this remark (*Times*, 3 Oct. 1924).

[78] Balfour, memo, 24 June 1916, Cab.37/150/17.

[79] UIL national directory minute book, 3 July 1916, NLI, MS 708.

[80] Campbell, memo, 19 June 1916, Cab.37/150/4.

which would be affected most directly, the question of exclusion from the home rule area replaced the rising as the main issue in discussion and debate. An east–west division emerged. Nationalists in the four counties which had already been scheduled for separation from the rest of Ireland in 1914 viewed the project more phlegmatically than those in the west, where there was a nationalist majority.[81] The trade unions fought against the scheme, while the *Irish Independent*, the newspaper with the largest circulation in Ireland, threw its weight against 'dismemberment'.

Opposition to the plan was led by the Catholic Church. Cardinal Logue pronounced that 'it would be infinitely better to remain as we are for 50 years to come, under English rule, than to accept these proposals'.[82] When Joe Devlin, the dominant figure among northern nationalists, visited the Ulster bishops he received little comfort from them. MacRory of Down and Connor would not accept the offer; McHugh of Derry rejected it contemptuously, described it as 'rot', and was prepared to go no further than the 1914 scheme of county plebiscites; and even though O'Donnell of Raphoe (one of the party's treasurers) was anxious to endorse the agreement, he concluded nonetheless that he could not do so and that county referenda were 'rational, democratic and defensible, but the present proposals were not'. Devlin warned that the only support was likely to come from Belfast, and that a conference would reject the scheme.[83] Members of the clergy organized anti-exclusion meetings and attacked the settlement when speaking to their parishioners after mass. Dillon wrote to T. P. O'Connor that 'the priests are working hard in Ulster. I hear they are at work all day long.'[84]

A convention was summoned in Belfast to represent Nationalists from the six counties which would be excluded from the home rule area. The meeting included one priest from every parish, all Nationalist members of elected bodies, and delegates from the UIL and AOH executives. The party leadership overcame the formidable opposition which it faced from its own followers; Fermanagh and Tyrone voted against the scheme, Derry was almost evenly divided, but support from the other three counties (Antrim, Down and Armagh) resulted in a large overall majority of 475 to 265. Opponents claimed later that the meeting was unrepresentative and that the tactics used, including a threat of Redmond's resignation, had been unfair.

On the other side of the Ulster divide the unionist population mourned the devastating losses which its division suffered at the battle of the Somme. At least 2,000 men were killed on the first day, more than died in all Irish political

---

[81] Eamon Phoenix, *Northern nationalism: nationalist politics, partition and the Catholic minority in Northern Ireland, 1890–1940* (Belfast, 1994), pp. 28–9, 35.   [82] *II*, 21 June 1916.

[83] Devlin to Redmond, 3 June 1916, JR, 15,181.   [84] Dillon to O'Connor, 19 June 1916, JD, 6741.

violence between 1916 and 1921. This sacrifice for the United Kingdom and the empire contrasted with what was seen widely as the renewed disloyalty of Irish nationalists.

Time passed and it seemed as if the home rule negotiations were making no progress. For the last time, southern unionists played an important role in British politics, and they launched a formidable attack on a scheme which Lord Lansdowne described (not unfairly) as 'a concession to rebellion'.[85] The Ulster unionists were satisfied at having ensured the permanent exclusion of six counties, but by 1916 their southern counterparts were even more horrified at the prospect of submission to the rule of a Dublin parliament than they had been before the war. Then they had dreaded control by Redmondites, while now they had to fear the prospect of an even more terrifying master: republican rebels. They schemed to wreck the proposed agreement. It became clear that if the plan were to be implemented it would provoke a political crisis in London and resignations from the cabinet. This would be far too high a price to pay for a dubious solution of the Irish question. As the difficulties and dangers became more apparent Asquith lost interest in settling his Irish problems, and he concentrated on saving his government. The delays which so frustrated Redmond and damaged his party were a source of satisfaction in Downing Street; they 'obviated premature and precipitate decisions' and helped ensure that, in the end, only one minister resigned.[86]

The Irish Party leaders gained nothing in return for antagonizing many of their followers. Lansdowne and his ally Walter Long succeeded in extracting further important concessions from the cabinet and in altering the terms of the settlement: not only would partition be made permanent (or, at least, it could not be ended without a new act of parliament), but future Irish representation in Westminster would also be diminished. When these terms were confirmed by the cabinet on 22 July the negotiations collapsed at once. Redmond declared in the House of Commons that the government ministers had 'disregarded every advice we tendered to them, and now in the end, having got us to induce our people to make a tremendous sacrifice and to agree to the temporary exclusion of six Ulster counties, they throw this agreement to the winds'.[87] The situation was almost exactly that which Dillon had hoped to avoid when he wrote to Redmond immediately after the rising, 'I would *far rather* face a frankly Tory Government – than be dragged after a hybrid Government for whose action you would be held responsible without having the power to control their proceedings.'[88]

In its pursuit of a home rule settlement the party had alienated many of its

---

[85] Asquith to George V, 27 June 1916, Cab.37/150/23.

[86] Asquith to George V, 5 July 1916, Cab.41/37/25.   [87] *Hansard*, 84, col. 1,434 (24 July 1916).

[88] Dillon to Redmond, 2 May 1916, JR, 15,182(22).

own followers; its reward was to be fooled and humiliated. Redmond berated British ministers for having deceived him, but many nationalists were inclined to despise him for having trusted them in the first place. The more he and his colleagues attacked the government's duplicity, the more they were derided for their own gullibility.

The policy of compromise had been gravely damaged. The republicans acquired much of the credit for reviving the prospects of home rule, and the Parliamentary Party was blamed for their collapse. While the negotiations were still in progress Maxwell reported that 'there is a growing feeling that out of Rebellion more has been got than by constitutional methods hence Mr Redmond's power is on the wane'.[89] The party's enemies rejoiced at its failure. Michael Collins, one of the interned rebels, wrote that he was 'in good form over the smashing of the HR proposals. Anything but a divided Ireland.'[90] In a similar mood Griffith described how he and his fellow-prisoners in Reading Jail 'buried the Partition Bill the other night with all solemnity, and a funeral address in Irish was delivered'. He believed that 'this partition plot will tend to unite those whom it was meant to further divide'.[91]

The *débâcle* of the home rule negotiations in the summer of 1916 had important long-term effects. The republicans had seized the initiative in Easter Week, but they were less well placed to revive their fortunes in the aftermath of their rebellion than was the Parliamentary Party. Its leadership and organization remained battered but intact, it still had considerable financial resources, and it could rely on press support. Yet it did nothing during the months in which it had the field to itself, before it had to face the separatist revival which began in early 1917. The party seemed content to let things drift. It held virtually no meetings, its leaders made few speeches (Redmond did not address a political gathering until October), and it attempted no reorganization until the end of the year. Martial law restrictions did not in themselves provide an adequate explanation for such torpor. Subscriptions fell sharply, those noted by the police dropping from £1,127 in the quarter ending in March 1916 to £674 in the quarter ending in June. They never recovered.[92] The UIL national directory, having endorsed the agreement on 3 July, did not convene again for another twenty-one months, until the conscription crisis in 1918.[93]

---

[89] Maxwell, memo, 16 June 1916, HHA, 42(152).

[90] Collins to Susan Killeen, 27 July 1916, cited in Tim Pat Coogan, *Michael Collins: a biography* (London, 1990), p. 52.   [91] Griffith to Lily Williams, n.d. and (?) 5 Aug. 1916, NLI, MS 5943.

[92] 'United Irish League meetings', CO.904/20/2.

[93] UIL national directory minute book, NLI, MS 708. (After the record of this final meeting on 30 Apr. 1918 the only other entry consists of two pages listing racehorses with names such as 'Mount Etna', 'Helter Skelter', 'Dwarf of the Forest' and 'Galloper King'.)

The party's morale was shattered, and as late as December the RIC inspector general was able to write that 'they have not got over the feeling of distrust occasioned by the failure of the Home Rule Conversations'.[94] It was as if the Nationalists had put all their efforts into this last attempt to win home rule, and when it failed they had nothing more to offer, they were left without a policy or a *raison d'être*. Redmond's own demoralization was particularly acute. When Walter Long and Lord Lansdowne killed the last serious chance of home rule they also killed the spirit and the will-power of the Irish Party.

The fate of the Redmondite National Volunteers reinforced this disillusionment. During the rising many of its members had offered their services to the crown forces and had lent some of their weapons to the army and police. These were not returned, and their commander complained to Maxwell that his men 'will not consider that they are well rewarded for their loyalty during the rebellion by being practically suppressed afterwards'.[95] Eventually some of them drifted into the waiting arms of their rivals, the Irish Volunteers.

Soon afterwards the party experienced another symbolic reverse when the House of Commons voted by 178 to 54 to harmonize Irish clocks with those in the rest of the United Kingdom; until then they had been twenty-five minutes behind Greenwich mean time. Dillon's protest that this difference 'reminds us that we are coming into a strange country' may not have helped his case, and, rightly or wrongly, Carson was blamed for this last conquest of Ireland.[96] Literally as well as metaphorically, the times were changing.

The Irish Nation League

Throughout the summer of 1916 short-lived attempts were made to exploit the home rulers' uncertainty and disillusion. These included the emergence and disappearance of dissident groups such as the 'Irish Ireland League' and the 'Repeal League'. One of the policies put forward by the latter was the coronation of Princess Mary, George V's daughter, as queen of Ireland in her own right.[97] A more significant indication of disarray was the formation of the Irish Nation League, a breakaway party which won support in those parts of nationalist Ulster which were to be excluded from the home rule area. Its history is no more than a minor theme, but the League's brief career illuminates both the decline of the Redmondites and the growth of the separatist movement. It

---

[94] IG's report, Dec. 1916, CO.904/101.

[95] Maurice Moore to Maxwell, 7 July 1916, NLI, MS 10,561(29).

[96] *Hansard*, 85, cols. 72–4, 2,227–8 (1, 17 Aug. 1916).   [97] *Irish Nation*, 30 Sept. 1916.

began as the only organized opposition to the partition clauses in the home rule negotiations, and it developed first as yet another schismatic Nationalist group, and then as a distinct party, until at last it was absorbed painlessly by Sinn Féin.

At a protest meeting in Derry on 20 July an organizing committee was formed to rally northern nationalists against the exclusion of the 'six counties'. The resulting Anti-Partition League spread rapidly throughout Derry, Tyrone and Fermanagh, even though the plans for partition collapsed only days after it was founded. Within a fortnight its name was changed to the 'Irish Nation League' and its objectives were widened to reflect the priorities of nationalists in other parts of the country. The new party did not want full separation from Britain, but it saw itself as a revived, purified and reinvigorated Parliamentary Party which might succeed where the Redmondites had failed. One of its members, Kevin O'Shiel, declared repeatedly that the League's aim was to give constitutionalism a last chance.[98] It soon established close contacts with the maverick MP Laurence Ginnell and with William O'Brien's All-For-Ireland League, a parliamentary faction centred on Co. Cork. Thereby it indicated the extent to which party members still viewed Irish politics within the framework of Westminster. Except for its absolute hostility to conscription and partition the party's aims were expressed in vague and uncontentious terms – such as 'to preserve and cherish the National ideals . . . to cultivate patriotism and good citizenship . . . to develop the natural resources of the country'.[99] At one of its meetings in Belfast a radical audience was disappointed by the mildness of the speeches.[100]

After an initial breakthrough in July and August 1916 the League lost its momentum and began a long period of stagnation; twenty-nine new clubs noticed by the police were formed in July and August, fourteen in September and only two in October.[101] It lacked the energy of other groups which emerged at the same time or shortly afterwards, and it did not fulfil the early hopes that it would become 'a vast national movement having its educational, economic, literary, and social sides'.[102] It was amateurish and had no organizers; its centre was not Dublin or any large town, but Omagh in Co. Tyrone; it waited nearly two months, until 10 September, before holding a meeting outside Ulster (although this gathering in the Phoenix Park was the first demonstration held in Dublin since the rising); it was unable to escape its origins as an anti-partition protest; and it was heavily influenced by the clergy. The League's dependence on support from the bishop of Derry is indicated by the fact that its only progress in Donegal

---

[98] *New Ireland*, 23 Sept. 1916.   [99] *II*, 4 Aug. 1916.   [100] IO's report (N.), Sept. 1916.

[101] IG's reports, Aug., Oct. 1916, CO.904/100–1.

[102] Kevin O'Shiel, *The rise of the Irish Nation League* (pamphlet, n.d. [1916]), p. 8.

was in the Inishowen peninsula, which came under his jurisdiction. The rest of the county formed the diocese of Raphoe, whose bishop's continuing loyalty to Redmond was widely shared or followed by his flock.[103]

The Nation League further weakened the UIL by drawing away some of the more active members who might have helped the party adapt to the new circumstances created by the rising. Yet it was more than a mere negative force. The League not only provided leaders and organizers who helped the separatists win the crucial Roscommon by-election in February 1917, but it also eased the path of many others who would have found the transition from the Parliamentary Party to Sinn Féin too drastic to be taken at one step. For example, *New Ireland* was a Redmondite paper which had supported the home rule negotiations in 1916, but it switched its support to the Nation League and from there graduated to full-blooded republicanism. One separatist priest saw the party as a form of purgatory, 'a place or state of punishment, where some Parliamentarians suffered for a time before they joined Sinn Féin'.[104] The League gathered together some of the more dynamic or idealistic elements in the constitutional movement and lured them gently towards the radicals until finally, swept along by the changes in public opinion, the party merged fully with the new Sinn Féin in September 1917.[105]

Prisoners and their comforters

The separatist movement was still battered and disorganized in late summer and autumn 1916, months when the Nation League was cautiously testing the waters. Almost all its prominent figures who survived the rising and the executions were either jailed or interned. As the republican Mary MacSwiney remarked, 'there is not a leader left . . . all the real brains of the organisation are dead or locked up'.[106] Those who had been most active in Easter Week were dispersed throughout several different prisons before being gathered together in Lewes Jail in Sussex. Griffith and others were sent to Reading Jail, and sooner or later most of the internees who were detained for a lengthy term were sent to Frongoch prisoner-of-war camp in North Wales. Many of these were soon discharged when the British authorities appreciated the excessive scale of the arrests. Over 800 had already been freed by mid-May, at a time when others were still being rounded up; by late July about 50 were released from Frongoch every

---

[103] CI's report, Donegal, Aug. 1916, CO.904/100.   [104] *II*, 15 Oct. 1917.

[105] For an assessment of the Nation League's impact, see Phoenix, *Northern nationalism*, pp. 43–5.

[106] MacSwiney to Peter MacSwiney, n.d. [June 1916], O'Brien and Ryan, *Devoy's post bag*, II, p. 493.

day; and a month later the total number of internees in the camp had fallen to 548.[107] A hard core remained until Christmas.

The detention of the most active radical leaders left a gap which could not be filled, but in the long run it was to be of enormous benefit to the separatist cause. During the months which the prisoners and internees were obliged to spend in each other's company their political beliefs were strengthened and they acquired a new sense of comradeship. Dedicated revolutionaries could not yet inspire nationalist Ireland with their ideas and enthusiasms, but they could at least inspire or instruct their fellow-detainees. The writer Darrell Figgis, who had been imprisoned in Reading, remarked later that it was 'extraordinary to think with what care men were brought from all over the country (many of whom began by disagreeing earnestly with the Rising) to receive one pattern of thought and to know one another and to learn of one another'.[108] The prisoners and internees acquired the habit of working together, and they elected representatives who were responsible to the British authorities for their conduct. A new national leadership emerged during these months; Michael Collins revived the IRB in Frongoch, while Eamon de Valera was the undisputed spokesman of the prisoners in Lewes Jail.

Eoin MacNeill was able to send a positive report of the routine in Lewes:

> I have plenty of interesting chats with fellow prisoners. De Valera enjoys scientific matters. Cosgrave is as much interested in the housing of the working classes as if he were at home in Dublin. FitzGerald talks about literature . . . With others I discuss matters of education. Every morning at exercise I have a small class of two or three in Irish language or Irish History; peripatetics in earnest are we. Nearly all the men form into small classes at the morning exercise, those who can teach the others. In cells most of us study, and in fact for part of the time prison becomes a sort of school.[109]

Not all the detainees' activities were so earnest. One of their pastimes in Reading was writing ballads, which led Ernest Blythe to protest

> To Reading Gaol I have been sent
> And must endure the punishment
> That every bloke is writing rhyme
> And I must praise it every time.[110]

---

[107] P. J. Earley to Mrs Bartels, 24 July 1916, Kate Kelly MSS, NLI, 8411; John J. Neeson to Mary MacSwiney, 15 Aug. 1916, O'Brien MSS, NLI, 8434.

[108] Darrell Figgis, *Recollections of the Irish War* (London, 1927), p. 168.

[109] MacNeill to Margaret MacNeill, 26 Mar. 1917, MacN, LA1/G/150.

[110] J. J. O'Connell, prison notebook, NLI, MS 19,924. Later Desmond Ryan asked 'God forgive us for all the poetry we wrote when under key' (*Remembering Sion*, p. 219).

Some internees needed to be warned against the temptations which were available in Frongoch, and one of their number wrote in shocked tones that 'if the report once got abroad that the Irish Prisoners of War were squandering . . . money in vicious gambling, an awful scandal would be cast upon all that which we hold most dear'.[111] In later months some even looked back fondly on the comradeship of the camp, and one released prisoner wrote to a former colleague that 'like yourself I could do with a spell of Frongoch just now. Office work is not as nice as the fatigues.' In similar fashion, when Collins was informed that some of the freed internees were still unemployed after they had returned to Ireland he suggested that they might be as well-off had they remained in Frongoch.[112]

As long as they were detained in Britain they were the objects of widespread sympathy. Agitation for their release mounted until eventually the government concluded, wrongly, that they were more dangerous in Frongoch than they would be in Ireland. At Christmas 1916 all except the court-martialled Easter Week prisoners were freed, and it was these newly released men who provided the impetus and leadership for the Sinn Féin revival of 1917.

Throughout the grim aftermath of the rising most of the prisoners and internees were able to retain their ideals and their sense of cohesion. This was facilitated by the efforts of charitable organizations which helped look after their own needs and those of their dependants in Ireland. The Volunteers had organized an insurance scheme long before the rising, and any contributor who was dismissed from his employment as a result of his Volunteering activities could draw up to £2 per week for at least three months.[113] (This was not an original idea, and a decade earlier the Dungannon clubs had devised a contributory insurance fund which would compensate its members for any arrest and imprisonment resulting from their membership.[114] The Ulster Volunteers acted in a similar fashion, and comparable schemes were a feature of many trade unions.)

The rebel leaders did not wish to impose on their families the martyrdom which they were prepared to risk for themselves, and they made their own financial arrangements shortly before Easter Week. They established a Volunteer Dependants' Fund which was managed by separatists, in particular by the wives and widows of imprisoned or executed rebels. It was hardly sur-

---

[111] W. J. Brennan-Whitmore to staff officer, no. II room, *c.* 30 June 1916, MacCurtain MSS, Cork Public Museum, L1966:186.

[112] [Illegible] to Seamus Fitzgerald, n.d., Fitzgerald MSS, CAI, PR6/16; Collins to James Ryan, 23 Aug. 1916, Ryan MSS, UCDA, P88/34.   [113] *Irish Volunteer*, 3 Apr. 1915.

[114] 'A system of insurance against the interference of the English government with the liberty of Irishmen', n.d., McG, 17,612.

prising that women were prominent in a charitable organization, and, when Collins was later appointed secretary seven of the twenty-two executive members present at the interview were women.[115] One of its members wrote shortly afterwards that 'the Leaders handed over to us any Funds they had on hand with instructions as to its disposal. We were therefore actively at work relieving distress even during Easter week, and have continued to do so since . . . in 3 weeks over £500 had been distributed.'[116] Kathleen Clarke claimed later that she had been left £3,000 by her husband and his colleagues.[117]

The National Aid Society, a more widely based organization, soon surpassed the Volunteer Dependants' Fund in the scale of its activities, and yet another body, the National Relief Fund, was founded in London before the rebels surrendered. Before the two Irish groups merged in August 1916 the National Aid Society's disbursements totalled £9,675 and those of the Volunteer Dependants' Fund came to £5,279.[118] The widespread arrests after Easter Week ensured that there would be a heavy demand on the society's resources, but money was plentiful and contributions poured in from every quarter, from unionists and home rulers as well as from republicans. They ranged in value from sixpenny offerings at the door-to-door collections which were made throughout the country to substantial cheques from sympathizers in America; £3,000 was sent from Melbourne, while John Murphy of Buffalo, who was instrumental in amalgamating the two Irish relief societies in early August, presented a cheque for £5,000.[119]

By the autumn the society's expenditure averaged between £1,200–£1,400 per week. Its commitments changed with circumstances; for example, when the last batch of Frongoch internees was released, and needed unemployment assistance, it was obliged to curtail its grants to those who had already been freed. There were some internal tensions, illustrated by a remark made about Kathleen Clarke, one of the society's founding members: 'some of them say "she thinks she is Kathleen ni Houlihan"'.[120] But initial problems were soon overcome and the society was managed in a businesslike fashion. Prison visits were arranged, and provision was made for the rebels' dependants; in August 1917 a sum of £20,000 was invested to provide for the families of seventy-eight Volunteers who

---

[115] Minutes, 13 Feb. 1917, NLI, MS 23,469.

[116] Sorcha MacMahon to Art O'Brien, 30 June 1916, NLI, MS 8435, letter 258.

[117] Clarke, *Revolutionary woman*, p. 132.

[118] Minutes, 22, 29 Aug. 1916, NLI, MS 23,469. These were significant amounts; £1 at the end of the First World War would probably be worth over £40 by the end of the twentieth century.

[119] IG's report, July 1916, CO.904/100.

[120] J. F. X. O'Brien, memo on discussion with Michael Davitt Jr, 7 May 1917, NLI, MS 13,477.

had been killed in the rising. In the course of the next three years the executive held 110 meetings and its expenditure totalled £138,000.[121] The auditing of accounts seems to have been managed as efficiently as the charitable work itself.

From the local police to the highest officials in Dublin Castle, the British administration watched the society's activities with fascinated suspicion. Henry Duke, the chief secretary, gave orders to the police to 'keep note of any information bearing on the origin and use of their funds, and to ascertain if possible whether they are being used for charity or for purposes of the Sinn Fein agitation'.[122] Accusations were made that resources were misapplied to promote political objectives, but no evidence of this was ever produced. Legal action was taken against the *Longford Leader* in response to its claim that money had been diverted from its proper destination, and the paper published a retraction.

But the British were right in seeing the society as a threat, even if they did so for the wrong reasons. It might not have provided the separatists with direct financial assistance, but it nonetheless assisted their revival. It helped maintain their morale, and it did much to keep together people who might otherwise have drifted away from the movement. It established a vital link between the old and the new phases or forms of Irish separatism. And, like the GAA and the Gaelic League, it provided cover for the radicals' activities. To take only the most obvious such example, in mid-February 1917 Michael Collins was appointed general secretary to the society, an office which he retained until he went on the run during the conscription crisis fifteen months later. He carried out his duties with characteristic efficiency, but he was able to exploit all the contacts he made in his new post for other purposes, such as reviving the IRB.

This charitable organization showed more drive and energy than any other separatist element in the second half of 1916; it had no counterpart among military or political groups, if only because these had been repressed by the British authorities and their leading figures interned or killed. But one other faction showed some feeble flickers of life towards the end of the year: Arthur Griffith's Sinn Féin party.

Sinn Féin without Griffith

The fact that first the Volunteers and then the Easter Rising were given the sobriquet 'Sinn Féin' was one of the principal reasons for the party's importance in later years. Even though many of the Volunteers themselves loathed and

---

[121] 'Report of the Irish National Aid and Volunteer Dependents' Fund', *Catholic Bulletin*, Aug. 1919, p. 436.   [122] Duke, minute, 29 June 1917, 'Sinn Fein funds', CO.904/23/6.

resented the name, it tended to be applied loosely and it could be difficult to avoid; as early as 1909 it had been used of the Transport Union, which was led by Griffith's *bête noire*, Jim Larkin.[123] Eoin MacNeill could declare bluntly that 'every man who stands for Ireland in preference to any other country, to any empire or to any combination of empires . . . is a Sinn Féiner'.[124] At the beginning of the Great War one of Griffith's supporters wrote, 'there is no organised party. Yet, Sinn Féin is much in the mouths of the Parliamentarians. Every Irish nationalist who is not of Redmond's party or O'Brien's party is dubbed a "Sinn Féiner" or a "Pro-German".'[125] Years later James Stephens suggested that, when the Parliamentary Party tried to take over the Volunteers in 1914,

> in order to discredit those who did not surrender, Mr. Redmond called them Sinn Féiners . . . by forcibly and in terms of contempt identifying the Volunteers with Sinn Féin Mr. Redmond did more for Mr. Griffith's organisation in one year than Sinn Féin could have accomplished in several years. It was a case again of one's battle being won by one's enemy.[126]

The independent nationalist MP Laurence Ginnell claimed in the House of Commons that this was done to discredit the Volunteers, and that the name was a term of opprobrium used for reasons 'corresponding to that which impels the people and the Press of this country [Britain] to call the Germans Huns'.[127] But not all separatists were so strict in rejecting the nomenclature, and (like counterparts at other times and in other places) many of them were prepared to adopt a name assigned by their enemy. Three of Count Plunkett's sons had fought in the rising, so he might be expected to use precise terminology, yet when he wrote to Asquith in June 1916 he referred to 'the Sinn Féin volunteers'.[128] Kathleen Clarke and other women prisoners taken to Dublin Castle described themselves as 'Sinn Féiners', even though she had reservations about the term.[129] One of James Ryan's undergraduate admirers wrote to him during his imprisonment requesting some of the 'Sinn Féin buttons' from his Volunteer uniform as souvenirs.[130] The purists might fret, but within a short time friend and foe alike referred to the insurrection as the 'Sinn Féin Rising'.

Griffith's party acquired an unearned prestige simply because it was the only

---

[123] Henry Patterson, *Class conflict and sectarianism: the Protestant working class and the Belfast labour movement, 1868–1920* (Belfast, 1980), p. 77.

[124] MacNeill, *Daniel O'Connell and Sinn Féin*, p. 5.

[125] De Róiste, diary, 30 Dec. 1914, CAI, U271/A/16.   [126] *Separatist*, 3 June 1922.

[127] *Hansard*, 82, col. 966 (11 May 1916).   [128] Plunkett to Asquith, 23 June 1916, HHA, 37(70).

[129] Clarke, *Revolutionary woman*, pp. 89, 91, 138.

[130] Madge Callanan to James Ryan, 8 June 1916, Ryan MSS, UCDA, P88/19.

group to call itself 'Sinn Féin', a name which was soon hallowed by its association with the rebellion. Consequently it was able to exert a stronger influence on the structure of the new separatist movement which was built up during the next eighteen months (largely through the efforts of the Volunteers) than the party's condition in the six or seven years before the rising would have indicated.

The decline which it had experienced from 1909–10 onwards had continued uninterrupted during the war. In 1915 Griffith's colleague Tom Kelly lamented that the party was 'on the rocks' and could not pay the tax or the rent on its headquarters.[131] In Carron (Co. Clare) a year later 'the old Branch of Sinn Fein' which had been active since the party's foundation was still kept alive and had about twenty loyal adherents. But its only activity known to the police was when the active members talked together on the road before or after mass.[132] Another illustration of the party's moribund state is given by a police report from Longford in April 1916: 'there are still two branches of Sinn Fein (National Council) in the County . . . These were formed in 1909, but latterly have practically ceased to exist in that no meetings were held and no officers appointed for the last four or five years.'[133] This report is exceptional in that it identified clearly, by use of the words 'National Council', precisely which 'Sinn Féin' was being discussed. Until the spring or summer of 1917 most police reports used the words 'Sinn Fein' as a vague and generic description; in August 1916, for example, the inspector general referred to 'the Sinn Fein or extreme group' which comprised the IRB, Cumann na mBan ('a society of female extremists'), the Volunteers and other bodies on his list, but he did not include the Sinn Féin party in his litany.[134]

The party remained quiescent throughout most of 1916, and not until September did it make any tentative efforts to exploit the new national mood. In that month Herbert Moore Pim resumed the editorship of the Belfast-based *Irishman* which he had founded the previous January. Pim had been interned after the rising and was released in August; he then directed the party's affairs until Griffith returned at Christmas. He claimed to act on the basis of his discussions in Reading Jail with Griffith and others who had remained in prison after his own release.[135] One of the more outlandish figures in the separatist movement, Pim had been an Ulster unionist until only a few years earlier, and then he converted simultaneously to Catholicism and radical nationalism. In 1918 he returned to his original unionist beliefs. An imposing figure with a large

---

[131] *FJ*, 14 Oct. 1915, cited in Kee, *Green flag*, p. 535.

[132] District inspector, Ballyvaughan to CI (Clare), 11 Nov. 1916, NAI, CSO regd. papers, 22,022/1916.   [133] CI's report, Longford, Apr. 1916, CO.904/99.

[134] IG's report, Aug. 1916, CO.904/100.   [135] *Irishman*, 4 Nov. 1916.

sallow face and a full, dark Assyrian beard, he was 'extremely handsome in a rather soft purring way'.[136] He wrote both mediocre romantic poetry (a not uncommon taste or habit at the time) and novels with titles such as *The man with thirty lives* and *The vampire of souls*. His brief prominence reflected the vacuum or lack of talent available to radical nationalists.

But under Pim's leadership Sinn Féin at least accepted that the rising had transformed Irish politics, and the party made few serious attempts to return to the patterns of earlier years. It now hoped to broaden the base of Griffith's narrow party, to expand so that it would coincide with the large, vague and amorphous 'Sinn Féin movement' embracing all the different separatist elements. In an article which he wrote in the *Irishman* Pim declared optimistically that 'the new Sinn Féiners represent three groups – Sinn Féin, or the policy of Hungary as employed against Austria; the men who represent the '67 tradition, and the recent converts to genuine Nationality'. He recalled a conversation in which both Pearse and MacNeill

> considered that it would be wise to adopt the Sinn Féin title which had been gratuitously bestowed upon all and sundry . . . It remains for those who represent the policy of Arthur Griffith to adapt their association to the present conditions, and embrace the other two sections . . . It remains for those whose hearts and consciences have been stirred by the recent events in Ireland to give the claims of Arthur Griffith's system their serious attention.[137]

Pim was perceptive in some respects, and he was a lively and aggressive journalist, but he was self-important, he inspired little trust, and he was a bad party leader. He bickered needlessly with the Irish Nation League, making repeated and unprovoked attacks on the party and its leaders. He resented their moderation and treated them with a mixture of intolerance and condescension; thereby he established a precedent which Count Plunkett would follow a few months later during his brief pre-eminence, but which would be abandoned by Griffith when he returned to Ireland and resumed control of the party.[138] Pim warned that 'the Nation League must conform to the Sinn Féin theory, as the Sinn Féiner is incapable of compromising', and that since the League had been 'founded by men who may have genuinely repented at the eleventh hour . . . Sinn Féin is wise and liberal enough to absorb the Nation League'.[139] (Even

---

[136] Obituary, *IT*, 15 May 1950; Joseph Connolly, *Memoirs of Senator Joseph Connolly (1885–1961): a founder of modern Ireland*, J. Anthony Gaughan (ed.) (Dublin, 1996), p. 134.

[137] *Ibid.*, 23 Sept. 1916, editorial.   [138] For Count Plunkett, see below, pp. 86–8.

[139] *Irishman*, 7 Oct. 1916, editorial; 18 Nov. 1916.

Griffith was less tolerant in late 1916 than he became in later years, and he wrote from Reading Jail that 'so far as it is a hinder to the disintegration policy this new Irish Nation League passes muster. Beyond that purpose however, it will be of no utility to Ireland.'[140])

The Leaguers remained conciliatory. They argued that there was no need for any controversy between the two parties, and that they might conclude a loose alliance in which points of difference could be left open until full agreement might be reached.[141] (This is what happened in the course of the following year, when various executives and joint committees were formed.) By Christmas the League had become even more adaptable, claiming that its programme was 'peculiarly Sinn Féin in spirit', and flirting with the idea of abstention from Westminster.[142] There was no response to such overtures.

Griffith was cut off from direct contact with his party, and in a letter from Reading Jail he commented ruefully that 'only in a general way do we know what is happening in Ireland. My well-meaning but feather headed friend Herbert Pim seems to be muddling up Sinn Féin a bit. However we must trust in God to take him in hand and show him how to unmuddle it.'[143] But throughout the second half of 1916 Pim alone did not represent Sinn Féin. The general council held meetings in Dublin which included father-figures such as John Sweetman (who had been the party president from 1908 to 1910), and the offices in Harcourt Street continued to function, even if at a low level of activity. Sweetman's predecessor, the *littérateur* Edward Martyn, wrote with engaging vanity to deplore the fact that the party 'is not in regular working order as in the days when I was President'.[144] Four-page halfpenny pamphlets were published with titles such as *Spectacles for Ulstermen* and *The invincible Sinn Féin 'tank'*. Pim urged the formation of 'constitutional Sinn Féin clubs', and by early December he was able to report activity in Cork, Limerick and Tipperary.

After the prisoners were released at Christmas Pim declared in the *Irishman* that 'Griffith will find the foundations of Sinn Féin as strong as he left them',[145] but in the light of the party's condition before the rising this was hardly a proud boast. Sinn Féin remained small and uninfluential, and in terms of membership it bore no relationship to the mass movement of the same name which would emerge within a few months. Its most important asset was still its name.

By the end of the year little had been done to channel or organize the change in public opinion which had taken place; radical nationalists were presented

---

[140] Griffith to James Whelan, n.d. [autumn 1916], NLI, MS 10,218.

[141] *New Ireland*, 21 Oct. 1916.   [142] *Ibid.*, 23 Dec. 1916.

[143] Griffith to Lily Williams, 29 Nov. 1916, NLI, MS 5943.   [144] *Irishman*, 11 Nov. 1916.

[145] *Ibid.*, 6 Jan. 1917.

with an opportunity to seize the political initiative, but they lacked energetic and imaginative leaders and they did not know how to respond. This mood of frustration and futility was well-illustrated by the West Cork by-election.

West Cork

The vacant seat had been held by William O'Brien's All-For-Ireland League against the Parliamentary Party in the general elections of January and December 1910. The 'parliamentary truce', which had existed since the beginning of the war, was a convention whereby vacant seats were normally uncontested. The party in possession nominated a candidate who would then be returned unopposed. Redmond followed this custom, and in any event he may have feared defeat; he was reported to have argued that any contest would display to the British government the extent of Sinn Féin strength in the constituency.[146]

The spread of separatist views was also illustrated by developments within the All-For-Ireland League. It was generally assumed that the main reason why O'Brien selected Frank Healy as his candidate was the fact of his deportation after the rising, and that this record, reinforced by his friendship with Griffith and his reputation of being a Sinn Féin sympathizer, would win over the extremist vote if he faced any challenge. Healy sat out the campaign in the sedate comfort of Bournemouth – where, one opponent claimed, he was able to enjoy six-course dinners in a first class hotel.[147] O'Brien misled his champion with the reassurance that 'the feeling among our friends in West Cork is wonderfully united and buoyant',[148] but the selection of an outsider from far-distant Queenstown (Cobh) provoked resentment among the local party workers. An independent All-For-Ireland candidate, Michael Shipsey, ran against Healy. This split in the enemy's ranks convinced West Cork Nationalists that they could win the seat, but Redmond still refused to approve a contest. At the last minute his instructions were defied and Daniel O'Leary, who had been defeated in the 1910 elections, ran as an unofficial UIL candidate. He began his campaign only nine days before the poll.[149]

Both All-For-Ireland candidates sought the votes of separatists, Healy stressing his internment and his subsequent deportation, and Shipsey announcing that he had been 'interested' in the Sinn Féin movement. (This was true;

---

[146] *Cork Constitution*, 6, 17 Nov. 1916, editorials.   [147] *Cork Examiner*, 14 Nov. 1916.

[148] O'Brien to Frank Healy, 22 Oct. 1916, O'Brien MSS, NLI, 8556(11).

[149] *Cork Constitution*, 7 Nov. 1916.

three years earlier he had written a series of articles for Griffith's newspaper.) T. M. Healy, canvassing on behalf of his namesake, promised the voters that 'if they elected O'Leary it meant conscription for Ireland; if they elected Frank Healy it meant no conscription, but amnesty for the prisoners.'[150]

During the campaign Pim urged Healy, who was the favourite to win the seat, that he should campaign on an abstentionist policy, 'working along with Sweetman and the rest of us on the General Council of Sinn Féin in Dublin'. When his overtures met with no response he wrote a letter to the *Irish Independent* in which he attacked Healy, declaring that 'no Sinn Féiner can vote to send a man to take an oath in Westminster. Better a corrupt Redmondite for a few months in his PROPER PLACE than a man who has been associated with Irish prisoners, even if by mistake, for a few weeks.'[151]

Three days before the poll the Sinn Féin executive in Harcourt Street reinforced Pim's public statement. It issued a manifesto attacking the All-For-Ireland League and quoting Parnell's advice that his followers should 'vote for open coercionists against rotten Whigs'. It claimed that if the League were to be routed, 'Sinn Féin will have virtually won West Cork at this election, and will possess West Cork at next election.'[152] The Volunteer leaders in Reading Jail rejected both Healy and Shipsey; an announcement was made 'by direction and on behalf of the Irish Prisoners of War in England . . . that neither Mr. Frank Healy, nor any of the other Candidates for parliament in West Cork, represent the views of either the interned prisoners or Sinn Féin'.[153] O'Brien had hoped to win separatist support, but his manoeuvre backfired. His choice of Healy split the party; he alienated the unionists, estimated at between 500 and 700, who had voted for his party in the past; and in the end his 'extremist' candidate was rejected by those whose assistance he had sought at the cost of provoking his other problems.

O'Leary won the seat by 116 votes, but his poll was 252 less than the combined votes for Healy and Shipsey, so everyone managed to draw encouraging conclusions from the result. The Parliamentary Party succeeded in gaining a seat where it had never expected to do so – and the *Freeman's Journal's* ungrateful reaction betrayed its astonishment: 'in the circumstances of the hour the result is less heartening than surprising'.[154] But this victory tended to engender an unwise complacency, a feeling that, at last, the country was 'coming to its senses again'; or that, in the words of the *Cork Examiner*, West Cork had returned 'to the National fold, to sanity, and to what is best in Irish politics'.[155]

---

[150] *Cork Examiner*, 15 Nov. 1916.   [151] *II*, 6 Nov. 1916.   [152] *Irishman*, 25 Nov. 1916.
[153] *Ibid.*, 18 Nov. 1916; *Cork Examiner*, 11 Nov. 1916.   [154] *FJ*, 17 Nov. 1916, editorial.
[155] *Cork Examiner*, 17 Nov. 1916, editorial.

The All-For-Ireland League consoled itself that, but for the split in its ranks, it would have held the seat comfortably. And Sinn Féin took full credit for the result, boasting that it had refused the assistance which the League had courted and needed. Nonetheless, the separatists still lacked the organization to take the positive step of nominating a candidate themselves. And in Cork city the more energetic spirits 'who have been in the limelight owing to the West Cork election' wanted a public meeting to launch the movement, but they were overruled by those who preferred 'genuine, quiet organising'.[156]

Transition

On the surface the second half of 1916 appears to have been a barren and unproductive period, fittingly rounded off by the inconclusive West Cork election. In mid-June Dillon had written to Lloyd George that 'for the moment the Party does not speak for Ireland', and there is *no leadership* in the Country'.[157] Six months later nothing had changed. The separatist movement 'was more a mood than an organisation, a repudiation of the old political Nationalism more than a promise to replace it'.[158] The Nation League was founded by dissident nationalists, but failed to fulfil its early hopes. Sinn Féin was revived by Pim, but had to wait until the following year before it made any noticeable progress. The Volunteers began an unobtrusive reorganization which was to lay the foundations of their future strength, but until the release of the Frongoch internees at the end of the year their activities too were on only a small scale. The most successful movement during these months, the Prisoners' Aid Society, was a charitable rather than a political organization.

Yet the period from April to December 1916 was one of transition, comparable to the interval between the leadership of Butt and Parnell in 1879–80. There was a dramatic increase in the number of people who sympathized with the Easter rebels and what they stood for. Tom Clarke's prophecy that 'we will die, but it will be a different Ireland after us', had already been vindicated.[159] This turning of the tide was basically an emotional reaction against what was seen as the excessive scale of the arrests and executions after the rising; it was an almost instinctive anti-British backlash by Irish nationalists. It was compounded by the failure of the home rule negotiations, by separatist propaganda, by the efforts

---

[156] De Róiste, diary, 20 Dec. 1916, CAI, U271/A/19A.

[157] Dillon to Lloyd George, 16 June 1916, LG, D/14/3/1.

[158] Fitzpatrick, *Politics and Irish life*, p. 142.

[159] Piaras Béaslaí, *Michael Collins and the making of a new Ireland* (Dublin, 1926), I, p. 122.

of newspapers such as the *Irish Independent* and the *Irishman*, by the Prisoners' Aid Society and by the release of internees from Frongoch. Among the many police references to this pattern is the comment from Queen's Co. (Laois) in July that 'Sinn Feinism appears to be the fashion at present'; in October a 'bad character' was arrested near Drogheda in possession of 393 carefully counted copies of a ballad entitled *Who fears to speak of Easter Week?;* while in December an estimated 2,000 people attended a separatist concert in Cork where, according to the police, they indulged in 'seditious songs, etc.'[160]

This transformation of public opinion, however incomplete, was the most important change in the period after the rising, and it was the fundamental reality behind the more exciting events of 1917. The new Sinn Féin which emerged in the opening months of that year enjoyed mass support even before it had developed an organization. The combined actions of the rebel leaders and the British authorities achieved for it in advance what would otherwise have been the hardest part of its task. Its main challenge was to build on its legacy.

In late 1916 this popular feeling was still largely blind. Many nationalists were inspired by negative views, they hated the government and rejected the Parliamentary Party, but they had as yet no satisfactory alternative. In August *New Ireland* lamented that 'we are sheep without a shepherd and even without a fold', and six months later it returned to this theme: 'since the rising Irish opinion has been somewhat chaotic. It has been "against the Party", it is true, but that is, perhaps, its only common denominator. There is very little that is positive or constructive in the fragmentary conditions of present-day Irish thought.'[161] Many people, and especially many young men, were waiting for a lead; once it was given they followed it with enthusiasm.

At the end of 1916 the army's intelligence officer for the Midlands and Connacht reported that Sinn Féin (in the broader sense of the term) 'given any chance or seeming apparent chance of success, would meet with support from the mass of the people, but lacking leaders, organization, and aid from abroad, it cannot effect much'.[162] The seeds which the Easter rebels had sown were nurtured carefully by the British authorities, but they germinated for many months, and it was not until the Roscommon election in the following spring that a more favourable political climate allowed the fruits of the rising to appear.

---

[160] CIs' reports, Queen's Co., July 1916, Louth, Oct. 1916, E. Cork, Dec. 1916, CO.904/100–1.
[161] *New Ireland*, 26 Aug. 1916, 17 Feb. 1917.   [162] IO's report (M. and C.), Dec. 1916.

3

ORGANIZERS AND CONVERTS, 1917

Soon after he displaced Asquith as prime minister in December 1916, Lloyd George decided to release all the remaining Irish internees; only those who had been tried and sentenced for their involvement in the Easter Rising remained in jail. This proved to be the first step in the revival of the separatist movement, and Redmond must soon have regretted his recent advice that 'they can do much more harm as prisoners in Frongoch than at liberty in Ireland'.[1] The combined efforts of political veterans such as Griffith and of younger activists such as Collins transformed Irish public life within the next six months. Herbert Moore Pim and others who had flourished in their absence were soon hustled back to obscurity.

Early in the new year the released prisoners and detainees began reorganizing the Volunteers, the body to which most of them had belonged before Easter Week. But they also reactivated the political wing of the separatist movement which had been dormant for many years. Gradually the tone of police reports became more apprehensive. In Clare, for instance, it was noted that 'in each place where an interned prisoner has returned, the Sinn Feiners have begun to meet, use seditious expressions and up to a certain point defy law and authority'.[2]

North Roscommon

The turning-point came with the North Roscommon by-election, a campaign which proved to be among the more important in modern Irish political history. The vacancy was caused by the death of James O'Kelly, one of the most colourful members of the Parliamentary Party. If his obituaries are to be believed, in the course of his varied career he studied in the Sorbonne and then

---

[1] Redmond to Asquith, 30 Nov. 1916, HHA, 37(137).

[2] CI's report, Clare, Feb. 1917, CO.904/102.

served as a member of the French Foreign Legion; he fought in Algeria and in Mexico, where he was wounded and captured in the service of Emperor Maximilian; having returned to Ireland, he was a member of the IRB supreme council at the time of the 1867 Rising; then, after rejoining the Foreign Legion, he fought against the Prussians outside Paris. In the New World he accompanied the US troops who fought against Sitting Bull, but his luck ran out briefly in Cuba where he was jailed by the Spaniards. He saved the life of the emperor of Brazil and searched for the Mahdi in the Sudan. After his second return to Ireland in 1879, he was elected MP for North Roscommon, and was a fellow prisoner of Parnell and Dillon in Kilmainham. He challenged one of his colleagues to a duel.[3]

Ill-health may have helped kill his early *Wanderlust*, and in the last years of his life one part of the world which he visited rarely, if ever, was North Roscommon. References were made to his poor health as early as the party convention of December 1909, at which he was unanimously re-selected for the constituency, and one speaker remarked then that he had never seen his MP.[4] (It seems, however, that his medical condition prevented him from travelling to Roscommon but not from attending the House of Commons.) O'Kelly had been returned unopposed for more than twenty years, so he may have assumed that his constituents felt none the worse for his absence. Yet, however uncharacteristic he may have been of his Irish (or British) fellow MPs, he had at least followed a path familiar to Irish nationalists as he drifted from physical force to constitutional politics.

Roscommon was already one of the most disturbed areas in Ireland and it experienced more agrarian unrest than almost any other part of the country. Farm labourers and others who were without land resented the large grassland areas devoted to raising cattle. It had ranked fifth among all the Irish counties in the number of its inhabitants who had been arrested after the rising, and it came first among those which had remained quiet during Easter Week.[5] The releases during the summer and at Christmas unleashed a set of agitators and activists who could exploit these favourable conditions.

The initiative in contesting the seat was taken by a group of Roscommon separatists who were led by a local curate, Fr Michael O'Flanagan. He was mercurial, dynamic and inconsistent. He had been elected to the Sinn Féin executive in 1910, and five years later he delivered an oration in Dublin as the body of O'Donovan Rossa, a Fenian veteran, lay in state. Despite this background he supported the partition clauses of the attempted home rule settlement in 1916.

---

[3] *FJ*, 23 Dec. 1916; *Roscommon Herald* and *Roscommon Messenger*, 30 Dec. 1916.

[4] *Roscommon Journal*, 1 Jan. 1910.   [5] MacGiolla Choille, *Intelligence notes*, p. 241.

He suggested that if southerners did not display more effort and imagination they would have to reconcile themselves to a permanently divided Ireland; he argued that since there were two Ulsters there must therefore also be two Irelands; and he described the island in heretical terms as 'an historic and social duality'.[6] More than once he was suspended from his clerical duties by the deeply unsympathetic Dr Coyne of Elphin, who ended one letter to his turbulent priest by describing himself as 'your grieved and afflicted Bishop'.[7]

O'Flanagan and his colleagues first approached Dr Michael Davitt, the son of the Land Leaguer, and when he declined the honour of challenging the Parliamentary Party they announced that they would have to ask 'old Plunkett'.[8] The man to whom they then turned was a improbable choice. George Noble Plunkett, a 65-year-old papal count, had written a study of Botticelli and had served as director of the National Museum of Science and Art in Dublin. He was a political neophyte, and from the standpoint of some separatists his past was dubious. Twice within recent years he had applied for the post of under-secretary in Dublin Castle, and he flew a flag from his house during George V's visit to the city in 1911; it was probably a mitigating circumstance that this was not the Union Jack, but the banner of the Holy Sepulchre of which he was a knight commander.[9]

Three of Plunkett's sons took part in the rising, two of them were imprisoned in its aftermath, and the third (Joseph, the signatory of the proclamation) was executed. His house in Kimmage had been used as an arsenal, and in the months before the insurrection he had carried messages to Germany from the rebels. After Easter Week he was dismissed from his museum post and deported to Oxford. Within days of his selection for Roscommon, the Royal Dublin Society expelled him from membership as a punishment for his connections with the rising nine months earlier; thereby its members reminded the country of his family's martyrdom.[10]

His scholarship won him respect in some quarters, and soon afterwards an admirer praised him as 'a nice, refined, educated gentleman of culture and especially gifted with a taste for the fine arts'.[11] Not all were so deferential, however, and the newly elected MP for West Cork described him as 'a Government official all his life, drawing a Government salary for looking after old fossils,

---

[6] *Leader*, 12 Aug., 9 Sept. 1916, pp. 17, 109. See below, p. 228.

[7] Coyne to O'Flanagan, 14 Jan. 1916, Joseph Brennan MSS, NLI, 26,185.

[8] J. F. X. O'Brien, memo on conversation with Michael Davitt Jr, 7 May 1917, NLI, MS 13,477.

[9] *Sinn Féin*, 15 July 1911.

[10] He was reinstated in May 1921. On that occasion the society displayed a shrewder sense of timing.

[11] *Roscommon Journal*, 14 Apr. 1917.

bones and stuffed birds in the Dublin Museum'.[12] Another critic claimed that he was 'not a place-hunter, but a place-holder . . . and only blossoms out as a quasi-extremist when the Government deprived him of office'.[13] But the most serious charge against him was his age, and he was dismissed as 'an amiable old Whig', as 'a very feeble old man and a delicate man', and as being so decrepit he could hardly speak, fit only to be in charge of a Christmas tree.[14] His strenuous activities for years to come would disprove such estimates of his strength; he became more radical as he aged, contested his final election nearly twenty years later (when he won only 4 per cent of the vote), and survived until 1948. Plunkett was an ambivalent figure. In the aftermath of the rising he was an obvious sympathy candidate, one who should be difficult to dislike or attack, but he was at best an unlikely champion of the 1916 legacy.

He was, however, fortunate in his opponents. Although some would-be successors had been nursing the constituency during O'Kelly's long illness, and although no less than eight of the twenty-one outdoor meetings held by the UIL between May and December 1916 took place in Roscommon,[15] the League revealed the sort of incompetence which might have been expected after so many tranquil years. Nearly a month elapsed before it selected its candidate, Thomas Devine, and he was given little more support from the Parliamentary Party than O'Leary had received in West Cork – even though the party truce now operated in the Nationalists' favour.

The seat was also contested by a third candidate, Jasper Tully, who provided himself with favourable publicity in the columns of his own newspaper, the *Roscommon Herald*. Tully was no slave to political consistency. He had represented South Leitrim for fourteen years until he was expelled from the Parliamentary Party, and the Nation League accused him of having offered to fight North Roscommon on its behalf before he ran as an independent. Within a few months he underwent yet another transformation and supported Sinn Féin in the South Longford by-election, but in Roscommon he was bitter in his attacks on Plunkett. Even the Redmondite *Roscommon Messenger* claimed that he would probably take more votes from the count than from his Parliamentary Party rival.[16]

The separatists' improvised and amateurish campaign in North Roscommon contrasted with the efficiency which they would soon display in the course of later elections. Plunkett may have been described as a 'Sinn Fein candidate',[17]

[12] *Roscommon Messenger*, 3 Feb. 1917.   [13] *FJ*, 6 Feb. 1917.

[14] *Roscommon Herald*, 27 Jan., 3 Feb. 1917; *II*, 30 Jan., 3 Feb. 1917.

[15] 'United Irish League meetings', CO.904/21/3.   [16] *Roscommon Messenger*, 27 Jan. 1917.

[17] *Ibid.*

but he was supported by individuals rather than by a party. An electoral machine was created, in large part spontaneously, during the interval between his nomination and polling day. O'Flanagan was the most active organizer and canvasser, and he was described as 'talking in impassioned language to the people at every village and street corner and cross-roads where he could get people to listen to him'.[18] He arranged the count's speaking programme in the days before the election.[19] Another prominent member of Plunkett's team was Laurence Ginnell, who co-operated with the separatists throughout the early months of the year, but who did not finally abandon Westminster and join Sinn Féin until July.[20] On 22 January Ginnell wrote that, so far, he and O'Flanagan were the only supporters who had spoken on Plunkett's behalf, and he added that their plan was 'to generate such enthusiasm as may shame any Roscommon man from opposing you'. He reassured the count that 'we have *all* the young, male and female'.[21]

The activists included Griffith and other members of the Sinn Féin party, J. J. O'Kelly, the editor of the *Catholic Bulletin*, and IRB members such as Seumas O'Doherty, who was appointed campaign manager. Many Volunteers canvassed for Plunkett, including some who had recently been freed from internment, although before doing so they had first to overcome their instinctive distaste for politics. Since they despised most of their contemporaries as weak, short-sighted compromisers it was difficult for them to put their faith in a change of heart by the Irish electorate. But they appreciated that another rising against the British was out of the question, at least in the immediate future, and many of them felt that under the circumstances they might as well exploit whatever opportunities were available. Until they were strong enough to challenge the British government again they could keep themselves busy by fighting a lesser enemy: the Redmondites. They conformed to a widespread pattern whereby revolutionaries often try to clear the battlefield by choosing moderate democrats as their first targets.

The Volunteers were determined to apply their military discipline to an unfamiliar type of campaign, and they acquired new skills and experience which they would later use in founding Sinn Féin clubs, organizing meetings and fighting other by-elections. There was some truth in Tully's jibe that Plunkett's supporters should be called Irish Volunteers rather than Sinn Féiners.[22] The Nation League was also active in North Roscommon, and its members concentrated on attacking the Parliamentary Party rather than on advocating the

---

[18] *IT*, 8 Feb. 1917.   [19] O'Flanagan to Plunkett, 27 Jan. 1917, CP, 11,374(15).

[20] On Ginnell see Bew, *Conflict and conciliation*, pp. 148–9, 179, 197.

[21] Ginnell to Plunkett, 22 Jan. 1917, CP, 11,374(15).   [22] *Roscommon Herald*, 3 Feb. 1917.

The old men were carried upon the backs
of the young

3.1 An image of N. Roscommon

merits of Count Plunkett. Despite their constitutional beliefs they were able to
co-operate harmoniously with the separatist Volunteers.

The greatest achievement of the campaign was the emergence of a sense of
cohesion and common purpose among a disparate group of people who, until
then, had often suspected or disapproved of each other. It was through the
informal and almost accidental process of working together in Roscommon
that they initiated the formal and deliberate policy of reviving the separatist
movement. An organization was developed and close links were established
between different parties and individuals.

The RIC county inspector warned that the separatist campaign was far more
vigorous than the efforts of the other candidates, and another observer compared Plunkett's election workers with the enthusiasts 'who must have carried

through the French revolution'.[23] These supporters canvassed for Plunkett as energetically as the appalling weather would permit. They had to battle through what was widely described as the greatest fall of snow that had taken place in living memory, and there were reports of drifts 10–11 feet (3 metres) high, of districts being cut off and of people missing or frozen to death. William O'Brien (a prominent trade union leader) recorded briefly in his diary his journey by car from Dublin with Collins and others: 'breakdown near Longford at 1 a.m. Mountains of snow everywhere. Roads almost impassable, and some quite so.'[24] Mrs Griffith's vicarious account provides more detail. She described Sinn Féiners going from town to town in the bitter cold, icicles hanging from their hair, one driver's gloves stuck to the steering wheel and the driver himself frozen so firmly that he had to be lifted off his seat.[25] Travellers armed themselves with shovels to dig their way through snowdrifts, Laurence Ginnell walked 11 miles (18 km) from Boyle to Elphin to make a speech, and young men carried elderly voters through the snow on polling day.[26] The campaign and its weather became honoured in political folk-memory.

The contest was one-sided, and the Volunteers' enthusiasm was not matched by any comparable energy on the part of their opponents. The Redmondites' main arguments were that the people should remain loyal to the party, and that Plunkett was not a figure who could be taken seriously. O'Flanagan reverted to his earlier demands for land distribution, and in this he was supported by Ginnell, but otherwise the Sinn Féiners' propaganda and speeches tended to be no more positive than those of the Nationalists. They either appealed for sympathy, arguing that the count was entitled to some reward for the sacrifices which he and his family had made on Ireland's behalf, or else they abused the Parliamentary Party, dismissing it as ineffective and discredited beyond redemption. Ginnell was reported as claiming that 150,000 Irishmen who had followed Redmond's advice and joined the army 'were feeding the worms in Gallipoli and Flanders'.[27] Some praised the rising and attributed to it Ireland's exemption from conscription, but apart from a few simplistic arguments they offered no definite set of aims or methods. One pamphlet gave as the first of several reasons for electing Plunkett, 'because he is an Irishman and a Count of the Holy Roman Empire, the highest honour the Pope could confer on a

---

[23] CI's report, Roscommon, Jan. 1917, CO.904/102; J. M. Wilson, memo citing 'a person of great judgment', 27–28 Mar. 1917, Patrick Buckland (ed.), *Irish unionism 1885–1923: a documentary history* (Belfast, 1973), p. 364.   [24] William O'Brien, diary, 2 Feb. 1917, NLI, MS 15,705.

[25] Maud Griffith to Kate Kelly, n.d., NLI, MS 8411.

[26] *Leader*, 17 Feb. 1917, pp. 39–40; *Catholic Bulletin*, Mar. 1917, pp. 150–1.

[27] 'Sinn Fein: meetings in 1917', CO.904/23/3, p. 4.

layman', while another urged the electorate to 'vote for Plunkett and you vote for a Seat for Ireland at the Peace Conference'. The last stanza of a song 'Hurrah! Hurrah! for Plunkett' (to the air of 'the Boys of Wexford') went as follows:

> Roscommon men awake and tell
> The cowards that they lie,
> When they proclaim your manhood tame
> Let this be your reply:
> 'Count Plunkett speaks for us to-day;
> Roscommon proudly hails
> The man exiled, by snobs reviled,
> Our prince of Irish Gaels.'[28]

In the circumstances of early 1917 a vague or even negative approach was both obvious and sensible. Some of the groups and individuals who supported Plunkett had virtually nothing in common, apart from their shared enmity towards the Parliamentary Party, and at this stage it would have been dangerous to advocate specific policies.

The count's first election manifesto, suppressed by the censor, was described as consisting simply of a long list of grievances without any positive content;[29] the second was published, but proved to be little more constructive. It was fortunate for Plunkett that he arrived in Roscommon only days before the poll, too late to do any damage to his own cause. As soon as he announced his policy, after he had been safely elected, it provoked controversy among his followers.

The Irish Party provided Devine with little assistance. The weather may have been partly responsible for this, and it was claimed that Redmond had sent sixteen MPs and between thirty and forty organizers to the constituency, but that snow had imprisoned them all.[30] Yet on the day before polling took place, John Dillon (whose family home was in Roscommon) quoted his latest reports which indicated that the party would probably win; 'on the whole Ireland is settling down and generally becoming sane again'.[31] He soon experienced what proved to be the first of many electoral disappointments at the hands of Sinn Féiners: Plunkett won by a surprisingly wide margin, receiving 3,022 votes to 1,708 for Devine and 687 for Tully.

The party was devastated by this defeat. The *Freeman's Journal* confessed that the result had been totally unexpected, while Maurice Moore warned Dillon that 'if something decisive be not done the revolution may go to the extreme of

---

[28] Leaflets and pamphlets, NLI, LO.P.116(78, 74, 76).

[29] 'Sinn Fein: meetings in 1917', CO.904/23/3, pp. 1–4.   [30] *Roscommon Herald*, 3 Feb. 1917.

[31] Dillon to Shane Leslie, 1 Feb. 1917, NLI, MS 22,836.

changing the whole party, leaders and all'.[32] Dillon replied indignantly that he would 'never be a party to any ridiculous and contemptible effort to curry popularity by deserting the policy I believe in', but nonetheless he regarded the election as opening up a new chapter in Irish history.[33] Not long afterwards he referred to the conflict which was taking place between 'the Irish revolution' and 'the Castle gang'.[34] Redmond's response was almost despairing, and he concluded that

> if, as would, perhaps be not unnatural, the people have grown tired of the monotony of being served for twenty, thirty, thirty-five, or forty years by the same men in Parliament, and desire variety and a change, speaking for myself, I have no complaint to make . . . Let the Irish people replace us, by all means, by other and, I hope, better men, if they so choose.

Even though Dillon and others dissuaded him from publishing this document, such fatalism was an ominous portent for the home rule cause.[35]

On the opposing side, O'Flanagan declared that what North Roscommon had done was so glorious, so great and so magnificent that no eloquence except the eloquence of silence would express his feelings.[36] From him, silence was an extraordinary tribute.

Uneasy allies

Shortly after the result was announced Plunkett and several of his most prominent supporters held a meeting in Boyle, the county town, and it was only then that he declared his intention to abstain from Westminster. In this way he followed the programme of Griffith's Sinn Féin rather than that of the Nation League. Some League members felt deceived, and they complained that the electorate had been unfairly disfranchised.

Before they parted the leaders arranged to contact each other again, and ten days later between fifteen and twenty representatives of different organizations and interests met in Plunkett's house in Dublin. They tried to agree on a policy which would unite and strengthen the radical nationalist forces.[37] Five of their number, Griffith, Plunkett, Seumas O'Doherty of the IRB, William O'Brien of

---

[32] *FJ*, 6 Feb. 1917, editorial; Moore to Dillon, 4 Mar. 1917, Moore MSS, NLI, 10,561(9).

[33] Dillon to Moore, 13 Mar. 1917, *ibid.*; Dillon to Leslie, 9 Feb. 1917, NLI, MS 22,836.

[34] *Hansard*, 90, col. 1,987 (26 Feb. 1917).

[35] Redmond, statement, 21 Feb. 1917, Lyons, *John Dillon*, p. 411.   [36] *FJ*, 6 Feb. 1917.

[37] F. J. O'Connor to Gavan Duffy, 7 Mar. 1917, GD, 5581.

the Trades Council and J. J. O'Kelly of the Nation League, formed a committee whose aim was to rationalize the activities of the various groups and societies. This body proved to be ineffective and it was ignored by Plunkett, the most energetic among the radical leaders at the time.

All parties and individuals shared the ideal of creating a united and widely based party which would coincide with the unorganized 'Sinn Féin' or separatist movement, and all were anxious to end the multiplicity of factions which had characterized separatism before the Easter Rising. Yet the next few months were marked by a series of bitter quarrels which at times made the achievement of such unity seem quite impossible. These all centred on Count Plunkett. Even without his vanity and his abrasive personality there would have been tensions between the various elements which had joined forces in North Roscommon. The Nation Leaguers were touchy and self-important, eager to take offence and resentful of Plunkett's ascendancy. Opposed to them were Volunteers such as Collins and Cathal Brugha who not merely despised the League, but who also regarded Griffith's Sinn Féin with deep distrust. However Plunkett accentuated these various differences, giving them a precise form and content.

His election victory made him the most prominent figure among radical nationalists, and to many outsiders he personified the Sinn Féin movement. Even Pim's *Irishman* described him as the new leader of the Irish race.[38] Plunkett failed to appreciate that his position was that of an ephemeral figurehead, and he took his new eminence far more seriously than his supporters had intended; he hoped to become the effective head of the Sinn Féin movement rather than serve in the symbolic role for which he had been chosen and for which he was admirably suited. Unfortunately for the separatist cause, his independence of mind was not matched by clarity of judgement. His scholarly life had left him ill-prepared for the compromises of party management, he lacked the diplomacy which his new position demanded, and twice within the next few months he came close to wrecking the precarious unity of the forces which combined against the Parliamentary Party.

The influence which he enjoyed in 1917 was in no way a tribute to his own merits or achievements, but was due simply to the lack of a determined rival. Griffith, whose main concern was with editing his newspaper *Nationality,* and who was disliked by many of the Volunteers, made no attempt to challenge Plunkett. When de Valera was released from jail the following June he proved to be a more natural and attractive leader, and the count's support vanished rapidly.

Given the impossibility of another rebellion, separatists disagreed on few

---

[38] *Irishman,* 31 Mar. 1917.

matters of principle. In 1917 the only contentious problems were whether they should aim at establishing an Irish republic, and whether their MPs should abstain from attendance at Westminster. The question of resorting to physical force in the future was not yet divisive – although some soldiers and politicians remained suspicious of each others' intentions. Attitudes and personalities were far more important and controversial, and it was according to such criteria that people were branded as 'moderates' or 'extremists'. To a considerable extent these distinctions were arbitrary, even meaningless, and they lacked the clarity and force of those which would later split the movement in two after the signing of the Anglo-Irish Treaty in December 1921. Sinn Féiners were categorized by the sentiments they expressed, the symbols they flaunted or the company they kept, rather by what they did in the present or had done in the past. Their opinions on the rising in 1917 seemed at times to be even more important than the actions which some of them had taken in 1916, or than the separatist beliefs which they held in earlier years when such opinions had been less fashionable.

The reflected glory of his sons, together with some fiery speeches of his own and a genuine distaste for any sort of compromise with Britain, made Plunkett the temporary spokesman of the radical republicans. There can be little doubt that many of them exploited him. On the other hand, new bonds were established, and the Roscommon campaign brought together three very different figures – Plunkett, O'Flanagan and J. J. O'Kelly – who over the next two decades would come to represent irreconcilable, fundamentalist republicanism.[39]

Although several of Griffith's principal lieutenants in the old Sinn Féin party, men such as Seán Milroy, W. T. Cosgrave and Páidín O'Keeffe, had all fought in the rising, and had thereby acquired a more impressive 'record' of militancy than some followers of Plunkett such as Rory O'Connor and Thomas Dillon, it was the former group which was regarded as moderate and which was suspected by many Volunteers. Similarly the Nation League was founded in opposition to the Redmondites' acquiescence in partition, but it was denounced for its timidity by O'Flanagan who had supported the scheme. As 1916 became the revolutionary Year One, Griffith's credentials as a leading radical nationalist since the beginning of the century tended to be ignored or forgotten. Some of his critics could not accept his commitment to the idea or the image of Grattan's Parliament, and they resented what they saw as his luke-warm attitude towards the rising. They tried to squeeze him out of the movement. Collins wrote to Thomas Ashe, in Lewes Jail, that on certain points Griffith 'was pretty rotten, and for that reason some of us have been having fierce rows with him'; he went

---

[39] Murphy, *Patrick Pearse*, pp. 78–9; Denis Carroll, *They have fooled you again: Michael O'Flanagan (1876–1942): priest, republican, social critic* (Dublin, 1993), p. 59. See below, pp. 442–6.

on to offer the reassurance 'for God's sake don't think that Master A G is going to turn us all into eighty-two'ites'.[40] In a similar fashion all the Nation Leaguers admired Griffith, even though he was the originator of the abstentionist principle which, when advocated by Plunkett, they denounced as 'suicidal'. The reason was simple: unlike his rival, Griffith was civil and tactful in his dealings with them, and on occasion he was prepared to compromise.

During his brief period as the leading figure in the separatist movement the count showed himself to be both dogmatic and exclusive, and he displayed an almost irrational hostility towards the members of the Nation League. Griffith was now more flexible than he had been in earlier years, and he preferred to reason with opponents, but Plunkett tried to browbeat and bully them into submission. He failed to realize that not all converts adopted their new beliefs with his own intolerant enthusiasm, that frequently time and patience were needed to complete a change of allegiance, and that while the Nation League might be absorbed slowly and painlessly into the separatist movement it could not be swallowed all at once. Within a short time of his election for Roscommon a series of conflicts developed between him and other sections of the Sinn Féin movement.

After Plunkett had decided belatedly against taking his seat in parliament he clung to the policy of abstention with a rigidity which appalled Griffith – who had developed the idea in the early years of the century, and had until now been its principal exponent. Griffith tended to distrust converts, especially when they were zealous. The Nation League maintained its belief that Irish MPs should withdraw from Westminster as a tactical move, rather than abstain permanently as a matter of principle, and in return the count tried to exclude it from the advanced nationalist movement. Aided by many of the younger Volunteers and Frongoch detainees he waged a vendetta against its members.

Personal dislikes soon proved as damaging to the unity of the Sinn Féin movement as were these differences of principle. The Nation Leaguers viewed Plunkett with open contempt and relished the quarrels which soon developed; they regarded him as incompetent, which he was, and as a fanatic, which he was not. Their letters are filled with denunciations of his character and actions. One of them wrote in disbelief of his monstrous behaviour in trying to establish himself as leader of the new movement and to 'strut in Griffith's mantle'.[41] They referred to his blundering and his insanity, and described him as foolish and

---

[40] Collins to Ashe, n.d. (Apr. 1917), cited in Seán Ó Lúing, *I die in a good cause: a study of Thomas Ashe, idealist and revolutionary* (Tralee, 1970), pp. 122–3. 'Eighty-two'ites' refers to those who shared Griffith's admiration for Grattan's Parliament of 1782.

[41] F. J. O'Connor to Gavan Duffy, 4 Apr. 1917, GD, 5581.

vainglorious, a usurper and dictator surrounded by unwise and dishonest flatterers.[42]

These squabbles placed Griffith in an awkward position. Naturally he agreed with Plunkett's stand on the abstention question, but in general he sympathized more with the Leaguers' cautious and comprehensive approach. While he was careful not to join them in an anti-Plunkett alliance, he remained in regular contact with several of their members. He was dismayed by the count's attitude of 'he who is not with me is against me', and was said to have described him as 'dogged, narrowminded and quite impractical'.[43] His admirer Darrell Figgis wrote of Griffith that he was 'very strong on holding to a general agreement, and sent me a message lately saying he felt he was fighting a very lone hand'.[44] Nonetheless, however faulty the count's tactics may have been, on the basic issue of abstention his (and Griffith's) attitude was more in tune with public opinion. The moderate Nation Leaguers failed to appreciate the extent to which the national mood had changed, and that in the circumstances of 1917 electors were now prepared to vote for abstentionist candidates. Their newspaper *New Ireland* acknowledged their misjudgement: 'the Roscommon election, we frankly admit, shows that the temper of Irish national opinion was underestimated by us'.[45] But League members were slow in putting this awareness into practice.

However vehemently the various separatist groups indulged in their political and personal differences, they maintained an even stronger common desire for unity and efficiency in their efforts to supplant the Parliamentary Party. The constant speculation about an early general election was a further stimulus to overcome their disagreements. These divisions rarely became public, and Griffith and Plunkett addressed crowds from the same platforms, yet disharmony at the top caused uncertainty at lower levels of the movement. During the months between February and May the spread of the Sinn Féin movement throughout the country received little help from its leaders, apart from their involvement in election campaigns. (It is possible, too, that some of their speeches may have seemed to lack any direct relevance to Irish circumstances; one issue of *Nationality* reported that Griffith had lectured to an immense and spell-bound crowd on 'the National Revival in Bulgaria', and that the following week Plunkett would talk on 'Some Irish artists'.[46]) F. J. O'Connor of the Nation League remarked that 'everybody feels that detached and isolated sections and

---

[42] Patrick McCartan to Gavan Duffy, 30 Mar.; F. J. O'Connor to Gavan Duffy, 6 Apr.; Gavan Duffy to O'Connor, 10 Apr.; O'Connor to Gavan Duffy, 4, 6 Apr.; A. J. Nicholls to Gavan Duffy, 14 Apr. 1917, GD, 5581.   [43] A. J. Nicholls to Gavan Duffy, 11 Apr. 1917, *ibid.*

[44] Figgis to Gavan Duffy, 1 Apr. 1917, *ibid.*   [45] *New Ireland*, 24 Feb. 1917.

[46] *Nationality*, 31 Mar. 1917.

parties are only wasting their energies and that they can accomplish little or nothing. They are missing opportunities and losing precious time.'[47]

The Plunkett convention

In mid-March Plunkett decided to convene a national assembly, and he summoned a meeting which would be held a month later in the Mansion House in Dublin. He sent a circular to various organizations and to every county and district council in the country. Exuding self-confidence, he declared that the duty had been cast on him of inaugurating a national policy, and that he would begin the task whereby Ireland would take control of its own affairs. The reaction in many quarters was predictably hostile. Seán T. O'Kelly, who remained on good terms with both radicals and moderates, reported that 'some wiser heads did their level best to dissuade him from circulating it'.[48] F. J. O'Connor commented that Plunkett was suffering from a swelled head, 'which is natural under the circumstances, as he has been everywhere as a demi god or superman', while the secretary to the archbishop of Dublin regarded him as a political fool and remarked that he was proving an awkward figurehead.[49] The archbishop himself believed that the manner in which the conference was presented to the country had done irreparable harm.[50] Patrick McCartan feared that it would take another Roscommon victory to undo the damage done by the count's manifesto, and police reports also indicated a lack of enthusiasm for him in different parts of the country.[51]

But his colleagues knew that they had to live with Plunkett, however tactless he might be; as J. J. O'Kelly remarked with understandable if exaggerated pessimism, 'the Count being the best man we were able to put up, we cannot think of turning him down now without the certainty of the new movement being practically stillborn'.[52]

When sending out his invitations, Plunkett had not appreciated that the local authorities were dominated by Redmondites, and since the great majority of them either ignored or rejected his proposal he was forced to modify his plans for the meeting. Newspapers reported that some local government representa-

---

[47] O'Connor to Gavan Duffy, 7 Mar. 1917, GD, 5581.

[48] O'Kelly to Gavan Duffy, 27 Mar. 1917, *ibid.*

[49] O'Connor to Patrick McCartan, 23 Mar. 1917; Michael Curran to Seán T. O'Kelly, 25 Mar. 1917, *ibid.*   [50] Michael Curran, statement, 1952, STO'K, 27,728(2), p. 193.

[51] McCartan to Gavan Duffy, 25 Mar. 1917, GD, 5581; CIs' reports, Kilkenny, King's Co. (Offaly), Sligo, Mar. 1917, CO.904/102.   [52] O'Kelly to Gavan Duffy, 30 Mar. 1917, GD, 5581.

tives had expressed sympathy with his idea of a conference, and such people were invited to attend in their own right. Sympathetic members of the clergy were invited to the Mansion House, and were urged to bring with them their 'fellow Priests of independent opinion'.[53] But despite his anxiety to secure a large attendance at his convention, Plunkett was not prepared to relent in his feud with the Nation League. His manifesto had been phrased in terms vague enough for its supreme council to consider acceptance, but in the course of a later acrimonious correspondence he confined participation to bodies whose policy included abstention from Westminster. No such requirement was made of other groups.[54]

The Mansion House convention of 19 April was the high-point of Plunkett's career as a national figure, and (appropriately) it came close to splitting the separatist movement in two. The preparations were so amateurish that the count had neglected to draw up an agenda; his son-in-law Thomas Dillon and his protégé Rory O'Connor were obliged to compile one shortly before the meeting. As delegates arrived, Dillon accosted them in search of acquaintances who might be willing to propose resolutions, and his political innocence was revealed by the fact that, unwittingly, he gave a strong representation to Griffith's Sinn Féin.[55] Only 68 of the 277 public bodies which had been circulated sent representatives to the conference, yet the Mansion House was filled with 1,200 people; not surprisingly, in the light of Plunkett's appeal to the clergy, many of those present were priests. Thomas Dillon issued invitations to his students in University College Dublin, while Collins, one of the count's supporters, had been allocated more than 30 per cent of the tickets to distribute.[56] Many Nation Leaguers attended in a private capacity.

Some members of the audience expected a breach between the Plunkett and Griffith wings of the movement, and a letter handed to the chairman illustrated these fears: 'it's said there is a "split" between the convention people and Arthur Griffith. I heard it from two priests. Should Arthur G. not be invited to the platform? In the name of God don't let it be said that there is a split'.[57] Griffith *was* invited to the platform, but the writer's apprehensions were justified and the two sides soon quarrelled fiercely.

After various uncontentious issues had been settled Plunkett confirmed his critics' fears. He denounced the evil of party organization and revealed his

---

[53] Plunkett, circular, Apr. 1917, CP, 11,383(3).

[54] Plunkett to J. J. O'Kelly, 11 Apr. 1917; F. J. O'Connor to Gavan Duffy, 4 Apr. 1917, GD, 5581.

[55] Thomas Dillon, 'Arthur Griffith and the reorganisation of Sinn Fein, (1917)', TCDL, MS 3738, p. 2.   [56] Note, n.d., CP, 11,383(1).

[57] 'C. MacG.' to Michael O'Mullane, 19 Apr. 1917, CP, 11,383(3).

plan for launching the 'Liberty League', a new movement which would challenge the Parliamentary Party. This body was to have about a thousand
branches, approximately one for every parish in the country, and any society
'of advanced thought' would have the right to be represented. Only those who
were committed to abstention from the House of Commons would be
welcome, and O'Flanagan warned delegates that they should not open doors
through which men would again steal into Westminster.[58] The count assured
the convention that his plan was not intended to damage any existing organization, but it was obvious that the new structure would duplicate rather than
complement the work done by Griffith's Sinn Féin, and that it would either
replace his party or else challenge it for the political leadership of radical
nationalists. Sinn Féin would receive the same dismissive treatment as the
Nation League.

   Griffith's colleague Seán Milroy outlined a rival scheme whereby organizations such as Sinn Féin, the Nation League, the Volunteers and the Labour Party
could co-operate under an executive on which they would all be represented;
through this body they could contest elections, present Ireland's case to the
postwar peace conference, and form a 'council of the Irish nation'. Others spoke
against Plunkett's proposal. Griffith warned that unless they banded together
against corruption the Parliamentary Party might be able to stage a comeback,
and he argued that there was no reason why men who did not see eye to eye
should not combine to pull down the common enemy. Pim, speaking on behalf
of the Sinn Féin party which Plunkett wished to marginalize, suggested that 'it
would be a pity to lose a name which had so distasteful a flavour in the mouth
of their Saxon friends'. Gavan Duffy of the Nation League pleaded on behalf of
the moderate elements that the convention should consider the views of the
middle-aged as well as the young – 'it was not fair to expect them to go the whole
hog at once'.[59] Plunkett's scheme was voted upon and accepted, but Milroy complained that the chairman had disallowed his rival motion. Griffith declared
that his party was not going to be absorbed by Plunkett's new organization, and
that 'Sinn Féin, for which we all stood when many of the men here to-day were
our opponents, still stands'.

   A split in the classic Irish tradition seemed imminent, there was much excitement in the hall, and 'those on the platform rose to their feet and conversed –
in some cases very heatedly – in small groups, while murmurs of protest
throughout the room testified that opinion was divided'.[60] However the assembly accepted unanimously the proposal of a Kerry priest that the matter should
be referred to Griffith and O'Flanagan, and the two men huddled together at the

---

[58] *II*, 20 Apr. 1917.   [59] *FJ*, 20 Apr. 1917.   [60] *Ibid.*

back of the platform. Freed from Plunkett's destructive influence they were able to agree on a formula almost identical to that proposed by Milroy a few minutes earlier.

It was decided that the different separatist and radical groups would preserve their distinct identities but they should 'get into contact with' an organizing committee. This body would represent the two rival factions. Griffith, Milroy, Tom Kelly and Stephen O'Mara were on one side, matched by Plunkett, his wife, O'Flanagan and Brugha on the other, and they were accompanied by William O'Brien the trade unionist, who was attached to neither group. (O'Mara, whose son James was one of Sinn Féin's principal benefactors, was by now aged 72, had been a Parnellite MP for a few months in 1886, and would end his career as a senator of the Irish Free State. At her husband's suggestion Countess Plunkett was included to represent the women of Ireland.)

This compromise was accepted with relief, and the gathering ended on a more positive note than many present had thought possible. Maud Griffith's account exudes an appropriate prejudice; she wrote that Plunkett suffered from a swelled head and 'was wanting (through innocence) to have a little following of his own, Fr O'Flanagan and Arthur had to settle it up for the public benefit'.[61] Plunkett's divisive actions had failed to provoke a split between radical and moderate elements in the movement, and the new committee provided a means of bringing them closer together. The convention also attracted much publicity, as well as providing more favourable opportunities for separatists from all over the country to establish contact with each other than had been possible in the blizzards of Roscommon.

Expansion

The new Mansion House committee proved to be more effective than its predecessor, the group which had been chosen two months earlier in the aftermath of Plunkett's election, and it enabled representatives of the different factions to co-ordinate their activities. But the feuding between 'radicals' and 'moderates' continued. Two weeks after the convention William O'Brien went to the first committee meeting with the intention of resigning his membership, but instead Griffith and O'Mara ensured that he was elected chairman; Plunkett had expected that he would occupy that post himself, and their manoeuvre caught him off guard.[62] This was only one of the setbacks which he encountered.

---

[61] Maud Griffith to Kate Kelly, n.d. (received 7 May 1917), NLI, MS 8411.
[62] William O'Brien, *Forth the banners go: reminiscences of William O'Brien* (Dublin, 1969), p. 150.

The balance of power between the two rivals soon changed, and during the weeks which spanned Plunkett's convention Griffith's position was strengthened immeasurably as his Sinn Féin party spread throughout the country. In February and March the police made occasional references to the foundation of Sinn Féin clubs, although the RIC's loose terminology limits the value of such reports. (It is only fair to add that until spring 1917 the general confusion concerning names and titles corresponded to a chaotic reality.) In mid-March the inspector general reported that 'Gaelic classes, concerts, dances, Sinn Fein clubs and GAA football matches are some of the most convenient means of collecting the rebels together and fomenting hatred of England'; the Sinn Féin party was regarded as being no more than one group among several.[63]

But from April onwards there were signs of a dramatic advance. Forty-one clubs were represented at the Mansion House convention (half of them from Dublin), sixteen were affiliated to the national executive at one meeting in April, while a week later *Nationality* claimed that there were Sinn Féin branches in every ward in Cork city and that all of them reported increased membership.[64] On 5 May the *Irishman* boasted that the party had about 150 clubs.[65] In June even the *Freeman's Journal* conceded that within the previous fortnight about seventy branches had been established throughout the country, and by the end of July the RIC (which would be likely to underestimate) had recorded a total of 336.[66]

From the precise details provided every week by *Nationality* it would seem that the party's 'take-off' came in late April and early May; by the end of the first week in May the paper claimed to have received requests for information from fifty-eight districts. In a mood of contagious enthusiasm new branches appeared all over the country; Sinn Féin was the fad or the craze of 1917. In Donegal the RIC county inspector suggested that the party's supporters were now less afraid to display their sympathies 'as their cause has received a certain political status', while a month later it was noted in West Galway that 'the older and more respectable people are getting afraid not to be Sinn Feiners'.[67] One Redmondite was reduced to suggesting that 'while this S.F. wave is passing over the land we should just hold tight and prevent ourselves from being carried away'.[68]

The new Sinn Féin branches were founded in various ways, and in the early months many of them were established as the result of private initiatives taken

[63] IG's report, Feb. 1917, CO.904/102.   [64] *Nationality*, 28 Apr., 5 May 1917.

[65] *Irishman*, 5 May 1917.   [66] *FJ*, 19 June 1917; IG's report, July 1917, CO.904/103.

[67] CIs' reports, Donegal, May 1917, W. Galway, June 1917, CO.904/103.

[68] Arthur Ryan to Maurice Moore, 11 Aug. 1917, NLI, MS 10,561(31).

by a few enthusiasts.[69] One of Plunkett's correspondents told him that 'there was a meeting of some of the most earnest workers from different parts of the County in Thurles, and it was decided unanimously to form Sinn Féin clubs in the various districts represented'.[70] In Carlow eleven separatists gathered to organize a Sinn Féin branch, formed themselves into a temporary working committee, wrote to Dublin for literature and membership cards, and convened a meeting at which new members would be enrolled.[71] A similar dynamism was reported from almost every part of the country, and sooner or later virtually all these branches affiliated with Sinn Féin headquarters at 6 Harcourt Street.

Sometimes clubs were formed by full-time party organizers, or as the result of the enthusiasm which followed their visits. In Cavan and Sligo numerous branches were established after Seán Milroy's tour in May. The effectiveness of these methods was noted by British observers, one of whom reported that the party

> owes its increasing strength to organisers who are allowed to go around the country forming new clubs and consolidating those already existing. The success of such organisers can be seen in the Co. Meath, which is now strongly Sinn Fein, thanks to the exertions of Sinn Fein organisers from Dublin.[72]

Prominent separatists were often present at the formation of a branch. At Caherciveen (Co. Kerry) about 500 Volunteers welcomed Austin Stack when he came to form a Sinn Féin club. Chaired by the local curate, he, Finian Lynch and Gearóid O'Sullivan (all released prisoners and senior military figures) addressed a crowded meeting. Then, after last mass on Sunday, a provisional committee was elected, a club was formed, and during the day about 200 members enrolled.[73] But even more important than such ceremonial occasions was the assistance given by already established branches to less advanced villages and townlands. Clubs founded others in geometric progression. One typical report concerned the Naas club's decision that 'every assistance should be accorded to the Eadestown men in the establishing of the branch, and in extending the organisation to the other neighbouring districts'.[74] In Co. Armagh

> excitement was caused in the little town of Moy on Sunday evening by the advent of a body of about 50 Sinn Féiners from Dungannon and Eglish, who paraded the town headed by a Sinn Féin flag, and proceeded to the

[69] For details of the clubs' activities see below, pp. 205–13.

[70] Pierce McCann to Plunkett, 25 May 1917, CP, 11,383(12).

[71] *Nationalist and Leinster Times*, 4 Aug. 1917.   [72] IO's report (M. and C.), Oct. 1917.

[73] *Kerryman*, 4 Aug. 1917.   [74] *Leinster Leader*, 23 June 1917.

Roman Catholic Reading Rooms, where a meeting for the purpose of inaugurating a Sinn Féin club was held.[75]

The rapid spread of Sinn Féin both assisted, and was assisted by, the by-elections which followed the separatists' victory in North Roscommon. The publicity, excitement and success associated with them inspired the party, even in areas far from the constituencies where contests took place.

South Longford

The first of these elections was held in South Longford, and the campaign had already begun by the time of Plunkett's convention in the Mansion House. The vacancy was long expected, as had been the case in Roscommon a few months earlier, and already in February the RIC noted that there was some Sinn Féin activity in anticipation of an election campaign.[76] John Phillips, the MP, died on 2 April, and within two days Griffith, Plunkett, Kelly, Collins, Rory O'Connor, William O'Brien and others met and decided to contest the seat.[77] Their candidate was Joe McGuinness, a Lewes prisoner who had been sentenced to three years' penal servitude after the rising. His brother Frank was a prominent figure among separatists in South Longford (although until Redmond's recruiting drive in 1914 he had been an active member of the UIL).[78] According to a later account, Griffith was unenthusiastic about Joe McGuinness's candidature and supported J. J. O'Kelly,[79] but any doubts which he might have had were mild compared with those shared by McGuinness himself and his colleagues in Lewes Jail.

On Easter Sunday de Valera wrote a long memorandum explaining why the prisoners had decided almost unanimously that separatists should not fight elections against the Parliamentary Party. He alluded to 'irrelevant items from the old Sinn Féin political policy, which, whatever their intrinsic merits, tend to alienate a number of Irishmen'. (Griffith's ideas concerning a dual monarchy and his past references to the king, lords and commons of Ireland must have been prominent among these items.) He wrote that if McGuinness were to be defeated, and if the prisoners were to be identified formally with his policy 'it would mean the ruin of the *hopes* – not to say the ideals – which prompted our comrades to give the

---

[75] *Armagh Guardian*, 26 Oct. 1917.   [76] CI's report, Longford, Feb. 1917, CO.904/102.

[77] William O'Brien, diary, 4 Apr. 1917, NLI, MS 15,705.

[78] Marie Coleman, 'County Longford, 1910–1923: a regional study of the Irish revolution' (Ph.D. dissertation, University College, Dublin, 1998), pp. 57, 70.

[79] O'Brien, *Forth the banners go*, p. 145.

word last Easter ... His defeat would mean our defeat – the irretrievable ruin of all our comrades died for and all that their death had gained.' His main concern was that the Volunteers should continue to be soldiers, and that, as a distinct organization, they should not be led into a political party. It would be satisfying to win the election, but to lose would mean bankruptcy, and he would have to be almost certain of success before agreeing to take the risk.[80]

However, de Valera realized that the prisoners were isolated in Lewes, and in a letter written at the same time to a friend in Ireland he confessed that the information which they received was meagre and almost contradictory.

> We are in a regular fog ... We have already had to come to important decisions on which the political situation had a most direct impact and intimate bearing – yet we had not the most necessary data for the forming of a clear solid judgment ... We are anxious to co-operate with you outside but we do not quite understand what you are doing.

Although the prisoners were willing to trust their comrades who were at liberty they did not even know whether these were united or divided into different camps. De Valera wondered 'whether it is good tactics (or strategy if you will) to provoke a contest in which *defeat* may well mean *ruin*', and he revealed some of the soldier's traditional suspicion of politics in his understandable anxiety lest 'what has been purchased by our comrades' blood should be lost on a throw with dice loaded against us'. He worried about Plunkett's programme and to what extent it was 'a reversion to the old Sinn Féin *political* movement' and stressed the need to avoid anything which 'would savour of old political parties and party divisions'.[81]

With only one or two exceptions the prisoners decided that it would be too dangerous to allow McGuinness contest the seat, and they turned down the proposal. When they learned that their objections had been overruled, and that his candidature was being continued despite their opposition, de Valera reported that 'some felt so strongly about it that they considered it our duty to repudiate it but the majority are in favour of letting it be for the present ... Nobody should think however that contesting elections is the policy which the men here would advocate if they had a say in the matter.' They thought that if the Parliamentary Party were left to itself it might crumble, but that its supporters might become more closely knit if they were attacked.[82]

One of those who disagreed with the majority of his colleagues was Thomas

---

[80] De Valera, memo, Easter Sunday 1917, EdeV.

[81] De Valera to Simon Donnelly, Easter Sunday/Monday 1917, *ibid.*

[82] De Valera to Donnelly, 28 Apr. 1917, *ibid.*

Ashe, the only prisoner who rivalled de Valera in military seniority. He argued that their colleagues at liberty in Ireland should be allowed discretion.[83] Ashe had an advantage over the others: a supply of coded messages from Collins in Dublin which kept him informed about the changing state of Irish public and political opinion.

Collins persisted in his support of McGuinness's campaign, despite the general disapproval of his military superiors, and when some of the Lewes prisoners conveyed their displeasure at his actions he referred to 'all their scathing messages . . . one gets so used to being called bad names and being misunderstood'. He was grateful for Ashe's support because it was the first encouragement which he had received.[84]

Already by this early stage Collins had begun to display those qualities – ambition, energy, efficiency, ruthlessness and charm – which would help make him the leading figure both in the war against the British and (somewhat ambivalently) in the subsequent consolidation of an independent Irish democracy. He would later add patience to his other qualities, but in 1917 he was an impetuous radical whose concerns were largely military.

The separatists' choice of Joe McGuinness, in contrast to that of Plunkett three months before, was a sign of their new confidence. They had abandoned their earlier ambiguity, and instead of running another sympathy candidate they had selected one of the Easter rebels as their champion. The battle lines were now clearly drawn, and the Redmondite *Longford Leader* compared McGuinness favourably to Count Plunkett: 'the Sinn Fein candidate in Longford is far more honest and tells us in advance what he means to do'.[85] Nationalist Ireland had a long tradition of electing political prisoners to parliament, and McGuinness could join a roll of honour which included William Smith O'Brien, O'Donovan Rossa, John Mitchel and Michael Davitt.

Despite the bond of a common enemy and the challenge of a new election campaign, tensions persisted within the separatist movement. One later account described an encounter which took place on the evening of Plunkett's convention. A group of Sinn Féiners sat together in the drawing-room of 6 Harcourt Street, Fr O'Flanagan reading out doggerel verse he had written to the air of 'the Rising of the Moon', when suddenly the door burst open. Accompanied by his ally Rory O'Connor, Collins entered, looked around truculently, and said loudly to Griffith 'I want to know what ticket is this Longford election being fought on . . . If you don't fight the election on the Republican ticket you will alienate all the young men'. An argument developed, even though

---

[83] Draft reply suggested by Ashe, n.d., *ibid*.   [84] Ó Lúing, *I die in a good cause*, p. 121.
[85] *Longford Leader*, 21 Apr. 1917, editorial.

Griffith was described as sitting silent and sphinx-like, and Collins rejected the craven suggestion that the most important objective was to win the election. The discussion waned after O'Flanagan, who had been a calming influence at the Mansion House not long before, resumed his role of peacemaker.[86] But such incidents did not disrupt the campaign, and, following the pattern of Roscommon, radicals and moderates co-operated with each other against the home rulers. According to newspaper and police accounts of the election, few of the Sinn Féin speakers stressed Collins's 'republican ticket'. It was quite enough that the party could appeal to what John Dillon would later describe as 'the hatred and distrust of the British Government – a sentiment which is in the blood and marrow of all Irish men and women'.[87]

Longford had a reputation of loyalty to Redmond, but in reality it had become even more alienated than many other parts of Ireland, and the Nationalists were debilitated by factions and feuds; the county's two MPs had loathed each other.[88] The party machine was exceptionally inefficient, and it was only on 25 April that Redmond ended the absurd situation in which three rival UIL candidates contested the seat; he chose one of them, Patrick McKenna, as the Parliamentary Party's sole nominee. McKenna was a formidable opponent. He was a radical who had long been regarded with suspicion by the police, he had enjoyed close links with the separatists in the past, and a decade earlier he had been one of the most prominent opponents of 'ranchers' in the county.[89] While there were still three home rule candidates in the field Frank McGuinness encouraged non-Sinn Féiners to vote for McKenna because he was the 'only one of the other three who had done a good day's work for Ireland'.[90] Some Nationalists were confident that they could repel the Sinn Féin challenge, and Dillon informed Redmond on 12 April that 'it appears to be quite certain that with a single candidate the Party could secure a sweeping victory'.[91] On the same day J. P. Farrell, the MP for North Longford, was able to assure Dillon that the Sinn Féin candidate 'is hopelessly out of it'.[92]

In South Longford the party aroused itself from its torpor for the first time since the home rule negotiations nearly a year earlier. The leadership had virtually ignored West Cork and North Roscommon, but Dillon, Devlin and many other prominent figures travelled from London or Dublin to speak in Longford.

---

[86] Michael J. Lennon, 'Looking backward', J. J. O'Connell MSS, NLI, 22,117(1).

[87] Dillon to T. P. O'Connor, 22 Sept. 1918, JD, 6742.

[88] Coleman, 'County Longford', pp. 31–7, 76, 92–4.

[89] Bew, *Conflict and conciliation*, pp. 156, 197.   [90] *Westmeath Examiner*, 21 Apr. 1917.

[91] Dillon to Redmond, 12 Apr. 1917, JR, 15,182(24).

[92] J. P. Farrell to Dillon, 12 Apr. 1917, JD, 6742.

With only one exception (South Armagh, the following year) more MPs campaigned there than in any of the other by-elections in 1917 and 1918. Dillon wrote to Redmond that 'we have the bishop, the great majority of the priests and the mob and four-fifths of the traders of Longford. And if in face of that we are beaten, I do not see how you can hold the party in existence.'[93]

Sinn Féin followed the pattern which it had already established in Roscommon; it took and held the lead, and it surpassed its opponents in both efficiency and numbers. The army intelligence officer for the Midlands noted that the Sinn Féiners were co-ordinated, and that they were not short of money or of organizers from other parts of the country.[94] *Nationality* launched what proved to be a most successful appeal for funds with which the separatists could fight the election; a total of £1,288 was raised, far more than was needed or used. The county inspector noted that 'they have a fleet of motor cars and are all put up in the best hotels in town and are spending money freely', while Redmondites taunted that they were funded by 'German gold'.[95]

A Sinn Féiner wrote to Plunkett that 'we got to know that our side was short of petrol and we were in a position to supply it so we sent 42 tins of it free of charge together with a motor on the day of the election'. He concluded proudly that it was an achievement 'which we think not bad coming from a small place like Castlerea [Co. Roscommon] with an MP living in our town'.[96] Limerick Sinn Féiners sent £50, two cars and eight men, while many supporters cycled the 77 miles (124 km) from Dublin to Longford; some of these covered an even greater distance when they got lost in Co. Leitrim.[97] McKenna complained that 'our opponents have been bringing their forces from all over the constituency in motors etc trying to intimidate the people'.[98] Already weeks before the election the *Irish Times* claimed that the Sinn Féin party was 'motoring daily in all directions', while later the *Irish Independent* reported that

> the Sinn Feiners have shown more remarkable organising powers. Their posters are displayed at every cross-road and village in the constituency and their colours float from tree tops and the roofs of houses. Pamphlets are being handed out by the thousand, giving quotations from the speeches of Messrs Redmond and Dillon on the questions of recruiting and conscription.[99]

---

[93] Lyons, *John Dillon*, p. 415.   [94] IO's report (M. and C.), Apr. 1917.

[95] CI's report, Longford, Apr. 1917, CO.904/102; *II*, 30 Apr. 1917.

[96] Thomas Egan to Plunkett, 12 May 1917, CP, 11,383(12).

[97] *Factionist*, 17 May 1917; Joe Good, *Enchanted by dreams: the journal of a revolutionary* (Dingle, 1996), p. 109.   [98] McKenna to Mr Mulvehill, 1 May 1917, CP, 11,379(14).

[99] *IT*, 19 Apr. 1917; *II*, 1 May 1917.

Copies of *Nationality* were distributed free before polling day. Sinn Féin posters and leaflets showing a convict in prison uniform, with the message 'put him in to get him out', had a widespread and enduring impact. Several separatists who had been deported in February, notably Darrell Figgis and Patrick McCartan, escaped from detention in England and returned to participate in the election. Almost all the Sinn Féin leaders took part, and a letter of Maud Griffith's gives an impression of the pace of the campaign. She wrote that 'we are all in a ferment over Longford, Arthur left this morning at 7 o'c by motor to address some meeting there, coming back tonight to see after the paper, then leaving again Tuesday morning to stay till the poll is announced on Thursday'.[100]

The issues which the separatists raised were not simply abstention from Westminster, McGuinness's status as a prisoner, the rising, or even (despite Collins's wishes) the republic. The Parliamentary Party was attacked for its failure to prevent the introduction of summer time (a recent wartime innovation), and Sinn Féin also claimed that it, and not the party, would be able to prevent the government's proposed land tax.[101] Numerous speakers argued that a victory by the home rulers would strengthen the case for both conscription and partition. In turn, McGuinness's supporters complained of warnings by Nationalists that if their candidate were to be defeated old age pensioners would suffer.[102] Redmondite canvassers often met with hostility, and at one meeting J. P. Farrell expressed regret that some of the old UIL members had turned their backs on the party.[103] But this must have been a feature common to all the separatists' victories in the by-election campaigns of 1917 and 1918. The electoral registers were out of date and many of the young radicals did not have the right to vote; the high poll for McGuinness and other Sinn Féin candidates was not the result of young voters making their presence felt, but of older voters changing their minds.

In a novel which he wrote in 1919 Brinsley MacNamara sent his fictional hero to campaign in the Longford election. The experience proved disillusioning, and the amateur politician found that

> there was nothing so very different from all that he remembered of a fight between a Nationalist and an Independent Nationalist in the days before Sinn Fein had dared to lift its head. The staunchest supporters of Joe McGuinness in the conduct of the campaign had once been staunch supporters after the same fashion of some nominee of Redmond's.[104]

---

[100] Maud Griffith to Kate Kelly, n.d. (received 7 May 1917), NLI, MS 8411.

[101] *Threatening a land tax* (pamphlet), EdeV.   [102] *II*, 4 May 1917.   [103] *II*, 30 Apr. 1917.

[104] MacNamara, *Clanking of chains*, p. 181.

The election was more closely fought than Roscommon, and there were reports of canvassers continuing their work until midnight and rousing farmers from their beds – a sign either of inexperienced enthusiasm or else of black propaganda, of campaigning under false colours with the aim of antagonizing electors rather than of persuading them. Violence and intimidation were widespread, speakers were stoned and pelted with eggs, and party workers were beaten up. If complaints against the other side's activities indicate the extent of intimidation, it would seem that the Sinn Féiners were more sinned against than sinning. The *Freeman's Journal* also reported that young men prevented their elders from voting, while the *Longford Leader* warned Redmondites against threats to parental authority:

> some of the young members of your household may try to put obstacles in your way to prevent you going to vote. If they won't get your breakfast in time or try to keep your best clothes hidden on you, don't be ashamed or afraid to turn out in your working clothes so long as you can make your way to the polling booth.[105]

Despite all the efforts of the Sinn Féin canvassers, despite the numbers of their supporters from Dublin and elsewhere, despite the weakness of the Parliamentary Party, and despite the discontent noted generally throughout the county, it is likely that McGuinness would have been defeated without the support of an unlikely ally: the Catholic archbishop of Dublin. The doubts expressed by de Valera on behalf of the Lewes prisoners were almost vindicated. On the day before the election Dr William Walsh attacked the idea of partition in a letter which he wrote to the Dublin *Evening Herald*, and he concluded by remarking 'I am fairly satisfied that the mischief has already been done, and that the country is practically sold.' News of this letter was telegraphed at once to Longford town. Sinn Féiners printed and distributed posters and leaflets in which Walsh's statement was accompanied by the gloss: 'this is a clear call from the great and venerated Archbishop of Dublin to vote against the Irish Party traitors and vote for Joe McGuinness!' These were distributed on polling day.

Initially McKenna was declared the winner and he was defeated only on a re-count after it was noticed that a bundle of ballot papers had been misplaced. As McGuinness's margin of victory was a mere thirty-seven votes, and since it is quite possible that Walsh's accusation may have swayed at least twenty electors, his action may have secured Sinn Féin's victory in South Longford. Intimidation may also have been used, and the RIC believed that at the declar-

---

[105] *FJ*, 10 May 1917; *Longford Leader*, 5 May 1917.

ation of the result a number of 'Liberty Hall men' who were present carried revolvers.[106]

The result was important, however narrow the margin of victory and however it might have been achieved. A Sinn Féin defeat in Longford would hardly have led to a Parliamentary Party victory in Clare two months later, but it might well have discredited the tactics of Griffith and the other political figures who led the separatist cause until the release of the Lewes prisoners. In this way it might have thrown the leadership of the movement into the hands of more extreme elements, some of whom remained dubious about the whole policy of contesting by-elections.

The Liberty League

A new problem risked undermining the separatist cause and intensifying the distaste which many Volunteers felt for the wiles of politics. During and after the Longford election campaign the rival factions were once more engaged in competing against one another, as well as in fighting their common Redmondite enemy. Plunkett and his radical advisers had not abandoned their attempt to gain control of the movement, and, despite the compromise settlement which had been reached at the end of the Mansion House convention, the count persevered with his idea of creating a new national organization. The aim behind this manoeuvre was to surpass Griffith in one of the areas where he had a decisive advantage, his leadership of a (relatively) organized party, and thereby achieve the ascendancy which had eluded him at the convention. Plunkett was probably right in his belief that the younger elements, and in particular the Volunteers, would be more likely to support him than Griffith. Gavan Duffy compared the count's followers to the radical 'mountain' in the French revolution.[107]

Plunkett went ahead with his old idea of establishing a 'Liberty League', a nation-wide system of clubs which would duplicate and rival the existing Sinn Féin structures. Even if he had acted earlier it is doubtful if such a new movement would have been successful. But by now (May–June 1917) it was too late to form a new separatist party unless it were either closely identified with the name 'Sinn Féin', or else were no more than an arm of the Volunteers – and not an independent force in its own right. Plunkett faced precisely such a takeover

---

[106] CI's report, Longford, May 1917, CO.904/103. Liberty Hall had been the headquarters of the Transport Union. It was destroyed in the rising.

[107] Gavan Duffy to P. S. O'Hegarty, 29 May 1917, GD, 5581.

bid from Mary MacSwiney who informed him that, at least in Cork, the only people who could be trusted with the organization of an independent Ireland were Volunteers and members of Cumann na mBan. Although on the surface he might not find them so capable, she assured him that they were known to be honest, and she warned that unless his executive were 'composed mainly of them and controlled by them it cannot succeed'.[108] But by this time Griffith's Sinn Féin had drawn too far ahead, and even if Plunkett had been prepared to adopt MacSwiney's course he would have been unable to overtake his rival. However he did his best.

The count issued another circular in which he urged his supporters to establish Liberty clubs in their districts, and a race developed between the two movements to found branches in every parish in the country. It was an unequal contest. He succeeded in arousing some enthusiasm, but the general level of response to his proposal remained discouraging. Along with numerous expressions of support, the replies which he received included many examples of confusion and misunderstanding. One correspondent informed Plunkett that in his travels throughout ten counties he found that 'at present all the young men are Sinn Féiners and a good many old men too'; he would be 'killed' if he tried to establish any other kind of club.[109] Another wrote that it was 'the general opinion that Sinn Féin Clubs would draw more members', but promised that if any district were found to be opposed to Sinn Féin 'we will get our friends . . . to start Liberty Clubs'.[110] A third raised an even more formidable objection: 'as many branches of Sinn Féin are now at work permit me to ask, is it wise to establish an organisation for the same objects as one already existing, and which is recognised not alone in Ireland but abroad as a power? . . . will it not bear the suspicion of rivalry and disunion?'[111] Others revealed that they did not share his concern with party labels. One told him that 'the Clubs here do not bear the name of Liberty Clubs but have the same object', while another assumed tactlessly that 'it would be immaterial which organization was established'.[112]

Plunkett provoked controversy as well as bewilderment. He was informed that separatists in Tralee 'nearly broke up our organisation here as a result of trying to decide between Liberty Club or Sinn Féin . . . it resolved itself into a question of Count Plunkett versus Arthur Griffith'. The result was a compro-

[108] Mary MacSwiney to Plunkett, 30 May 1917, CP, 11,383(6).

[109] Owen Hegarty to Plunkett, 21 May 1917, CP, 11,383(5).

[110] Patrick McDonagh to Plunkett, 22 May 1917, CP, 11,383(8).

[111] Seamus Breathnach to Plunkett, n.d., CP, 11,383(6).

[112] Mary Clancy to Plunkett, 27 May 1917, CP, 11,383(5); Seán Ó Súilleabháin to Plunkett, 31 May 1917, CP, 11,383(9).

mise in which the members decided to call themselves the 'Casement Club' and establish direct contact with the Mansion House committee.[113] Liam de Róiste wrote from the Sinn Féin branch in Cork deploring the committee's inaction and the prospect of a split in the national movement. He concluded that until the present differences had been settled 'this Executive claims the right to direct and control the organisations in Cork city and county, as the best means of preventing a break up of the forces here making for Irish Sovereign Independence'.[114] The inspector general of the RIC hoped that the Sinn Féin movement might split into moderate and radical elements, the latter led by Plunkett.[115]

The Liberty clubs were unable to compete with Sinn Féin. They lacked all their rival's advantages – a start of several months (or years), a tradition, a well-known name, a central office with two paid full-time organizers, and two newspapers, *Nationality* and *The Irishman*. Their power was negative. They could prevent Griffith's Sinn Féin from becoming the only representative of political separatism, and perhaps they could even prevent it from supplanting the Parliamentary Party as the main voice of Irish nationalism, but they could not replace or marginalize it. As both parties gained support the chances of conflict between them increased. Plunkett had no wish to divide and deadlock the movement in this way, and the backing of those new clubs which he had established, together with the fact that he was still widely regarded as the principal figure in the separatist cause, placed him in a strong position if he chose to compromise. Eventually he gave way and abandoned his Liberty League.

The two parties merged after extended negotiations in late May and early June, the details of which remain obscure. According to one account the amalgamation was decided upon at a meeting of the Mansion House committee which met in Cathal Brugha's house in Rathmines. A long argument over what form a new, united party should take came to a hasty end as most of those present rushed to catch the last tram home, but before they left they agreed that Plunkett's clubs would join with Sinn Féin, and that half of the old executive would retire to make way for an equal number of members from the Liberty League.[116]

The party would retain its dual monarchist policy, and Griffith would remain as president until October when a convention of all the amalgamated Sinn Féin

---

[113] E. O'Connor to Plunkett, 22 May 1917, CP, 11,383(9).

[114] De Róiste to Mansion House committee, 2 June 1917, CP, 11,383(6).

[115] IG's report, May 1917 (written 9 June), CO.904/103.

[116] Thomas Dillon, 'Birth of the new Sinn Féin and the ard fheis, 1917', *Capuchin Annual*, 1967, pp. 395–6.

clubs would review the situation. *Ex officio* the members of the Mansion House committee would form part of the new executive, and its other members included Collins and Rory O'Connor. Any other party which might join later would also be entitled to representation, and during the summer and autumn the committee's numbers were augmented as de Valera, Cosgrave, Markievicz and others were co-opted after their release from prison. Until the convention met nearly five months later this group led the Sinn Féin party or movement.

By now the Nation League had come to accept the principle of abstention from Westminster, and it joined the new united Sinn Féin after three months of intermittent and leisurely negotiations. It vanished from sight as completely as the Liberty clubs had already done. The ease with which it finally merged with the two main branches of political separatism vindicated Griffith's conciliatory approach towards its members earlier in the year, in contrast to the abuse and excommunications of Count Plunkett. The League retained its air of lofty superiority to the end, and one of its members believed that it would 'be better for the country that some Nation Leaguers should be on the controlling body as a steadying factor'.[117] At least they were able to contribute their political experience together with their self-confidence.

East Clare and Kilkenny

For a brief two weeks Griffith was able to enjoy his position as unchallenged leader of a united movement. Plunkett continued along his flamboyant path during this period; he was detained after addressing a proclaimed meeting, and the ensuing scuffle resulted in the death of the only government official to be killed in Ireland between April 1916 and January 1919. However both he and Griffith were eclipsed when the Lewes prisoners, the surviving heroes of Easter Week, returned to Dublin on 18 June.

Lloyd George was anxious to placate American opinion and to weaken the impact of the anti-war Irish lobby in the United States. To this end he summoned an 'Irish Convention' which would represent all sides and all factions in the country; it was argued that such a body might draft a united report which could then be implemented by the government. In order to create a general mood of goodwill and reconciliation all the remaining prisoners were freed. For many of them a 'life sentence' had ended after only thirteen months in jail. The cabinet agreed that 'the real question for decision was whether the amnesty would or would not give the Convention a better chance, and that this was the

---

[117] George Murnaghan to Gavan Duffy, 6 July 1917, GD, 5581.

only ground on which it should be considered'.[118] (A mere three weeks later, however, the leading figures in Dublin Castle agreed that if Sinn Féin won the forthcoming East Clare by-election it was questionable whether the convention would have any useful results.[119])

The Lewes prisoners were the natural leaders of the movement which had flourished as a result of their rebellion. They began to assert themselves in the course of the next few months, once they appreciated what had been achieved in their absence and once they had overcome their soldiers' aversion to political activity. The successes of the first half of 1917, the by-election victories, the conversion and organization of public opinion, and the painful emergence of a united political party, all encouraged the surviving leaders of the Easter Rising to work through the framework which had already been developed, rather than build any new structures of their own. The conflict between Griffith and Plunkett which had cast its shadow over most of the period had only just been settled, and the Sinn Féin house had only just been put in order, when the prisoners returned to Ireland.

The timing was perfect. Instead of having to sort out the chaos created by incompetent deputies – or so the situation might have appeared to them had they been released even three weeks earlier – de Valera, Ashe and the other imprisoned leaders came into the fullness of their inheritance. They found a united, efficient and energetic party awaiting them. If the unification of Sinn Féin had been delayed until after the release of the prisoners, it is virtually certain that Griffith, Plunkett and others who had been active in early 1917 would have been discredited. In that case, the influence of the Volunteers and the extremists on the joint executive would have been considerably greater. It is also possible that the divisions between rival sections might have persisted longer and might have been harder to resolve.

The newly released Volunteers had no time to familiarize themselves at leisure with the arts and skills of politics; together with the veterans of Roscommon and Longford, they were thrown at once into another by-election campaign. Major Willie Redmond (the party leader's brother) was killed at Messines on the Western Front, and his death created a vacancy in East Clare. This was one of the constituencies which were most likely to elect a Sinn Féiner, or simply to defeat a Parliamentary Party candidate no matter what form the opposition to him might have taken.

Clare was the most unruly and rebellious area in Ireland, and to an even greater extent than Roscommon it was a source of anxiety to Dublin Castle. In

---

[118] Cabinet conclusions, 14 June 1917, Cab. 23/3, WC.163(19).
[119] Notes of discussion, 3 July 1917, Cab. 23/3, WC.175, appendix II.

early 1917, 154 of the 220 people who needed police protection throughout the country lived in Clare and Galway.[120] As far back as 1909 Clare had the third highest number of paid-up members of Griffith's Sinn Féin party of any county in Ireland.[121] The UIL was in decline, and while the local press reported 147 meetings in Clare during 1913, the figures fell to 44 in 1914, 10 in 1915, and 1 in 1916 before the Easter Rising.[122] In November 1916 T. M. Healy remarked that both the MPs for the county would be rejected by their electors if the present mood persisted,[123] and in late May 1917 the Ennis rural district council passed a resolution calling on Major Redmond to resign.

The local Nationalist paper, the *Saturday Record*, claimed that by the time of Willie Redmond's death Sinn Féin had formed election committees which tapped the remotest parts of the constituency. This was followed by 'a descent on the district of the outside organisers from Dublin, Belfast and Cork, all adepts in the inner intricacies, machinery and manipulation of up-to-date electioneering, who held the field with practically no opposition for a fortnight'. A grudging tribute was paid to the 'really perfectly organized machinery at the headquarters in Ennis'.[124]

Within a week of the vacancy a convention of 200 people (including 60 priests) had selected de Valera as the Sinn Féin candidate, and his widely anticipated release from jail two days later was the signal to turn the East Clare campaign into a triumphant procession. Several other names had been considered. Later it was claimed that the clergy had canvassed for Eoin MacNeill but that de Valera's supporters lobbied more effectively, and that the Volunteers refused to accept MacNeill because of his countermanding order on Easter Sunday.[125] Peadar Clancy, the only Clareman sentenced to death after the rising, was described during the campaign as the first candidate selected by the Sinn Féin constituency committee.[126] Thomas Ashe was encouraged to stand, but declined because of the persistence shown by de Valera's supporters and his own reluctance to cause disunity.[127]

East Clare with its 9,000 voters was one of the most populous constituencies in Ireland (outside Ulster, which was under-represented), and it was also one of the largest. Its rail network was poor and many of its villages were isolated,

---

[120] IG's report, Mar. 1917, CO.904/102.   [121] *Sinn Féin*, 28 Aug. 1909.

[122] Fitzpatrick, *Politics and Irish life*, p. 114.

[123] Healy to William O'Brien, 3 Nov. 1916, NLI, MS 8556(11).

[124] *Saturday Record*, 14 July 1917.

[125] Joe Barrett, memo, 17 Apr. 1963, EdeV; Michael Brennan, *The war in Clare, 1911–1921: personal memoirs of the Irish War of Independence* (Dublin, 1980), p. 25.

[126] *Clare Champion*, 30 June 1917.   [127] Ó Lúing, *I die in a good cause*, pp. 129–30.

ensuring that the contest would be dominated by cars to an even greater extent than had been the case in Longford. Sinn Féin's campaign was boosted when West Cork Volunteers supplied 100 gallons (450 litres) of petrol which had been washed ashore in metal drums from a torpedoed transport ship.[128] No election had been contested since 1895 and the UIL machine was understandably decrepit; the Redmondites fought with less enthusiasm than they had displayed in Longford, and their defeat was widely expected. The county inspector remarked later that only the Sinn Féiners had been active during the campaign.[129]

De Valera's opponent, Patrick Lynch, was described memorably as being a strong candidate because 'he has defended one half of the murderers in Clare and is related to the other half'.[130] He received little support from his prospective colleagues. Joe Devlin remarked that the party would not intervene in Clare 'as Mr Redmond feels very sore at the way in which his brother was treated by them', and Dillon reinforced the view that they should distance themselves from Lynch.[131] Later, however, he wrote to Redmond that he and Devlin were inclined to withdraw their opposition to involvement in the contest; Nationalists from Clare and Limerick had demanded that party members should be allowed to help Lynch's campaign.[132] Urgent appeals were sent to Dublin for cars and speakers. Redmond was warned that the party was faced with desperate opposition, and that the bishop and a section of the clergy, particularly the younger priests, were 'moving heaven and hell' to secure de Valera's election.[133] The leaders relented, grudgingly. Afterwards, Devlin admitted that he had sent forty cars to Clare for the election at a cost of between £500 and £600, and had not charged the constituency organization for their use, but he repudiated any other expenditure. Dillon complained that 'the impertinence of Lynch in demanding his expenses is really intolerable'.[134]

Sinn Féin was organized and aggressive. Its self-confidence was shown by repeated defiance of the British authorities, particularly through the military activities of the Volunteers, and by the provocative tone of many speeches. Some

---

[128] Liam Deasy, *Towards Ireland free: the West Cork brigade in the War of Independence, 1917–1921* (Cork and Dublin, 1973), pp. 37–8.   [129] CI's report, Clare, July 1917, CO.904/103.

[130] Annie O'Brien to Redmond, 19 June 1917, JR, 15,263(2).

[131] Devlin to Henry Moloney, 16 June 1917, Moloney MSS, Public Record Office, Northern Ireland, T.2257/11; Dillon to Redmond, 21 June 1917, JR, 15,182(24).

[132] Dillon to Redmond, 26 June 1917, *ibid.*

[133] John Moroney to Redmond, 4 July 1917, JR, 15,263(2).

[134] Devlin to Redmond, 1 Aug. 1917, JR, 15,181(3); Dillon to Redmond, 3 Aug. 1917, JR, 15,182(24).

separatists abandoned the guarded language and the relative restraint of Roscommon and Longford, and those who wanted a republic expressed their demands quite openly. De Valera, in particular, alarmed some supporters by his vehement speeches.[135] He told audiences that 'you have no enemy but England, and you must be prepared to fight against England', and 'although we fought once and lost, it is only a lesson for the second time'.[136] But at times he was ambivalent, and he was able to declare that 'every vote you give now is as good as the crack of a rifle in proclaiming your desire for freedom'.[137] At one meeting, denying that he was an anarchist and an atheist, he was reported as saying that 'all his life he had been associated with priests', they knew him, and they were behind him in the election.[138]

There was a divergence in emphasis between the moderate and the republican elements in Sinn Féin. The 'Griffithites' tended to be more cautious. They stressed themes such as Irish nationality, they demanded complete independence and representation at the post-war peace conference, and they denounced over-taxation, the Parliamentary Party, loyalists and British oppression. An audience in Tulla was assured that Sinn Féin was as constitutional as Parnell and the Land League had been.[139] The radicals referred frequently to 'the republic' and 'the enemy', to fighting, arming, drilling and reviving the Irish Volunteers. But the difference was one of degree rather than of kind, and the lines between the groups were not clear-cut. De Valera and Griffith provided the two poles, the one frequently stressing his republicanism and the other never going into details about systems of government, while the rest of the Sinn Féin leaders came somewhere between them.

The party's propaganda stressed other issues, in particular those of pensions and the threat of conscription. One pamphlet was headed 'This concerns OLD AGE PENSIONERS', while another declared that 'John Redmond supports Conscription'. A third began with 'a Business Proposition. Ireland is now being taxed to the tune of over Thirty Millions each year. Ireland cannot escape that as long as she is held captive by England,' and it continued by claiming that through an appeal to the peace conference Ireland could demand that her tax per capita be reduced from £8 to £2.10s (£2.50p).[140]

It was during the Clare election that the Volunteers re-emerged in public as

---

[135] For a somewhat different interpretation of de Valera in East Clare, see David Fitzpatrick, 'De Valera in 1917; the undoing of the Easter Rising', in John P. O'Carroll and John A. Murphy (eds.), *De Valera and his times* (Cork, 1983), pp. 101–12.

[136] 'Sinn Fein: meetings in 1917', CO.904/23/3, pp. 41–2.   [137] *Clare Champion*, 14 July 1917.

[138] *FJ*, 6 July 1917. See below, pp. 00–00.   [139] *Clare Champion*, 23 June 1917.

[140] Pamphlets, EdeV; NLI, LO.P. 116(49 and 62).

a powerful element in Irish life. They paraded through the streets, formed escorts for de Valera, acted as a private police force, and generally succeeded in making the RIC redundant. The county inspector was alarmed at the fact that 'almost every young man carries a revolver',[141] and the campaign introduced into the constituency a new element of lawlessness which worsened steadily throughout the autumn and winter. Clare enhanced its position as the most disturbed area in Ireland, and eventually, in February 1918, it became the first county to be placed under military rule since the aftermath of the rising.

Intimidation was widespread. On election day in Feakle

> the High Sheriff and his assessor . . . were held up on their customary tour of the polling stations by a motor car drawn across the road at the entrance to the village. They were challenged as to whether they were voters for Mr Lynch, but when their identity was made clear, a way was instantly made and they went into the booths.[142]

Few incidents were as dramatic as this, but numerous complaints were made about Sinn Féin abuses and about sons voting in place of their dead fathers. (This would, of course, have been fully in accordance with Irish electoral practice.) On the other hand, a unionist, George O'Callaghan-Westropp, was able to praise the general level of discipline during the campaign and he provided Clare with the ultimate accolade: 'the tone and conduct of the election would have done honour to South County Dublin'.[143]

To an even greater extent than had been the case in Roscommon and Longford, the Sinn Féin campaign was conducted in a military fashion. For example, Patrick Brennan of the Volunteers reported his 'measures for protection': about 200 men, armed if possible with sticks and hurleys, were positioned strategically throughout Ennis, and arrangements were made for communications and the provision of food.[144] De Valera's papers include a note in his own hand giving a list of instructions for polling day: two cars with armed guards were to accompany ballot boxes to Ennis after the polls closed; a staff of capable men was to check the voters' lists; and the first of several numbered points read 'no Drink'.[145] One minor example of the discipline which characterized the campaign was noted long afterwards: the Irish language writer Padraic Ó Conaire went to Clare and remained sober throughout the election.[146]

Virtually all the young people supported Sinn Féin, including the greater

---

[141] CI's report, Clare, June 1917, CO.904/103.   [142] *Saturday Record*, 14 July 1917.

[143] *IT*, 17 July 1917.   [144] Patrick Brennan, report, n.d. (July 1917), EdeV.

[145] De Valera, note, n.d. (July 1917), *Ibid*.

[146] Sidney Arnold to Michael J. Lennon, 15 Nov. 1952, NLI, MS 22,288(II).

part of the young clergy. So did the county newspaper, the *Clare Champion*. The election result was seen as a foregone conclusion, even though no-one expected that the margin of victory would be so wide; de Valera received 5,010 votes and Lynch 2,035. The *Freeman's Journal* conceded that East Clare had declared for revolution by an overwhelming majority, and T. M. Healy rejoiced with a sense of historical perspective: 'since we put out the Liberals in June 1885, I have not felt so flippant'.[147] There were celebrations in Clare and throughout the country; one touching example came from a seven-year-old boy in Tarbert (Co. Kerry) who wrote to de Valera that 'we had candles lighting in every window the night you were elected'.[148] The following stanza comes from one of the many poems which commemorated the victory:

> De Valera! my ideal of what noble man should be
> Calm, reservéd, warm, impulsive, and strong-hearted as the sea,
> Laughter-loving, glad and pensive, sad and happy all combined,
> Scorning all the hollow shamming of the modern human mind,
> True to principle and honour, yet as playful as a child,
> As a father, soldier, scholar, always gentle, always kind.[149]

De Valera was now the people's hero; Griffith or Plunkett had never inspired such verse. His election was the decisive turning-point in his rapid evolution from military to political republicanism, and he soon acquired a mastery of his new trade. He revealed himself to be a man who 'could blend . . . superficial inflexibility with profound opportunism';[150] he became a shrewd, skilful, revered and autocratic leader. His many strengths were undermined by deviousness, self-importance and narrowness of vision, but in the short run only his virtues were apparent.

The excitement of the Clare campaign distracted attention from Sinn Féin's caution in deciding not to challenge the Parliamentary Party when the South Dublin seat fell vacant; it was an unpromising area which had elected a unionist as recently as January 1910. The next contested by-election, in Kilkenny city, was little more than a formality. Like Clare, Kilkenny was out of sympathy with the Nationalists, and to a considerable extent it had already been won over to separatist views. In March the *Irishman* reported that two of the county's three newspapers had changed their political allegiance, and that all its five boards of guardians and district councils had repudiated Redmond;

---

[147] *FJ*, 12 July 1917, editorial; Callanan, *T. M. Healy*, p. 533.

[148] Denis Quill to de Valera, 14 July 1917, EdeV.

[149] Unsigned poem, n.d., EdeV. In a typescript variant the final words are 'always gentle, loving, mild'.   [150] David Fitzpatrick, *The two Irelands, 1912–1939* (Oxford, 1998), p. 105.

'what Roscommon did yesterday, Kilkenny would do to-morrow, if it got the chance'.[151]

The Sinn Féin candidate was W. T. Cosgrave, a long-serving Sinn Féin member of Dublin Corporation who had fought in the Easter Rising. As if to launch his campaign, the *Kilkenny People*, which had been a subject of police complaints for the past year, was suppressed and some of its staff were arrested. At the beginning of August the RIC reported that separatism was making considerable progress and 'all the young people are rampant Sinn Fein but the older and representative citizens keep aloof from it'. The Nationalists were in a minority and so far they had offered no opposition.[152]

The constituency was compact, its electorate was one of the smallest in Ireland, and the campaign was subdued. Even after the result had been declared, when accusations of intimidation might have been expected, the *Freeman's Journal* remarked that 'one of the most remarkable features of this election was the great order'.[153] (The defeated candidate himself was less temperate in his comments, describing the result as 'a victory for intolerance, low, mean, lying and scurrilous abuse, terrorism and intimidation of the grossest type'.[154])

Volunteers armed with sticks and accompanied by bands paraded through the streets in support of Cosgrave, while de Valera and others made inflammatory speeches and demanded a republic. Even though the party leadership descended on the city in force, the campaign cost little in comparison with those which had preceded it; the relevant figures were Longford, £491, Clare, £766 and Kilkenny, £210.[155] The Parliamentary Party made little effort and the national press reported only three of its MPs campaigning in the constituency. Cosgrave won by 772 votes to 392, and afterwards one British military observer remarked that the same result appeared likely in any constituency which would become vacant.[156]

The by-elections

Sinn Féin's election campaigns have generally been seen as the first fruits of the party's revival. More importantly, however, they were also one of the causes of this revival, and were one of the means whereby the separatists were guided into political and constitutional channels. In 1917 Sinn Féiners needed activity,

[151] *Irishman*, 31 Mar. 1917.   [152] CI's report, Kilkenny, July 1917, CO.904/103.

[153] *FJ*, 13 Aug. 1917.   [154] *Kilkenny Journal*, 15 Aug. 1917.

[155] 'Cash account of national executive and various elections, 30th Sept., 1918', RB, 8786(1).

[156] IO's report (S.), Aug. 1917.

3.2 Stepping-stones

excitement and success, and all of these were provided by the election campaigns. The movement was able to spread its wings and test its strength. It could
evaluate and adapt the different tactics which it used, it acquired publicity, and
its leaders were able to influence and be influenced by public opinion.
Throughout the country there were reports of how election successes invigo-
rated the separatists, and one typical example of this pattern was Maud
Griffith's reaction to Longford: 'the victory put great heart and hope into all'.[157]
In West Cork in July 1917 the RIC inspector noted that the only political feature
during the month had been the rapid growth of the Sinn Féin movement, and
that the Longford and Clare election results had been chiefly responsible for
this.[158]

The elections were both an encouragement and a vindication, showing the
separatists that the people supported them and their policies – or, at least, their
image. Griffith believed that Sinn Féin should win mass support through political agitation and organization, and that it should build an efficient party

[157] Maud Griffith to Kate Kelly, 22 May 1917, NLI, MS 8411.
[158] CI's report, W. Cork, July 1917, CO.904/103.

machine capable of utilizing the change in public opinion. His approach seemed to have been confirmed by events.

Things might have turned out differently. Volunteers might have taken to the hills and guerrilla warfare might have begun earlier than 1919, or else a number of mutually hostile parties might have dissipated their efforts, as seemed about to happen (thanks to Count Plunkett) on two different occasions during 1917. But localized violence would probably have antagonized the public unless nationalists had first been strengthened in their new separatist loyalties, and this task was achieved in the 'political phase' of 1917–18. The by-elections alone did not cause the emergence of the new Sinn Féin party, but they provided it with a decisive initial impulse and encouraged the development which it took. Without this stimulus, and without the enthusiasm which the campaigns inspired and channelled, political reorganization would have been slower and less certain.

More than any other factor it was these four by-elections in 1917 which facilitated the drastic change in the scale and efficiency of the Sinn Féin effort. Roscommon broke the vicious circle whereby organization could best be furthered by political activity, and political activity by organization. Responding to a local initiative, a miscellaneous group of individuals and factions developed a machine which flourished, despite the problems which it encountered, and which soon overcame the experienced UIL. The process snowballed, and each victory facilitated the next. The RIC inspector general, observing de Valera's campaign in Clare, remarked that 'such is the impetus gained by Sinn Féin from the victories at Roscommon and Longford that his success is not improbable'.[159] In each county where an election took place Sinn Féin's strength increased as dramatically as that of the UIL declined, but the impact was also nation-wide and not merely local.

The by-elections provided both a need and an opportunity for co-operation among the various elements of the heterogeneous Sinn Féin movement, and gradually a broad consensus emerged. The Nation League was weaned away from its early commitment to Westminster, while the Volunteers and the other physical force elements accepted the principle (or the practice) of contesting elections. They helped build a popular political movement as well as form an army of the elite. Politicians and soldiers learned from the events of 1917, and the by-elections were the most important of these events. Both the zealots and the mass of the people moved in each other's direction, and the result was a rough-and-ready compromise between them.

The elections also fulfilled another important, although negative function. The Parliamentary Party was defeated on its own ground by the electioneering

---

[159] IG's report, June 1917, *ibid.*

methods in which it had proved so adept for so long. After the Clare result, the *Freeman's Journal* lamented 'the severity of the blow that has been struck at the national cause in the only form in which that cause could triumph within the present generation'.[160] In Easter Week the party had been outmanoeuvred when the republicans transferred the rivalry between them to the military battlefield, an arena where the parliamentarians were at a natural disadvantage. In 1917 the Redmondites were routed on the constitutional front where their own defensive positions and their enemies' inexperience should have enabled them to hold their ground. When put to the test these defences were far weaker than most observers had expected.

It was the defeat of the Parliamentary Party in four successive contests which transformed public disillusionment, widespread even before the rising and the home rule negotiations, into a massive exodus of its members. The by-elections and their consequences also helped ensure that there would be a new party in which these political refugees could take shelter; they began the process of clearing the ring between Irish separatism and the British government. As Liam de Róiste remarked in his diary, 'all that seemed so sedate, so settled, so steady, so unchangeable a few years ago is gone. We live in a new era.'[161]

The October convention

But after the last of the elections was over and Kilkenny had been won, Sinn Féin still had unfinished business ahead of it. The spread of the party during the summer and autumn was not impeded by any further quarrels among the leaders, but the compromise settlement which had merged the Liberty clubs and Sinn Féin still left the united party with a president (Griffith) and a programme (monarchist) unacceptable to many of the Volunteers. Despite his official position, Griffith remained in the background, as he had done during Plunkett's period of pre-eminence. He seems to have had no strong desire to remain leader of the movement, provided that it followed a course which he approved. His hostility towards Plunkett was partly the result of personal dislike, and of pique at what he regarded as the count's usurpation of a position to which he had no right. It was also based on a well-merited contempt for Plunkett's political abilities. But he admired de Valera and believed that his prominence in Easter Week gave him a claim to high office which Plunkett lacked. In July he wrote in *Nationality* that 'in choosing Eamon de Valera as its representative, East Clare has not only chosen a true and gallant Irishman – it

---

[160] *FJ*, 12 July 1917, editorial.   [161] De Róiste, diary, 8 Aug. 1917, FO'D, 31,146(1).

has chosen a man with the mind and capacity that Ireland will need at the Peace Conference – the mind and capacity of the Statesman'.[162]

It became clear that de Valera would challenge Griffith for the presidency of the new, united party, and that both men would have a substantial body of support. Griffith decided not to contest the election. This was arranged in the course of a private discussion with de Valera which took place in a Grafton Street café,[163] but he did not announce his decision until the convention met a week later. British observers were unaware of this agreement and they expected a split in the movement, as they had already done twice before, first when Plunkett summoned his convention, and again when he launched his Liberty clubs. De Valera was elected president unanimously, while Griffith and O'Flanagan were chosen as his vice-presidents; Griffith received three times more votes than Count Plunkett who was the third (and unsuccessful) candidate. With this result the disputes over Sinn Féin's leadership came to an end, and they did not reappear until the treaty debates four years later.

Wisely, the party's policy had been left vague. This was partly because many separatists had only hazy ideas about their ultimate objectives, and partly also because they wished to avoid controversial issues until they had consolidated their hold over Irish public opinion. But by October the inchoate movement which had existed at the beginning of the year had been transformed into a united party, and its members could now afford the luxury of working out their policies in some detail. The question of abstention from Westminster had been settled, social issues were ignored, and the only remaining problem of any immediate importance was whether or not Sinn Féin should commit itself to the aim of an Irish republic.[164]

Few members of the old Sinn Féin party were committed royalists, and few even regarded an Irish kingdom as a positive aim worth striving for. Yet many of them believed strongly that to commit the party to a republican policy would not only alienate unionists, but would also make any ultimate agreement with Britain more difficult – if not impossible.[165] They felt that a republic could be achieved only as the result of an improbable defeat of the British army by rebel Irish forces. But in 1917 the moderates who held such views were restrained and on the defensive, aware that Pearse's proclamation in Easter Week had made the radicals even more determined and had made 'the republic' a popular slogan. In late summer and autumn the committed republicans voiced their demands

---

[162] *Nationality*, 21 July 1917, editorial.

[163] Earl of Longford (Thomas Pakenham) and Thomas P. O'Neill, *Eamon de Valera* (London, 1970), pp. 67–8.   [164] The party's policy will be examined in more detail below, in pp. 240–7.

[165] See below, pp. 118, 243.

more forcefully than ever before, and the Volunteers' new prominence also weakened the moderate and pacifist elements within the party. The differences between the two groups brought about the final clash between rival elements in the Sinn Féin movement before its new structure was completed.

There are no surviving records of these negotiations. At the October convention and in the treaty debates Brugha claimed that the leaders had needed three nights to decide on the new constitution, and according to later accounts the two sections quarrelled bitterly while it was being drafted. Griffith, Milroy and other 'old Sinn Féiners', while no longer adhering rigidly to a dual monarchy as outlined in *The resurrection of Hungary*, were nonetheless reluctant to acquiesce in the radicals' demands. Volunteers such as de Valera, Brugha, Collins and McGuinness insisted on a republic. After one fierce quarrel de Valera brought back some exasperated negotiators who had walked out of the room and they continued arguing until 1 or 2 a.m.[166]

Eventually they reached agreement on a 'compromise' formula suggested by de Valera, a settlement which gave the republicans all they wanted while at the same time conciliating the moderates and enabling them to save face. The party would commit itself to securing a republic and later, once freedom had been attained, the people could choose between a monarchy and a republic. The concession was irrelevant, since most moderates did not object to the *idea* of securing a republic, but doubted the wisdom of demanding it or the possibility of achieving it. According to a later account, Brugha remarked that Griffith had been forced to accept the republic or else walk the plank.[167] Physical force was not a controversial issue. Griffith expressed reservations as to the circumstances in which its use would be legitimate, but (as in the past) he foresaw the possibility that it might be necessary. In 1917 only the most zealous separatists were dissatisfied with this; and, after all, any future rising would be carried out by the Volunteers rather than by Sinn Féin.

At least 1,700 delegates were present at the October convention, most of them young men aged between eighteen and forty, and more than 1,000 branches were represented. By now the total number of clubs, whether affiliated or not, was over 1,200 – averaging one for virtually every Catholic parish in the country. This was the 'natural' spread of an Irish nationalist party; for example, it has been estimated that Parnell's National League totalled 1,285 branches in 1886, and the UIL 1,256 in mid-1912.[168] Only delegates from affiliated clubs

---

[166] Dillon, 'Arthur Griffith and the reorganisation of Sinn Féin', p. 4.

[167] William O'Brien, *Forth the banners go*, p. 155.

[168] Conor Cruise O'Brien, *Parnell and his party*, p. 133; 'United Irish League: miscellaneous cases', CO.904/20/2.

were admitted, and others were turned away. The proceedings were well organized, the agenda was distributed before the meeting, and business was conducted efficiently. Free accommodation was provided for those unable to meet
the expenses of two days' residence in Dublin.

In theory the convention was the effective governing body of the party. Its
purpose was to decide issues such as Sinn Féin's aims and constitution, organizational structure, and leadership. It elected an executive whose task would be
to implement its decisions. In practice the convention's function was essentially
one of ratification, of putting a gloss on agreements which had already been
reached in June or in the course of the intervening months. At the end of the
agenda a notice read, 'it may be well to explain for the guidance of Delegates that
Resolutions proposed by the executive are *all* Resolutions that the Executive,
after the fullest deliberation, have agreed to *unanimously*'.[169] But as one delegate
forecast, 'behind the formulas and declarations will be the question of
control',[170] and ambitious politicians manoeuvred to expand their power.

The new constitution was accepted without difficulty and de Valera's scheme
of organization for the party was approved with only two dissenting votes.[171]
The convention thus acted as a rubber stamp for the decisions of the executive.
But it had another purpose, more important than its official duties: it gave the
new movement a sense of its own strength and unity, and it gave the party a tone
– serious, moderate and comprehensive. The crucial exception to this moderation was its commitment to republicanism, a point which de Valera stressed in
his speech. He declared that they had nailed the republican flag to the mast and
would never lower it, and that it was as a republic that they had a chance of
international recognition. Having secured that recognition, they 'would agree
to differ afterwards', and they could choose their system of government by ref-
erendum.[172]

A few delegates made personal attacks on Eoin MacNeill, but these were
uncharacteristic of the meeting and they failed to win widespread support.
Markievicz, Kathleen Clarke and Helena Molony denounced him for his efforts
in trying to prevent the rising, but their move backfired when de Valera, Griffith
and Seán Milroy all made forceful speeches in his favour. De Valera urged the
delegates to 'show by your votes that MacNeill deserves honour from his countrymen'. Since MacNeill headed the list of members elected to the executive, and
with 888 votes was 205 ahead of Brugha, his nearest rival, it is probable that the
women's attacks had gained him sympathy.

---

[169] *Sinn Féin. Tenth convention. Thursday, October 25th, 1917* (Dublin, 1917), p. 5.

[170] De Róiste, diary, 27 Sept. 1917, FO'D, 31,146(1).   [171] See below, pp. 170–3.

[172] *II*, 27 Oct. 1917.

Liam de Róiste recorded afterwards that Markievicz 'was strong about the men who have been talking about MacNeill but who had not the courage to stand up there and say what they were saying in private. They left it to the women.' Some of her own critics then conveniently 'discovered things to her disadvantage – she was in a lunatic asylum when she was 14 and again when she was 20!'[173]

The convention discussed various other matters such as the Irish language, the threat of a food shortage, links between Irish and British trade unions, and schemes of organization. Little support was given to those who opposed the name 'Sinn Féin', or to extreme demands such as that all future Sinn Féin candidates should be men who had fought in Easter Week and that Sinn Féin members should be able to use guns.

Over a hundred candidates competed for the twenty-four posts on the party's new executive. When it was announced that the moderate and extremist elements had run rival lists of candidates, speakers from the floor and from the platform attacked such a manoeuvre; de Valera read out a resolution from Sinn Féin prisoners in Mountjoy which deplored this tendency and hoped piously that 'beginning a new Ireland, it will not be necessary to resort to such measures any more'.[174] O'Flanagan pointed out that the two lists circulated represented the candidates of the extreme left and the extreme right, and that his own name featured on both. Later accounts credited Collins and Figgis with organizing these rival 'tickets'. Similar lobbying had taken place before the convention, and de Róiste complained of efforts to pack branch meetings at which delegates were to be chosen.[175]

These attempts to control the party were unsuccessful, and the executive which was elected was a motley but representative group. Some of its members were chosen because of their local prominence, their Volunteering or other activities, their participation in the rising, or the publicity they had gained in the previous few months through speechmaking or party organization.

In his presidential address Griffith had told the delegates that 'differences on minor points must be subordinated to the great issues and responsibilities cast upon you'. And so they were. Although the account of the proceedings in the *Irish Independent* editorial was inclined to gush, it was nonetheless substantially accurate. Contrasting the convention with UIL assemblies, it claimed that the Sinn Féin meeting

---

[173] De Róiste, diary, 27, 28 Oct. 1917, FO'D, 31,146(1).   [174] *II*, 26 Oct. 1917.

[175] De Róiste, diary, 18 Oct. 1917, FO'D, 31,146(1); Robert Brennan, *Allegiance* (Dublin, 1950), pp. 154–5. See below, p. 195.

was much more deliberative and business-like; the platform did not mono-
polise the time; delegates were free to speak; if there was any cliquism it was
pretty well concealed; a statement of accounts was presented – and there
were no batons. There seemed, in fact, to be a sense of power in the ordering of the proceedings which quite accorded with the strength of the movement.[176]

The Sinn Féin convention in October 1917 ratified and consolidated the new
united party which had developed during the previous six months. The 'Sinn
Féin movement', a sentiment or attitude which was almost as vague as nationalism or separatism, had been transformed into an organized political force.

Earlier in the year F. J. O'Connor of the Nation League complained that
'there is no National Party, no Leader, or Leaders, no settled Programme', while
the *Round Table* observed that 'there is no such thing at present as a Sinn Fein
party. But there are numerous little groups each a trifle uncertain of the other,
each groping for a policy.'[177] These groups came close to splitting the movement
into warring factions at precisely the same time that their combined hold over
the country was being consolidated.

By the autumn all had changed, and only two separatist bodies remained, the
Volunteers (together with their women's auxiliary, Cumann na mBan) who
embodied the military wing, and Sinn Féin, by now the more important of the
two, which represented the political side of the movement. The squabbling
which had marred the earlier months of the year had ended, and Sinn Féin's
hold over the country at large was consolidated. There was some exaggeration,
but also much justice, in *Nationality*'s claim that 'in nine months the country
has been won and organised for Sinn Féin'. (The article went on to declare that
the same energy would be directed to educating the country in every aspect of
Sinn Féin policy.)[178] The movement's problems were of its own creation, but at
least they had been overcome before the party had to face serious outside opposition, and the happy ending to the Sinn Féiners' dissensions obscured their
irresponsibility. The party was energetic and efficient in 1917. It was also lucky.

---

[176] *II*, 26 Oct. 1917, editorial. 'Batons' was an allusion to the notorious UIL 'baton convention' of
1909.   [177] O'Connor to Gavan Duffy, 4 Apr. 1917, GD, 5581; *Round Table*, Mar. 1917, p. 374.
[178] *Nationality*, 3 Nov. 1917.

4

REVERSES AND VICTORY, 1918

Sinn Féin's series of achievements throughout 1917 bred a confidence which bordered on complacency. Some observers imagined that the party's momentum would continue without challenge or interruption until it reached its natural conclusion in the long-overdue general election. But the pattern of events in 1918 differed from any such expectations. Although the year *did* end in victory for Sinn Féin and in its final destruction of the Parliamentary Party, this triumph was secured only after it had suffered a number of minor setbacks at the hands of the home rulers and after it had withstood a massive counter-attack by the British authorities.

Three defeats

The first three parliamentary seats to fall vacant after the Sinn Féin October convention were all situated in Co. Armagh. Local Sinn Féiners decided to avoid involvement in North-and Mid-Armagh, constituencies which were so safely Unionist that neither had been contested by Nationalist candidates since 1886. But they could not so easily ignore the challenge posed by the vacancy in the south of the county. This was created by the death of Charles O'Neill, the last surviving MP associated with Butt's establishment of the home rule movement in 1870.[1] The constituency was strongly nationalist, and in the last general election the Parliamentary Party had defeated an O'Brienite All-For-Ireland opponent by a margin of three to one. Unlike many other northern seats it could in theory be won by the Sinn Féiners, and a campaign there would also provide them with the opportunity to test their fortunes in Ulster for the first time.

Nonetheless, South Armagh presented them with serious problems. The party had failed to attract much support, morale was low, and the new standing committee was informed that there were only eight branches in the constit-

---

[1] *Newry Reporter*, 17 Jan. 1918.

uency.[2] The AOH (controlled by Joe Devlin) was strong in the area, and Hibernian halls were the principal local meeting places. Dillon remarked soon afterwards that 'South Armagh is almost the most favourable seat for us in Ireland.'[3] The Parliamentary Party's confidence was displayed by its decision to hold the election as quickly as possible, before Sinn Féin would have time to organize its forces.

The Nationalist candidate, Patrick Donnelly, was a Newry solicitor who was well known in the constituency. Patrick McCartan, his Sinn Féin opponent, suffered from a double disadvantage: he was a stranger from (relatively) distant Tyrone, and he was then in the United States where he represented Sinn Féin – while also working as a doctor in a New York hospital. The Unionists honoured the party truce and withdrew their candidate, but they did so too late for his name to be removed from the ballot paper. In the event he received only forty votes. The rival nationalist parties devoted considerable effort and resources to the contest, and some Sinn Féin departments were later criticized for their extravagance during the campaign.[4] It was claimed that the election provoked more activity than Roscommon or Longford had done the previous year, and that on one day a record total of 200 speakers addressed meetings in the constituency.[5] Both sides organized their campaigns from outside South Armagh, the Parliamentary Party from Newry and Sinn Féin from Dundalk. This latter choice added point to Donnelly's accusation that Sinn Féin was carrying out an 'invasion of Ulster' (thereby echoing, no doubt unconsciously, Protestant dismay at the southern onslaughts of O'Connell in the 1840s and Parnell in the 1880s).

Sinn Féiners arrived from Kerry, Tipperary and elsewhere, and uniformed officers commanded groups of young Volunteers. De Valera's followers sang 'Clare's dragoons' as they marched through the streets, and one account related how Claremen armed with hurleys routed stone-throwing Redmondites. Another described 'scores of electioneering experts, organisers, and orators' arriving at the respective party strongholds by every train.[6] Rival groups clashed in the streets, provoking the commander of the Cork Volunteers in the constituency to report that 'we had a few scraps and they are tough boys the "wee lads of the North"'.[7] Unmilitary campaigners seemed out of place, and Laurence Ginnell's traditional politician's uniform of silk hat, frock coat and umbrella made him look incongruous, 'a barnyard hen in a flock of hawks'.[8]

---

[2] SCM, 17 Jan. 1918.   [3] Dillon to T. P. O'Connor, 19 Jan. 1918, JD, 6742.

[4] SCM, 21 Feb. 1918.   [5] II, 28 Jan. 1918.   [6] Clare Champion, 23 Feb. 1918; II, 24 Jan. 1918.

[7] Tomás MacCurtain to Seán Hegarty, 27 Jan. 1918, Terence MacSwiney MSS, Cork Public Museum, L.1955:75.   [8] FJ, 2 Feb. 1918.

Platform speakers indulged themselves. Against de Valera's boast that truth and tolerance were the weapons of Sinn Féin, Joe Devlin was able to retort that 'Nationalists stood for a gospel of love, of generosity, of conciliation and of goodwill.'[9] Seán MacEntee complained that the older generation in South Armagh was Redmondite and he advised the young men 'not to plough, sow or reap for fathers who would be so base as to betray Ireland', while Devlin appealed to the people's sense of gratitude towards the old leaders who had guarded them for thirty years.[10] Dillon must have been one of the first in the country to pose a question which, because it was so widely applicable, would become a much-loved taunt in the repertoire of Irish political abuse; on one occasion he asked 'where was Dr. McCartan during Easter Week? Could they not have selected a man who really stood to the fight?'[11] Following the pattern of the 1917 by-election campaigns, both sides claimed credit for averting the threat of conscription. One of McCartan's leaflets cited a complaint by Brigadier-General Page-Croft that only Sinn Féin influence prevented thousands of splendid young Irishmen from joining the army, and it urged the electors to 'keep on preventing and vote for McCartan'.[12] On the other hand, the Sinn Féin candidate was criticized frequently for having helped the Larne gun-runners in 1914.

Cardinal Logue was a determined opponent of Sinn Féin. He believed that, with the exception of the United States, republics were characterized by instability and corruption, and he dismissed the aim of an Irish republic as 'a dream which no man in his sober senses can hope to see realised . . . The thing would be ludicrous if it were not so mischievous and fraught with such danger.'[13] His pronouncements were circulated by the Parliamentary Party, just as Archbishop Walsh's letter had been distributed by McGuinness's supporters in South Longford. However this did not prevent the cardinal from being given pride of place, even ahead of episcopal sympathizers such as Walsh, O'Dwyer of Limerick and Fogarty of Killaloe, in a leaflet printed for the election which was entitled *Irish bishops recommend Sinn Féin.*[14]

The result of the poll was a clear victory for the Nationalists, who held the seat by 2,324 votes to 1,305. They had been expected to win, but there was some surprise at the extent of their triumph. McCartan claimed later that he learned of his nomination in a New York newspaper, had never heard of what had happened in the election until he saw the result in the press, and was grateful for

---

[9] *Newry Telegraph*, 2 Feb. 1918.   [10] *Armagh Guardian*, 1 Feb. 1918; *II*, 1 Feb. 1918.

[11] *FJ*, 28 Jan. 1918.   [12] *Conscription?* (leaflet), NLI, MS 10,494(10).

[13] David Miller, *Church, state and nation in Ireland, 1898–1921* (Dublin, 1973), p. 399.

[14] Leaflet, NLI, LO.P.116(98).

what, in the circumstances, was a remarkable vote on his behalf.[15] Griffith was less phlegmatic. He complained that Sinn Féin had been beaten on a five-year-old register 'by a combination of forces of English ascendancy and rotten place-hunters'; and, since he argued that most of the unionist electorate had supported Donnelly, he was able to calculate that McCartan had secured a majority of forty-six among the nationalist voters.[16] The RIC believed that one third of the unionists in the constituency had voted for the Parliamentary Party,[17] but even if this were true it would not have decided the result.

The reality was that, although Sinn Féin performed better than the All-For-Ireland League had done in the general election of December 1910 (their shares of the poll were, respectively, 35.5 and 25.7 per cent), it had clearly been beaten. There were good reasons for its defeat, but there was little point in trying to claim that the result was a moral victory. The party's new executive, the standing committee, responded more positively when it decided soon afterwards to train special staff for election work.[18]

South Armagh had provided the Parliamentary Party with a badly needed boost, although this triumph was unable to dent Dillon's natural pessimism. Shortly after the result, he wrote despondently about the prospect of a general election – always providing, he added, that there remained any party and any cause left to fight for.[19] A few weeks later John Redmond died, weary and disillusioned, and after eighteen years as his deputy Dillon succeeded him as leader of the party – for what proved to be the last few months of its life.

Redmond's son William, an army officer fighting on the Western Front, chose to inherit his father's seat in Waterford city. De Valera approved of his rival's consistency in wearing his Irish Guards uniform during the campaign,[20] but this preference for khaki may also have been a shrewd political move. Probably more than was the case in any other city or town outside Ulster, Waterford's economy depended on the army and on the munitions industries which had boomed as a consequence of the war. Uniforms were more popular there than elsewhere in nationalist Ireland, and approximately 35 per cent of the city's male population of military age had joined the army during the first sixteen months of the conflict.[21] One speaker was able to ask what chance would Waterford have had of securing loans or grants without a voice in parliament throughout the past twenty-seven years.[22] This background, combined with the

[15] *II*, 22 Apr. 1918.   [16] *II*, 4 Feb. 1918; *Nationality*, 9 Feb. 1918.

[17] IG's report, Jan. 1918, CO.904/105.   [18] SCM, 1 Mar. 1918.

[19] Dillon to T. P. O'Connor, 13 Feb. 1918, JD, 6742.   [20] *II*, 15 Mar. 1918.

[21] Thomas P. Dooley, 'Politics, bands and marketing: army recruitment in Waterford city, 1914–15', *Irish Sword*, 18, 72 (1991), p. 205.   [22] *Waterford Evening Star*, 18 Mar. 1918.

Redmond family's popularity and the probability of a large sympathy vote, encouraged the Nationalists to rush the election as they had already done in South Armagh.

The campaign was even rougher than usual, and party workers on both sides armed themselves with sticks; the Claremen who had marched in South Armagh were now matched in Waterford by Devlinites organized from Belfast. As the underdogs, Sinn Féiners were the principal victims. They were attacked with stones and bottles, their club was besieged, and even the unsympathetic RIC reported more assaults on them than on the Nationalists.[23] Prominent among their opponents were the 'separation women', whose Dublin sisters were chronicled by Sean O'Casey, and who associated the war with their new (relative) prosperity. Devlin assured an audience that the Irish Party would secure shorter hours for the workers, and would try to make for them a heaven upon earth. Voters were told that if they wanted to find the party's monument, 'you will get it in the £3,000,000 a year which we have secured for old age pensions'.[24]

One 'young lady, who was stated to have Sinn Fein tendencies' voted on polling day, probably the first woman in Ireland to do so in a parliamentary election; the Representation of the People Act had granted female suffrage only a few weeks earlier, and although it had not yet come into effect her name appeared on the register by mistake.[25]

The result of the election was a second defeat for Sinn Féin: the Parliamentary Party held the seat by 1,242 votes to 764, but the RIC commented that in such a strongly Redmondite city a Sinn Féin vote of 35 per cent must be seen as representing progress.[26] Herbert Moore Pim did not agree. Within three months he had reconverted to his earlier unionist beliefs, but Captain Redmond's victory provoked him into one of his last pronouncements as an Irish nationalist – a tirade in the spirit of an Old Testament prophet. He deplored the 'abiding and horrid infamy' of the result, declaring that it had been a national sin 'more grievous in its effects than a mortal sin, [which] goes down for generations tainting the soul of a people, and causing torment, and horror, persecution, famine, and pitiable and mean exhibitions of weakness'.[27] Waterford city had much to answer for.

William Redmond had been MP for East Tyrone since 1910, and by resigning his seat so that he could succeed his father in Waterford he created yet another vacancy. Once more it was in an area where Sinn Féin was weak. There were reports that the constituency executive had intended not to contest the

[23] CI's report, Waterford, Mar. 1918, CO.904/105.

[24] *II*, 21 Mar. 1918; *Waterford Evening Star*, 21 Mar. 1918.   [25] *Ibid.*, 23 Mar. 1918.

[26] CI's report, Waterford, Mar. 1918, CO.904/105.   [27] *Irishman*, 30 Mar. 1918.

4.1 Sinn Féin propaganda. 'Separation women'

seat, but that in the end it yielded to local demands.[28] The unionists formed a large minority (in the last election, in December 1910, their candidate had won 48.8 per cent of the vote), and although they stood aside officially from the contest, in practice they sided against Sinn Féin.[29] Once again the candidate (this time Seán Milroy) was from outside the constituency, and once again, as in South Armagh, Joe Devlin took command of the Parliamentary Party's campaign. The Nationalists' choice of a candidate who had opposed the 1916 exclusion scheme may have been a sign that they were uncertain of the voters' loyalty.[30] One of the more memorable remarks of the campaign was by Russell

---

[28] *II*, 25, 26 Mar. 1918; de Róiste, diary, 26 Mar. 1918, FO'D, 31,146(3).   [29] *FJ*, 29 Mar. 1918.

[30] Phoenix, *Northern nationalism*, p. 47.

McNabb, who told an audience that 'the Devlins were nothing more or less than a lot of shoeboys, stableboys, and bottle washers in the history of their country'; in turn, the Nationalist candidate dismissed Sinn Féiners as 'lunatics who had never done one honest day's work for Ireland'.[31] The normal civilities were observed. Sinn Féin knew that it was doomed to defeat and, sure enough, it lost by 1,802 votes to 1,222.

Nationality claimed predictably that, since the Parliamentary Party had been saved by unionist voters, the result was therefore yet another triumph for Sinn Féin.[32] Such excuses can have convinced only the hardened and uncritical faithful. Home rulers rejoiced, and according to the *Freeman's Journal* the Sinn Féiners' commitment to the principle of abstention had led them to conclude that 'not only is it unnecessary to sit in Parliament, but it is even unnecessary to be returned to it'.[33] After three defeats in rapid succession, the party's invulnerable image was by now a thing of the past, and the pamphlet circulated during the Clare election, which boasted that Sinn Féin 'is an invincible force, and its effects follow each other with regularity and rapidity', must have had a dated appearance.[34] By April 1918 the momentum of 1917 could be seen in a somewhat different light; in the seven by-elections between North Roscommon and East Tyrone, Sinn Féin received 13,569 votes and the Parliamentary Party 10,964. Sinn Féin won 55.3 per cent of the total, a clear overall victory but hardly a rout of its opponent.

There was much truth in the Sinn Féiners' claim that all three seats which they had lost in early 1918 were unrepresentative of the country in general, and there is no doubt that they had been unlucky in their recent battlefields. But in so far as there was any truth whatever in Dillon's claim that 'Sinn Fein was on the *rapid* down grade, in fact a slump had set in',[35] it was saved, as extreme movements in Ireland have so often been saved, by the actions of the British government. The cabinet's decision to impose conscription on Ireland radicalized public opinion and transformed the balance between the rival nationalist parties.

Conscription

From the very beginning of the war there were widespread fears that Irishmen would be conscripted, and many nationalists were determined to resist such a

---

[31] *Dungannon Democrat*, 10 Apr. 1918; *Tyrone Courier*, 4 Apr. 1918.
[32] *Nationality,* 13 Apr. 1918.   [33] *FJ,* 5 Apr. 1918, editorial.
[34] *Sinn Féin releases the prisoners,* NLI, LO.P.116(69).
[35] Dillon to Asquith, 30 June 1918, HHA, 37(211).

threat. In October 1914, an 'Irish Neutrality League' was formed, with James Connolly as president and Griffith a committee member, and inevitably one of its aims was to prevent the conscription of Irishmen into the British army.[36] The following year the separatist newspaper *The Spark* summed up a widespread view among nationalists when it declared that 'in Ireland the proposal would be as obnoxious as the attempted suppression of the drink industry', and it quoted approvingly the advice given by a Westmeath curate as to how the people should respond to the conscriptionists' arrival: meet them with a deputation of snipers.[37] Redmond's unpopularity was aggravated by his support for the government's voluntary enlistment campaign and by the War Office's reluctance to form nationalist Irish as well as unionist Ulster regiments.

Conscription was imposed on Britain for the first time in January 1916, but Ireland remained exempt. This was seen as an 'unconscious repudiation of the Union', and it provoked protests from Conservatives and unionists.[38] As the war dragged on, the Irish reprieve appeared increasingly anomalous, and RIC reports confirmed a widespread and growing apprehension that the island would be brought into line with the rest of the United Kingdom. The county inspector in Kilkenny remarked in September 1916 that the fear of conscription was growing, 'as is also a bitter opposition should it come . . . the young farmers, shop assistants, artisans, etc. dread the idea of conscription'.[39] His counterpart in West Galway reported that conscripts 'might be more of a danger than anything else in Irish Regiments', and General Maxwell believed that Sinn Féiners would welcome such a move by the government since it would drive the other parties into their ranks.[40]

All nationalists agreed on the question. Although Redmond had campaigned for voluntary enlistment in the British army, and although he believed that Ireland had identified itself thoroughly with the empire in the war, he insisted nonetheless that 'until we have some real proof that this [i.e., conscription] is necessary from a military point of view – for my part I remain anchored in my hostility to a system of compulsion'.[41] Later he warned that conscription would be resisted in every village in Ireland, and his National Volunteers trained in readiness for the day when they would have to fight it.[42] Arthur Griffith,

---

[36] *Sinn Féin*, 17 Oct. 1914.   [37] *Spark*, 23 May, 14 Nov. 1915.

[38] A. J. P. Taylor, *English History, 1914–1945* (Oxford, 1965), p. 56; John O. Stubbs, 'The Unionists and Ireland, 1914–18', *Historical Journal*, 33, 4 (1990), pp. 875–6.

[39] CI's report, Kilkenny, Sept. 1916, CO.904/101.

[40] CI's report, W. Galway, Oct. 1916, CO.904/101; Maxwell, memo, 26 Sept. 1916, Cab.37.155/40.

[41] *Hansard*, 77, cols. 1,006–7 (5 Jan. 1916).

[42] *FJ*, 7 Oct. 1916; circular, 16 Oct. 1916, CO.904/23/5, p. 73.

regarded in some quarters as a pacifist pure and simple, wrote from Reading Jail that the British could never impose conscription if Ireland resisted, 'and Ireland must fight Conscription with tongues, pens, sticks, stones, pitchforks, swords, guns and all the other resources of civilisation'.[43] The RIC inspector general reported the belief that Ireland's exemption from the Military Service Act was due to the Volunteers' threats of resistance.[44]

During the 1917 by-elections both sides had exploited the people's fears. In East Clare Patrick Lynch argued that, in the absence of Irish representation in parliament, a conscription bill could be passed at once without any opposition, while de Valera's headings for a speech in Lisdoonvarna began: 'show how Easter Week stopped Conscription and kept the young men in Ireland to work the land'.[45] A priest told his audience that, but for rebels such as de Valera, 'the bones of the young men of Ireland would be bleaching to-day in the blood-sodden soil of France'.[46] Some months later an army intelligence officer noted that Sinn Féin's main attractions were its promise to prevent conscription and its assurance that it would guard against any imposition of fresh taxes.[47]

The Irish public was quite right to be apprehensive. Lord Lansdowne, the leader of the House of Lords, advised the cabinet of a growing feeling in Ireland 'that it is utterly wrong that the sacrifices which this war has entailed should fall wholly upon those Irishmen who have volunteered to come forward for the defence of the Empire'.[48] A few months later, soon after he had replaced Asquith as prime minister, Lloyd George wrote to the chief secretary asking for his latest views on the practicability and advisability of extending conscription to Ireland. 'The military authorities are worrying me on this subject, and it is clear we shall soon have to discuss the best methods of utilising the man power of Ireland.'[49]

He was informed that about 134,000 Irishmen had joined the forces since the beginning of the war, and that an estimated 161,000 remained available. But 40,000 of these had gone to work in England, in munitions factories and elsewhere, with a guarantee against liability for military service. The report concluded that 'with a national settlement in Ireland conscription could be applied without grave risks and that without such a settlement it could be done but at the cost of much disturbance and some bloodshed now and new and intensified animosities henceforward'.[50]

---

[43] Griffith to Lily Williams, 29 Nov. 1916, NLI, MS 5943.

[44] IG's report, Aug. 1916, CO.904/100.   [45] Pamphlet, EdeV; de Valera, memo, n.d., EdeV.

[46] Clare Champion, 30 June 1917.   [47] IO's report (M. and C.), Jan. 1918.

[48] Memo., 4 Nov. 1916, Cab.37/157/8.

[49] Lloyd George to Henry Duke, 26 Jan. 1917, LG, F/37/4/8.

[50] Duke to Lloyd George, 30 Jan. 1917, LG, F/37/4/10.

4.2 Anti-recruitment propaganda

Despite all the public alarm and private discussion it was not until the spring of 1918 that the question became urgent. When the Bolsheviks surrendered at Brest-Litovsk, 1 million German soldiers were moved from Russia to the Western Front. In the massive Ludendorff offensive which followed this transfer, the reinforced German armies were able to smash through allied lines and break the military deadlock which had persisted – at a horrendous cost in human lives – since September 1914. At one stage it seemed as if they might even capture Paris.

In its response to this crisis the British government decided to draft more men into the army by raising the age of exemption from forty-one to fifty-one. This made Irishmen's immunity seem even more glaring and unjust. The British press was overwhelmingly in favour of extending conscription equally throughout the United Kingdom; the *Observer*, for example, grumbled that Ireland's exemption had spread a spirit of irresponsible Bolshevism, that Sinn Féiners claimed the position of a privileged race compared with Englishmen, Scotsmen and Welshmen, and that they felt they had no duties to mankind.[51] The cabinet would have been obliged to create at least an impression of activity, if only to placate British public opinion, but most of its members were genuinely anxious to extract more soldiers from Ireland. In the ensuing discussions they concerned themselves seriously with Irish affairs for the first time since the home rule negotiations in the summer of 1916.

The minister for national service told his colleagues that if conscription were applied to Ireland with the new age limit of fifty-one, as was planned for the rest of the United Kingdom, the army command would be able to replenish its forces with 200,000 men. Such a figure seemed almost irresistible at a time when the government was desperate for manpower. Walter Long advised the prime minister that 'the Irish will talk, shout, perhaps put up a fight or two, but they know they are beaten, and if we sit tight, make no concessions, you will soon have 200 to 300,000 fine fighting Irishmen in the ranks'.[52] Thomas Jones (assistant secretary to the cabinet) recorded in his diary that the cabinet secretary had tried to persuade Lloyd George to take a more conciliatory line with Ireland 'but the P.M. was quite implacable'.[53]

Many of the experts counselled against such a move. Henry Duke warned that an attempt to impose conscription 'would consolidate into one mass of antagonism all the Nationalist elements in Ireland, politicians, priests, men and women', while General Joseph Byrne, the inspector general of the RIC, believed that they would do well if half of the conscripts became efficient

---

[51] Cited in *II*, 1 Apr. 1918.   [52] Long to Lloyd George, 10 Apr. 1918, LG, F/32/5/20.
[53] Thomas Jones, *Whitehall diary*, I (Oxford, 1969), p. 57 (10 Apr. 1918).

soldiers.[54] It was suggested (and promptly rejected by the military present at the cabinet meeting) that Irish conscripts might shoot their officers.[55] The Irish attorney general argued that to impose conscription would lead inevitably to a rebellion and to animosities which would endure for half a century, while Carson warned that the price would be too high.[56]

The Liberal element in the government intended that conscription should be linked to a new home rule measure. Naturally the Conservatives were wary of any revival of home rule, and inevitably the question of Ulster emerged once more, but at least there was the potential for a deal. In an exchange between two members of the war cabinet, one accepted conscription to ensure home rule, the other home rule to ensure conscription.[57] The new home rule bill was to be drawn up by Walter Long; since he had been Carson's predecessor as leader of the Irish unionists, his appointment illustrates the shift in the cabinet's balance of power from Liberals to Conservatives.

'To die on their own doorstep'

In such circumstances of national crisis and the risk of military defeat it was natural that the British government should regard the prospect of violence in Ireland as a relatively minor matter. Irish considerations took second place to measures which were deemed necessary to win the war. It is hard to disagree with the reaction of Lord Midleton, the leader of the southern unionists, after he had met Lloyd George and other cabinet members: 'the Government have in this case as in many others been so busy with other troubles that they have not had time to think out their scheme'.[58] From his prison cell Michael Collins was equally scathing, writing that the British 'can hardly be serious' and speculating that their motives might be bluff or sheer desperation.[59] The Military Service Bill was duly introduced, and the reaction which it provoked surpassed the fears of the pessimists in the cabinet. The whole of nationalist Ireland shared the views ascribed to the population of North Tipperary: 'hostility, indignation,

---

[54] Duke, memo, 27 Mar. 1918, Cab.24/46, GT. 4052; cabinet conclusions, 27 Mar. 1918, Cab.23/5, WC.375(2).   [55] *Ibid.*, 28 Mar. 1918, Cab.23/5, WC.376(5).

[56] James O'Connor, memo, 2 Apr. 1918, Cab.24/47, GT. 4129; cabinet conclusions, 28 Mar. 1918, Cab. 23/5, WC.376(5).

[57] G. N. Barnes and Lord Robert Cecil, cabinet conclusions, 6 Apr. 1918, Cab.23/6, WC.385.

[58] Memo., 2 May 1918, Midleton MSS, PRO.30/67/38.

[59] Collins, diary, 8 Apr. 1918, '"Oh! Lord the unrest of soul": the jail journal of Michael Collins', *Studia Hibernica*, 28 (1994), pp. 16–17.

and fury'.[60] Two years earlier, as Ireland was exempted when conscription had been imposed on Britain, a Sinn Féin member wrote that, in the event of the measure being extended to Ireland, 'the whole nation would have been banded together'.[61] Now that ideal was realized, with the inevitable exception of unionist north-east Ulster.

Once again the RIC reports provide a survey of national opinion. In King's Co. it was reported that 'at first the people almost went crazy', while in Fermanagh the county inspector observed that the priests, anticipating that large numbers would be killed, exhorted the people to go to the sacraments.[62] In parts of North Tipperary the police had to be kept in their barracks at night to defend them in case of attack.[63] Even the normally sober and moderate writer George Russell ('AE') claimed that 'our people look on this last act of British power with that dilated sense of horror a child might feel thinking of one who had committed some sin which was awful and unbelievable, as the sin against the Holy Ghost'.[64] The *Times* complained that 'the Convention might never have sat in Trinity College for all that one hears of it to-day, and Home Rule seems as remote as the Corn Laws'.[65] Apart from the unionists, all groups in Ireland co-operated against conscription, and not since the days of O'Connell had Catholic Ireland been so united.[66]

The Irish Parliamentary Party spoke and voted against the bill in the House of Commons. Dillon warned that the measure would open up a second front in Ireland, while one of his colleagues announced that he would tell the young men of Ireland 'it is better for them to die on their own doorstep than on the plains of France and Belgium on behalf of a gang of traitors and hypocrites'.[67] The newly elected MP for East Tyrone declared that, after only twenty-four hours in the House of Commons, he would be unable to return to his constituency and resist the arguments which his defeated Sinn Féin rival would now use against him.[68] Even though the Irish Nationalists received some support from Labour and opposition Liberal MPs, the House of Commons approved the bill by 301 votes to 103. The clause applying conscription to Ireland passed by 296 votes to 123.

---

[60] CI's report, N. Tipperary, Apr. 1918, CO.904/105.

[61] De Róiste, diary, 8 Jan. 1916, CAI, U271/A/19.

[62] CIs' reports, King's Co., Fermanagh, Apr. 1918, CO.904/105.   [63] IG's report, Apr. 1918, *ibid.*

[64] *Conscription for Ireland – a warning to England* (pamphlet, Dublin, 1918).

[65] *Times*, 24 Apr. 1918.

[66] Pauric Travers, 'The priest in politics: the case of conscription', in Oliver MacDonagh, W. F. Mandle and Pauric Travers (eds.), *Irish culture and nationalism, 1750–1950* (Dublin, 1983), p. 161.

[67] Dillon, Thomas Lundon, *Hansard*, 104, cols. 1,500, 1,423 (10, 9 Apr. 1918).

[68] Thomas Harbinson, *ibid.*, col. 1,542 (10 Apr. 1918).

The party then returned to carry on the anti-conscription fight in Ireland, prompting taunts that it was now, far too late, showing signs of conversion to Sinn Féin ideas, and in particular to the policy of abstention from Westminster. Many people believed that its claims to hold the balance of power in parliament had been exposed by an anti-Irish combination of the main British parties. Such a division along national lines had been prophesied repeatedly by Griffith, most recently in the claim that 'the one place that England can never be defeated is on the floor of the British House of Commons'.[69] He seemed to have been vindicated in his argument that Ireland would have to fight its battles at home, rather than in London. With this move to Dublin the Nationalists abandoned one of the policies which had sustained them over many decades. At the same time, Dillon rejected with contempt any question of linking home rule with conscription; in this casual and incidental manner the Parliamentary Party turned down the last of all the home rule proposals made by British ministers. One of Devlin's speeches revealed the extent to which moderate nationalism had been weakened: 'I know perfectly well that anything we say is unheeded here ... As long as we spoke in a constitutional way in this House we did not count. It takes a rebellion and things of that sort to bring home the grim realities of the Irish situation.'[70]

The Irish Labour movement threw its weight behind the campaign against conscription, and its one-day general strike in protest was successful everywhere outside unionist north-east Ulster. Shops and pubs were closed, no trains ran and no post was delivered. It was a warning of the passive resistance which would accompany conscription. There was even a report from Ballycastle (Co. Antrim) of co-operation by both communities in opposing the measure, 'with Orangemen, Hibernians, and Sinn Féiners marching alternately to such tunes as "the Boyne Water" and "A Nation Once Again"'.[71]

But no-one had any illusions that Irish nationalists would confine themselves to passive resistance, and the initiative for leading the fight against conscription was taken by the Volunteers. The probability of violence made their training, their military experience in the rising, and their (very limited) supplies of guns and ammunition suddenly seem appropriate to the new circumstances. They prepared for another rebellion in the confidence that this time, in contrast to Easter Week, they would enjoy mass support and they would lead a genuine national insurrection. The *Irish Independent* warned that the rising of 1916 was but a trifling incident compared with what would happen if conscription were to be imposed.[72] In Cork there were rumours that Gurkha troops had been sent

---

[69] *Nationality*, 5 Jan. 1918, editorial.   [70] *Hansard*, 105, col. 96 (15 Apr. 1918).

[71] *II*, 18 Apr. 1918.   [72] *II*, 13 Apr. 1918, editorial.

to Ireland, that British planes might bomb cities, and that machine gunners might mow down people in the streets.[73] Not long afterwards G. K. Chesterton remarked of the British that 'bad as we were, we managed to look much worse than we were. In a horrible unconsciousness we re-enacted history through sheer ignorance of history. We were foolish enough to dress up, and to play up, to the part of a villain in a very old tragedy.'[74]

The Volunteers were ordered to stop drilling and marching; they should save their energies for real military challenges. Similarly there was a sharp decline in agrarian agitation, while arms raids became more widespread. Republican prisoners, including Collins, were even directed to recognize the courts and pay bail; they would be foolish to remain in jail, unable to participate in the expected new rebellion.[75] In country districts many young men were reported to be sleeping out at night.[76] The government was warned that the situation was 'one of passive rebellion, everyone doing their usual work, and trying to get arms, ammunition, binoculars etc. by force or theft . . . There have been many thefts of gelignite and other explosives.'[77] A group of Volunteers near Bandon made a desperate attempt to acquire weapons, and tried to dig up rifles which had been buried carefully in an airtight casket after the Fenian Rising in 1867. They failed, because in the course of the intervening half-century the features of the land had changed.[78]

Sinn Féin had an important function as the civil wing of this planned insurrection, and it engaged in an intensive campaign of recruitment and propaganda. If a rebellion took place much of the harvest would be lost, and the party tried to organize the people so that they might avoid the hunger which would otherwise accompany the outbreak of fighting. Parish committees were advised to buy up stocks of non-perishable food and disperse it for storage so that it could be distributed to those unable to afford its purchase. They were to liaise with the St Vincent de Paul Society and other charitable organizations.[79] *Nationality* even offered patriotic Irishwomen a recipe for making 'conscription bread' in the absence of normal ingredients.[80] Passive resistance might take forms such as the refusal to pay instalments on land annuities or to purchase any commodity (except for necessary foods) on which the government levied indirect taxes.[81]

---

[73] De Róiste, diary, 23 Apr. 1918, FO'D, 31,146(3).

[74] G. K. Chesterton, *Irish impressions* (London, 1919), pp. 121–2.

[75] Collins, diary, 17–20 Apr. 1918, *Studia Hibernica*, pp. 29–33.   [76] IO's report (S.), May 1918.

[77] C.-in-c., coast of Ireland, memo, 6 May 1918, Cab.24/50, GT. 4447.

[78] Dorothy Price, 'History of Sinn Féin movement in W. Cork, 1915–1918', NLI, MS 15,344, p. 18.

[79] SCM, 2 May 1918.   [80] *Nationality*, 11 May 1918.

[81] *Ard-chomhairle* decision, 4 Apr. 1918, SCM, 6 May 1918.

Patriotic orators aroused the population, and their tone is indicated by an account in the *Tyrone Constitution*: 'the speeches delivered on the occasion were most violent, bitter and seditious, and from start to finish breathed of nothing but hatred of England. Still they appealed to the sentiments of the crowd of Sinn Feiners, who cheered each pronouncement with great enthusiasm.'[82] In East Cork the police noted that Sinn Féin had 'enlisted under its banner the whole of the Nationalist population', and in the west of the county, in Castletownbere, communal hostility to conscription overrode the dislike which many people felt for the republican movement.[83] The Sinn Féin club in Letterkenny reported that its membership had increased by 75 per cent since the conscription crisis began, and that on the evening of its largest protest meeting sixty-nine new members had joined.[84] In Sligo 103 new clubs affiliated within a few weeks, and some old branches reported a fourfold increase in membership; it was claimed that in the course of one month party headquarters had sent out 50,000 membership cards.[85] (Some values, however, remained sacred. An anti-conscription meeting in Naas was postponed for two hours because it clashed with a football final.[86])

Sinn Féin was fortunate that the threat of conscription came sufficiently late in the war to enable it, rather than the Parliamentary Party, to identify itself with the national outburst of Anglophobia. Things might have turned out very differently if the crisis had come in 1916 or even early in 1917, in time to rescue the Redmondites. But by now the separatists were ideally placed to harness a wave of emotion which was even stronger than that which had followed the rising.

In the face of such an emergency the politicians were prepared to put aside their differences and co-operate in what was effectively a coalition government of nationalist Ireland. A 'Mansion House conference', established to co-ordinate resistance, was chaired by the lord mayor of Dublin and comprised two delegates each from four main *blocs*: de Valera and Griffith on behalf of Sinn Féin, Dillon and Devlin from the Parliamentary Party, T. M. Healy and William O'Brien as dissident MPs, and Thomas Johnson and 'the other' William O'Brien representing the labour movement. In effect, Sinn Féin had a majority on this committee; O'Brien the trade unionist had been interned after the rising, and he was active in the Sinn Féin interest in 1917, canvassing in Roscommon and subsequently serving as a member of the committee which was established at Plunkett's convention. Healy and O'Brien (the parliamentarian) were so dominated by hatred of their former colleagues that they tended almost instinctively

---

[82] *Tyrone Constitution*, 19 Apr. 1918.

[83] CI's report, E. Cork, Apr. 1918, CO.904/106; Peter Hart, *The I.R.A. and its enemies: violence and community in Cork, 1916–1923* (Oxford, 1998), p. 60.   [84] *Irishman*, 11 May 1918.

[85] *Sligo Champion*, 11 May 1918.   [86] *Leinster Leader*, 4 May 1918.

to side against them and with Sinn Féin. However, O'Brien (MP) was inclined to overestimate his contemporaries and underestimate the younger generation. He wrote to Healy that 'de Valera is personally a charming as well as honest man, but he is too good for this rough world of old Parliamentary hands, and will no doubt subside into a meek instrument of Dillon's'.[87] O'Brien was a poor prophet.

There was disagreement within Sinn Féin as to whether or not de Valera and Griffith should join the Mansion House conference. The minutes of the party's standing committee declared initially that the decision was taken 'unanimously', but this word was later crossed out. Rather than record that the two men were to meet with representatives of other parties, the minutes were also altered to read that they would 'be at liberty to accept the invitation' to a meeting.[88] It is one of the relatively few occasions when divisions within the committee were indicated in this manner. Cathal Brugha, an honest and courageous man with a strong but narrow mind, distrusted any form of compromise and objected even to a temporary collaboration with the Parliamentary Party. His letter of resignation was the first item on the standing committee's agenda. He had attended no meetings so far (although illness may have been an explanation for his absence), and doubtless he felt more useful as well as more comfortable in the company of fellow soldiers than among politicians who, in times of national emergency, were prepared to join forces with their rivals. His plans for opposing conscription included a scheme for assassinating members of the British cabinet.[89] Collins shared his suspicion of co-operation with the Parliamentary Party, whose leaders he described as traitors to their native land; he believed that 'even unity can be purchased at too high a price' and that only the Volunteers stood between Ireland and conscription.[90]

The Church and the pledge

The Catholic Church was disturbed by the prospect of conscription, and it was dismayed by the probability that, if imposed, it would lead to a bloody conflict throughout the country. From the beginning it played a leading part in the campaign against the government's measure, hoping thereby to deflect agitation into peaceful channels. On the same day that the government announced its

---

[87] O'Brien to Healy, 2 May 1918, O'Brien MSS, NLI, 8556(19).   [88] SCM, 10 Apr. 1918.

[89] Ernie O'Malley, *On another man's wound* (London, 1936), p. 93; Florence O'Donoghue, 'Cathal Brugha' (lecture, 1966), FO'D, 24,913, p. 13; Good, *Enchanted by dreams*, pp. 131–42.

[90] Collins, diary, 12, 15 Apr. 1918, *Studia Hibernica*, pp. 23, 27.

plans, the hierarchy's standing committee met in Maynooth. It described the idea of conscription as 'a fatal mistake, surpassing the worst blunders of the past four years', a measure which would provide a forceful argument in favour of 'desperate courses'.[91] The bishop of Cork warned young Volunteers against unauthorized directives from Dublin, where extremists might give orders for an ineffectual rising.[92]

At separate meetings on 18 April the Mansion House conference and the Catholic hierarchy discussed the organization of a nation-wide anti-conscription pledge. The idea had originated with the administrator of Armagh cathedral, and he made clear the source of his inspiration: 'following the eminent example set us a few years ago by Sir Edward Carson, the priests and people of this Cathedral Parish of Armagh will hold a series of meetings on next Sunday for the purpose of founding a Solemn League and Covenant against Conscription'. However, he insisted that Carson's resort to arms was a pattern which should not be followed.[93]

De Valera's skilful tactics disproved William O'Brien's low estimate of his abilities, and he showed himself quite able to survive in the 'rough world' of politics. Before the hierarchy's meeting he had communicated with Archbishop Walsh, and the two men agreed that Walsh would persuade his fellow bishops to postpone any decision concerning conscription until they had heard from the politicians.[94] A delegation from the Mansion House conference then went to Maynooth and addressed the hierarchy. De Valera argued in favour of armed resistance. The politicians' formula declared that conscription amounted to a declaration of war on the Irish nation; that if they accepted it the people would surrender their liberties and acknowledge themselves to be slaves; and that they should pledge themselves to oppose it by the most effective means at their disposal.

The bishops described the conscription act as 'an oppressive and inhuman law which the Irish people have a right to resist by every means that are consonant with the law of God', and they decreed that masses of intercession should be said throughout the country. At every mass on the following Sunday details would be provided of public meetings at which the pledge would be administered, and the clergy were requested to announce that collections to finance the anti-conscription campaign would be held outside church gates;[95] 10 per cent of the proceeds were be forwarded to the Mansion House conference in Dublin and the balance would be retained locally. The combined

---

[91] *II*, 10 Apr. 1918.   [92] De Róiste, diary, 21 Apr. 1918, FO'D, 31,146(3).   [93] *FJ*, 13 Apr. 1918.
[94] Travers, 'Priest in politics', p. 165; Tim Pat Coogan, *De Valera: long fellow, long shadow* (London, 1993), pp. 107–8.   [95] *II*, 19 Apr. 1918.

opposition to the Military Service Act was later described as a 'parliament of priests and people'.[96]

Sinn Féin was determined to be involved as closely as possible with both the pledge and the national collection. Every branch in the country was instructed to co-operate in preparing and organizing both activities, and it was suggested that the simplest means of supplying paper for signatures would be to buy quantities of school exercise books.[97] In the eyes of many cautious and moderate nationalists the party's close association with the Catholic Church made it seem more respectable and less dangerous. Revolutionaries had cause for satisfaction when the unionist *Irish Times* complained that the Church had associated itself with the party of revolution.[98] Clerical involvement also provoked different forms of resentment. In an extreme case, one Sinn Féin club protested that the local parish priest had not only appointed his own parochial committee and ignored all the lay participants in the campaign, but he had also decided to control the disposal of the sums collected, and even questioned the Mansion House conference's right to receive 10 per cent of the total.[99]

Hundreds of thousands of people signed the anti-conscription pledge, and they responded extravagantly to the national defence fund. It was hardly surprising that the wealthier sections of the population, who were doing very well out of the war, were prepared to invest heavily in order to maintain the satisfactory *status quo*. Big farmers were prepared to pay substantial sums of money to keep their sons out of the trenches, and they were also anxious to retain their labourers on the land. In Armagh the RIC reported that farmers were subscribing to the fund as they had never contributed to any cause in the past, while a levy of £1 per member imposed on Limerick pork butchers was expected to raise a total of about £300.[100] The poor were as generous as the rich, and the Aran islands contributed the impressive sum of £400.[101] Eoin MacNeill was sent £20 15s (£20.75p) from Rathmore in Kerry, comprising 10 per cent of the collection from 'one of our three parishes', and the half-parish of Clostoken in Galway raised a similar total: £230.[102] By late June nearly £250,000 had been subscribed.

At the end of the day, when the crisis was over and the government had abandoned its plans for imposing conscription, the question arose of what should be

---

[96] *Kerryman*, 7 Dec. 1918.   [97] *II*, 20 Apr. 1918.   [98] *IT*, 1 May 1918, editorial.

[99] Liam Ua Murgán to Archbishop Walsh, 25 May 1918, AW, 379/7.

[100] CI's report, Armagh, Apr. 1918, CO.904/105; *II*, 24 May 1918.

[101] CI's report, W. Galway, July 1918, CO.904/106.

[102] W. J. Besance to MacNeill, 31 May 1918, MacN, LA1/H/24; *Précis* of captured documents, NLI, MS 10,494(1), p. 2.

done with the money. The Mansion House conference allocated a portion of the fund to care for the families of those who had been arrested because of their opposition to the measure. Some of it was returned to the donors. It was claimed that the bishop of Cork wanted part of the fund to be spent on building a new cathedral in his city, and it was also suggested afterwards that some of it had gone to the Chinese missions.[103] In 1921 de Valera and Devlin agreed to use anti-conscription money in their joint fight against unionist candidates in the elections for the first Northern Irish parliament.[104]

Parish committees controlled the 90 per cent of the fund which remained in local hands and which was not forwarded to Dublin. In 1919 they were encouraged to hand the money over to the Dáil, the newly elected Irish parliament. In many cases, village meetings voted to relinquish their claims in this way; in Barefield (Co. Clare), for example, only about a tenth of the 127 subscribers 'consented' to receive back their money.[105] Some people resisted such pressures. In Ballinacarrow (Co. Sligo) the club praised the 'admirable spirit of the subscribers towards the anti-conscription fund in devoting it to the purpose advocated by the priests and people of the parish, except a few, whose nationality is equal to the miserable mite they were entitled to'.[106] The police watched closely, and the inspector general reported in June 1919 that £21,000 had been sent to the Mansion House conference, £164,000 returned to the subscribers or applied with their consent to Church charities, £17,000 handed over by the subscribers to Sinn Féin collectors 'who attended when the money was being returned,' while £5,000 was still in the hands of the trustees.[107]

Management of these funds was only one example of clerical involvement in the campaign against conscription. The RIC inspector general exaggerated when he claimed that 'the clergy assumed command of the movement',[108] but the Church's actions were both crucial and controversial. An intelligence officer claimed that 'a sort of Holy War against the British Army is being preached', and in Mayo the crisis was described as a conflict between Church and state.[109] Lloyd George saw the question in terms of a challenge by the Catholic Church to imperial and parliamentary supremacy, while for Walter Long the hierarchy had declared war on the British government.[110]

---

[103] *II*, 6 Jan. 1919; J. J. O'Kelly, evidence, 27 Apr. 1948, SFFC, 2B/82/118(39), p. 49.

[104] See below, p. 336.   [105] *Clare Champion*, 5 Apr. 1919.

[106] *Sligo Champion*, 3 May 1919.   [107] IG's report, May 1919, CO.904/109.

[108] IG's report, Apr. 1918, CO.904/105.

[109] IO's report (M. and C.), Apr. 1918; CI's report, Mayo, Apr. 1918, CO.904/105.

[110] Cabinet conclusions, 19 June, 29 July 1918, Cab.23/6, WC.433(2), and Cab.23/7, WC.453(7); Kendle, *Walter Long*, p. 165.

The authorities also faced an unprecedented problem: in this crisis they could not rely on the loyalty of the RIC. There was no register of the Irishmen who would be available for conscription, and any such list would have to be compiled by policemen using their local knowledge. This would make them obvious targets for retribution. Bonar Law was warned that if conscription were to be linked to home rule, as the government seemed to intend, 'the RIC etc. will hesitate to enforce conscription if they know that the Government of the country is to be handed over at the same time to those who are passionately opposed to it'.[111] Zeal would not be rewarded. It was suggested that any attempts to arrest priests opposed to conscription might have results so disastrous as to break up the force.[112] Complaints were made about several priests who preached sermons in which (it was claimed) they warned that policemen who assisted conscription would incur the consequences of mortal sin. In Mayo large numbers of the younger policemen were expected to resign if they were required to enforce the act, and most people in Clare refused to speak to members of the RIC or provide them with food and turf.[113]

The 'German plot'

The government was faced with the united opposition of nationalist Ireland. It soon realized that conscription could be enforced only at the cost of rebellion and bloodshed, and that at least in the immediate future more troops would have to be moved into the island than could be extracted from it. Lloyd George and his colleagues chose to play for time and they delayed extending the military service law to Ireland, but they also decided to take action against those groups which they blamed for their humiliation: Sinn Féin and the Volunteers. This reaction gave less than full justice to other bodies, such as the Parliamentary Party, which were also involved in the campaign of resistance.

The arrest of Sinn Féin leaders had been under discussion long before the Germans' offensive in March and the resulting conscription crisis. On 26 February the home secretary referred to legal difficulties in connection with the chief secretary's proposal for interning certain Sinn Féiners.[114] A month later General Bryan Mahon, the commander-in-chief in Ireland, advised that if conscription were to be imposed the first step should be to get all the known oppo-

---

[111] Robert Cecil to Bonar Law, 8 May 1918, BL, 83/3/21.

[112] Arthur Samuels (Irish attorney general), memo, 10 May 1918, Cab.24/51, GT. 4541.

[113] IG's report, CIs' reports, Tyrone, Mayo, Clare, Apr. 1918, CO.904/105.

[114] Cabinet conclusions, 26 Feb. 1918, Cab.23/5, WC.354(8).

4.3 Anti-conscription postcard

sition leaders out of the way at once.[115] For weeks nothing was done, even though by now a pretext had been provided: a 'German agent' had been arrested after landing on the Clare coast. He was a member of Casement's Irish Brigade who had been sent by submarine to contact Sinn Féin leaders and to make arrangements for supplying troops and weapons. The unfortunate man was so innocent of Irish realities that he had planned to meet not only Dillon but also John Redmond – who was strongly anti-German and who had, in any case, died a month earlier. Some of the British authorities found it hard to take him seriously.[116] Then, at the beginning of May, Dublin Castle was purged of 'moderates' and the lord lieutenant, chief secretary and inspector general were all replaced. On 8 May the cabinet instructed Lord French, the newly appointed viceroy, to investigate Sinn Féin's links with Germany, and it agreed with Walter Long's demand that 'the most drastic steps should be taken to stamp out pro-German intrigues' in Ireland.[117]

On the night of 17–18 May seventy-three prominent Sinn Féiners were arrested, and more were imprisoned in the course of the next few days. This was intended to be a sudden and crippling blow at the separatist movement, but in fact it had long been expected by its victims. At the beginning of March, before the conscription crisis broke, the party's standing committee decided on a plan

---

[115] *Ibid.*, 27 Mar. 1918, Cab.23/5, WC.374(12), appendix.
[116] O'Halpin, 'British intelligence in Ireland', p. 65.
[117] Cabinet conclusions, 10 May 1918, Cab.23/6, WC.408(11).

of action which would be followed in the event of its members' arrest, and shortly before they were rounded up they arranged for substitutes to take their place.[118] By now Collins's spy network was active, and he was able to inform his colleagues of what was intended.[119]

The committee discussed the matter and decided that, rather than go underground and be arrested one by one, its members would wait and allow themselves be imprisoned *en masse*. In this way their detention would make a greater impact. According to Figgis, they were told that that the G men (detectives who specialized in political work) had instructions to report at 10 p.m. for all-night duty, and that Dublin Castle yard was filled with lorries.[120] Mrs Griffith wrote soon afterwards 'we were expecting it for some time that day. Arthur heard he was to be taken so waited in town after sending me letter by hand, a meeting was held at Harcourt St. to make all arrangements to carry on and when no one appeared, the men left for their homes . . . All were prepared.'[121] A few separatist leaders decided to go on the run, among them Brugha and Collins, as well as Harry Boland who was to be a central figure in directing the Sinn Féin party during the next few months. Guilelessly, Lord French informed Lloyd George that 'the secret was well kept and the whole of them were taken by surprise'.[122] In contrast to the pattern of two years earlier, the prisoners were supported by cheering crowds as they were taken to their ship in Kingstown.

Dillon was enraged by what soon became known as the 'German plot' arrests. He had attacked conscription just as forcefully as the Sinn Féiners had done, he had shared platforms and attended committee meetings with de Valera, and yet he and his colleagues were left unscathed, unmartyred, as if they were beneath Lloyd George's notice. (They were. By failing even to discuss the Parliamentary Party, let alone arrest its leaders, the British showed clearly that it was not regarded as a threat.) He claimed that the government, 'with a stupidity amounting to malignity' had deliberately adopted a policy of destroying Irish moderates and throwing the country into the hands of the 'Revolutionary Party'.[123]

Cabinet ministers had accused Sinn Féin of treasonable contacts with the enemy, and now they felt obliged to produce the evidence. This proved to be disappointing. Much of it consisted of public speeches, and in the words of the *Irish Independent*, it was 'a curious sort of conspiracy that is proclaimed from the house tops'.[124] The British claims referred to three and a half years of con-

[118] SCM, 1 Mar., 17 May 1918.   [119] Coogan, *Michael Collins*, p. 90.

[120] Darrell Figgis, *A second chronicle of jails* (Dublin, 1919) p. 13.

[121] Maud Griffith to Kate Kelly, n.d. (received 28 May 1918), NLI, MS 8411.

[122] French to Lloyd George, 19 May 1918, LG, F/48/6/12.   [123] *II*, 23 May 1918.

[124] *II*, 25 May 1918, editorial.

tinuous contact with Germany, but the bulk of the evidence related to preparations for Easter Week. Yet many of the Sinn Féin leaders had been released from jail in June 1917 and had then been invited by the government to attend the Irish Convention. It seemed inconsistent to arrest them now for offences carried out before they had been amnestied. A key document was dated 17 June, the very day on which de Valera and several of his colleagues had been released from prison; if they *had* resumed contact with the Germans, they did so with remarkable speed.

There was some embarrassment at the paucity of evidence. Edward Shortt, the new Irish chief secretary, was reduced to confessing to Lloyd George that although he could not claim that each person arrested had been in personal contact with German agents, 'we know that some one has, and each of the interned persons has said or done something which gives ground for the suspicion that he or she is in it'.[125] Weeks before the arrests Bonar Law wrote to Carson, 'we have nothing I am told which would be proof in a Court of Law',[126] and little new material seemed to have been acquired in the interval. Even the most careful presentation could not do much to flesh out such a skeletal plot. There was widespread scepticism in Britain, and total disbelief in nationalist Ireland where the idea of a 'German plot' was seen as outlandish and comical. The theme was taken up a year later by an Irish satirical journal which reported its discovery of an infernal plot in which Sinn Féin was in league with the devil himself.[127] Perhaps the strangest aspect of the whole affair is that Lloyd George and at least some members of his cabinet do seem to have believed sincerely in the existence of a German plot.

The arrests dealt a heavy blow to Sinn Féin. All its officers were arrested except Fr O'Flanagan, who was one of the vice-presidents, and Harry Boland, who had recently been appointed an honorary secretary. Only nine of the twenty-one members of the standing committee remained at liberty and many of the party's files were seized, but all its funds remained intact. For the rest of the year the party was harassed continually, its offices raided, its property confiscated and its members imprisoned. But although Sinn Féin survived and flourished in the months ahead, and although it often gave the impression of carrying on normally after it had been beheaded, the long-term consequences of the arrests were severe. The new members of the standing committee were less weighty figures than those whom they replaced. Moderates such as Arthur Griffith disappeared from national life for nearly a year, and the dominant figures in Sinn Féin were now O'Flanagan and Boland, both of them on the

---

[125] Shortt to Lloyd George, 20 May 1918, LG, F/45/6/3.
[126] Bonar Law to Carson, 28 Apr. 1918, BL, 84/7/25.   [127] *Irish Fun*, May 1919, p. 2.

radical, republican wing of the party. T. M. Healy remarked somewhat unfairly of the Sinn Féiners some time later, 'they are so headless, folly is sure to come uppermost'.[128] The *ard-chomhairle* (the new governing body) decided to confine the party's activities to four principal areas, in place of the sixteen which had been decided upon at the end of 1917.[129]

Politicians suffered more severely than the military, and soldiers like Collins, Brugha and Richard Mulcahy were able to evade capture and carry on their military preparations more or less as before. The Volunteers began to overshadow Sinn Féin, and the pattern of the years before the rising was soon repeated. The arrest of the party's leaders can be seen as one of the events which helped shorten the 'political phase' of the Irish revolution and which made a resumption of violence more probable.

East Cavan

In the short run, however, the German plot arrests benefited Sinn Féin. Two days after the conscription bill was passed by the House of Commons, Samuel Young, the 96-year-old member for East Cavan, died after a long illness. Both sides had been prepared for the vacancy, and as early as May 1917 the RIC noted that Seán Milroy had been organizing the constituency in preparation for a by-election.[130] (Because of his extreme age and poor health Young had not visited Westminster for some time. Milroy suggested mockingly that Sinn Féin should have the right of succession to his seat, since the MP 'was making a fairly good attempt at being a Sinn Feiner, inasmuch as he had not gone to the English Parliament for the past two or three years'.[131]) In early February 1918 the standing committee had singled out East Cavan as one of three areas in the country which needed particular attention,[132] and within days of Young's death Sinn Féin selected Arthur Griffith as its candidate.

From an early stage there were demands that a divisive contest in Cavan should be avoided. The threat facing the country, and the spirit of co-operation which the two parties had displayed in the Mansion House conference, were arguments used in favour of a compromise. Since the Parliamentary Party had recently stood aside at a by-election in King's Co., Dillon demanded that Sinn Féin should now act in a similar fashion, and he viewed its determination to

---

[128] Healy to William O'Brien, 3 Sept. 1918, O'Brien MSS, NLI, 8556(20).

[129] Hon. secretaries' report, *Ard-Fheis Sinn Féin*, 1918, RB, 8786(1). For the *ard-chomhairle* see below, p. 172.   [130] CI's report, Cavan, May 1917, CO.904/103.

[131] *Anglo-Celt*, 8 Sept. 1917.   [132] SCM, 6 Feb. 1918.

fight as 'wanton provocation'.[133] However the King's Co. seat had been held by
an independent, and the wartime party truce would by itself have provided adequate grounds for the Nationalists' abstention. Furthermore, attacks on Griffith
which had appeared in the *Freeman's Journal* immediately after his nomination
made an agreement more difficult: his withdrawal would have the appearance
of defeat.[134] Even though some of the more republican elements in the
Volunteers might have dismissed him as a moderate, the home rulers regarded
him with particular distaste and could not forget the long years which he had
devoted to attacking them. Dillon remarked later that Sinn Féin could not have
put forward a more offensive and scurrilous critic of the Parliamentary Party,
one who had 'poured forth a torrent of the most disgusting and infamous abuse
and calumny of the Irish Party'; no other choice could have been more calculated to add bitterness to the contest.[135]

The Church was particularly anxious to secure national unity in the fight
against conscription, its leaders urged Griffith to stand down, and the local
bishop proposed a compromise candidate. However, the furthest Sinn Féin was
prepared to go was to suggest that the nationalist population could hold an
informal ballot after Sunday mass, and that the winner should go forward as the
sole anti-conscription candidate.[136] This was a meaningless concession. Such a
procedure would be no less divisive than a conventional by-election, and the
proposal was rejected by the Parliamentary Party.

In contrast to the pattern of the three campaigns earlier in the year the
Nationalists delayed moving the writ for the election. Polling did not take place
until two months after Young's death. The arrest of the Sinn Féin leaders, and
particularly of Griffith himself, relieved the pressure on him to stand aside and
allow an uncontested election. He was now seen as yet another martyr for old
Ireland, a victim of the British government's spite who had been jailed in
revenge for its inability to impose conscription. The Nationalist candidate was
tainted by being allowed to enjoy his incriminating liberty. Sinn Féiners revived
the slogan of South Longford, 'put him in to get him out', and pictures of
Griffith in prison uniform were distributed widely.

Now the Parliamentary Party, in its turn, came under pressure to withdraw
its candidate. Dillon received conflicting advice about what he should do, but
ultimately he decided, as Sinn Féin had done earlier, to remain in the fight. He
complained later that, without the arrests, 'we had S.F. absolutely beaten. The
tide had turned decisively against them, and we would have won East Cavan by
a *decisive* majority.' (He argued, implausibly, that in such a case it would have

---

[133] Dillon to Archbishop Walsh, 23 Apr. 1918, AW, 397/7.   [134] *FJ*, 23, 24 Apr. 1918, editorial.
[135] *II*, 13 May 1918.   [136] *Nationality*, 11 May 1918.

THE EAST CAVAN HANDICAP.

4.4 Griffith and Dillon

been the end of Sinn Féin as a progressive and dangerous force in Irish politics.)[137] As usual, the party's candidate appealed to past achievements, and he
reminded electors 'how it came about that the price of flour was increased from
6/8 per stone to 22/6 per stone and on to 32/6 per stone. I think you know that
it was not Griffith who did that.'[138] Sinn Féin also stressed economic issues, and
at a meeting in Bailieborough one speaker claimed that after the Roscommon
victory old age pensions had been increased by 50 per cent, from 5s to 7s 6d.[139]

Sinn Féin's campaign revealed signs of poor organization. Three weeks after
Griffith's selection, Kevin O'Shiel, the election agent in Ballyjamesduff, com-

---

[137] Dillon to T. P. O'Connor, 18 June 1918, JD, 6742.

[138] John F. O'Hanlon, 'Views in brief' (leaflet), MacN, LA1/H/24(18). The decimal equivalent of
these figures is 33p, £1.12 and £1.62.

[139] *Meath Chronicle*, 8 June 1918. The decimal equivalent is 25p and 37.5p.

plained that he had not yet received any lists of voters arranged by townlands, nor, in contrast to the home rulers, had he been sent any literature for distribution. His other needs varied from dispatch riders to 'up Griffith' slips and songs for schoolchildren.[140] The candidate himself displayed characteristic energy in the period before his imprisonment, and despite his numerous other responsibilities he visited the constituency five times in little over three weeks.[141]

The German plot arrests evoked widespread sympathy and revitalized the party's efforts. Sinn Féin speakers drew enormous crowds, and they hammered home their most powerful argument: the one-sided nature of the British action proved that only Sinn Féin and the Volunteers had opposed conscription in an effective manner. Dillon was ridiculed for putting forward a candidate who sought election to the parliament from which all the party's existing MPs had just returned to Ireland.

Soon after the North Roscommon election Fr O'Flanagan had been forbidden to attend political meetings, but he now defied his bishop, returned joyously to the public platforms, and became the most active figure in the Sinn Féin campaign. In one speech, resisting any temptation towards accuracy, he told his audience that Redmond had induced 167,000 Irishmen to join the army and that most of these had been killed.[142] On another occasion, it was reported from Ballyjamesduff that a victim of paralysis had been visited by O'Flanagan and that, a few days after receiving the priest's blessing, the man was able to walk a short distance.[143] With such advantages Sinn Féin could not lose, and when the election finally took place on 20 June Griffith won by 3,785 votes to 2,581. Clerical supporters played a prominent role in Sinn Féin meetings, and Dillon complained later that the result was a consequence of moral intimidation, a victory for the priests.[144]

Preparations

East Cavan was the last Irish by-election of the parliament which had been elected in December 1910. It enabled Sinn Féin to regain its momentum of 1917 and to recover from its setbacks in the three recent campaigns. Other circumstances continued to help the party, above all the fact that the dread of conscription had not been removed. In principle the government had simply postponed

---

[140] Kevin O'Shiel, notes, 13–15 May 1918, NLI, MS 22,964.

[141] Maura McNally, 'The 1918 East Cavan by election' (MA dissertation, University College, Dublin, 1978), p. 37.   [142] *Dundalk Examiner*, 15 June 1918.   [143] *II*, 19 June 1918.

[144] McNally, 'East Cavan', pp. 57–63; Dillon to T. P. O'Connor, 22 June 1918, JD, 6742.

implementing the Military Service Act, and it warned that conscription would be enforced if a renewed voluntary recruiting scheme failed to extract sufficient troops. To no-one's surprise this new measure failed, and by the end of September less than 8,000 had responded to an appeal for 50,000 recruits.[145]

The British authorities continued to deliberate on the matter, and Bonar Law denied publicly that the government had abandoned its plans.[146] Lord French continued to have as his objective 'the complete removal of useless and idle young men between the ages of 18 and 24 or 25 by the enforcement of *Conscription . . .* it is good that it should come, as being the only means of eradicating the main root of all the evil'.[147] Only a month before the war ended the chief secretary felt obliged to echo his predecessor's warnings against the measure: there were enough arms in Ireland to start a conflagration, and while the young men were hot-headed and dangerous, 'by far the greater danger will come from the women. Very many of them are of the type of the militant suffragette.'[148] Long cautioned that if conscription were to be imposed there would be a risk of parliament losing its nerve after a few women and priests had been killed.[149] Even while the German armies retreated cabinet ministers continued to devote attention to the scheme for conscripting Irishmen to fight them.[150]

In Ireland the immediate threat of compulsory military service might have been dispelled by the time of the German plot, but deep fears and passions persisted until the end of the war. In East Galway one farmer was unable to persuade anyone to save his hay because he had refused to sign the anti-conscription pledge.[151] A doctor with a large practice attended British soldiers, with the result that his civilian patients went elsewhere; 'nothing was said to him by anyone, his business simply had vanished'.[152] Sinn Féin and the Volunteers incited alarm and prepared for resistance, and they warned the public not to relax or to assume that the crisis had passed. In the autumn, both the *Irishman* and the *Irish Independent* advised that conscription might be imposed in November, and even after the armistice had been signed the Volunteers' journal *An tÓglách* included a reference to 'daily rumours with regard to Conscription'.[153]

[145] IG's report, Sept. 1917, CO.904/107.   [146] *Hansard*, 106, col. 1,759 (6 June 1918).

[147] French to George V, 13 July 1918, LG, F/48/6/17.

[148] Shortt, memo, 7 Oct. 1918, Cab.24/66, GT. 5918.

[149] Long, memo, 9 Oct. 1918, Cab. 24/66, GT. 5926.

[150] Alan J. Ward, 'Lloyd George and the 1918 conscription crisis', *Historical Journal*, 18, 1 (1974), p. 125.   [151] CI's report, E. Galway, June 1918, CO.904/106.

[152] IO's report (M. and C.), June 1918.

[153] *II*, 21 Sept. 1918; *Irishman*, 28 Sept. 1918; *An tÓglách*, 15 Nov. 1918.

Sinn Féin was able to maintain a national mood of unease and suspense, thereby bridging a potentially awkward gap between the excitement of the German plot arrests and the beginning of the general election campaign. The government's ban on public meetings provoked resentment and widespread defiance, particularly and triumphantly by the GAA.[154] Dillon commented, not unfairly, that the Sinn Féiners' hopes 'are built on the fear of conscription, and on the continuation of the policy of suppressing meetings'.[155] The longer that attention was focused on conscription the more irrelevant the Parliamentary Party seemed to be; disregarded by the British government, it was ignored in turn by most of the Irish people.

For years there had been speculation about a wartime election, but once the Representation of the People Bill had been enacted in February 1918 it seemed likely that the poll would take place before the end of the year, no matter how long the war might continue. After the failure of the Ludendorff offensive, and particularly after the success of the allies' counter-attack in August, an autumn or winter election seemed virtually certain. Lloyd George showed no sign of expecting the war to end soon, and as late as August 1918 he referred in cabinet to the possibility of its continuing until 1920,[156] but he could nonetheless appeal to the voters at a time when Britain and its allies held the initiative. The Germans collapsed with unexpected speed and they surrendered a mere three months later.

An election was long overdue. It was ironic that the House of Commons which had been elected in December 1910, and which soon afterwards reduced the maximum interval between elections from seven years to five, became the longest-serving Westminster parliament since the reign of Charles II. Because of the war it had simply prolonged its own life, year after year.

The Representation of the People Act widened the franchise, extending the vote to men of twenty-one and granting it to women for the first time – although only to those who were aged over thirty and who were either themselves householders or else were married to householders.[157] (In independent Ireland women did not get the vote on the same terms as men until 1922, and in the United Kingdom not until 1928.) They could also run for election to parliament. There was a threefold increase in the number of those entitled to vote, and in Ireland the figure rose from 698,000 to 1,931,000. In historical terms this was a profound change: the 1884 Reform Act had widened the electorate from

---

[154] Mandle, *Gaelic Athletic Association*, pp. 183–5.

[155] Dillon to T. P. O'Connor, 22 Aug. 1918, JD, 6742.

[156] Cabinet conclusions, 15 Aug. 1918, Cab.23/7, WC.459.

[157] Since 1898 some women had been eligible to vote in local elections.

8 to 31 per cent of the population aged twenty and over, and now the proportion was increased to 75 per cent.[158] The fact that so many electors had never
voted before made it more likely that they would break with the political habits
of their fathers, or else (because the old system had enfranchised householders
and denied the vote to many of the poor) that they would reject the opinions of
their wealthier neighbours. It has been estimated that only about 360,000 had
voted previously in a parliamentary election.[159]

Some of the old surviving rotten boroughs were eliminated, including Newry,
whose 12,841 voters totalled less than a tenth of East Belfast's 135,788. Ulster had
been under-represented at the time of the previous revision in 1885 and it now
received four extra members, while the cities benefited at the expense of the
countryside; Dublin and Belfast were awarded three and five new seats respectively. Ireland was already over-represented in parliament as a result of the dramatic decline in its own population and the steady increase in Britain's, and this
inequity was increased by the addition of two extra seats. In terms of population
the island should have had 66 MPs, and not its new total of 105. (If the pattern
had been reversed, Griffith would have enjoyed playing with such figures and
exposing a further example of British discrimination against Ireland.)

It was against this background that, from mid-summer onwards, Sinn Féin
began preparing for the long-awaited opportunity to deliver the *coup de grâce*
to the Redmondites and secure the election of a parliament dominated by its
own members. Its standing committee approved schemes whereby organizers
would visit each constituency to instruct party members in the details of the
new franchise and in the conduct of elections.[160] Even though many Sinn Féin
members had until recently been active in the Parliamentary Party or the UIL,
the fact that most Irish elections were uncontested meant that they could have
acquired little experience in gaining and disciplining support against a serious
opponent. They had much to learn. Each constituency was to pay the organizer's salary while he was in its area, collections were to be made for the election fund, and local committees were warned that (in contrast to the pattern of
the recent by-elections) they would be left on their own and could not rely on
any outside help.[161] The names of candidates chosen locally were to be submitted to the party's standing committee for its approval, although in some cases
its wishes or directives were ignored.

---

[158] Richard Sinnott, *Irish voters decide: voting behaviour in elections and referendums since 1918*
(Manchester, 1995), p. 25.

[159] John Coakley, 'The election that made the first Dáil', in Brian Farrell (ed.), *The creation of the
Dáil* (Dublin, 1994), p. 36.   [160] SCM, 11 July 1918.

[161] 'Sinn Féin notes', *Kerryman*, 24 Aug. 1918.

The process of selecting candidates lasted from August until the end of November, and occasionally it was marked by quarrels. There was resentment in West Clare at the choice of Brian O'Higgins (sometimes referred to as 'the Meath poet'), and there was even talk of the Clare Volunteers putting forward an independent candidate. They produced a handbill which denounced the 'politicians' who had made the selection, and demanded that Patrick Brennan, one of their own, should contest the seat.[162] Later Brennan warned that his decision against challenging O'Higgins should not be interpreted as an expression of satisfaction with the way in which the decision had been made.[163] In Mallow the constituency executive selected Diarmuid Lynch as the candidate. Afterwards, while Fr O'Flanagan was (characteristically) addressing a crowd from a window, William Kent entered the room and protested to the delegates that the selection had been made behind the backs of his family 'who were the first in North-East Cork to fight for Ireland'. After a long discussion the executive decided that Kent's brother David (who had already been chosen for the seat eighteen months earlier) should have full power to nominate a candidate, and that the executive would abide by his decision.[164] People can hardly have been surprised when David Kent selected himself, and Lynch was transferred to neighbouring South-East Cork.

Elsewhere the process could be equally informal. North Wexford chose as its candidate John Sweetman from Meath, who had been president of Griffith's Sinn Féin between 1908 and 1910. When he read of this in a newspaper he declined the position on grounds of age (he was seventy-four), and his cousin Roger Sweetman from Wicklow was nominated in his place. The new candidate proved to be a man of limited experience, and when he spoke at a Sinn Féin meeting shortly afterwards he confessed that it was his first appearance in public life. It may have been no coincidence that the chairman of the meetings which made both these selections was yet another cousin, the radical Dom Francis Sweetman of Mount St Benedict school in Gorey; obviously the seat was to be kept in the family.[165] Perhaps in a protective spirit, Fr Sweetman continued to preside at meetings addressed by his untrained relative.

Others were unhappy at being chosen, and in Cork city Liam de Róiste regarded his selection as a most unwelcome order. In the privacy of his diary he complained that he was not a politician, that he disliked the whole paraphernalia of party politics, and that 'what is asked of me is, in my mind, as big a sacrifice as could possibly be asked'.[166] But he was prone to self-pity. Decades

---

[162] De Róiste, diary, 10 Oct. 1918, CAI, U271/A/21.   [163] *Clare Champion*, 9 Nov. 1918.

[164] *FJ*, 5 Nov. 1918.   [165] *Enniscorthy Guardian*, 9, 16 Nov. 1918.

[166] De Róiste, diary, 5 Sept. 1918, CAI, U271/A/21.

later, Páidín O'Keeffe reminisced that Louth Sinn Féiners had urged the standing committee 'whatever you do don't send us a gunman';[167] they were granted their wish and were sent J. J. O'Kelly, who fitted that description but who later became one of the most extreme republicans.

The standing committee decreed that only candidates with a command of the Irish language should be nominated for Gaeltacht districts. This rule was taken seriously, several names were vetted, and in one case the candidate was referred back because the committee remained unconvinced by claims of his fluency.[168] Cumann na mBan urged that some female candidates should be chosen, and in this respect Sinn Féin showed itself more radical than any other party in Ireland or Britain; it selected three women, and although one of them, Hanna Sheehy-Skeffington, declined the nomination, her colleague Countess Markievicz went on to become the first woman elected to parliament in the United Kingdom. The only other female candidate in the election was Sinn Féin's Winifred Carney who contested the unionist stronghold of Belfast, Victoria, and won a mere 4 per cent of the votes. (The first to be nominated had been Helena Molony of Labour, but she refused to stand even before her party decided not to contest the election.[169])

Sinn Féin made a point of contesting seats in parts of Ulster where the Parliamentary Party had never ventured, and only the unionist strongholds of North Down and Trinity College were to be left unchallenged. The party ran thirty-four candidates who were in jail, six who were evading arrest, and four who were in the United States.[170] Even if abstention from parliament had not been a central aspect of Sinn Féin's policy, its MPs would have been unable to attend Westminster in large numbers. In mid-September one candidate, Liam de Róiste, remarked that he was the only one so far selected who had never been in prison or on the run. This defect was soon remedied, the police moved to arrest him, and within ten days he was in hiding.[171] Later the *Irish Bulletin* could boast with only slight exaggeration that, apart from the two envoys in France and the United States, every one of Sinn Féin's elected representatives had been in jail.[172] Collins and Harry Boland were accused of controlling nominations and of excluding their opponents, while Richard Mulcahy thought it likely that he and Joe McGrath had been selected as candidates because of their IRB connections.[173] At a meeting of the Dáil in 1919 Tom Kelly, one of the old Griffithite

[167] O'Keeffe, interview, 1964, RM, P7/D/47, p. 7.   [168] SCM, 3 Oct. 1918.

[169] *Roscommon Journal*, 30 Nov. 1918.   [170] *II*, 21 Nov. 1918.

[171] De Róiste, diary, 15, 24 Sept. 1918, CAI, U271/A/21.   [172] *Irish Bulletin*, 13 Aug. 1920.

[173] O'Keeffe, interview, 1964, RM, P7/D/47, p. 2; Mulcahy, 'Memoirs', RM, P7b/134, p. 46; see Clarke, *Revolutionary woman*, p. 164.

Sinn Féiners, teased his colleagues, 'I fear that the majority of you here are "gunmen".'[174]

The party's manifesto was drawn up by a sub-committee consisting of O'Flanagan, Kelly and Boland (the two honorary secretaries), and Robert Brennan (the director of elections).[175] This programme repeated the demand for an Irish republic, demanded the withdrawal of Irish representatives from Westminster, and called for the establishment of a constituent assembly. It also committed the party to using 'any and every means available to render impotent the power of England to hold Ireland in subjection by military force or otherwise'.[176]

The British authorities were forceful in their treatment of Sinn Féiners. Police broke up a meeting which was held to select a candidate in Cahir (Co. Tipperary), and its activities were concluded in a wood outside the town.[177] The party's headquarters in Harcourt Street was raided four times, and the British arrested three successive directors of elections, Seán Milroy, Dan McCarthy and Robert Brennan. The imprisonment of party activists, the dispersal of meetings, the removal of posters and the seizure of leaflets all disrupted the campaign, but at the same time these measures provided Sinn Féin with favourable publicity and gave it the halo of martyrdom. The standing committee urged that, since large meetings would be banned, party members should engage in canvassing. It was claimed that in East Clare most of the work had been done in the form of campaign literature, and that 'there was scarcely a house or voter, but had been smothered with leaflets'; perhaps this was redundant effort in a constituency where no contest took place.[178]

Seán T. O'Kelly, the director of organization, reported in October that many clubs which had been dormant for one reason or another were now wide awake, and that members were aroused by the prospect of an early poll.[179] New branches were formed during the campaign. In Longford the RIC noted that Sinn Féin had been losing ground, but that the general election was exactly what was needed to infuse new life.[180] It was widely remarked, particularly by the police, that Sinn Féin had the support of the younger voters; the pattern established during the by-elections was maintained.

---

[174] De Róiste, diary, 10 Apr. 1920, CAI, U271/A/30. Kelly had been in jail since the previous December, so his remark must date from 1919.   [175] SCM, 30 Sept. 1918.

[176] *Nationality*, 19 Oct. 1918.   [177] *Nationalist and Leinster Times*, 21 Sept. 1918.

[178] *Clare Champion*, 26 July 1919.

[179] Report of director of organization and plebiscite, *Ard-fheis Sinn Féin, 1918*, RB, 8786(1).

[180] CI's report, Longford, Nov. 1918, CO.904/107.

Opponents

The Parliamentary Party's condition was very different. Its morale had been eroded by the failure of the 1916 home rule negotiations, by Sinn Féin's spread and consolidation in 1917, and by the recent conscription crisis. In July, Dillon remarked that the party must decide on some new policy, but he showed no signs of knowing what this might be.[181] Soon afterwards its MPs abandoned their short-lived practice of abstention and returned to Westminster for a few last, undistinguished months.

Dillon was left on his own, and Joe Devlin, who earlier in the year had fought so energetically in Armagh, Waterford and Tyrone, did not take part in the general election campaign. In his correspondence Dillon referred to Devlin's depression, and as late as 28 November he complained that there had been no word from his deputy since the contest began; his absence was a dreadful blow.[182] It was suggested elsewhere that Devlin had no wish to involve himself in the impending disaster, and his disloyalty to Dillon was noted at a meeting of the British cabinet.[183]

Many MPs decided that the Irish Party's cause was hopeless and that they should desert their sinking ship. Some of them pleaded private grounds for their unwillingness to run for re-election, and others argued that it would be impossible to make good the party's lack of organization before polling day. In Limerick the MP's reasons for standing down included an admirable concern that the peace and harmony of the city would not be endangered – as well as an awareness that his own supporters lacked organization and enthusiasm.[184] A colleague explained that, having always been returned unopposed, 'after so many years' friendly association with all classes in Cavan I cannot see my way to be a leader of strife'.[185] But the most remarkable excuse of all was that offered by the fastidious Swift MacNeill in South Donegal. He announced that, having represented the constituency since 1887, and having been unopposed since 1895, to enter a contest now would be 'moral torture'. He continued, 'I have too long been member for this constituency to be able consistently with sincerity or self-respect to solicit as a favour votes to secure my election to Parliament.'[186]

In Leitrim a form of musical chairs was played, in which, apparently, the loser was the player who actually ended with the seat rather than without it. Thomas Smyth stood down in favour of Francis Meehan who was rejected by a

---

[181] Dillon to W. G. Fallon, 1 July 1918, Fallon MSS, NLI, 22,578.

[182] Dillon to T. P. O'Connor, 18 Aug., 28 Nov. 1918, JD, 6742.

[183] Cabinet conclusions, 21 Nov. 1918, Cab.23/8, WC.505(11).

[184] *Limerick Leader*, 6 Dec. 1918.   [185] *FJ*, 23 Nov. 1918.   [186] *FJ*, 8 Nov. 1918.

conference which selected Thomas Fallon who also retired.[187] Gerald Farrell was finally chosen, only to be humiliated when he won a mere 15 per cent of the votes against his Sinn Féin opponent. Of the sixty-eight Irish Party MPs who held seats at the time of the dissolution of parliament, thirty-two chose to withdraw from public life, while another three tried their luck in different constituencies. All of these were unsuccessful.

Dillon despised his colleagues' timidity and he reacted with growing despair as his party was overwhelmed. In early September he complained that 'nothing has been done yet here in preparation for the General Election and it is immensely difficult to get anything started', and ten weeks later he longed for 'a decent machine, and an organisation half or one quarter as effective as the Sinn Feiners'; with these, he claimed, the party could save forty or fifty seats.[188]

The Nationalists' election programme was unimpressive. Their only remaining objective had been the achievement of home rule, and despite its enactment four years earlier their goal still seemed as elusive as it had been in the past. Lloyd George, in a letter to Bonar Law which was published soon afterwards, made the obvious point that in the present circumstances an attempt to introduce home rule could not succeed.[189] The cause had also been tainted by its recent link with conscription. There was at least some element of justice in the claim by The Freeman's Journal that Nationalists were being punished for their own achievements, and that Sinn Féin's appeal would be less powerful if the country still suffered from the grievances which the party had removed.[190] Their manifesto looked back to the past and urged that Ireland should carry on the policy which had gained so much since the new departure of 1879. It was now on the threshold of final victory. And its enemies were denounced, along with their policies of an Irish republic and an appeal to the postwar peace conference.

Sinn Féin faced problems from Labour as well as from the parliamentarians. The Labour Party had been founded in 1912, but it remained inactive for several years and (like Griffith's pre-war party) it had contested only one by-election. Any serious involvement in politics would have risked alienating either the Protestant workers in the north, who were committed to maintaining the union with Britain, or else their Catholic and nationalist counterparts in the south. The Labour movement had been deeply divided by the participation of Connolly and the Citizen Army in the Easter Rising, and it manoeuvred warily to avoid further antagonizing any of its component parts. For example, when the trade union leader William O'Brien was elected to the Mansion

---

[187] *II*, 27 Nov. 1918.   [188] Dillon to O'Connor, 5 Sept., 22 Nov. 1918, JD, 6742.

[189] *II*, 18 Nov. 1918, article entitled 'home rule betrayal by premier'.

[190] *FJ*, 11 Oct. 1918, editorial.

House committee in April 1917 he accepted the position hesitantly and soon felt obliged to resign. He explained that since 'most of the members of the rank and file of the Irish Labour Party up to recently gave their adhesion to the Redmondite Home Rule Party', and since a considerable minority still held such views, his prominence in the Sinn Féin movement might be divisive.[191] Nonetheless, by late 1918 demands were made in some quarters that the party should contest the first general election to be held since its foundation six years earlier.

The separatists were prepared to be flexible, and at the end of 1917 Thomas Johnson, the Labour leader, was informed that 'Sinn Féin is out for a deal on the Dublin seats.'[192] The party continued to display a limited degree of sympathy in the course of the following year, and at a meeting of the standing committee it was proposed that if a 'good man' were put up by Labour for a vacancy in Dublin's Wood Quay municipal ward, the party should offer him its support.[193] But soon afterwards a deputation from the Sinn Féiners in Wood Quay protested against such a move and argued in favour of running their own candidate. After some discussion the committee decided to leave the matter to the club.[194] Similarly in Cork city, there was a feeling that 'it is Sinn Féin that should win, and as Sinn Féin', rather than vicariously in the form of a sympathetic Labour candidate.[195] The College Green constituency party later displayed mutinous tendencies, refusing to carry out instructions regarding the 'adjustment of the Labour Question'.[196]

In August, Boland was instructed to arrange a compromise between the standing committee and 'representative Labour men' concerning the election and other matters.[197] These talks proved fruitless. He reported back that Labour intended to contest fifteen seats and would not – as required by Sinn Féin – agree to abstention from Westminster on principle; it insisted that its MPs should abstain as a matter of mere expediency. The committee decided to maintain Sinn Féin's policy of running candidates in every constituency, while remaining prepared to modify it if occasion arose. Boland, Brennan and Kelly were 'empowered to negotiate with Labour in respect of three seats', and the discussions continued. There was little doubt about the damage which Labour could inflict in a contest between the two parties, and the standing committee was warned that if enough trade union candidates intervened in the campaign they could deprive Sinn Féin of up to twenty seats.[198]

[191] O'Brien to Thomas Dillon, 28 May 1917, O'Brien MSS, NLI, 15,653(3).
[192] Brian Farrell, *The founding of Dáil Éireann* (Dublin, 1971), p. 36.   [193] SCM, 23 July 1918.
[194] *Ibid.*, 1 Aug. 1918.   [195] De Róiste, diary, 6 Sept. 1918, CAI, U271/A/21.
[196] SCM, 24 Oct. 1918.   [197] *Ibid.*, 16 Aug. 1918.   [198] *Ibid.*, 12, 19 Sept., 7 Oct. 1918.

By this stage, however, Labour had run into difficulties. The Dublin Trades Council decided to contest four constituencies,[199] but Belfast Labour rejected the party's policy, and anti-nationalist Labour and trade unionist candidates ran for election. As he travelled around the country William O'Brien encountered pessimism and apathy. In Meath, for example, the Labour Union decided to stand aside, and when he arrived in Cork he discovered that the meeting to select a candidate would not take place.[200] His colleague P. T. Daly, who had formerly been prominent in the IRB, lobbied against Labour's involvement in the election.[201] When a conference was held to decide whether Labour would contest the South Kilkenny seat, the Thomastown Sinn Féin branch urged those of its members who also belonged to the Transport Union to ensure that '*genuine* Sinn Féiners who put the cause of an Irish Republic first and above all other causes' should be chosen as representatives.[202]

Labour offered a radical programme. Among other objectives it declared that it would gain for the workers the collective ownership and control of the whole produce of their work; adopt the principles of the Russian revolution; secure the democratic management of all industries in the interest of the nation; and abolish all privileges which were based on property or ancestry. But its election manifesto conceded that the predominant issue of the day was not of its own choosing.[203] The party would secure at most a few seats in Dublin by concluding a deal with Sinn Féin, while at the same time it would be branded as the subordinate partner in this new alliance and it would alienate Protestant trade unionists in the north east.[204] By fighting independently it would provoke a mutiny in its own ranks.

A special party conference in Dublin decided against contesting the elections by the decisive margin of ninety-six votes to twenty-three.[205] Gavan Duffy's suggestion to his colleagues on the Sinn Féin standing committee that they reciprocate by giving at least ten seats to Labour was chivalrous in its generosity. Naturally it was rejected, and the committee decided to contest them all.[206]

Labour's abstention removed what would otherwise have been the most

---

[199] *II*, 25 Sept. 1918.   [200] William O'Brien, diary, 29 Sept., 19 Oct. 1918, NLI, MS 15,705.

[201] Farrell, *Founding of Dáil Éireann*, pp. 37, 40.

[202] John O'Carroll to James O'Mara, 26 Oct. 1918, JO'M, 21,546(2).   [203] *II*, 29 Sept. 1918.

[204] Michael Gallagher, 'Socialism and the nationalist tradition in Ireland, 1798–1918', *Éire-Ireland*, 12, 2 (1977), p. 101.

[205] *II*, 2 Nov. 1918; on Labour's withdrawal, see Michael Laffan, '"Labour must wait": Ireland's conservative revolution', in Patrick J. Corish (ed.), *Radicals, rebels and establishments* (Belfast, 1985), pp. 214–16.   [206] SCM, 7 Nov. 1918.

serious obstacle to a Sinn Féin triumph, but another, more localized problem still remained. The party's recent by-election defeats had illustrated clearly its relative lack of support in Ulster. Extra resources were made available in an effort to overcome this weakness, and in late November Jennie Wyse Power, financial director for the north-east, was sent to Belfast with the sum of £2,250 to help finance the campaign.[207] When the party's election expenditure was calculated in April 1919, it was revealed that £3,200 out of a total £8,267 had been spent in unionist Ulster.[208]

Sinn Féin faced an immediate problem in the areas where the combined nationalist forces were in a small overall majority. If it and the Parliamentary Party fought each other in these constituencies, as would be the pattern in the rest of the country, they would split the nationalist vote and allow unionist candidates to take the seats. Here too, as in the case of its dealings with Labour, the standing committee was open-minded. It was willing to accept the idea of local plebiscites (as had been proposed during the Cavan election, although for a different reason) and to accept the verdict of a majority of the nationalist population as to which party should challenge the unionists; in effect, these contests would fulfil the same function as American primary elections. Matters could be left in the hands of the local constituency organizations.[209] In the event only one such plebiscite was held, in North Fermanagh where Sinn Féin won by 3,737 votes to 2,026.[210]

Lengthy discussions followed, and Sinn Féin expressed its willingness to accept a compromise proposed by the bishop of Derry. This was to the effect that a meeting should be held in a central Ulster town such as Dungannon; each of eight constituencies should be represented by two home rulers, two Sinn Féiners and two priests; and the delegates should try to reach an understanding which would avert an internecine conflict.[211] But the Parliamentary Party was less ready to give way. The pessimistic *Freeman's Journal* remarked that there was little to choose between the unionists and Sinn Féin since, if either party won, the nationalist population would not be represented in Westminster. The party was to play the role of the lady of Riga who went for a ride on a tiger; its members were to 'commit suicide to save themselves from slaughter'; and the paper boasted that Dillon preferred to go down fighting than submit to such an ignoble fate.[212] (These views were matched on the other side by the *Irishman*,

---

[207] *Ibid.*, 25 Nov. 1918.   [208] *Ard-fheis* report, II, 10 Apr. 1919.   [209] SCM, 16 Oct. 1918.

[210] *Fermanagh Herald*, 7 Dec. 1918.   [211] *FJ*, 16 Nov. 1918.

[212] *FJ*, 22 Nov. 1918, editorial. The Limerick (an unworthy specimen) went as follows: 'There was a young lady from Riga/ Who went for a ride on a tiger/ They came back from the ride/ With the lady inside/ And a smile on the face of the tiger.'

which argued after the election that if all seats had been contested 'the worst that could have happened would have been the return of eight orthodox Orangemen in place of eight green Orangemen'.[213])

Once again, as in the conscription crisis some months earlier, the Catholic hierarchy intervened. Logue and the other northern bishops were appalled at the prospect of unionist candidates winning what should have been safe nationalist seats. They proposed a conference between the two sides which would be chaired by the lord mayor of Dublin, and they suggested an equal division of the eight constituencies in question. This idea provoked strong disagreement among the members of the Sinn Féin standing committee. Piaras Béaslaí argued that 'if we agree we lose the support of every decent man in Ireland', while George Murnaghan put forward the view of those whom he described as 'the Sinn Féin bishops': that the party would be ruined if it rejected the proposals and Dillon accepted them. (It may be significant that Béaslaí was a Volunteer and Murnaghan a former member of the Nation League; some divisions between radicals and moderates still survived.) At Collins's suggestion it was finally agreed to convene a meeting of representatives from the eight constituency executives; in effect, the standing committee evaded the issue.[214]

This meeting decided in favour of acceptance by a narrow majority, but local home rulers maintained their opposition to the withdrawal of any of their candidates. From the opposite standpoint Collins shared their reservations, and he wrote to Austin Stack suggesting that 'we must not I think even if we divide the seats advise support' (presumably of a Parliamentary Party candidate).[215] To stand down in favour of Nationalists might be an unfortunate necessity, but to canvass for them would carry anti-unionist solidarity too far.

An equal division of the seats was finally accepted by both sides, and once again it was Collins who made the proposal to the standing committee,[216] but this agreement came too late for the names of the eight 'rejected' candidates to be removed from the ballot paper. Each party urged its candidates not to campaign in the four constituencies which had been allocated to the other, and despite their shared unease both sides advised their supporters to vote for the agreed anti-unionist champion. This proved particularly difficult to enforce in the case of some home rule candidates who, like Sinn Féin members when faced with their own party headquarters' generosity towards Labour, were reluctant to abandon seats which they believed they could win.

---

[213] *Irishman*, 21 Dec. 1918.   [214] SCM, 28 Nov. 1918.
[215] Collins to Stack, 28 Nov. 1918, NLI, MS 5848.   [216] SCM, 4 Dec. 1918.

Triumph

The 1918 general election was the most widely contested for a quarter of a century, since that of 1892 which had been fought in the bitter aftermath of the Parnell split. Sinn Féin supporters were active, despite the restrictions imposed on their meetings; speakers harangued crowds, canvassers distributed leaflets, and the party's spirits were raised by the government's repressive measures. It was claimed that O'Flanagan addressed ninety-seven meetings in the course of a month.[217] Many parliamentarians ran only a token campaign, and from Kilkenny it was reported that the sitting MP had done no canvassing; 'not even a poster has been seen in his favour'.[218]

Several of the defeated Nationalist candidates commented on the good nature of the campaign and the fairness of the results, but the election was marked nonetheless by widespread violence and personation. Speakers were stoned and meetings were disrupted. In East Cork, the police divided the population into two neat categories: 'the community generally is engaged in either intimidation or being intimidated'.[219] Dillon warned an audience in Ballaghdereen that Claremen (those scourges of South Armagh earlier in the year) were on their way to bully the Mayo electors.[220] In Wexford many people were injured as rival mobs bludgeoned each other with sticks, Fr O'Flanagan was howled down by Redmondites, and the meeting ended with a police baton charge.[221] Even less politically active clergy were not immune, and in some instances their speeches were heckled and their houses were stoned. In Mayo, for example, a Sinn Féin priest was prevented from speaking and was told 'when you are on the right side we will hear you'.[222] There were reports of conflict between the generations, and complaints were made that 'sons are frightening their fathers as to what will happen if the fathers don't vote Sinn Féin'.[223] Vilification and scare stories were frequent, and in Connemara an audience was warned by its MP that 'the result of Sinn Fein was that men with blackened faces went into the houses of the people and stole their property'.[224]

In their speeches Nationalists tended to stress reforms such as the land acts and old age pensions, and naturally they claimed that all the credit for these measures belonged to the home rule movement. Audiences were reminded that 'the Party had won for the farmers their homes and land, and now that they [the electors] had won their holdings, and had little more to get, they would be thor-

---

[217] *II*, 9 Apr. 1919.   [218] Fr M. Fitzpatrick to James O'Mara, 10 Dec. 1918, JO'M, 21,546(1).
[219] CI's report, E. Cork, Nov. 1918, CO.904/107.   [220] *II*, 13 Dec. 1918.   [221] *FJ*, 29 Nov. 1918.
[222] *Limerick Leader*, 29 Nov. 1918.   [223] CI's report, Mayo, Nov. 1918, CO.904/107.
[224] *II*, 25 Nov. 1918.

oughly ungrateful if they did not support the Party'.[225] They were assured that 'the evictor was now a thing of the past . . . The mud-wall cabins had been replaced by 50,000 labourers' cottages.'[226] The party boasted repeatedly that it had won the land for the people, and one answer which it received was that, thanks to its advice, many good men had been given land: a soldier's grave.[227] In similar fashion, Dillon declared in Swinford that there were now only two parties, and was met with the retort 'the other one is in jail'.[228]

Sinn Féin's propaganda emphasized the heroism of the Easter rebels and stressed the demand for a republic, it took all the credit for averting conscription, and it denounced British oppression. One of Robert Barton's campaign leaflets attacked the government 'which in one year batoned and bayoneted 10,000 men and women of your own flesh and blood'.[229] A ballad, to be sung to the tune of 'Paddies evermore', proclaimed that

> When Conscription hovered o'er the land,
> Sinn Féin was all we had.
> The Party could not raise a hand
> To save one stalwart lad.[230]

The fall of so many European monarchies towards the end of the First World War made Sinn Féin's demand for an Irish republic seem less absurd or unrealistic than might have been the case a year or two earlier; it was pointed out, for example, that the pope had sent his best wishes to the new republic of Finland. But not all Sinn Féiners flaunted republican views, and three years later Roger Sweetman, the incongruous candidate for North Wexford, claimed that in his election campaign he had never used the word 'republic' and had demanded only 'full independence'.[231] The Parliamentary Party's adherence to its belief in attendance at Westminster was much derided, particularly in the light of its futile protest against conscription. As in the past, its MPs were accused of selling their country for a salary of £400 a year (a mere £65 of which, it was claimed, went in taxation).[232] The RIC inspector general remarked philosophically that 'the language used, though disloyal and bitterly anti-English, was, on the whole, not worse than might be anticipated'.[233]

The Volunteers were active during the campaign. In West Galway the police commented on Sinn Féin's remarkable organization, its pickets on all polling

---

[225] *Limerick Leader,* 25 Nov. 1918.   [226] *FJ,* 10 Oct. 1918.

[227] *Nationalist and Leinster Times,* 30 Nov. 1918.   [228] *II,* 27 Nov. 1918.

[229] *Irishmen!* (leaflet), Barton MSS, NAI, 1093(11).

[230] *Roscommon Journal,* 7 Dec. 1918, supplement.   [231] *II,* 29 Dec. 1921.   [232] *II,* 2 Dec. 1918.

[233] IG's report, Nov. 1918, CO.904/107.

booths, and the guards who accompanied the ballot boxes to Galway court-house. They then kept watch throughout the two weeks' interval between polling day and the count on 28 December. (The delay was caused by the need to bring home the soldiers' ballot papers from France and the Middle East.) For the first time, electors in every constituency voted on the same day. At polling stations in Sligo members of Cumann na mBan performed their accustomed supportive tasks; 'their duty was to provide, at stated intervals, food and refreshments for the men at work in the various booths'.[234] Personation was a commonplace occurrence, and many enthusiasts voted repeatedly on behalf of the tardy, the absent and the dead. In Cork city people regarded it as a good joke.[235] However, in most cases it was probably unneces-sary, and as one RIC inspector remarked, 'Sinn Féin organizers were satisfied that they would have a large majority without resorting to any of the usual electioneering subterfuges.'[236]

The results, although not surprising in their broad outlines, caused an upheaval in Irish politics comparable to that of the Parnellite landslide in 1885; 80 seats were contested by 187 candidates, 77 of whom were Sinn Féiners, 56 Nationalists and 35 Unionists. They were accompanied by 6 independent nationalists, 4 independent unionists, 8 Ulster Labour candidates of different sorts, and 1 unqualified independent. O'Brien's All-For-Ireland League had vanished. Perhaps the single most revealing proof of the Parliamentary Party's demoralization was its abandonment of 25 safe nationalist seats which it had held or challenged at the last election. Large parts of the country experienced no contest at all; none took place, for example, in Cavan, Cork (except for Cork city), Kerry and King's Co. Of the 24 Munster constituencies, 17 returned Sinn Féin candidates unopposed, and throughout the country the electorate in the uncontested areas totalled 475,000. Nonetheless the Parliamentary Party managed to hold on to its former vote; where it failed decisively was in attract-ing new votes in a vastly enlarged electorate – as Sinn Féin and the Unionists succeeded in doing.[237]

Sinn Féin won seventy-three seats (although the total of its elected candi-dates was sixty-eight, since five of them represented two constituencies), while the Unionists won twenty-six and the Parliamentary Party six. Sinn Féin engaged in thirty-seven straight fights with the Nationalists and won thirty-five of them; only in Waterford city and Falls (Belfast) could Captain Redmond and Joe Devlin hold out against the tide. Apart from Trinity College, one other seat

[234] *Sligo Champion*, 21 Dec. 1918.   [235] De Róiste, diary, 15 Dec. 1918, CAI, U271/A/23.
[236] CI's report, Longford, Dec. 1918, CO.904/107.
[237] Farrell, *Founding of Dáil Éireann*, pp. 48–9.

was lost by the party in the three southern provinces – Rathmines, where the Unionist Maurice Dockrell obtained more votes than his Sinn Féin and Parliamentary Party opponents combined. Sinn Féin performed less impressively in constituencies along the east coast than elsewhere outside Ulster, but only in Louth was there any serious prospect of it losing the seat; its candidate, J. J. O'Kelly, secured a mere 50.6 per cent of the vote. For old Sinn Féiners one of the most satisfying results must have been in Leitrim, where the defeat of 1908 was avenged and C. J. Dolan's brother won the seat by the largest majority of any constituency in the country. Dillon fought on to the end in East Mayo but he lost to de Valera by a margin of two to one, while Sinn Féin gained almost exactly two-thirds of the vote in the seven Dublin city constituencies.

Sinn Féin was not the only victor in 1918; the Unionists also triumphed, increasing the number of their seats by eight. For nearly six years they had represented only a minority of the Ulster constituencies, but now, as the result of a redistribution which matched the population balance more evenly, they held twenty-three out of the provincial total of thirty-seven. Their opposition to all forms of Irish nationalism was strengthened accordingly. But in other respects, too, the pattern in Ulster differed from that in the south. In many parts of the province the Parliamentary Party polled remarkably well, and in some cases it performed even better than its Sinn Féin challenger; the precedent of the Armagh and Tyrone by-elections was followed. In Falls, Devlin secured 72 per cent of the vote in a straight fight with de Valera. Among the seats won by the Unionists, the ratio of the minority nationalist vote in Duncairn was nearly 10:1 in favour of the Parliamentary Party, while in South Derry it was ahead of Sinn Féin by 3,981 votes to 3,425. In East Donegal, one of the four seats later allocated by Logue to the Parliamentary Party, the *Freeman's Journal* reported in November that the Nationalists were hopeful, since Sinn Féin had held no meetings and its canvassers had met with little success.[238]

Even in those constituencies where Sinn Féin gained more votes than its rival the margin of victory was often relatively slight. The balance was 5,787 to 4,752 in South Donegal, and in the west of the county 6,712 to 4,116. The result in East Down was the most remarkable of all. It was one of the four seats which Logue had assigned to Sinn Féin, but there, despite Dillon's painfully extracted acceptance of the compromise agreement, the home rule candidate refused to withdraw. Against such a background, repudiated by his own party leadership, defying the cardinal (who complained about 'the treachery of National Party followers'[239]), and ensuring that the unionist would win the seat because of a

238 *FJ*, 23 Nov. 1918.
239 Logue to Archbishop Walsh, 29 Dec. 1918, Logue MSS, ADA, Walsh 1909–21, 9a.

split nationalist vote, he nonetheless secured 30 per cent of the poll against his Sinn Féin rival's 27 per cent.[240]

The reasons for this regional discrepancy are not hard to find. Dillon was only one of numerous observers who pointed out how flabby and disorganized the Irish Party had become throughout most of the country, and in many constituencies MPs had been returned unopposed for decades. The record was held by West Donegal which had never yet been contested since its creation as a separate entity in 1885, but other parts of the country were habitually inert at election time. The last fight in West Clare took place in 1895, and in East Waterford, South Westmeath and West Wicklow in 1892. North-East Cork had been contested only once in thirteen general and by-elections.[241] In December 1910 two-thirds of the Redmondite MPs (forty-nine of seventy-three) had been elected unopposed. Thanks to the Parliamentary Party's position of unchallenged dominance, to its position as the only party in a one-party nation, it had faced no serious opposition. Its machinery, so formidable in Parnell's campaigns, had rusted and crumbled; it had become complacent and vulnerable.

Things were different in divided north-east Ulster. There the Nationalists faced a powerful and organized Unionist enemy, and in many constituencies every election was, if not a matter of life and death, at least a question of win or lose.[242] Seats changed hands on the narrowest of margins, and the party was alert, organized and responsive to its constituents. In Joe Devlin it had an energetic young leader (however inactive he might have been in the general election campaign). The party was able to resist the Sinn Féin challenge and, ultimately, to overcome its new rival; while in the south the Parnellite Party was wiped out in 1918, it survived in the new Northern Irish state, it adapted to new circumstances, and until the general election of 1969 it remained the principal voice of the nationalist minority.

Apart from its mixed fortunes in Ulster, various statistics or lines of approach might seem to dent the image of a Sinn Féin triumph. It secured a respectable but not overwhelming 60 per cent of the contested seats, 48 out of 80. It won a mere 474,859 of the 1,011,248 votes cast in the 'ordinary' (non-university) constituencies, while the Unionists won 289,025 and the Parliamentary Party 220,226; the respective proportions were 46.9, 28.5 and 21.7 per cent. The inherent injustice of the British 'first past the post' electoral system might seem

---

[240] On East Down see Phoenix, *Northern nationalism*, p. 52.

[241] For election details see B. M. Walker (ed.), *Parliamentary election results in Ireland, 1801–1922* (Dublin, 1978).

[242] See Michael Laffan, *The partition of Ireland, 1911–1925* (Dublin, 1983), p. 36.

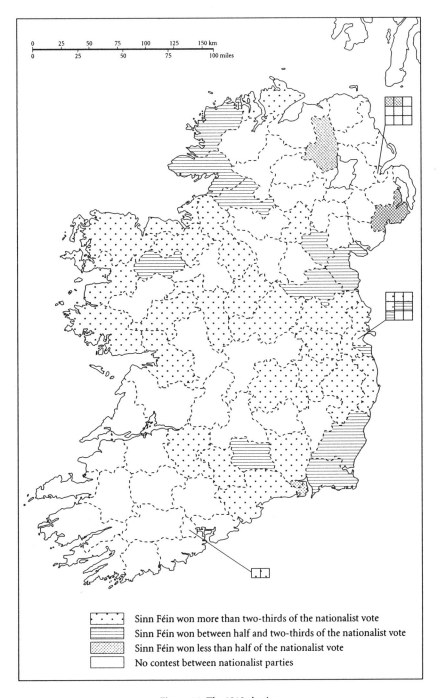

Figure 4.1 The 1918 election

to have come to its rescue by enabling it to win nearly three-quarters of the seats with less than half of the votes.

Nonetheless the results probably underestimate the scale of Sinn Féin's achievement, rather than exaggerate it. Most of the twenty-five uncontested seats were situated in those areas where the party was already dominant; for example, with the exception of South Longford, all those areas which it had already won in by-elections no longer needed to be fought again. Counties such as Clare and Kerry, which were already Volunteer strongholds and had a high Sinn Féin membership per head of population, would undoubtedly have augmented the separatist vote had the Parliamentary Party not stood aside. In most cases, it was precisely because they were aware of Sinn Féin's strength in their constituencies that the outgoing MPs chose not to stand again. In comparative terms the Unionists' high total vote and national percentage are somewhat misleading; they reflect the fact that the party was challenged in almost every constituency which it won, and as a result its followers trooped *en masse* to the polling stations. So in contrast to the accurate reflection which was provided of Unionist strength, Sinn Féin's real support was undoubtedly far greater than was indicated by its national percentage of votes. And even if allowance is made for widespread personation, it is likely that in almost all cases Sinn Féin would have won fairly without recourse to such measures.

One tribute stands out among all those paid to Sinn Féin in December 1918. Even before the results were announced and the full extent of the Parliamentary Party's *débâcle* had become clear, Dillon wrote that his own fight in East Mayo was 'a microcosm of the conditions all over the country – Absolute lack of organisation and helplessness on our side – against the most perfect organisation and infinite audacity on the other'. Many Sinn Féiners would have savoured the second part of this backhanded compliment as much as the first.[243]

The party's achievement in combining so effectively its different (and at times still mutually suspicious) component parts, in disciplining and channelling its support, came to a grand climax in December 1918. But its greatest problems still lay in the future.

---

[243] Dillon to T. P. O'Connor, 20 Dec. 1918, JD, 6742. Some might have taken equal pride in his concluding reference to 'ferocious intimidation'.

5

The party: structures and members

By the end of 1918 Sinn Féin had achieved most of its important objectives – except, of course, the achievement of an independent Irish republic. It had converted and organized nationalist opinion, defeated the Parliamentary Party, and secured the election of a large Sinn Féin majority among Irish MPs. These representatives could now proceed to establish a parliament and government in Dublin. The new scheme of organization approved by the October 1917 convention had been in operation for a year. The party had expanded to the natural limit of its membership, it had reached its peak, and it would soon decline.

Between 1919 and 1921 British censorship and suppression, followed by the hazards and horrors of war, would limit Sinn Féin's effectiveness and undermine its organization. The activities of the Volunteers would relegate it to a subordinate position, and the party would even be displaced as the main civilian expression of Irish separatism. Its moment of triumph in December 1918 is an appropriate point at which to examine Sinn Féin under various headings: how it was organized; the extent to which its aims and structures responded to Irish realities; who its members were; what they did; and how party membership affected their lives.

Theory

In some respects Sinn Féin's constitution and its scheme of organization were abstract constructs, irrelevant to the party's real life and inappropriate to the circumstances of the time. They impinged only marginally on the activities of individual branches or of most members. Yet they deserve a brief appraisal. They reveal what many people (and in particular the party's leaders) believed Sinn Féin should represent, and how they thought it should conduct its affairs. When the party fell to pieces in the split of 1922, its constitution and rules were important weapons which were exploited by both sides in the struggle for power which followed.

169

Until the convention in October 1917 the movement or party was run by *ad hoc* groups which functioned without great ceremony. The first of these was the committee formed after the Roscommon election. This was followed by the Mansion House committee which met in the aftermath of the Plunkett convention, and it in turn was succeeded by the coalition which brought together Griffith's Sinn Féin, the Liberty League and, ultimately, the Irish Nation League.[1]

The party convention of October 1917 not only replaced Griffith as president by de Valera and committed the party to the goal of a republic, but it also approved a new party structure which had been outlined by the leaders.[2] With some minor alterations this remained intact until the party disintegrated in 1922. The constitution was modelled closely on that of Griffith's pre-rising party, with the crucial difference that the form of government which was to be achieved was now republican rather than monarchist. There followed a long list of ideals and objectives, such as summoning a constituent assembly, developing a consular service, and establishing a system of arbitration courts. In the course of the next few years several of these aims were achieved, and others were seen to be less appropriate to a party than to a government or its civil service. They were all removed in October 1921.

The new party organization was an elaborate pattern of assemblies and committees, of interlocking and overlapping bodies, and at the 1917 convention several party members complained that it was unnecessarily complex. (So, too, did later observers. These included the judge and counsel in the Sinn Féin funds case who, thirty years later, struggled to disentangle the party's structures. The judge described it as 'a curiously muddled document, barely grammatical and without any orderly or systematic arrangement'.[3])

The new scheme operated as follows. At the lowest of six levels were the individual clubs or branches, the numbers of which varied considerably between about 1,200 and (at least in theory) about 1,800. Their members elected representatives to two different higher bodies, although often the same people served for both purposes. One pair of delegates represented each club at the second stage or level, that of the constituency executives (or *comhairlí ceanntair*). These were responsible for organizing the party at constituency level and for raising any necessary funds. They were to meet at least once every three months, and each had its own standing committee.

The constituency executives (which numbered about 100) in turn selected one representative each who, along with a second group of delegates chosen by

---

[1] See above, pp. 85–90, 93, 105–6.   [2] *Sinn Féin scheme of organisation, rules etc.* (pamphlet, Dublin, 1917).   [3] T. C. Kingsmill Moore, judgment, 26 Oct. 1948, SFFC, 2B/82/117(32), p. 9.

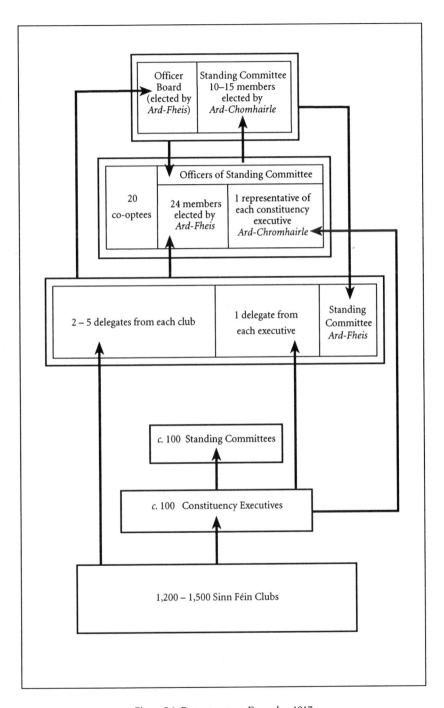

Figure 5.1 Party structure, December 1917

all the clubs in the country, comprised the party convention, or *ard-fheis*. The branches sent between two and five representatives each, depending on the size of their membership, although they had to pay £1 for every extra nominee above the basic number of two. The *ard-fheis* normally comprised between 2,000 and 3,000 delegates, it was expected to meet annually, and it was the party's supreme legislative body. The *ard-fheis* alone could change the Sinn Féin constitution, and it could do so only by a two-thirds majority. It elected the party's officers (its president, two vice-presidents, two honorary secretaries and two honorary treasurers) and these in turn were *ex officio* members of the *ard-fheis*.

By its very nature the *ard-fheis* was unwieldy, and it delegated its authority to smaller groups. In the intervals between its annual meetings almost all its powers were exercised by the penultimate layer of the structure, the *ard-chomhairle*, or governing body. This met quarterly, and it consisted of one representative from each constituency, twenty-four members chosen by the *ard-fheis*, and (coming in the opposite direction, descending from above) the officer board of the standing committee. It could co-opt up to twenty members, and it also elected members of the standing committee. The *ard-chomhairle* convened the *ard-fheis* and laid down the rules governing its procedure, but it was bound by decisions taken by an *ard-fheis* and it could not change the party's constitution.

At the sixth and uppermost level came the standing committee, which consisted of the officer board (elected by the *ard-fheis*) together with between ten and fifteen members chosen by the *ard-chomhairle*. The committee was expected to meet weekly, it exercised all the *ard-chomhairle's* powers except any which were specifically withheld from it, but it could not modify any decisions taken by either of the two larger bodies. Between 1918 and 1922 it conducted the regular business of the party, subject to the intermittent (and increasingly rare) intervention of the *ard-chomhairle*. (See figure 5.1.)

Sequentially, within a month of every annual *ard-fheis* the constituency executives were obliged to hold conventions and elect delegates to the *ard-chomhairle*. It would then convene and elect members of the standing committee (other than the officers, who had already been chosen by the *ard-fheis*).

The structure differed from that of a pyramid, which narrows as it rises towards the summit and in which each higher layer reposes on that below. Constituency executives bypassed the *ard-fheis* to elect members to the *ard-chomhairle*, while the *ard-fheis* leapfrogged over the *ard-chomhairle* and elected members of the standing committee. In the opposite direction there was also a downward flow of representation; the officer board belonged *ex officio* to the *ard-chomhairle*, and the outgoing standing committee was likewise entitled to automatic membership of the *ard-fheis*. In many respects Sinn Féin's structure in 1917 was borrowed from that of the old, pre-rising party, although from the very beginning the circumstances in which it operated were quite dissimilar. These differences increased steadily as time went by. The new Sinn Féin adapted from Griffith's party its triple structure of a large legislative assembly, a small executive and an intermediary body which helped bridge the gap between them.

The scheme proposed by de Valera in October 1917 had no less than thirty-three different headings, but he remained dissatisfied with it and sought to make the party's structure even more abstruse. He wanted the counties to send separate representatives to the *ard-fheis*, quite distinct from those selected by the constituency executives. He was defeated on this point, but he did not abandon the idea and four years later he tried again to create a different form of 'county' structure for the party. Fr O'Flanagan was sensible on this question, but he craved a different form of complexity and in 1917 he suggested an executive of between 200 and 300.[4]

An alternative structure had been proposed to the October convention by Cathal Brugha and seconded by Michael Collins – a revealing alignment – but it received only two votes in an assembly of over a thousand delegates. Their plan was simpler than de Valera's, although between the constituency executives and the national convention (their equivalent of the *ard-fheis*) they too included a middle layer elected by Sinn Féin clubs organized on a county basis.[5]

Practice

De Valera's scheme, adopted by the 1917 convention, was an interlocking system which involved endless meetings, elections and delegations, endless rubbing together of different elements and different levels. It was democratic almost to excess. In principle it survived as long as the party did, and the only significant change made to it was in 1919, when the election of *ard-chomhairle* members by the *ard-fheis* was abandoned. De Valera explained then that 'he was against 2,000 people electing 24, for it was not always possible to know the merits of these 24'.[6] (Soon afterwards the syndicated 'Sinn Féin notes' elaborated on this point: 'experience has shown that those likely to catch the fancy of the Ard Fheis

---

[4] 'Sinn Fein convention, 1917, report, etc.', CO.904/23/5, p. 26.

[5] *Scheme of organisation proposed by Cathal Brugha* (pamphlet, Dublin, 1917).

[6] *II*, 9 Apr. 1919.

by a brilliant speech during the proceedings were elected irrespective of their executive ability', and that the system was vulnerable to sections of the assembly running 'ticket' lists of candidates.[7]) In future each constituency executive would send a delegate – who could not be a Dáil (or parliamentary) deputy – to the *ard-chomhairle*, and this body, having co-opted twenty new members, would then elect the standing committee.

A second modification made at the 1919 *ard-fheis* revealed yet again the deep suspicion of politics and politicians which was so widespread among the Volunteers. De Valera proposed a divorce between the party and the parliamentary apparatus which would ensure that Sinn Féin could not be used as a political machine by members of the Dáil. According to his scheme no member of the cabinet (except the president and the minister for home affairs) could be elected by the *ard-chomhairle* to the standing committee, and not more than one-third of the committee's members could also belong to the Dáil. The other cabinet ministers would be entitled to attend and speak, but could not vote. He assured delegates that the amendment would not affect his own position, since according to the constitution he would be obliged to resign the presidency the following October after he had served two years in office.[8] (The restriction on his tenure was abolished a few months later.) One consequence of this decision was that ministers who were hitherto members of the standing committee would no longer be eligible for membership, and could attend merely as non-voting observers. Collins, the minister for finance, remarked soon afterwards 'I am only an onlooker at the Standing Cttee now.'[9]

This change illustrates the concern that Sinn Féin should remain protected from contamination, that it be preserved as a noble and apolitical movement, or popular front, rather than be allowed degenerate into a mere, base party. The distinction between the party on the one hand, and the parliament and government on the other, anticipated the theory and some of the practice of the Soviet Union and its East European satellites. Another example of this attitude, from a lower level within the party, came in the form of a proposal from North Offaly at the *ard-chomhairle* meeting in August 1919: no Sinn Féin member holding office on any public board should be an officer or committee member of his club, or (except as a co-optee) represent it on the constituency executive. This was to prevent Sinn Féin clubs from being 'machined' as those of the UIL had been.[10] At the October 1921 *ard-fheis* further and long-overdue changes were made to its constitution and its scheme of organization. The constitution was amended so that the party swore its undivided allegiance to the Dáil, and

---

[7] *Meath Chronicle*, 26 Apr. 1919.   [8] *II*, 9 Apr. 1919.
[9] Collins to Stack, 11 May 1919, NLI, MS 5848.   [10] *Nationality*, 30 Aug. 1919.

various relics of the pre-rising Sinn Féin were dropped.[11] Basically, however, the system survived as long as the party.

It took some time to build the new structures. This was the task of the executive elected by the October convention, and it met on nine occasions before it disappeared as a separate entity. Before it dissolved it had ensured the establishment of 86 constituency executives. (There was a theoretical maximum of 101, but some constituencies lacked the minimum number of branches or members needed to establish an executive.)[12] When the new *ard-chomhairle* met on 17 December 1917 it elected fifteen members to join the officer board (which had already been chosen by the *ard-fheis*) on the new standing committee. Local organizations were adapted to the revised party structures; in Kildare, for example, the executive divided in two so that each of the county's constituencies would have a separate organizing body, as was demanded by the new scheme.[13]

In practice things worked out very differently from the ideal which de Valera had outlined at the October convention. After his election as president he tended to act in an autocratic manner, ignoring the executive and alienating old party members by his appointment of 'directors' to manage specialized aspects of its activities.[14] Sinn Féin's work was disrupted by the British authorities, it was banned for nearly two years, and a structure which seemed cumbersome even at the best of times was unable to cope with the confusion and dislocation caused by the Anglo-Irish War of 1919–21. Never again after October 1917 would there be a normal *ard-fheis* which could be attended by all qualified members; some of them were in jail at the time of the 1918 and 1921 conventions, while those held in April 1919 and in February/May 1922 were extraordinary meetings, summoned for special purposes. The October 1919 *ard-fheis* was banned by the British authorities, and although it convened in secret it was attended by only a small proportion of the delegates. None was held in 1920.

The *ard-chomhairle* functioned regularly for some time. In its first year it held three regular meetings (in December 1917, and in March and August 1918) as well as two special sessions which were summoned in response to the conscription crisis and the German plot arrests. It made decisions on issues such as breaking up grasslands in the west and on measures to avert conscription. It did not ratify all the replacements which the standing committee had made to fill

---

[11] See below, p. 345.   [12] *Report of hon. secretaries. Ard-Chomhairle, 19/12/1918*, CP, 11,405.

[13] *Leinster Leader*, 17 Nov. 1917.

[14] Seán T. O'Kelly, 'Memoirs', STO'K, 27,707, p. 191. This is the original text of O'Kelly's memoirs which were later translated into and published in Irish.

the gaps in its ranks caused by the arrests of May 1918; members of the larger group took seriously their own right to make such appointments. Collins felt that the *ard-chomhairle* could exercise a welcome degree of control over the dangerous signs of moderation revealed by the standing committee and by party headquarters. He wrote to Stack in August 1918 that

> things are happening in S.F. circles that are somewhat calculated to upset one . . . The Ard Comhairle is tomorrow and I shall give you an account of it. There are certain resolutions being proposed with a view to unearth and destroy any attempt at compromise. The S.F. organisation lacks direction at the present moment. The men who ought to be directing things are too lax and spend little or no time at No 6 [Harcourt Street].[15]

The following day the *ard-chomhairle* resolved that there should be no departure from the Sinn Féin objective of an independent Irish republic – which was probably the issue alluded to by Collins.[16]

But the balance of power within the party shifted towards the standing committee which, as time went on, was increasingly able to act without much or any intervention from the *ard-chomhairle*. All significant matters discussed by the larger body were proposed to it by the committee – which, by no coincidence, drew up the *ard-chomhairle*'s agenda. As early as August 1918 only sixty-five executives sent delegates to the *ard-chomhairle*, and its efficiency soon declined; at two successive meetings, in May and August 1919, less than half the constituencies were represented.[17] It soon vanished, and was revived only after the truce in July 1921.

It was the standing committee, and party headquarters over which it kept direct control, which held the party together at national level and helped provide it with a sense of direction. In the four and a half years between January 1918 and June 1922 the committee held a total of 160 meetings. During its first two years it convened regularly and conducted its affairs with impressive efficiency. From the beginning it tended to act like a cabinet which presided over different government ministries; it decided in March 1918, for example, that 'all land questions in future to be dealt with by the Sinn Féin Department of Agriculture, before being submitted to Standing Committee'.[18] To some extent it shared the fate of the party's more cumbersome structures and its effectiveness was seriously impaired during the Anglo-Irish War. Nonetheless it could still carry out its most important tasks – as was shown by its ability to

[15] Collins to Stack, 19 Aug. 1918, NLI, MS 5848.   [16] *II*, 22 Aug. 1918.

[17] *Ibid.*; *Ard-chomhairle*, 6 May, 21 Aug. 1919, résumés of proceedings, RB, 8786(1).

[18] SCM, 1 Mar. 1918.

organize the selection of candidates in April–May 1921 and to run an election campaign.

Money

One of the standing committee's principal responsibilities was management of the party's finances. When it first convened in January 1918 it inherited a treasury which would have been the envy of Sinn Féin's founding fathers a year earlier. Apart from the Prisoners' Aid Society, the separatists had virtually no money during the second half of 1916 and in early 1917. According to Fr O'Flanagan, when Griffith was released from jail some friends presented him with £150 which he could use to re-establish his newspaper. He believed that the most urgent need was to win an election, and so he offered the money to finance the campaign in North Roscommon; however two other separatists lent a further £400 towards the cost of the election, with the result that Griffith was able to keep his gift and revive the paper soon afterwards. Later it was claimed that James O'Mara gave Griffith £500 at this time.[19] (O'Mara, a wealthy Limerick bacon-curer and sausage-manufacturer, a former MP and a future Dáil deputy, was the Maecenas of the Sinn Féin movement, and from the Leitrim campaign to the treaty split he was generous in his response to requests for money.)

This shoestring budgeting soon came to an end. A Sinn Féin fund was established in May 1917 to help organize clubs and meet other expenses; within a week the contributions reached £70, and four months later they passed £2,000.[20] The Sinn Féin branches provided most of the party's money, and by the time of the convention in October 1917 affiliation fees came to £1,010, and subscriptions to £1,988. Other sources totalled £1,527, a remarkable £1,290 of which consisted of contributions to help fight the Longford election.[21] (The party's financial report of September 1917 listed the expenses of this campaign as a mere £491, and the profit could be used for other, later by-elections.[22])

Contributions ranged from £50 provided by the Cork executive to innumerable offerings of a shilling or even less, and their total was doubtless increased by the fact that every donation, however small, was acknowledged sooner or later in the pages of *Nationality*. Many clubs collected special sums to help fight elections. In a Tipperary branch, for example, it was decided to send Griffith £30

---

[19] *Fr O'Flanagan's suppressed speech* (pamphlet, n.d. [1918]); Lavelle, *James O'Mara*, pp. 120–1.
[20] *Nationality*, 2 June, 6 Oct. 1917.   [21] *II*, 26 Oct. 1917.
[22] *Cash account of national executive and various elections, 30th Sept. 1917*, RB, 8786(1).

for the East Clare campaign, and one brave member offered to make good the balance if the collection fell short.[23] The party's election fund in Cork city raised £1,600 during the year.[24] Party members were urged to exploit all possible occasions for raising money – such as hurling and football matches, dances and pilgrimages to local shrines – and the police noted that the numerous Sinn Féin lectures and concerts served not only to propagate party doctrine but were also a fruitful source of revenue.[25]

Three main areas of expenditure were listed in the financial accounts presented to the October 1917 convention: organization, £1,011; office expenses, £417; and printing and stationery, £378. Salaries and other administrative costs rose as the party expanded and consolidated, and by June 1919 £65 per week was paid to the thirteen employees in party headquarters and to the three provincial organizers.[26] These organizers' salaries and expenses were a source of some controversy, but everyone who canvassed and carried out other election work did so without financial reward.

Much of Sinn Féin's income never featured in such lists because it was collected and used at local level. In July 1919, for example, the East Clare executive reported that it had received £703 from clubs and had spent £523 of this sum.[27] The standing committee tried to ensure that branches forwarded all their funds to headquarters, except for a small amount which they could use to cover their working expenses.[28] A report from the chief secretary's office, which was based on information supplied by the RIC, suggested that £2,924 had been submitted to Sinn Féin headquarters by local branches by October 1917, while £3,665 was believed to be in the hands of clubs throughout the country.[29] These figures are most unlikely to be accurate in detail, but they may be substantially correct. Furthermore, the close links and the overlap between Sinn Féin and the Irish Volunteers ensured that the outlay of each organization on activities in which both were involved might be deceptively small.

When the standing committee took over responsibility for the day-to-day management of the party's affairs it continued its predecessor's habits. It launched a special collection for the South Armagh election on the pattern of that for South Longford in the previous year. (This, too, made a profit.) It engaged in endless battles with clubs to extract affiliation fees and levies, and to

---

[23] *Tipperary People*, 6 July 1917.

[24] 'Sinn Féin Cork city election fund', de Róiste MSS, CAI, U271, Acc. 89/19.

[25] *Programme of immediate work for cumainn* (pamphlet, n.d. [1917]); IG's report, Jan. 1918, CO.904/105. [26] *Cash account of national executive*, RB, 8786(1); SCM, 5 June 1919.

[27] *Clare Champion*, 26 July 1919. [28] SCM, 1 Mar. 1918.

[29] Gen. Joseph Byrne, report, n.d. (Oct. 1917), 'Sinn Fein funds', CO.904/23/6.

secure the repayment of loans. It struggled with the East Cavan executive, pointing out that while the by-election's costs were likely to be £1,600, only £480 had been received in subscriptions. A committee member visited the constituency but failed to extract an adequate amount, so East Cavan Sinn Féiners were finally instructed to make house-to-house collections and to appeal publicly for funds.[30]

This might seem a miserly approach, since the party was not short of money. Before the 1918 general election campaign its income was declared to be £17,360 and its expenditure £9,718; nearly half of the balance belonged to the election fund.[31] John Dillon complained in the course of the summer that there seemed to be no limit to Sinn Féin's financial resources.[32] September 1918 was the high-water mark of the party's prosperity, and even after the election, despite all the expense which it had involved, the Sinn Féin national organization was still in credit to the sum of £3,900.[33] Some of its propaganda actually made money, and in July 1919 the standing committee was told that two pamphlets published the previous year were expected to yield a profit of £100.[34]

In January 1919 the general election payments book was seized in the course of a British raid on Harcourt Street,[35] and the standing committee was forced to reconstruct its accounts. At first its efforts to discover the real costs of the election came to nothing; each constituency was asked to supply a statement of its expenses and forward the balance in hand to headquarters, but only in North Kerry was any notice taken of this request. Paid organizers had to be dispatched throughout the country to find out the details.[36] One rebuke to a party activist in Kilkenny began brutally: 'complaints have been raised here of your doings in Graiguenamanagh at the recent elections, where without any authority you incurred large expenses'. In turn this provoked an angry protest about unfairness and insolence.[37] Slowly, month by month, bills came in from the constituencies. Even though headquarters had paid off many of these expenses in the meantime, by September 1919 the party still owed a total of £1,360. It had no money, and the Dáil ministry was asked to liquidate its election debts.[38] One claim for the 1918 election was still unresolved six years later.[39]

---

[30] SCM, 8 July, 25 July, 1 Aug. 1918.   [31] FJ, 30 Oct. 1918.

[32] Dillon to T. P. O'Connor, 2 June 1918, JD, 6742.

[33] Treasurers' report, Ard chomhairle of Sinn Fein. 20th February, 1919. Résumé of proceedings, RB, 8786(1); SCM, 19 Dec. 1918.   [34] SCM, 5 June 1919.   [35] II, 13 Jan. 1919.

[36] Treasurers' report, Ard chomhairle, February 1919, RB, 8786(1).

[37] Director of elections to T. P. McMahon, 29 Jan. 1919; McMahon to James O'Mara, 5 Mar. 1919, JO'M, 21,546(2).   [38] SCM, 25 Sept. 1919.

[39] Standing committee minutes, 22 Dec. 1924, NAI, 2B/82/117(23), p. 102.

A sign of things to come was Gavan Duffy's proposal in December 1918 that the sum of £50,000 would be needed for presenting Ireland's case at the peace conference which would soon convene in Paris; already, the previous summer, £100 had been allocated to foreign propaganda, but now a wholly new level of expenditure was envisaged.[40] One member of the standing committee suggested that, as a step towards raising this money, a levy of one penny per head should be imposed on everyone who had voted for Sinn Féin in the recent election. The committee floated towards even more unrealistic heights of optimism by deciding that this sum should be raised to one shilling (i.e., twelve pence).[41]

But within a few months a new agency, the Dáil ministry, had begun to make its presence felt. From this stage onwards the new Irish government, rather than the party, was able to concern itself with such financial problems and it paid most of the bills for the separatist movement. By then, Sinn Féin, as it had existed in its days of glory between early 1917 and early 1919, had begun to disappear.

Headquarters

In its early months the new Sinn Féin party often grew spontaneously, with little guidance from 6 Harcourt Street. But once the party's 'natural spread' had been reached by the late summer or autumn of 1917, most branches were eager or willing to link up with the national movement. Through newspapers, leaflets and speakers they were encouraged to establish contact with headquarters. By October more than 1,000 of the 1,200 clubs had affiliated and paid their fees – a proportion which would be regarded with admiration and disbelief in later years. The advantages of being able to combine with other branches became more apparent, and (apart from demands for money) party headquarters did not curb their freedom or interfere excessively in their activities. Nonetheless, it was able to impose a basic degree of discipline and uniformity, even of harmony, on what had been a diverse and spontaneous movement.

The instructions sent by the party leaders to the local branches included the following demands: to acquire funds for electoral work and propaganda; to influence the local press; to obtain copies of the voters' register and prepare for the next election; to win over doubters by reason and argument; to purchase Irish goods; and (of course) to send money to headquarters. Sinn Féin members were exhorted constantly to greater effort. Griffith's influence can be seen in the encouragement to support Irish manufactures and to investigate each region's industrial resources and potential.[42] But despite the wishes of some members

---

[40] SCM, 19 Dec. 1918, 27 June 1918.   [41] *Ibid.*, 19, 31 Dec. 1918.   [42] *Nationality*, 5 Jan. 1918.

(and of others outside the party, particularly among the Irish Volunteers) the clubs' activities remained largely political.

Through its newspapers and through the speeches made by its leaders, the national organization encouraged tolerance and comprehensiveness; the party was not to be an elite like the Volunteers. An article in the *Irishman* sought 'the formation of Sinn Féin clubs – not exclusive clubs, but clubs where men who now see the folly of their ways shall receive a welcome from those who have borne "the burden and heat of the day"'.[43] It was inevitable that the majority of Sinn Féin members would be ex-Redmondites, and converts were not to be made to feel guilty about their past beliefs.

A principal function of party headquarters was to organize new branches and constituency executives in areas where they had not yet been established. The expansion which characterized 1917 had been patchy, and some parts of the country were relatively inactive; this was particularly the case in north-east Ulster. In late September there were complaints that Galway city was still without a club, and south Wexford also seems to have been slow; a proud boast of dramatic progress within a few weeks during September and October 1917 reads more like an admission of tardiness.[44]

From the summer of 1917 onwards, Harcourt Street was overwhelmed with requests for affiliation, advice and information. The demand for speakers was so great that *Nationality* insisted on three weeks' notice from clubs which wanted party leaders to address them on Sundays.[45] Some branches showed an impressive determination to annex the leading figures of the movement. A letter sent to Eoin MacNeill read as follows:

> You have been appointed a member of the newly formed Rathmines and Rathgar Branch of Sinn Féin, and in addition you have been selected as Delegate to Convention.
>
> I trust you will excuse the liberty we are taking, we are quite unscrupulous . . . When we secure a suitable meeting place I hope to invite you to meet your fellow members.[46]

The demands made on the party leaders were illustrated by Mrs Griffith as she described her husband's busy pace: 'he has so little time rushing about the country working for the convention, which passed off very well indeed, after next week I hope to have him some time, it is now 9 months since he's been

---

[43] *Irishman*, 17 Feb. 1917.

[44] *Galway Express*, 22 Sept. 1917; *Enniscorthy Guardian*, 13 Oct. 1917.

[45] *Nationality*, 28 July 1917.

[46] Edward Dalton to Eoin MacNeill, 13 Sept. 1917, MacN, LA1/H/20.

home a weekend'.[47] Dan McCarthy, the election agent, was reported to have set up election committees in thirty-three towns, as well as in various city wards.[48] But as the party consolidated its position it became less dependent on the initiative and the over-work of individual leaders.

The standing committee's minute book, which runs for an unbroken period of over four years, is one of the main sources of information on the party's activities. The committee conducted routine business, organizing elections, raising money and (to the best of its ability) maintaining discipline. It was assailed with minor queries and problems. A complaint was made about unpatriotic behaviour in selling eggs to England, while another concerned the absence of Corkmen among those elected to the committee; advice was sought on paying a dog tax; and an investigation was launched into a reported outbreak of leprosy.

The committee's powers were limited. Its prohibition of arms raids on private houses was often ignored, and it was unable to enforce any sanctions when Limerick city refused to withdraw its preferred general election candidate in deference to the committee's choice. Its letters and directives often met with little response from clubs and executives throughout the country, and it was harassed by the British authorities. Nonetheless, it presided over a relatively efficient organization and ran a successful general election campaign. It was able to initiate worthwhile minor ventures, such as an employment bureau which tried to find posts for Sinn Féiners who had been dismissed because of their political views; in its first six weeks of operation the bureau secured jobs for seventy-three people.[49]

At the beginning, in early 1918, the standing committee developed extravagant ambitions and established a series of sub-committees which were the equivalent of government departments; their responsibilities included agriculture, industry, trade and commerce, public health, national finance and foreign affairs, along with such obviously 'political' matters as organization and elections. All this came to an end with the German plot arrests and the ensuing repression of the party; henceforth its responsibilities were to be limited to four areas: organization, elections, propaganda and food (which was a pressing issue at a time of anticipated shortages and rumours of a new famine).[50] This was the sort of retrenchment which is natural in times of adversity. Even such a limited range of activities provided the committee with much to do, particularly in the months before the general election campaign, although once the campaign was over it sought to expand its activities once more. Soon, however, it encountered new obstacles which imposed drastic limitations on its powers.[51]

---

[47] Maud Griffith to Kate Kelly, 2 Nov. 1917, NLI, MS 8411.

[48] *Report on the organization of Sinn Féin*, 19 Dec. 1917, CP, 11,405.   [49] *II*, 31 Oct. 1918.

[50] SCM, 23 May 1918.   [51] See below, pp. 284–7.

From late 1919 to late 1921 the party underwent a period of hibernation comparable to that experienced by the separatist movement after the Easter Rising, and during this period most of the elaborate organization created in 1917 either collapsed or faded away. But both the national headquarters and many individual branches continued to function discreetly, and the party's framework was reconstructed speedily at the end of the Anglo-Irish War. A successful but short-lived attempt was made to repair the damage which had been done and to restore the structural *status quo ante*. By the end of 1921 the headquarters was functioning normally, money was plentiful, and (at least nominally) Sinn Féin was more popular than ever before. The revival was shattered by divisions over the party's aims, and in particular over whether or not it should compromise its republican ideals. These disputes reinforced the persistent tensions between the 'civilian' and 'military' wings of the movement.[52]

It was only at this stage, as the party fell apart, that its constitution, its structure and the policies of its leaders encroached to any serious extent on the lives of its ordinary members. Until then most of them had joined Sinn Féin for emotional rather than rational reasons, had been involved in the party's local activities without being preoccupied with its national policies, and had experienced an organization far more varied and human than that which was indicated by its rules, its constitution, or directives from headquarters. The party's members and the activities in which they engaged are subjects which are both more important and (fortunately) more interesting than a framework which was always complex and at times could appear abstract or unreal.

Members

What is in some ways the most fundamental question of all about the Sinn Féin party – how many members did it have? – is perhaps the most difficult to answer. The average membership of a club, and the total membership at national level, are impossible to calculate with any degree of accuracy. While (intentionally or incidentally) hundreds of branches provided details about themselves in a collection of documents captured by the British in 1918, only a tiny fraction of these revealed their numerical strength. The numbers given ranged from 175 to an apologetic 21 (from an area in Cavan where the AOH was strong), and the average was 98; but even though the sample might be representative, its size, a mere nine clubs, is so small as to make it of little value.[53] Some branches must have been diminutive. The townland of Curry in Sligo boasted that it had five

---

[52] See below, pp. 196, 279–81, 300.   [53] *Précis* of captured documents, NLI, MS 10,494.

active Sinn Féin clubs, and that it enjoyed the reputation of being the best-orga-
nized parish in Ireland;[54] this may well have been true, since, with a population
of 304 recorded at the previous census, few of its adult inhabitants can have been
excluded from the party. The Volunteers represented only a small minority of
Irish nationalists, but, at least for a while, in some parts of the country, Sinn Féin
embraced virtually the whole adult population.

In February 1918 the Sinn Féin club in Mullinabreena (Co. Sligo) listed all
its members, and 126 of these can be traced in the 1911 census.[55] An examination of the returns reveals that only 3 of them were women; 1 was a Protestant;
65 were farmers, 49 farmers' sons and 3 agricultural labourers, while other categories (author, postman, etc.) accounted for 1 each; 13 were illiterate, 10 spoke
both Irish and English, and only 1 (out of about 500 people whose forms were
examined) wrote in Irish. The average age was a surprisingly elderly 42.3, and
the age structure was as follows:

under 20	5
20–29	29
30–39	27
40–49	26
50–59	19
over 60	20

The RIC provided monthly statistics on Sinn Féin membership, but these must
be treated with great caution; the county inspectors admitted repeatedly how
little they knew about the activities of a hostile and secretive population. Within
months of the rising it was reported from South Tipperary that 'it is impossible
to say to what extent the Sinn Fein party are actually increasing, it is most
difficult to get any information about them'. These problems persisted, and in
early 1917 it was believed that Sinn Féiners in West Galway were meeting
secretly, 'but no informant of the slightest use can be got for any money'; by
1918 in Kilkenny it was 'impossible for the Police to obtain any information of
what may be going on'; in Mayo, Sinn Fein's 'workings andc. are kept very secret
and there is little leakage of information locally'; and in Kerry in 1919, 'the Sinn
Fein organisation is being conducted in such secrecy that it may now be claimed
as a secret organisation . . . The police experience the greatest difficulty in
getting information in even the most trivial matters.'[56]

---

[54] *Sligo Champion*, 2 Feb. 1918.

[55] *Ibid.* 16 Feb. 1918. I am grateful to Paul Rouse for his assistance in this research.

[56] CIs' reports, S. Tipperary, Aug. 1916, W. Galway, Feb. 1917, Kilkenny, May 1918, Mayo, Dec.
1918, Kerry, Jan. 1919, CO.904/100, 102, 106, 107, 108.

These reports are characteristic of many others. In December 1917 the inspector general estimated the number of branches as being 'over 1,000', and gave a total membership of 66,000 – resulting in an implausibly low average membership of less than 66 per club; the same month Sinn Féin itself provided a total of 1,240 branches and gave the details for every county in Ireland.[57] (These are used in Figure 5.2.) For what it may be worth, in August 1920 the RIC noted 61 clubs in Kerry, with a total membership of 6,530 – yielding an average membership of 107.[58]

Any figure suggested for party membership must be hypothetical, and Griffith's estimate of a quarter of a million by October 1917 was almost certainly optimistic.[59] A reasonable guess would probably be that membership averaged somewhat over a hundred members per club. In October 1917 the treasurer of the South Leitrim executive reported that the county's population was 60,000, with 20 clubs and about 2,000 members.[60] The party's *Scheme of Organisation* laid down that every club with a paid-up membership of 150 or more should be entitled to an extra delegate at the *ard-fheis*, with proportionate increases for membership of 200 and 250;[61] obviously a membership of more than 150 was regarded as exceptional. With between 1,200 and 1,300 branches throughout the country, the national total would probably be in the region of between 120,000 and 130,000 members. Naturally, the figure varied over time, almost certainly reaching a high point during the conscription crisis (1,700 clubs) and falling in 1920–1. The party claimed to have nearly 2,000 branches in August 1919, but by then many of them were merely nominal.[62]

Regionally the party was strongest in the south-west and in north-east Connacht, together with neighbouring Cavan and Longford. It tended to flourish in areas which were distant from Dublin, had a recent tradition of

---

[57] IG's report, Dec. 1917, CO.904/104; 'Report on organisation of Sinn Fein', CP, 11,405. David Fitzpatrick's stimulating article, 'The geography of Irish nationalism, 1910–1921' relies heavily on these RIC figures, ascribing to them a greater accuracy than their compilers appear to have done (C. E. Philpin (ed.), *Nationalism and popular protest in Ireland* (Cambridge, 1987, pp. 419–23). [58] 'Crime special. County of Kerry', cited in *Irish Bulletin*, 16 Sept. 1920.

[59] *II*, 26 Oct. 1917. This total was accepted in Michael Laffan, 'The unification of Sinn Fein in 1917' (*IHS*, 17, 67 (1971), p. 368), but it is too high. The author, much older and a little wiser, now repents of his youthful credulity and hereby disowns the figure.

[60] Hugh Harte to hon. sec., national council, 18 Oct. 1917, *précis* of captured documents, NLI, MS 10,494(3), p. 76. [61] *Sinn Féin. Scheme of organisation, rules &c.* (Dublin, n.d. [1917]).

[62] *Ard-Fheis Sinn Féin, 1918, report of director of organisation and plebiscite; Ard-Fheis Sinn Féin, 6th October 1919, report of hon. secretaries*, RB, 8786(1).

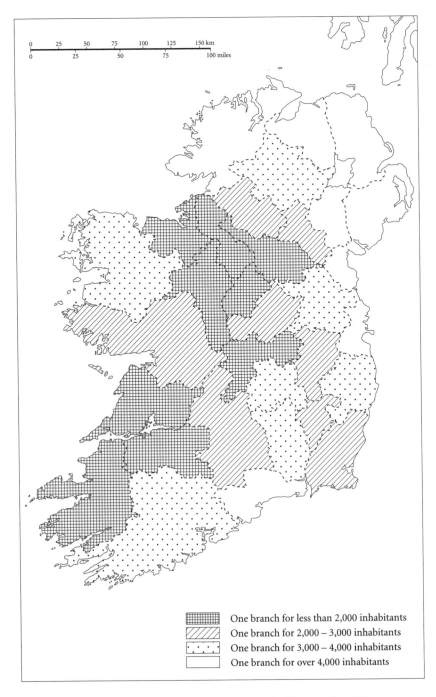

Figure 5.2 Ratio of inhabitants to each Sinn Féin club, December 1917

Table 5.1 *Ratio of inhabitants per county to each Sinn Féin club, December 1917*

Clare	1,427	Galway	2,939
Leitrim	1,478	Laois	3,035
Longford	1,565	Mayo	3,203
Roscommon	1,648	Kilkenny	3,407
Cavan	1,657	Meath	3,426
Sligo	1,756	Cork	3,564
Limerick	1,788	Tyrone	3,567
Kerry	1,878	Wicklow	3,794
Offaly	1,960	Donegal	4,435
Tipperary	2,032	Louth	5,305
Monaghan	2,041	Waterford	6,997
Westmeath	2,068	Armagh	8,019
Wexford	2,494	Derry	11,719
Kildare	2,562	Dublin	12,236
Fermanagh	2,576	Down	14,593
Carlow	2,589	Antrim	48,401

Source: Report on Organisation of Sinn Féin (December 1917), Plunkett MSS, NLI, 11,405)

agrarian unrest or political confrontation, and had a high percentage of the population working on small farms.[63]

In the list of clubs compiled by the executive in December 1917 the figures for the provinces were: Munster, 435 branches, Leinster, 293, Connacht 267 and Ulster 245. If the figures are adjusted to take account of population size, three of those counties where electoral contests had taken place during the year feature among the four where the party was strongest. (The other is Leitrim, which had already been contested in 1908 and had long been a stronghold of radical nationalism.) Kilkenny came twentieth out of the thirty-two counties, but there the by-election campaign was brief and was confined to the city (see Table 5.1).[64] Recent activity, excitement and publicity (which were all the result of a random feature, parliamentary vacancies) form a pattern which matches the prevalence of party branches. There was no correlation between arrests after the rising and membership in late 1917.

The ten counties where the ratio was lowest were all in Ulster or on the east

---

[63] For studies of regional patterns see Tom Garvin, *The evolution of Irish nationalist politics* (Dublin, 1981), p. 109; E. Rumpf and A. C. Hepburn, *Nationalism and socialism in twentieth-century Ireland* (Liverpool, 1977), pp. 43–57; Peter Hart, 'The geography of revolution in Ireland 1917–1923', *Past and Present*, 155 (1997), p. 170.   [64] See above, pp. 112–13.

coast. The figure for Dublin is probably misleading, since the density of population would necessitate fewer clubs than in rural districts. Cork's low total seems anomalous in the light of its radical traditions, its subsequent support for Sinn Féin, and the fact that (particularly in the west of the county) it was heavily over-represented in the leadership of Sinn Féin and the Volunteers.[65] Perhaps the discrepancy can be explained, at least in part, by the fact that Cork (an abnormally large and varied county) was the only area outside unionist Ulster where the Parliamentary Party had faced serious opposition in the recent past. At the last general election, in December 1910, William O'Brien's All-For-Ireland League won eight of the nine seats in Cork city and county, while in the rest of the country only two independent nationalists were elected – and in both cases they were returned unopposed. To an extent which was comparable with parts of Ulster, Sinn Féiners in Cork encountered an opponent whose complacency had been punctured and whose efficiency had been improved by the experience of recent combat. The All-For-Ireland League still held the loyalties of many Cork opponents of the Parliamentary Party in 1917, as was proved by the combined votes for its two rival by-election candidates in November 1916, but it did not take long for the county to 'fall into line'.

By the end of 1918 Sinn Féin supporters probably comprised a large majority of the nationalist population, but party members and voters differed widely in the length and depth of their commitment. The most active members tended to be young men from labouring and small farming backgrounds, from the lower-middle and working classes. A wide range of sources confirms the youth of Sinn Féin activists; one typical newspaper account referred to a large attendance at the inauguration of a Sinn Féin club in an Armagh village, 'ninety per cent of whom were young men from 18 to 25 years of age'.[66] In areas of agrarian unrest such as Roscommon, many of the landless men turned to Sinn Féin, just as they had earlier turned to the UIL, until the party demonstrated clearly its lack of interest in their lack of land.[67] Some of them would have gone to the United States had emigration not ceased shortly after the outbreak of war in 1914. This blocking of the normal outlet or safety valve of discontent is a principal explanation of the rise and spread of Sinn Féin. The party was able to draw on a reservoir of underemployed young men and women, and it appealed particularly to those who, in normal circumstances, would have had the energy and initiative to try their luck abroad.

As was one of the intentions behind the government's ban on emigration, many of the young men trapped in Ireland joined the army to fight in France

---

[65] Tom Garvin, 'The formation of the Irish political elite', in Farrell, *Creation of the Dáil*, p. 54.
[66] *Armagh Guardian*, 26 Oct. 1917.   [67] See below, pp. 257–8, 315–17.

Table 5.2 *Emigration figures for the years spanning the First World War*

1912	29,344	1915	10,659	1918	980
1913	30,967	1916	7,302	1919	2,975
1914	20,314	1917	2,111	1920	15,531

Source: W. E Vaughan and A. J. Fitzpatrick (eds.), *Irish historical statistics: population, 1821–1971* (Dublin, 1978), p. 263.

and elsewhere. The total number of recruits exceeded the 'excess' population. But recruitment tended to be disproportionately heavy from the unionist population and from towns and cities, while large areas of the countryside remained relatively unaffected.[68] Ulster had the highest provincial rate of enlistment (of both Catholics and Protestants) and Connacht the lowest, while the counties along the western coast from Mayo to Cork produced very few recruits. Numbers fell as the nature of the conflict in the trenches became more widely known, and there was relatively little enlistment between 1916 and 1918, the years in which Irish nationalism was radicalized.[69]

By the end of the war parts of rural Ireland contained large numbers of 'surplus' people who would have gone elsewhere if they had been able to do so, and who felt cooped up, frustrated and embittered. Emigration resumed only slowly after peace was restored, while in 1919 tens of thousands of demobilized soldiers returned home – and found few jobs awaiting them. Both among those who stayed in Ireland during the war and (to a much lesser extent) among those who came back from the Western Front after the armistice, Sinn Féin and the Volunteers provided outlets for the energetic and the resentful.

Observers on both sides were well aware of how discontent was spread by a growing pool of underemployed young men whom 'the Government will neither conscript nor permit to emigrate'.[70] Those with long memories might have recalled that emigration to the United States had fallen sharply during the years between 1875 and 1879, fuelling the agrarian unrest of the Land League years.[71]

---

[68] Patrick Callan, 'Recruiting for the British army in Ireland during the First World War', *Irish Sword*, 17, 66 (1987), pp. 49–50; Martin Staunton, 'The Royal Munster Fusiliers in the Great War, 1914–19' (MA dissertation, University College, Dublin, 1986), pp. 10–13.

[69] David Fitzpatrick, 'The logic of collective sacrifice: Ireland and the British army, 1914–1918', *Historical Journal*, 38, 4 (1995), pp. 1020, 1025.   [70] IO's report (S.), Mar. 1918.

[71] Vaughan and Fitzpatrick, *Population, 1821–1971*, p. 262.

One hopeful police inspector remarked after the end of the war that 'the young men who in the ordinary course would have emigrated to America have had to remain at home and are the source of all the trouble. With emigration re-opened and facilitated a good deal of the trouble would disappear.'[72] From the opposite standpoint, *An tÓglách* fulminated against the resumption of emigration after the war, a 'cowardly desertion' which should be curbed by the sternest measures: 'It will be the duty of the Volunteers to deal in the severest manner with any young man who attempts to emigrate without a permit from the Irish Republic.' Emigration agents who issued tickets were to be regarded as enemies, and Irishmen who left the country were seen as being little better than degenerates.[73] At least in theory, each male emigrant was a potential soldier lost by the Volunteers. (Years earlier Pearse had argued along similar lines: 'let us plainly tell the emigrant that he is a traitor to the Irish State'.[74])

Few surviving internal records give details of members' class, status or occupation, and the information which we possess is impressionistic rather than quantifiable. Some of the evidence for such matters comes from police reports or from other hostile witnesses. Occasionally these accounts reveal almost as much about the writer as about his subject; an example is the RIC inspector general's description of the Sinn Féin candidates in the 1918 election as comprising 'a few doctors, solicitors, farmers and shopkeepers, together with clerks, ex Post Office clerks, students, teachers, commercial travellers, a labourer and other persons of insignificance'.[75]

Yet, however blind or biased individual policemen or intelligence officers might have been, the cumulative effect of all their reports over several years is convincing – especially since it is reinforced by miscellaneous scraps of evidence from a wide range of other sources. Police and army reports feature comments such as 'the lower classes in this District are most hostile towards the Government', or the Sinn Féin movement was 'confined almost entirely to the labouring and small farming classes', or 'shopboys are Sinn Fein and disloyal almost to a man, and many of the artisans and small shopkeepers'.[76] These are characteristic remarks, inadequate but nonetheless revealing. Similarly, Sinn Féin established an employment agency which secured places for dismissed shop assistants, labourers, domestic servants, clerks and civil servants.[77]

---

[72] CI's report, W. Cork, Dec. 1918, CO.904/107.

[73] *An tÓglách*, 15 Sept. 1920, 1 Apr. 1921; Dept. of Defence, manifesto, 5 June 1920, MacSwiney MSS, CAI, PR4/3/18.

[74] *An Claidheamh Soluis*, 18 July 1903, cited in Edwards, *Patrick Pearse*, p. 78.

[75] IG's report, Nov. 1918, CO.904/107.

[76] IO's report (S.), Sept. 1917; CI's report, Kildare, June 1918, CO.904/106; IO's report (M. and C.), Dec. 1917.   [77] *Irishman*, 9 Nov. 1918.

In late 1916 the military intelligence officer for the southern district commented on the disloyalty of national schoolteachers who were 'well-educated, poorly paid, and, as a result, discontented and good subjects for the Sinn Fein movement'.[78] Numerous complaints of this sort were made. At the time of the conscription crisis the lord chief justice remarked that 'the late backbone of the Irish disaffection, namely, farmers and their sons, had given place to a body composed of shop assistants, clerks, Government officials, school teachers, andc.' He regarded this new enemy as being much more formidable than its predecessor.[79] Shopkeepers, so influential in the United Irish League, were somewhat less prominent in the ranks of its rival.

As in most other revolutionary groups, the driving force behind Sinn Féin and the Volunteers tended to consist of the young, the energetic and those with least to lose by any change; 33 per cent of the members of the first Dáil were aged under 35, and the figure for its successor was 38 per cent. The percentages for those under 45 were 73 and 75.[80] (By way of contrast, the average age of Nationalist and Unionist MPs elected in December 1910 was 50 and 51 respectively, and this average had risen considerably by 1918.[81]) A correspondent of Count Plunkett's wrote that his local Sinn Féin club was 'mostly confined to the juniors' but that he hoped to attract some older members, while in the general election campaign the new Nationalist MP for South Armagh lamented that 'the youthful Sinn Fein votes outnumber ours very much'.[82] Many students were separatists, and the RIC inspector who described University College, Galway as 'this Sinn Fein college' and as 'a hotbed of Sinn Feinism' could have made the same remark about other institutions.[83] Party activists often tended to be single. When a hundred members joined a new club in Clare, it was noted, almost in surprise, that the most encouraging feature of the occasion was the number of married men in attendance.[84] The frequency of weddings after the truce in July 1921 was a source of some comment.

The more dedicated members of Sinn Féin tended to come from lower down the social scale than those of the Parliamentary Party, and the police felt able to dismiss the fifty members of the new Sinn Féin club in Mullingar (Co.

---

[78] IO's report (S.), Sept. 1916.

[79] Cabinet conclusions, 28 Mar. 1918, Cab.23/5, WC.376(5). On teachers in Irish society and politics, see Garvin, *Nationalist revolutionaries*, pp. 24–9.

[80] J. L. McCracken, *Representative government in Ireland: a study of Dáil Éireann, 1919–48* (Oxford, 1958), p. 30.

[81] F. S. L. Lyons, *The Irish Parliamentary Party, 1890–1910* (London, 1951), p. 158.

[82] J. Miller to Plunkett, 23 May 1917, CP, 11,383(11); Phoenix, *Northern nationalism*, p. 51.

[83] CI's report, W. Galway, Feb. 1917, CO.904/102.   [84] *Clare Champion*, 7 July 1917.

Westmeath) as young shopboys; 'no person of any importance' had joined it.[85] But the difference tended to be one of degree rather than of kind, and there were many middle class and professional people in the party's ranks, as well as among the Volunteers. In June 1918, a raid on the Dublin Total Abstinence Association League interrupted a session of illegal drilling, and twenty-three young men were arrested. They were described as being, in many cases, 'well dressed, of fine physique, and apparently men of education, such as medical or university students'.[86] Complaints were made that Sinn Féin clubs were an outlet for the feelings of not only the shopboys who featured in police reports, but also of 'farmers' sons, schoolteachers and younger clerics'.[87] According to a list of the officers of the South Donegal constituency executive in January 1920, the president was an auctioneer, the treasurers a draper and a tailor, one of the secretaries a secondary school teacher (the other's occupation is not recorded), while the vice-president's address was given as 'Inver Creamery'.[88] The occupations of the Sinn Féin candidates for the Mountjoy Ward in the Dublin local elections of 1920 were: widow, electrician, shopkeeper, general printer, provision merchant, brass finisher and engineer.[89] In Navan (Co. Meath) the candidates consisted of two drapers, two labourers, a chemist, a tailor, a clerk, a shopkeeper and a sawmill manager.[90] The members of the first and second Dáil were largely an urban, middle-class group; 65 per cent of deputies of the first Dáil and 58 per cent of the second belonged to the professional and commercial classes (which comprised a mere 6 per cent of the population in the 1926 census) while farmers (31 per cent of the population) were represented by a mere 10 per cent of TDs.[91]

Sinn Féin was more solidly Catholic than was the Irish Parliamentary Party which, right to the end, included a considerable number of Protestants among its MPs. In July 1916, Tomás MacCurtain was able to record with satisfaction that there were three Protestants among a total of twenty-seven Irish prisoners in Reading Jail,[92] but the disproportionately Catholic membership of the Sinn Féin party did provoke some unease. When Lord Midleton's sister, Albinia Brodrick, joined the movement she not only Gaelicized her name to Gobnait Ní Brudair, but she also provoked one Quaker observer to remark that Brodrick

---

[85] CI's report, Westmeath, May 1917, CO.904/103.   [86] II, 14 June 1918.

[87] IO's report (M. and C.), Sept. 1917.   [88] 'List of Sinn Féin officers', Jan. 1920, NLI, MS 5649.

[89] 'Sinn Féin and Labour candidates', Jan. 1920, NLI, IL.B.300, P.5(39). 'Engineer' may be an ambiguous term.

[90] Oliver Coogan, *Politics and war in Meath, 1913–23* (Dublin, 1983), pp. 200–1.

[91] McCracken, *Representative government*, pp. 33–4.

[92] MacCurtain, diary, 16 July 1916, Cork Public Museum, L.1945:225.

was 'so full of affection towards her "beloved people and their religion" that I'm in a fright now for fear she may turn Catholic herself, like Casement and Madame de Markievicz. I do dislike to have things look as if no one could be a Sinn Féiner without being a Catholic.'[93]

When delegates at the October convention elected the party's executive they chose a group whose members were young and who came from varying backgrounds. The average age was thirty-eight, and only two were over fifty while five were still in their twenties. They included four women, three priests, a university professor and lecturer, two teachers, two doctors, an ex-MP, a draper, a grocer, a solicitor's clerk, a sweet manufacturer, an electrical engineer, a salesman, a farmer, and several civil servants, writers and journalists as well as two widows of 1916 leaders. There were three Protestants (Ernest Blythe, Darrell Figgis and Kathleen Lynn) in a total of twenty-four – although there would have been four had it not been for Markievicz's recent conversion to Catholicism. The great majority had been educated by the Christian Brothers or in the national schools, although a few were former pupils of the Jesuits. Seven of those shot after the rising had been taught by the Brothers, as were twenty members of the first Dáil and twenty-seven of the second.[94] They were also cosmopolitan, and about half of the leaders of the 'revolutionary generation' had lived outside Ireland for significant periods, usually in Britain or America.[95]

The separatist leaders were a varied, interesting and formidable group. One of their number was Joe McGuinness, whose brother (and campaign manager) had advised voters during the Longford by-election that it was dangerous to return intellectuals to parliament, since they were out for themselves; 'the man who knew no more than two and two made four was the better man'.[96] This advice was not followed by the delegates at the October convention when they elected a new generation of leaders.

Volunteers

Members of Sinn Féin were characterized less by class and education than by their support for the Gaelic League, the GAA and (most decisively of all) the Irish Volunteers. The overlap between the party and the army was always considerable

---

[93] Rosamond Jacob to Hanna Sheehy-Skeffington, n.d. [1919], HSS, 22,689.

[94] Barry M. Coldrey, *Faith and fatherland: the Christian Brothers and the development of Irish nationalism, 1838–1921* (Dublin, 1988), pp. 251–2.

[95] Garvin, 'Formation of the Irish political elite', in Farrell (ed.), *Creation of the Dáil*, p. 56.

[96] *FJ*, 23 Apr. 1917; *Anglo-Celt*, 28 Apr. 1917.

and in some areas it was nearly total. Almost all the political leaders had Volunteer connections, and they had behind them (at the very least) a prison sentence, or (ideally) a record of action in 1916. Of the sixty-eight Sinn Féin candidates elected to the first Dáil, forty-six had been arrested in the aftermath of the rising (including some, like MacNeill and Griffith, who had not joined in the fighting), while only three had never been jailed or interned. All but four surviving members of the first Dáil were re-elected to the second, and the newcomers were as closely linked to the Volunteers as were their predecessors. Similarly, six of the twenty members elected to the Volunteer executive of 27 October 1917 had been elected to the Sinn Féin executive the previous day.[97]

Many Volunteers resented Griffith's pre-rising Sinn Féin party because they regarded it as moderate and monarchist. An extreme example of such views was provided by the *Irish Nation* in October 1917:

> the policy of Arthur Griffith is not a bit more popular in Ireland to-day than it was from 1905 up to the rebellion . . . Its exponents are making headway in the country because they are supposed to stand for the principles of the men who died at Easter, otherwise they would not win a solitary constituency. This is the real Sinn Féin, the Hungarian policy is merely a parody.[98]

Most of the Volunteers had not joined the old Sinn Féin, and de Valera's connection with the party began only in July 1917 when he was co-opted to its national council, or executive.[99]

Yet despite their collective suspicion of politics and politicians, the Volunteers, including some of their most radical members such as Collins, proved themselves to be effective organizers and canvassers during the 1917 by-elections. This may be at least in part because, by the standards of military organizations, their own structures and procedures were remarkably democratic; companies elected their officers, who in turn elected the battalion commanders.[100] Many Volunteers were probably already experienced in soliciting votes.

In the October, convention 'moderates' such as Tom Kelly and Walter Cole of the old Sinn Féin, and Stephen O'Mara and Kevin O'Shiel of the Nation

---

[97] Richard Mulcahy, 'The Irish Volunteer convention 27 October 1917', *Capuchin Annual*, 1967, pp. 408–9.   [98] *Irish Nation*, 20 Oct. 1917.

[99] Páidín O'Keeffe to de Valera, 21 July 1917, EdeV.

[100] Augusteijn, *From public defiance to guerrilla warfare*, p. 60; Kevin B. Nowlan, 'Dáil Éireann and the army: unity and division (1919–1921)' in T. D. Williams (ed.), *The Irish struggle, 1916–1926* (London, 1966), p. 69.

League, were replaced by young men who first entered public life when they resorted to arms in Easter Week. In Cork city the Volunteers acted decisively in support of Tomás MacCurtain, their brigade commandant, and one of the out-manoeuvred moderates complained that

> there was an influx of new members on the nights meetings were held to nominate persons for the National Executive and appoint delegates. In most cases the 'onslaught' was successful as the older members did not wish to have dissensions . . . Every man who is not a Volunteer or in the good graces of the Volunteers is to be pushed aside from responsible positions in Sinn Féin.[101]

But it is easy to exaggerate the significance of these disagreements and of the elections to the executive in October 1917. The result cannot be seen as a sudden coup. Volunteers had been the most active element in Sinn Féin throughout the previous six months, and it would have been surprising if they had not formalized their actual leadership of the party. Many 'old Sinn Féiners' were prominent in the military force, and an overlap between politicians and soldiers existed long before the rising. Griffith himself was a member of the Volunteers, and it has been claimed that he actually wished to take arms in Easter Week until he was persuaded by some of the rebels not to do so.[102] He had been an IRB member, and it seems likely that he left the organization merely because of disagreement over a question of discipline.[103] His close supporters in the old Sinn Féin who had fought in 1916 would not have been opposed in principle to a 'takeover' by politically active Volunteers. Some of the moderates were later to occupy leading positions in the movement, and Páidín O'Keeffe never relinquished his old post of party general secretary.

The radicals did not enjoy a sweeping victory. The existence of an IRB 'ticket', supposedly orchestrated by Collins, was exposed at the convention and the manoeuvre was unsuccessful; moderates such as Griffith and MacNeill won the highest number of votes, while Collins himself tied for last place among those who were elected.[104] MacCurtain was defeated, despite the measures which Volunteers were accused of having taken on his behalf in Cork. (The republicans seem to have taken their revenge in later years. In his memoirs Figgis complained that Collins and Boland packed the *ard-fheis* of April 1919

---

[101] De Róiste, diary, 18, 20 Oct. 1917, FO'D, 31,146(1).

[102] Ó Lúing, *Art Ó Gríofa*, pp. 265–6; Edwards, *Patrick Pearse*, p. 306; Oliver St John Gogarty, *Free State*, 19 Aug. 1922.

[103] P. S. O'Hegarty, *Studies*, Sept. 1922, p. 354; George A. Lyons, *Forum*, Jan. 1950, p. 8.

[104] See above, p. 120.

with IRB men, and that he and other moderates were voted off the executive.[105]) However, not all Sinn Féiners were Volunteers, and not all Volunteers were radical republicans. Frequently the lines of division in 1917 (and even more clearly, those in 1921) crossed rather than paralleled the rift between the old Sinn Féin party and its detractors.

Many of the soldiers felt superior to those whom they often regarded as mere civilians – and sometimes even dismissed as cowards. They shared the attitude expressed by Ernest Blythe before the rising when, after enthusing about 'the red tillage of the battlefield', he concluded that 'none is worthy of the name of Nationalist or citizen or man but the soldier'.[106] The people may have comprised the body of the nation, but the army was its soul. Years later, colleagues of Liam de Róiste in Cork believed that in the past Irish politicians had usually been weaklings who broke up Volunteer movements, while in South Meath a Sinn Féin organizer reported that 'prominent Volunteers seemed to encourage amongst their men a feeling of contempt for the political side of the movement, and put it down as constitutionalism'.[107]

But the overlap between the two bodies was so thorough as to create widespread confusion. At times the public needed to be reminded of each organization's particular responsibilities and of the principal differences which persisted between them. One such explanation was that the Volunteers did the fighting while Sinn Féin 'was the constitutional section of the advanced movement'.[108] In many areas Sinn Féin clubs were urged to establish Volunteer units, but the distinction between them was often blurred, and sometimes the creation of two distinct and separate bodies seemed redundant at local level. Sinn Féin club treasurers frequently served as quartermasters of the local Volunteer company, leading to disputes concerning their disposal of common funds.[109]

Particularly in the early years one organization often covered both political and military activities, and documents seized from Sinn Féin headquarters in May 1918 include letters which boasted that 'all the young men drill three times per week' and that the 'Club is making great headway – "drilling every night"'.[110] The North Mayo executive informed Figgis, one of the party's honorary secretaries, that instructions from brigade headquarters were being carried out, and requested that he send two or three rifles and bayonets with ammunition.[111] At

[105] Figgis, *Recollections*, pp. 245–7.   [106] *Irish Freedom*, Dec. 1913.

[107] De Róiste, diary, 10 Oct. 1918, CAI, U271/A/21; Seamus Ó Dubhghaill, report, 9 Aug. 1919, Collins MSS, IMA, A/0326 II.   [108] Art O'Connor, cited in *Leinster Leader*, 30 June 1917.

[109] Seán Moylan, statement, 1953, STO'K, 27,731, p. 42.

[110] *Précis* of captured documents, NLI, MS 10,494(1), pp. 4, 17.   [111] *Ibid.*, p. 26.

local level there was obviously scope for further education in the differences between the military and civilian wings of the movement. In early 1922, when one Sinn Féin club in Wicklow was canvassed to vote against the treaty, the secretary replied in apparent puzzlement, 'as a matter of fact, we have no club, that is, in a sense, we never had any membership of old people and when our company of Volunteers was properly organized most of the young fellows were busy enough. However we managed to carry out any work that fell to our lot.'[112] The East Clare Volunteers were given equal rights with Sinn Féin members in selecting candidates for the local elections.[113] In many instances the same person represented both organizations at their respective conventions in October 1917; the Volunteers were able to hold their assembly in the shadow of Sinn Féin's, thereby ensuring a representative gathering (although with only one quarter as many delegates).[114]

The Volunteers – and in particular the 1916 rebels – were more glamorous than civilian Sinn Féiners. In East Limerick it was resolved that only men of Easter Week should be selected as parliamentary candidates, and this decision was symptomatic of a widespread attitude.[115] In the absence of such a military record a term of imprisonment could provide another passport to popularity, and in West Cork the RIC county inspector decided not to arrest two seditious speakers who, he felt, were anxious to become leaders. He reported that 'neither has influence or following at present. Sentence by Courtmartial turns them ipso facto into heroes . . . and really dangerous men.'[116] Speechmaking had an obvious appeal for some, but other less public forms of political activity were often seen as lacking the attraction of guns, danger and sedition.

Frequently the division was made on grounds of age: old men could help by joining Sinn Féin, young men by joining the Volunteers. A small Volunteer company in Tipperary, which was left with only ten men after the rising, was further depleted when two of its oldest members resigned to join Sinn Féin.[117] In many districts the Volunteers were an extension of a youth subculture, at odds with parental authority and with the middle-aged in general;[118] some of them might not have been attracted by a political party in which their elders remained influential. One result of this tendency was that the party became

---

[112] Seamas Ó Tuathail to Déogréine Barton, 24 Jan. 1922, RB, 8786(2).

[113] *Clare Champion*, 8 Feb. 1919.   [114] Richard Mulcahy, 'Memoirs', RM, P7b/134, p. 37.

[115] *Tipperary People*, 14 Sept. 1917.   [116] CI's report, W. Cork, Oct. 1917, CO.904/104.

[117] Joost Augusteijn, *From public defiance to guerilla warfare: the radicalization of the Irish Republican Army – a comparative analysis, 1916–1921* (Amsterdam, 1994), p. 58. (This reference is to the original edition of the book, and not to the different (1996) version which is cited elsewhere in this work.)   [118] Hart, *I.R.A. and its enemies*, pp. 180, 183.

more inclined towards caution and conservatism, and the natural differences between the two bodies widened even further.

But since Sinn Féin was a larger organization than the Volunteers, and since relatively few women joined the party's branches, a preponderance of older men could hardly explain Sinn Féin's greater numerical strength. Many young but unromantic or unheroic males must have contented themselves with belonging only to the political organization and not to its military counterpart. Even in the quiet years of 1917 and 1918, let alone in 1920 and 1921, Volunteering demanded greater commitment and involved greater risk; far more people were prepared to vote and even canvass for independence, or for an Irish republic, than were prepared to risk discomfort, danger and death for their political beliefs.

In October 1917 Markievicz rejected the idea that all young men should bear arms and insisted that only those who wanted to fight should become Volunteers. Others should join Sinn Féin. She made it clear that she did not want to have 'a lot of young men hunted into my organisation who were not prepared to fight'; such people, she felt, could find work in a political party. From a different standpoint, Griffith agreed with her. Another speaker declared that the Volunteers had been able to get along very well without much help from Sinn Féin, and that 'we don't want politicians meddling with a military organisation'.[119]

There were territorial disputes between the two organizations, and complaints of poaching or theft. There was also mutual support, and a feeling, which was never completely eroded by the Volunteers' sense of superiority, that each was a different wing or branch of the same movement. The very fact that men like de Valera and Collins held important offices in both bodies was a consolidating element which often had its counterpart at the level of the local party club and Volunteer unit.

The clergy

Many priests sympathized with the Sinn Féin party, despite its military colouring, and their support was both courted and cherished. Their involvement in politics often represented little more than yet another example of the deference shown to the clergy by a pious people, and parish priests and curates were frequently appointed to the presidency of their local clubs as a mark of respect and affection. Particularly in poorer and more rural districts the priest was seen as

---

[119] 'Sinn Fein convention 1917', CO.904/23/5, p. 16.

the obvious leader of the community, and nothing seemed more natural than that he should occupy any position of prominence in the locality.

De Valera made a point of stressing his relationship with the clergy, of appearing to be more Catholic than the Redmondites, and at one gathering in his constituency he was described as arriving on the platform with 'his sombre bodyguard of priests'.[120] As several contingents of Sinn Féiners marched into Ennis during the Clare campaign they were led by members of the clergy.[121] A survey of Sinn Féin clubs in the same county over a three month period reveals that of 20 clubs whose chairmen were identified in the county newspaper, 12 were presided over by parish priests or curates.[122] Of the 87 constituency executives throughout the country whose presidents are listed on a document surviving from January 1920, priests held the presidency in no less than 24. 10 of these were in Ulster and 7 in Connacht. It is also significant that only 21 other priests were mentioned in the total of 469 offices whose holders' names appear in the volume; if the clergy held any positions in the party, they tended disproportionately to assume the most senior and honorific posts.[123] This clerical influence must have helped counteract that of the local Volunteers, just as the bishops' intervention at national level had restrained some of the more militaristic elements during the conscription crisis.

Many of the clergy had strongly nationalist views, and in East Galway the county inspector referred in passing to 'one of the very few non-Sinn Fein priests in this Riding'.[124] A *Times* special correspondent was able to remark casually that one Irish nationalist 'was typical of Sinn Fein, because he was young, because he was a priest, and most of all because he was a schoolmaster'.[125] But in general the clergy tended to reinforce their parishioners' views rather than take the initiative, and their opposition was not always effective. Joseph MacBride reported from Mayo that, immediately after a mass at which the priest had denounced Sinn Féin from the altar, half the congregation went directly to the party's meeting.[126]

One newspaper item illustrates vividly the influence which a strong-minded or much-loved priest could wield in a small community: the Ballyrush club in Co. Sligo regretted the departure of its president, Fr O'Reilly, and announced that it would dissolve the following Sunday.[127] In a similar fashion the entries in the Naas branch's minute book conclude sadly with a reference to its president:

---

[120] *Saturday Record*, 13 Oct. 1917.   [121] *II*, 30 June 1917.

[122] *Clare Champion*, 7 July–29 Sept. 1917.   [123] 'List of Sinn Féin officers', NLI, MS 5649.

[124] CI's report, E. Galway, Jan. 1919, CO.904/108.   [125] *Times*, 13 Dec. 1919.

[126] MacBride to Maurice Moore, 9 Oct. 1917, Moore MSS, NLI 10,561(22).

[127] *Sligo Champion*, 27 July 1918.

'Fr Doyle to go to sanatorium'.[128] When Fr O'Flanagan was suspended from his duties in 1918 the doors of the village church were locked against his successor, who was forced to climb in through a sacristy window, and parishioners made a round trip of 6 miles (9.5 km) to a neighbouring village to hear mass on Sundays. (This was a recurring theme in his life; when he had been transferred from his first parish in 1915, after his demands for land reform had caused offence in certain quarters, his parishioners had been equally unwilling to accept the new incumbent.[129])

Among the clergy (as among the laity) there tended to be a difference along generational lines; the parish priests (and *a fortiori* the bishops) were inclined to support the Parliamentary Party, while their curates tended to side with Sinn Féin. But even within the hierarchy there was a degree of sympathy for the new movement. O'Dwyer of Limerick became a hero among separatists for his defiant and contemptuous open letter to Maxwell in the aftermath of the rising; Walsh of Dublin intervened to damage the Parliamentary Party in the Longford election; and Fogarty of Killaloe, one of the treasurers of the Dáil loan, made speeches such as that in which he denounced the death of Thomas Ashe as 'the sort of cruelty we were accustomed to hear of as possible only in the ancient Bastille, or the dungeons of Naples, or the bleak prisons of Russia'.[130] Before the 1918 election a reference was made in the standing committee to four bishops in the province of Armagh who 'were on the side of Sinn Féin'.[131] At the popular level one prelate could be played against another, and when a priest cited the support of O'Donnell of Raphoe for the Parliamentary Party candidate in 1918, he was met with cheers for Fogarty of Killaloe.[132] In June 1921 de Valera directed that if the bishops succumbed to republican pressure, and if a forthcoming statement of theirs could be interpreted favourably, the Dáil's publicity department should ensure that newspaper headlines would read 'The Irish Bishops Recognise The Republic'.[133] The hierarchy remained cautious and the headlines never appeared.

Nuns were far less prominent in Irish public life than priests, and they were not active in Sinn Féin or in other parties. There is virtually no surviving evidence of their political views. However, the words of the patriotic ballad 'Who fears to speak of Easter Week' were written by Mother Columba Gibbons, a

---

[128] Club minutes, 15 Mar. 1922, NLI, MS 13,561(5).

[129] *II*, 25, 29 July 1918; Carroll, *They have fooled you again*, pp. 39, 84.

[130] *Irish bishop speaks. The death of Thomas Ashe. The bishop of Killaloe's protest* (handbill, 1917), TCDL, MS 2074.   [131] SCM, 28 Nov. 1918; see above, p. 161.   [132] *II*, 9 Dec. 1918.

[133] De Valera to publicity department, 19 June 1921, 'Epitome of documents seized', CO.904/23/7, p. 21.

member of the Loreto order,[134] and she may have been representative of many of her sisters.

Women

The military nature and leanings of the Sinn Féin party influenced the role which women played within its ranks. The Volunteers were an all-male force, and, at least by implication, their women's counterpart, Cumann na mBan, was seen as an appendage. Its rules laid down that branch members 'should keep in touch with their local Volunteer Battalions, appear at the parades, and identify themselves with Irish Volunteer work in every suitable way'.[135] Several of them, most notably Countess Markievicz, were prominent in military affairs to a greater extent than was possible in civilian or political life in the years before women secured the vote. In a pamphlet which dates from 1917 the organization declared that its activities included supporting female candidates and reminding the country that under the 1916 proclamation women were entitled to the same rights of citizenship as men.[136] It urged that women should be selected as candidates in the 1918 election campaign.

Sinn Féin had always been emancipated on the issue of female suffrage. Griffith had supported the cause before the war, although, characteristically, he was anxious that it should not distract attention from the predominant 'national' question.[137] Disillusioned with male politicians, he even declared that he would not repine if Ireland were to become a 'gynocracy.'[138] Before the 1911 local elections he advised that 'the women candidates everywhere should be voted for'; female representatives of all parties had always shown themselves genuinely interested in discharging their duties honestly.[139] Markievicz remained in the party after other radicals withdrew, on the grounds that it was the only organization which admitted women, while Jennie Wyse Power became a vice-president in 1911.[140] The Easter rebels were no less radical, and their proclamation was addressed to both 'Irishmen and Irishwomen'.

---

[134] F. X. Martin, '1916 – myth, fact, and mystery', *Studia Hibernica*, 7 (1967), p. 114.

[135] *Cumann na mBan (The Irishwomen's council)* (pamphlet, n.d. [*c.* 1915]), p. 4.

[136] *Cumann na mBan* (pamphlet, n.d., [1917?]).

[137] On Griffith's concern that the manner of seeking female suffrage should not 'injure the nation', see *Sinn Féin*, 5 Apr., 5 July 1913.   [138] Glandon, *Arthur Griffith*, p. 139, n. 54.

[139] *Sinn Féin*, 27 May 1911, cited in Murray, 'Citizenship, colonialism and self-determination', p. 216.

[140] Davis, *Arthur Griffith*, p. 68; Margaret Ward, *Unmanageable revolutionaries: women and Irish nationalism* (London, 1983), p. 67.

Like its predecessor, the new post-rising Sinn Féin party opened its ranks to men and women on equal terms, and this was confirmed by a resolution passed at the 1917 convention. By the standards of the time (and also of later times) women were remarkably well represented on the standing committee and in various party offices; at different stages Kathleen Lynn was vice-president, Hanna Sheehy-Skeffington director of organization, Áine Ceannt director of communications and Jennie Wyse Power honorary treasurer. Every successive standing committee of Sinn Féin had either three or four women members. They tended to be more conscientious in their attendance than the men, and on a few occasions at the height of the Anglo-Irish War in 1920 they formed a majority of those present at meetings.

One woman was elected to the first Dáil and six to the second, a figure which would not be surpassed until 1981. All five women members of the Dublin Corporation elected in January 1920 were Sinn Féiners, and in Cork the only female candidate (for a corporation of fifty-six members) was also a member of the party; she was elected. Markievicz was appointed minister for labour in the first Dáil government, although de Valera dropped her from the cabinet when its numbers were reduced in August 1921. (No woman would be appointed again to an Irish cabinet until 1979.) In a circular which the party sent to constituency executives before the 1921 elections, enclosing a sample ballot paper to illustrate the working of PR, three of the six 'candidates' were women.[141] There were some reservations about such liberal attitudes, and in 1918 Fr O'Flanagan, the party's acting president, doubted the wisdom of choosing female candidates; he feared that it might cause confusion and 'raise a side question from the one of Ireland's right to independence'.[142] But this was a minority view among the more prominent figures in the movement.

Most party members were more conservative in this respect than their leaders, and from their earliest years women were conditioned to act as supportive observers. For example, it was noted that shortly after the rising young girls in Cork sang

> Here's to the Sinn Feiners. The Sinn Feiners are men.
> If I were a boy I would Sinn Fein with them.
> As I'm a girl, I must lead a girl's life.
> But I'll do my very best to be a Sinn Feiner's wife![143]

There was widespread uncertainty among women sympathetic to Sinn Féin as to whether they were actually eligible for party membership, and queries on this

---

[141] Páidín O'Keeffe, circular, 14 Apr. 1921, RB, 8786(2).

[142] De Róiste, diary, 15 Sept. 1918, CAI, U271/A/21.

[143] 'Nan' to Terence MacSwiney, 12 July 1916, MacSwiney MSS, UCDA, P48b/8.

point were often sent to headquarters. More surprisingly, members of Cumann na mBan posed the same question. In return, *Nationality* referred to the opinion, apparently still prevalent in some places as late as 1919, that the Cumann was a women's auxiliary to Sinn Féin.[144] A report from Roscommon referred to Sinn Féin and Cumann na mBan branches as if they belonged to complementary organizations.[145] (However at national level there might have been some cause for confusion; until late 1918 Cumann na mBan's offices were located in the Sinn Féin headquarters on Harcourt Street.[146]) On numerous occasions Sinn Féin reminded women that they were eligible and welcome to join the party; at a meeting of the standing committee after the 1921 general election Hanna Sheehy-Skeffington asked de Valera to issue such an appeal, and he agreed to do so provided that she would draft it. Soon afterwards the committee decided to appoint 'four Lady Organisers, one for each Province'.[147]

There was much opposition to any involvement by women in the man's world of politics, and conservative, male-dominated bodies were suspicious of female self-assertiveness. The GAA requested the Sinn Féin standing committee to prevent the holding of 'flapper' meetings throughout the country, and a copy of its letter was sent to constituency executives.[148] In October 1921 it was noted at the *ard-fheis* that, for the first time in many instances, women had finally joined Sinn Féin clubs even though local prejudice still militated against them.[149] Casual remarks revealed deep-rooted attitudes, as in the announcement that a Sinn Féin branch in Clare had been reorganized and it was expected that 'every man in the parish' would join it at once.[150] In many districts Sinn Féiners practised sexual segregation, and separate women's clubs were established. This was possibly an extension of the military division between the Volunteers and Cumann na mBan, although it may also have been a reflection of the same attitude which allowed (or enforced) separate male and female Irish language classes. In Kilinumry (Co. Sligo), for example, the club discussed starting 'a Ladies' Auxiliary'.[151] Several such women's clubs were established, almost in a defiant tone, and they were probably the result of exclusion caused by male prejudice.

In 1918, just as women had gained the vote, and when their involvement in political affairs might seem less likely than a few years later, a list of Sinn Féin election officers in West Wicklow revealed seventy-four offices occupied by men and only two by women.[152] Of sixty-one Sinn Féin clubs listed by the RIC in

---

[144] *Nationality,* 8 Feb. 1919.   [145] *Roscommon Journal,* 3 Nov. 1917.

[146] Marie O'Neill, *From Parnell to de Valera: a biography of Jennie Wyse Power, 1858–1941* (Dublin, 1991), pp. 105–6.   [147] SCM, 31 May, 4 July 1921.   [148] *Ibid.,* 8 June 1920.

[149] *II,* 28 Oct. 1921.   [150] *Clare Champion,* 2 Feb. 1918.   [151] *Sligo Champion,* 16 Mar. 1918.

[152] 'Election 1918', RB, 8786(1).

Kerry in August 1920, only eighteen had women members; they normally made up about a quarter of the total of the 'mixed' clubs in this list, and the proportions varied from ninety-six men and one isolated woman in Portmagee, to those of a small but advanced club in Fenit where the sexes enjoyed a greater degree of equality: the membership comprised sixteen men and nine women. The total figures were 6,124 men and 406 women, but these, coming as they do from the RIC, must be treated with caution.[153]

At local level, as opposed to that of the national leadership, women rarely reached the top. In the same list of constituency executives which revealed that 45 out of 469 offices in constituency executives were held by priests, it was also disclosed that a mere 9 of these posts were occupied by women. Déogréine Barton was president of her executive in West Wicklow; six of her fellow-officers were from Leinster and the remaining two from Ulster.[154] A general and predictable pattern was that women tended to fare better in the towns than in the countryside. As one example, on the pro-treaty wing of Sinn Féin in 1922 five of the twenty-nine club officers in Clontarf were women, although they did not occupy any of the more senior positions.[155] The *Freeman's Journal* observer at the February 1922 *ard-fheis* noted that practically all the female delegates came from the cities and towns and that

> while in town clubs women often share the officer posts with men, in the country they are seldom even members. This is probably due, not so much to sex antagonism as to the fact that farmers' wives and daughters have to work too hard and too continuously on the farms to have time for politics.[156]

Obviously this reasoning did not apply to the farmers or their sons.

All in all, whatever might be the later pattern shared by its pro- and anti-treaty successor parties from 1922 onwards, in the question of women's involvement in Irish public life the united Sinn Féin party tended to be on the side of the revolutionaries and not of the conservatives. Its lead may not have been followed widely, but it led.

Roots and branches

All Sinn Féiners, men and women, soldiers and civilians, clergy and laity, co-operated together within a framework of about 1,200 clubs scattered through-

---

[153] 'Crime special. County of Kerry', Aug. 1920, *Irish Bulletin*, 16 Sept. 1920.

[154] 'List of Sinn Féin officers', NLI, MS 5649.

[155] 'Clontarf committee', 30 Mar. 1922, RM, P7/A/71.   [156] *FJ*, 21 Feb. 1922.

out the country. One of the main tasks of dedicated party members was to educate and indoctrinate their neighbours. In 1916 the majority of Irish nationalists had not supported the Easter rebels' actions or objectives. Despite all the failings and failures of the Parliamentary Party most Irish nationalists remained faithful to it until 1917 or 1918, even if their enthusiasm had faded long before the conscription crisis finalized their transfer of loyalties.[157] One result of such a rapid change of opinion was that a large majority of Sinn Féin members were recent initiates who had been converted by the rising and its aftermath, and who had been blown into the party by a gust of emotion. They were often fervent, but they were also normally uninformed about all but the most general of separatist ideas.

Most inaugural meetings of Sinn Féin clubs consisted of an explanation of the party's programme by someone who was prominent either in the district or at national level, and this was usually followed by the enrolment of new members and the selection of officers. Many subsequent branch meetings centred on speeches, lectures or debates on aspects of Sinn Féin policy. In Grange (Co. Sligo) the secretary reported that newly registered members were ordered to distribute leaflets concerning a proposed tax on farmers.[158] Debates were held on subjects such as 'physical force versus passive resistance' and 'republicanism versus monarchism'. A paper on 'the Resurrection of Hungary' was read in Kells (Co. Meath), another on O'Connell and Sinn Féin in Navan, and in Maryborough (Portlaoise, Co. Laois) 'the Abstention Policy' was chosen as the subject for discussion at the club's next meeting.[159] The heroic past – and particularly the recent past – was a frequent theme of lectures and discussions; for example, in a lecture in Courtown Harbour (Co. Wexford) Pearse was held up as an example of a patriot 'who had lived every hour of his life for the land of his love'. The talk was followed by singing and a dance.[160] Many branches ran classes on the Irish language, or on songs and dancing, while some set up lending libraries; by November 1917 the library in Scarriff (Co. Clare) comprised nearly a hundred books, and the club provided Irish language classes almost every night.[161]

Branch meetings frequently took place after Sunday mass, and the church could also serve other purposes; the club in Maugherow (Co. Sligo) announced in the local newspaper that the date of the next meeting would appear on the chapel gate, while in Kilmacanogue (Co. Wicklow) it was decided that a circular

[157] On the continuity of personnel between the Parliamentary Party and Sinn Féin, see Fitzpatrick, *Politics and Irish life*, pp. 118, 123, 137–8.   [158] *Sligo Champion*, 4 Aug. 1917.

[159] *Meath Chronicle*, 28 July 1917, 2 Feb. 1918; *Leinster Leader*, 23 June 1917.

[160] *Enniscorthy Guardian*, 19 Jan. 1918.   [161] *Clare Champion*, 10 Nov. 1917.

from the constituency executive should be read after mass.[162] In Kilrush (Co. Clare), after a report that more than half the members were absent from an evening meeting, it was decided to return to the earlier pattern of gathering immediately after the last mass on Sunday.[163]

At least in the towns Sinn Féiners seem to have had little difficulty in finding temporary venues where they could hold their meetings, although some of them continued to use reading rooms or temperance halls. Public houses were available as an alternative for those who were prepared to mix drink and politics. Sometimes they captured the enemy's positions, and after vanquishing the local AOH in Mountmellick (Co. Laois) they converted the Order's hall to their own use.[164] In a Sligo village, negotiations with the local UIL branch resulted in its transferring its band instruments to the Sinn Féin club without imposing any conditions;[165] this may have been facilitated by the county's tradition of intimidation. The Gaelic League and the GAA also continued to provide shelter as well as cover.

In the countryside party members were often forced to improvise, but normally efforts were made to find suitable permanent quarters. In the Castlebar district of Mayo, for example, Sinn Féiners built meeting halls 'of one sort or another', most of them erected by voluntary labour.[166] Not all the labour was voluntary, and a Sinn Féin court in Kinvara (Co. Galway) sentenced a convicted defendant to a week's hard labour at construction work on a new party hall.[167] In one instance, which exudes an un-republican air of deference, forty younger members of a club spent the day digging the potatoes of a local farmer 'as a small token of gratitude to him, for allowing them the use of his spacious house in Ballagh [Co. Roscommon] as a Sinn Féin Hall'. When their work was completed they were 'sumptuously entertained to the small hours of the morning', so perhaps the honours were even by the time the revels ended.[168]

Meetings seem to have been run democratically, and, with occasional and natural exceptions in the early days, officers and committees were elected by the club members. The party rules of October 1917 laid down that all elections should be held by secret ballot. The degree of competition for such posts is impossible to estimate with any accuracy, and accounts of several people competing for a small number of posts are matched by others which refer to the unanimous re-election of the officers and committee.

---

[162] *Sligo Champion*, 2 Mar. 1918; club minutes, 14 Aug. 1918, NLI, MS 15,730.

[163] *Clare Champion*, 24 May 1919.   [164] *Nationalist and Leinster Times*, 2 June 1917.

[165] *Sligo Champion*, 3 Nov. 1917.   [166] *Mayoman*, 9 Aug. 1919.

[167] *II*, 25 Mar. 1918. For the Sinn Féin courts, see below, pp. 311–14.

[168] *Roscommon Journal*, 17 Nov. 1917.

In Athy (Co. Kildare) the *Leinster Leader* published the contents of the club's minute book for six weeks in the heady days of May and June 1917. They give a good illustration of the party's workings at branch level.[169] After a local separatist, P. P. Doyle, had received a letter from the secretary of the Kildare Sinn Féin provisional committee, he summoned a preliminary meeting in the town on 19 May. This first gathering did little more than discuss the prospect of acquiring rooms. A second, more representative meeting went further and took the decision to establish a club, while a third elected a committee of ten members and a president (not Doyle). Eamonn Fleming, one of Sinn Féin's itinerant organizers, made a speech and was questioned sharply by some of those present on aspects of party policy. There were objections to the old Sinn Féin's 'king, lords and commons' constitution, the party's reliance on the peace conference which would follow the war, and its policy of abstention from Westminster. It was decided that the branch's committee should meet weekly and its members fortnightly at the newly acquired Sinn Féin rooms. (Until then they had gathered in the urban council room.) Soon afterwards the committee appointed a librarian, established an amusements and sports sub-committee, and drafted a code of rules for the club which would be submitted to the next general meeting. On that occasion members discussed the question of holding a large assembly in the town.

The workings of the Athy Sinn Féin branch are better illustrated than those of any other for this period, but innumerable references in provincial newspapers confirm that they are broadly representative of the country at large. All over Ireland club members performed more or less the same interacting functions of constructing a local party machine, boosting their own morale, and propagandizing the movement. Except in those few areas where parliamentary vacancies occurred there was little else of a purely political nature that they could do, or needed to do, other than prepare for the next general election.

Most branches formed election committees, and East Cork lost no time by choosing its candidate as early as May 1917.[170] An important part of the members' activities was to compile lists of the inhabitants of each townland so that they could influence the revision of the electoral register. When the franchise was widened in 1918 they had to ensure that the register included the names of all Sinn Féin supporters in the district who were newly entitled to vote. Such mundane activity did not always appeal to some party members, and they

---

[169] *Leinster Leader*, 30 June 1917.

[170] Jeremiah Lane to Plunkett, 14 May 1917, CP, 11,383(6). After some internal wrangling the selected candidate, David Kent, was returned unopposed in December 1918. See above, p. 153.

needed encouragement to busy themselves with useful but unexciting activities. As one writer put it, 'you may get a thousand to make a parade, and ten to assist in the registration room . . . The work on our register *now* means the success or non-success of the self-determination idea.'[171] Constituency executives were urged to buy the electoral register, make a dozen typescript copies of it, townland by townland, and to mark the electors 'for', 'against' and 'doubtful'.[172] A branch in Sligo boasted with justifiable pride that it had submitted ninety-one names for inclusion on the register and had secured the franchise for eighty-two of its nominees.[173]

One source gives a revealing indication of what Sinn Féin headquarters and many of the branches actually did during the months between the October convention and the German plot arrests. When 6 Harcourt Street was raided in May 1918 much of the party's incoming correspondence was seized and examined by the British authorities. The originals have disappeared, but Dublin Castle made a *précis* of every captured letter and this document has survived.[174] The fact that the letters have been processed by another (enemy) hand lessens their value in some respects, and can result in confusion or distortion – and at times also elements of humour which may not have existed in the original. For example, an account from Achill (Co. Mayo) reads, 'they have pledged to shoot any spy, traitor, or slacker to their cause. Father Egan is to be their leader. He wants to get tobacco badly.' The reader longs to know more about Fr Egan, but this remark can hardly be classified as an insight into the workings of the Sinn Féin party.

Many other documents have the ring of truth, however brutally their contents may have been summarized; for example, the election agent Dan McCarthy reported that he was 'stranded in Baltinglass [Co. Wicklow] with only a few bob in his pocket', while one of his colleagues was 'on the rocks' in Dundalk and as a result he was sent £4 from headquarters. Trivial items of correspondence give a convincing feel of an organization in which leaders and led spoke a different language – or, at least, chose different topics of conversation. Yet, even if they have to be interpreted with caution, the summarized letters illustrate the party's nature and workings in a far more vivid and convincing manner than does its complex scheme of organization. They provide an insight into aspects of Sinn Féin activity in particular and Irish life in general during the early months of 1918.

Numerous correspondents asked for copies of the party rules, membership cards and leaflets; some sought advice about associating with the police and

---

[171] *Nationality*, 6 July 1918.   [172] Darrell Figgis, *Nationality*, 15 Sept. 1917.

[173] *Sligo Champion*, 31 Aug. 1918.   [174] *Précis* of captured documents, NLI, MS 10,494.

with Redmondites; others protested at *Nationality*'s failure to publish their subscriptions, or complained about delays in replying to their earlier letters. There were references to disorganization; from Westport (Co. Mayo) came the plea 'for goodness sake to send an organiser at once', while it was reported that in Bray (Co. Wicklow) only one member had turned up to a club meeting. There were begging letters, such as a request for tickets to a hurling match, or an inquiry from a branch secretary who asked whether an old second-hand bicycle might be available for party work. One correspondent sought information about where he might acquire make-up for amateur theatricals. There were grumbles, such as the charge that club officials 'have too much talk and no interest in their work'. There were attempts at concealment, as in the case of the doctor of divinity from Maynooth who wanted his £25 subscription for the Armagh election fund to be acknowledged as coming from 'Some Ecclesiastical students'. A few letters were sent by informers, such as that written by the club president who, having been exposed as an ex-policeman, complained that the secretary would have joined the police too if he had not been rejected on medical grounds. An indignant correspondent from Co. Derry wrote 'demanding the name of the person who reported he was convicted of keeping a sheebeen'.

There were reports of quarrels and splits. Clubs in Leitrim seemed to be unusually disputatious, while Roscommon showed a concentration of letters concerning the division of grazing land. Protests were made about cattle-driving. News of the formation of a branch came from 'labouring men' in Galway, while the club in Roscrea (Co. Tipperary) asked whether it might amalgamate with the Transport Workers. In the words of the official *précis*, several letters were from a man 'who thinks he is a poet, [and] wants to be paid for the "Flowing Tide", which he has written for Clare election'. The correspondent who 'wants a situation for his boy in the Sinn Fein offices' displayed signs of the jobbery which more self-righteous party members associated with the Redmondites. The most unusual letter came from a man who, presumably, never spent long enough in any one place to strike roots: 'a travelling circus man stage name Presto wants to become a Sinn Feiner'.

The branches' activities were varied, and they provided a focus for non-political activities. Meath had a Sinn Féin dramatic club, and in Tuamgraney (Co. Clare) 'a week hardly passes but there is a dance or a demonstration of some kind which tends to keep the spirit very much alive'.[175] In Celbridge (Co. Kildare) hurling, football and camogie clubs functioned as 'adjuncts to the political club', while in Dunmanway (Co. Cork) a hurling club was transformed

---

[175] *Clare Champion*, 17 Nov. 1917.

into a Sinn Féin branch.[176] The party's standing committee, emphasizing its astonishment and disappointment, reprimanded the club in Bagenalstown (Co. Carlow) for spending its surplus funds on an outing for the members.[177] (Some months earlier the same branch had shown less sign of frivolity when it condemned unanimously and emphatically 'the action of the local aristocratic dancing jingoes in introducing into our decent little town that immodest dance, the "Rag-time"'.[178])

An article in the *Tipperary People* entitled 'Sinn Féin co-operative tillage' described how over 250 Sinn Féiners, superintended by a priest, dug and gathered 1 acre (0.4 hectare) of potatoes on behalf of one of their colleagues who had been sentenced to a year's imprisonment for drilling with his fellow Volunteers. They also pulled and pitted 3 acres of mangolds belonging to another political prisoner.[179] There are many other such reports, particularly of cutting turf on behalf of the families of those in jail. In Mayo the Kilmeena Sinn Féin branch sent 17 tons of potatoes to nearby Westport for sale or distribution to the poor; their largesse was transported in twenty-one carts whose horses were decorated with tricolours as they entered the town in procession.[180] In Moylough (Co. Sligo), arrangements were made to assist a farmer whose two cows had been killed in a thunderstorm.[181] The club in Mountrath (Co. Laois) organized a sweepstake on the county hurling final in aid of the general election fund, and a Sinn Féin demonstration in honour of St Kieran of Clonmacnoise was attended by crowds drawn from six neighbouring counties.[182] A Sinn Féin demonstration in Roscommon was on such a grand scale that the procession which included 'horse, foot and cycle corps' extended for almost a mile.[183] A hundred cyclists from Tuam (Co. Galway) travelled to meetings in nearby Belclare and Kilbeg, and – apart from any enlightenment which might have resulted – such an excursion was probably great fun.[184] Along with their political impact the clubs served a valuable social function in bringing people together, providing them with a sense of community, and often simply giving them something to do in their leisure hours.

Time and time again dedicated party workers complained of the difficulties which they faced in maintaining their colleagues' energy and commitment. Elections provided a focus, but they were rare, and members' enthusiasm often

---

[176] *Leinster Leader*, 16 Mar. 1918; CI's report, W. Cork, Feb. 1918, CO.904/105.

[177] SCM, 18 July 1918.   [178] *Nationalist and Leinster Times*, 23 Mar. 1918.

[179] *Tipperary People*, 26 Oct. 1917.   [180] *Nationality*, 16 Feb. 1918.

[181] *Sligo Champion*, 8 Sept. 1917.

[182] *Nationalist and Leinster Times*, 2 Mar. 1918; *II*, 11 Sept. 1917.

[183] *Roscommon Journal*, 3 Nov. 1917.   [184] *II*, 10 Aug. 1917.

proved to be fickle and transient. At least to a certain extent there was value in activity for its own sake. A futile plebiscite, demanding that Ireland should be allowed present its case at the peace conference, kept many clubs busy amassing signatures in early 1918; in Bray it was noted that this exercise had been interrupted several times, but was being pushed to a conclusion.[185] A Galway RIC county inspector commented revealingly that drilling 'collects idle and reckless young men together; presently they begin to feel their strength . . . the marching and stamping about excites them and frightens other people'.[186] In a similar mood the inspector general complained that drilling 'fosters an arrogant spirit, and a sense of power amongst the young men engaged in it, which is very embarrassing to the Police'.[187] Apart from its intimidatory effect, activity of this sort gave the participants a feeling of self-confidence and purpose.

The party's structure was horizontal as well as vertical, and members of different clubs met each other frequently – thereby complementing and reinforcing the contacts between Dublin headquarters and the local branches. Regional executives were formed, enabling clubs to co-ordinate their activities, assist their counterparts in neighbouring districts, exchange views and information, and in the process acquire a greater sense of comradeship and solidarity. In at least some parts of the country the pattern of establishing constituency executives had been under way for many months before the party's new leadership assumed the task in November 1917. In its early days headquarters was too busy and too inexperienced to take such initiatives, and while it gave this development its blessing it was unable to provide much guidance. As early as May 1917 a county convention was summoned to organize the Sinn Féin cause in Kilkenny, the North Meath constituency executive was founded a month later, while by the end of June eleven clubs (and three parishes which were still without branches) were represented in the South Sligo Sinn Féin alliance.[188] Three hundred representatives attended a convention of party branches in Limerick.[189] By mid-July twenty-five clubs in Cavan sent representatives to a Sinn Féin conference, and those present agreed to form an executive which would prepare for the general election.[190]

In a few cases these constituency executives had to be restructured in mid-1918 when parliamentary seats were redistributed;[191] some constituencies were merged, while in other cases their boundaries were re-drawn. Further changes

---

[185] *Irishman*, 20 July 1918.   [186] CI's report, W. Galway, Feb. 1918, CO.904/105.

[187] IG's report, Mar. 1918, *ibid.*

[188] T. Hennessy to Plunkett, 21 May 1917, CP, 11,383(10); *Meath Chronicle*, 16 June 1917; *Sligo Champion*, 18 Aug. 1917.   [189] *Factionist*, 28 June 1917.   [190] *II*, 17 July 1917.

[191] SCM, 2 May 1918.

were needed when proportional representation was introduced, and these were implemented under far more difficult circumstances when the next general election was held in May 1921.[192]

Sinn Féin was fashionable throughout 1917 and 1918, a circumstance which it could exploit but which also left it open to exploitation. One illustration of this danger is a letter sent to the party headquarters from 'the Wanderers' Gaelic Club' asking could it retain its existing name while affiliating with Sinn Féin; the Wanderers may have remained more committed to sport than to politics.[193] Yet identification with the party was not always transformed into membership, and in the immediate aftermath of de Valera's election the branch in Inagh (Co. Clare) complained that there were still 'scores of fellows in the parish sporting Sinn Féin badges who have not yet joined the Club.'[194] Such attitudes provided a challenge to the party's activists, and it was a problem which would become more acute over the years.

Sinn Féin had to fight against apathy, particularly in the drab aftermath of periods of excitement and expansion. Many people drifted into the party because they were bored, and they may have drifted out again for the same reason. If Sinn Féin could not find outlets for its members' energies and enthusiasms there was a risk that new recruits who joined the party in search of novelty and excitement would find they had simply exchanged one kind of tedium for another. From New Ross (Co. Wexford) came a request to party headquarters that either Eoin MacNeill or Seán Milroy should attend a local concert 'as their presence is desirable owing to the people's indifference'.[195] In Sligo a warning was given to 'milk-and-water members to attend next meeting to render an account of their absence; if not extreme steps will be taken'.[196] In many cases commitment and enthusiasm simply evaporated.

Branches did try to impose discipline on their members, and at least some of these efforts were successful. This was a source of deep regret to the British authorities, and as early as January 1917 it was noted that Sinn Féiners in Belfast and Dundalk were 'very sober, a state of affairs which is to their credit but renders it difficult to get information'.[197] A year later the intelligence officer for the Midlands and Connacht lamented that drunkenness was almost unknown amongst those deeply implicated in Sinn Féin activities, and it appeared to be dealt with severely. This was 'foreign to the usual state of things in similar move-

---

[192] See below, pp. 335, 337.

[193] Secretary, Wanderers' Gaelic Club to secretary, national council, Sinn Féin, 11 Sept. 1917, *précis* of captured documents, NLI, MS 10,494(1), p. 39.   [194] *Clare Champion*, 25 Aug. 1917.

[195] *Précis* of captured documents, NLI, MS 10,494(3), p. 100.   [196] *Sligo Champion*, 19 Jan. 1918.

[197] IO's report (N.), Jan. 1917.

ments'.[198] A Sligo club expelled three members for an offence which can easily be visualized: they had assaulted a temperance procession on St Patrick's Day.[199] In other respects, too, attempts were made to keep followers in line. The Sinn Féin branch in Kildare town decided to prevent any repetition of the disturbances which followed the result of the Kilkenny by-election, and it reported that in doing so it was imitating the example of other districts.[200] Newspaper accounts of club meetings referred occasionally to expulsions.

Speeches by Sinn Féin leaders and articles published in *Nationality* depicted a calm, contented and united party whose members were concerned only with abstract and long-term goals. But at the lowly level of 1,200 or more branches throughout the country such statements concealed a more interesting and varied reality.

Throughout 1917 and 1918 Sinn Féin pulled itself up by its own shoelaces. Club members were enrolled, organized and instructed in policy by recent converts who knew little more about separatist beliefs and (in some cases) little more about party management than did the newcomers themselves. Attitudes were formed, and propaganda was written and distributed, at the same time that a new party was being hammered into shape. Often this was done by inexperienced, amateur politicians who improvised as they went along. Although the formation of the mass Sinn Féin party can appear in retrospect as a natural and logical process, it is remarkable that order emerged so quickly from such chaos. Everyone played the Sinn Féin tune by ear, and apart from background low-key rumblings the result was surprisingly free of discord.

---

[198] *Ibid.* (M. and C.), Dec. 1917. [199] *Sligo Champion*, 30 Mar. 1918.
[200] *Leinster Leader*, 18 Aug. 1917.

6

POLICY: BELIEFS AND ATTITUDES

After the 1918 general election Fr O'Flanagan is said to have remarked that 'the people have voted Sinn Féin. What we have to do now is to explain to them what Sinn Féin is.'[1] Long before the party's triumph one of its main tasks was to enlighten or inform the electorate, and it had a substantial body of beliefs or attitudes which could be fed into its propaganda machine.

Many of these were unimpressive. Griffith and other, lesser writers were publicists rather than intellectuals, and they said little that was new. With the exception of Connolly, who applied Marxist ideas to Irish conditions, they did not engage in the sort of intellectual debates which preoccupied many of their counterparts in other countries. They preached the merits of a republic but did not discuss such 'republican' concepts as the rights and duties of the citizen. Their arguments simply justified the struggle against Britain, and they tended to reinforce or rationalize the assumption that an elect few had a right or a duty to dominate the masses; the Irish nation was not the Irish people, but rather those members of Sinn Féin who had the self-confidence (or arrogance) to speak on its behalf. This elitism can be discerned in most aspects of the party's policy.

People joined Sinn Féin in their tens of thousands because they were attracted by its image, not because they believed in its ideology. They joined because their Anglophobia surfaced after the Easter Rising and during the conscription crisis. They joined because they were distrustful of Britain or disillusioned with the Parliamentary Party; because they were frustrated, bored or intimidated. Basic concepts such as 'we'll be masters in our own house' or 'we'll drive the British out' had an obvious attraction. As well as appealing to idealism and self-sacrifice, Sinn Féin could exploit xenophobia, resentment and greed. For many, freedom from Britain would be a panacea. One West Cork republican outlined to the novelist Edith Somerville the Nirvana that would be attained after independence: 'no polis and no taxes'.[2] Beyond this simple vision

---

[1] P. S. O'Hegarty, *The victory of Sinn Féin* (Dublin, 1924), p. 32.
[2] Hart, *I.R.A. and its enemies*, p. 136.

was a determination that Ireland would be run in a fairer, more competent and more 'Irish' manner. Sinn Féin built on these foundations, and it elaborated a set of policies which formed a coherent, propagandistic whole.

The post-rising party represented a range of different interests, objectives and methods, and its adherents ranged from the impassioned and self-sacrificing to the cynical and opportunistic. Nonetheless many aims and assumptions were either shared or else were easily absorbed by the different elements which combined to form the new Sinn Féin in 1917–18. The creation of a single united party brought with it little ideological conflict or reassessment. Most separatists clung to their old beliefs, and in particular they retained their convenient devotion to the image of an abstract 'Ireland' which existed quite independently of the people who happened to live on the island. There would also be no modification of their refusal to be distracted by any causes or problems, however attractive or pressing they might be, which would deflect attention from the supreme objective of achieving full independence from Britain. These assumptions and objectives were transmitted to 'the nation of converts' which joined the party in 1917 and 1918.

Abstractions

Before the Easter Rising, nationalists had indulged frequently in religious imagery. Nationality was spiritual, not material, and the cause of Irish freedom was a cause of God; the national idea was 'a holy and a sacred thing'; and Wolfe Tone was described as 'the first great Apostle and Martyr of the complete Nation'.[3] Patrick Pearse, a late but passionate convert, regarded national freedom as being marked 'like a divine religion', by unity, sanctity, catholicity and apostolic succession; his generation received the national demand as a trust from their fathers and 'we have not the right to alter it or to abate it by one jot or tittle'. He continued:

> the man who, in return for the promise of a thing which is not merely less than Separation, but which denies Separation and proclaims the Union perpetual . . . is guilty of so immense an infidelity, so immense a crime against the Irish nation, that one can only say of him that it were better for that man (as it were certainly better for his country) that he had not been born.[4]

---

[3] *Spark*, 2 Jan. 1916; *Irish Freedom*, Nov. 1910, Nov. 1914, editorials. See Michael Laffan, 'The sacred memory: religion, revisionism and the Easter Rising', in Judith Devlin and Ronan Fanning (eds.), *Religion and rebellion* (Dublin, 1997), pp. 176–9.

[4] Pearse, 'Ghosts', *Political writings*, pp. 226, 230–2.

Within one paragraph he used the words 'faith', 'dogma' and 'Credo'.[5] By the standards of his time Pearse would have made a good preacher; he would have inspired and terrified his congregation with his 'rich vocabulary of baptism, vocation, holiness, prophecy, service and martyrdom'.[6]

The IRB looked to the past for example and inspiration, and many of its members gloried in the idea of self-sacrifice. Ernest Blythe claimed that

> if the succession of martyrs fail while the nation is enslaved she shall yield up her soul to the conqueror . . . As in the national language is all sanity and strength, so in the fresh blood of the martyrs is all hope and pride and courage . . . Let the little-hearted talk of living for Ireland, but be well-assured that it is a finer thing to die for Ireland and more profitable than to win great victories.[7]

The religious rhetoric which had characterized separatism before the rising was enhanced by the heroism and bloodshed associated with Easter Week; there was now an even greater tendency for its spokesmen to think, talk and write in terms of spiritual nationalism, to use the language of 'a cult rather than a party'.[8] Many separatists were religious men who had found a vocation in revolution.[9] De Valera claimed that faith could not be divorced from politics, and that if the Sinn Féin movement were to succeed it 'must have religion'.[10] The *Irishman* was particularly addicted to spiritual terminology. It declared that 'you cannot teach a man that he may deny his national faith without making it easier for him to lose his faith in religion'; the compromise over the Ulster seats in 1918 was 'a deadly sin'; and Sinn Féin 'on the summit of its Calvary . . . knows that the Resurrection Morn shall come'.[11] At a meeting in a Sligo village, which was convened with the purpose of 'disseminating the Sinn Féin doctrine', one speaker announced appropriately that he had come to preach the gospel of Sinn Féin.[12] Figgis compiled the *Sinn Féin catechism*, while a separatist priest wrote a pamphlet entitled *The faith and morals of Sinn Féin*. A leading article in the Volunteers' journal *An tÓglách* was headed 'the Holy War'.[13] Some of the fighting men thought as instinctively in these terms as did the writers and politicians; one member of a flying column in West Cork in 1921 described his group as being 'the happiest people in Ireland

---

[5] *Ibid.*, p. 227.

[6] Seamus Deane, *Celtic revivals: essays in modern Irish literature, 1880–1980* (London, 1985), p. 69.

[7] *Irish Freedom*, Oct. 1913.   [8] Fitzpatrick, *Politics and Irish life*, p. 132.

[9] Good, *Enchanted by dreams*, p. 86.   [10] *II*, 3 Nov. 1917.

[11] *Irishman*, 24 Feb. 1917, 21 Dec. 1918, 12 Oct. 1918.   [12] *Sligo Champion*, 2 Feb. 1918.

[13] *An tÓglách*, 13 May 1921.

today . . . The reason is, I suppose that we are passing on a sacred Spiritual tradition.'[14]

Perhaps the clearest example of such imagery comes from a member of an
Irish-American delegation (and former Redmondite fund-raiser) who assured
members of the Dáil in 1919 that 'you will tread your way of the Cross; you will
march through your Garden of Gethsemane; the crown of thorns will be placed
on Ireland's brow; there will be a Calvary; but the stone will be rolled away on
an Easter morning'.[15]

C. S. Andrews's memoirs, although written many decades later, nonetheless
capture the mood and flavour of these years. In one vivid passage he explained
that

> our Ireland was an Ireland which had nothing to do with economics, prop-
> erty, or with how people lived or loved or prayed. It had in fact become a
> political abstraction, and from Caitlín Ní Uallacháin, Roisín Dubh and the
> Sean Bhean Bhocht proceeded the Republic. The fact that we had never
> seen any of these mythical personalities did not dismay us. We had been
> taught to believe profoundly in God and the Holy Spirit, neither of whom
> we had ever seen; our whole upbringing had been based on mysteries, glo-
> rious, sorrowful and joyful.[16]

Even Arthur Griffith, normally so blunt and down-to-earth in his attitudes and
expressions, rejected the idea

> that a nation was nothing more than a collection of human beings, and that
> the interests of the nation were nothing more than the interests of the said
> human beings – a body without a soul . . . When we say we love Ireland we
> do not mean by Ireland the peasants in the fields, the workers in the facto-
> ries, the teachers in the schools, the professors in the colleges – we mean
> the soul into which we were born and which was born into us.[17]

For dedicated Sinn Féiners who revered an abstract 'Ireland' just as they might
revere a Christian saint, it was easy to regard themselves as belonging to a
priestly caste. They were distinct from the masses, and were ranked above
them.

This tendency to idealize a metaphysical image of the nation was not
confined to Ireland, and it was prevalent throughout Europe in the decade
spanning the First World War. Continental European nationalists would have

---

[14] Florence O'Donoghue to 'G', 6 May 1921, FO'D, 31,176.

[15] Michael J. Ryan, *DE, 1919–21*, p. 108 (9 May 1919).

[16] C. S. Andrews, *Dublin made me* (Dublin and Cork, 1979) p. 99.   [17] *Sinn Féin*, 26 Apr. 1913.

appreciated Ernest Blythe's distinction between an ideal Ireland and the Irish people who had only a life-interest in the country; 'they are trustees for citizens unborn, and to sell, surrender or partition they have no shadow of right'.[18] Clemenceau was described by Keynes as having 'one illusion – France; and one disillusion – mankind, including Frenchmen'.[19] Charles de Gaulle, who belonged to the same generation as the Irish revolutionary leaders (he was born a month after Michael Collins), described in the famous opening passage of his *War memoirs* his image of France in terms of 'the princess in the fairytales or the Madonna in the frescoes', and he believed that any mediocrity in its acts and deeds should 'be imputed to the faults of Frenchmen, not to the genius of the land'.[20] Living people could be (and often were) unworthy of their abstract nations.

In the Irish context, as in that of many other countries, such views were associated with feelings of virtue and superiority; the patriot was often a smug prig. In 1917 a pamphlet described a 'shoneen', or someone who despises his native land, as a person whose traits included the following: he neglected to learn his country's language, history, song and story; he wasted on drink his money which, if well-spent, would make his home happy and his family comfortable; and he sold or bought immoral postcards, corrupt newspapers, dirty novels, 'the offscourings of a pagan civilization which the Godless Saxon dumps into this holy isle'.[21] An editorial in *Nationality* informed readers that 'there are no skeletons in our cupboards, no blood-stains on our hands: no mask of hypocrisy on our face. We are Irish.'[22] The conclusion explained all.

Heavy demands were made on the people fortunate enough to be Irish, and a pamphlet by Robert Lynd, *The ethics of Sinn Féin*, imposed an exacting rigour. The Irish people must keep their conduct above reproach and make their characters as nearly perfect as possible; they were exhorted to 'choose the Ireland that you think is best, and fashion yourself in its likeness'; they were 'to become, so far as it lies in their power, a comely and heroic and self-sacrificing and loveable race'.[23] The Sinn Féin image of Ireland was of a virtuous, honourable and wronged people, and many party members and supporters tended to fall into the obvious trap of self-righteousness. Even while the civil war discredited their cause, one of them confessed that 'an assumption made by many Sinn Féin

[18] *Irish Freedom*, Apr. 1914.

[19] J. M. Keynes, *The economic consequences of the peace* (London, 1919) p. 29.

[20] De Gaulle, *War memoirs*, I (London, 1955), p. 9.   [21] *Irish Republic*, 21 July 1917.

[22] *Nationality*, 8 Feb. 1919, editorial.

[23] Robert Lynd, *The ethics of Sinn Fein* (Limerick, 1912), pp. 3, 4, 7. See Goldring, *Pleasant the scholar's life*, pp. 43–6.

6.1 The new broom

public men was, and still is, that only they are honest in public life; all others are intriguers, jobbers and self-seekers'.[24]

In so far as they looked at the customs of other countries and tried to learn from the outside world – rare practices which were not widely recommended – they had to live up to the most exalted standards. Living composers were to be encouraged, because otherwise 'we shall never approach to the ideal towards which no nation should fail to move – Grand Opera'.[25] From the tone it is clear that grand opera was valued in national and not in musical terms. (Pearse had expressed similar views but he did so more lyrically: in an independent Ireland art and literature would flourish, and the voice of the people 'will make such music as has not been heard since Greece spoke the morning song of the free people'.[26])

---

[24] De Róiste, diary, 5 July 1922, CAI, U271/A/45.   [25] *Irishman*, 10 Nov. 1917.

[26] *Spark*, 9 Apr. 1916, cited in Edwards, *Patrick Pearse*, p. 338.

The past

Even before 1916 such a concept of exalted destiny had been rooted in an image of Irish history. Now there was a recent and powerful addition to that image: the rising itself. Pearse and his colleagues joined the Valhalla of patriots whose members they themselves had praised in prose and verse. Historical references recurred time and time again to inspire or outrage Irish nationalists, to confirm them in what they believed or rejected, to prove that Ireland's right to freedom was 'supported by her meritorious record when independent'.[27]

In the 1918 general election Robert Barton's campaign literature included a leaflet which lingered over the Celtic past, in particular over those centuries when

> their nation was a society bound together in a spiritual union – by the love of one undivided country . . . To make a common history for the whole people, the legends of ancient heroes were searched out . . . Scholars laboured incessantly to make the Irish speech worthy of their people and of their history.

The author praised a national altruism which endured over the centuries: 'since the time of St. Patrick, whenever they have taken a part in affairs outside their own land, it has only been at a spiritual call – a call of religion, of learning or of liberty'.[28]

Sinn Féiners brooded over 700 years of conquest and conflict. Inevitably Griffith and his followers recalled Grattan's Parliament, that period, as one of them reminded his readers, 'when Ireland got control of her affairs in 1783, [and] she doubled her revenue in ten years. This is a financial achievement without equal in the world's history.'[29] They lingered over Britain's responsibility for the horrors of the great famine. One writer declared that 'never before in the history of the world has such a deliberate process of depopulation been carried out with such scientific economic thoroughness'; de Valera cited John Mitchel's claim that it was a time when the English ate the surplus food; and an account which was headed 'Destruction of the White Race in Ireland' claimed that when the British government took steps to destroy the menace of the country's increasing population 'the peasantry of Ireland were artificially starved out of their holdings and the country turned into a grazing wilderness'.[30] Parnell

---

[27] Laurence Ginnell, *The Irish republic. Why?* (New York, 1919), p. 8.

[28] *Ireland a nation* (leaflet, 1918), Barton MSS, NAI, 1093/11.

[29] Herbert Moore Pim, *Three letters for unionists only!* (Dublin, n.d. [1917?]), p. 4.

[30] *Nationality*, 15 Feb. 1919; *II*, 7 Dec. 1917; *The first of the small nations* (n.d., ?1919), p. 13.

was annexed to the Sinn Féin cause without difficulty, and his commitment to the House of Commons was either elided or dismissed as a product of transient circumstances.

It is hardly surprising that the treaty debates of 1921–2 provided the clearest examples of forays being made on the Irish past to reinforce present beliefs, of disinterring the bones and summoning up the spirits of patriotic heroes. Count Plunkett represented the views of many with his credo 'I am faithful to the dead', while Mary MacSwiney, at the climax of one of her lengthy diatribes, made four separate references to 'the name of the dead' or 'the martyred dead'.[31] The *Donegal Vindicator* had as its test of the treaty's terms: 'how does Kevin Barry sleep in his prison grave to-night? Does MacSwiney know tranquillity?'[32] The *Connachtman* published a different result of the Dáil vote on the treaty from that recorded elsewhere: the result was a deadlock, with sixty-four votes ranged against sixty-four, in which the fifty-seven living anti-treaty members had been reinforced by the seven signatories of the Easter Week proclamation.[33]

Griffith too was able to presume the support of his long-dead hero, and was confident that the treaty had 'translated Thomas Davis into the practical politics of the day', while a pro-treaty pamphlet quoted Pearse to the effect that Davis's acceptance of repeal (of the Act of Union) in no way derogated from his status as a separatist.[34] One Dáil deputy protested that 'the bones of the dead have been rattled indecently in the face of this assembly', while another mused about his own status, wondering whether he should be disqualified from speaking in the debate on the grounds that he was still alive.[35]

But the litany of the patriots was too strong an incantation to be discarded lightly. A few months later the republican *Plain People* denounced the Free State constitution as 'a trampling on the ideals of Art MacMurrough, of Aodh Ruadh, of Sean O'Neill, of Eoghan Ruadh, of Tone, and Emmet, and Mitchel, and O'Leary, and Pearse . . .'[36] Many other examples could be chosen to illustrate the argument that the Irish nation was 'a divine geographical entity – situated, for the most part, six feet underground'.[37] In almost every case the past was ransacked in a crude fashion to reinforce views held about the present or the future; the sanction which it provided came from history 'not as chronological narrative but as symbolic pattern, in which certain utopian moments are extracted from the flow'.

---

[31] *DE, treaty debate*, p. 29 (19 Dec. 1921); *DE, private sessions*, p. 255 (17 Dec. 1921).

[32] *Donegal Vindicator*, 9 Dec. 1921, editorial.   [33] *Connachtman*, 14 Jan. 1922.

[34] *DE, treaty debate*, p. 23 (19 Dec. 1921); *Means to an end!* (pamphlet), Blythe MSS, UCDA, P24/620(2).   [35] Finian Lynch, Michael Hayes, *DE, treaty debate*, pp. 57, 129 (20, 22 Dec. 1921).

[36] *Plain People*, 18 June 1922.

[37] British and Irish Communist Organisation, *Aspects of nationalism* (Belfast, 1972), p. 36.

Nationalists could redirect the energies of the past into new patterns, and they 'reserved the right to reinterpret the past in the light of their desired future, which they recruited against a despised present . . . History thereby became a form of science fiction.'[38] It was far too useful to be left to mere scholars.

By constructing a suitable image of the past, and by venerating the (carefully chosen and useful) dead, Sinn Féiners reinforced the bonds between the abstract nation and religious belief or practice. They could more easily ignore the living Irish people and rationalize their own elite status.

Only on rare occasions were attempts made to evaluate the historical record or to question cherished myths. One such effort was made by J. J. O'Connell, who believed that Irish history was generally written in an uncritical and sentimental manner.[39] In late 1916 he tried to guide his fellow-prisoners in Reading Jail towards historical sophistication. He told them that 'if we wanted to learn anything we should face facts, and not be always casting about for some excuse for all our failures and defects'. One of his audience, George Nicholls, responded in appropriate verse to the news that there never had been such a regiment as Clare's dragoons:

> He said that Clare's Dragoons were not
> And those who sang of them sang rot,
> And should for ignorance be shot,
> Or dangled from a hempen rope . . .
> And when he hears it said the rout
> At Kinsale was just brought about
> By treason he says 'cut it out
> And study records of the time.
> It really makes me sick to feel
> You nothing know of Great O'Neill
> And other warriors of the Gael
> That you do prate so much about'.
> Though truth be bitter, falsehood sweet,
> For Irishmen 'tis always meet
> To separate the chaff from wheat
> And not through pleasant falsehoods grope.[40]

Lessons such as O'Connell's made understandably little impact, even when given to students as admirably receptive and creative as George Nicholls. In the

---

[38] Declan Kiberd, *Inventing Ireland: the literature of the modern nation* (London, 1995), p. 293.

[39] J. J. O'Connell, 'History of Irish Volunteers', Ch. 8, p. 7, Hobson MSS, NLI, 13,168.

[40] O'Connell, prison notebook, NLI, MS 19,924.

circumstances of the time it was only natural to value fervour more highly than balance or accuracy. In Ireland, as elsewhere, 'getting its history wrong is part of being a nation'.[41]

Unionists and others

With relatively few exceptions Sinn Féiners did not look around them to see how other societies conducted their affairs. Pearse quoted with approval Geoffrey Keating's description of Ireland as *domhan beag innti féin* (a little world in herself),[42] and the vision of many Irish nationalists was blinkered by their obsession with the problems of their own island.

Griffith was fascinated by foreign illustrations and examples, but these were always used to reinforce his one, unvarying message: that if other small countries could exist as independent states, Ireland could do so too. He knew the answer long before he asked his questions. Some of his analogies were false. His hero-worship of the Hungarians led him to disguise from his readers, and perhaps even from himself, their treatment of the subject nations which they ruled; once they were given the opportunity to do so, they repressed the Croats, Romanians and Slovaks even more forcefully than they themselves had earlier been repressed by the Austrians. In some respects the Hungarians had more in common with the Anglo-Irish ascendancy than with the mass of the Irish people. His use of Friedrich List to buttress his argument in favour of economic independence was selective beyond the point of dishonesty.[43] For all the international flavour of his journalism, and despite the imposing array of statistics and parallels with which he impressed or bewildered his readers, Griffith was a narrow nationalist. He was able to mock 'silly Irish people who believe that Ireland has a duty to look after other people's affairs and not to attend to her own', and he declared that

> if there be men who believe ... that the path to redemption for mankind is through universalism, cosmopolitanism or any other ism than national-ism, I am not of their company ... I am not concerned with the interests of humanity at large. I am concerned with the interests of my own people.[44]

But Griffith's was not an isolated voice, and his was simply the most articulate expression of a widely held attitude. D. P. Moran's *The Leader* was equally

[41] Ernest Renan, cited in E. J. Hobsbawm, *Nations and nationalism since 1780: programme, myth, reality* (Cambridge, 1990), p. 12.   [42] 'Ghosts', *Political writings*, pp. 227–8.

[43] See above, p. 19.

[44] Griffith to Lily Williams, 29 Nov. 1916, NLI, MS 5943; *Sinn Féin*, 25 Oct. 1913.

representative in not wishing Irish papers to devote columns to foreign affairs; 'what do we know or care of the passing show in France, Spain, Italy, Sweden, or any other foreign country?'[45] This mood was fully in tune with many of the equally narrow nationalisms which flourished and festered after the First World War, with the *sacro egoismo* of continental statesmen and agitators.

Irish nationalists, unable to challenge Britain's power and success, preferred instead to dismiss their enemy as crude and materialistic. Sinn Féiners, like others before them, emphasized the dichotomy between 'inner purity and external corruption'; alien strength was countered by native spirituality as Ireland was 'plundered, oppressed and outraged by a morally inferior people'.[46] Enemy soldiers were dismissed as 'pale, puny, anaemic products of English factory towns . . . creatures rather to be pitied than hated, as the pitiful products and slaves of a capitalistic Imperialism built on the exploitation of the many for the benefit of the few'.[47] Comments or judgements on Britain ranged from raw loathing to crass exaggeration; John MacBride declared a few years before the rising that 'my command of the English language is not sufficiently wide to allow me to put into words the intense hatred and detestation I have for England', while de Valera later claimed that had Ireland been ruled by kaiser, emperor or czar, rather than by the British, its population would have doubled or tripled.[48] Writing about Irish representation at Westminster Bishop Fogarty of Killaloe referred to 'the leprosy of anglicisation'.[49] But the most vivid expression of a common opinion was that of the Sinn Féin general secretary, Páidín O'Keeffe, who explained to a British interviewer that 'Sinn Féin was Revenge . . . By Hell, Revenge, that's what Sinn Féin is.' (Another, neater version is that he summarized Sinn Féin's policy as being 'vingeance, bejasus'.)[50]

All this involved no more than embellishing time-honoured stereotypes, it consisted merely of adjusting a collection of models, of dispensing praise and abuse. It demanded no thought, and its function was simply to raise the separatists' morale and harden their determination. When Sinn Féiners cherished such views or images it became easier for them to support the idea of killing Irish policemen or British soldiers. But the party's attitude towards Irish (and specifically Ulster) unionists fell into a different category.

Irish unity was taken for granted; it was a given fact determined by geography and (somewhat less conclusively) by history and sentiment. 'The frontier of

[45] *Leader*, 20 Aug. 1921.   [46] Goldring, *Pleasant the scholar's life*, p. 116; *Spark*, 21 Feb. 1915.

[47] *An tÓglách*, 30 Nov. 1918.   [48] *Irish Freedom*, Nov. 1912; *Nationality*, 19 July 1919.

[49] Fogarty to James O'Mara, 21 Nov. 1918, JO'M, 21,546(1).

[50] *Separatist*, 19 Aug. 1922. See Donagh MacDonagh, 'Ballads of 1916', *Bell*, 2, 1 (1941), p. 22; Sean O'Faolain, *Vive moi! an autobiography* (2nd edn, London, 1993), p. 144.

6.2 'The conscripts' chorus', an Irish view of Britain

Ireland has been fixed by nature.'[51] Such assumptions posed grave problems, and the awkward presence of a million Ulster unionists obscured the clarity of theories and maps. Although nationalists believed in an undefined Irish race which they assumed was the Catholic and Celtic people of Ireland, 'they also accepted the idea of an Irish nation (which included, whether they liked it or not, the Irish Protestants)'.[52] Many of them would seem to have been happier with the idea of race than of nation; the Irish soul was Catholic and Gaelic.[53] In the years before and after the rising the separatist movement retained lingering or hidden traces of sectarianism, an assumption that in a free Ireland Protestants would be absorbed into the Catholic community.[54] Understandably, perhaps, the unionists were often regarded as enemies, and even the moderate Irish Nation League viewed with dismay the prospect of partition which would leave 'the graves of Patrick, Brigid, and Colmcille, and many another sacred shrine within enemy territory'.[55]

In looking at Ulster Sinn Féin was faced with a dilemma: should the union-ists be attacked or cajoled? Many separatists shared a simplistic approach to northern Protestants; they regarded the unionists both as dupes of the Conservative Party and as paradoxical allies of Irish separatists. Robert Lynd

---

[51] Griffith, *Resurrection of Hungary*, p. 79.   [52] Boyce, *Nationalism in Ireland*, p. 251.

[53] R. F. Foster, *Modern Ireland, 1600–1972* (Harmondsworth, 1988), p. 479.

[54] Richard Davis, 'Ulster Protestants and the Sinn Féin press, 1914–22', *Éire-Ireland*, 15, 4 (1980), pp. 70–1.   [55] The Irish Nation League, *The bishops and the crisis* (pamphlet, n.d. [1916]).

wrote of the Orangemen that they were a source both of eager hope and melancholy despair; hope because they were sincere, passionate and extreme, despair because they did not 'forget the childish quarrels of vanished ages'.[56] Ulster unionists were praised repeatedly for their armed defiance of Asquith's government, and they were supposed to be reassured by messages such as that of Herbert Moore Pim: 'I know you detest compromise. And Sinn Féin kills compromise in a nation.'[57]

It was as if Sinn Féiners expected unionists to reciprocate the admiration which separatists felt for them (or for their tactics). *Irish Freedom* was able to claim naïvely or blindly that there were no irreconcilable differences between Irish parties that could not be settled by one day's friendly negotiations, if England would only keep its distance; 'the Ulster Volunteers are a guarantee that Ulster will not be coerced; the Irish Volunteers are a guarantee that Ireland cannot be divided'.[58] Griffith claimed that the basis of the Ulster unionists was the same as that of 'every armed Nationalist movement in Ireland this last hundred years . . . Who can prevent the mind of the armed Ulstermen from travelling slowly but certainly to the logical conclusion of their attitude and action?'[59] Similarly, Casement, in his speech from the dock, referred to the nationalists' welcome for Carson's defiance of the British government and declared that 'we aimed at winning the Ulster Volunteers to the cause of a united Ireland . . . Our hope was a natural one, and if left to ourselves, not hard to accomplish.'[60] Yet despite all this rhetoric few attempts were made to reconcile the opposing interests of north and south. Before the war the Sinn Féin party had outlined a number of concessions which might induce the unionists to accept an all-Ireland government, but they were ignored.[61] Separatists' admiration rarely took the positive form shown by Patrick McCartan, a prominent Sinn Féiner and IRB member, who offered his car to help the Larne gun-runners.[62]

There were limits to the esteem in which unionists were held, and in any event Carson's Volunteers lost much of their appeal when they flocked to join the British army in August 1914. Northern objections and objectives were not taken seriously. Seán Milroy represented a nationalist consensus in his blunt warning that 'Ireland is not going to let Ulster go. Ireland cannot do without Ulster; and Ulster cannot do without Ireland.'[63] Diarmuid O'Hegarty, secretary

---

[56] Riobárd Ua Fhloinn [Robert Lynd], *The Orangemen and the nation* (Belfast, 1907), p. 1.

[57] Pim, *Three letters for unionists only!*, p. 8.   [58] *Irish Freedom*, June 1914, editorial.

[59] *Sinn Féin*, 28 Mar. 1914, editorial.   [60] Brian Inglis, *Roger Casement* (London, 1973), p. 407.

[61] Maye, *Arthur Griffith*, pp. 167–8.

[62] Davis, 'Ulster Protestants and the Sinn Féin press', p. 66. See above, p. 124.

[63] *Irishman*, 16 June 1917.

to the Dáil cabinet, referred to rumours of proposals such as a settlement by county option and then dismissed these ideas: 'our position is that these things do not merit discussion or even reference. The Republic IS, and it has got to stay and make itself felt.'[64] Unionists had some justification when they claimed that Sinn Féin was imperialistic.

De Valera was prepared to give credit to the Protestants of the north for holding out for their aspirations and interests, but he told them that they were only a small minority and that if they did not come in on the Sinn Féin side they would have to go under; Ulster 'should not be petted and the interests of the majority sacrificed to please her'.[65] He regarded the Ulster unionist as a brother, but continued 'if my brother stepped in the way of Ireland's freedom I would endeavour to sweep him from the path'.[66] Kevin O'Higgins illustrated a common view in his (historically defensible, but politically ungenerous) description of the unionists as an alien minority introduced by ruthless confiscation and systematic plantation. The Ulster problem was an English creation, and the British government

> fanned the flames of religious bigotry until they blazed with a fierce and evil glow unknown in any other quarter of the world ... The leaders of Sinn Féin will never temporise with or pander to the forces of disloyalty in Ireland whether before or after the recognition of the Irish Republic. They will never admit the right of any portion of Ireland to secede from the Irish nation. If those who were planted in Ireland three centuries ago on the confiscated territory of the native Irish are not prepared to live in loyalty and obedience to the Government of Ireland then they can leave the country and the Irish government will be prepared to acquire their interest not by confiscation but by purchase.[67]

The issue was seen in stark terms. There were only two parties in Ireland, the Old Irish and those who stood for England; Ulster unionists must either accept that they were part of the Irish nation or else proclaim themselves an English garrison.[68] The unionists were often viewed as puppets manipulated by Bonar Law and Lloyd George, or as 'a parasitic growth upon the trunk of British

---

[64] O'Hegarty to Gavan Duffy, 27 Aug. 1919, Gavan Duffy MSS, NAI, 1125/2.

[65] *Saturday Record*, 7 July 1917, supplement; *II*, 6 July 1917.

[66] *Saturday Record*, 21 July 1917; see John Bowman, *De Valera and the Ulster question, 1917–1973* (Oxford, 1982), pp. 31–7.

[67] *Nationalist and Leinster Times*, 12 July 1919. His views changed; see, for example, *DE, official report*, 1, col. 482 (20 Sept. 1922).

[68] De Valera, *II*, 18 Feb. 1918; Griffith, cited in 'Sinn Fein meetings', CO.904/23/3 (13 Sept. 1917).

policy', rather than as a separate community in their own right.[69] Before the war, *Irish Freedom* could declare blithely that 'nothing separates Ulster from the rest of Ireland but prejudice, ignorance and unreasoning fear', as if such obstacles could be removed easily.[70] After the rising 'Ulster' was seen as a barrier used by the British to block Sinn Féin's advance, and the opposition of a million northern Protestants was dismissed as 'really a question of ignorance in Ulster about the fundamental facts of the life both of Ulster and the rest of Ireland'.[71] As late as 1921 Collins believed that 'the old Pale finds its present-day counterpart in Belfast and its surrounding country. All that must be redeemed for Ireland.'[72]

A year later the party's officer board advised 'the Irish of the six northern counties to continue refusing to recognize [the] Northern parliament and government';[73] clearly, the Ulster unionists did not count as 'Irish'. For the *Irish Bulletin* it was significant that disorders in Belfast and other areas of the northeast began in the same month as the British authorities intensified their campaign against the IRA elsewhere in Ireland, 'and it has been clear from the beginning that the two movements were directed by the same minds'.[74] Irish nationalists recognized all too rarely the ability and willingness of Ulster unionists to act in what they perceived to be their own interests, without any need for prodding by London politicians. One exception to this tendency came from the radical and erratic Fr O'Flanagan. In late 1916 he conceded that the 'two-nation theory' had a basis in fact; 'if you want to know a man's nationality, there are many tests, but one test is final – ask him!', and he wrote later that the Ulster unionists 'have never been absorbed into the soul of Ireland . . . If the North East really wishes to stay out, by all means let it stay out until the majority of its people become convinced that they can best pursue liberty and happiness by coming in.'[75] Critics quoted these remarks and he was careful not to repeat them.

Some of the suggestions as to how the unionists might be won over were worthy, but naïve. In his *Ethics of Sinn Féin*, Lynd reflected that 'if the average professing Nationalist had been a perceptively finer character than the average professing Unionist . . . all the noble men and women in Ireland would by the law of their natures have been attracted to the national banner'.[76] *Irish Freedom* acknowledged the justice of some unionist objections, as in the corruption in

[69] Callanan, *T. M. Healy*, p. 571.   [70] *Irish Freedom*, Apr. 1912.

[71] *Ard-Fheis Sinn Féin, 16th October, 1919, hon. secretaries' report*, RB, 8786(1).

[72] Collins to de Valera, 15 Jan. 1921, NAI, DE, 2/266.

[73] Officer board, minutes, 21 Apr. 1922, NAI, 2B/82/116(12).   [74] *Irish Bulletin*, 2 Sept. 1921.

[75] *Leader*, 12, 26 Aug. 1916, pp. 17, 60; see Carroll, *They have fooled you again*, pp. 45–50, and above, p. 79.   [76] *Ethics of Sinn Féin*, p. 6.

appointments by local boards, and in 'the abiding vices of most of us, unpunctuality, unreliability, irresponsibility . . . all these must go also'.[77] It was not a policy which could guarantee speedy results.

While some Sinn Féin propaganda tended to dismiss Ulster's relative prosperity as a myth, Pim attempted in his usual coarse manner to appeal to what he saw as the unionists' commercial instincts. He assured them that, in contrast to supporters of the Parliamentary Party who could be instantly recognized as 'oily, red-faced, false-eyed, cunning, half-washed, peering creatures . . . national degenerates', Sinn Féiners were 'clean, clever, hard-headed, sensible, shrewd, monied people . . . keen business men, who regard the independence of Ireland as a business proposition'.[78] It is hardly surprising that Sinn Féin propaganda failed to impress the unionists.

Others among the (few) Ulstermen who were prominent in Sinn Féin could also show themselves blind to the daily realities of life in their province. Shortly before the election of the Northern Irish parliament in May 1921, Eoin MacNeill lamented that the Belfast republicans 'have inherited and failed to cast off the old traditions of regarding their local opponents as the principal enemy', and he deplored 'the absence or weakness of the clear national ideal'.[79] Sinn Féiners either gazed at or away from London, but they glanced only rarely at Belfast. Even when they made a sustained effort in the north, as in the 1921 election, some did so out of a sense of obligation or even with signs of distaste; after the poll but before the results had been announced, Páidín O'Keeffe wrote to de Valera, 'I hope we are finished with the North now; in my opinion they have got the last chance.'[80]

A few Sinn Féin leaders were more subtle. Erskine Childers, for example, was prepared to grant the unionists local power in a federalized Ireland. Such a settlement, involving unionist control of education in any devolved area, would be opposed by the Irish Catholic Church (which took a more rigid view in such matters than did its weaker or more flexible counterparts in other countries). The prospect of disagreement with the Church over such an issue did not discourage him. He was also prepared to placate Belfast industry by concluding a free trade treaty with Britain for a certain number of years.[81] This represented a modification of Griffith's protectionist principles which had made little appeal to a north-east Ulster dependent on its trade with Britain. Perhaps in a similar fashion, de Valera told a private meeting of the Dáil that 'if the Republic were

---

[77] *Irish Freedom*, Mar. 1913, editorial.   [78] Pim, *Three Letters for unionists only!*, p. 2.

[79] MacNeill, memo, 12 May 1921, MacN, LA1/G/179.

[80] O'Keeffe to de Valera, 26 May 1921, EdeV.

[81] Childers to Gavan Duffy, 5 Mar. 1920, GD, 5582.

recognised, he would be in favour of giving each county power to vote itself out of the Republic if it so wished'.[82] But only a month earlier Lloyd George had made it perfectly clear that there would be no such recognition of an Irish republic.

One prospect which Sinn Féiners were not prepared to confront, or even to contemplate, was that by now the Irish unionists could be regarded only to a limited degree as 'agents of the Tories'. Once the Conservatives had entered the cabinet in 1915 their need of the unionists vanished, even though in most cases they retained a sense of obligation and even of goodwill towards their Ulster allies. Southern unionists displayed their independence of mind by wrecking the proposed home rule settlement in 1916, which had been supported by most of the Tory leadership, and soon afterwards the northerners showed themselves equally determined in the Irish Convention of 1917–18.

The unionists remained intransigent, and some Conservatives came to regard them as an embarrassment, but unpopularity did not deter the Ulstermen from pursuing their interests with characteristic tenacity. They dismissed suggestions that they might be conceded local autonomy or financial privileges within an all-Ireland context; still less were they concerned with any reformation of character on the part of Irish nationalists. Their objections to home rule, and *a fortiori* to the idea of a republic, went deeper than most Irish nationalists were able to imagine. Collectively they suspected, and in many individual cases they loathed, both Catholics and Catholicism. Such views were fuelled by a scorn for what they saw as the improvidence of their nationalist fellow-islanders, and by fear of high taxation under a Dublin parliament. They dreaded the thought that the Ulster Catholics, underdogs for more than three centuries, might exploit a Dublin government to acquire an equal status in their province; or, even worse, that they might begin to enjoy in their turn the sort of local hegemony that the unionists themselves had exercised for so long.

These attitudes were totally at variance with the doctrines and assumptions of Irish nationalism. The prominence of Protestants in the nationalists' ranks, from Tone and the United Irishmen to Parnell and the home rulers, and the emphasis given to a geographic rather than a historic or confessional image of the community or the nation, accustomed them to the belief that 'Irish domicile *per se* created Irish nationality'.[83] Sinn Féin's ideology blinded it to unacceptable realities. In theory its nationalism was inclusive, but it made no attempt to embrace the unionists' culture, accommodate their interests or calm

---

[82] *DE, private sessions*, p. 29 (22 Aug. 1921).

[83] Oliver MacDonagh, *States of mind: a study of Anglo-Irish-conflict, 1780–1980* (London, 1983), p. 18.

their fears. In practice it was southern, exclusive, Gaelic and Catholic in its attitudes and personnel.

The Ulster unionists' hostility could not be disposed of simply by reason and goodwill; nor, in the light of the support which they continued to receive from the Conservatives, was it likely that they could be overcome by force. The problems which resulted were so grave, and apparently so insoluble, that in general most Sinn Féiners preferred not to think about them. The quantity of statements and documents dealing with the unionist minority was remarkably small, and the quality of the arguments was unimpressive. Most separatists acted, and apparently even thought, in terms of a homogenous nationalist Ireland; the first task was to achieve independence, and the Ulster question, along with various other problems, could then be solved more easily. The few actions which were taken by Sinn Féin, the IRA and the Dáil proved to be disastrous.

The boycott of Belfast goods imposed by the Dáil in January 1921 was an understandable reaction to the discrimination and attacks suffered by the nationalist minority in the north-east, but the measure failed to take account of economic realities and it was self-destructive in its effects. When Catholics were expelled from their workplaces in 1920, and were replaced by Protestants, there were no other jobs available for them in a time of deepening economic recession; and to eject Protestants in turn from their newly acquired posts would be politically unacceptable to unionists and their Conservative supporters.

The solution which was adopted by the Dáil, and which was implemented in part by Sinn Féin, did more credit to their hearts than to their heads. In the words of an official proclamation, 'it should be explained to shopkeepers that trading with Belfast means endorsing the Orange atrocities'.[84] Imposing a series of barriers to Belfast's trade with nationalist Ireland did undoubtedly result in financial losses to some unionist firms, but it did not bring about the reinstatement of any expelled Catholic workers. In the long term it increased even further Belfast's economic dependence on its British markets, and it added an economic partition of Ireland to deepen the political and administrative divisions which Lloyd George's government was busily entrenching at precisely that time. (However, this was not simply a policy imposed by blinkered southerners. When the party's standing committee met Ulster delegates to the Sinn Féin *ardchomhairle*, they too were unanimous in their support of the Belfast boycott.[85])

A few discerning critics denounced the boycott, but they were in a small minority at a time when the dominant reaction was simply a desire to *do* something. In the same issue of *Old Ireland* in which P. S. O'Hegarty declared that

---

[84] Proclamation, Mar. 1921, NAI, DE, 2/110.   [85] SCM, 12 Aug. 1921.

'England, not Ulster, is the enemy to be fought', that the boycott accepted partition, and that it would have deplorable consequences, another (anonymous) writer argued that the boycott 'is the only weapon left us by England, who backs Belfast with her soldiers . . . if Sinn Féin were forced to use that weapon it could smash Belfast in a month'.[86]

Nationalist Ireland was outraged when the island was divided by the 1920 Government of Ireland Act, but the attention of the Dáil, Sinn Féin and the IRA remained fixed resolutely on their struggle in the south. Before and during the treaty negotiations the question of partition was not taken seriously by the Irish leaders, and its main function was described brutally by de Valera at a meeting of the Irish cabinet: 'if a break is inevitable, Ulster would be the best question on which to break'.[87] The cabinet had not yet formulated its Ulster policy when it sent the delegates to London, and partition was to be no more than a tactic in the negotiations.[88] In the course of the public debates on the treaty only 9 pages (of 338) were devoted to the north; otherwise the concern of virtually all the deputies was with the degree of independence which would be available to the rest of the country.[89] But these debates represented the caring, all-Ireland face of the Dáil, and in the private sessions both pro- and anti-treaty deputies showed still less interest in Ulster problems; even when isolated remarks and sentences are included in the total, the question still occupied less than 3 pages out of 181.

Separatists denounced Redmond and his party as 'partitionists', but their own record in tackling internal Irish divisions was no better. During the civil war the Belfast-born Seán MacEntee wrote from prison to his wife that 'in regard to Partition I am simply disgusted at the way in which the Republicans are using the plight of our people in the North as a propagandist weapon, while in their hearts they care as little about them really as the Treatyites do'.[90] This was a fair assessment. Sinn Féiners' attitudes towards Ulster were characterized by ignorance and hypocrisy. Like other aspects of the party's policy, they served to reinforce party members' confidence in their own assumptions and their indifference to hostile groups or unpleasant realities.

Perceptions of other 'outsiders' went beyond mere folly or neglect. Plunkett fulminated against the Jews who, he claimed, resorted to sweated labour,

---

[86] *Old Ireland*, 21 Feb. 1921, pp. 37, 40–1.   [87] Cabinet minutes, 13 Nov. 1921, NAI, DE, 1/3.

[88] See Laffan, *Partition of Ireland*, pp. 80–3.

[89] Maureen Wall, 'Partition: the Ulster question (1916–1926)', in Williams, *Irish struggle*, p. 87. The private Dáil sessions had not yet been released when this book was published.

[90] MacEntee to Margaret MacEntee, n.d., [late 1922/early 1923], MacEntee MSS, UCDA, P67/74(83).

engaged in political and commercial jobbery, published pornographic journals and (working together with the trusts and the Freemasons) had initiated and directed the First World War. Part of his explanation for their behaviour lay in the fact that 'their codes of honour and morals are not Christian'.[91] In a similar mood a *Prospectus of the Sinn Féin clubs* (apparently never published) complained that Ireland was not allowed to vote money towards a Catholic chapel for the National University. This was in contrast to the pattern in India where the viceroy had recently opened a university which taught 'the Brahmin doctrine of cow-worship', and to the establishment of a university in Khartoum, 'where Moslem "theologians" are subsidised to teach polygamy to the young Arabs'. Accompanying the mutterings about Jews, Masons and Orangemen was the complaint that according to the plans for home rule the sovereign independence enjoyed by the 'Nigger state of Liberia' was too lofty an ideal for the Irish people to cherish.[92]

On occasion such views were put into practice, if on a limited scale. Local Volunteer units in areas such as Mayo were tempted to uphold moral standards and eradicate foreign elements from 'Gaelic culture', attacking certain books and non-Irish fashions, music and dances, while in Cork the IRA drove 'tramps' out of one district after another.[93] Whatever might be the party's theories and principles, in practice the policy of Sinn Féin, of 'we ourselves', could at times be narrow and exclusive.

Language

The positive side of Sinn Féin's rejection of Britain, of its blindness to Ulster unionism, and of its intermittent intolerance towards other groups, was its belief in the ideology of Irish-Ireland – and in particular its commitment to the revival of the Irish language. One writer in *Irish Freedom* declared that 'Ireland can, if necessary, get along for another hundred years without Ulster, but she cannot get along for a week if the language is finally overwhelmed.'[94] Ulster and Ireland were obviously separate or separable entities. Griffith's *Sinn Féin* conflated the real and the ideal in its claim that

---

[91] Plunkett to de Valera, 2 July 1921, EdeV. Historians and others have often chosen to linger over Griffith's anti-Semitic remarks, expressions of a youthful bigotry which he outgrew, and to ignore the more vigorous and enduring prejudices displayed by many of his contemporaries. See Maye, *Arthur Griffith*, pp. 362–72.   [92] 'Prospectus of the Sinn Féin clubs' (typescript), CP, 11,405.

[93] Augusteijn, *From public defiance to guerrilla warfare*, p. 310; Hart, *I.R.A. and its enemies*, pp. 150, 311.   [94] 'Sarsfield', *Irish Freedom*, Feb. 1913.

from whatever sources our origins sprang, to-day we are all Irishmen and Irishwomen with a common language and a common history. That most of us neither know that language nor that history is our misfortune and our shame, but it cannot affect the immutable fact of our nationality.[95]

Many years later, de Valera told the Gaelic League *ard-fheis* that, if he could choose between having freedom without the language and the language without freedom, he would rather have the latter.[96] So, at least in theory, the country's freedom and unity were to be subordinated to the revival of the 'national language' which by now was spoken by a mere 13 per cent of the nation.

The 1891 census figures had revealed a drastic decline in the number of people who could speak Irish, and the shock which they provoked was one impetus towards founding the Gaelic League; yet in the course of the next twenty years the minority able to speak the language decreased by another 14.4 per cent, while the number of monoglot Irish speakers fell by 56 per cent.[97] To an ever-increasing extent English was becoming the mother tongue of the Irish people, and many Sinn Féin activists argued that this trend should be reversed. The more dogmatic among them believed that only the small minority who spoke (or tried to speak, or wished to speak) the Irish language represented the abstract 'Ireland'; here too their ideology facilitated their dismissal of the masses and strengthened their faith in themselves. The words 'Sinn Féin' could refer to a small as well as to a large group.

There was a dual inspiration or driving force behind this linguistic nationalism. For many people its central aspect was their deep love of the Irish language, of what MacNeill described as its beauty and power,[98] and this commitment was accompanied by a sense of loss, of rootlessness and of cultural and national impoverishment at the prospect of its final disappearance. Douglas Hyde claimed that Irish had never been approached, either in age, variety or value, by any vernacular language in Europe, while at a less exalted level it offered the young Frank O'Connor an escape from a life of drudgery and humiliation which – for him – was symbolized by the English language.[99] If English snobbery would always result in the rejection of the Irish people, they could at least build up a Gaelic counter-culture.[100] Such views were accompanied by a repu-

---

[95] *Sinn Féin*, 26 Sept. 1909, editorial.   [96] *Connaught Telegraph*, 13 Aug. 1921, editorial.

[97] *Census of Ireland, 1911. General report*, p. 291.

[98] Brian Ó Cuív, 'MacNeill and the Irish language', in F. X. Martin and F. J. Byrne (eds.), *The scholar revolutionary: Eoin MacNeill, 1867–1945* (Shannon, 1973), p. 10.

[99] Janet and Gareth W. Dunleavy, *Douglas Hyde: a maker of modern Ireland* (Berkeley, 1991), p. 164; Frank O'Connor, *An only child* (London, 1961), p. 175.

[100] Garvin, *Nationalist revolutionaries*, p. 87.

diation of English as an alien influence, as yet another example of British conquest and oppression, and by a corresponding belief by many people in Irish 'as
the most distinctive symbol of their nationality'.[101] It could serve as a barrier
against alien influences, and according to Terence MacSwiney 'our frontier is
twofold, the language and the sea'.[102] It permitted a new self-confidence to
people who lacked it, and Thomas MacDonagh believed that 'the Gaelic Revival
has given to some of us a new arrogance'.[103]

There was probably little or no exaggeration in Eamonn Ceannt's claim that
90 per cent of those who had assisted in the work of the Gaelic League, as well
as all its outside supporters, acted solely 'from motives of nationality'.[104]
Driven by both pride and resentment, many nationalists hoped for a cultural
revolution. Ernest Blythe demanded that the Gaelic League should be as much
against English as for Irish; the country must be relieved as quickly as possible
from the degradation of having a foreign tongue spoken as the vernacular on
its soil.[105] Pim's *Irishman* dismissed English as the language of newspapers such
as the *Daily Sketch* and the *News of the World*, and insisted that it must not
'shoulder out the unsullied speech of the Gael' from Irish churches.[106]
Anglicization had turned Ireland into a 'population of semi-slaves'.[107] Irish revolutionaries had so little respect for the mass of the people that they must have
found it easy to dismiss the national linguistic preference for English as lazy
and unpatriotic.

Many of those who wished to weaken or sever Ireland's cultural links with
Britain hoped that the ensuing renaissance would be accompanied by a national
insurrection, and that this would drive out not only the English language, but
also British institutions, and values, and the soldiers who upheld them. They
saw this as a natural progression. It was no coincidence that several of the Easter
Week rebel leaders should have been committed to the language revival, and
that two of them (Pearse and Ceannt) were prominent in the League. Of a
hundred variables tested in one survey, the best single predictor of republican
violence between 1916 and 1923 was the percentage of national schools in
which Irish was taught for fees. But the links between language and political loyalties were less strong.[108] Even if only in a vague and indirect manner, 'Irish-
Ireland' ideas influenced many activists in the revolutionary movement, and in

---

[101] De Valera, *II*, 18 Feb. 1918.

[102] Terence MacSwiney, *Principles of Freedom* (Dublin, 1921), p. 131.

[103] Thomas MacDonagh, *Literature in Ireland* (Dublin, 1916), p. 167.

[104] *Sinn Féin*, 15 Feb. 1913.   [105] *Irish Freedom*, Feb. 1914.   [106] *Irishman*, 25 Nov. 1916.

[107] O'Rahilly, *An Claidheamh Soluis*, 7 Feb. 1914.

[108] Hart, 'Geography of revolution in Ireland', p. 170.

consequence they had an influence after 1922 which would have appeared totally disproportionate only a few years earlier.

About half of those who would later serve as government ministers or senior civil servants in the first fifty years after independence had been members of the Gaelic League in their youth.[109] They benefited from discrimination on their behalf by ideologically minded governments. In 1919 the *Leader* advised that people would have to use Irish for their own advancement, and three years later it returned triumphantly to the theme:

> One revolution had we here,
> But soon another will appear,
> When shoneens will to Irish fly
> To get a finger in the pie.[110]

This policy was soon implemented; independent Irish governments fulfilled the wishes of the zealot who called for 'language bigots to go out into the highways and byways and speak the language, and shove it down the throats of all and sundry, whether they want it or not'.[111] The same desire to get on in the world, 'to get a finger in the pie', which had led to the decline of the language in the eighteenth and nineteenth centuries would now be used to revive it in the twentieth. It was significant that the truce in July 1921 was followed by a remarkable increase in the sale of Irish grammars, dictionaries and textbooks.[112]

In so far as Sinn Féin had an ideology and wished to transform Ireland and the Irish people, its ideology was linguistic nationalism. The country would manifest its independence by changing its language for a second time and by reverting to Irish as its vernacular tongue. This vision of Ireland was narrower than that shared by most other forms of Irish nationalism, and (quite reasonably) its adherents made little attempt to appeal to the Ulster unionists – who, with only a handful of exceptions, had no enthusiasm for a Gaelic Ireland. The fact that 'compulsory Irish' would drive yet another wedge between Catholic nationalists and Protestant unionists was a matter which, logically enough, caused little concern.[113] Although Sinn Féiners desired national unity, from time to time they acted in such a way as to prejudice its achievement: 'the greater in particular their insistence upon the Catholic-Gaelic foundation of Irish

---

[109] Garvin, *Evolution of Irish nationalist politics*, p. 102.
[110] *Leader*, 22 Mar. 1919, p. 151, 4 Nov. 1922, p. 297.   [111] *Irish Freedom*, Nov. 1911.
[112] O'Hegarty, *Victory of Sinn Féin*, p. 64.
[113] See Bew, *Ideology and the Irish question*, pp. 84–90.

nationhood, the more acute the Northerners' feeling that they were, and indeed were deemed to be, alien to it'.[114]

The separatists' language policy revealed an underlying insecurity. It was often based on an assumption that the Irish people should speak Irish because only then would they become significantly different from the British – and only then would the anti-British revolution be justified. After independence they would have to be made 'free' to justify the effort in freeing them.

Particularly in the short term it would be difficult to implement such a linguistic ideal. *Nationality* printed Irish conversation lessons in early 1918, and in the South Sligo constituency it was proposed that all clubs should send at least one member to an Irish language class; those who belonged to this core group would soon in turn be able to teach their colleagues.[115] There are a few such examples, but not many, and in general, party members were willing to leave the task of reviving the language to the Gaelic League or to the future government of an independent Irish state. There was little response when members were encouraged to write to each other and to party headquarters 'in Irish, rather than in the language of the enemy'.[116] (In the bitter aftermath of the treaty debates Cathal Brugha went further when he condescended to speak to his opponents in English, 'the language of their masters'.[117]) De Valera began one speech by remarking that he would be ashamed to address his audience in the language of the foreigner, but after a brief introduction in Irish he triumphed over his shame.[118]

One of the resolutions at the October 1917 convention proposed that Irish should be the language of the party's executive, and that people who could not speak Irish should not be eligible for election to the executive or should not be nominated as candidates for parliament. Communications were to be banned unless addressed in the national language. Another resolution demanded that Irish should 'be made imperative' for all party members. These proposals were rejected on the grounds that they were not sensible and could not be acted upon immediately.[119] But such voices were prophetic of the future, and in later decades a privileged and illiberal establishment would impose the task of learning 'compulsory' Irish on a passive, acquiescent but unenthusiastic majority.

Irish-speaking candidates were chosen for the Gaeltacht areas in the 1918

---

[114] Nicholas Mansergh, *The prelude to partition: concepts and aims in Ireland and India* (Cambridge, 1978), p. 19.   [115] *Sligo Champion*, 23 Feb. 1918.

[116] *Work for a Sinn Féin branch* (pamphlet, Dublin, n.d. [1917]), p. 4.

[117] *DE, 1921–22*, p. 465 (19 May 1922).   [118] *Clare Champion*, 30 June 1917.

[119] *II*, 27 Oct. 1917.

general election, and it was suggested that this practice should be extended to the local government elections. The Gaelic League argued that it would be disastrous if non-Irish speakers and election literature in English were to be 'let loose' in Irish-speaking districts. Efforts were made to implement such ideas, but the standing committee turned down later proposals that the League might be involved in the choice of Sinn Féin candidates.[120] This preference for Irish speakers reduced drastically the pool of talent available for election, and when Liam de Róiste wished to retire from public life in 1922 he feared (rightly) that he would be forced to run for office once more because Irish-speaking candidates like himself were difficult to find.[121] In a similar mood, J. J. O'Kelly, minister for Irish in the first Dáil cabinet, lamented that 'men with a knowledge of Irish were almost impossible to get'.[122]

When the Dáil assembled in January 1919 the proceedings of its first meeting were held entirely in Irish, except for the English and French translations of its declaration of independence and its democratic programme. The result was that few deputies or members of the public understood what was happening, although from press accounts it appears that their incomprehension did not lessen the dignity of the occasion; indeed its dignity might well have been enhanced. There was something theatrical, even incantatory about the ceremony, and one observer remarked that if any speaker had descended to the use of English 'it would have broken the charm and the spell and put the whole proceedings out of tune'.[123] Others made snide remarks, and one critic claimed that 'two-thirds cannot speak Gaelic, yet the debates are to be held in that tongue, and a deaf and dumb legislature proposes to administer laws for a confused people'.[124]

Such forecasts were disproved by later events, and apart from occasional set-piece speeches almost all the subsequent proceedings of the Dáil would be conducted through English. This was particularly the case when important issues such as the treaty were discussed. De Valera displayed a notable cynicism when he began his speech in the treaty debates with an apology (in Irish) that his command of the language was inadequate for him to persevere, and then explained away (in English) his change of language by claiming that he did so because otherwise some deputies would not understand him.[125]

Messages summoning deputies to Dáil meetings were printed in Irish but were accompanied by an English translation.[126] Yet even the basic task of writing

---

[120] SCM, 16 Sept. 1918, 20 Apr. 1920.　　[121] De Róiste, diary, 30 Apr. 1922, CAI, U271/A/43.

[122] DE, private sessions, p. 40 (22 Aug. 1921).　　[123] Leader, 1 Feb. 1919, p. 629.

[124] Daily Mail, cited in II, 24 Jan. 1919.　　[125] DE, treaty debate, p. 7 (14 Dec. 1921).

[126] E.g., summons, 28 July 1919, CP, 11,374(19).

these Irish messages proved to be too great a burden, and before the cabinet secretary circulated formal letters to newly elected deputies in 1921 he had first to
ask one of their number to translate them into the official national language.[127]
Not surprisingly, he turned down a request that he supply the Irish form of
names which could be used when issuing emigration permits.[128] When de
Valera communicated with Lloyd George in 1921 his letters were first translated
into Irish by J. J. O'Kelly, and then the original English version was labelled
'official translation'.[129] As a gesture towards the language the first Dáil cabinet
included a minister for Irish, whose responsibilities also included education.
Tragically for the history of independent Ireland, even when a separate
Department of Education was established in 1921 it retained its predecessor's
priorities, and over many decades it subordinated the educational needs of Irish
children to the dictates of linguistic nationalism.

The Sinn Féin leadership shared and reflected the movement's concerns,
weaknesses and preference for gestures rather than for action. In the four and a
half years of its existence, from January 1918 to June 1922, the standing committee held 160 meetings, the minutes of which cover more than 540 pages; yet
only one brief passage of less than seven lines is written in Irish.[130] Occasionally
a form of pidgin was employed, as in the entry which began 'the Standing
Committee met again on the 12adh Bealtaine 1921'. The 'formal' role of the language is illustrated by the habit of using the Irish version of members' names in
attendance lists, and thereafter reverting to the English – so that within a few
lines 'Siobhán Bean an Phaoraigh' became 'Mrs Wyse Power'. Although
'cumann' was the official term for a Sinn Féin branch, it was rarely used except
in lists or official documents. The fact that almost every speaker at the *ard-fheis*
in 1922 used the English word 'club' provoked a sharp comment about party
members' ignorance of the language which they asked other people to learn.[131]
Similarly, while these members might be referred to in the Irish form (normally
although not always as 'Sinn Féinidthe'), even language enthusiasts such as de
Valera and MacNeill used the popular term of 'Sinn Féiner'. One London sympathizer used another variant: Sinn Fenian.[132]

At local level most people were satisfied with gestures towards using the language. For example, after Sinn Féin's victory in the 1920 local elections the new
town councillors of Ballyshannon (Co. Donegal) pledged their allegiance to the

---

[127] O'Hegarty to Piaras Béaslaí, 12 May 1921, NAI, DE, 2/1.

[128] Stack to O'Hegarty, 15 June 1921; O'Hegarty to Stack, 16 June 1921, NAI, DE, 2/8/27.

[129] J. J. O'Kelly, *Stepping-stones* (Dublin, n.d. [1939/40], p. 16.

[130] SCM, 10 Mar. 1922. The subject matter was appropriate: the use of Irish in the press.

[131] *II*, 22 Feb. 1922.   [132] Margaret Kendrick to de Valera, 6 Aug. [?1917], EdeV.

Dáil and decided unanimously that street names should be marked exclusively in Irish because 'it would be the language of future generations'.[133] As in other areas, the leaders' initiatives sometimes met with an apathetic reaction from their followers; in 1922 the pro-treaty faction of Sinn Féin sent samples of hand-bills in Irish to all its directors of elections, but the response was disappointing.[134] However, the pattern was not always one of young Irish-speaking zealots jolting their more sluggish Anglophone elders into tardy action, and on occasion the linguistic roles were reversed. When Florence O'Donoghue was on the run during the closing months of the Anglo-Irish War, he and his companion were billeted with an old man and woman, neither of whom could speak English. Since the young Volunteers had little or no Irish the two pairs were virtually unable to communicate with each other.[135]

In 1919 Desmond FitzGerald expressed an opinion which conflicted with many Sinn Féin assumptions and attitudes. He claimed that 'the Irish language was dying. It had been dying ever since Easter Week, dying ever since the Dáil came into existence', and that 'English was more the language in Ireland than French was in France'. He argued that the separation of Ireland from Britain was more urgent in cultural than in political terms, but that modern dances would be cultivated in a free Ireland, and that while the kilt might be Celtic, the Irish people would have to abandon the idea of wearing it. Ireland needed outside influences, and where these were necessary they should be sought on the Continent of Europe rather than in Britain; Irish people should go into the world and choose what was best and most adaptable.[136]

FitzGerald's views had no appeal to the predominant Irish-Ireland tendency in the separatist movement, to elements which had little concern with Continental Europe and which were committed to the kilt, Irish dances, and above all, the national tongue. His was a lone voice against a consensus. A commitment to reviving the language, varying in intensity from the vague to the dedicated, was a distinguishing feature of the movement and the party.

The republic

Other areas of belief and attitude proved more controversial, and none was more divisive than the question of the 'republic'; along with the related issue of

---

[133] *Donegal Democrat*, 11 June 1920.

[134] Propaganda sub-committee minutes, 9 May 1922, FG, p. 37.

[135] O'Donoghue to 'G', 28 May 1921, FO'D, 31,176.

[136] *Nationalist and Leinster Times*, 31 May 1919.

civil–military relations it would tear apart the country and the party in 1922.[137] Before 1916 republicans were no more than a small minority among Irish nationalists. But having seen their flag raised in Dublin in Easter Week, having been inspired by it, and in some cases having fought under it, they were even less inclined towards compromise than they had been in earlier years.

After the outbreak of the First World War the IRB's newspaper had claimed, probably on tactical grounds, that the German kaiser was a high-souled patriot and that if all kings were like him there would be no republican governments.[138] An anonymous IRB member had written that 'Fenian propagandist work in the 'sixties was entirely separatist, with practically no reference to Republicanism.'[139] However this flexibility was matched by sterner declarations such as the following: 'our aim is the establishment of an Irish Republic, for the simple and sole reason that no other ending to our quarrel with England could be either adequate or final . . . To compromise is to surrender the nation, the national life, every noble tradition, every heroic aspiration in our people.'[140] Just as the appeal of the Irish language was enhanced by the fact that the British people spoke English, so Ireland must be a republic because Britain was a monarchy.

Pearse and other rebels might have been prepared to accept the idea of a German monarch,[141] but their own actions lessened the chances of such open-mindedness being acceptable to those who came after them. Their successors interpreted the proclamation in a more literal and fundamentalist sense, as a decision or a doctrine on which there could be no turning back, as an ideal which pushed many of them into entrenched positions from which retreat would be difficult or impossible. The executed leaders were seen as having died not simply for an independent Ireland, but specifically for an Irish republic, and their collective commitment became sacrosanct. As Patrick McCartan remarked some years later, it was not for dominion home rule or a dual monarchy that Pearse and Clarke gave their lives in Easter Week.[142]

De Valera appeared to show signs of moderation when he ruled out the idea of a king belonging to the House of Windsor, while conceding that 'if there is to be a monarchy in this land it will be an Irish monarchy'.[143] However, even

---

[137] See below, pp. 351–60.   [138] *Irish Freedom*, Oct. 1914.   [139] *Ibid.*, Dec. 1910.

[140] *Ibid.*, Nov. 1912, editorial.

[141] Edwards, *Patrick Pearse*, pp. 223–4; F. X. Martin, 'The 1916 Rising – a coup d'état or a "bloody protest"?', *Studia Hibernica*, 8 (1968), p. 106; FitzGerald, *Memoirs*, pp. 140–1.

[142] *II*, 4 Oct. 1921. Along similar lines, in the treaty debates Piaras Béaslaí could not imagine anyone dying for de Valera's formula of external association (*DE, private sessions*, p. 231 (17 Dec. 1921)). See below, pp. 363–4.

[143] 'Sinn Fein convention 1917', CO.904/23/5, p. 51; see above, p. 118.

such limited flexibility was uncharacteristic of many separatists, and in general the demand for a republic hardened in the years after 1916. In his memorandum and letter written from Lewes Jail, at the time of the Longford by-election campaign, de Valera referred to 'Ireland's freedom', 'absolute independence' and 'the Independence position', and he described the prisoners as 'soldiers of the Irish nation', but he never mentioned the word 'republic'.[144] Yet soon after his release, having realized how opinion had changed during the year of his imprisonment, he felt able to make repeated demands for an Irish republic. His longhand notes for one speech in Clare refer not only to Ireland's claim of absolute independence and the demand for a sovereign state, but also to the proclamation of the republic in Easter Week; 'to that govmt when in a visible shape I offered my allegiance and to its spirit I owe all my allegiance still'.[145]

Already during the Clare campaign the *Freeman's Journal* declared that de Valera must wield a potent spell; 'at a wave of his hand, the Constitutionalists of April have become the red revolutionists of July', the Girondins had been transformed into Jacobins.[146] The *Round Table* commented that the question of the Irish republic was the one definite point on which de Valera was pledged to his followers.[147]

Others had made such demands long before the Lewes prisoners were released, and Collins had been one of the more vociferous republicans. His reasons would seem to have been nationalistic rather than ideological, and he remarked later, 'we repudiated the British form of government, not because it was monarchical, but because it was British'.[148] Even Griffith's Sinn Féin appreciated that the times had changed and that the policy of the 'king, lords and commons' might have an even narrower appeal than in former years. It accepted that the aims as well as the tactics of separatism had been radicalized. Throughout 1917 there were only two references in *Nationality* to the old Sinn Féin beliefs: a declaration that the party's objective remained essentially that which had been pursued by Deák in Hungary between 1850 and 1867, and a contrast between Greek republicanism and the Gaelic idea of monarchy.[149] Griffith was not prepared to swim against the strong new tide, and Grattan's Parliament was now effectively ignored. At the end of 1918 one of his models disappeared as the Austro-Hungarian dual monarchy collapsed and was replaced by a series of successor states; much of its territory was carved up between three new republics, Austria, Czechoslovakia and Poland. According to some definitions the pre-

---

[144] Memo., Easter Sunday/Monday, letter to Simon Donnelly, 28 Apr. 1917, EdeV.

[145] Notes, July 1917, EdeV.   [146] *FJ*, 6 July 1917, editorial.

[147] *Round Table*, Sept. 1917, p. 767.   [148] Michael Collins, *The path to freedom* (Dublin, 1922), p. 71.   [149] *Nationality*, 26 May 1917, 8 Sept. 1917, editorials.

rising Sinn Féin was not a separatist body, but such an accusation could not be thrown against Griffith and his colleagues after 1917. Even his newspaper was able to declare that 'nothing short of the establishment of an Independent Irish Republic will satisfy the aspirations of the people of Ireland'.[150]

The republican demand was popular among ordinary party members as well as among the leaders. In late 1917 a meeting of twenty-two Sinn Féin clubs in south Sligo approved 'the full Republican programme', while a year later the RIC inspector general warned that 'practically the entire Nationalist youth of both sexes in the country have become obsessed with the idea of an Irish Republic and with the policy of abstention from the House of Commons'.[151]

The October 1917 convention formally replaced the party's monarchism with a commitment to the goal of a republic, along lines suggested by de Valera in a speech which he had made in Rathfarnham a month earlier. Then he had declared that 'they would have to proclaim themselves as Irish Republicans – words that would be understood in America, Russia, and France as no others could be', and that once freedom had been obtained they could choose between a monarchy or a republic.[152] This concession was virtually meaningless, since by now there were few committed monarchists left among those who were dubious of the republican aim: those moderates for whom, as Blythe remarked during the treaty debates, republicanism was 'not a national principle but a political preference . . . a means to an end and not an end in itself'.[153] Their objections lay rather in the wisdom of seeking a republic, and the probable bloody and frustrating consequences of persisting with such a demand.

This adoption of the new constitution was a fateful step. As with other aspects of its programme the 'republican policy' justified the leaders in ignoring or dismissing the views of most Irish people. It committed the party to a policy which some of its members would take literally, but which most of the party – to judge by the expression of its internal divisions in 1921, and by the election results in 1922 – regarded as an admirable and worthy ultimate objective which could nonetheless be sacrificed in a compromise settlement. In the words of one later commentator:

> to some who held what I may call the transcendental view, the Republic was an article of faith: others considered that at that juncture in world affairs there were sober and valid reasons for thinking that an independent republic could be obtained; still others – and those perhaps a majority – regarded

[150] *Nationality*, 17 May 1919, editorial.
[151] *Sligo Champion*, 27 Oct. 1917; IG's report, Nov. 1918, CO.904/107.   [152] *II*, 24 Sept. 1917.
[153] *DE, treaty debate*, p. 192 (3 Jan. 1922). See above, pp. 117–18.

the republic only as the best and most dramatic symbol of independence; a few accepted it cynically as a convenient piece of political clap trap.[154]

The demands for a republic were made with increasing vigour. Seán T. O'Kelly rejected the idea of a dominion settlement and remarked to William O'Brien that while 'it may be that some day the "half-loaf" policy might again be adopted by the majority of nationalists but just now there seems no likelihood of such measures being listened to'.[155] In the 1918 general election campaign, which was already under way when O'Kelly wrote, numerous speakers declared that a vote for Sinn Féin was a vote for the republic. (This was not always the case, and in Cork radical Volunteers complained that the magic words 'Irish republic' had not been mentioned at a public meeting. The rival view, heretical in its pragmatism, was expressed succinctly: 'what we wanted to do now was to win the election, to get votes: not lay down principles'.[156] There should be no dictation by the Volunteers.)

Electors may have voted for Sinn Féin for reasons other than its republican programme; they may have wished to spite the British government or punish the Parliamentary Party, or they may have believed that there was no acceptable alternative. But they had little control over how their votes would be interpreted, and committed republicans viewed the result as an endorsement of their beliefs and methods. (Mary MacSwiney, however, admitted later that while Sinn Féin had committed itself to a republic in the 1918 election, the result 'was rather a vote against the Party than for a Republic definitely'.[157])

Dan Breen complained at the lack of support for his guerrilla group in the months after the ambush at Soloheadbeg, and that 'the people had voted for a Republic, but now they seemed to have abandoned us who had tried to bring that Republic nearer, and who had taken them at their word'.[158] It was his right to interpret their word, or their wishes. Three years later the same message was repeated to the electors: 'on your suffrage the Republic of Ireland was constitutionally founded . . . You who vote for Sinn Féin candidates will cast your votes for nothing less than for the legitimacy of the Republic.'[159] An uncontested election in most of the country ensured that, at least in 1921, few people risked having their votes used in this manner to justify measures which they might later feel tempted to reject.

---

[154] Kingsmill Moore, judgment, 26 Oct. 1948, SFFC, 2B/82/117(32), p. 9.

[155] O'Kelly to O'Brien, 19 Sept. 1918, O'Brien MSS, NLI, 11,439(6).

[156] De Róiste, diary, 2 Dec. 1918, CAI, U271/A/23.

[157] *DE, private sessions*, pp. 251–2 (17 Dec. 1921).

[158] Breen, *My fight for Irish freedom* (Dublin, 1924), p. 52.

[159] De Valera, manifesto, *Irish Bulletin*, 4 May 1921.

The Dáil duly re-proclaimed the republic of Easter Week, and Cathal Brugha, a man passionately committed to the idea of the abstract republic, ensured that an oath of allegiance to it and to the Dáil would be taken by all deputies and Volunteers.[160] The increasing use of the initials IRA (Irish Republican Army) in place of the old name, the Irish Volunteers, was yet another example of this trend. The Volunteers' journal rejected any compromise such as colonial home rule; 'we have pinned our flag, the tricolour of the Irish Republic, to the mast, and we will stand or fall by it'.[161]

It is probable that many Sinn Féin supporters regarded 'the republic' as a slogan or a battle cry, rather than as a concrete objective which must be attained; in the words of one British intelligence officer, it was 'a kind of pious opinion which must be expressed at every meeting, but which nobody from de Valera down ever hopes to see realised'.[162] There were occasional voices of caution. Two days after the Dáil had solemnly re-proclaimed the republic Griffith wrote from Gloucester Jail warning that it 'would not be advisable . . . to go into the details of an Irish Constitution at present: just keep the straight question of Irish independence first'.[163] Few of his colleagues who were at liberty paid any attention to him.

Even though crowds might sing 'we'll crown de Valera',[164] the president of Sinn Féin was elected president of the Dáil and *príomh aire*, or (as he referred to himself on occasion) 'Chief Minister of the Government'.[165] On one page of the official record he was described variously as president of the ministry, as *príomh aire* (first minister), and as president of the Dáil.[166] He soon became known as 'president', and throughout his visit to the United States he allowed himself be addressed as 'President of the Irish Republic'.[167] He became accustomed to the title, and his personal authority became intertwined with the republican idea. Nonetheless it was not until August 1921 that the Dáil formally elected him president of the republic, and a few months afterwards, in the course of the treaty debates, he described it as the most glorious title that any man could have.[168]

---

[160] *DE, 1919–21*, p. 151 (20 Aug. 1919).

[161] *An tÓglách*, 31 Jan. 1919. The republican tricolour was a relatively new symbol; see Liam de Paor, *On the Easter proclamation and other declarations* (Dublin, 1997), pp. 49–51.

[162] IO's report (S.), Jan. 1918. [163] Griffith, memo, 23 Jan. 1919, CP, 11,405.

[164] *Sligo Champion*, 24 Aug. 1918. (The lines went: 'When we were little children Johnny Redmond was a fool/ He bade us to be satisfied with something called Home Rule./ But we have learned a thing or two since we went to school,/ And we'll crown de Valera King of Ireland' (Ryan, *Remembering Sion*, p. 240).) [165] De Valera to Páidín O'Keeffe, 9 Feb. 1921, EdeV.

[166] *DE, 1919–21*, p. 34 (1 Apr. 1919). [167] Coogan, *De Valera*, p. 207.

[168] *DE, private sessions*, pp. 54–6, 217 (23 Aug., 16 Dec. 1921).

The opening of serious negotiations with the British government imposed on the Sinn Féin leaders a new need for realism, and the result was a remarkable discretion on the question of the republic. Throughout the crucial months between July and December 1921 it was almost a taboo subject.[169] It was only after the treaty had been signed, and the unsought objective of a republic had not been achieved, that the more radical members of the cabinet and the Dáil raised demands which they had failed to make in public until then.

They were able to buttress their case by referring to various sacred texts: the Easter Week proclamation, the Sinn Féin constitution of 1917 (which could be altered only by a two-thirds majority), the 1918 election manifesto, the Dáil's republican proclamation of 1919, and the 1921 election manifesto, as well as the oaths to the republic taken by members of the Dáil and the army. Some republicans may have wished to lock the Irish people into a set of demands which would give them no excuse for second thoughts, for wriggling out of what they might come to regard as rash commitments, for displaying yet once more their feeble preference for a quiet life rather than one of heroism, sacrifice and suffering. If so, they did their job well.

The British government was equally rigid, doctrinaire and ideological in its commitment to a monarchy and its refusal to tolerate the idea of an Irish republic. George Russell's *Irish Statesman* commented in 1919 that 'to some English minds there is something almost blasphemous, something bordering on the indecent, in the claim that Ireland is entitled to be a Republic'.[170] Britain had, of course, sound strategic reasons for fearing that such an unmistakable sign of full Irish sovereignty might stimulate demands for independence throughout the empire. These attitudes were reinforced by the powerful lobby in the House of Commons, in the army and among the British public, which was passionate in its commitment to the image and institution of monarchy. For example, in the mid-1930s a serving British prime minister (and former leader of the Labour Party) described a reception for dominion premiers in the following terms: 'the Empire was a great family, the gathering a family reunion, the King a paternal head. We all went away feeling that we had taken part in something very much like a Holy Communion.'[171]

The difference between the two sides lay not in any imagined contrast between British moderation and Irish fanaticism, but simply in the two countries' relative fire-power. Because of its military and economic strength Britain

---

[169] See below, p. 347.   [170] *Irish Statesman*, 27 Sept. 1919, p. 328.

[171] David Marquand, *Ramsay MacDonald* (London, 1977), p. 774, cited by David Cannadine in Eric Hobsbawm and Terence Ranger (eds.), *The invention of tradition* (Cambridge, 1983), p. 152.

could impose a modified form of its beliefs on Ireland. In the 1921 settlement many felt that there was something almost vindictive in the British insistence that members of the Irish parliament should swear an oath to the king; it was comparable to the Romans forcing defeated enemies to pass under the yoke.[172] (On the other hand it could be argued that Lloyd George sought not only to out-manoeuvre the Irish delegates, but also to deceive British public opinion and conceal from it the extent of the concessions which he had made. For him, as for his opponents, symbolic victories were important.) In the end, after the treaty was signed, most of the Irish people were prepared to do what the radicals had always feared: compromise on an issue which they regarded as being of relatively little importance.

Violence

An Irish republic could be achieved only by force; on this point there was virtual unanimity on all sides in both Ireland and Britain. Only rarely were there signs of confusion, as in the syndicated 'Sinn Féin Notes' which declared that 'an independent Irish Republic is the objective. Passive Resistance combined with an appeal to the Peace Conference is the method of achievement.'[173] Far more characteristic was de Valera's warning that only when Britain's losses through holding Ireland began to balance its gains would it begin to listen to the claims of justice.[174] Yet despite the exhortations of their leaders, and despite assurances that the nation was committed to republicanism, Irish nationalists remained divided on the question of using force in the years after the Easter Rising just as they had been divided before it.

Nonetheless, there was a significant shift after 1916, and the distinctions between separatists now tended to reflect differences of degree rather than of kind. Pearse had lamented that the generation which was then growing old had almost forgotten its heroes, and had come to believe that where these heroes 'had trodden hard and bloody ways: we should tread soft and flowering ways'. Freedom was not a status to be conceded, rather a glory to be achieved.[175] His actions and those of his fellow rebels in Easter Week revived the memory of heroes and increased admiration for the hard and bloody ways.

Soon after the end of the rising, James Stephens used language which Pearse would have admired when he wrote that

---

[172] Owen Dudley Edwards, *Eamon de Valera* (Cardiff, 1987), p. 104.

[173] 'Sinn Féin Notes', *Meath Chronicle*, 18 Jan. 1919.   [174] *FJ*, 1 Apr. 1921.

[175] Pearse, 'How does she stand?' and 'Ghosts', *Political writings*, pp. 66, 225.

if, after all her striving, freedom had come to her as a gift, as a peaceful present such as is sometimes given away with a pound of tea, Ireland would have accepted the gift with shamefacedness, and have felt that her centuries of revolt had ended in something very like ridicule. The blood of brave men had to sanctify such a consummation if the national imagination was to be stirred to the dreadful business which is the organizing of freedom.[176]

Pride in the rebels' courage and anger at their fate helped to glorify the idea of armed resistance. As the internees and prisoners were released, particularly in the two waves of December 1916 and June 1917, they made a point of justifying their own and their comrades' actions. De Valera was said to have told a crowd of young men that they should acquire rifles and shotguns, and that if nothing better were available 'you can get the old weapons of your fathers, the pike, a very good weapon at close fighting'.[177] Even Sinn Féiners on the moderate wing of the party advocated rebellion if conscription were to be imposed on the country; Griffith declared that if it were attempted he would advise the people to resist, and would take his place in such a resistance.[178] But his emphasis remained different. An editorial in *Nationality* declared that Britain should 'be fought with all things – with coal, iron, leather, woollens, as well as with the weapons of the spirit'.[179] Some Volunteers might have been surprised that guns and bullets did not feature on this list.

Irish separatists were able to point out that violence and bloodshed were not confined to Ireland; until November 1918 the country was one of the more peaceful areas of Europe, while tens of thousands of Irish volunteers who enlisted in the British army were killed fighting on the Western Front. A cartoon by Grace Plunkett contrasted the '68 Irishmen killed fighting (without pay) for the freedom of a small nation' with the 'millions of Irishmen in the army on the advice of John Redmond slaughtered in British blunders at Gallipoli, Verdun, Mons, Cambrai, the high seas etc.'[180] De Valera's papers contain a note in his own hand for a speech to be made in the Clare election campaign. It reads: 'Physical force – only, No . . . Wm Redmond. *Flanders.*'[181] The violence and the killings in Ireland between 1916 and 1923, however great the suffering they might have caused, were on a tiny scale compared with those of Continental Europe between 1914 and 1918. De Valera's predecessor as MP for East Clare was one of many millions of victims.

---

[176] Stephens, *Insurrection*, p. xii.   [177] 'Sinn Fein meetings in 1917', CO.904/23/3, p. 89.

[178] *II*, 25 Sept. 1917.   [179] *Nationality*, 5 Jan. 1918.

[180] 'Whose is the policy of bloodshed', NLI, ILB.300, P.5(4).

[181] De Valera, notes, n.d., EdeV.

A moderate Sinn Féiner complained that elements in the party rejected de Valera's political policy and refused to consider or discuss anything except fighting.[182] But those who so wished could assign to the Volunteers the responsibility for all questions relating to force and armed resistance. They could argue that, as party members, they represented only the political arm of the movement, and that all violent actions were carried out by the military arm; they could stress the constitutional nature of the party, even though the demarcation lines between the two bodies were much clearer in theory than in practice.[183] In this, as in other matters, Sinn Féin was able to face in different directions and to change its arguments according to audience or circumstances. During the campaigns of 1917 and 1918 voters were reassured that there would not be another rebellion. In the general election they were deemed to have voted both for the image of the 1916 Rising and, more immediately, for the 'peace party' which had averted the threat of conscription and direct Irish involvement in the Great War.

Some party members were clearly dismayed by the turn of events between 1919 and 1921. One Dáil deputy, Roger Sweetman, opposed the IRA's policy and resigned his seat in protest at measures taken in the name of the Irish republic. But Griffith maintained a discreet silence, and as acting president of the underground government during some of the bloodiest phases of the Anglo-Irish war he seems to have made no effort to prevent attacks on the British army and the police. Collins and others were prepared to act behind his back, and he may have preferred that they should do so.[184] Sinn Féin supported the army, its 'other arm' which operated under the nominal guidance or direction of the Dáil cabinet. Its members praised the strength of that arm, but some of them averted their eyes from the blood on its hand.

This support for violence contrasted with the pacifism of Griffith's pre-rising party and conflicted with the wishes of most of the people. It provided the clearest illustration that separatism was basically unconcerned with public opinion. Ultimately it relied on force; the strong, the determined and the ruthless would have their way, and they would liberate or dominate the weak.

---

[182] De Róiste, diary, 10 Mar. 1918, FO'D, 31,146(3).   [183] See above, pp. 196–8.

[184] See Richard Davis, 'The advocacy of passive resistance in Ireland, 1916–1922', *Anglo-Irish studies*, 3 (1977), p. 44. Griffith has been compared to a man who laboured for ten years writing a play which no-one would stage. Later it became a popular success, but in a form which bore little resemblance to his original creation. He himself then bcame a leading actor in the distorted version of his own play. (Terence de Vere White, 'Arthur Griffith', in Conor Cruise O'Brien (ed.), *The shaping of modern Ireland* (London, 1960), p. 63.)

The peace conference

Other aspects of Sinn Féin's policy proved transient and were less statements of fundamental principles than reactions to changing circumstances or to short-lived opportunities. From late 1916 to early 1919 a frequently expressed demand was that Ireland should be represented at the peace conference which would follow the war. One basis of this claim was Ireland's belligerent status during the rising, when the Easter Week proclamation acknowledged the assistance of 'gallant allies in Europe', but this was no longer emphasized with the same degree of conviction after Germany's defeat in November 1918.

The policy of an appeal to the peace conference had considerable attractions for the Irish leaders; in particular it distracted attention from the disfranchise-ment of the Irish electorate which followed from Sinn Féin's refusal to take its seats in Westminster. Abstention was a logical and natural tactic, given the policy of the separatist movement, but it conflicted with Irish electors' tradi-tional expectations of their representatives. It provoked both unease and oppo-sition. Many nationalists felt that its defects were exposed when Sinn Féin could do no more than watch powerlessly as the Government of Ireland Bill was enacted in Westminster, and as the country was partitioned with hardly an Irish voice raised in protest.[185] Griffith and others probably felt that little damage had been done by abstention, and that things would have been no worse if eighty-five Irish nationalists had been present to vote against the government. If so, they may possibly have been right. Nonetheless this disfranchisement left northern nationalists politically impotent, helpless and voiceless while they were cut off from the rest of the country.

With the promise of an appeal to the peace conference Sinn Féin was able to deflect criticisms of its insularity. It could argue that it was merely by-passing Westminster, which had always been dominated by Ireland's enemies, and was appealing from a more advantageous platform to an audience which was likely to be more responsive and impartial: the free nations of the world. This retreat from a pure 'Sinn Féin' policy might lessen the impact of abstention for those who doubted the wisdom of Ireland relying solely on its own resources. But the retreat was merely tactical, and was not necessarily at odds with Sinn Féin prin-ciples; it could be argued plausibly that Ireland, having first recognized its own independence in the 1918 election, proceeded logically to seek recognition of this independence from the rest of the world.

During and after the war Sinn Féin propaganda laid considerable emphasis on the peace conference; the Irish people were informed that 'nothing else polit-

---

[185] See below, pp. 332–3.

ical now matters'; 'the objective now was to make Ireland an international question'; 'the great goal of our political endeavour is now the Peace Conference'.[186] But Griffith had few illusions about being able to achieve his aim of international recognition, and in a letter from Reading Jail in late 1916 he wrote of the conference that 'if we don't get in – which I suspect is possible – we shall stand on the stairs and harangue the world outside'.[187]

Seán T. O'Kelly headed the Irish delegation when the peacemakers convened in Paris in January 1919. In the course of the next few months vast sums were spent on entertainment and publicity, and O'Kelly was criticized and envied for his extravagance, but no international recognition ensued. Like various other delegations from small nations whose time had not yet come (including the Vietnamese, who were represented by Ho Chi Minh) the Irish were forced to operate on the margins of the great debates and decisions. But they made informal contacts with other outcasts, such as fellow subjects of the empire from India, Egypt and South Africa,[188] and they were able to establish their credentials as members of an anti-British 'international'.

All this activity was viewed sceptically by those Volunteers who were determined that there should be no distraction from the home front, and Piaras Béaslaí remarked that to concentrate Irish eyes on the peace conference would be as dangerous as concentrating them on Westminster.[189] Some months later Collins wrote to Stack along similar lines: 'our hope is here and must be here. The job will be to prevent eyes turning to Paris or New York as a substitute for London.'[190] (By this time de Valera had begun his eighteen-month tour of America in what turned out to be a successful fund-raising campaign, but a vain attempt to win recognition.[191]) Even Griffith's *Nationality* was sceptical about the peace conference, and long before the negotiations came to an end it suggested that the statesmen gathered in Paris were doing their utmost 'to make the world safe for hypocrisy'.[192]

Sinn Féin's attitude to the Irish Convention was quite different. Lloyd George summoned this assembly in the summer of 1917 with the hope that it should represent all shades of Irish opinion, and with the assurance that the government would implement its conclusions if substantial agreement were reached. This was a perfectly safe undertaking, particularly since the word 'substantial'

---

[186] *Nationality*, 3 Mar. 1917, editorial; Griffith, *II*, 1 Aug. 1917; *Sinn Féin national fund trustees' appeal* (leaflet, n.d.), RB, 8786(1). [187] Griffith to Lily Williams, 29 Nov. 1916, NLI, MS 5943. [188] *II*, 5 June 1919. [189] *II*, 12 Feb. 1919. [190] Collins to Stack, 20 July 1919, NLI, MS 5848. [191] See Carroll, *American opinion*, pp. 149–62; Donal McCartney, 'De Valera's mission to the United States, 1919–20' in Art Cosgrove and Donal McCartney (eds.), *Studies in Irish history presented to R. Dudley Edwards* (Dublin, 1979), pp. 307–23. [192] *Nationality*, 19 Apr. 1919, editorial.

would be defined by the government.[193] Sinn Féin refused to participate, although one of its members, Edward MacLysaght, attended and kept party leaders informed of the proceedings. The Mansion House committee argued that the government's commitment to the Ulster unionists made any settlement impossible, and that the convention's failure was therefore ensured in advance.[194] Redmond did not share the separatists' healthy scepticism; he was more trusting, or hopeful, or desperate, and in the end he was disappointed once again. The convention's failure completed the destructive work of the 1916 home rule negotiations. As far as Sinn Féin was concerned, its main importance was that it provided the occasion for the release of the Lewes prisoners in June 1917.[195]

Class conflict

All these aspects of policy or strategy, all these various beliefs and attitudes, pro-voked relatively little controversy until December 1921, when the party split abruptly and decisively over the question of the republic. But there was one other area of policy where Sinn Féin feared divisions, and where it displayed considerable determination and consistency in avoiding them. This was in its attitude towards social conflicts, towards the clashes of interest between farmer and labourer or between employer and employee. In such matters the new Sinn Féin party took on board much of the ideological or tactical baggage of its pre-rising predecessor – and also, in this as in several other areas, some of the atti-tudes and habits of the Irish Parliamentary Party. It maintained continuity with the leaders of the Easter Rising who, with the exception of James Connolly, had broken with the pattern of earlier rebellions in 1798, 1848 and 1867, and had refrained from attacking the 'establishment'. The rebels 'did not deliberately antagonise any section of Irish life, whether Irish Parliamentary Party, Catholic bishops and clergy or any of the other customary targets of revolutionaries'.[196] Their successors followed this example, although naturally they excepted the Redmondites.

Sinn Féin's tendency to speak in terms of an abstract Ireland and a mono-lithic Irish people, an attitude revealed by its geographical determinism and its denial of the separate traditions of the Ulster unionists, was extended with a

[193] R. B. McDowell, *The Irish Convention, 1917–18* (London, 1970), p. 78.   [194] *II*, 24 May 1917.

[195] See McDowell, *Irish Convention*, pp. 82–4; Edward MacLysaght, *Changing times: Ireland since 1898* (Gerrards Cross, 1978), pp. 73–86.

[196] Wall, 'Background to the rising', in Nowlan, *Making of 1916*, p. 181.

remorseless and formidable logic into other areas of its policy. The party and the Dáil cabinet were equally determined to ignore (or, if necessary, to suppress) internal conflicts between different groups or elements within Irish nationalism, to prevent disagreements or clashes which might distract attention from the 'foreign enemy'.

The pre-rising Sinn Féin, while enlightened on the question of women's suffrage, was nonetheless concerned lest it become a divisive issue.[197] Similarly, Griffith, although sympathetic towards the poor, shared the anger felt by members of the Parliamentary Party at what they saw as Jim Larkin's negative and disruptive tactics, his division of Irish nationalists into two rival camps, and his deflection of people's interests from the one supreme goal of national autonomy or independence. His newspaper *Sinn Féin* argued in October 1913 that 'a wise state will, when it is necessary, tax the community to provide work for the workless' and that it was the duty of the organized nation to protect labour; but it also declared that while Sinn Féin would not tolerate injustice or oppression, neither would it associate itself with class war. He rejected socialism as a remedy, and declared that it was 'not Capitalism, but the abuse of Capitalism, [which] oppresses Labour; and not in the destruction of the Capitalist, but in his subjection to the law of the State, interpreting the conscience and the interest of the Nation, will Labour be delivered from its oppression and restored to all its rights'.[198]

Griffith provided other examples of his determination to put the abstract 'nation' before the poor of the nation. During the 1913 lock-out he was moved to a tirade of abuse at the trade unionists' unpatriotic activities, in the course of which he wrote:

> it has been recently discovered that the Irish workingman is not an Irish workingman at all. He is a unit of humanity, a human label of internationalism, a Brother of the men over the water who rule his country. There is nothing to divide him from them except a drop of water. Race, tradition, nationality are non-entities, and History and its formative influences on character and outlook a figment.[199]

This outburst was provoked by the decision of the Dublin workers to accept £5,000 worth of food from British trade unionists.

But such views were by no means confined to Griffith and his party, and they were shared by many among the IRB elements which had broken with him in 1910. It is simplistic to establish a neat division between reactionary constitutional Sinn Féiners and socially progressive 1916 rebels. *Irish Freedom*

---

[197] See above, p. 201.   [198] *Sinn Féin*, 25 Oct. 1913.   [199] *Ibid.*, 4 Oct. 1913.

complained that 'for some time now Labour has talked of and considered nothing but its rights. Yet its rights are as nothing compared to its duties . . . so long as Labour accepts the Nation, Labour must subordinate its class interests to the interests of the Nation . . . The greatest right of labour is the right to stand by the flag.'[200] One writer believed that 'every stoppage of trade here means the impoverishment of Ireland and the enrichment of England . . . the gain to the workers has never balanced the loss to the nation'.[201] Seán MacDermott, although critical of the employers in the 1913 lock-out, and although ready to praise some of Larkin's achievements, nonetheless saw him as a danger in other respects:

> he talks nationalism, but only in so far as he thinks it is likely to help along his Socialist programme . . . Socialism and the Sympathetic Strike are dangerous ruinous weapons in Ireland at the present time . . . all this talk about the friendliness of the English working man and of the Brotherhood of Man, the English food-ships etc. have a very bad unnational influence.[202]

Pearse, too, opposed any leader who deflected attention from the national aim 'except with the object of strengthening his forces for the main fight – the fight for nationhood'. He believed that Parnell would not have been justified in devoting an hour of his time or a penny of his funds to the land war except as a means to an end.[203] Later de Valera warned that Sinn Féin would not be turned into a labour movement. Labour was class-based, and while a national movement such as Sinn Féin was concerned with raising the centre of gravity of the whole nation, labour's aim was to raise the centre of gravity of only one of its parts.[204] The party's *ard-chomhairle* was told in August 1919 of the need for all classes to live in harmony; 'consequently the Labour troubles give much concern. Every effort should be made to prevent strikes, lock-outs, etc., and, when these cannot be prevented, persevering efforts should be made to bring about settlement and reconciliation.'[205]

Such attitudes provoked disagreement and anger. Despite their co-operation on other issues Connolly was forceful in his rejection of some ideas put forward by nationalists such as Griffith. Years earlier he had written:

> when a Sinn Feiner waxes eloquent about restoring the Constitution of '82, but remains silent about the increasing industrial despotism of the capital-

---

[200] *Irish Freedom*, Dec. 1911, editorial.   [201] *Ibid.*, Nov. 1913.

[202] MacDermott to Joe McGarrity, 12 Dec. 1913, McG, 17,618.

[203] Pearse, 'Psychology of a Volunteer', *Political writings*, p. 105.   [204] *II*, 2 Apr. 1918.

[205] 'Hon. secretaries' report to *ard-chomhairle*', *Nationality*, 30 Aug. 1919.

ist; when the Sinn Feiner speaks to men who are fighting against low wages and tells them that the Sinn Fein body has promised lots of Irish labour at low wages to any foreign capitalist who wishes to establish in Ireland, what wonder if they [the workers] come to believe that a change from Toryism to Sinn Feinism would simply be a change from the devil they do know to the devil they do not know![206]

Ernest Blythe was another who took a more aggressive stance, arguing that it was the poor who would always be ready to fight for Ireland, and that 'the men who cannot devise a social policy when Ireland is enslaved will never devise one when she is free . . . Like the Language Revival, the work of social reconstruction is best done now.'[207] There was also support for the idea of a social policy on the grounds that, rather than dissipate effort, it would add to the strength of the separatist movement.[208]

Connolly and Blythe may exemplify a radical attitude more congenial to the values of later generations, but Griffith, with all his acerbity, represented more accurately the prevailing spirit of his own times. James Stephens remarked in 1916, that, with the obvious exception of Connolly, the rebel leaders' reputation was that of people who were not particularly interested in the problems of labour.[209] After the rising, with only very few dissenters, it was Griffith's views which predominated among Sinn Féiners and republicans. This was not necessarily because he had converted most of his contemporaries, but because his opinions were more acceptable than Connolly's to other 'single-minded' nationalists. There was a general agreement that all internal disputes must be postponed until full independence had been achieved, and that then, freed from British incompetence and malevolence, the Irish people could resolve their problems without much difficulty. Naturally Sinn Féin's enemies were quick to exploit the party's lack of urgency or precision on social questions. Joe Devlin, for example, described himself as being too devoted to the working class to wait fifty years for its grievances to be solved.[210]

The party was careful not to produce a social policy, although it was ready to contemplate economic and social change in the national interest. Griffith was an economic optimist, and he saw no reason why Ireland should not be prosperous and contented once it had escaped from all the restrictions associated with the Act of Union. His economic ideas were a reflection of his nationalism, and not *vice versa*. His arguments have been described as being dominated by

---

[206] *Irish Nation*, 23 Jan. 1909, cited in Desmond Ryan (ed.), *Socialism and nationalism: a selection from the writings of James Connolly* (Dublin, 1948), pp. 88–9.   [207] *Irish Freedom*, Mar. 1913.
[208] *Ibid.*, Jan. 1913.   [209] Stephens, *Insurrection*, pp. 96–7.   [210] *FJ*, 31 Jan. 1918.

'a paranoid vision which ascribed all the world's ills to Britain and an Utopian fantasy about the absence of any genuine conflict of interest within Ireland due to the limitless resources supposedly available to an independent Irish state'.[211] He expected, for example, that 'in a free Ireland the counties of Cavan and Leitrim would form the centre of one of the greatest industrial districts of the world', and argued that the country had 'room and abundance' for another 16 million people; it had enough coal to supply its needs for the next two or three centuries.[212] (Pearse too had believed that in a free Ireland the population would rise to 20 or even 30 million, even though it would continue to depend on agriculture and rural industry.[213])

Irish firms should be protected against foreign competition, but Griffith's concern with building up industry was based on political rather than on social or economic criteria:

> a mere agricultural state is infinitely less powerful than an agricultural-manufacturing state. The former is always economically and politically dependent on those foreign nations which take from it agriculture in exchange for manufactured goods . . . An agricultural nation is a man with one arm who makes use of an arm belonging to an arm belonging to another person, but cannot, of course, be sure of having it always available.[214]

He ignored the awkward fact that Ireland already possessed a booming centre of modern heavy industry, the Lagan Valley, which flourished on free trade with Britain. Its prosperity seemed to vindicate List's inconvenient assumption that the United Kingdom was an economic unit.

Sinn Féin's economic programme was published in late 1917, and its twenty-two points included the following aims: industries should be encouraged; land purchase should be completed and absentee landlordism curtailed; a mercantile marine and a tariff commission should be established; a department of public health should be created; and a distinct Irish currency should assert Ireland's 'separate national existence in International Trade and Finance'. All this was, as its title indicated clearly and honestly, an economic rather than a social policy; it was directed at increasing national wealth, an object which would unite and inspire all except the most austere Sinn Féiners, rather than with redistributing it, an aim which would create fierce divisions. Only three

---

[211] Patrick Maume, 'The ancient constitution: Arthur Griffith and his intellectual legacy to Sinn Féin', *Irish Political Studies*, 10 (1995), pp. 132–3.

[212] *Nationality*, 29 Sept. 1917; 12 July 1919, editorial; 22 Dec. 1917.

[213] *Spark*, 9 April 1916, cited in Edwards, *Patrick Pearse*, p. 338.   [214] *Nationality*, 24 Mar. 1917.

clauses in the programme could be seen as socially progressive and as likely to risk perturbing party members or alienating outsiders. One of these aimed at subordinating the country's wealth and resources to the people's needs and welfare; another demanded equal educational facilities for all classes; and the third sought a more equitable distribution of taxation.[215] Elsewhere it was suggested that Ireland's annual contribution to imperial taxation would be cut by £4 million if alcohol consumption were halved – and as a first step to sobriety, temperance should be enforced in Sinn Féin club buildings.[216]

Before the war Griffith favoured the nationalization of Irish railways and canals in the cause of economic efficiency, and later his newspaper argued that in Meath, where the number of cattle had declined, the grass farms of the county should be broken up.[217] But change was acceptable or welcome only when it would not be divisive. It is true that *some* concern was shown for the needy and the vulnerable. In January 1919, Griffith suggested that the Dáil should aim at replacing the existing workhouse system with a better and more humane structure based on the extension of outdoor relief; hostels and houses should be provided for the aged and infirm, and the Scottish poor law system could be used as a model.[218] In general, however, the poor were expected to display the Christian virtue of patience.

After the rising, as before it, Sinn Féin's attitude had its critics. Occasionally members made rabble-rousing speeches, such as J. J. Walsh's declaration that 'the day an Irish Republic was formed, the landlords would be put against the wall and there would be an end of landlordism once and for all'.[219] But Walsh was prone to make unusual suggestions, such as that Bolshevik literature should be distributed to British troops in Ireland,[220] and he was not always taken seriously. Edward MacLysaght argued that the party should organize agricultural labour throughout the country; such a policy would help Sinn Féin as well as the labourers, while also denying Joe Devlin an opportunity to win support.[221] But more characteristic of the party was the vote in the Naas Sinn Féin club on 'Capital versus Labour from the Sinn Féin point of view'. Most of those present voted in favour of capital.[222]

Between 1881 and 1911 the number of farm labourers fell by 40 per cent, and by the 1920s they were employed by only one-fifth of the farmers in the

---

[215] *Sinn Féin economic programme* (pamphlet, n.d. [1917]).

[216] *How to form Sinn Féin clubs* (pamphlet, n.d. [1917]).

[217] *Sinn Féin*, 26 Apr. 1913; *Nationality*, 27 Oct. 1917.

[218] Griffith, memo, 23 Jan. 1919, CP, 11,405.   [219] *Anglo-Celt*, 14 July 1917.

[220] SCM, 9 Jan. 1919.   [221] MacLysaght to Eoin MacNeill, 11 Sept. 1917, MacN, LA1/H/20.

[222] *Leinster Leader*, 15, 22 Dec. 1917.

country.[223] Political and even numerical weight had shifted to those with small holdings of land, and the party was unwilling to alienate this new power in Ireland. It would not antagonize the 'haves', whose votes and financial contributions it needed, in an effort to win the support of the 'have nots', whose influence was in steady decline. In contrast to the pattern of earlier decades, land hunger would now divide rather than unite Irish nationalists. Urban unrest was equally menacing, and nationalism 'not only absorbed pre-war social radicalism, but apparently negated it'.[224]

The Sinn Féin leadership resisted all temptations to involve itself in social disputes where it would be obliged to take sides and antagonize one or another group of its supporters. Class tensions could still tear the movement apart. When social issues emerged in the course of the party's campaigns (and the question raised most frequently was that of old age pensions) consistency was not highly prized. In the Roscommon by-election, for example, O'Flanagan supported the land-hungry and the cattle-drivers, while a few months later in South Longford it was the UIL which opposed the ranchers and Sinn Féin which secured their support.[225] Such flexibility revealed the party's opportunistic lack of a policy. Where commitment to detailed programmes ran the risk of creating internal divisions it was wiser to keep quiet, and nothing would be changed until the British had been driven out. In early 1918 de Valera was recorded as warning a meeting of the *ard-chomhairle* that

> we ought not attempt to regularise the land campaign. It would take all our time and we have not the whole country at our back . . . Capital was being made against us about [the] Russian revolution and similar things in Ireland . . . concentrate on the political machine point. Other things to be thrown over if necessary.[226]

Three years later he expressed confidence that 'the common patriotism of all sections will prove superior to all special class interests'.[227] When the party became popular and respectable in 1917, and was joined by many of the bourgeoisie, its natural conservatism was reinforced. As Aodh de Blácam wrote in 1921, 'we have had for three years the curious situation of a government with conservative objects working in a revolutionary atmosphere and by revolutionary methods'.[228]

---

[223] Emmet O'Connor, *Syndicalism in Ireland, 1917–1923* (Cork, 1988), p. 34; *Census of population, 1926. General report* (Dublin, 1934), p. 27.   [224] Foster, *Modern Ireland*, p. 446.

[225] Bew, *Conflict and conciliation*, p. 214.   [226] De Róiste, diary, 10 Mar. 1918, FO'D, 31,146(3).

[227] De Valera, statement, 9 Apr. 1921, NAI, DE, 2/102.

[228] A. de Blácam, *What Sinn Féin stands for* (Dublin, 1921) p. 133.

The Dáil's democratic programme of January 1919 was drafted jointly by Seán T. O'Kelly of Sinn Féin and Thomas Johnson of Labour. The imbalance of power between the two sides ensured that the document was pruned of much of its socialist content, but some of the original radical elements survived. The programme decreed that every citizen was to be entitled to an adequate share of the produce of the nation's labour; the government would concern itself with the well-being of the children, and would care for the aged and the infirm; and it would seek 'a general and lasting improvement in the conditions under which the working classes live and labour'.[229] Such sentiments can be seen as a debt of honour to the Labour Party, as a gesture of appreciation for its recent abstention from the general election. They were also, perhaps, an attempt to win over support which Labour might otherwise gain in future, but without thereby committing Sinn Féin to any unpopular measures.[230]

Only in one area was Sinn Féin forced to come to grips with social realities and conflicts. It established a legal system whose function was to take away business from the crown courts, provide the movement with valuable publicity, and prevent any deflection of energies from the struggle with Britain. Here, predictably, the party showed itself cautious and conservative, and despite its involvement in curbing social unrest in some parts of the country its principal aim was to avoid unwelcome distractions. But here, in contrast to most other aspects of its policy, it was forced briefly to confront the realities of Irish life. Here, at least to an extent, theory was put into practice.[231]

Propaganda

One of the main challenges facing Sinn Féin was to instruct the people in the details (and sometimes also in the broad outlines) of the party's attitudes and beliefs; to explain and justify an emphasis on policies such as the republic, the Irish language or the resort to force, which were demanded by no more than a lobby or pressure group. Here the party triumphed; it excelled in publicity.

Separatist propaganda had been dealt a serious blow by the censorship restrictions which were first imposed soon after the outbreak of war in 1914,

---

[229] *DE, 1919–21*, p. 23 (21 Jan. 1919).

[230] See Patrick Lynch, 'The social revolution that never was', in Williams, *Irish struggle*, pp. 45–8; Farrell, *Founding of Dáil Éireann*, pp. 57–61; Arthur Mitchell, *Revolutionary government in Ireland: Dáil Éireann, 1919–22* (Dublin, 1995), pp. 15–16; Seán T. O'Kelly, 'Memoirs', STO'K, 27,707, pp. 215–16.   [231] The practice will be examined below, pp. 310–18.

and these were tightened in the aftermath of the rising.[232] Griffith was forced to devote much of his time and ingenuity to circumventing government controls; for example, shortly after *Nationality* was re-founded a colleague remarked of him in passing that 'Monday was one of his busy days with the Censor.'[233] Long afterwards, one Sinn Féin journalist reminisced about how the censor had been distracted from dangerous proofs by a discussion of subjects close to his heart: the iniquities of income tax and the fortunes of his racehorses.[234] Despite the efforts of the British authorities, leaflets and photographs, pamphlets and ballads began circulating soon after Easter Week, and as early as June a complaint was made in Meath that 'copies of Republican documents which are sold by authority are having a wide circulation and are doing considerable harm in as much as they create sympathy with the leaders of the rebellion and are leading people who were not Sinn Feiners to hold Sinn Fein ideas now'.[235]

At this stage propaganda was disorganized and piecemeal, but it soon became more efficient and more centralized. Leaflets and pamphlets were reinforced by newspapers such as *The Irishman* and *Nationality*, and by mid-1917 they were reported as being passed from hand to hand.[236] Within weeks of its reappearance in February *Nationality* took the lead among separatist newspapers, and from May 1917 onwards it received the most impressive proof of its effectiveness: police demands that it should be banned. The paper was soon able to claim (although without producing details) that its circulation was second only to that of the *Irish Independent*.[237] In early 1918 the Sinn Féin club in Louisburgh, a small town in Mayo with a population of 1,410 people, requested three dozen copies of *Nationality* every week.[238] One of Lloyd George's cabinet colleagues noted that, while walking in Co. Carlow, he had bought *Nationality* in a 'Sinn Fein shop'.[239] Until his arrest in May 1918 Griffith was closely involved with the newspaper, although after his release the pressure of other work prevented him from resuming his editorship until July 1919, by which time he was already the acting head of the new, 'rebel' Irish government. But throughout its life-span of nearly three years it was characterized by his style and preoccupations.

Much separatist propaganda was bilious, turgid or maudlin; for example, shortly before the rising the 'Stars of Freedom' were described as

---

[232] See Glandon, *Arthur Griffith*, pp. 147–52, 159–60.

[233] F. J. O'Connor to Gavan Duffy, 4 Apr. 1917, GD, 5581.

[234] David Hogan, *The four glorious years* (Dublin, 1953), pp. 40–1.

[235] CI's report, Meath, June 1916, CO.904/100.

[236] CI's report, W. Galway, July 1917, CO.904/103.   [237] *Nationality*, 22 Sept. 1917; 6 Apr. 1918.

[238] *Précis* of captured documents, NLI, MS 10,494(1), p. 24.

[239] H. A. L. Fisher, diary, 26 Sept. 1918, Fisher MSS, Bodleian Library, Oxford, Fisher, 9, p. 129.

still flickering with the same undying splendour as of yore, those wondrous beacon lights of mystic lustre . . . Their brilliance dimmed only when tyranny asserted itself, and attested to its own wrongfulness by wresting from the Hand of God that power which is His Own Divine Right.[240]

In a later pamphlet readers were assured that 'one spark of political truth will be sufficient to light the furnace of Sinn Féin, in which all that is foul and hideous can be consumed, and by which the machinery of national endeavour shall be set in motion'.[241] Much bad poetry was perpetrated, and the following stanza is representative of hundreds, if not thousands:

> Oh, think ye, Men of Erin! Oh, think upon the past!
> Since first the chain of slavery around your necks was cast –
> Who forged the galling chain? Who robbed and rieved your land?
> 'Twas England of the wily ways. 'Twas England's bloody hand! [242]

It was probably fortunate that Griffith's colleagues did not respond to his exhortation that they should 'mobilise the poets. Let them address [President] Wilson, and let them remind him in their best verse that he has the opportunity and the duty of giving the world true peace and freedom.' Yeats was among those whom he named in this context.[243] In a similar mood it was proposed that authors such as Oliver St John Gogarty, Daniel Corkery and T. C. Murray should write plays illustrating British methods in Ireland which could be performed in America.[244]

But despite his occasional lapses and his blind spots, Griffith's writing was normally blunt and down-to-earth. He was once more in jail when, during the May 1921 elections, de Valera was sent some draft pamphlets and dismissed them as unworthy; 'they are all froth, except a few paragraphs. Solid stuff, like A. G.'s, is what we want.'[245] Griffith and his writings *were* solid, and he confined himself to the prose of Irish nationalism, while leaving the poetry to others. When Liam de Róiste received a telegram which purported to be from Griffith, he doubted whether Griffith was really the author: 'he would not use so many words'.[246]

He was merciless in his statistical analysis and his provision of lists, moving

---

[240] Eilís Ní Colmáin, *The Gael*, 29 Jan. 1916.

[241] *The invincible Sinn Fein 'tank'* (Pamphlet, n.d. [1916]), p. 4.

[242] 'To the men of Ireland', *Irish Republic*, 13 Oct. 1917.

[243] Griffith, memo, 23 Jan. 1919, CP, 11,405.

[244] Minister of labour to director of publicity, 20 June 1921, 'Epitome of documents seized', CO.904/23/7, p. 26.   [245] De Valera to Páidín O'Keeffe, 1 Mar. 1921, EdeV.

[246] De Róiste, diary, 28 Jan. 1922, CAI, U271/A/42.

triumphantly from one set of figures to the next. He examined the relative extent of Irish and English taxation in proportion to population ('on the basis of National Wealth and Population to-day, the Irishman is paying £27 in taxation for every £15 the Englishman pays'), and deplored the country's economic problems; Ireland had lost one-sixth of its population since Dillon entered parliament, more than the total number of British, dominion and colonial troops killed in the World War.[247] He attacked the Nationalists and their leaders with particular ferocity. In one article he accused Dillon of reproaching the British government; 'would it be a service to England, he asked, if the Irish Parliamentary Party disappeared! At last, the party that has masqueraded as National to the eyes of the Irish people blurts out the truth that its existence is a service to England.'[248] He warned that

> England having destroyed our constitution, suppressed our Parliament, loaded her debt on to our shoulders, ruined our trade and commerce, turned our tillage-fields into cattle-ranches, trebled our taxation and halved our population – all within a century – wants what is left of us to fight for her supremacy over the world.[249]

He catalogued the number and population of the American states whose legislatures supported Irish independence, and in May 1919 *Nationality* devoted four columns of tables comparing Ireland with countries such as Poland, Finland and Estonia.[250] Some of his readers must have been baffled by much of his paper.

The British government's double standard in its dealings with Irish nationalists and unionists was a time-honoured subject which still provided rich material. Seditious speeches made by unionist politicians before and after the war were printed in loving detail, and there must have been considerable satisfaction when the police seized pamphlets which consisted entirely of 'rebel' declarations by once-more respectable unionists.[251] James Good commented on the absurdity whereby 'the Lord Chancellor of Ireland, as a member of the Irish Executive, solemnly labels his own speeches seditious literature'.[252] Attention was drawn to the treatment of Thomas Ashe and how it differed from that

---

[247] *Nationality*, 7 Apr. 1917, 30 Nov. 1918.   [248] *Ibid.*, 3 Mar. 1917, editorial.

[249] Griffith, *When the government publishes sedition* (pamphlet, Dublin, n.d. [?1915]), p. 11.

[250] *Nationality*, 9 Aug. 1919, 3 May 1919.

[251] *II*, 2 July 1919. See Thomas Johnson, *A handbook for rebels* (Dublin, 1918); J. J. Horgan (ed.), *The complete grammar of anarchy, by members of the war cabinet and their friends* (Dublin, 1918) which was 'respectfully dedicated to Sir Edward Carson'.

[252] James Good, *Ulster and Ireland* (Dublin, 1919), p. 206. See also *Irishman*, 23 Sept. 1916.

meted out to Carson, Bonar Law, and F. E. Smith; all four men had threatened rebellion under certain circumstances, all engaged in hypothetical treason, but only Ashe died from maltreatment in a British jail.[253]

Nationality ran articles on themes such as zinc deposits, the need for a mercantile marine, afforestation, the cement industry and Ireland's position in naval strategy. Much space was given to Irish history, while over-taxation was an issue to which Griffith returned with almost obsessive regularity. Not surprisingly, it was a theme which provoked much public interest. In Drumcliffe (Co. Sligo) it was decided to distribute copies of the paper among club members 'as it was the only means of showing the people how they have been misrepresented and over-burdened by taxation'.[254] International affairs were viewed from a predictable standpoint, with generous coverage given to news such as the arrest of Egyptian nationalists by the British. And like other Sinn Féin papers and pamphlets, *Nationality* provided organizational details, giving progress reports, lists of new clubs, acknowledgements of contributions and other such matters. Throughout the summer of 1919 each issue provided a progress report on de Valera's American tour.

Some Sinn Féin pamphlets were weighty publications. One of them, *Ireland's case against conscription*, was almost a scholarly monograph, with thirty pages of references supporting fifteen of text.[255] Normally, however, they were short and easily digestible. Much Sinn Féin propaganda consisted of the 'progressive simplification of consciousness in which ideas were turned into slogans, and the slogans turned into occasions for action'.[256]

Sinn Féin's efforts were reinforced by the favourable treatment which the party received from publications such as the *Irish Independent* and the *Catholic Bulletin*. The former was owned by William Martin Murphy, and the positive coverage which it gave to Irish separatism was little more than a means whereby Murphy was able to vent his spite against his former colleagues in the Parliamentary Party. The latter was edited by J. J. O'Kelly ('Sceilg'), who was active in the Nation League and Sinn Féin, and from July 1916 onwards it ran a series of hagiographical articles on the Easter rebels.[257]

The owners and editors of most provincial newspapers were generally unsympathetic towards radical nationalism, but they were nonetheless prepared to satisfy the demands of the growing number of readers who abandoned the Parliamentary Party between 1916 and 1918. The *Irishman* urged Sinn

---

[253] *Nationality*, 6 Oct. 1917, editorial.   [254] *Sligo Champion*, 1 Sept. 1917.

[255] De Valera, *Ireland's case against conscription* (Dublin, 1918).

[256] Thompson, *Imagination of an insurrection*, p. 67.

[257] For the *Catholic Bulletin* see Murphy, *Patrick Pearse*, pp. 66–7.

Féiners to influence local newspapers through deputations to their editors or proprietors, and by the end of 1917 an army intelligence officer noted revealingly that the 'Local Press has been, as a whole, captured by Sinn Fein – that is, it produces what will be acceptable to its readers.'[258] In 1918 the syndicated 'Sinn Féin Notes' were circulated to forty newspapers and were printed by most of them.[259]

Particularly after *Nationality* had been suppressed in September 1919, the *Irish Independent* became the paper which provided Sinn Féin with its most sympathetic coverage – with the result that, together with the *Freeman's Journal* (which had long ago abandoned its Redmondite loyalties), it was held responsible for the disturbed state of the country. In August 1920 the RIC county inspector reported from West Galway that 'the mainstay of the Sinn Fein movement in this County is the Irish Daily Independent. It is this paper which creates, fosters and foments hatred of the English Government from day to day, from week to week, from year to year. It never lets it alone.'[260]

Sinn Féiners also exploited modern techniques. They used cinemas to illustrate the prisoners' return to Dublin in June 1917, and Thomas Ashe's funeral three months later. On the first of these occasions a dynamic newsreel producer ensured that the film was processed, printed and distributed to cinemas within a few hours, and one result of his efficiency was that some of the men newly released from Lewes were able to watch 'their own film'.[261] By 1919 use of the new medium had progressed to the extent that a film entitled *Sinn Féin Review*, 2,200 feet (670 metres) long and representing 'events of Sinn Féin interest since 1916' was shown in various parts of Ireland.[262] A more traditional form of propaganda, but one which remained enormously effective, was song. Old patriotic ballads were joined by new additions to the repertoire such as *Kevin Barry* or *Who fears to speak of Easter Week?*[263] But other compositions had little chance of popularity, and the opening lines of *The Gaelic Athlete* were worthy of William McGonagall: 'Come, join me in singing the praise of the men/ Of the Gaelic Athletic Association . . .', while *The Sinn Feiners' election song* (set to the tune of *The boys of Wexford*) included righteous Griffithite sentiments which were also unlikely to appeal to the masses:

---

[258] *Irishman*, 17 Feb. 1917; IO's report (M. and C.), Dec. 1917.

[259] 'The Department of Publicity. History and progress' (Aug. 1921), Blythe MSS, UCDA, P24/19.

[260] CI's report, W. Galway, Aug. 1920, CO.904/112.

[261] Kevin Rockett, Luke Gibbons and John Hill, *Cinema and Ireland* (London, 1988), p. 34.

[262] *II*, 17 Apr. 1919.

[263] See Eimear Whitfield, 'Another martyr for old Ireland: the balladry of revolution', in David Fitzpatrick (ed.), *Revolution? Ireland 1917–1923* (Dublin, 1990), pp. 60–8.

The Spaniards, Bulgars, Swedes and Danes
Have claims less high than we,
Yet suffer they no foeman's chains, -
Those nations can be free![264]

However valuable songs and verse might have been in spreading the Sinn Féin message, the party still depended on prose. Between 1917 and 1919, and again after 1921, speeches were a normal way of spreading propaganda, although during the Anglo-Irish War orators were forced to be more circumspect.

In January 1918, *Nationality* looked back on the previous twelve months and reflected that 'the year of Sinn Féin propaganda has closed in success'.[265] But from 1919 onwards the party's publicity was subjected to far more drastic restrictions than in the past, and it was correspondingly less effective. Raids and arrests became more frequent, and finally the paper was suppressed in September 1919. By this time, however, the war circumstances of the years 1919–21 were reflected by the influential *Irish Bulletin*, which provided meticulous (if partisan) details of British repression and atrocities, and the Dáil cabinet had begun to take over much of Sinn Féin's propaganda work.[266] But by then the party's newspapers, pamphlets and posters had achieved most of their objectives.

Many of Sinn Féin's policies may have been unoriginal or unremarkable, but its formidable propaganda machine was one of the two principal means whereby the separatist movement radicalized most Irish nationalists. The other was its use of force.

---

[264] *Latest ballads of Sinn Féin* (pamphlet), pp. 7–8.   [265] *Nationality,* 5 Jan. 1918, editorial.
[266] See below, p. 309.

7

WAR AND REPRESSION
1919–1921

Sinn Féin's achievements of the previous two years reached their apogee on 21 January 1919 with the formal opening of the first Dáil Éireann, or Irish parliament. The Act of Union was formally repudiated, the Irish republic which had been proclaimed in arms in 1916 was now confirmed by a democratically elected assembly, and (at least in theory) the newly elected MPs could proceed to legislate for their country. The Sinn Féin deputies could choose a government and begin to implement Griffith's long-term programme.

While these events were taking place in the Mansion House, a group of nine Volunteers waited in ambush by the side of a road at Soloheadbeg in Tipperary. They then seized a cart laden with gelignite, and in the course of their action they killed the two RIC constables who guarded the consignment. The operation was on a small scale and it was bungled; the gelignite was taken, but the detonators were left behind. The killing of the policemen may have been unintentional, and may have been another sign of an operation which had gone wrong.[1] However, this incident came to be seen in retrospect as the opening round in the Anglo-Irish War, or the War of Independence, which would last until the truce of July 1921. The achievements of the triumphant Sinn Féin party and of the newly elected Dáil would be overshadowed by those of the IRA, as the Volunteers were now more often called. As one movement reached its crescendo, a new theme could already be discerned.

The reality was less simple and less neatly symbolic; for nearly two years Ireland had experienced a steady increase in violence, and the country was not plunged overnight from peace into war by the ambush at Soloheadbeg. Since the rising and the subsequent executions several people had been killed in scuffles and clashes between nationalists and crown forces, even though, until then, only one such victim had been in government service. The shooting of the two RIC men marked a natural escalation of the violence and conflict which had long been a feature of Irish life; it was yet another provocation by the Irish Volunteers which

---

[1] Breen, *My fight for Irish freedom*, p. 41; Andrews, *Dublin made me*, p. 115.

in turn elicited a further, drastic response on the part of the British authorities, and it locked the country even more firmly into its spiral towards war. But Ireland had been sliding in that direction long before January 1919.

Skirmishes

Many Volunteers longed to resume the struggle which had been interrupted when Pearse ordered the rebels to lay down their arms. Radicals such as Collins were determined to avoid the mistakes which had been made in Easter Week: they would fight the next round by different methods and under different rules. In particular, they would follow the advice of John MacBride, who had told the fellow members of his garrison that they must never allow themselves be trapped inside a building again. Some of those who had not taken up arms in 1916 continued to feel guilty and defensive about their inactivity; Austin Stack (whose record in Kerry had been unimpressive) confessed that, 'I am ashamed of my abortive efforts to serve my country'; and when Terence MacSwiney was arrested in February 1917 his captors recorded that they had discovered documents including notes for a speech 'showing why they did not fight at Easter'.[2]

Towards the end of 1916 Brugha and others began the process of reviving the Volunteers. In November he presided over a conference in Dublin at which about fifty members were present, and a month later the release of the Frongoch detainees provided many units with experienced leaders. Their resolve had been hardened by defeat and internment. Following the pattern established when the Volunteers were originally founded in 1913–14, their re-formation after the rising was the work of a dedicated elite with a long tradition of radical activity. Existing IRB circles often formed the core of new or revived companies.[3]

In May 1917 an army convention elected a new executive whose first task was to continue the reorganization which was already under way; it would then try to complete the work of the Easter rebels. But the national leadership warned that it could provide local units with little assistance, and that each county would be responsible for training and arming its own soldiers. Members were also assured that 'they will not be called upon to take part in any forlorn hope' and that orders to take the field would not be issued without reasonable hope of success.[4] In the new circumstances created by the rising and its aftermath, the

---

[2] Stack to John Daly, 14 June 1916, cited in J. Anthony Gaughan, *Austin Stack: portrait of a separatist* (Dublin, 1977), p. 66; IG's report, Feb. 1917, CO.904/102.

[3] Augusteijn, *From public defiance to guerrilla warfare*, pp. 52–3, 58.

[4] Circular, 22 May 1917, EdeV.

Volunteers' official policy would be closer to the attitudes represented by MacNeill in 1916 than to those of Clarke and MacDermott. A day after the Sinn Féin convention in October 1917 de Valera was elected president of the Volunteers, so at the highest level there would be unity of command of the two separate bodies in the one person. This was a logical if paradoxical application of Griffith's dual monarchy theories. A GHQ was established in Dublin in March 1918.

The Volunteers were far less numerous than Sinn Féin, but their revival paralleled that of the party during 1917 and the spread of each movement facilitated that of the other. Reports of drilling, of arms raids and of secret meetings between Volunteer activists became more frequent. A police patrol was attacked in West Cork 'by a dozen or so, of Sinn Feiners, who had just been turned out of the local public house', and in Cork city 140 men were interrupted in their drill practice when the RIC raided the Volunteers' hall.[5] Soldiers home on leave from the Western Front frequently lost their rifles, either through theft or sale, although the value of such weapons was limited because they lacked ammunition. Three soldiers gave their rifles to Sinn Féiners in Ennis after they had met Countess Markievicz on a train, and at the Sinn Féin October convention one Volunteer boasted that 'we can get arms enough from drunken soldiers without Sinn Fein assistance'.[6]

There were frequent disturbances and shootings, and in one incident a man was shot dead when police fired into a crowd outside a barracks in Ballybunion (Co. Kerry).[7] In June 1917 a policeman was killed in Dublin during disturbances which followed speeches by Plunkett and Brugha. Members of a Sinn Féin club in Sligo objected when the local parish priest organized an entertainment in his school; they boycotted the gathering, barricaded roads 'and appear to have discharged firearms'.[8] This wave of violence contrasted with the traditional pattern familiar to the courts, and, in Galway, Lord Justice Molony commented on the new social problem whereby a 100 per cent decrease in drunkenness coincided with a 300 per cent increase in crime.[9] (The first of these remarkable figures may be partly explained by the fact that it was now more expensive to get drunk than it had been before the war; the price of a pint of Guinness increased threefold between 1914 and 1918.)

Arrests were widespread, although it was feared that this policy might backfire if suspects were tried in court. The authorities tended to prefer court-

[5] CIs' reports, W. Cork, E. Cork, Dec. 1916, Mar. 1917, CO.904/101–2.

[6] Staunton, 'Munster Fusiliers', p. 8; 'Sinn Fein convention 1917', CO.904/23/5.

[7] IO's report (S.), July 1917; *Nationality*, 27 Oct. 1917.

[8] *Précis* of captured documents, NLI, MS 10,494(1), p. 35.   [9] *II*, 22 Mar. 1918.

martials which were seen to be 'expeditious and attract little public attention', while prosecution before magistrates 'too often assumes the importance of a state trial, inflammatory speeches are made by local solicitors, popular demonstrations are organized for the occasion, necessitating the drafting of a large force of Police into remote villages, and the sentences, limited by statute, are scarcely adequate.'[10] Severe punishments were imposed for mild offences such as singing songs or carrying flags. The government's policy has been well described as 'mild coercion – repression too weak to root out opposition, but provocative enough to nurture it'.[11]

Of all the actions which rebounded on the British authorities, the most important was probably the death of Thomas Ashe in September 1917. He went on a hunger-strike in protest at his treatment in Mountjoy Jail, and died as a result of incompetent force-feeding. He was instantly canonized by nationalist opinion, and his funeral became one of the great set-piece occasions at which republicans had always excelled. Tens of thousands of mourners filed past his coffin, and Collins, who had delivered the brusque and blunt funeral oration, reported afterwards that 'Dublin is in the hands of the Volunteers again this week. No living person ever witnessed such a crowd as thronged the streets.'[12] Eighteen months later the chief secretary remarked that Ashe's death had done 'more to stimulate Sinn Feinism and disorder in Ireland than anything I know'.[13]

By early 1918 a military intelligence officer admitted that considerable areas of the south had degenerated into a state of anarchy, and that in Thurles (Co. Tipperary) Volunteers had carried out large-scale operations such as occupying the railway station.[14] Even before the conscription crisis police were being concentrated in fortified positions, and many outlying posts had been abandoned. The breakdown of law and order was illustrated by a claim made in the Wexford quarter sessions: the court was told that when the Sinn Féiners 'painted the sergeant's pig in republican colours they would do anything'.[15] Clare was proclaimed a special military area, permission was needed to enter and leave the county, mail was censored, and in some districts a curfew was imposed. But where Clare led, other parts of the country soon followed, and within a short time West Cork and part of Kerry were also designated special areas. As early as February 1918 troops were sent to Galway, Mayo, Roscommon, Sligo and

---

[10] IG's report, Oct. 1917, CO.904/104.
[11] Charles Townshend, *The British campaign in Ireland, 1919–1921* (Oxford, 1975), p. 1.
[12] Collins to Gearóid O'Sullivan, 28 Sept. 1917, NLI, MS 23,466, p. 309.
[13] Ian Macpherson to Lloyd George, 27 Feb. 1919, Cab.24/76, GT. 6906.
[14] IO's report (S.), Feb. 1918. [15] *II*, 9 Jan. 1918.

Tipperary.[16] The spread of the Sinn Féin party took place against a background of intermittent unrest and violence – following the patterns already established by the O'Connellite and Parnellite movements in the previous century.

During the summer of 1918 many football matches and other sports fixtures were banned. The foreign circulation of twenty-eight Irish papers was prohibited, while in the course of one week six provincial newspapers were suppressed.[17] Figures supplied by Sinn Féin (and therefore to be treated with caution) listed seven civilians 'wantonly murdered without provocation' by the army and police in 1917, and six in 1918. Other statistics indicated the increase in violence, if in a partisan manner:[18]

	1917	1918	1919
Arrests	349	1,107	959
Raids on private houses	11	260	13,782
Assaults by police and military	18	81	476

As a sign of things to come, early in 1918 Sinn Féin clubs throughout the country were asked to provide the names of 'sympathetic medical practitioners'.[19] Trouble lay ahead.

The Volunteers flourished during the conscription crisis, when a military confrontation suddenly appeared likely. Tens of thousands of young Irishmen made it clear that they would prefer to die in Ireland for their own country's rights (particularly the right not to fight in Britain's war) rather than to die in France or the Middle East for the freedom of other small nations (but not their own). Violence continued after the crisis ended, and the Volunteers became more daring than they had been in the past. In Co. Cork, after two RIC men had enforced a ban on a local *feis*, one had his arm fractured, the other was shot in the neck and their car was thrown over a cliff. Their rifles and ammunition were seized.[20] On armistice night, triumphant British soldiers fought republicans, as a result of which, Collins boasted, 120 officers and soldiers were injured and 5 killed. (No such deaths were announced by the military authorities, but both Collins and *An tÓglách* claimed that publication of these details was forbidden by the censor).[21]

---

[16] IG's report, Feb. 1918, CO.904/105; Stubbs, 'Unionists and Ireland', p. 891.

[17] *Two years of English atrocities in Ireland* (pamphlet, 1919), p. 8; *Nationality*, 13 Apr. 1918.

[18] 'Notes of progress of militarism', Mar. 1920, Monteagle MSS, NLI 10,914. The high figure for arrests in 1918 was a consequence of the 'German plot'.

[19] E.g., *Précis* of captured documents, NLI, MS 10,494(1), p. 4.   [20] *Cork Examiner*, 9 July 1918.

[21] Collins to Stack, 28 Nov. 1918, NLI, MS 5848; *An tÓglách*, 30 Nov. 1918.

After Soloheadbeg

Lloyd George's cabinet took some time to appreciate the scale of its Irish problems, and early in 1919 Winston Churchill, the secretary for war, still believed that 'there was no place in the world where there was less danger at the present time'.[22] Already by this stage, however, a process of provocation and retaliation had begun. Although the ambush at Soloheadbeg did not disturb a tranquil and settled country, it did incite the British authorities to take more drastic measures than those which had already been adopted after other, less serious incidents. Fairs and markets were banned for a period of three months, with the result that the whole population suffered. These restrictions provoked complaints, among them an angry protest which was made from Clonmel (Co. Tipperary): its inhabitants should not be punished for a crime which had been committed 20 miles away.[23]

The more dedicated rebels were concerned by their colleagues' ebbing enthusiasm, and the pessimists even feared that the Irish Volunteers might disintegrate. But in at least some cases the repressive measures taken by Dublin Castle bonded them together and forced them to become more disciplined. Thereby the British fulfilled the forecast made by the impatient Sean Treacy at the end of the previous year: 'if this is the state of affairs, we'll have to kill someone, and make the bloody enemy organise us!'[24] The resumption of fighting was the action of a small and unrepresentative minority. Cathal Brugha later dismissed Ernie O'Malley's claim that the people had not been consulted, and pointed out that 'if so, we would never have fired a shot. If we gave them a good strong lead, they would follow.'[25] He was right, and ultimately most of the nationalist population *did* follow.

The majority of the IRA's early victims were Catholic Irish policemen who were often popular and respected figures in their communities. Some of them were unarmed and were shot in the back; many people regarded their deaths as squalid murders. In some cases during the early months of confrontation there seems to have been genuine sorrow and anger when they were killed, but elsewhere people lapsed easily into the traditional Irish stance of being 'agin the government'. After an attempted rescue at Knocklong railway station, in the course of which two policemen were shot dead, the RIC complained that the local people 'remain perfectly callous and give no assistance in tracing

---

[22] Cabinet conclusions, 4 Feb. 1919, Cab.23/9, WC.526(3).

[23] *Nationalist and Munster Advertiser*, 1 Feb. 1919.

[24] Desmond Ryan, *Sean Treacy and the 3rd. Tipperary brigade* (Tralee, 1945), pp. 55–6.

[25] Ernie O'Malley, *The singing flame* (Dublin, 1978), p. 25.

the murderers'.[26] Within months a ballad sheet was in circulation celebrating the attacks at Soloheadbeg and Knocklong.[27] Another attempt to rescue a wounded prisoner in Limerick workhouse hospital resulted in the death of the prisoner and one of his guards. It was the Volunteer's funeral which drew large crowds, and thousands of his colleagues marched in the procession behind his coffin, accompanied by the clergy, the mayor and members of the corporation.[28]

As a result of this incident, Limerick city was proclaimed a special military area, and a system of permits was imposed with the intention of controlling travel into and out of the city. In practice Limerick was cut in two. The measure provoked not only outrage and a sense of grievance, but also an organized pattern of defiance. The trades council (rather than the Sinn Féin party) called a meeting at which it was decided that workers should not be forced to suffer the inconveniences imposed by the proclamation; 15,000 people joined in a general strike, and a committee (the 'Limerick soviet') was elected to run the city.[29] Its methods were efficient, orderly and non-revolutionary, and its chairman declared that the confrontation with the British authorities was a labour rather than a political dispute.[30] The soviet arranged for the collection of food and for its distribution at fixed prices, published a daily news-sheet, and even printed its own money. Relays of boats with muffled oars ran food supplies through the British blockade.[31]

In comparison with later events it was a good-humoured conflict. Crowds attended a hurling match which was held outside the city limits, and when they tried to return they were stopped by armed soldiers who insisted that they accept military permits. They rejected this demand, and then flaunted their defiance by marching up and down the Clare side of the Shannon. Some of them later crossed the river by boat to avoid the British controls on the bridges, while others boarded the Ennis train, 'stampeded' through the police defences at Limerick station, and entered the city in triumph.[32]

This confrontation aroused widespread indignation throughout the country, and the *Irish Independent* complained that 'the action of the authorities amounts to a provocation which accentuates the resentment of the people against the Government . . . Limerick, a singularly crimeless city before the unfortunate occurrence of a few weeks ago, is besieged and treated as if all its

---

[26] IG's report, May 1919, CO.904/109.

[27] *II*, 5 Sept. 1919, referring to a copy of the ballad seized on 1 Aug.   [28] *II*, 11 Apr. 1919.

[29] James Kemmy, 'The Limerick soviet', *Saothar*, 2 (1976), p. 47.   [30] *II*, 23 Apr. 1919.

[31] Liam Cahill, *Forgotten revolution: Limerick soviet 1919; a threat to British power in Ireland* (Dublin 1990), p. 74.   [32] *FJ*, 23 Apr. 1919.

inhabitants were diabolical criminals.'[33] The national Labour movement supported its Limerick colleagues, although not to the extent which would have been necessary to prolong their resistance, and the soviet did not spread to other areas as its organizers had hoped. The strike lasted for twelve days before it collapsed, and the military authorities withdrew their proclamation a week after normal work had been resumed. The police welcomed this victory over Irish nationalism, and they seemed to be unaware of the extent to which the measures taken by the crown forces had provoked deep resentment.[34] This defeat was followed by recriminations, but the population of Limerick resisted any temptation to blame its inconveniences on the Volunteers; the British army had offered itself as a new and more acceptable target of public anger.

Many Sinn Féiners were uneasy at the Labour movement's prominence in the Limerick soviet, and they did not want to enhance their ally's power and status. The strike did not form a model for later acts of defiance. Both the Dáil and the party seem not to have encouraged more widespread trade union action.[35] (They were also perturbed by the widespread agrarian unrest; in Cork and Kerry, for example, bands of agricultural labourers marched through the countryside, taking men from their work in the fields.[36] Here, too, as in the strike of engineering and power workers in Belfast, the Sinn Féin party chose to keep its distance.[37])

Slowly the scale of violence increased, and in May *Nationality* pointed out that four men had been shot by the RIC within the previous month.[38] More policemen were killed, and their deaths provoked less sympathy than had been extended after earlier attacks; it was reported that in Thurles a crowd laughed and jeered as one inspector lay dying in the street.[39] Clare was once again proclaimed a military area. After a British soldier was killed in the course of an arms raid in Fermoy (Co. Cork) the attackers delayed pursuit by felling trees across a road and cutting telephone wires. Although the incident was described by one policemen as having 'more of the savour of a wild colt cinema thrill than a happening in a quiet country town',[40] its aftermath discouraged any such escapist fantasies. All meetings within a 3 mile radius were banned, and the dead man's comrades engaged in an even more direct form of reprisal – thereby establishing a pattern which would be followed on numerous occasions during the next two years. Their target was the local population, and they sacked the town, demolishing more than fifty shop fronts, smashing windows and looting. They

[33] *II*, 23 Apr. 1919, editorial.   [34] IG's report, CI's report (Clare), Apr. 1919, CO.904/108.

[35] Cahill, *Forgotten revolution*, pp. 106, 110.   [36] IG's report, Mar. 1919, CO.904/108.

[37] See above, pp. 252–5, 257–9.   [38] *Nationality*, 10 May 1919.   [39] *II*, 25 June 1919.

[40] *II*, 9 Sept. 1919.

paid particular attention to jewellers' premises. Their commander objected to what he saw as an unreasonable attitude by the inhabitants of Fermoy, and he remarked that 'the people seemed to think that the soldiers should sit down and make no reprisals'.[41] In response to a complaint about broken windows he retorted angrily, 'damn the windows! You have got no industry. You are simply living on the Army and but for them you would be taking in each other's washing. When this thing happens and you lose a few hundred or a few thousand pounds you come and cry for protection.'[42]

These British retaliatory measures provoked widespread inconvenience (and in several cases, such as that of Fermoy, also financial loss), but the RIC inspector general was nonetheless forced to admit that 'the general public is apparently prepared to suffer rather than openly condemn the criminal acts of the republican fanatics'.[43] The pattern of 1916 was now repeated in 1919. At first the IRA's attacks were often unpopular; they were seen as hopeless ventures which could only damage the nationalist cause, and they disrupted people's comfortable routines. Soon they came to be tolerated, and even admired. The Limerick pattern was followed elsewhere, and in many cases the local resentment which had initially been aimed at the rebels was refocused on the British authorities; it was their repressive measures and their policy of collective punishment, rather than the earlier provocations, which became the target of public dislike. The radicals enticed and compelled a dubious population into supporting measures which, in most cases, it had at first opposed; they were indifferent to the wishes or the disapproval of the Dáil, the Irish cabinet and politicians in general. Some of the soldiers had slipped the civilian leash.

Even former politicians whose lives had centred on Westminster for many decades came to accept the efficacy of violence. T. M. Healy wrote of the British that, 'nothing but the threat or use of force will move them to do anything', while John Dillon later asked himself 'can there be any doubt that if murder and guerrilla war ceased in Ireland the Irish Question would within a few weeks be laid on the shelf and forgotten?'[44] Such remarks represented the views of many moderate nationalists who were committed to politics and to constitutional procedures, but who no longer believed that their preferred methods would produce any significant results. 'The old fantasy proclaimed since the days of Strongbow that the Irish were fighting England for their freedom at last became a sort of reality.'[45]

---

[41] *Cork Examiner*, 10 Sept. 1919.   [42] *IT*, 10 Sept. 1919.

[43] IG's report, Sept. 1919, CO.904/110.

[44] Healy to William O'Brien, 21 July 1919, O'Brien MSS, NLI, 8556(23); Dillon, diary, 18 Feb. 1920, Virginia Glandon, 'John Dillon's reflections on Irish and general politics', *Éire-Ireland* 9, 3 (1974), p. 31.   [45] Kee, *Green flag*, p. 708.

Dublin became a battleground. Collins formed his 'squad' which was both ruthless and effective in shooting dangerous 'G men' (the 'political' section of the police force). His system of spies and informers enabled him to single out zealous detectives and have them killed. The accuracy of his information was illustrated neatly by Walter Long's remark that 'the best Secret Service man we had . . . was shot near Glasnevin some time ago'.[46] In the first months of 1920 the squad killed both the Dublin assistant commissioner responsible for combating 'political crime' and the man who seems to have acted as the unofficial head of Castle intelligence.[47] A centuries-old pattern whereby the British authorities infiltrated Irish rebel or nationalist movements was now reversed.

In August 1919 between twenty and thirty men attacked a police hut in Clare, and by November the Volunteers had reached the stage of burning down their first (unoccupied) police barracks. In all, sixteen policemen and one soldier were killed during the year, although the IRA's most exalted target, Lord French, narrowly escaped assassination. In one abandoned attempt on his life, the team lying in wait by the front gate of Trinity College consisted of so many Sinn Féin Dáil deputies as to provoke the suggestion that it was a test parade for the TDs.[48] But the viceroy escaped uninjured when those hunting him finally made what he described as their 'murderous attack with bombs and revolvers', and ambushed his motorcade near Phoenix Park.[49]

Only a few dedicated radicals were involved in these early incidents. Dan Breen and his unit carried out the attacks in Soloheadbeg and Knocklong; many of the rest were the work of Collins's squad (aided, in the case of the attempt on French's life, by Breen, on one of his visits to Dublin). The numbers of those involved increased rapidly during 1920, but they always remained a tiny percentage of the total Volunteer force. Ultimately the British repressive measures forced the active members of IRA units to become full-time professional fighters, to go on the run, and to form 'flying columns' which engaged the crown forces in intermittent combat. 'The more the government hounded the Volunteers, the more like revolutionary soldiers they became.'[50] Most of the country was relatively unaffected by the war, but large areas of Munster – particularly Cork and Tipperary – were scenes of regular attacks and counter-attacks.

The Volunteers' principal target was the RIC. The police were hemmed into their barracks, and by the end of 1919 one of them reported from West Galway,

---

[46] Thomas Jones, *Whitehall diary*, III (Oxford, 1971), p. 19 (31 May 1920).

[47] O'Halpin, 'British intelligence in Ireland', pp. 72–3.

[48] Patrick O'Daly, statement, c. 1965, RM, P7/D/8, p. 22. TD was the normal term for a Dáil deputy, or Teachta Dála.   [49] French, diary, 19 Dec. 1919, NLI, MS 2269.

[50] Fitzpatrick, *Politics and Irish life*, p. 217.

'so closely are we watched that it is unsafe to weaken one district in order to help another'.[51] The Sinn Féin party aided the IRA in demoralizing the RIC, and a circular from headquarters advised all clubs to appoint deputations which would lobby the parents and other near relatives of policemen. They were also urged to co-operate in finding jobs for members of the force who resigned their positions.[52]

Civilian involvement in the conflict also took different forms. In most cases the forces of the crown were unable to identify or respond to their attackers. They tended to lash out wildly, with the result that many non-combatants and passers-by were injured or killed. The *Times* commented at the end of 1919 that the penalties fell on the wrong people, that their only effect was to irritate, and that 'the population in southern Ireland is between two coercions, each imposing restrictions upon ordinary liberty . . . of the two powers Sinn Fein has the more terror. That perhaps should be neglected. The serious part is that on the whole Sinn Fein has more moral authority.'[53]

French expressed the hope that the Sinn Féin movement was breaking up into moderate and extreme parties, but British actions tended to consolidate Irish nationalists rather than divide them.[54] On the same day when Edward Shortt, a former chief secretary, suggested to the cabinet that 'no-one would be relieved more than the Sinn Feiners if the Irish Volunteers were proclaimed', a message from the viceroy made it clear that he did not recognize any such distinction. He remarked of Co. Tipperary that 'Sinn Feiners in that district are an organised club for murder of police.'[55] It seemed unlikely that he would encourage any serious attempts to divide moderates from extremists. Soon afterwards the Sinn Féin party, the Volunteers, Cumann na mBan and even the Gaelic League were banned throughout the whole of Tipperary; *Nationality* described the League's inclusion in this list as marking the first English proclamation against the teaching of the Irish language for two centuries.[56] In their reactions and in their responses to their Irish problems the British tended (as so often) to oversimplify, to treat the various aspects of separatism or republicanism as one undifferentiated mass, to regard them as a monolithic 'Sinn Fein movement'. By doing so they helped bring about such a blending of moderates and extremists. They helped create the monster which they feared.

---

[51] CI's report, W. Galway, Dec. 1919, CO.904/110.

[52] O'Keeffe to Sinn Féin club secretaries, July 1920, and Markievicz, circular, Sept. 1920, RB, 8786(1). See J. Anthony Gaughan, *Memoirs of Constable Jeremiah Mee, R. I. C.* (Dublin, 1975), pp. 314–22, and see below, pp. 291, 312–13.   [53] *Times*, 12 Dec. 1919.

[54] French, memo, 15 May 1919, Cab.24/79, GT. 7277.

[55] Cabinet conclusions, 26 June 1919, Cab.23/15, WC. 585A.   [56] *Nationality*, 12 July 1919.

British attitudes and actions remained inconsistent, and the government had only limited control over its forces in Ireland. In November 1920 Lloyd George was furious when Griffith was arrested, and he described the action as 'a piece of impertinence' on the part of the authorities in Dublin; but he felt unable to order Griffith's release. The cabinet decided to take no action against de Valera when he returned to Ireland in December after eighteen months in the United States, although Hamar Greenwood, the chief secretary, made it clear that his safety could not be guaranteed.[57] Eventually he was arrested by chance – and was promptly freed on the orders of the cabinet. Like their Irish counterparts, the British military and civilian authorities often found it difficult to work together.

Soldiers and politicians

Despite the considerable overlap of membership between the Sinn Féin party and the army, their identities and functions remained separate. The Volunteers cherished their distinctiveness. Some of them tended to display the elitism which can be a characteristic of some professional soldiers, and they regarded politicians not simply as mere civilians, but as a particularly low form of civilian life.[58]

The language of the Volunteers, and in particular of their journal *An tÓglách*, was forceful and unambiguous. Its very first issue declared that the Volunteers were a military body, pure and simple, and that its members were the agents of the national will, the captains of its mind.[59] It exhorted them to think in terms of violence and bloodshed; they were informed that 'people who are not prepared to fight for their liberty do not deserve to get it', and 'the nation for which no shots ring out and for which no steel is reddened will lie like a bone in a kennel . . . it can never experience aught but a change of masters'.[60] In the event of conscription being imposed they were urged to wage 'ruthless warfare' and were told to 'eliminate all talk and all thought of passive resistance. Because passive resistance means in effect no resistance at all.'[61] There was predictable approval for the view expressed in Shaw's *Major Barbara*, that 'nothing is ever done in this world until men are prepared to kill one another if it is not done'.[62]

---

[57] Jones, *Whitehall diary*, III, p. 46 (20 Dec. 1920).   [58] See above, p. 196.

[59] *An tÓglách*, 15 Aug. 1918.   [60] *Ibid.*, 30 Nov. 1918, 15 Apr. 1919.

[61] *Ibid.*, 14 Oct. 1918. Mulcahy later thought that this article was probably written by Ernest Blythe 'from the calm detached atmosphere of a jail' ('Memoirs', RM, P7b/134).

[62] *Major Barbara*, Act III; *An tÓglách*, 29 Oct. 1918.

The soldiers' glamorous image was enhanced by the execution of republican prisoners such as Kevin Barry; by dramatic escapes, such as that of de Valera from Lincoln Jail, or of twenty Volunteers who climbed down a rope from the walls of Mountjoy during daylight; and by the inability of the British authorities to capture wanted rebel leaders. Ernie O'Malley claimed in his memoirs that, by the end of the Anglo-Irish War, he could go to dances and hear people singing about his own exploits.[63] Collins inspired widespread devotion, and even his enemies regarded him with respect: he became 'almost as much a legend alive as Pearse was dead'.[64] After he had organized an escape from Kilmainham, the British commander-in-chief, Nevil Macready, remarked that 'it was very cleverly done, and I rather admire Michael'.[65] Among the stories concerning him which floated about Dublin Castle were: 'M.C. has, I hear, grown a beard: He is the idol of the young men'; 'Michael slept with a girl, address known, once a week'; and 'Michael is often disguised as a priest with a remarkably high collar.'[66] A student in University College, Dublin reported in her diary what must have been one of innumerable stories circulating about him: 'we heard Michael Collins was killed in the battle of Roscarberry while leading his men on a white charger'.[67] How could a mere Sinn Féin politician, concerned with drab details such as voters' registers and election expenses, hope to compete with such a legend?

Substantial rewards were made available for the capture of prominent IRA leaders; the figure of £10,000 each was mentioned in the case of Brugha, Collins and Mulcahy, and £3,500 for lesser figures such as Cosgrave and Stack. But this was done discreetly, since public knowledge that a price had been placed on their heads would make 'greater heroes than ever of these people in the eyes of their followers'.[68]

From the British point of view one pattern was even more dangerous than that of making heroes of the Irish leaders: that of turning them into martyrs. This was a fate which some of them appeared determined to embrace. Most influential of all was the seventy-three-day hunger-strike of the lord mayor of Cork, Terence MacSwiney. He had decided to win a moral victory against the British, either by forcing them to back down or else by sacrificing his life. He was also anxious to

[63] O'Malley, On another man's wound, p. 311.

[64] Thompson, Imagination of an insurrection, p. 108.

[65] Macready to John Anderson, 16 Feb. 1921, Anderson MSS, CO.904/188(1).

[66] Mark Sturgis, diary, 1, 3 Sept. 1920, 21 Jan. 1921, PRO.30/59/1 and 3.

[67] Celia Shaw, diary, Jan. 1921, NLI, MS 23,409.

[68] Macready to Anderson, 5 Mar. 1921, Anderson to Macready, 8 Mar. 1921, Anderson MSS, CO.904/188(1).

atone for the shame of Cork's failure to rise in 1916, and during his protest he wrote to Brugha, 'ah, Cathal, the pain of Easter Week is properly dead at last'.[69] Churches were filled with people praying for his deliverance, on one occasion a crowd of 40,000 gathered in Cork to recite the rosary for him, and a miracle was reported outside Mountjoy Jail in Dublin. When his body was returned to Cork, eight bishops and hundreds of priests accompanied his cortège.[70] Religious practice seemed to reinforce the demand for Irish independence.

Apart from the greater risks which they ran, there were other reasons why the military might feel superior to civilians. The Volunteers had a strong case when they claimed that they were not only the right arm of the republic but that they had also been the republic in embryo. After the first meeting of the Dáil, An tÓglách declared that 'without our National Army the Republic would not exist'.[71] Three years later Seán MacEntee made the same point: 'the Dáil was the creation of the Army and the Army was not the creation of the Dáil'. (The previous day one of his colleagues, Seán Moylan, had put matters even more bluntly when he told his fellow TDs that 'there would be none of us here if there were not gunmen'. Collins endorsed his remark.)[72]

As a consequence of this exalted status, the Volunteers were expected to keep their distance from other bodies, however worthy they might be. In early 1917 a circular instructed them that, although they were encouraged to join other organizations, they should obey only the orders of their own executive; in this way they would avoid any misunderstanding 'such as occurred on the last occasion'. They were reminded of the dangers of politics, and of how, when Parnell had induced the Fenians to join him, the result was the virtual abandonment of physical force as a policy.[73] They were informed that there was no lack of political workers in the country, and that it was easier to find men who would be active in the political arena than it was to find good Volunteer officers; they should not allow themselves be distracted by political activities.[74] At the Sinn Féin convention in October 1917 it was announced that the Volunteers did not want politicians interfering in military matters, and that the soldiers were able to take care of themselves.[75] But IRA men were

---

[69] MacSwiney to Brugha, 30 Sept. 1920, MacSwiney MSS, UCDA, P48b/416.

[70] John Newsinger, '"I bring not peace but a sword": the religious motif in the Irish War of Independence', Journal of Contemporary History, 13, 3 (1978), p. 623.

[71] An tÓglách, 31 Jan. 1919.   [72] DE, 1921–22, pp. 341, 303 (28, 27 Apr. 1922).

[73] 'Óglaig na hÉireann (Irish Volunteers)', (circular, 22 May 1917), NLI, MS 10,494(10).

[74] An tÓglách, 14 Sept. 1919.

[75] De Róiste diary, 27 Oct. 1917, FO'D, 31,146(1); 'Sinn Fein convention 1917', CO.904/23/5, p. 16. De Róiste thought that Collins made this remark.

beset by temptations, and sometimes it appeared as if they were prepared to do anything except fight the British. *An tÓglách* complained later that, in areas where few or no engagements against the crown forces had taken place, Volunteers were busily arresting criminals, closing public houses and suppressing poteen stills. It seemed as if they were allowing police work to monopolize their attention and distract them from their main responsibility of waging war.[76]

Sinn Féin's fortunes were affected by the rapid increase in the scale and impact of the Volunteers' activities, and party members were soon overshadowed by the soldiers who, in many cases, viewed them with condescension and scorn. Once again, as with the spread of violence, this was a pattern which preceded 1919. Three later memoirs illustrate the feelings shared by some of these young warriors. Dan Breen boasted that the first Volunteer parade in his part of Tipperary came as an even greater shock to the local Sinn Féiners than it did to the British. (The politically minded had their revenge, and Breen admitted that work for the 1918 general election had a serious effect on the Volunteers' morale; many of them had ceased to be soldiers and had became politicians.)[77] Ernie O'Malley's comrades in the IRA sneered at those Gaelic Leaguers and members of Sinn Féin clubs who did not belong to the military wing of the movement.[78] Long afterwards, C. S. Andrews recalled how men in his Volunteer company regarded Daniel O'Connell as a coward and, even worse, as a politician; and all politicians were low, dirty and treacherous. His colleagues did not take the Sinn Féin club seriously, seeing it merely as a useful means of raising money and as a cover for Volunteer activities.[79]

There was no shortage of contemporary comment to illustrate these attitudes. Collins shared the widespread distaste for the corrupting influence of politics; he wrote to Stack about how he was having a quiet laugh at the political eagerness of some of the 'I'm only a fighting man' fraternity as the 1918 general election drew near.[80] (He himself was elected an MP in 1918, as were ten others of the twenty members of the Volunteer executive who took office a year earlier; the corresponding figure for the second Dáil would rise to thirteen.[81]) Some months later, after the constitutional changes in April 1919 which had barred him (*ex officio*, as a cabinet minister) from membership of the standing committee, he complained that 'we have too many of the bargaining type already'. He expressed doubts as to whether

---

[76] *An tÓglách*, 1 Sept. 1920. On such non-military distractions, see below, pp. 314–18.

[77] Breen, *My fight for Irish freedom*, pp. 9, 32–3.   [78] O'Malley, *On another man's wound*, p. 57.

[79] Andrews, *Dublin made me*, pp. 100–01.   [80] Collins to Stack, 28 Nov. 1918, NLI, MS 5848.

[81] Mulcahy, 'The Irish Volunteer convention', p. 408.

our movement or part of it at any rate is fully alive to the developing situation. It seems to me that official SF is inclined to be ever less militant and ever more political and theoretical . . . There is I suppose the effect of tendency of all Revolutionary movements to divide themselves up into their component parts. Now the moral force department have probably been affected by English propaganda.[82]

One apprehensive Griffithite Sinn Féiner anticipated that the party would be disparaged as a kind of parliamentary movement, as a lesser body than the Volunteers; 'this was attitude of some formerly and I feel almost certain it will be taken up again . . . force is being exalted to a principle. The means has become the end.'[83] Sinn Féin was regarded by many as an organization more suitable for women than for men – and such a designation was not intended as a compliment. Rather than combine Sinn Féin with the IRA, some wished to merge it with Cumann na mBan. Plunkett felt that 'the Volunteer movement should draw in every young man, and the Sinn Féin organisation every young woman', while the intemperate *Irish Nation* bragged that the Volunteers were a man's force, while the Sinn Féin of which Arthur Griffith was the father was an old woman's organization.[84] A notice in the *Clare Champion* indicates the way in which the soldiers tended to see themselves as a group apart from the rest of the community: when a Sinn Féin branch was formed in Ennis (and was described, perhaps optimistically, as a 'non-drinking club') its committee comprised 'six representing the volunteers, and six the general public'.[85]

Sometimes the soldiers' dislike and suspicion were reciprocated. For example, at the end of 1918, Tomás MacCurtain wrote that he and other Volunteers had been sleeping out of doors and that

> Sinn Féin people pay little attention now to anyone on the run from the peelers. Nobody asks us any question about the state we're in . . . We have to do something and without delay. There is no use relying on Sinn Féin people or on anyone else. Maybe they'll do something when we and our families are in the poorhouse.[86]

There were a few examples of soldiers feeling inferior to politicians. Ernie O'Malley (of all people!) complained to George Plunkett that, except in the large centres, IRA officers and men did not possess sufficient status. Frequently

---

[82] Collins to Stack, 18 May 1919, NLI, MS 5848. For these changes, see above, p. 174.

[83] De Róiste, diary, 9 Jan. 1917, CAI, U271/A/29(A).

[84] *Roscommon Herald*, 13 Oct. 1917; *Irish Nation*, 27 Oct. 1917.

[85] *Clare Champion*, 1 Sept. 1917.

[86] MacCurtain, diary, 31 Dec. 1918, Cork Public Museum, L.1945:228.

'a non-Volunteer will point, with pride and awe to the local President of the Sinn Féin Club; he would not dream of doing so where the local Volunteer Captain was concerned'.[87] But such views were rare.

The Volunteers kept their distance from the Dáil and its cabinet, as well as from the party. Nonetheless they tended to regard the Dáil with a vague, benevolent deference, provided that it made no serious attempts to limit their freedom of action. (In general they were left in peace; the minutes of 129 cabinet meetings between April 1919 and December 1921 contain only 26 reference to military affairs.[88]) They viewed its message to the free nations of the world – which included a reference to the state of war between England and Ireland – as a welcome justification of their actions. The fighting men were reassured that

> never before have they secured so complete and authoritative national sanction for the work in which they have been engaged. They, as agents of the national will, have had that will expressed by the highest national authority in just such terms as every Volunteer would wish to hear it expressed . . . the authority of the nation is behind them, embodied in a lawfully constituted authority whose moral sanction every theologian must recognise.[89]

On Brugha's proposal, the army, along with Dáil deputies and others, took an oath to 'support and defend the Irish Republic and the Government of the Irish Republic, which is Dáil Éireann'. He explained (ironically in the light of his own later actions in 1922) that he regarded the Volunteers as a standing army, and that as such they should be subject to the government.[90] His aim may have been not merely to consolidate civilian authority, but also to limit the power of the IRB within the army – particularly since his rival Collins had recently been elected president of the brotherhood's supreme council.[91] A month later the IRB in turn accepted the Dáil as the government of the country, and in similar fashion it followed the Dáil's example by acknowledging de Valera as president of the Irish republic in August 1921.[92]

But the Dáil did not reciprocate fully, and as late as January 1921 it avoided taking responsibility for the army's actions. It finally recognized the state of war

---

[87] O'Malley to Plunkett, 5 Dec. 1919, EO'M, P17a/158.

[88] Charles Hannon, 'The Irish Volunteers and the concept of military service and defence 1913–1924' (Ph.D. dissertation, University College, Dublin, 1989), p. 191.

[89] *An tÓglách*, 31 Jan. 1919.   [90] *DE, 1919–21*, pp. 151–3 (20 Aug. 1919).

[91] Coogan, *Michael Collins*, p. 115.

[92] John O'Beirne-Ranelagh, 'The IRB from the treaty to 1924', *IHS*, 20, 77 (1976), pp. 31–2.

with Britain six weeks later.[93] The deputies knew that they had little or no power over the active elements of the IRA, and that by refraining from futile attempts to control or direct the military organization they avoided a battle which they would almost certainly have lost.[94] The former Nationalist MP Stephen Gwynn commented to Mark Sturgis, a Dublin Castle official, that 'Dáil Éireann no more controls the gunmen than you control the police.'[95]

Richard Mulcahy, the chief of staff, was later reported to have told the active service units from the Dublin battalions that if an attack could be traced to them they might be disowned by the Dáil government. As one of them commented, 'we accepted these terms, although they opened up very unpleasant possibilities for us, for we would then be outlawed by the British, repudiated by our own Government, and also might suffer the censure of the Church'.[96] Mulcahy believed strongly that the army should be subordinated to the civilian government – but that the IRA in turn should be protected from interference by TDs.[97] (His attitude resembled that of de Valera and others who wanted to shield the party from members of the Dáil. Legislators were not trusted.)

De Valera's division between the party and the state apparatus, and his exclusion of most members of the cabinet from the Sinn Féin leadership, were moves which had important consequences. Not only did they deprive the party of some of the most talented and dynamic figures within its ranks, but they also tended to drive a wedge between it and the militant elements in the Volunteers. This change was implemented in May 1919, and it coincided with a period when Collins's life became busier and more endangered. Nonetheless it is significant that he attended fifteen of the twenty-three standing committee meetings held between 7 November 1918 and 15 April 1919; thirty-two months and another seventy-five meetings elapsed before he reappeared, in the aftermath of the treaty. Except in the prelude to the 1918 general election he had never been closely involved in the party's activities, but, as a result of de Valera's action he was virtually excluded from them until his election as a vice-president at the October 1921 *ard-fheis*.

Already in March 1919 Collins had tried to over-rule the Sinn Féin standing committee's cautious acceptance of a British ban on demonstrations; this prohibition was intended to prevent celebrations welcoming de Valera's return to Dublin after the 'German plot' prisoners had been released. According to one account, he declared that the sooner fighting was forced and a general state of

---

[93] *DE, 1919–21*, pp. 249, 264, 278–9 (25 Jan., 11 Mar. 1921).

[94] Fitzpatrick, *Politics and Irish life*, p. 211.   [95] Sturgis, diary, 9 Dec. 1920, PRO.30/59/3.

[96] Ryan, *Sean Treacy*, p. 117.

[97] Maryann Gialanella Valiulis, *Portrait of a revolutionary: General Richard Mulcahy and the founding of the Irish Free State* (Dublin, 1992), p. 62.

disorder created throughout the country, the better; Ireland was likely to profit more from such conditions than by maintaining things as they were. He also made clear his contempt for the Sinn Féin executive, and told its members that they had been summoned only to confirm what 'the proper people' had decided. These were the Volunteers, who 'were ready to face the British military, and were resolved to force the issue. And they were not to be deterred by weaklings and cowards.' Griffith rejected this usurpation of civilian authority, making it clear that he would accept the decision of the standing committee and of no other body.[98] De Valera acquiesced in the ban, and (perhaps surprisingly) he was supported in this by Brugha. Collins was left virtually isolated, and with confessed exaggeration he compared Sinn Féin's withdrawal to O'Connell's defeat at Clontarf in 1843.[99] But this was no more than a temporary setback, and soon his wish for confrontation was fulfilled.

Suppression

The Anglo-Irish War glorified conflict and heroes, making politicians seem safe, tame and dull, but it also crippled Sinn Féin in an even more direct manner. The fear and repression which accompany most wars, and in particular all guerrilla wars, drove the party underground. The raids and arrests of 1918 had been damaging but they were not systematic, and Sinn Féiners had managed not merely to survive but even to triumph in the general election at the end of the year. The repression of 1919–21 was of a totally different order. As two rival armies fought each other on Dublin streets and country lanes there often seemed to be little for politicians and other civilians to do except keep their heads down and wait for the shooting to stop.

Despite disagreements within the British cabinet, the Sinn Féin party was banned first regionally and then throughout the whole country. In May 1919 the viceroy, Lord French, and Ian Macpherson, the chief secretary, argued that it was essential to suppress the 'Sinn Fein organisation' which, in their view, comprised Sinn Féin clubs, the Volunteers, Cumann na mBan and the Gaelic League. Carson expressed doubts about such a move, and Bonar Law also demurred; he suggested to Lloyd George that to suppress Sinn Féin would in effect put an end to the whole political life of southern Ireland, and he believed that this could not be done effectively.[100] In the circumstances of the time such

---

[98] Figgis, *Recollections*, pp. 243–4.   [99] Collins to Stack, 26 Mar. 1919, NLI, MS 17,090.
[100] Bonar Law to Macpherson, 15 May 1919, BL, 101/3/69; Bonar Law to Lloyd George, 18 May 1919, LG, F/30/3/63.

common sense was unlikely to triumph. The cabinet's Irish expert, Walter Long, was able to assure his colleagues that, once Sinn Féin leaders had achieved their aim of an Irish republic, they would 'take immediate steps, following upon the appointment of the new Irish Government, to bring about union with the Republic of the United States of America'.[101] Long was an irascible, humourless man, and this remark appears not to have been intended as a joke. At a lower level the inspector general of the RIC learned with interest two months later, on the basis of a captured copy of *The constitution of the Irish Volunteers*, that 'there is no appreciable difference between the I.R.B. and the Irish Volunteers except that the latter are a military organisation'.[102] Dependent on such a level of understanding, the cabinet and the Castle were unlikely to display wisdom or moderation.

Many leading figures in the Sinn Féin movement were already in jail or in hiding. One symptomatic item discussed by the standing committee in May 1919 was the appointment of a general secretary to replace Páidín O'Keeffe while he was on the run.[103] Between July and September 1919 the party was suppressed in the most 'disturbed' counties of Cork, Clare and Tipperary, and in the following month this ban was extended to Dublin city and county – apparently in a move to prevent the forthcoming *ard-fheis* from taking place. Griffith, who was acting president during de Valera's absence in the United States, simply advanced the date of the convention by two days and summoned a hurried meeting with a reduced attendance of about 500. The *ard-fheis* concluded its business in the early hours of the morning.[104] British forces blockaded the Mansion House on the date which had been scheduled, but discovered that they were too late. The Dáil had already been suppressed on 12 September.

Finally, on 26 November, the Sinn Féin party was proscribed throughout the whole country, along with the Gaelic League, Cumann na mBan and the Volunteers. *Nationality* and other papers were closed down, and even the *Freeman's Journal* was banned for six weeks in December 1919 and January 1920. The list of sympathetic provincial newspapers silenced by the British authorities grew even longer. Many people both inside and outside the country agreed with Griffith's response: 'the English Government in Ireland has now proclaimed the whole Irish nation, as it formerly proclaimed the Catholic church, an illegal assembly'.[105] These measures weakened the moderate and

---

[101] Long, memo, 24 Sept. 1919, Cab.24/89, GT. 8215.   [102] IG's report, Oct. 1919, CO.904/110.
[103] SCM, 29 May 1919.
[104] Diarmuid O'Hegarty to Seán T. O'Kelly, 30 Oct. 1919, Gavan Duffy MSS, NAI, 1125/2; *FJ*, 17 Oct. 1919.   [105] *II*, 27 Nov. 1919.

political elements within the republican movement and strengthened those who were committed to a military solution; the radicals could argue, not unreasonably, that British actions left the Irish with no alternative to violence.

Arrests became more widespread, and they were accompanied by a range of petty restrictions. Curfew was enforced in many areas, so that from February 1920 public lighting was extinguished in Dublin at 11.30 p.m. and the streets were empty by midnight. The curfew hour was lowered, until by the summer it came into force at 8 p.m. Social habits were adjusted accordingly, and in University College, Cork students held their dances in the late afternoons, creating an artificial night by fitting blackout curtains to the windows.[106] Because cars had been used in most arms raids, from November 1919 onwards all owners and drivers of cars and lorries were obliged to secure special permits. The Union of Motor Drivers forbade its members to apply for licences, and for three months a politically motivated strike caused widespread social and economic disruption. Even Cardinal Logue travelled in a horse-drawn carriage as a protest against the restrictions.[107] A *Times* special correspondent remarked that the government was 'pushed into sheer absurdities of repression in order to combat the claims which impeach its authority'.[108]

For several months railwaymen refused to carry British troops, armed police or their weapons, with the result that passenger services were disrupted or virtually ceased throughout much of Ireland. At an early stage in the dispute party headquarters asked Sinn Féin clubs to collect money for the railwaymen's fund; this would be forwarded to Thomas Johnson of the Labour Party, and Sinn Féin functioned merely as an auxiliary.[109] A total of £120,000 was contributed. Even though the workers abandoned their strike after months of deadlock, it had, nonetheless, provided valuable support for 'the moral authority of the alternative system established by Sinn Féin'.[110] By the end of 1920 permits were required for practically every journey beyond a 20 mile radius, and later in Cork all use of bicycles was prohibited.[111]

Most people did not follow the railwaymen's example and instead, cautiously, they tried as best they could to lead ordinary lives and avoid being caught up in the war. At the beginning of 1921 the chairman of North Tipperary county council reported that 'young men will not jeopardise their lives. Middle

---

[106] O'Faolain, *Vive moi!*, p. 141.   [107] CI's report, Armagh, Nov. 1919, CO.904/110.

[108] *Times*, 9 Dec. 1919.

[109] O'Keeffe, 'Munitions of war fund' (circular, 28 June 1920), HSS, 22,691(3).

[110] Charles Townshend, 'The Irish railway strike of 1920: industrial action and civil resistance in the struggle for independence', *IHS*, 21, 83 (1979), p. 282.

[111] De Róiste, diary, 16 Apr. 1921, CAI, U271/A/37.

aged and old men will not jeopardise their cash.'[112] Later it was noted that, throughout the conflict, the phlegmatic people of North Kildare had 'not worried very much about anything except the price of cattle and the odds at the Curragh'.[113] Only a small minority of the population was active in its hostility to British rule. Stack might tell the Dáil that 'Ireland could well afford to lose some of the 180,000 young men saved [from conscription] in the last few years and could suffer to lose fifty or a hundred million pounds' property',[114] but not many were so sanguine, or so indifferent to the pleasures of peace.

Many British ministers and officials doubted the wisdom of their repressive policy, but this did not affect significantly the measures taken by the police and the army. Sinn Féin was forced to operate as an underground party. At the national level the *ard-fheis*, having met secretly despite the suppression of October 1919, did not convene again for two years, and similarly the *ard-chomhairle* showed no sign of life. It should have held quarterly meetings, but none took place between August 1919 and August 1921.[115] The disruption was so thorough that when its members finally reassembled after the truce they were told that their last gathering had been in May 1919; a sitting which was held three months later was quite forgotten.[116]

Despite its small size even the standing committee was affected by British restrictions, and the infrequency of its meetings indicates the extent to which normal civilian life was suspended. It was expected to convene weekly, and it performed most creditably during its first two years when it met fifty-five times in 1918 and forty-six in 1919. In the first half of 1920 the figure dropped to sixteen, and in the second half of the year to seven. During the first six months of 1921 it held nine meetings, but four of these took place within a nine-day period in May when it ratified candidates for the general election campaign. In November 1919 it had failed to reach a quorum, so at the next meeting, 'in view of the exceptional circumstances', the requirement was reduced from seven members to five.[117] Even so, on several occasions during the next year less than five members attended, and on 14 July 1920 only one person turned up. Finally, on 14 October, it was decided that the committee would not reconvene until there was a special reason for it to do so, and it lay dormant throughout most of the savage winter which followed. The next meeting did not take place until 10 February 1921.

---

[112] Seán O'Byrne to Local Government Department, 2 Jan. 1921, DELG, 27/13.

[113] Unsigned letter to Darrell Figgis, 13 Oct. 1921, DELG, 13/11.

[114] *DE, 1919–21*, p. 247 (25 Jan. 1921).

[115] *Ard comhairle, hon. secretary's report*, 23 Aug. 1921, RB, 8786(2). See above, pp. 175–6.

[116] *Ibid.*   [117] SCM, 13 Nov. 1919.

Nonetheless the Sinn Féin headquarters continued to function, however minimally, and the party's main activities between mid-1919 and mid-1921 were described as being to implement Dáil decrees, help impose the Belfast boycott and collect funds for the IRA and the munition workers' strike.[118] British measures forced the party to become more decentralized. In December 1919 branches were reminded that their activities should be focused on their constituency executives, and that no correspondence should be sent to 6 Harcourt Street except by hand or by some other such safe means; in turn the executives were directed to supply headquarters with local addresses 'which would not be suspect'.[119] In summer 1920 headquarters sent propaganda to the constituency executives, and club members were expected to distribute these at chapel gates on Sundays, at football matches, markets and other venues.[120]

At local level Sinn Féin was harried as well, and in the martial law counties any meeting of more than eight people was declared illegal. The RIC reports made occasional references to the party's activities; the police dispersed a group of well-known Sinn Féiners who attempted to summon a meeting of the East Cork constituency executive in their hall in Midleton, while in West Galway they noticed that, although no Sinn Féin meetings were held, leaders and organizers were forever on the move.[121] On nine separate dates between February and September 1920 party headquarters supplied a total of twenty branches in West Wicklow with receipts for their £3 affiliation fees; obviously both 6 Harcourt Street and individual clubs were able to carry on at least some of their routine business.[122] Terence MacSwiney convened a meeting of the Mid-Cork executive, and on rare occasions large gatherings were held, such as that of 160 Sinn Féiners in the Longford Temperance Hall.[123] In Dublin, the Pembroke constituency executive decided to reconstitute its officer board on a more regular basis by asking the clubs to hold new elections.[124]

Records of such occasions were few, although their absence does not necessarily indicate complete hibernation, and in mid-1920 the RIC (not necessarily a reliable authority in such matters) described only seven out of sixty-one Sinn

---

[118] *Ard comhairle, hon. secretary's report,* 23 Aug. 1921, RB, 8786(2).

[119] Tom Kelly and Hanna Sheehy-Skeffington, circular, 10 Dec. 1919, RB, 8786(1); SCM, 30 Oct. 1919.   [120] Páidín O'Keeffe, 'Help to spread the light' (circular), 28 June 1920, HSS, 22,691(3).

[121] CIs' reports, E. Cork, Oct. 1919, W. Galway, Jan. 1920, CO.904/110–11.

[122] O'Keeffe to Déográine Barton, 19 Sept. 1921, RB, 8786(2).

[123] MacSwiney to Mid-Cork executive, 16 June 1920, MacSwiney MSS, CAI, PR4/6/43; CI's report, Longford, July 1920, CO.904/112.

[124] A. MacLochlainn to Desmond FitzGerald, 24 June 1920, NAI, DE, 4/12/36.

Féin branches in Kerry as being 'inactive'.[125] Many sources of information concerning the party were no longer available as a result of censorship, and in other cases the clubs' silence may have been tactical; they would not have wished to draw attention to themselves. Nonetheless the evidence from the period after the truce in July 1921, when people were able to talk and write freely about what they had or had not done during the previous two years, points overwhelmingly to a virtual stoppage of most clubs' earlier activities.

This is illustrated vividly in the case of Clare. It was claimed that the Ennis branch held no meetings and that 'our men' were driven from their society room, the landlord took possession of the houses in which meetings had been held in the past, records and minutes were concealed, and many documents were lost. No list of members was available when one was required in October 1921, and the new secretaries 'had to obtain from persons whom they knew had been members, the names of such other members as they could recollect'.[126] At the height of the Anglo-Irish War the chief secretary felt able to reassure Lloyd George that the Sinn Féin cause and organization was breaking up, and his optimism was at least partly confirmed when, in August 1921, W. T. Cosgrave could refer in passing to 'the almost complete disappearance of the Sinn Féin Organisation'.[127]

The few independent initiatives credited to the party (or to people associated with it, rather than with the Volunteers) tended to have unfortunate consequences. In the aftermath of Bloody Sunday, in November 1920, a Dáil deputy (Roger Sweetman of Wexford) broke ranks with his colleagues, wrote to the press deploring the methods of warfare which were being used, and called for an end to the bloodshed. He proposed an immediate conference 'without prejudice to the general settlement, which will eventually have to be negotiated between Dáil Éireann on the one hand and the British Government on the other'.[128] (Later he resigned his seat in protest at the killings of Bloody Sunday and other IRA operations, declaring that he wished 'to see nothing done which they as moderate men could not stand over in the main'. On the same occasion a less temperate view was expressed by Joseph MacDonagh: 'it would be well worth while if the whole country was burned provided they won through'.[129]) A few days after Sweetman's initiative a group of Galway county councillors discussed the prospects of peace and the idea that the Dáil should negotiate a truce. This was reported (and distorted) in the press. Both of these incidents created

---

[125] 'Crime special. County of Kerry', *Irish Bulletin*, 16 Sept. 1920.

[126] *Clare Champion*, 4 Feb. 1922.

[127] Greenwood to Lloyd George, n.d. [Nov. 1920], LG, F/19/2/31; *DE, 1921–22*, p. 36 (17 Aug. 1921).

[128] *II*, 30 Nov. 1920.   [129] *DE, 1919–21*, pp. 243–4 (25 Jan. 1921).

an impression of failing Irish will-power in the war against the British forces. But worst of all was the intervention of Fr O'Flanagan.

A vacuum in the Sinn Féin leadership enabled O'Flanagan to take an unwise initiative. De Valera was president of both the party and the Dáil, and after his departure in June 1919 Griffith succeeded him on a temporary basis in both these offices. By December 1920 de Valera was still in the United States, Griffith had recently been arrested, and Collins in turn had succeeded Griffith as acting president of the Dáil. O'Flanagan was now the acting president of Sinn Féin, even though his influence was minimal and he had attended only two of the twenty-three standing committee meetings which were held during the year. Leadership of the party and the state apparatus was divided, for the first time since the Dáil government began functioning effectively in April 1919. It was against this background that O'Flanagan sent a telegram to Lloyd George. The message ran: 'you state that you are willing to make peace at once without waiting for Christmas. Ireland also is willing. What first step do you propose?'[130]

Lloyd George was anxious to find out if this statement represented party policy, and at a cabinet meeting he suggested that, because of the position which O'Flanagan held, the initiative was more likely to have been taken on behalf of Sinn Féin than in a personal capacity.[131] Others lost no time in making it clear that this was not the case. O'Keeffe announced that no meeting of the standing committee had been held since Griffith's arrest the previous month, and that O'Flanagan's telegram was therefore 'simply a statement of personal opinion, and has not the sanction of the Sinn Féin executive'. He added that only the Dáil had the authority to speak for Ireland.[132] De Valera also disowned the turbulent priest, Collins remarked that O'Flanagan spoke only for himself and that his voice seemed to be very unsteady, and from jail Griffith deplored his imprudence.[133] De Valera was later urged to sack O'Flanagan from the party; he would be less dangerous outside than inside.[134] Only Seán Milroy (a member of Sinn Féin but not of the Dáil) saw any merit in his suggestion.

The British viewed O'Flanagan's initiative as a further sign of Irish weakness, and at this stage Lloyd George was not prepared to make serious concessions to those whom he continued to regard as 'gunmen'. Despite the mortification which O'Flanagan had caused his colleagues, he persevered in his search for peace, and he actually met Lloyd George and Carson in London. By now,

---

[130] *II*, 6 Dec. 1920.

[131] *Hansard*, 135, col. 1,715 (6 Dec. 1920); cabinet conclusions, 6 Dec. 1920, Cab. 23/23, C.66(20)2.

[132] *II*, 8 Dec. 1920.

[133] Collins to Art O'Brien, 14 Dec. 1920, NAI, DE 2/234B; Griffith to Collins, 7 Dec. 1920, EO'M, P17a/158.   [134] P. J. Little to de Valera, 19 Feb. 1921, EdeV.

however, it was obvious that he represented no-one but himself.[135] Lloyd George remarked dismissively that O'Flanagan could not deliver the goods, and others were equally unimpressed; Hamar Greenwood, the chief secretary, regarded him condescendingly as 'a good fellow, a fine nature, but fearfully ignorant'.[136] With this one inglorious exception the party and its leaders left all initiatives to the Dáil government and the IRA.

Escalation

While Sinn Féin was bludgeoned into quiescence, and the Irish cabinet, the Dáil and even some county councils were driven underground, the active elements among the Volunteers (always a small minority of the total) struggled with the crown forces. These were forced to abandon large areas of the country. The campaign by which the police were boycotted, already under way in 1917, was intensified in later years; only after they had been ostracized and turned into 'outsiders' did widespread attacks on them begin.[137] In Wexford in June 1920 it was reported that the RIC could not obtain transport and that some of its members were forced to commandeer their food, while from Galway came the complaint that policemen's lives were scarcely bearable, they were 'shunned and hated and rejoicing takes place when they are shot. They have to take the necessaries of life by force. Their wives are miserable, and their children suffer in the schools, and nobody cares.'[138] One county inspector reported that half the policemen were informers to Sinn Féin and the other half ready to become assassins; but some chose a different, less dramatic course, and the *Irish Bulletin* was able to claim that by July 1920 resignations from the RIC averaged forty-six per week.[139] Increasingly, the main function of the police was to protect themselves rather than the public, and there was much truth in the claim of *An tÓglách* that 'the old "R.I.C." force, England's right arm and eyes and ears in Ireland has largely ceased to be effective for work on its former lines'.[140]

Dublin Castle lost control over much of the countryside. When the crown forces entered the Dingle peninsula in Kerry they 'had practically to assume the

---

[135] Carroll, *They have fooled you again*, pp. 119–23.

[136] Jones, *Whitehall diary*, III, p. 49 (30 Jan. 1921); H. A. L. Fisher, diary, 12 Jan. 1921, Fisher MSS, Bodleian Library, Oxford, Fisher 17, p. 8.

[137] Augusteijn, *From public defiance to guerrilla warfare*, p. 220.

[138] CIs' reports, Wexford, June 1920, W. Galway, Aug. 1920, CO.904/112.

[139] Warren Fisher to Lloyd George, 21 July 1920, LG, F/17/1/6; *Irish Bulletin*, 4 Aug. 1920.

[140] *An tÓglách*, 1 June 1920.

dimensions and attitude of an invading column', while some months later the RIC reported that the Dungloe district of Donegal, one-sixth of the county, seemed to have become a miniature republic.[141] The *Irish Times* lamented in May 1920 that 'the forces of the Crown are being driven back on their headquarters in Dublin by a steadily advancing enemy... the King's Government virtually has ceased to exist south of the Boyne and west of the Shannon', and it went on to claim that the district of Millstreet (Co. Cork) 'is entirely subservient to the bold and not unchivalrous law-givers of the Republican movement'.[142] Macready wrote to Greenwood that for many years the principal source of information for the police was 'corner boys and loafers and such like, who gave information to the RIC, and indeed acted as their jackals'. This group had now changed sides.[143]

In July 1920 the British cabinet decided that the time had come to take the offensive. Following the pattern of the conscription crisis two years earlier, the government ignored the good advice which it was given by most of its Irish experts; Lloyd George remarked that it could not persevere with its Restoration of Order Bill if the public learned of the weight of argument against its intended measures.[144] The British launched a counter-attack which undid many of the IRA's achievements. The new troops who were poured into Ireland included the Black and Tans and the Auxiliaries, who soon acquired a well-deserved reputation for brutality. They 'pushed violent response to the level of counter-terrorism'.[145] Martial law was imposed throughout the whole of Munster, as well as in Kilkenny and Wexford, even though the military authorities argued that such a localized enforcement was worthless.

Attempts were made to inject life and intelligence into Dublin Castle, a system described as comprising 'some thirty-six Departments, many of them hardly on speaking terms with each other', and in which the viceroy himself lamented that 'the place seems to be honeycombed with spies and informers and men who cannot be trusted'.[146] Warren Fisher, the permanent secretary to the Treasury, was imported from London, and he wrote a devastating assessment of the incompetence which he found. He saw the Castle officials as almost woodenly stupid and quite devoid of imagination, and complained that they listened only to the ascendancy party:

---

[141] IG's reports, Oct. 1920, Apr. 1921, CO.904/113 and 115.

[142] *IT*, 1 May 1920, editorial. For republican law-givers, see below, pp. 314–18.

[143] Macready to Greenwood, 17 July 1920, LG, F/19/2/12.

[144] León Ó Broin, *W. E. Wylie and the Irish revolution, 1916–1921* (Dublin, 1989), p. 95.

[145] Townshend, *Political violence in Ireland*, p. 350.

[146] R. B. Haldane, cited in Jones, *Whitehall diary*, I, p. 83 (10 Apr. 1919); French to Ian Macpherson, 11 Dec. 1919, Strathcarron MSS, Bodleian Library, Oxford, MS Eng. Hist. C.490(173).

7.1 'Peace offering to Ireland'

The phrase 'Sinn Fein' is a shibboleth with which everyone not a 'loyalist' is denounced, and from listening to the people with influence you would certainly gather that Sinn Fein and outrage were synonyms . . . In fact the ruling caste reminds one of some people in England – mainly to be found in Clubs and amongst retired warriors and dowager ladies – who spend their time in denunciation of the working classes as 'socialists'.

The government, 'by refusing to discriminate and by using the label "Sinn Fein" to cover murderers and criminals on the one hand and everyone whose political persuasion it dislikes on the other' was simply antagonizing the majority of the population. He insisted that 'Sinn Fein *is* a political party, however much people may dislike it', and he denounced its proscription as 'indescribable folly'.[147]

Fisher's criticisms were reiterated by the chief secretary when, a month later, he described the outlawing of the party as a great embarrassment; the law was flouted daily because the administration could not suppress all expressions of Sinn Féin sentiment. The stifling of the mere expression of political views and

---

aspirations, 'however obnoxious', was inconsistent with general government policy.[148] Nonetheless, Sinn Féin remained banned. A few months later an entry in the diary of a Dublin Castle official summed up precisely the sort of attitude which Fisher rejected with such distaste; Mark Sturgis wrote 'I almost begin to believe that these mean, dishonest, insufferably conceited Irishmen *are* an inferior race and are only sufferable when they are whipped – like the Jews.'[149]

During its last twelve months the war was waged savagely by both sides. Pitched battles were fought, and the toll of death and destruction mounted steadily: 29 people were killed and over 100 wounded on Bloody Sunday, 21 November 1920. Soon afterwards 17 Auxiliaries were killed at the battle of Kilmichael (Co. Cork), and in early December British forces burned much of the centre of Cork city. Between January 1919 and June 1920, 60 policemen and soldiers were killed by the IRA, but the figure for July 1920 to July 1921 was 495. In a time of growing brutality and anarchy O'Flanagan had to warn against terrorist acts 'carried on in the name of Dáil Éireann, of the Irish republic or in any name they thought would carry them to the prosecution of their selfish end'.[150] Many IRA members, like their counterparts in the British forces, chose to put their faith in terror.[151]

The police and (to a lesser extent) the army were not the only victims of the Volunteers, or of nationalist violence in general. Critics were harassed, and when the *Irish Independent* described the assassination attempt on Lord French as a deplorable outrage its printing machinery was wrecked in retaliation. Loyalists were robbed, made homeless and even murdered. In the summer of 1920 Protestant traders in Boyle were intimidated, and in the following year unionists were killed on the Monaghan–Fermanagh border.[152] A sectarian campaign was waged in Co. Cork. Of more than 200 civilians who were shot by the IRA in the county between 1920 and 1923, 70 were Protestants; this was five times the proportion of Protestants in the civilian population, and only 15 per cent of the houses burned by the IRA belonged to Catholics.[153] In Leitrim the police reported that after a Protestant farmer was dragged from his home at night he was shot and his body mutilated – as a penalty for refusing to pay an IRA levy.[154] By the end of the Anglo-Irish War the police in Kerry noted what

---

[148] Greenwood to Bonar Law, 22 June 1920, Cab.27/108, SIC 1.

[149] Sturgis, diary, 3 Sept. 1920, PRO.30/59/1.   [150] Carroll, *They have fooled you again*, p. 115.

[151] Hart, *I.R.A. and its enemies*, pp. 96–103.

[152] Edward Micheau, 'Sectarian conflict in Monaghan', in Fitzpatrick (ed.), *Revolution?*, pp. 113–15.

[153] Peter Hart, 'The Protestant experience of revolution in southern Ireland', in Richard English and Graham Walker (eds.), *Unionism in modern Ireland: new perspectives on politics and culture* (London, 1996), p. 89. See also Hart, *I.R.A and its enemies*, chap. 12.

[154] CI's report, Leitrim, Apr. 1921, CO.904/115.

'appears to be a determination to burn out all the old Gentlemen's country houses . . . to keep old families from returning after "Peace" and to grab their demesne lands'.[155] As always happens in such conflicts, the vulnerable were exploited and private scores were settled in the name of principle or patriotism. Warfare produced thugs as well as heroes.

After his return to Ireland in December 1920 de Valera suggested that the IRA should 'ease off as far as possible consistent with showing the country that they were in the same position as before'.[156] The active army units paid no attention to such advice from the political leadership and they maintained their momentum. The *Irish Bulletin* claimed that while the number of attacks during March and April 1920 were 13 and 15, the figures for the same months in 1921 were 122 and 211.[157] (But this increase must be seen in perspective, and one British officer remarked that the total casualties inflicted on British troops during the last and bloodiest eighteen months of the war 'were little, if any more, than many a battalion suffered in a single morning during the War in France'.[158]) From a different standpoint, the number of Irish people who died as a result of violence between 1919 and 1921 amounted to less than 5 per cent of the Irish soldiers killed during the Great War, and it has been estimated that the death toll in Anglo-Irish conflict between December 1918 and July 1921 was about 1,400.[159] (If the Easter Rising is added, the total between 1916 and 1921 would still be less than 2,000.) Lloyd George's government changed its policy more in response to international hostility, and to the shame and revulsion felt by British public opinion, than as a consequence of military weakness or defeat.

Murder became commonplace, whether it was carried out by the crown forces, by the IRA, or as a result of private hatreds. People were beaten and shot, tortured and terrorized. Houses were burned down in reprisal for attacks by the IRA, and co-operative creameries became a popular target of the British forces. One revealing entry in a British officer's notebook listed the Sinn Féin sympathizers in the village of Doon (Co. Limerick) and remarked ominously that they all owned the houses in which they lived.[160] Presumably they had no fire insurance and were accordingly all the more vulnerable to 'reprisals'. An RIC county inspector reported that, in retaliation for the murder of a district inspector, 'fifteen houses of known rebels resident in the area of the 3rd

---

[155] CI's report, Kerry, May 1921, *ibid.*   [156] *DE, 1919–21*, p. 241 (25 Jan. 1921).

[157] *Irish Bulletin*, 20 May 1921.

[158] Brigadier-General J. Brind, memo, 1 Oct. 1921, PRO, WO.32/9533.

[159] Liam Kennedy, *Colonialism, religion and nationalism in Ireland* (Belfast, 1996), p. 192; Fitzpatrick, 'Militarism in Ireland'. p. 405.

[160] 'Captured British army documents' n.d. [? July 1921], EO'M, P17a/9.

Tipperary Brigade (I.R.A.) have been officially destroyed'.[161] But the British establishment was aware of where such a policy would lead, and as one MP put it, 'the military having burned a cottage, the Sinn Feiners had burned a mansion'.[162]

Perhaps the most damning indictment of all was a letter written in December 1920 by an Auxiliary who had participated in the burning of Cork city. After confessing that 'we did it all right never mind how much the well-intentioned Hamar Greenwood would excuse us', he continued

> in all my life and in all the tales of fiction I have read I have never experienced such orgies of murder, arson and looting as I have witnessed during the past 16 days with the R.I.C. Auxiliaries. It baffles description . . . Many who witnessed similar scenes in France and Flanders say, that nothing they had experienced was comparable to the punishment meted out to Cork.[163]

In one of hundreds of incidents related by the *Irish Bulletin*, a party of Auxiliaries sought revenge after four of their men had been wounded in an IRA attack near Headford (Co. Galway). That night lorry-loads of troops arrived in the village. Most of the inhabitants fled, but their attackers, equipped with petrol, burned down eleven houses and shops and then, on their way back to barracks, they dragged a man from his house and shot him in a field.[164] In Dublin Castle, Sturgis wished, in vain, that 'these lorry loads of police could be restrained from this idiotic blazing about as they drive along'.[165] During the first three and a half months of 1921, 124 members of the army and police forces were convicted of criminal offences.[166] The *Clare Champion* was almost convinced that 'civilization, as we understand it, has broken down', and one Sinn Féin TD, Liam de Róiste, took refuge in a lunatic asylum where he felt safer than in the allegedly sane world outside.[167] He and his party seemed irrelevant to the horrors around them.

But at least in military terms these British measures proved effective. By the end of the war 19 IRA brigade commanders, 90 battalion commanders and 1,600 company officers had been interned, and it was reported from Leitrim that 'the police are receiving information through country people – a source

[161] CI's report, S. Tipperary, May 1921, CO.904/115.

[162] Walter Guinness, cited in Jones, *Whitehall diary*, III, p. 72 (2 June 1921).

[163] 'Charlie' to his mother, 16 Dec. 1920 (captured document), FO'D, 31,226.

[164] *Irish Bulletin*, 'Acts of aggression', week ending 22 Jan. 1921.

[165] Sturgis, diary, 3 Nov. 1920, PRO.30/59/2.

[166] Townshend, *British campaign in Ireland*, p. 143.

[167] *Clare Champion*, 29 Jan. 1921, editorial; de Róiste, diary, 22 May 1921, CAI, U271/A/37.

which for a long time past had completely dried up'.[168] This was symptomatic of a new development: the crown forces now evoked even more fear than the IRA. The British cabinet was reassured that the practice of unauthorized reprisals had succeeded in driving a wedge between moderates and extremists.[169] One of the Volunteers on the run in West Cork conceded that the policy was 'really quite a good one' from the enemy's point of view, yet only weeks before the truce Lord Birkenhead was forced to admit that British military methods had failed to keep up with and overcome those of the IRA.[170]

Throughout Britain there was grave disquiet at the conduct of the army, the police and their auxiliaries in Ireland. It was suggested at a cabinet meeting that if the report on the burning of Cork city were to be published while parliament was sitting the result 'would be disastrous to the Government's whole policy in Ireland'.[171] Early in 1921, Lloyd George complained that 'the charges of drunkenness, looting and other acts of indiscipline are in too many cases substantially true' and that 'Sinn Fein atrocities have been almost forgotten owing to the flood of stories which have been spread of unjustifiable actions taken by the Police.'[172]

The words 'Sinn Féin' might be used loosely to cover all Irish nationalists, and in particular the IRA, but there was universal recognition that the real contestants were the two rival governments and the armies which, intermittently, they controlled. The Volunteers saw the Sinn Féin party as being, at best, an ancillary to the fighting forces, and at worst a distraction, an outmoded or superseded phase of operations. To many nationalists the political phase of the Irish revolution seemed to be no more than a distant memory. Few people remembered that until the Easter Rising British rule in Ireland had been characterized by moderation and forbearance; the republicans' policy of radicalizing Irish nationalists by goading the crown forces into repressive measures had succeeded beyond all possible expectations.

The truce

By July 1921 the IRA was on the defensive and the British government was subject to intense moral and political pressure. For different reasons both sets of

---

[168] Charles Townshend, 'The Irish Republican Army and the development of guerrilla warfare, 1916–1921', *English Historical Review*, 94, 371 (1979), p. 342; CI's report, Leitrim, Dec. 1920, CO.904/113.   [169] Cabinet conclusions, 1 Oct. 1920, Cab. 23/22, Conf.53A(20).

[170] Florence O'Donoghue to 'G', 15 June 1921, FO'D, 31,176; Townshend, *Political violence in Ireland*, p. 356.   [171] Cabinet conclusions, 29 Dec. 1920, Cab.23/23, C.79A(20).

[172] Lloyd George to Greenwood, 25 Feb., 21 Apr. 1921, LG, F/19/3/4 and 17.

national leaders were prepared to negotiate a truce. The Volunteers, bloodied but undefeated, were able to claim credit for forcing Lloyd George to do what he had so often vowed not to do: negotiate with Irish 'gunmen'. Everyone knew that this change of heart had been brought about by dead bodies, and not by living voters or Dáil deputies or party canvassers. By offering dominion status the British were now prepared in effect to concede what Griffith had demanded for so long, but they did so because Irish rebels had employed means which he had always believed would be futile. As had happened in 1916 (and in the case of the Ulster Volunteers, between 1912 and 1914), the use or even the threat of violence was seen to achieve results. T. M. Healy remarked enviously that 'the Sinns won in three years what we did not win in forty . . . in broad outline they have got what was denied us by Gladstone, Asquith and [Campbell-] Bannerman'.[173]

The natural consequence was to enhance the Volunteers' status and influence in comparison to those of their political counterparts; earlier tendencies to disparage the party's functions were now reinforced or confirmed. The soldiers were lionized, they posed and paraded, they were the heroes of the hour, and it was not only in Co. Cork that they were seen as 'the lads who beat the Black and Tans'. Local leaders grew self-important and felt able to defy their superiors. This could be seen as a natural development; the decentralized nature of the war against the British had devolved authority to regional commanders who were understandably reluctant to relinquish their new power and influence. Richard Mulcahy, the IRA chief of staff, sympathized with one of Liam Lynch's difficulties as commander of the 1st Southern Division: 'the trouble about [Tom] Barry is that he is utterly undermined by vanity . . . He was very petulant and childish in some of his statements. He practically said that if he spoke a word that five Brigade Commdts. would withdraw from the Division.'[174]

As Volunteering became a safe and prestigious summer pastime, and as new recruits poured into the IRA's ranks, parallels were drawn with its short-lived popularity during the conscription crisis of 1918.[175] Freed from effective interference by the RIC and the British army, Volunteers could act with an impunity which encouraged arrogance and bullying. In Tipperary it was noticed that, now that all the fighting was over, 'so many braves are so keen on soldiering', while IRA members in Kerry were reported to have commandeered cars and bicycles; 'they say they are entitled to some consideration for having fought for the Freedom of Ireland'.[176] In Mayo there were complaints that the local IRA

---

[173] Callanan, *T. M. Healy*, pp. 561–2.

[174] Mulcahy to Lynch, 7 Oct. 1921, RM, P7/A/26, p. 87. This file contains numerous complaints about Volunteers' behaviour.   [175] O'Malley, *Singing flame*, p. 34.

[176] CIs' reports, N. Tipperary, Kerry, Aug. 1921, CO.904/116.

had imposed a tax of one penny on a bottle of stout. The Dáil Local Government Department inspector described this as an incentive to profiteering which would 'fleece the public', and Brugha issued a circular prohibiting such levies or forced collections by the Volunteers: 'no pressure of any kind is to be used to make unwilling persons subscribe to our funds'.[177] Similarly, in parts of Wicklow the IRA imposed a levy on every householder and occupier, and the Volunteers showed themselves efficient in making collections.[178] It was not only enemies and victims who noted such behaviour. *An tÓglách* was clearly concerned by these developments, and it warned the soldiers against adopting 'an aggressive or intolerant attitude towards civilians and the non-combatant elements of the nation'; they should avoid the dangers of hero-worship and should not develop swelled heads.[179]

There was nothing surprising in this. Some of the active Volunteers must have found the relaxation of tension which followed the truce an incitement to wild and irresponsible extravagance. In the course of their struggle many of them experienced an exhilaration and a degree of fulfilment which would be impossible to maintain in the peacetime world. Fear, excitement and discipline all tended to vanish together in July 1921. Shortly before the truce Florence O'Donoghue quoted a colleague in his flying column near Dunmanway expressing concern that 'we'll all wake up some morning to find ourselves members of the civil population, with peace made and our occupation and our power gone. Then I'll go back to the poorhouse, and I suppose you'll start selling collars again.'[180] It is little wonder that normality held so little appeal for so many Volunteers.

Long afterwards the Sinn Féin secretary general remarked that 'with the truce the troubles began. Fellows went mad with joy.'[181] One visitor to Dublin in September 1921 found that on both sides the civilians were anxious for peace, but that 'the young soldiers at the Castle talked the same language as the young soldiers of the Irish Republican Army. Both still believed in force . . . Both seemed to take more pleasure in contemplating the destruction of their enemy than in the victory of their cause.'[182] In similar mood Eoin O'Duffy told

---

[177] Chief of inspection to Brugha, 17 Oct. 1921, DELG, 21/19; Brugha, circular, 26 Oct. 1921, FitzGerald MSS, UCDA, P80/20.

[178] Thomas Fleming to Déogréine Barton, 17 Sept. 1921, RB, 8786(2).

[179] *An tÓglách*, 14 Oct., 11 Nov. 1921. See Hannon, 'Irish Volunteers', pp. 275–9.

[180] O'Donoghue to 'G', 8 May 1921, FO'D, 31,176.

[181] Páidín O'Keeffe, interview, 1964, RM, P7/D/47, p. 4.

[182] Harold Spender, 'Ireland under the truce', *Contemporary Review*, Nov. 1921, pp. 587–8. Gunmen on both sides inhabited a 'gangsterish culture of violence' (Hart, *I.R.A. and its enemies*, p. 111).

the Dáil some weeks later that 'the chief pleasure I felt in freedom was fighting for it'.[183]

At least in some quarters, the republican soldiers' traditional suspicion and scorn of political activity had been heightened by the course of the Anglo-Irish War. Tomás Derrig epitomized a widespread view when he harangued one meeting, boasting that the IRA had borne the brunt of the battle while the Sinn Féin clubs had collapsed, and that in many cases their failure was the result of apathy and indifference.[184] Áine Ceannt was faced with obstruction or opposition when she tried to develop a system of communication whereby the party could evade British censorship. The organizer sent by Sinn Féin headquarters was regarded as unacceptable throughout most of Co. Cork, while in many other areas the IRA was uninterested and saw no need to help its civilian counterpart.[185] Seán Milroy complained to Brugha, the minister for defence, about 'an atmosphere of aloofness on the part of the Volunteers, and an implied attitude that the Sinn Féin Clubs were not serving any useful purpose and that it was a waste of time and energy to trouble about them'.[186]

Some Volunteers tried to institutionalize their *de facto* control over their neighbourhoods. In Ennis the commander of the Mid-Clare brigade warned the county council that if his brigade's nominees for the posts of rate collector were not accepted, anyone else who attempted to collect rates would be shot.[187] Many nationalists were inclined to make little distinction between native and foreign authority, and they seemed to take the view that all central government was unwelcome. In Louth one Dáil deputy objected to the intervention in county council meetings of the Local Government Department's inspector, and he pointed out that on an earlier occasion he had thrown the Dublin Castle inspector out of the council chamber for intervening in a similar manner. The clear implication was that, if he thought it necessary or desirable, he would repeat his earlier action.[188]

The Dáil cabinet and its bureaucracy were unable to fill the vacuum created by the collapse of British authority. Many people regarded them with suspicion, and a distrust of administrators, government and politicians, which had originally been directed at the British regime, was transferred to the Dáil authorities

---

[183] *DE, treaty debate*, p. 227 (4 Jan. 1922). Despite such views O'Duffy voted for the treaty.

[184] *Connaught Telegraph*, 19 Nov. 1921.

[185] Áine Ceannt, report, 15 Nov. 1921, NAI, D/T, S12,110.

[186] Milroy to Brugha, 22 Oct. 1921, EdeV.

[187] Kevin O'Higgins to W. T. Cosgrave, 26 Sept. 1921, DELG, 5/18.

[188] Mary E. Daly, *The buffer state: the historical roots of the Department of the Environment* (Dublin, 1997), p. 69.

once they showed signs of evolving into a real government.[189] The Castle official who liaised with the IRA during the truce remarked that 'while we watch them and they watch us and the Truce itself paralyses our forces, lawlessness akin to anarchy is spreading'.[190] Strikes and soviets advertised unrest. The Farmers' Union complained that in Wexford

> farmyards are being burned practically daily; fairs and markets are still being held up; roads are being blocked by means of tree-felling; farm produce is being looted; cattle are being driven in thousands by men on bicycles and many of them are being injured. Unorganised workers are being dragged from their employment.[191]

Three Wexford Dáil deputies, Richard Corish, Seán Etchingham and James Ryan, were reported to be 'prominent in interference and opposition' to the Department of Local Government, and Mayo TDs also indulged in 'free lance' hostility to central control.[192] Leitrim established itself as the most ungovernable part of the country, and when a Dáil local government official attended an anti-rates meeting he was obliged to defend himself by firing over people's heads. The cabinet was warned that local government in Leitrim might collapse, and it was urged that at least forty young men should be sent to the county to collect rates 'by any means they deemed necessary'. However, there were fears that such an expedition might constitute a breach of the truce with the British.[193]

Leitrim continued to pose problems for Dáil administrators, and some Sinn Féin branches shared the IRA's dislike of central authority. By early 1922 it was reported that the clubs had taken over the county council's control of the appointment of road workers and foremen – except in those areas where they had not yet decided whom they would select. Every Sinn Féin club in Leitrim acted as its own county council.[194] To a lesser extent this pattern was reported from other parts of the country.

Kevin O'Higgins, who substituted for Cosgrave as minister for local government, warned that Sinn Féin should not try to control or interfere with the activities of TDs or local government representatives; like any other organization the

---

189 Tom Garvin, 'Great hatred, little room: social background and political sentiment among revolutionary activists in Ireland, 1890–1922', in Boyce (ed.), *Revolution in Ireland*, p. 106.

190 Sturgis, diary, 22 Nov. 1921, PRO.30/59/5.

191 Michael O'Hanlon to cabinet members, 15 Dec. 1921, cited in Gaughan, *Austin Stack*, p. 129. On Wexford see O'Connor, *Syndicalism in Ireland*, pp. 139–40.

192 Kevin O'Higgins to Diarmuid O'Hegarty, 5 Oct. 1921, NAI, DE, 2/468.

193 Daly, *Buffer state*, p. 89.

194 Eamonn O'Carroll to Local Government Department, 28 Feb. 1922, DELG, 16/9.

party could make representation to the government, but it should not dictate to local authorities in matters such as appointments.[195] Some of the Dáil's ministers and bureaucrats had never felt much sympathy towards politics, and their prejudices seemed vindicated in the aftermath of the truce. They watched as local politicians followed the example given to them by many soldiers, discovering the joys of jobbery and acquiring power which they could abuse. The standing committee shared this disapproval and rejected as improper the action of the Rathmines executive 'in giving official support to a person selling a position'.[196] In the circumstances of the time this was a counsel of perfection, and the party leaders did not always provide good example. During the truce Count Plunkett pointed out to de Valera that Fr O'Flanagan had suffered for the cause and suggested that he might be compensated by appointment as an endowed professor of 'Economics, Civics, or such like' in the National University. Fortunately, perhaps, de Valera had other plans for O'Flanagan.[197]

The new self-confidence of the Volunteers took other forms and had other consequences. In a paradoxical reversal of the 1918 pattern some units now began a pattern of conscripting all the young men of the neighbourhood into their ranks and giving them military training. It was intended that they should be prepared for battle if (as was widely expected) the London negotiations collapsed and fighting was resumed. By October this form of conscription was nearly at an end in Kildare, but only because all the likely victims had already been recruited.[198]

Between July and December the nominal total of Volunteer membership rose from about 30,000 to about 75,000.[199] Of the 1,000 IRA men who belonged to the battalion in Bandon (Co. Cork) after the truce, only a fifth had been available for duty a few months earlier.[200] The new recruits (the 'Trucileers'), whether conscripts or volunteers, were understandably resented by those who had been in action or on the run before hostilities ended in July. The RIC could do no more than observe these events. The county inspector in Kildare noted an 'extremely bitter feeling between the old soldiers and the new which must sooner or later come to a head', and he continued, that the principal reason was 'greed and anxiety as to who is to get the "plums" amongst the new jobs to be given, when the country is "free"'.[201]

A disillusioned official from the Dáil's Department of Local Government

---

[195] O'Higgins to Páidín O'Keeffe, 4 Sept. 1921, RB, 8786(2).   [196] SCM, 10 Oct. 1921.

[197] Plunkett to de Valera, 10 Oct., de Valera to Plunkett, 11 Oct. 1921, EdeV.

[198] CI's report, Kildare, Oct. 1921, CO.904/116.

[199] Sheila Lawlor, *Britain and Ireland, 1914–23* (Dublin, 1983), p. 122.

[200] Hart, *I.R.A. and its enemies*, p. 227.   [201] CI's report, Kildare, Sept. 1921, CO.904/116.

described himself as thoroughly sick and disgusted with Kerry. He reported that the county abounded in cliques and factions, and that its people ('the wolves of Kerry') were liars, blackmailers and masters in intrigue. He warned that he could foresee anarchy unless an iron discipline was maintained, and suggested that 'perhaps some of our warriors in Kerry would wish to set up a Mexico here so that they may be free to continue the noble profession of arms'.[202]

The months between the truce and the treaty completed the pattern of the Anglo-Irish War. After the grim experiences of guerrilla warfare, with its accompanying fear, misery and bereavement, it was only when the fighting came to an end that parts of Irish society became thoroughly militarized for the first time. If war had helped depoliticize nationalist Ireland, it seemed as if the coming of peace brought little improvement. It also seemed as if a civil war of sorts was already under way even before the London negotiations began or the treaty was signed.

This breakdown in discipline was an important contributing factor to the conflict between the civilian authorities and the bulk of the army which developed between March and June 1922. But it is only a partial explanation. The most committed of the republican commanders during the civil war, Liam Lynch, was also one of those most determined to impose order on the troops under his command.[203] De Valera and Brugha were stern in upholding the government's authority, at least until they lost control of the cabinet and the Dáil. Ideological factors and personal interests, and in particular the refusal by many soldiers and by some politicians to compromise their belief in an abstract Irish republic, would soon transform a conflict between local and central power. These issues reinforced the tensions which had already emerged between democrats and bureaucrats on the one hand, and freedom-fighters on the other.

If any of these components had been absent, the cease-fire of July 1921 might indeed have brought the peace which was craved by the vast majority of the population. But ultimately the people's wishes were overruled by men with guns who ensured that the truce brought no more than a respite, and that one form of conflict would soon be replaced by another.

---

[202] Eamonn Coogan, 'Report, Killarney', 12 Dec. 1921, DELG, 12/16. Throughout the previous decade Mexico had been ravaged by rebellion and civil war.

[203] Valiulis, *Portrait of a revolutionary*, p. 101; Florence O'Donoghue, *No other law (the story of Liam Lynch and the Irish Republican Army, 1916–1923)* (Dublin, 1954), p. 181.

8

MINISTERS AND BUREAUCRATS, 1919–1921

Military events dominated the years after January 1919, but they represented only one aspect of the separatists' struggle against British rule. The other consisted of political, administrative and judicial campaigns, and in these areas the Sinn Féin party might have been expected to remain predominant. But here, as in the armed conflict against the forces of the crown, politicians were regarded merely as auxiliaries of their more important allies, although here their relegation was a cause of much greater surprise and disillusionment. The high hopes for the party's future which many felt in the aftermath of its triumph were soon to be disappointed.

In December 1918 such problems still lay in the future, and Sinn Féin was rightly exultant. Its vindication of the Easter Rising, its destruction of the Parliamentary Party, its ability to win a conclusive victory in the general election despite the imprisonment of its leaders, all filled it with confidence and enthusiasm. The standing committee revived its extravagant ideas of a year earlier and planned to establish a series of departments dealing with areas such as public health, the Irish language, national finance and foreign affairs.[1] New pamphlets were prepared, and two special organizers were appointed to improve the party's efficiency in Ulster. When the standing committee met with a group of the newly elected MPs all those present agreed on the importance of maintaining Sinn Féin's political organization; in particular its electoral machinery should be conserved.[2] It seemed as if parliament and party would work in tandem.

The first Dáil

The formal gathering of Dáil Éireann in the Mansion House on 21 January 1919 brought the efforts of the previous two years to a triumphant climax. With

---

[1] SCM, 13 Feb. 1919.   [2] *Ibid.*, 1 Jan. 1919.

due solemnity the republic of Easter Week was re-proclaimed and ties with Westminster were broken. An estimated 2,000 people were present, but most Irish MPs were in prison and those who attended the meeting were outnumbered two to one by journalists. Although the assembly was composed in large part of former rebels, and although it made a point of demonstrating its adherence to revolutionary objectives, its proceedings were moderate and constitutional. The *Times* correspondent remarked that the occasion was prosaic, orderly and dignified, and that not a word was uttered which could provoke discord or ill-feeling.[3] Writing from Gloucester Jail, Griffith described the Dáil's impact as splendid, and he urged that the country should be kept calm and disciplined, that it should avoid provocation by the 'Castle gang'.[4] Brugha presided over a temporary cabinet until de Valera returned to Ireland some weeks later and was then elected president.

Even before the Dáil held its first meeting, some prominent Sinn Féiners had begun to distance themselves from the party, and Collins remarked dismissively that 'the Sinn Féin organisation would be informed in due course of the programme of the leaders'.[5] This attitude soon became more widespread. As the Dáil began to function on a regular basis, and as its cabinet began to acquire greater experience and authority, the inequality of their relationship with the Sinn Féin party became steadily more apparent. Just as Sinn Féin was treated as an adjunct of the Volunteers during the Anglo-Irish War, the party was also superseded and overshadowed in what had been until then its unchallenged sphere of influence: civil affairs. Perhaps in a different manner from that which had been intended, the *Times* was prophetic when it claimed that 'history will probably date the definite decline of the Sinn Fein movement from the day when its National Assembly was opened in Dublin'.[6] Similarly, Kevin O'Shiel may have exaggerated when he said that 'Sinn Féin had now ceased to exist, because its place had been taken by the government of the new Irish Republic', but there was nonetheless an element of truth in his remark.[7]

At the party's *ard-fheis* three months later, in April 1919, the honorary secretaries reported that 'heretofore the Sinn Féin Executive has been looked upon as the de jure Government of the country'. Those days were now over, although an important if less exalted function was outlined for it instead. De Valera believed that the sooner 'a certain distinction' was drawn between the Dáil and the party the better, and he announced that Sinn Féin would be a sort of civil army which would carry out the decrees of the cabinet; government decisions 'would have to be more or less jointly agreed upon between the Dáil and the

---

[3] *Times*, 22 Jan. 1919.   [4] Griffith, memo, 23 Jan. 1919, CP, 11,405.   [5] *II*, 13 Jan. 1919.
[6] *Times*, 23 Jan. 1919.   [7] *FJ*, 8 Jan. 1919.

Standing Committee, if they were to be really effective and work without trouble'.[8]

On the same occasion Griffith reminded deputies that they were members of the Dáil because Sinn Féin had made them so. He went on to declare that since the party represented 'the civil side of the administration' the Dáil would request it to carry out government policies; if the standing committee objected to doing so, the Dáil would find out if there were other mechanisms for putting its plans into operation.[9] The irascible Seán MacEntee objected to such ideas and argued that since the Dáil was the *de jure* government its decisions should be supreme. His colleagues did not share this high-handed approach, and as the *Irishman* pointed out, since the Dáil was not yet the *de facto* government it could implement its decisions only with the goodwill of other bodies.[10] A modicum of tact was still necessary. Soon afterwards the syndicated 'Sinn Féin Notes' summarized the new relationship:

> the Sinn Féin Standing Committee is the executive machinery in civil affairs for the Dáil, but not merely that, inasmuch as the Standing Committee must sanction any proposal of the Dáil before carrying out such proposal . . . In military affairs the Volunteers will stand in the same relationship to the Dáil as Sinn Féin does in civil matters.[11]

Later, in September 1919, the party's director of organisation warned (or perhaps reassured) members that Sinn Féin was not a mere political machine, and that the scope of its activities would widen as the Dáil's functions became more apparent to the country.[12] The party would become the civilian half of a movement which would operate under the direction of the cabinet – and thus it would balance the Volunteers, who functioned as the military half. Yet even this intention was not realized.

The Dáil cabinet and ministries were the principal concern of leaders such as de Valera (when he was not in America), Collins (when he was not preoccupied with military affairs) and Griffith, who was acting president of the party and the Dáil from June 1919 until his arrest in November 1920. In so far as circumstances allowed, the cabinet began to implement Griffith's programme and tried to function as a normal government. It developed its own separate bureaucracy, which eventually expanded to about 300 full-time employees and was reinforced by 2,000 others who provided voluntary labour.[13] The government was careful to avoid taking over *en bloc* Sinn Féin's structures or person-

---

[8] *II*, 9 Apr. 1919.   [9] *Ibid.*   [10] *Irishman*, 19 Apr. 1919.   [11] *Meath Chronicle*, 26 Apr. 1919.

[12] *Ard-fheis Sinn Féin, 16th October, 1919, reports of officers and directors*, RB, 8786(1).

[13] Mitchell, *Revolutionary government*, p. 156.

nel, although it used the Volunteers as a police force to impose its decisions. One natural consequence of these developments was that new administrative structures began to encroach on functions which had hitherto been exercised by Sinn Féin and its standing committee.

During 1918 the party had been energized by the conscription crisis and the general election campaign, and when these external stimuli were removed it was left deflated and aimless. In mid-1919 the RIC county inspector for West Cork remarked that 'the Sinn Féin party seems to live by advertisement',[14] but after the election was over little advertising was needed and the party seemed at a loss for something to do. Subsequent events seemed to have borne out a forecast of the party and its members which had been made at the end of 1917: 'unless constant excitement is given them, their interest in it will tend to die away'.[15]

Frequent complaints were made about Sinn Féiners' inactivity. At the 1919 *ard-fheis* it was claimed that clubs were displaying a 'lamentable lack of duty' and were not sending fees to party headquarters as they had done in the past.[16] The director of organization commented that increased membership did not imply increased efficiency, and that the party's expansion had been too rapid for the education of its new recruits.[17] Throughout the early summer there were numerous references to poor attendance at meetings, and in Wexford it was observed that the clubs' activities were limited to holding fund-raising concerts.[18]

At the *ard-chomhairle* in August 1919 an impressive increase in the number of branches was reported: the total now stood at 1,822. But 39 per cent of these had not bothered to affiliate with headquarters and thus were not entitled to send representatives to the *ard-fheis*; a mere 3.5 per cent of members had paid their fees, and in many cases membership fees for 1918 had not been forwarded.[19] Soon afterwards the party acted realistically when it abolished individual members' fees.[20] An appeal was made to the constituency executives 'who, for some time past, have not been displaying the energy required'.[21]

A month later, some branches in Roscommon were forced to amalgamate, while in Kilmacanogue (Co. Wicklow) the club minutes recorded sadly that 'there was no business to be transacted. Members occupied their time reading

---

[14] CI's report, W. Cork, May 1919, CO.904/109.   [15] IO's report (M. and C.), Dec. 1917.

[16] Secretaries' report, extraordinary *ard-fheis* (8 Apr. 1919), RB, 8786(1).

[17] *Nationality*, 19 Apr. 1919.   [18] CI's report, Wexford, June 1919, CO.904/109.

[19] *Annual ard comairle of Sinn Féin, August 21st, 1919. Report on organisation*, RB, 8786(1).

[20] *Report on twelfth annual ard fheis. 16th October, 1919*, RB, 8786(1).

[21] *Nationality*, 30 Aug. 1919; *Annual ard chomhairle of Sinn Fein, 21st August 1919, résumé of proceedings: hon. secretaries' report*, RB, 8786(1).

some Sinn Féin literature.'[22] The minutes (and in all probability, the club along with them) soon faded away, and the solitary entry after September 1919 referred to the death of Terence MacSwiney a year later. Branches in Mayo were exhorted to 'set to work with more energy and enthusiasm than they have shown since the General Election', but in many cases inquiries from headquarters were ignored by the local clubs.[23] All this took place at a time when the party, although it was subject to police obstruction and interference, enjoyed far more freedom than in the period which would follow its suppression in autumn 1919.

The area from which Sinn Féin might have hoped for salvation proved in many respects to be not merely a disappointment, but also a threat. The Dáil undermined the party and relegated it to a subordinate role. The suspicion with which many republicans had always viewed political activity could now be expressed openly, and the years of the first Dáil were characterized by an austere policy of distancing the state apparatus from the party, of imposing distinctions between the spheres of politics and administration. Diarmuid O'Hegarty, secretary to the Dáil cabinet, declared that the government's constructive work would create a stronger impression on the people than political work; it would prove that the Dáil had 'stepped away from the beaten path of party politics and their shibboleths, and that it is functioning as any progressive Government would be expected to function'.[24] The sentiment was worthy, but the tone was dismissive and disparaging.

Shortly before both the parliament and the party were suppressed, Seán Milroy urged deputies to show greater attention to Sinn Féin's needs in their constituencies. He claimed that many of them were reluctant to do so, and that they did not seem to appreciate the sacrifices which had been made to secure their election. Although he refrained from using the word 'ingratitude', it was implicit in his remarks.[25] Another reason for this detachment, however, was distrust of the deputies themselves. De Valera told the party's *ard-fheis* in April 1919 of the leaders' intention that Sinn Féin could not be used as a political machine by members of the Dáil.[26] Republicans remembered how the Parliamentary Party had exploited the UIL.

From the very beginning the cabinet was determined that, as in the relationship between the party and the Volunteers, there should be no overlap of

---

[22] Club minutes, 20 Aug. 1919, NLI, MS 15,730.

[23] *Mayoman*, 6 Sept. 1919; *Ard-fheis Sinn Féin, 16th October 1919, report of director of organisation*, RB, 8786(1).

[24] Diarmuid O'Hegarty to Gavan Duffy, 27 Aug. 1919, Gavan Duffy MSS, NAI, 1125/2.

[25] *DE, 1919–21*, pp. 143–4 (19 Aug. 1919).   [26] *II*, 9 Apr. 1919. See above, p. 174.

responsibility or function between the party and the government. Demarcation lines should be drawn clearly, and any use of Sinn Féin personnel or structures for Dáil purposes should be the result of definite agreements for limited periods.

As early as mid-April 1919 the standing committee decided that, at least for the immediate future, it would place its staff at the disposal of the Dáil ministry.[27] Not long afterwards it asked the cabinet to take over its propaganda department for at least six months, and an agreement was soon reached whereby Sinn Féin would pay the staff's salaries, the government would be responsible for half of the running expenses, and each side should pay for its own output.[28] In similar fashion, the finance ministry recruited some Sinn Féin staff to assist in organizing a national loan, and when they were no longer required the party's standing committee confessed that it could not take them back; it had no funds with which to pay them.[29] The cabinet was inclined to supervise the party's activities, and Collins, the minister for finance, was directed 'to see that the Cttee. appointed by Ard Comhairle of Sinn Féin gets to work on [a] Co-operative Bank Scheme'.[30] Two months later *Nationality* reported that the Dáil was directing most activities hitherto run by Sinn Féin, and that the party's sphere of responsibility had in effect shrunk to elections, party organization, and its share of their joint propaganda.[31]

The missing element, which explained much of Sinn Féin's malaise, was the absence of elections. Most of its past achievements had centred on the task of winning parliamentary seats, but at least for the foreseeable future this phase in its career was over. In some respects it was almost as if Sinn Féin had been a mirror image of the Parliamentary Party, and when its enemy disappeared, it vanished too. In February 1919 the standing committee had decided, with apparent eagerness, to contest the vacancy in North Derry, and it rejected by seven votes to two the suggestion that it should postpone a decision until local party members had been consulted. A sum of £300 was allocated to the director of elections for the purpose.[32] The contest was hopeless, the Sinn Féin candidate (Patrick McGilligan) lost to the Unionist by a margin of more than two to one, and North Derry was noteworthy only as being the last by-election which the party ever contested. Apart from compiling electoral registers and preparing for the next general election (which was not due until the end of 1923) none of Sinn Féin's activities was immune from the Dáil ministry's steadily expanding range of interests. In early 1919 the party began canvassing for the

---

[27] SCM, 15 Apr. 1919.   [28] *Ibid.*, 19 June, 3 July 1919.   [29] *Ibid.*, 8 Apr., 29 June 1919.
[30] Cabinet minutes, 26 June 1919, NAI, DE 1/1.   [31] *Nationality*, 30 Aug. 1919.
[32] SCM, 18 Feb. 1919.

local elections which were expected to be held during the summer, but they were postponed until 1920; by the time they were held the party had been banned and its activities curtailed. At the end of the year Plunkett remarked to de Valera that 'the clubs are a bit lax since the elections' – but these had been held twelve months earlier.[33]

Republican courts

Sinn Féin was obliged to hand over to the Dáil one of the most remarkable of its achievements: the establishment of arbitration courts which were organized by the party's clubs and constituency executives. For many years Griffith had urged that British institutions should be disregarded, that an Irish executive and legislature should administer the country, and that as one central aspect of such a policy an independent national system of courts should be established.[34] The formation of a separate legal structure would advertise the people's repudiation of British rule, deprive the crown courts of much business, and weaken Dublin Castle's authority. It would involve the creation of an alternative network of power.

Such a move would also lessen the danger of class conflict disrupting the party's efforts; there would be no diversion of energies or divisions within its ranks. Social tensions were less acute than they had been in the past, and in 1917 one British intelligence officer noted with relief 'the lack of any really material grievance to agitate about, such as the land question was 30 years ago'.[35] Nonetheless, many farm labourers wanted land of their own and some of them were ready to seize it if they could. Their appetites were sharpened by the fact that the activities of the Congested Districts Board in purchasing and redistributing land had been curtailed or ended by the impact of the First World War. Some sections of the population had not benefited from the social revolution of the past few decades, and the growing unrest after 1918–19 provided them with an opportunity to improve their lot; in some cases they did so by bullying or robbing their neighbours. The Anglo-Irish War undermined and splintered the forces of stability.[36]

The Sinn Féin leadership did not wish to become involved in any social conflict, and at one of its earliest meetings the party's standing committee forbade clubs to engage in serious projects of cattle driving without first inform-

[33] Plunkett to de Valera, 3 Dec. 1919, EdeV.

[34] *Resurrection of Hungary*, p. 94; *The 'Sinn Féin' policy* (Dublin, 1906), pp. 22–3.

[35] IO's report (S.), Dec. 1917.   [36] O'Connor, *Syndicalism in Ireland*, p. 60.

ing the local constituency executive and receiving its endorsement.[37] When the Landless Men's Association wrote to Plunkett in the summer of 1917 he was reported as replying sternly, telling its members that they could not get land until they would have an independent Ireland; he could not see his way to doing anything about their plight at present.[38] At times headquarters felt obliged to follow local initiatives, as when clubs decided to impose a ban on foxhunting until the 'German plot' prisoners would be released, but it is significant that they were prompted from below.

The party's fears were illustrated by an RIC report from Kerry in summer 1919: 'the farmers who previously took the lead in Sinn Feinism were helpless when the labourers organised and they had to fall back on the police for protection. They no longer meet with labourers at S.F. clubs.'[39] Similarly, Brian O'Higgins, the TD for West Clare, saw unjust land claims as 'useful only to the common enemy' and as a distraction from the aim of defeating British rule.[40] Naturally this aspect of class conflict was welcomed by the British authorities, and the following year the chief secretary remarked of labour and agrarian unrest in Connacht that 'a part of this movement is not doing the Government any harm'.[41] Even though Sinn Féin and the Dáil were reluctant to involve themselves in disputes which might distract attention from the 'national struggle', the consequences of aloofness might be even more damaging.

In late 1917 a system of Sinn Féin arbitration courts began to spread throughout parts of the country, and they helped mitigate the problems which Plunkett and others seem to have dismissed so lightly. The first such court to be recorded was established in Killaloe (Co. Clare), and it was presided over by a former commissioner of the peace who had been dismissed from his post by Dublin Castle.[42] Already by this stage a military intelligence officer had warned that the condition of the country made it almost impossible to expect a conviction from an ordinary petty sessions bench, no matter how conclusive the evidence might be, and that a policy of refusing to recognize British law was being put into effect.[43] The pattern established in Killaloe was soon followed widely, and within a few weeks reference was made to the successful operation of Sinn Féin courts 'in some parts of the country' with the recommendation that these examples should be imitated.[44]

[37] SCM, 15 Feb. 1918. [38] *Roscommon Messenger*, 14 July 1917.

[39] CI's report, Kerry, Aug. 1919, CO.904/109.

[40] Wright McCormick, *Irish republican arbitration courts* (New York, 1920), p. 3.

[41] Jones, *Whitehall diary*, III, p. 17 (31 May 1920).

[42] *Tipperary People*, 5 Oct. 1917; *Nationality*, 13 Oct. 1917. [43] IO's reports (S.), July, Sept. 1917.

[44] *Nationalist and Leinster Times*, 20 Oct. 1917, 'Queen's Co. notes'.

Sinn Féiners were encouraged to establish such courts 'after the manner of O'Connell'.[45] (O'Connell's scheme for arbitration by popularly elected judges had operated to a limited extent, and another precedent available to nationalists was the Land League courts of 1880.[46]) Efforts were made to keep these new structures under tight control. The East Clare constituency executive, although it had not yet considered the land question, and although it accepted that the main objective was to win full independence, nonetheless concluded that it could not neglect 'other questions of importance to National life'. Despite the reservations of a priest who felt it was a pity to involve Sinn Féin in land disputes, the executive tried to control and channel cattle-drives. But party members were asked to take no steps without outlining their planned course of action to their clubs, and these in turn were expected to submit each case to the appropriate constituency executive.[47]

Land was not the only source of conflict. In Ireland, as elsewhere, the years after the First World War were characterized by a wave of industrial unrest. The number of strikes peaked in 1919–20, and their geographical spread was greater than ever before.[48] In some cases, most notably in Limerick, strike committees used the newly fashionable revolutionary terminology and called themselves 'soviets' (see above, pp. 272–3). They had little in common with their namesakes in Moscow or Petrograd, and Ireland experienced less class conflict than Italy or other European countries, but conservative elements in society found the strikers' imagery almost as alarming as their actions.

This development, like the land agitation, provided Sinn Féin with both a threat and an opportunity, and here too it tried to act as mediator. In turn, the party's involvement posed a danger to the British authorities; for example, when Figgis was sent to Clonmel to settle a long-lasting brewery strike the RIC saw this and other such actions as 'exercising a deplorable effect on Government prestige'.[49] But attempts to mediate often failed, as when the party tried unsuccessfully to settle a bakers' strike in Mayo where the employers were all Sinn Féiners.[50]

The emergence of new legal structures was facilitated by the isolation and demoralization of the RIC. A pattern of boycotting policemen was widespread by summer 1917.[51] As early as April, the *Factionist* threatened to expose people who associated with them, while six months later it was reported that no-one

---

[45] Pim, *Three letters for unionists only!*, p. 11.

[46] J. P. Casey, 'The genesis of the Dáil courts', *Irish Jurist*, 9 (1974), p. 326; Samuel Clark, *Social origins of the Irish land war* (Princeton, 1979), pp. 313–15.   [47] *Clare Champion*, 9 Mar. 1918.

[48] See David Fitzpatrick, 'Strikes in Ireland, 1914–21', *Saothar*, 6 (1980), p. 30.

[49] IG's report and CI's report, S. Tipperary, July 1920, CO.904/112.

[50] CI's report, Mayo, May 1919, CO.904/112.   [51] See above, pp. 276, 291.

liked to be seen speaking to members of the force and that the people seemed to regard them as informers or enemies.[52] From 1919 onwards the IRA's campaign drove them out of many parts of the country; by August 1920, Kildare's quota of police barracks had been reduced from the normal twenty-four to about six, and West Galway's from sixty to twenty.[53] The retreat of the RIC to larger and more easily defensible barracks left parts of the countryside without any police force, so the Sinn Féin and Dáil courts also served to fill a vacuum which had been created by the actions of the Volunteers. And since many of the crown forces resorted to criminal measures in their fight against the IRA, the republicans could often portray themselves as the only representatives of law and order. (The Irish experience in this regard was not unique. More than twenty years later the French resistance sapped the power and authority of the Vichy authorities by a combination of threats, persuasion and protection; in some respects it acted as a police force, and it enlisted the population in its rival power structure.[54])

The origins of the Sinn Féin courts went back long before the 1918 election, but the new government and its bureaucracy soon intervened to appropriate the results of the party's efforts. In summer 1919 the Dáil decreed the establishment of national arbitration courts in every county.[57] In some areas no Sinn Féin courts had been organized and it was necessary to create a completely new system, but elsewhere the Sinn Féin model was either replaced or subsumed into a new structure. The party acquiesced in its lowly status, and when the North Longford executive asked headquarters for information on the procedures of setting up such courts, the matter was referred to the Dáil.[58] In the one area where Sinn Féin had become involved in the realities of Irish social conflict, its experience and its responsibilities were soon snatched away.

Other elements of the crown legal system came under pressure. The *Irish Bulletin* was able to list 348 magistrates (about 5 per cent of the total) who had resigned as commissioners of the peace in the course of August 1920. This was not the result of spontaneous decisions; plans had been made to ensure a 'compulsory' mass resignation.[55] The IRA also patrolled the roads and prevented litigants from attending crown courts.[56]

---

[52] *Factionist,* 26 Apr. 1917; CIs' reports, W. Galway, Clare, Oct. 1917, CO.904/104.

[53] CIs' reports, Kildare, W. Galway, Aug. 1920, CO.904/112.

[54] H. R. Kedward, *In search of the maquis: rural resistance in southern France, 1942–1944* (Oxford, 1993), pp. 96–9.

[55] *Irish Bulletin,* 15 Sept. 1920; Terence MacSwiney to Daniel Corkery, 14 July 1920, MacSwiney MSS, CAI, PR4/4/62.

[56] Conor A. Maguire, 'The republican courts', *Capuchin Annual,* 1969, p. 380.

[57] *DE, 1919–21,* pp. 122, 140 (18 June, 19 Aug. 1919).   [58] SCM, 19 June 1919.

Austin Stack, the minister for local government, had reservations about the party's involvement in the new legal system. He accepted that the parish and district courts operated effectively in Clare and Galway, but in mid-1920 he noted disapprovingly that their arbitrators had been appointed by the Sinn Féin constituency executives; they had not been elected by the local population, as was laid down in the Dáil scheme. Because these courts were successful he was prepared to wait until the end of the year before organizing the election of arbitrators by popular vote.[59] It was clear that the Sinn Féin courts were regarded merely as an initial phase which was to be transcended as quickly or as conveniently as possible. The Dáil's official account of its own legal system played down the Sinn Féin party's involvement and claimed (wrongly) that only in West Clare were crown courts deserted before the establishment of the Dáil system in spring 1920.[60]

The new courts were used widely and their powers were extended. The law was 'frozen' at 21 January 1919, except for any legislation enacted by the Dáil, and in a petty-minded spirit it was decreed that Brehon, Roman, French and other law codes could be cited, but not legal texts published in Britain.[61] Trials took place, those convicted were punished, and the courts' sentences were enforced by the IRA. In one case in Tipperary the suspect was pursued and arrested by the Volunteers, guarded for a week during which he was kept busy spreading farmyard manure, tried by a court held at midnight in a bog, and sentenced to two years' expulsion from the province of Munster.[62] Dancing in public houses was prohibited by the Volunteers in Louth, while in one incident in Tyrone, which must have been a cause of great outrage and scandal, 80 gallons (360 litres) of illicit whiskey were confiscated and emptied into a river.[63]

In 1920 land agitation was more widespread than for many years past. The value of land and of agricultural produce had risen dramatically during the war, thereby widening the gap between the haves and the have-nots. The number of the latter had also increased in many rural areas as a result of the government's wartime ban on emigration and the unequal pattern of army enlistment. Cattle-driving and attacks on landlords became more widespread; one landowner was driven naked through a crowded fair in Roscommon town, and another was shot dead in Athenry.[64] In a particularly gruesome incident, a herd who did not follow his colleagues' example, and refused to leave an estate where agitation

---

[59] Stack, 'Parish and district courts', 16 June 1920, NAI, DE, 2/38; Gaughan, *Austin Stack,* p. 108.

[60] *Constructive work of Dáil Éireann,* I, pp. 7, 15.

[61] Mary Kotsonouris, *Retreat from revolution: the Dáil courts, 1920–24* (Dublin, 1994), p. 30.

[62] *II,* 3 June 1920.   [63] *Irish Bulletin,* 27 Aug. 1920.

[64] *Constructive work of Dáil Éireann,* I, p. 12; *FJ,* 4 Mar. 1920.

had festered for several years, was attacked by a group of about twenty men, tied to a tree and then beaten and stoned to death.[65] A Galway priest who was active in collecting for the Dáil loan wrote to Collins complaining that 'things are very bad in S. Connemara. The Volunteers according to my information claim to do all kinds of things in the name of the Irish Republic', and as a result of boycotting and intimidation 'our work there is killed'.[66]

There was widespread dismay at such unrest, and the official Dáil report concluded:

> all this was a grave menace to the Republic. The mind of the people was being diverted from the struggle for freedom by a class war, and there was a likelihood that this class war might be carried into the ranks of the Republican Army itself, which was drawn in the main from the agricultural population and was largely officered by farmers' sons.

It boasted that, where land agitation had been raging, the arbitration courts had saved society from anarchy; and anarchy was clearly a frightening prospect for the Irish revolutionaries.[67] Like the Dáil and its bureaucracy, the party was actively involved in trying to quell the unrest, and the standing committee declared that the names of Sinn Féin and the Dáil should not be used in connection with land seizures.[68] This involvement of the party and the government in social conflicts can be compared with the Church's participation in the fight against conscription. In both cases the principal motive was to tame a public mood which might assume dangerous proportions and might result in uncontrollable violence. By the time that the political revolution began, during the First World War, those who were anxious to maintain the status quo were both more numerous and more powerful than their opponents. They blocked any organized challenge to their interests. To the embarrassment, despair and frequently the disbelief of later historians of the Left, the Irish revolution took nationalist, political and military forms, but it did not seriously attempt – let alone achieve – a change in the social balance of power.

In Kerry a dispute provoked by labourers' demands for additional land had reached the level of burning houses and crops. When Art O'Connor, the acting minister for agriculture, paid a visit in February 1920 his response was worthy of a Dublin Castle official. He declared that 'the commotion showed all the symptoms of finally taking the form of a civil war of a kind which would undoubtedly have spread to the calm parts of the country, and probably in the ultimate from small beginnings involve the [Dáil] Government itself in general

---

[65] *Mayoman*, 5 June 1920.   [66] 'Gaillimh' (Fr T. O'Kelly) to Collins, 29 Feb. 1920, NAI, DE, 2/25.
[67] *Constructive work of Dáil Éireann*, I, pp. 12, 16 .   [68] SCM, 11 May 1920.

ruin'. He lectured both farmers and labourers on their duty to the state, and he concluded severely that the people confused licence with liberty.[69] The *Irish Bulletin* was equally firm. It was dismayed by what it saw as 'a lawless invasion of private rights, the revival of ancient and unwarrantable claims, gross intimidation, cattle-driving, fence-levelling and an "ugly rush" for land. The mind of the people was being diverted from the struggle for freedom into a class war.'[70]

O'Connor met with the East Galway Sinn Féin executive, and agreement was reached on a provisional constitution for arbitration courts in the constituency;[71] subsequently the party's direct involvement in the Dáil's legal system was minimal, and here, as elsewhere, new structures were established which were responsible to the government. A special land commission was established which adjudicated claims, valued and divided land, and fixed prices when this was required. Between May 1920 and June 1921, according to the *Bulletin*, it heard 299 cases in 23 different counties affecting a total of 63,150 acres (25,580 hectares). In one case, heard by Kevin O'Shiel in Roscommon, the court was told how a landowner was dragged from his house and invited to sign away much of his property for what he regarded as a derisory price. Some of his kidnappers pointed revolvers at his head while others began digging a grave on the lawn in front of him; their counsel later assured the Dáil court that this action should be seen as 'inducement' rather than 'duress'.[72]

The *Irish Statesman* could soon refer casually to Sinn Féin as the *de facto* government in three quarters of Ireland, while the London *Daily News* commented that 'Sinn Fein law has a sanction behind it such as no other law in Ireland has had for generations . . . Even Unionists are astonished and pleased by it.'[73] By August 1920 the police reported that in West Galway

> the local government of the County is in the hands of Sinn Fein . . . Lunatics are committed to the Asylum by Sinn Fein magistrates . . . Agrarian unrest has diminished as disputes are referred to Sinn Fein Arbitration Courts . . . Sinn Fein has taken possession of the County.[74]

Walter Long passed on to his cabinet colleagues an account by a Limerick unionist which conceded that

[69] *A brief survey of the work done by the Agricultural Department, 1919–21*, NAI, DE, 2/64, pp. 7, 10.

[70] *Irish Bulletin*, 4 Aug. 1921.   [71] *Work done by the Agricultural Department*, p. 11.

[72] Kevin O'Shiel, 'No contempt of court', *IT*, 21 Nov. 1966.

[73] *Irish Statesman*, 5 June 1920, p. 532; Dennis Kennedy, *The widening gulf: northern attitudes to the independent Irish state, 1919–49* (Belfast, 1988), p. 43.

[74] CI's report, W. Galway, Aug. 1920, CO.904/112.

Sinn Fein rules the County – and rules it admirably . . . The fact is that everybody is going over to Sinn Fein, not because they believe in it, but because it is the only authority in the County; and they realise that if their lives and property are to be secured, they must act with Sinn Fein.[75]

In all these instances 'Sinn Fein' obviously refers to the whole separatist movement, and not simply to the party.

There were frequent boasts of the republican courts' effectiveness in dispensing justice, but some of their efforts to resolve disputes proved unsuccessful. It is also clear that litigants were often prepared to resort to other measures if their cases failed. In North Roscommon occupiers of grazing lands were driven off by the RIC and then appealed to the Sinn Féin constituency executive, but when it ruled in the owner's favour the men concerned refused to be bound by the decision. They seem to have had their way, for soon afterwards the owner complied with Sinn Féin regulations authorizing the compulsory acquisition of the land in dispute.[76]

Many Sinn Féin members paid no attention to party or governmental policy and acted solely in their own interests. In 1919, for example, one branch in Co. Sligo responded in a firm manner to the news that a ranch was being sold privately: 'we wish to inform all intending purchasers that we require all the ranches in the district for distribution among all the small-holders and landless young men. We are prepared to pay a reasonable price for the land, and we will allow no grazier to purchase or hold it whoever he may be.'[77] Individual Sinn Féiners in their hundreds or their thousands saw the disturbed times and the separatist movement as providing opportunities for bettering themselves. For them, if not for their leaders, revolution involved redistribution. Art O'Connor reported that claimants sometimes tried to seize holdings not much larger than their own, and he conceded that 'many unjust acts undoubtedly have been done in the name of Sinn Féin'.[78] But the Sinn Féin tricolour was no more than a flag of convenience; any movement or party would have served the same purpose, and many who were dissatisfied or greedy soon became disillusioned with what they saw as the social conservatism of Sinn Féin and the Dáil.

Others were unimpressed for different reasons. The courts' police forces often failed to command or deserve respect, and Collins later referred scornfully 'to the wretched Irish Republican Police system, and to the awful personnel that was attracted to its ranks . . . The lack of construction and the lack of control in this force have been responsible for many of the outrageous things which have

---

[75] Long, memo, 30 June 1920, Jones, *Whitehall diary*, III, pp. 24–5.   [76] *II*, 26 Feb., 7 Mar. 1918.
[77] *Sligo Champion*, 1 Nov. 1919.   [78] *Work done by the Agricultural Department*, p. 12.

occurred throughout Ireland.'[79] On occasion the IRA resorted to its own form of martial law – as in court-martialling the committee of a creamery on the grounds that an employee had been dismissed for absenting himself on Volunteer activities.[80]

Many of the courts were forced to limit or to end their activities as a result of British repressive measures in late 1920 and early 1921. After the truce they could be revived without fear of British interference, but 'non-military' violence increased rather than diminished. Often the Dáil courts were unable to restore order or impose justice. In 1922 they were wound up by the new provisional government in a brusque and bureaucratic manner; once Irish nationalists had begun to control the apparatus of the state they could dispense with their earlier revolutionary measures.[81]

Subordination

The legal system developed by Sinn Féin provided the Dáil with one of its most important propaganda successes, but the new government had other uses for the party. At the most basic level, some of the rooms in its headquarters were taken over by the Dáil bureaucracy, while its network of branches and its system of communication were exploited by the different government departments to gather and circulate information. When the Dáil's secretary outlined its policy of boycotting the police, Sinn Féin decided to draw up a circular and distribute a copy to every club in Ireland; at one of its last meetings before the truce in July 1921, the standing committee decided that provincial organizers should help bring as many cases as possible before the republican courts; in that year the party dispensed Dáil leaflets through its constituency executives – including 225,000 dealing with the 'English Trade Boycott'.[82] The standing committee and party headquarters became the Dáil cabinet's post office or messenger boy.

Sinn Féin was passive, and acquiesced in its own relegation. A letter concerning the Belfast boycott provoked a discussion which ended in the flabby conclusion that the party had neither initiated the boycott nor discussed it, and when the standing committee was asked about the land fever in Galway, Griffith

---

[79] Collins to Mulcahy, 7 Aug. 1922, cited in Michael Hopkinson, *Green against green: the Irish Civil War* (Dublin, 1988), p. 91.

[80] Seán Ó Buachalla to Collins, 19 June 1921, and subsequent correspondence, NAI, DE, 2/240.

[81] See Tom Garvin, *1922: the birth of Irish democracy* (Dublin, 1996), pp. 170–1.

[82] SCM, 1 May 1919, 7 June 1921; Secretaries' report, *ard-fheis*, 1921, RB, 8786(2).

replied that the problem was under consideration by the Dáil cabinet.[83] Such attitudes revealed a worthy reluctance to interfere in the sphere of action of a democratically elected parliament and government; it gave little indication of the initiative and the energy which had characterized Sinn Féin in the recent past. In similar fashion, as early as the 'Limerick soviet' of April 1919, the initiative in a civilian aspect of the fight against British rule was taken by the trade union movement and by the Labour Party, rather than by Sinn Féin (as would probably have been the case in earlier years).[84]

The party also faced financial problems and it was forced to economize. Many of its clubs and members no longer paid their dues. Seán Milroy, the director of organization, warned the standing committee that while Sinn Féin needed to display greater efficiency, it had no money to lend to those constituencies in need of organizers.[85] In its turn the committee approached the cabinet and asked for a loan. At Griffith's request the Dáil approved a grant of £1,300 to meet the party's general election expenses,[86] but henceforth the government would normally do no more than lend Sinn Féin money for special purposes. It would not make gifts or grants. The party's poverty created problems of discipline, and the Limerick city executive threatened to withhold its affiliation fee unless it was paid £150 for cars sent to Waterford at the time of the general election, nineteen months earlier. (The committee reacted angrily and threatened the executive with suspension.)[87]

The Dáil, by contrast, was able to raise considerable sums. De Valera's eighteen-month tour of the United States was a triumph in financial terms, if not in other respects. Irish-Americans were impressed by the dramatic progress which had been made since the rising and they were prepared to contribute generously to finance further advances. The first day's collection in Brooklyn raised $150,000, a total of $2.4 million was pledged by New York city, and by May 1920 $3 million had been secured.[88]

In Ireland Collins claimed to have succeeded in raising more than £370,000 from the constituencies, despite a formidable range of obstacles which were placed in his path.[89] Not all the contributions were voluntary, however, and at least in some areas people were pressurized or forced to subscribe.[90] Munster was particularly generous, followed by Connacht, while there was a relatively poor response from Dublin, north-east Ulster and former Redmondite

---

[83] SCM, 5 Feb., 27 Apr. 1920.   [84] See above, pp. 272–3.   [85] SCM, 10 July 1919.

[86] *DE, 1919–21*, p. 162 (27 Oct. 1919).   [87] SCM, 20 July 1920.

[88] Sean Nunan to Collins, 20 Jan., 17 May 1920, NAI, DE, 2/292. In 1920 $4 equalled £1.

[89] Collins to Bishop Fogarty, 20 Sept. 1920, NAI, DE, 2/527.

[90] See, for example, de Róiste, diary, 20 May 1920, CAI, U271/A/30.

strongholds.[91] In mid-1920 Diarmuid O'Hegarty was able to write that the loan was oversubscribed by £50,000, and that the cash receipts to date approximated £300,000.[92] The British authorities managed to capture only £23,000 of this sum.[93] The RIC inspector general complained that the country was flooded with loan literature, some of which had been seized by the police, while in East Cork 'leaflets were distributed by unknown cyclists'.[94] The cabinet's finance committee announced that each TD should organize the loan in his constituency, and that if he were imprisoned or abroad the task should be carried out by the local Sinn Féin executive.[95] The party was to be no more than a reserve or a second-best.

Thanks to this Irish and American generosity, the Dáil and its cabinet were not short of funds, and allocating these resources gave the TDs something to do. When they convened in June 1920 (after an interval of eight months) they were able to enact ten decrees, all of them involving expenditure; this was in contrast to the pattern of the Dáil's meetings in 1919, when, lacking money with which it could implement its wishes, its activities had been concerned largely with procedure and propaganda.[96] Naturally, the largest share went to the Department of Defence, and in the eight months between May and December 1920 it received £16,000 out of a total of £41,000.[97]

In financial as in other matters the Dáil ministers turned their backs on Sinn Féin, the means by which they had risen to their present eminence. When Cosgrave, the minister for local government, informed the standing committee that his department would supply the party with a grant of £300 for electoral purposes, the statement was crossed out in the minute book and in the next entry it was repudiated as incorrect.[98] Eighteen months later Collins wrote to de Valera protesting that the same department had behaved in a grossly corrupt manner by sending out a party notice from its office; 'a department spending public funds in whipping a party together cannot have full cognisance of its responsibility'. De Valera agreed in principle, although he felt that this reaction was too harsh.[99] A few days later he directed the cabinet secretary to warn departments not to send

---

[91] Mitchell, *Revolutionary government*, pp. 64–5.

[92] O'Hegarty to Gavan Duffy, 5 July 1920, Gavan Duffy MSS, NAI, 1125/2.

[93] Collins, *DE, treaty debate*, p. 381 (9 Jan. 1922).

[94] IG's report, CI's report, E. Cork, Oct. 1919, CO.904/110.

[95] *Report of Finance Department* (n.d. [autumn 1919]), NAI, DE, 2/7.

[96] Ronan Fanning, *The Irish Department of Finance 1922–58* (Dublin, 1978), pp. 22–3.

[97] *Self-determination and loan accounts, 1st May 1920 to 31st December 1920*, NAI, DE, 2/7.

[98] SCM, 17, 31 Dec. 1919.

[99] Collins to de Valera, 17 June 1921; de Valera to Collins, 18 June 1921, 'Epitome of documents seized', CO.904/23/7, pp. 32, 34.

letters dealing with Sinn Féin matters, and to remind them that government offices should be confined *strictly* to government work.[100] The principle was sound; the party might work for the state, but the state must not work for the party.

In a similar vein, the *Irish Bulletin* remarked later that Sinn Féin had no function in the government of Ireland, which was entirely in the hands of the Dáil; 'the Sinn Féin Organisation is purely a political organisation . . . The Sinn Féin Organisation has neither executive nor administrative authority. Dáil Éireann does not consult it in any matters of government, except for suggestions as to procedure or to seek its co-operation to enforce the law.'[101] Collins was anxious to keep the bureaucracy free from contamination by the Dáil as well as by the Sinn Féin party, and he expressed strong reservations when two members of the staff of the Department of Local Government were elected to the second Dáil in May 1921. He saw this development as 'leaving us open to charges of jobbery, and with good reason', and in his complaint to de Valera he described it as indefensible. But the cabinet reached no firm decision when it discussed the matter the following day.[102]

Even if these principles might be carried to excess, and even if administrators might sometimes exude whiffs of self-righteousness, at a time when a new state was being formed in exceptionally difficult circumstances such a high-minded horror of corruption deserves respect. But those who worked only for the party, and not for the Dáil, cannot but have had mixed feelings as they saw the results of their labours appropriated with so few signs of appreciation and with so many signs of condescension or distaste.

After mid-1919 Sinn Féin was marginalized by the Dáil and its bureaucracy, as well as being suppressed by the British and disparaged by many in the IRA. But like the party, the Dáil too was affected by British repressive measures and it was convened only rarely. Already, within months of its first meeting, there were mutterings about how power rested in the hands of a small clique, complaints that the cabinet and party headquarters were unwilling to pass on information, and even claims that the 'bossism' of Sinn Féin surpassed that of the Parliamentary Party.[103] A grumpy TD described the ministers as dictators and complained that the functions of ordinary deputies ended with their election and their endorsement of pious resolutions. Collins was probably the unnamed member of the cabinet who was described as an 'ambitious lad who is forcing his way forward on the strength of the fact that he has made a corner in several movements'.[104]

---

[100] Diarmuid O'Hegarty, circular to ministers, 20 June 1921, NAI, DE, 2/2.

[101] *Irish Bulletin*, 3 Nov. 1921.

[102] Collins to O'Higgins and de Valera, 24 May 1921, NAI, DE, 2/443; cabinet minutes, 25 May 1921, NAI, DE, 1/3.   [103] De Róiste, diary, 22, 23, 29 Mar. 1919, CAI, U271/A/24.

[104] J. J. Walsh to Hanna Sheehy-Skeffington, 5 May [1919], HSS, 22,689.

Deputies' ability to influence the cabinet declined even further. In its eight 'legal' months, between January and September 1919, the Dáil met thirteen times, while in the following twenty months between September 1919 and May 1921, when it was driven underground, it met on only eight occasions. Attendance was kept low for fear of mass arrests. One TD complained in February 1921 that he had not been summoned to a meeting since the previous August, and he suggested sourly that 'private members are to abstain from Dublin as well as Westminster'.[105] Before the truce in 1921 the average attendance at meetings was twenty-four. In these circumstances it was unable to act as a legislative body in any real sense, and much of its activity consisted simply of approving proposed expenditure and departmental reports. As one deputy remarked, 'meetings of the Dáil were got through hurriedly, and there could be very little discussion on many important subjects'.[106] Members of the cabinet and their officials paid little more attention to the parliament than they did to the party.

The ministries operated from purchased or rented offices scattered throughout the city; the Propaganda Department used fourteen different locations, while Mulcahy, the minister for defence, had over twenty offices and hideouts in different parts of Dublin.[107] Dáil ministers and bureaucrats pedalled their bicycles from one building to another, and 'an entire Department might find it necessary to make a hurried removal through a skylight or down a drainpipe at a moment's notice'.[108] On other occasions they could meet more comfortably in the drawing rooms of wealthy supporters such as Walter Cole. Collins did his best to run a tight ship, but his success was limited, and in January 1921 he complained that only two departments, Agriculture and Trade, had submitted their estimates for the next six months.[109] He showed characteristic impatience in disparaging the Labour Ministry which 'works in continuous fear of a raid. Nobody ever seems to be there.'[110] (The department had operated under difficult circumstances; the minister, Countess Markievicz, had been arrested in September 1920, and within ten weeks her successor, Joe McGrath, had followed her to jail.[111])

---

[105] Joseph MacDonagh to Diarmuid O'Hegarty, 17 Feb. 1921, NAI, DE, 2/234A.

[106] Seán MacEntee, *DE, 1919–21*, p. 214 (17 Sept. 1920).

[107] Mitchell, *Revolutionary government*, p. 54; Valiulis, *Portrait of a revolutionary*, p. 51.

[108] Hugh Kennedy, cited in Fanning, *Irish Department of Finance*, p. 18.

[109] Collins, statement, 23 Jan. 1921, NAI, DE, 2/7. See Andrew McCarthy, 'Michael Collins: minister for finance, 1919–22', in Gabriel Doherty and Dermot Keogh (eds.), *Michael Collins and the making of the Irish state* (Cork, 1998), p. 67.

[110] Collins to de Valera, 'Epitome of documents seized', 7 June 1921, CO.904/23/7, p. 32.

[111] Richard Cotter (departmental secretary), report, 19 May 1921, NAI, DE, 2/5.

Even the Dáil cabinet was affected by the scale and severity of the British repression. Between its first sitting on 26 April 1919 and the truce in July 1921, it held 102 meetings, an average of almost one a week, but in the course of three and a half months between 18 December 1920 and 6 April 1921, it met only five times. Yet despite these restrictions it functioned effectively enough to usurp the position which Sinn Féin had occupied in 1917 and 1918. The party was left with little to do except make its staff and experience available to the offspring which had supplanted it, and to concentrate on precisely that sort of activity which it had been told repeatedly was no more than a minor part of its responsibilities: election work. But with no general election in the offing, and with the few parliamentary vacancies left uncontested, the only challenge it faced before May 1921 was the local elections of 1920.

Great importance was attached to these, however, since control of the county councils and other local government bodies would help the Dáil cabinet to organize civilian resistance to British rule and to implement many of its policies. Until then, every Sinn Féin campaign had been waged with the aim of establishing a future independent Irish parliament, but in 1920 the party's objective was to seize control of local bodies which had, for the most part, been controlled by Irish nationalists for more than twenty years. It could try to implement the views of a party member who had urged that 'we must reinstate that derided parish pump in the national life from which a futile political generation expelled it'.[112] (He need not have worried; the parish pump would have a new lease of life after independence.)

The 1920 local elections

No local elections had been held for six years, and they were long overdue. They provided the occasion for an experiment which was to condition every subsequent election in independent Ireland: the replacement of the British 'first past the post' system by proportional representation (PR). Under the 1914 Home Rule Act it had been intended that nearly 20 per cent of Irish MPs would be elected in this manner.[113] The immediate background to its imposition in 1920 was the bankruptcy of Sligo Corporation, followed by the Sligo Corporation Act of 1918 which allowed special elections to be held for this one borough. When voting took place under the PR system the results were remarkable. One month

---

[112] Sean MacCaoilte, *Nationality*, 24 May 1919.
[113] Government of Ireland Act, 1914, § 9, *Law reports, public general statutes* (London, 1914), pp. 411, 438–40.

after Sinn Féin's landslide victory in the 1918 general elections, the Sligo
Ratepayers (a combination of Nationalists and Unionists) won 8 seats, Sinn
Féin 7, Labour 5 and independents 4; the first preference votes were, respec-
tively, 823, 674, 432 and 279; and a unionist headed the poll on the first count.[114]

It seemed as if PR might be able to undo some of the effects of the 1898 Local
Government Act, and that it might limit or even prevent a sweeping victory by
Sinn Féin in the south – as well as by Unionists in the north-east. One RIC
county inspector noted that Sinn Féiners would be likely to control local
government unless PR were introduced before the elections took place, and that
'they greatly fear the example of Sligo town'.[115] As so often before and since,
Britain was ready to pursue a Palmerstonian policy of radicalism abroad and
conservatism at home. PR gave a fairer representation to minorities and this
benefit would be imposed on Ireland, but Britain would retain its own primi-
tive and unrepresentative method of election; British voters would continue to
be regarded as illiterate (or innumerate) and would mark their ballot papers
with an 'X' rather than number them 1, 2, 3 . . . As recently as February 1918,
the House of Commons had rejected a Lords' amendment to the franchise bill
according to which 100 Westminster MPs would be elected by PR. Nonetheless,
with almost indecent haste, it was decided to apply the 'Sligo system' to the
whole of Ireland. By acting in this way Lloyd George's government followed a
pattern already established elsewhere; in Belgium and Denmark, for example,
forms of proportional representation had been used to block the advance of the
Left.[116]

The measure was intended simply to damage Sinn Féin, and not to engender
a more sophisticated pattern of voting on the part of Irish voters. The authorities decided to do no more than train the returning officers in the intricacies of
the new system, and the education of the electorate had to be carried out by Sinn
Féin and the Proportional Representation Society. The society held model elections in many towns, distributed 125,000 leaflets, and provided slides for display
on cinema screens during the week before polling day.[117]

The old Griffithite Sinn Féin had believed in proportional representation,[118]
and (despite justified cynicism concerning the reasons for introducing the new
system) the April 1919 ard-fheis was almost unanimous in support of the
measure. The party sent its election agent on a tour of the constituencies, and
local officers who had been trained in the complexities of PR were in turn able

[114] *II*, 18 Jan. 1919; *Nationality*, 22 Mar. 1919.   [115] CI's report, Dublin, Feb. 1919, CO.904/108.

[116] Maurice Duverger, *Political parties* (London, 1954), pp. 246–8.

[117] *Representation: the Journal of the Proportional Representation Society*, May 1920, pp. 62–3.

[118] See, for example, *Sinn Féin*, 29 June 1912, editorial.

to inform club secretaries and voters.[119] But as a banned organization it could wage only a subdued campaign.

In such a contest it was inevitable that candidates would be selected locally, without intervention from party headquarters, and the only demand made on them by Harcourt Street was that they should pledge allegiance to the Irish republic. The standing committee would become involved only if the constituency executive rejected a candidate who had been chosen by the electoral area, and the committee would then have the final decision.[120] As in the 1918 parliamentary elections there was a preference for Volunteers; in East Clare the executive had agreed unanimously that all candidates for local office should be active members of the force.[121] It was claimed that in Cork city the selection of candidates provoked disputes, resignations and virtual expulsions, and that splits between rival factions seemed likely to result in 'independent Sinn Féin' candidates running for office. One branch was swamped and dissolved by Volunteers who expressed their contempt for Sinn Féin as a mere political organization.[122] The Cork Sinn Féin executive ordered that the Volunteer brigade council should exercise a veto over nominees for the district and county councils. Collins and Liam Lynch (the commander of the 1st Southern Division) were dubious about this, and both men believed that the IRA had sufficient responsibilities without involving itself in such questions. Collins believed that 'it is important that persons selected and elected should hold our views on matters of national principle, and perhaps more so of policy. All we can do is influence people who in doing this, must not be taken away from our Volunteer work.'[123]

Any available headquarters staff were transferred temporarily to the elections department.[124] In Co. Dublin the police noted that 'ordinary Sinn Feiners' were concentrating on electioneering, although the community in general did not appear to be unduly interested.[125] One observer commented that 'P.R. has apparently taken the gizz out of elections and reduced them rather to mathematical propositions.'[126] Party members organized 'lightning meetings' in front of unsuspecting audiences and dispersed before they could be arrested by the police, but candidates tended to devote most of their efforts to canvassing rather than to making speeches.[127] The conduct of the campaign varied from one

---

[119] *II*, 3 Jan. 1920.   [120] SCM, 20 Nov. 1919.   [121] *Clare Champion*, 26 July 1919.

[122] De Róiste, diary, 2, 21 Dec. 1919, CAI, U271/A/29.

[123] Lynch to Collins, 29 Mar., 12 Apr. 1920, Collins to Lynch, 10 Apr. 1920, Collins MSS, IMA, A/0499/xv, xxi, xxiii.   [124] SCM, 4 Dec. 1919.

[125] CI's report, Dublin, Dec. 1919, CO.904/110.   [126] *New Leader*, 24 Jan. 1920, p. 271.

[127] *Evening Telegraph*, 13 Jan. 1920.

region or district to another. Sinn Féin was the only party to hold meetings in Derry, and was able to do so without police or army interference, but in Cork ex-soldiers attacked Sinn Féiners who were armed with sticks, and in the ensuing battle guns and knives were used.[128]

Sinn Féin's programme was worthy but unremarkable. It demanded efficient and honest administration, appointments based on merit, open competitive examinations for all clerical posts, improvements in health services and in the provision of housing, and a policy of spending the rates within Ireland on goods produced under trade union conditions.[129] (This last point was doubtless a sop to the party's Labour allies.) Its propaganda could be colourful, as in lines from one pamphlet distributed in Cork city:

> Those false creatures you elected, never voiced the least protest
> When the fiends incarnate murdered, Ireland's bravest, and her best
> All elections were suspended, for our British tyrants knew
> That our people were disgusted with the rotten servile crew
> Now the time has come to deal with all the foul and loathsome pack
> They have clung to office too long, give the whole damn lot the sack.[130]

The elections were divided into two phases. Those in the cities and towns were held in January 1920, and the rural areas followed them five months later. In all, 126 urban centres voted in the first round, and, in another contrast with the general election which had been held little more than a year earlier, only 9 of the councils or corporations were uncontested. The electorate was more restricted than for parliamentary elections, and the Dublin municipal register listed only 95,000 voters in contrast to the 124,000 who had been eligible to vote in December 1918.[131] This reduction would almost certainly have weakened Sinn Féin. Nearly 70 per cent of the electorate voted, an impressive figure considering that the motor permits dispute was still in progress, and parties were forced to curtail the already well-established pattern of driving voters to the polling stations. Derry city maintained its reputation for a high turnout with a poll of 93.5 per cent. The fact that spoiled votes amounted to only 2.8 per cent of the total was a formidable tribute to the scheme of education carried out by Sinn Féin and by the Proportional Representation Society.

The results damaged both the victors of December 1918. Following the Sligo pattern, Sinn Féin's share of the seats in nationalist Ireland fell drastically; it won

---

[128] *Derry People*, 17 Jan. 1920; *Cork Examiner*, 16 Jan. 1920.

[129] *Municipal elections, 1920: Sinn Féin Manifesto* (pamphlet).

[130] 'Cork municipal elections, January 1920' (pamphlet), de Róiste MSS, CAI, U271/H/3.

[131] *Evening Telegraph*, 7 Jan. 1920.

only forty-two out of eighty seats for Dublin Corporation, in Cork thirty of fifty-six, in Limerick twenty-six of forty, in Waterford nineteen of forty, and in Galway ten of twenty-four.

Similarly in north-east Ulster the Unionists lost fifteen seats on Belfast city council, winning only thirty-five out of sixty, while Labour gained twelve and Sinn Féin and the Nationalists five each. The result was a council more balanced politically and socially than in the past or the future.[132] (After partition the new Unionist government promptly restored the old, unrepresentative wards.) For the first time control of Derry city passed to its Catholic majority, although by a small majority: nineteen Unionists opposed ten Sinn Féiners, ten Nationalists and one independent nationalist. Derry elected its first Catholic mayor since the seventeenth century. (As in Belfast, this pattern did not endure. The Unionists were able to restore minority rule in 1924, and to maintain it until the Northern Irish state began to collapse in 1968.) The Unionists gained 46 per cent of the Ulster seats, while Joe Devlin's Nationalists performed considerably better than Sinn Féin, winning 15 per cent of the first preference votes as opposed to their rival's 9 per cent.[133] Armagh reverted to an earlier tradition of uncontested elections and all its seats were filled by agreement; five Sinn Féiners were returned, along with five Nationalists and eight Unionists, and all three groups included Labour representatives.[134]

At national level the figures were as follows: Sinn Féin won 550 seats, Labour 394, the Unionists 355, and the Nationalists 238, independents 161 and municipal reformers 108.[135] Two-thirds of the women elected (twenty-eight out of forty-three) were Sinn Féiners.[136] Minority elements such as ex-soldiers secured representation, and Kilrush (Co. Clare) was probably an extreme case in returning seven Nationalists, five Labour candidates and no Sinn Féiner.[137]

PR achieved the intended result of ensuring that seats would be proportionate to votes, and it removed the unfair advantage which the British system gave to locally preponderant groups. Sinn Féin studied the results carefully. Harry Boland wrote that the party was particularly anxious to analyse both the voting patterns and the attitudes of Sinn Féin and Labour towards one another.[138] The victory was expensive, and nearly five months after the municipal election one Dublin club was still struggling to meet the costs of the campaign.[139]

---

[132] Ian Budge and Cornelius O'Leary, *Belfast: approach to crisis* (London, 1973), p. 139.

[133] *Representation*, May 1920, p. 66.   [134] *Irish News*, 15 Jan. 1920.   [135] *IT*, 20 Jan. 1920.

[136] *II*, 21 Jan. 1920.   [137] Fitzpatrick, *Politics and Irish life*, p. 121.

[138] Extract from letter, 30 Jan. 1920, NAI, DE, 2/81.

[139] Sean O'Callaghan to Anna O'Rahilly, n.d. [June 1920], Sighle Humphries MSS, UCDA, P106/215.

In June the electorate for county and rural councils and for boards of guardians was three times larger than for the urban centres in January. By now Sinn Féin and the Volunteers were able to bring pressure to bear on other parties, and – following the pattern of 1918 – many seats were uncontested. There is little surviving evidence for the conduct of the election, but there are several explanations for the absence of extensive coverage or comment: many candidates were returned without a contest; the main party in the country was banned; and press censors were vigilant.

In February the standing committee decided to send 1,000 copies of its manifesto to directors of elections, and each constituency was asked to print enough duplicates for its needs. The powers and functions of county councils were explained in the 'Sinn Féin Notes' which were distributed to local papers, but shortage of funds prevented the Proportional Representation Society from maintaining the level of activity which it had displayed during the urban elections in January.[140] Sinn Féin headquarters received a 'very satisfactory report' showing that few contests would take place in Munster,[141] and in most counties more than half the candidates were returned unopposed. In many areas Sinn Féin concluded an alliance with Labour and ran a joint panel of 'Republican' candidates in which it predominated by a ratio of seven to one.

Sinn Féin operated under serious disadvantages, but these were lessened by the fact that the elections took place at a time when the RIC was demoralized and the IRA's influence was at its height. The police ascribed the party's victory in Cavan and Monaghan to good organization and intimidation, while in the south, west and midlands the Volunteers kept discipline in the absence of the police.[142] In these circumstances it was hardly surprising that Sinn Féin candidates fared so well. In Cork the RIC had traditionally escorted the returning officers, their clerks and the ballot boxes to the counting centres, but this responsibility was now taken over by Volunteers riding bicycles.[143] For different reasons the conduct of the poll in Mayo became known as the 'bicycle election'. In some districts of the county voters were informed that they need not inconvenience themselves by going to the polling stations in person; the chore of voting could satisfactorily be delegated to others. On election day Volunteers duly cycled from one village or townland to another, casting numerous votes under a variety of names. Elsewhere some republicans felt able to flaunt their defiance of the authorities in a different manner, and in Glenealy (Co. Wicklow) the first vote was cast by a Sinn Féin candidate who had been on the run for the previous nine months.[144]

---

[140] SCM, 26 Feb. 1920; *FJ*, 9 June 1920.   [141] *FJ*, 18 May 1920.

[142] IG's report, June 1920, CO.904/112; *Representation*, Aug. 1920, p. 115; *II*, 7 June 1920.

[143] *Cork Examiner*, 3 June 1920.   [144] *FJ*, 3 June 1920.

The election resulted in a Sinn Féin landslide. In the provinces of Munster and Connacht every single county council member was a member of Sinn Féin or the Labour Party. The Unionists lost control of Tyrone, and the *Belfast News-Letter* described the result as the most severe blow which the Unionists of the county had ever sustained, 'as all the leading Boards will now pass under the control of the Sinn Feiners'. At least in Omagh there was a simple explanation for this defeat:

> the Sinn Fein–Nationalist combine indulged in a barefaced system of impersonation. Men and women hitherto looked on by their Unionist neighbours as respectable and honest lost themselves in the swirling pools of corruption and fraud, and were guilty of the most reprehensible acts . . . Women were perhaps the greatest offenders. Some of them seemed to possess an elaborate wardrobe for the day, and having voted as Mrs. So-and-So in one dress, donned another, and presented themselves with the greatest confidence to vote as Mrs. Somebodyelse.[145]

Fermanagh County Council had been controlled by nationalists since 1902, and in 1920 Sinn Féin gained five seats compared with six won by Devlin's Nationalists and nine by the Unionists. Only in Ulster and in Louth did the Nationalists gain a sizeable proportion of the vote, and their failure to win seats in their former strongholds of Waterford and Wexford was almost certainly the result of intimidation.

Of the 263 county council seats in Munster and Connacht, Sinn Féin won 258 and its Labour ally 5; in Leinster the figures were Sinn Féin 192; Labour 37 and others 24; and in Ulster the Unionists won 81, Sinn Féin 79, Nationalists 26 and Labour and independents 2 each.[146] The RIC verdict on the results in Longford was that 'the local councils in this county are now in the hands of the rabble'.[147]

Administration

Outside the four north-east counties with Unionist majorities the newly elected councils recognized the Dáil's authority. With varying degrees of speed and enthusiasm they began to distance themselves from the Dublin Castle authorities and to implement Dáil policies.[148] In one sense they followed the example of the Unionist county councils which had already anticipated partition by

---

[145] *Belfast News-Letter*, 4 June 1920.   [146] *FJ*, 12 June 1920.

[147] CI's report, Longford, June 1920, CO.904/112.   [148] See Daly, *Buffer state*, pp. 52–4.

seceding from the long-established nation-wide General Council of County Councils and setting up their own separate association.[149] More directly, they implemented Griffith's policy as outlined in 1904.[150] It was at this time that General Macready examined some captured correspondence which laid down the Dáil government's policy for establishing its authority, and remarked that 'it is almost word for word what Arthur Griffith foreshadows in that book of his, "The Resurrection of Hungary".[151]

Like the Sinn Féin party at local level, the new councils were often run by IRA men – as illustrated by the subsequent fate of the chairman of Limerick County Council, John Wall, who was killed fighting crown forces in May 1921.[152] Clare County Council convened in secret, and with good reason: its chairman was a local IRA commander, and almost all its members were on the run. One of its meetings was held in the county mental hospital, a second took place at night in an empty house where most council members sat on bags of hay, while during a third the members could enjoy the comfortable surroundings of the thick carpets, antique furniture and silver candlesticks of Knoppogue Castle.[153]

By transferring their allegiance to the Dáil the county councils lost approximately 15 per cent of their revenue, which until then had come in the form of grants from Dublin Castle. As a result they were forced to make sacrifices. Among the savings proposed to the Dáil by Austin Stack, the minister for home affairs, were economies on road works, on the treatment of venereal diseases and on child welfare; £10,000 could be saved by returning certain groups of asylum inmates to their homes.[154] Collins discussed the idea of raising money by taking over the issue of dog licences, and he even contemplated licensing the distilling of poteen.[155] Everyone suffered in this conflict, and even in one of the quieter parts of the country the people 'were faced with bad roads, dismissed roadmen, few trains, diminished business and an empty county exchequer'.[156] Not surprisingly, the weakest members of society were the principal victims, and while 'equality of sacrifice' was an ideal advocated by Kevin O'Higgins it was one which he could not implement in practice. Surveyors might earn nearly six times more than roadworkers, but they were less vulnerable to casual dismissal.

[149] *Irish News*, 10 Jan. 1920; John McColgan, *British policy and the Irish administration, 1920–22* (London, 1983), pp. 38–9.   [150] *Resurrection of Hungary*, p. 94.

[151] Macready to Anderson, 5 Aug. 1920, Anderson MSS, CO.904/188(1).

[152] *Limerick Leader*, 11 May 1921.   [153] *Clare Champion*, 11 Feb. 1922.

[154] *DE, 1919–21*, p. 219 (17 Sept. 1920).

[155] Collins to Terence MacSwiney, 12 July 1920, MacSwiney MSS, CAI, PR4/2/19.

[156] CI's report, King's Co., Nov. 1920, CO.904/113.

They retained their jobs, while by March 1921 only 400 out of approximately 8,500 road workers were still employed.[157]

The county councils had an unenviable task as they manoeuvred between two rival masters, Dublin Castle and the Dáil Department of Local Government. Both authorities brought pressure to bear on rate-collectors and other employees, with the result that, 'not knowing which persecutor would prevail, many collectors retreated into canny inactivity'.[158] Ratepayers too were understandably reluctant to commit themselves to either of the rival authorities (let alone run the risk of having to satisfy both), and often they decided to wait and see what would happen. Many of them were unionists and had little sympathy with the new administrators. Some defaulters expressed their objections in forceful terms; a Tipperary landowner explained that, knowing the present composition of the local bodies, he expected that whatever money he paid 'would be forthwith squandered', while a formidable Cork Protestant wrote in response to a demand for £48 rates:

> I would remind you that your armies have cruelly murdered my son, burned down the house on which the rates are assessed and sold for your own purpose all my property in the gardens, and that a sum of £29,000 has been awarded to me in compensation and is a charge upon the rates in question . . . If however you will see that the compensation of £29,000 is immediately paid to me, I will have no objection that you should deduct £48 alleged to be due for rates.[159]

The war caused universal inconvenience, but it posed particular problems for local government officials.

Councils transferred their allegiance at varying speeds, and Kinsale (Co. Cork) did not recognize the new authority until as late as October 1921.[160] Central control of local government was necessarily indirect, and in late 1920 the Dáil's department complained that its information concerning the administration of Carlow 'consisted of quite vague rumours from adjoining counties'.[161] Yet however patchy the pattern might have been throughout nationalist Ireland, sooner or later the Dáil's administrative machine was able to intervene in the details of the people's lives. In Tullamore (Co. Offaly), for example, a £10 fine was imposed on a shopkeeper for the offence of selling English-made jam.

---

[157] Thomas Foran to Local Government Department, 16 July 1921, DELG, 27/30; n.d. [Oct. 1921], DELG, 17/15.   [158] Fitzpatrick, *Politics and Irish life*, p. 193.

[159] Daly, *Buffer state*, p. 87; Ethel Peacocke to Local Government Department, 1 Feb. 1922, DELG, 6/44.   [160] Cosgrave to inspector, Kinsale urban district, 25 Oct. 1921, DELG, 6/44.

[161] Local Government Department to Tomás Bolger, 8 Dec. 1920, DELG, 3/6.

He denied the accusation, and when his premises were inspected it was discovered that his stock included Scottish marmalade, purchased ten months earlier. This was clearly a lesser offence, and his fine was halved.[162]

The files of the Department of Local Government indicate an administrative machine which operated with a surprising degree of efficiency. Against formidable odds, many county councils showed impressive skill and tenacity in limiting the decline in the services which they provided – a decline which was made inevitable by financial constraints and by the ravages of warfare. The relative success of the Dáil government's local administrators further marginalized the Sinn Féin party; more than ever it appeared (correctly) to be simply a means towards an end. To many in the separatist movement the means seemed to be ever more redundant and unworthy as they achieved successes in other areas and as the end, independence from Britain, appeared to be within sight at last.

But in the short term the results of the 1920 campaigns and the capture of local government machinery marked another triumph for Sinn Féin, even if a relatively easy and undemanding one. There was a temptation on the part of some party members to relax, and Páidín O'Keeffe had to rebuke those who seemed to think that there was little need for further effort now that the local elections were over.[163] However, the intensification of the war between the active IRA units and the combined forces of the British army, the RIC, the Black and Tans and the Auxiliaries provided many Sinn Féiners with a reason or an excuse to take what they could regard as a well-earned rest and to concentrate on other matters.

The 'Partition Act'

The next challenge which faced the Sinn Féin party came in May 1921, and it consisted of general elections for two separate 'devolved' parliaments in Dublin and Belfast. These were an indirect result of the timetable imposed by the Home Rule Act of September 1914. Lloyd George and his colleagues were faced with the prospect of home rule coming into effect once the war had ended and the ensuing peace treaties had been concluded. They would also have to confront the Ulster question once again. Understandably, perhaps, they played for time and adopted the solution chosen by so many governments in comparable circumstances: they appointed a committee which could take the burden from their shoulders. This body was given the task of recommending measures which

---

[162] Tomás Ua Duinn to Local Government Department, 29 Nov. 1921, DELG, 15/11.

[163] O'Keeffe, 'Affiliation fees' (circular, 18 Sept. 1920), NAI, 1094/1/4.

might solve the Irish question. It was chaired by the cabinet's alleged authority on Ireland, Walter Long; in the past his advice on Irish affairs had almost always been wrong, but this was not held against him.

The outcome of lengthy deliberations and negotiations was the Government of Ireland Act of 1920. Anxious to be free of their day-to-day responsibilities for local Irish problems, and tied to the interests of Ulster unionists by the Conservative majority in the cabinet, the government decided on a policy of Irish 'home rule all round'. Two pairs of devolved (or home rule) parliaments and governments would be established, one for each 'majority area'. Nationalist Ireland would no longer be denied what it no longer wanted, while unionist Ulster would be forced to accept what it had always opposed. The British cabinet and parliament established the boundary between the two parts of Ireland in a manner which avoided the inconvenience of consulting the inhabitants in disputed areas. It simply gave the Ulster unionists what they demanded: the largest possible area which they believed they could control. By the standards which were applied elsewhere in Europe in the early 1920s, Ireland was partitioned in an unjust and undemocratic manner. A principal attraction of the new scheme for the government was that both parts of the island would remain firmly anchored in the United Kingdom, and yet all Irish groups would be able to deal with their local problems without involving British ministers or MPs. Ireland could be dropped from Westminster's agenda.

Following the precedent of the recent local elections, the PR system would be used in voting for the new Dublin and Belfast parliaments. This decision was opposed by the unionists. They feared that PR might blunt the sectarian divisions which, if perpetuated, should guarantee them permanent supremacy within their carefully chosen frontiers. They had already begun to display that obduracy and lack of far-sightedness which would characterize so much of their future behaviour.

The Dáil cabinet and the Sinn Féin party, preoccupied as ever with the problems of the south, paid little attention to these developments; the standing committee's decision some months earlier to allocate £1,000 for 'organising Ulster' was an uncharacteristic sign of concern.[164] As the new measure progressed through parliament Liam de Róiste provided a narrow Cork perspective in anticipating that 'whatever the outcome of it, the Bill has no interest for Irish people. It has no relation to realities in Ireland.'[165] But the indifference towards the north displayed by southern leaders throughout 1919 and 1920 was soon replaced by anxiety; it became clear that the Government of Ireland Bill would come into effect after all, the island would be divided in two, and elections

---

[164] SCM, 26 Aug. 1920.   [165] De Róiste, diary, 11 May 1920, CAI, U271/A/30.

would be held for both new parliaments. In early 1921 Collins confessed that 'up to recently I was strongly of opinion that it was never intended to set up the Northern Parliament, but I have changed this view now'.[166] (Devlin was better informed, and in April 1920 he feared that Ulster nationalists 'have depended too much on the insincerity of the Government and have lulled themselves into the mistaken belief that the Government proposals will not materialise'.[167])

In early 1921 northern nationalists sought advice as to how they should react, and their initiative provoked the party into belated activity.[168] De Valera, who had finally returned to Ireland after eighteen months in the United States, asked O'Keeffe to provide him with a statistical study of the local election results in the Northern Ireland area, together with an estimate of the parliamentary seats which might be won by Sinn Féin and Nationalist candidates. He also announced that it would be necessary to prepare at once for an election in the north.[169] (His attitude towards his party colleagues may be indicated by the fact that, before raising this matter with them, he had already discussed it with Joe Devlin.[170])

De Valera also wrote to Collins assessing various options which were available to the Dáil government. He felt that unless Sinn Féin was certain of winning at least ten seats in the new Northern Irish parliament (almost one-fifth of the total) he would be inclined to boycott the election; any lower figure would create the impression 'that these counties were practically a homogenous political entity, which justified partition'. He appreciated that letting the election go by default might be seen as an abandonment of the north, and he argued that Sinn Féin would make a greater impact if its elected MPs abstained from the new Belfast parliament.[171] Another reason which he gave in favour of entering the contest revealed neatly the 'southern-centred' approach of Sinn Féin leaders and their negative attitude towards Ulster: abstention might throw Sinn Féin supporters into the Nationalist camp, 'a result which might later have a dangerous reactionary effect, by contagion, on the South'.[172] Collins dismissed the idea of abstention as too passive, and felt that it would be regarded as a 'mock heroic' gesture.[173]

The Dáil cabinet decided to contest the Northern elections and to negotiate an electoral agreement with Devlin and the Nationalists as quickly as pos-

---

[166] Collins to de Valera, n.d. (mid-Jan. 1921), EdeV.

[167] Devlin to Bishop O'Donnell, 2 Apr. 1920, O'Donnell MSS, ADA, IV, political.

[168] George Murnaghan to Máire MacEoin, for communication to Griffith, 4 Jan. 1921, NAI, DE, 2/266.   [169] De Valera to O'Keeffe, 13 Jan. 1921, EdeV.

[170] Devlin to Cardinal Logue, 7 Jan. 1921, Logue MSS, ADA, V, political.

[171] De Valera to Collins, 13 Jan. 1921, EdeV.   [172] De Valera to cabinet, 17 Jan. 1921, EdeV.

[173] Collins to de Valera, 15 Jan. 1921, NAI, DE, 2/266.

sible.[174] For a short while Sinn Féin was obliged to forgo its customary indifference and to devote most of its attention to Ulster affairs. If the party contested only one set of elections it would effectively recognize partition, so this decision in respect of the northern parliament also involved running candidates in the south. All the members returned to both 'partition parliaments' would constitute a new, second Dáil.

The party's manifesto was drafted by de Valera, and it stressed the right of self-determination, the protection of minorities and the principle of devolved administration. It also informed the electors that votes for Sinn Féin were votes 'for the legitimacy of the Republic; for Ireland against England, for freedom against slavery, for right and justice against force and wrong . . . against the enemy from without . . . and against the traitorous or pusillanimous within'.[175]

PR involved the creation of new electoral areas – in effect, the merging of several old constituencies into fewer, larger entities. De Valera therefore proposed that 'single-seat' executives should combine to form new bodies, and that these would be responsible for the multi-member constituencies created by the new scheme. These changes in the constituency structure were an *ad hoc* measure, a reaction to an immediate challenge; they were 'purely temporary and are made solely for more efficient working of this Election'. The newly merged constituency executives would dissolve into their old component parts as soon as the campaign was over – even though the party had committed itself to the PR system which would involve using such larger constituency units in the future.[176] Summer 1921 was not a suitable time for making long-term or structural changes.

De Valera was concerned by Sinn Féin's unpreparedness and remarked that 'the whole machinery has to be reassembled under conditions of extreme difficulty'. He admitted that, as president, he should give the party his personal attention, but his duties as chief minister of the government occupied so much of his time that 'only a small fraction is available for Sinn Féin'. Other members of the officer board, particularly Stack and O'Keeffe, would have to take the necessary steps.[177] In recent years Stack's involvement with the party had been minimal, he had not attended a single meeting of the standing committee since April 1918, and he was also an inefficient cabinet minister. But it was perhaps of greater importance that he could be trusted to represent de Valera's interests. His appointment as Sinn Féin's director of elections did not augur well for the campaign.

[174] Cabinet minutes, 6 Feb. 1921, NAI, DE, 1/3.

[175] SCM, 13 Apr. 1921; *Irish Bulletin*, 4 May 1921.

[176] O'Keeffe, circular, 14 Apr. 1921, RB, 8786(2).   [177] De Valera to O'Keeffe, 9 Feb. 1921, EdeV.

The 1921 elections

Only at this stage was the party's standing committee woken from its torpor. Its members had not even discussed the problems posed by Fr O'Flanagan's initiative in December, but when de Valera wrote to the committee appealing for assistance in organizing Sinn Féin, Ulster and the rest of the country, his letter provided the agenda for its first meeting in nearly four months.[178]

De Valera and Devlin agreed to co-operate in fighting the Unionists. This was a far easier matter to arrange in 1921 than it had been three years earlier; the Nationalists rejected the 'Partition Act' as vehemently as did Sinn Féin, and PR would also limit the risk that rivalry between the two parties would result in the loss of nationalist seats to the unionists. This time there would be no need for Cardinal Logue to appear as a *deus ex machina* and impose a last-minute compromise as he had done in 1918. Both parties agreed on a policy of 'self-determination' for Ireland, and their candidates were pledged to abstain from the proposed Northern Irish parliament. Each would put forward a maximum of twenty-one candidates, and each would encourage its followers to give their lower preference votes to the other. De Valera suggested that they divide equally the remaining money in the anti-conscription fund; this posed problems, however, since only the lord mayor of Dublin knew how much remained in the account, and he was absent in the United States.[179] It was hardly surprising that tension persisted between the two sides, and de Valera complained that the Nationalist party was making no effort to ensure that its second preferences would be passed on to Sinn Féin. Devlin rejected this accusation.[180]

The suppression of the party and the imposition of martial law in the southern counties prevented Harcourt Street from giving any substantial aid; constituencies were to be responsible for their own expenses, and the leadership could offer no more than to provide the necessary organizers. But the Dáil cabinet curtailed its parsimony for the occasion and decided to allocate £4,000 to Sinn Féin. O'Keeffe objected to such extravagance, and with characteristic belligerence proposed that if Ulster nationalists were not prepared to finance the elections the government should wash its hands of them; 'there were 80,000 Catholic families in the North, and they should be easily able to raise £20,000 for the election'. MacEntee retorted that Belfast republicans were in a state of destitution since the previous July.[181]

---

[178] SCM, 10 Feb. 1921.

[179] Summary of correspondence, 25 Apr.–19 May 1921, 'Epitome of documents seized', CO.904/23/7, p. 65.   [180] *Ibid.*

[181] *DE, 1919–21*, pp. 266–7 (11 Mar. 1921). In July 1920 sectarian violence had erupted once again in Ulster, and many nationalists were expelled from their jobs and their homes.

Throughout the campaign Sinn Féin was subjected to pressure from the British authorities, its organizers were arrested, and its candidates' houses were searched for election literature. At times the party was in disarray. Páidín O'Keeffe, a man of short temper and large vocabulary, was described as swearing at Sinn Féiners in the 'old' pre-PR constituencies in Kildare because of their inability to hold a joint convention. He announced that, if he were able to do so, he would allocate all the seats in the new Kildare-Wicklow constituency to the better-organized Wicklow side. As one Sinn Féiner remarked, 'Paudeen would have no one's way but his own.' The sitting deputy, Donal Buckley, who was presumed by party headquarters to be the North Kildare secretary, did not even know the names of the clubs in the constituency.[182] A telegram was sent to George Murnaghan in Tyrone instructing him to nominate five candidates, and a similar arrangement was made for Co. Derry.[183] Problems ensued, and an extra candidate was imposed by party headquarters on a reluctant Tyrone-Fermanagh constituency.[184] In Armagh some clerical elements opposed (in vain) plans for nominating Michael Collins.[185]

Two deputies had died in prison and three more had resigned their seats, but only one other, J. J. Clancy of Sligo, was not renominated.[186] In 1918 his selection had been unanimous, and subsequently he enjoyed an honourable record of arrest and deportation. But he had stood down as chairman of the county council some months earlier, apparently because of his reluctance to agree to the IRA's demands that it should be paid for its work in collecting rates.[187] The RIC county inspector commented that he had not been selected 'because his views were not considered extreme enough – he did not approve of police murders &c.'[188] Party headquarters was unhappy at the refusal of the Sligo executive to reappoint him, and demanded to know the reason for its action.[189] Similarly, the committee was dissatisfied with the explanation supplied for the selection of the IRA leader, Seamus Robinson, rather than Brighid Dooley in East-Tipperary–Waterford. As late as nomination day she was listed as a candidate, so her replacement was obviously a last-minute affair, but here, too, headquarters was unable to influence the decisions of locally dominant Volunteers.[190]

---

[182] C. M. Byrne to Déogréine Barton, 1 May 1921, RB, 8786(2). Buckley, as Domhnall Ua Buachalla, was later governor-general of the Irish Free State.   [183] SCM, 12 May 1921.

[184] Eamonn Donnelly to de Valera, 24 May 1921, EdeV.

[185] O'Keeffe to de Valera, 5 Apr. 1921, EdeV.

[186] Pierce McCann and Terence MacSwiney had died, while Diarmuid Lynch, James O'Mara and Roger Sweetman had resigned.

[187] Michael Farry, *Sligo 1914–1921: a chronicle of conflict* (Trim, 1992), pp. 212–13.

[188] CI's report, Sligo, May 1921, CO.904/115.   [189] SCM, 10, 12 May 1921.

[190] *Ibid.*, 31 May 1921; *FJ*, 13 May 1921.

The new southern Irish parliament would have 128 members, and Sinn Féin candidates would also be returned in some northern seats, so the second Dáil would be considerably larger than its predecessor. Active or imprisoned Volunteers were selected to an even greater extent than in 1918. Of the 125 Sinn Féin candidates who were elected to the second Dáil, 47 were in jail and 52 others were 'wanted' by the police. (Diarmuid O'Hegarty pointed out that 'not more than about forty or fifty will be in jail leaving about ninety available', and that it would be difficult to bring together so many deputies without attracting attention.[191]) Death sentences had been passed on 15 of them and 112 had served at least one term of imprisonment.[192] Piaras Béaslaí later described members of the second Dáil as 'politicians by accident', and two of his colleagues remarked that, had they not been in prison or an internment camp when the election was called, they would probably not have been chosen as candidates.[193]

Liam de Róiste complained that his nomination had been opposed at the Cork convention because of his alleged support for the peace proposals which had been made some months earlier. He denied the accusation.[194] (In a Dáil debate he had objected to what he described as unfair attacks on Roger Sweetman, the deputy who had criticized the IRA's tactics and had resigned his seat in protest.[195]) De Róiste claimed that the Cork meeting was under the impression that Dublin had forbidden his nomination. De Valera was concerned at this news, protested he had heard of no such instruction, and declared that it was 'a mistaken policy to appear at the present time to be forcing out everybody who ventures to disagree with our attitude'. He continued, 'it will look very bad to have him thrown out by a Convention which, under the present circumstances, will scarcely be regarded as sufficiently wide in its constitution'. De Róiste was selected after all, and he speculated that his letter to de Valera might have encouraged Cork Sinn Féiners to overrule the Volunteers who had opposed his nomination.[196]

External problems were solved more easily than those within the party. Sinn Féin conferred with Labour in the hope that its abstention pattern of 1918 would be repeated. De Valera was 'desperately afraid of MacEntee in any bargaining – he doesn't know where to stop', and suggested that Stack might handle the negotiations with Belfast Labour.[197] Any concessions which either man

---

191 O'Hegarty to de Valera, 9 May 1921, NAI, DE, 2/1.   192 *Irish Bulletin*, 29 June 1921.

193 Béaslaí, *DE, private sessions*, p. 232 (17 Dec, 1921); Patrick Hogan, *ibid.*, p. 236 (17 Dec. 1921); Joe McGrath, *DE, treaty debate*, p. 305 (7 Jan. 1922).

194 De Róiste to de Valera, 23 May 1921, 'Epitome of documents seized', CO.904/23/7, p. 14.

195 *DE, 1919–21*, p. 242 (25 Jan. 1921). See above, p. 289.

196 De Valera to Stack, 7 May 1921, EdeV; see also de Róiste, diary, 3–13 May 1921, CAI, U271, A/37.

197 De Valera to Stack, 22 Apr. 1921, EdeV.

might have made in the course of these discussions were to no avail; Labour ran candidates in Belfast but abstained everywhere else. Captain Redmond also announced that 'this was not the time to stir up strife' and stood down in Waterford, while John Dillon, now in retirement, joined him in urging abstention. Every single constituency for the new southern Irish parliament was uncontested; Sinn Féin won 124 seats, and 4 independent unionists were returned for Trinity College. One RIC county inspector explained that all the Sinn Féin candidates were elected unopposed because 'no one wished to get shot by offering himself as an opposition candidate'.[198] The reality was more complex. In the circumstances of the Anglo-Irish War it is probable that most Irish nationalists would also have interpreted any opposition to Sinn Féin as a gesture of support for the British army and the Black and Tans. The elections in the south were no more than a formality, and one Sinn Féin candidate remarked that 'there is not the shadow of a shade of a sign of them'.[199] Yet even such a nominal campaign had beneficial side-effects, and shortly before the truce it was noticed that the Dublin city and county executives were operating more effectively since the election than they had done during the previous twelve months.[200]

In a break with its past habits the party devoted most of its attention to Ulster, and a hundred speakers were sent to the north.[201] Its leaders were on the run and were unable to appear in public – with the exception of the ever-energetic Fr O'Flanagan who spoke at seven meetings on one day.[202] De Valera outlined a scheme whereby Sinn Féin and the Dáil would each contribute £1,000 to supply anti-partition propaganda among unionists, but by polling day this was seen as wasted effort. It was then appreciated, too late, that 'the only effect that all our literature and leaflets etc. will have upon them is to bring them out to vote against us in great numbers'.[203]

In the election for the Northern Irish parliament the fifty-two seats were contested by seventy-seven candidates – forty Unionists, twelve Nationalists, four independent Labour, one independent and twenty Sinn Féiners. (Eight of these were in jail and seven on the run.[204]) Unionists professed to be indignant at the Sinn Fein challenge, and James Craig defied 'any authority, whether it be the British government or de Valera, to take away from us a Parliament once it is rooted in Ulster soil'.[205] His colleague Dawson Bates claimed that 'Sinn Féin

---

[198] CI's report, Waterford, May 1921, CO.904/115.

[199] De Róiste, diary, 25 Apr. 1921, CAI, U271, A/37.   [200] SCM, 7 June 1921.

[201] O'Keeffe to de Valera, 21 May 1921, EdeV.   [202] Carroll, *They have fooled you again*, p. 134.

[203] SCM, 13 Apr. 1921; Eamonn Donnelly to de Valera, 24 May 1921, EdeV.

[204] *Irish Bulletin*, 24 May 1921.   [205] *FJ*, 7 May 1921.

meant the driving out of the Protestants of Ireland . . . the present movement was one of the biggest attempts ever made against the Protestant religion and all it stands for since the days of the Reformation.'[206] The Belfast shipyard workers were offered political reassurance in familiar terms: although 'Rome was behind the great war, and Rome was behind the present movement in Ireland . . . they would put a band of steel around the six counties that neither de Valera, the priests, nor Cardinal Logue would ever break.'[207] Nationalist voters were warned of the horrors which would follow partition, and in Omagh a parish priest forecast that 'under a Belfast Parliament Catholics would be taxed to build schools for the wealthy Protestants of Belfast . . . It had also been hinted that divorce – an abomination to modest ears – would be legislated for.'[208]

Resources were divided unequally in the election; almost all the cars belonged to unionists, and it was claimed that on polling day Sinn Féiners scattered nails and tacks on the roads.[209] However, at least some Sinn Féin motorists ventured forth, and in a letter to de Valera on polling day Eamonn Donnelly described how 'cars were set on and drivers taken off and beaten'.[210] Complaints of personation were made in Belfast, and MacEntee, pointing out that in some districts 99.5 per cent of the electors had voted, proposed the motto 'long live the dead'.[211]

The turnout was 89 per cent, and every seat was contested; the percentage of invalid votes fell to a mere 1.01 (from 2.79 at the January 1920 local elections).[212] In a polarized campaign all Labour and independent candidates were defeated, and while every one of the forty Unionists was returned, Sinn Féin and the Nationalists won only six seats each. Three of the Sinn Féin victories were in Fermanagh and Tyrone – where 54.7 per cent of the electorate voted against the new Northern Irish state at the first available opportunity. In Belfast, where gerrymandering was more refined than elsewhere, nationalists won 23 per cent of the votes and secured 6 per cent of the seats.[213] Devlin had expected the combined nationalist seats to total between fifteen and twenty, and O'Keeffe had hoped that twelve Sinn Féin candidates would be elected, along with five Nationalists, so there was deep disappointment at the result.[214] At least Sinn Féin could take some comfort from the fact that its share of the first preference vote was nearly double that of the Devlinites – 20.4 per cent to 11.9 per cent – but this pattern would be reversed in later contests.

[206] *Belfast News-Letter*, 3 May 1921.   [207] *II*, 18 May 1921.   [208] *II*, 23 May 1921.

[209] *Belfast News-Letter*, 25 May 1921.   [210] Donnelly to de Valera, 24 May 1921, EdeV.

[211] *FJ*, 27 May 1921.   [212] *Representation*, July 1921, pp. 21–2.   [213] *Irish Bulletin*, 3 June 1921.

[214] Phoenix, *Northern nationalism*, p. 129; O'Keeffe to de Valera, 21 May 1921, EdeV.

Neighbourhood loyalties remained important. Many electors voted for de Valera or Griffith, but then deserted Sinn Féin and gave their second preferences to Nationalist candidates who were local men.[215] Following the pattern of 1918, all Sinn Féin's six MPs elected to the northern parliament lived in the south – even though they included two Ulstermen. Five of them also represented seats in the new Dublin parliament, and the only Belfastman in the Dáil, Séan MacEntee, was elected for Co. Monaghan. Sinn Féin held 130 seats in the second Dáil, as opposed to 73 in the first, but there was no increase in the number of deputies who came from Northern Ireland.[216] In the light of the treaty split a few months later it was significant that while the six Nationalist MPs refused to take their seats in the Belfast parliament, they also chose not to regard themselves as members of the Dáil; Sinn Féin theory encouraged them to do so, but only if they took an oath to the Irish republic.

In all, the propaganda for the elections was estimated to have cost Sinn Féin £5,770, a sum which burdened the party with further debts.[217] But this consisted merely of the figure at national level. As in 1918, each candidate had to pay a deposit of £150, and this was forfeited by all those who were elected and then abstained from parliament. Sinn Féin, with a total of 130 seats in Dublin and Belfast, thereby lost £19,500. Except in unionist Ulster most of this money was funded locally. After the elections the standing committee agreed to repay the loan of £5,000 provided by the finance ministry to run the campaign in the north-east, and it also decided to dispense with the services of the party's election agent because there was no more work for him to do.[218] The Sinn Féin party became once more the Cinderella of the separatist movement.

Revival

The elections of May 1921, although coinciding with the bloodiest phase of the Anglo-Irish War, helped indirectly to bring the fighting to an end. For years the British government's hands had been tied by the Conservative Party's obligations to the Ulster unionists. But now, with the unionists satisfied, with their Conservative mentors ready to display some flexibility towards nationalist Ireland, and with British public opinion alienated by the way in which the war was being fought, Lloyd George was at last ready to begin serious negotiations with the Dáil government. The formal opening of the Belfast parliament provided George V

---

[215] *Representation*, July 1921, p. 20.   [216] Mitchell, *Revolutionary government*, p. 284.

[217] Unsigned note, 'Epitome of captured documents', CO.904/23/7, p. 48.

[218] SCM, 31 May 1921.

with the opportunity to make a plea for peace in the south; discussions soon followed, and a truce came into effect on 11 July.

The Dáil and Sinn Féin could now emerge from hiding into what was, in many respects, a new Ireland. Police reports were no longer dominated by terror and death, and they reverted to conventional themes – as in Monaghan where 'a man broke a window in the town saying he wanted to be locked up. He has been.'[219] Sinn Féin could operate with even greater freedom than in the relatively easygoing days of 1917 and 1918. But one feature of the war years remained constant: the political organization remained subordinated to the government.

Throughout the lifetime of the first Dáil, from January 1919 to May 1921, the party's relationship with the parliament and cabinet had been astonishingly and unnaturally normal. The usual pattern in democracies is for parties to flourish in opposition. Political leaders, deprived of state power, devote their efforts to winning or regaining such power through their parties. Once that objective has been achieved, the party recedes into the background of their busy lives, and the politician (by now, if successful, the minister) moves onto a different level of activity and responsibility. Only loss of power (or the prospect of such loss through an election defeat) restores his earlier devotion to the party and its members, a restoration which, from his point of view, should be mercifully brief.

That this pattern should have applied in the circumstances of the years between 1919 and 1921, when parliament, cabinet, ministries and party were in hiding, when all the usual comforts and satisfactions of office were lacking, is yet further proof of the relativity of power. Even when both were on the run and in fear of their lives, a minister could feel that he lived on a more exalted plane than a mere party official. Sinn Féin, like other, more conventional parties in other, more conventional circumstances, was seen by ambitious politicians as no more than a stepping stone or as a ladder which would help them rise to higher places.

While the Irish leaders concentrated on their negotiations with the British cabinet, the Dáil administration exploited the new opportunities for extending its control over local government. The RIC watched this pattern with dismay. One county inspector remarked that the Sinn Féin organization was very active, and 'only its murders are at an end', while another was driven to despair: 'the authority of the Crown is simply sneered at, and all that the Servants of the Crown can do is to watch all they have suffered for trampled in the mud and smile'.[220]

---

[219] CI's report, Monaghan, Aug. 1921, CO.904/116.

[220] CIs' reports, Mayo, Aug. 1921, CO.904/116, E. Cork, Nov. 1921, CO.904/152, Cork (1).

The Dáil courts were revived, and in the absence of any serious British interference they became more effective than ever before.[221] General Macready complained in late August that 'to-morrow in Dublin scores of dairymen are being tried before Sinn Fein Courts for adulteration of milk ... [the Volunteers] patrol the streets, make arrests, and sometimes prevent arrest by RIC and Military Police'.[222] In Tipperary the police observed that control of the country was rapidly 'slipping into the hands of those who were the hunted a couple of months ago', and that people who were convicted by 'Sinn Fein courts' were either tied to chapel railings or else were forced to leave their homes.[223] By mid-October it was claimed that throughout Laois all the parish courts were functioning again, and higher courts were also sitting regularly.[224] The results were frequently unpopular. The RIC, watching powerlessly from the sidelines, reported that in West Cork the IRA's licensing restrictions had greatly disgusted publicans and their patrons.[225] Nonetheless, at a time of near anarchy in some parts of the country, the republican police and courts were often unable to restore order or impose justice.

Apart from their involvement in such activities, most Sinn Féiners were content to relax and celebrate. O'Keeffe reported at the end of July that everything possible was being done to overhaul the party's machinery, and that the breathing space provided by the truce had already had good results.[226] For some time there was little to show for such efforts. Then, on 5 August, the standing committee asked TDs to help reorganize their constituency executives, and it approved the payment of twenty organizers who would assist in the task of reviving the party during the next two months. The merger of the old (pre-PR) constituency executives, which had been implemented for the May elections, was now undone; perhaps understandably, the party still made no effort to adapt its structures to the new electoral boundaries.[227] The British cabinet, concerned that Sinn Féin would use the truce to consolidate its authority, was warned that the party intended to establish branches throughout Ireland.[228]

In the course of the following month local newspapers reported meetings of clubs and executives, and when the *ard-chomhairle* convened for the first time

---

[221] Gaughan, *Austin Stack*, p. 123.

[222] Macready, memo, 29 Aug. 1921, Anderson MSS, CO.904/188(1).

[223] CIs' reports, N., S. Tipperary, Aug. 1921, CO.904/116.

[224] *Nationalist and Leinster Times*, 15 Oct. 1921.

[225] CI's report, W. Cork, Aug. 1921, CO.904/116.

[226] O'Keeffe to Diarmuid O'Hegarty, 27 July 1921, NAI, DE, 2/2.

[227] SCM, 5 Aug. 1921; O'Keeffe, circular to TDs, 25 Aug. 1921, NLI, MS 11,405.

[228] Cabinet conclusions, 25 Aug. 1921, Cab.23/26, C.72(21)1.

since August 1919 an intensive campaign of reconstruction was launched. Hanna Sheehy-Skeffington, the director of elections, reported that the activities of many branches had dwindled or ceased, and the standing committee decided to appoint full-time secretaries who would organize each county. Thereby it added a new 'county' layer to the existing old and new constituency executives; the party's structure was to become even more complex. Perhaps unrealistically, the clubs and executives themselves were expected to raise the £10,000 which would be needed to pay for their own reorganization.[229] Shortly afterwards Stack announced his intention of setting up county administrative committees 'as a local Cabinet to represent the National Cabinet'.[230]

In the favourable circumstances of late 1921 the party's position was soon transformed. By the time the *ard-fheis* met in late October the number of affiliated and paid-up branches was 1,373, while a mere two months earlier it had been a miserable 89.[231] (Nonetheless, the total for 1920 was given as 1,162 – almost certainly an accurate figure since each club was recorded as having paid its £3 fee. However some of this money may have been paid retrospectively, after the truce.[232]) In December it was reported that twenty-one out of a possible maximum of twenty-three clubs in south Mayo had affiliated with party head-quarters.[233] The Naas branch provided a model of energy and efficiency. At its first meeting on 2 October an officer board was appointed, delegates to the constituency executive and the *ard-fheis* were chosen soon afterwards, and 250 new members joined after a public rally. All this took place within a fortnight. A dance and a football match raised £110 (which, significantly, was handed over to the army), and the club engaged in activities such as examining voters' lists, enforcing the Belfast boycott, organizing lectures and classes, and lobbying local government bodies. By mid-January there had been five full meetings of the club, fifteen of the executive, and the total membership was 410.[234] All this seemed reminiscent of the good old days of 1917–18. Yet while Naas showed such dynamism, the local constituency executive in North Kildare drew up a list of nine moribund clubs which had not yet been revived.[235] Although impressive in many respects, the party's revival remained patchy.

[229] Hanna Sheehy-Skeffington, *Report on organisation*, RB, 8786(2); SCM, 6 Sept. 1921.

[230] Stack to Déogréine Barton, 7 Oct. 1921, RB, 8786(2).

[231] *Tuairisc na runaithe, ard-fheis 1921. 1920–1921. Summary monies received up to the 12th August, 1921*, RB, 8786(2). Fifty-two of these eighty-nine clubs were in Leinster, twenty-eight in Munster, eight in Ulster and one in Connacht.

[232] *Sinn Féin ard-fheis, 27adh Deireadh Foghmair 1921; hon. secretaries' report*, RB, 8786(2)

[233] *Mayo News*, 10 Dec. 1921.

[234] Naas club, 'Report to comhairle ceanntair', 15 Jan. 1922, NLI, MS 13,561(1).

[235] 'Joint officer board meeting', 17 Jan. 1922, NLI, MS 13,561(6).

One newspaper account of the October 1921 *ard-fheis* illustrated Sinn Féin's lowly image and status. The meeting was contrasted unfavourably with its predecessors: in 1921 there was little of the earlier animation and bustle, it was noted that women and priests were much in evidence, and none of the romantic figures, 'no wounded warriors' or few of the younger men were to be seen. It was presumed that many of them had more serious work in hand, that 'with the eyes of the nation turned to the councils in Downing St., and with the Volunteers and Cumann na mBan busy in their own spheres, the activities of the purely political wing of the Sinn Féin Organisation must needs become somewhat humdrum'.[236]

At the *ard-fheis* de Valera proposed a long-overdue amendment to the party's constitution. This took the Dáil's existence into account, and deleted superfluous clauses such as Sinn Féin's aim of establishing a constituent assembly. It is perhaps surprising that such an obvious change was not implemented in April 1919, along with the separation of 'party and state' and the ending of the *ard-fheis*'s right to elect members of the standing committee. As a result Sinn Féin would henceforth give its 'undivided allegiance and entire support to Dáil Éireann, the duly elected Parliament of Ireland'. This natural and sensible measure would assume an unexpected significance in the political battles which began a few months later.

Delegates were told that in future Sinn Féin's main function would be 'to hold itself in readiness for any emergency, to see to the putting into effect of the decrees of Dáil Éireann, and generally, to take all possible steps towards strengthening the government of the Republic'. The party's political character was played down, and 'clubs that meet only for election purposes are neglecting the greater part of their work'.[237] Some people still retained the wish that Sinn Féin should be a broad national movement rather than a mere political party. It might have re-emerged as a mass movement in the months after the truce, but it still occupied a modest place in the minds of both the soldiers and the political leaders.

---

[236] *II*, 28 Oct. 1921.   [237] *Ibid.*

9

THE TREATY AND THE SPLIT, 1921–1922

The Sinn Féin party was not involved in the treaty negotiations. This was a natural and obvious corollary of its relegation by the Dáil and the Irish cabinet; both in practice and in theory it was no more than a political party which offered its support to a government in office – even if that government operated under unusual circumstances and exercised only limited powers. Between October and December 1921 Sinn Féin members waited on the results of the discussions in London with the same hope, impatience and apprehension as did the rest of the country.

Manoeuvres

Almost everyone in Ireland wanted peace, and most nationalists would have been content with a compromise settlement; after all, until only a few years earlier the overwhelming majority of Sinn Féiners had either supported or acquiesced in the home rule policies of John Redmond. Moderates might have felt reassured by Lloyd George's offer of dominion status and by de Valera's declaration in the Dáil that 'we are not Republican doctrinaires'.[1] On receipt of the British invitation to talks in London de Valera did not reassert his republican beliefs; instead, he invited Irish unionists to meet him, on the grounds that his response to Lloyd George's initiative would affect the minority population on the island no less than the majority. When entering these discussions he described himself not as president but as 'spokesman for the Irish Nation'; Griffith later drew attention to this point.[2] His public attitude seemed to indicate a moderate, consensual approach.

---

[1] *DE, 1921–22*, p. 9 (16 Aug. 1921).

[2] De Valera to James Craig and others, 28 June 1921, *Dáil Éireann. Official correspondence relating to the peace negotiations, June–September, 1921* (Dublin, 1921), p. 4; *DE, 1921–22*, p. 303 (27 Apr. 1922).

When exploratory meetings were held in London in mid-July de Valera raised the Irish demand for a republic, but Lloyd George was decisive in rejecting the idea. (He viewed de Valera as maladroit and as an unskilful negotiator, but he was often dismissive of Irish leaders and he described Collins as a 'rather stupid man'.[3]) Later, in the course of eight letters and telegrams to the prime minister, de Valera made only two references to this objective. In one of these he simply remarked on the fact that the Irish people had 'set up a Republic'. In the other he pointed out that the British were not expected to give formal or informal recognition to the republic as a preliminary to negotiations; in similar fashion the Irish should not be expected to surrender their own positions in advance of the talks.[4] (By way of contrast, Lloyd George referred repeatedly to dominion status, the commonwealth and allegiance to the king.) De Valera never rejected the prime minister's insistence that there could be no settlement except on the basis of southern Ireland becoming a dominion.[5]

There is no record of the matter being discussed in the Irish cabinet or mentioned in the instructions which were given to the delegates. De Valera was committed to an imaginative and far-sighted scheme of his own creation, that of an 'external association' between Ireland and Britain, but he failed to communicate to his colleagues the strength of his feelings on this subject. Nor did he emphasize the form of government which an Irish state would adopt. It seemed as if the Sinn Féiners' principal aim was to avoid any formal or direct link to the monarchy – and in particular to ensure that no oath of allegiance should be taken to the king. Even the most extreme of all Dáil deputies, Mary MacSwiney, never believed that the negotiations would end in British recognition of an Irish republic.[6]

Yet from the standpoint of Irish politics (as distinct from that of Anglo-Irish negotiations) mere vagueness concerning objectives might indicate that the Dáil government was still determined to achieve a republic. This had been Sinn Féin's objective since 1917, and other recent developments indicated that the Irish leadership might not be as flexible as many people hoped. It was only after de Valera's meetings with Lloyd George, after he had been informed bluntly that a republic could not form part of any peace settlement, that he and Brugha proposed a change in his title: he should be acknowledged formally as president of

---

[3] Jones, *Whitehall diary*, III, p. 110 (7 Sept. 1921); *The political diaries of C. P. Scott* (London, 1970), p. 405 (29 Oct. 1921).

[4] De Valera to Lloyd George, 30 Aug., 19 Sept. 1921, *Dáil Éireann. Official correspondence*, pp. 16, 22.   [5] Frank Pakenham (Earl of Longford), *Peace by ordeal* (London, 1935), p. 90.

[6] *DE, private sessions*, p. 124 (14 Dec. 1921).

the Irish republic, and not merely of Dáil Éireann.[7] Thereby they raised the stakes and created a new obstacle to any settlement with Britain. While the negotiations were still taking place in London de Valera began speaking strongly against any idea of accepting the crown, even though he accepted that those who were opposed to a policy of 'the isolated Republic' comprised a majority of the nation.[8]

Ominously, the two most committed republicans in the cabinet, Brugha and Stack, followed his example and refused to go to London. Both were rigid men who would have been unskilled negotiators, and de Valera explained afterwards that despite Brugha's good qualities he was 'a bit slow at seeing fine differences and rather stubborn'.[9] These ministers represented the determined minority which rejected compromise and which was indifferent to the cost of continued warfare – an attitude which was far more widespread in the army and the political leadership than among the civilian population.

Some of the more dedicated republicans regarded the Irish people with deep distrust, and Mary MacSwiney wrote to de Valera hoping that 'there will be no talk of an election because there is no doubt that there would be found weaklings who might reduce our majority. *An Dáil* has its mandate and can answer for the Nation.'[10] She was confident that 'we can trust the majority of the members of an Dáil to have no compromise',[11] and she believed that others (outside this Dáil majority) could not be trusted. The people had no right to change their minds and abandon their republic – just as, in years gone by, Griffith had argued that they had no right to abandon their separate parliament.[12] Even before the truce came into effect Count Plunkett was said to have informed Brugha that he would oppose any serious negotiations. He wanted 'the continuance of a rigorous campaign to bring England to a better mind. We must not lose the advantages won for us by hard fighting and self-sacrifice.'[13] Shortly before the treaty was signed Stack remarked that 'the London business is about over with no great good done – and no harm'.[14] His tone was casual, and the prospect of renewed conflict appears not to have perturbed him. Some

---

[7] *Ibid.*, pp. 54–6 (23 Aug. 1921). Three days later this decision was ratified at a public meeting of the Dáil.   [8] De Valera to McGarrity, 27 Dec. 1921, McG, 17,440.   [9] *Ibid.*

[10] MacSwiney to de Valera, 4 Aug. 1921, MacS, P48a/115(49).

[11] MacSwiney to Harry Boland, 4 Aug. 1921, MacS, P48a/115(56)/3.

[12] Maume, 'Ancient constitution', pp. 135–6.

[13] Plunkett to Brugha, 9 July 1921 (printed leaflet, no provenance), NLI, ILB. 300.P3.

[14] Stack to Mary MacSwiney, 5 Dec. 1921, MacSwiney MSS, UCDA, P48a/37(4). According to J. J. O'Kelly, Stack held such views at the time of de Valera's visit to London in July (*Stepping-stones*, p. 15).

weeks later he longed for the simplicities of wartime; 'I would give eyes, ears, hands, arms, anything, everything to get back to the military position.'[15] Outside the ranks of the IRA few others looked back so fondly on the recent war.

Months afterwards, an opponent of the treaty deplored the president's inconsistency and pointed out that, after preparing for a compromise with Lloyd George, he had then rushed back to the rock of republicanism; while the plenipotentiaries were in London he 'became subjected to the will of Cathal Brugha and Austin [Stack]'.[16] De Valera seems to have feared and resented Collins's combination of ambition and efficiency, and in a mutually dependent relationship he both influenced and was influenced by the suspicion of Collins which was shared by Brugha and Stack.[17] Principle was reinforced by self-interest.

A further sign of trouble to come was his attempt to restructure the army in late 1921. He and Brugha tried to insert the incompetent but loyal Stack as deputy chief of staff, with the aim of ensuring that their own faction of the cabinet would be better able to control the Volunteers. This plan was rejected by the GHQ staff, some of whose members distrusted the cabinet and several of whom were themselves politicians; six of the thirteen members of the general staff were also Dáil deputies. The army was embroiled in political controversy long before the treaty, although, ironically, those politicians who were anxious to establish their control over the military later took arms against a civilian government, while most of the general staff who resented their interference would later support democracy and majority rule.[18]

One more problem was created for the future. By a unanimous vote the Dáil had granted plenipotentiary powers to the delegates, but privately they were issued with other, contradictory instructions: before finalizing an agreement they were directed to refer any draft settlement to 'the Members of the Cabinet in Dublin'.[19] In the absence of three ministers who formed part of the delegation (Griffith, Collins and Barton) this section of the cabinet would be dominated by those who had refused to take the responsibility of negotiating with the British. In the private Dáil debates de Valera interpreted 'plenipotentiary' as meaning 'men sent over to make peace [who] come back and their actions were

---

[15] Gaughan, *Austin Stack*, p. 181.

[16] Joseph Connolly to Joe McGarrity, 8 July 1922, McG, 17,654(1).   [17] Garvin, *1922*, pp. 57, 96.

[18] Cabinet minutes, 15 Sept. 1921, NAI, DE, 1/3; Coogan, *Michael Collins*, pp. 249–51; Mitchell, *Revolutionary government*, pp. 317–9; Valiulis, *Portrait of a revolutionary*, pp. 104–9; Hannon, 'Irish Volunteers', pp. 258–64.

[19] *DE, private sessions*, p. 96 (14 Sept. 1921); 'Instructions to plenipotentiaries from cabinet', 7 Oct. 1921, *ibid.*, appendix 6, p. 289; Coogan, *De Valera*, pp. 255–6.

ratified or not',[20] yet in practice he saw their position in a different light and he was determined to be involved – even at a distance – in any final settlement. (The attempt to ensure that a decision would not be reached in Downing Street could also be seen as a deserved tribute to Lloyd George's negotiating skill and cunning. Keynes, who had observed the prime minister during the 1919 peace conference, described him exotically as 'this syren, this goat-footed bard, this half-human visitor to our age from the hag-ridden magic and enchanted woods of Celtic antiquity . . . a vampire and a medium in one'.[21])

This action by the cabinet in overruling the Dáil was characteristic of the executive's cavalier attitude towards the legislature. It also amounted to a deception of most Irish nationalists, who imagined that the delegates *were* plenipotentiaries and who learned of these conflicting instructions only when the treaty split revealed the divisions within the national leadership.

The London negotiations lasted from 11 October to 6 December. The Irish delegates, led by Griffith and Collins, fought hard to achieve 'essential unity' and to minimize the role of the crown in southern Irish affairs. They proved more successful in the second of these aims than in the first. In the end they chose to ignore both the cabinet directive and Griffith's recent promise not to sign any draft treaty before referring it back to Dublin; they exercised the plenipotentiary powers conferred on them by the Dáil, and concluded a settlement with the British.

Purists and pragmatists

The agreement granted Ireland dominion status, although with some restrictions or qualifications. A mere two years earlier the British cabinet described this degree of independence as something which 'had never been contemplated', and almost to the end of the Anglo-Irish War Lloyd George remained fiercely opposed to it.[22] At no stage had recognition of an Irish republic been a serious possibility; instead, the new dominion would be entitled the 'Irish Free State' – a literal interpretation of the Irish word *saorstát*, which was in turn a translation of the English word 'republic'. While the republic proclaimed in 1916 was described in Irish as *poblacht*, on its re-proclamation in 1919 it was called *saorstát*; the two words were clearly synonyms. In one of his meetings with de Valera the previous July, Lloyd George had cleverly drawn attention to

---

[20] *DE, private sessions,* p. 83 (26 Aug. 1921).

[21] J. M. Keynes, *Essays in biography* (London, 1933), pp. 36–7.

[22] Mansergh, *Unresolved question,* pp. 146, 159, 173.

the literal meaning of the word *saorstát* which was employed in communications from the Irish government.[23] The term was already in use, and on occasion during the truce the Dáil courts were described as acting in the name of 'Saorstát na hÉireann (Free State of Ireland)'.[24] One Irish-speaking Dáil deputy announced that since he had taken his oath of allegiance to the *Saor Stát* he was being consistent in voting for the settlement. If the debate were being held in Irish rather than in English there would be no disagreement over the meaning of words.[25]

The crucial aspect of the treaty concerned the role of the king and the oath which would be taken to him by members of the Dáil; the Anglophobic obsession with 'the crown' outranked all other questions.[26] The relevant article laid down that all deputies must swear an oath of allegiance to the constitution of the Free State and an oath of fidelity to the king. George V would be head of state of both Britain and Ireland, and Mary MacSwiney pointed out – quite accurately – that in accepting this agreement Griffith had simply reverted to his earlier support for a dual monarchy.[27] The treaty conceded all that the constitutional Sinn Féiners had sought before 1916, but a rebellion and a guerrilla war were needed to bring about what they had hoped to achieve by political means.

The question of 'Ulster' was postponed, and the frontier between the two parts of Ireland would be decided by a boundary commission. This article of the treaty was not a divisive issue in 1921–2, even though its loose wording would later allow the border to remain unchanged.

Collins's support of the treaty was of vital importance, particularly since in the past, in 1916 and 1919, he had been among those who were determined to defy the wishes of the people. He agreed to a compromise settlement in 1921 less because a large majority desired peace than because he and some of his colleagues believed that it was the best deal which could be secured for nationalist Ireland. But when he and other leading military figures were converted to moderation, and then encountered opposition among the more uncompromising elements in the IRA, they were encouraged or even forced to court public opinion; they were enabled to become democrats. The mass of the population which wanted peace could now enjoy the protection of at least some members of the army, while the radicals who had always distrusted the people were now divided.

Many in Sinn Féin and the IRA rejected the settlement because they were

---

[23] Thomas Jones to Churchill, 29 Jan. 1929, *Whitehall diary*, III, p. 89; de Valera, *DE, private sessions*, p. 115 (14 Dec. 1921). See de Paor, *On the Easter proclamation*, p. 35.

[24] *Evening Telegraph*, 8 Oct. 1921.   [25] Liam de Róiste, *DE, treaty debate*, p. 158 (22 Dec. 1921).

[26] Foster, *Modern Ireland*, p. 506.   [27] *DE, treaty debate*, p. 113 (21 Dec. 1921).

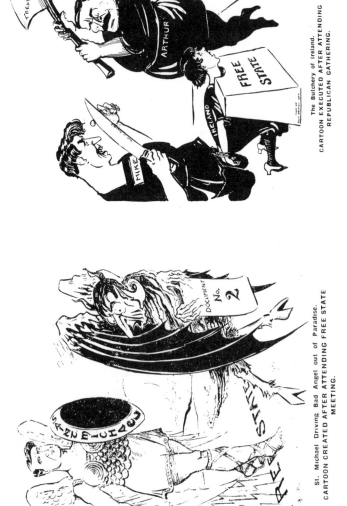

St. Michael Driving Bad Angel out of Paradise.
CARTOON CREATED AFTER ATTENDING FREE STATE MEETING.

The Butchery of Ireland.
CARTOON EXECUTED AFTER ATTENDING REPUBLICAN GATHERING.

9.1 Rival images of the Treaty

committed to the ideal of an abstract republic, but de Valera took a different position. Unlike some of the extremists in the army he had always been prepared to moderate his views, and it seems reasonable to claim that he joined Stack and Brugha in opposing the treaty not because it was *a* compromise, but because it was not *his* compromise.[28] He resented the fact that a decision had been taken without his approval, and as a sardonic French observer remarked, 'he thought that his conscience was outraged, while only his vanity was wounded'.[29] Long afterwards, Ernest Blythe claimed that de Valera rejected the treaty because he was not permitted to change it in some way and deny Collins the credit for having won it.[30]

Only days after the agreement was signed de Valera held a private meeting with Barton, Childers and Gavan Duffy. He was dissatisfied with an alternative to the treaty which they had discussed, and Childers recorded in his diary his own astonished reaction to the president's plans: it was a 'revelation to me to find that he was thinking more of one which he could get extremist support for than moderate support! His nerve and confidence are amazing. Seems certain of winning.'[31] In the circumstances of December 1921 extremist support was not hard to find.

As Liam de Róiste remarked, war had welded the people together but even the mere prospect of peace with Britain divided them.[32] A Dublin Castle official concurred: 'we who told "London" over a year ago that if they would put the cards down they would either win a complete acceptance or at worst split S.F. from top to bottom did not quite know how right we were to be proved'.[33] The disruption provoked by the treaty illustrated with exceptional and tragic clarity the differences between two traditions of Irish nationalism. A quarter of a century later T. C. Kingsmill Moore, the high court judge presiding over a law case involving the party's funds, remarked that if the British had offered either a little more or a little less the Irish would have been unanimous in accepting or rejecting the proposed treaty; yet in a way which was probably fortuitous, the terms were precisely such as to accentuate fundamental divisions within their ranks. His remarks are worth quoting at some length:

---

[28] Ronan Fanning, *Independent Ireland* (Dublin, 1983), p. 3.

[29] Simone Téry, *En Irlande: de la guerre d'indépendance à la guerre civile (1914–1923)* (Paris, 1923), p. 142.

[30] Blythe, statement, 1972, cited in Glandon, *Arthur Griffith*, p. 200. One of de Valera's supporters remarked of him that 'he never saw a draft submitted by anybody but he must alter it' (Brennan, *Allegiance*, pp. 163–4).   [31] Childers, diary, 9 Dec. 1921, TCDL, MS 7814.

[32] De Róiste, diary, 17 Dec. 1921, CAI, U271/A/41.

[33] Sturgis, diary, 22 Dec. 1921, PRO.30/59/5.

In favour of acceptance were those of a sanguine and prospective nature, men who thought more of securing their opportunities than insisting on what they considered to be their rights; the moderates whose outlook suggested and whose experience confirmed the thesis that all life is an illogical compromise between logical extremes and that the grave of every great controversy is accordingly a great compromise: the cautious who weighed the certainty of half a loaf against the possibility of no bread: the practical and pragmatic whose minds were concerned with things rather than words. Against them were gathered those whose traditional suspicion of England led them to suspect a snare in every phrase: those who could not brook the idea of compromise in matters which they considered to [be] sound in principle and not in political expediency; the Puritans of politics who were willing to face martyrdom for the rigidity of their code. To a degree each side respected the opinions of its opponents. But there came the sticking point. While the supporters of the Treaty saw the Republic as a desirable consummation likely to be achieved in the fullness of time, but not essential to the reality of independence, to their adversaries its present existence and the need to preserve it were articles of faith which to abandon would be a major heresy . . . one fact has emerged beyond question, and that is the sincerity of those who demand the republic and nothing but the republic. To them it was not a matter of argument but of conviction transcending all considerations of reason. There was an element almost of religion in their attachment to the Republic.[34]

The obsession with the symbolic, almost doctrinal question of the oath might reasonably have been expected of an obscure faction which was far removed from any prospect of exercising real power. It might seem less appropriate to a parliament which was engaged in discussing whether it would or would not ratify a peace treaty. But Dáil deputies were not the only legislators to be preoccupied with the problem, and in the House of Commons the treaty was criticized harshly because it contained no oath of allegiance to the king.[35]

The Irish cabinet divided almost evenly on the issue, with four members supporting the treaty and three (including the president) opposed to it. The Dáil then debated the question in public and private sessions, and these occupied a total of fifteen days between 14 December and 7 January. The main issues in the debates were the position of the king and the right of the delegates to sign the treaty without referring it back to Dublin. Its supporters defended the agree-

---

[34] Kingsmill Moore, judgment, 26 Oct. 1948, SFFC, 2B/82/117(32), pp. 20–1.

[35] See, for example, *Hansard*, 149, cols. 95, 105, 147 (14 Dec. 1921).

ment as the best which could have been reached under the circumstances, and they claimed that, in Collins's phrase, it gave Ireland the freedom to achieve freedom. Senior IRA officers warned the Dáil of the army's weakness if the struggle against the British were to be renewed.[36] Critics of the treaty accused the delegates of having betrayed the republic, and they displayed throughout the debates a deep suspicion of British intentions; as one (pro-treaty) deputy put it, 'mistrust of English rulers is bred in our bones from the reading of the history of our land'.[37]

Little was said about Ulster or partition. Sinn Féin, the Dáil and the cabinet had all displayed scant interest in northern affairs over the years, and this was reflected by the readiness with which they accepted that the question should be handed over to a boundary commission. Lack of criticism of the treaty's Ulster clauses 'can be ascribed to support of them, inability to devise a better alternative, or simply the belief that there was no solution to partition'.[38]

Some of the speakers were lucid and passionate, while others were hypocritical and self-righteous. Rarely were the debates enlivened by humour. One deputy illustrated the difference between the treaty's oath of allegiance to the constitution and its oath of fidelity to the king by pointing out that 'when a man gets married he promises to be faithful to his wife which is a very different thing from owning allegiance to her (A voice, "Wait until you get married")'.[39] Kevin O'Higgins suggested that if the man in the street were told he was to be sacrificed in order to hand on a tradition to posterity, he might ask plaintively what had posterity ever done for him.[40] Seán Etchingham rejected claims that under the treaty the Irish people would march into the empire with their heads up: 'rather into it with their hands up'.[41] (Months later Markievicz provided a variation of this image; 'Arthur Griffith had said they were going to march into the British Empire with their "heads up". I say with tails down, like a pack of cringing curs.'[42]) There were frequent lapses into bathos, as in the case of the deputy who told his colleagues that 'there is a tide in the affairs of nations as in the affairs of men which when taken at flood time often results in a great advantage to the country'. He was redeemed by another heckler who shouted 'it takes you out to sea sometimes'.[43]

---

[36] John M. Regan, 'The politics of reaction: the dynamics of treatyite government and policy, 1922–33', *IHS*, 30, 120 (1997), pp. 547–8.

[37] Liam de Róiste, *DE, treaty debate*, p. 160 (22 Dec. 1921).

[38] Joseph M. Curran, *The birth of the Irish Free State, 1921–1923* (Alabama, 1980), p. 135. See above, pp. 225–32.   [39] Gearóid O'Sullivan, *DE, private sessions*, p. 245 (17 Dec. 1921).

[40] *DE, treaty debate*, p. 47 (19 Dec. 1921).   [41] *Ibid.*, p. 54 (20 Dec. 1921).

[42] *Western People*, 1 Apr. 1922.   [43] Alec MacCabe, *DE, private sessions*, p. 206 (16 Dec. 1921).

A few people changed their minds, and among those who voted for the treaty was the deputy who, only a few months earlier, had urged that the Irish people should entrench themselves somewhere as a republic, even on the Aran Islands.[44] On the other hand, Markievicz was characteristically consistent and implacable when she announced that she would not work with anyone who considered the case of Ireland from a lower standard than her own, while Mary MacSwiney (who described herself fairly as 'a doctrinaire republican') declared that 'when you sent the delegates to London you didn't send them to compromise'. For her the question was enviably simple: 'the issue is not between peace and war; it is between right and wrong'.[45]

Some TDs stressed the inviolability of their oath to the republic, which had been taken at Brugha's instigation in August 1919. Griffith claimed that he had a collection of seven different oaths to the king which had been sworn by Dáil deputies opposed to the treaty, and that it was 'damnable hypocrisy' to stress the sanctity of one in contrast to all others. But Brugha himself would have been quite unimpressed by such arguments, making it clear that he had no interest in any other broken oaths and that 'the only oath that concerns me is the Oath of Allegiance to the Dáil'.[46] Republican deputies seemed to be less concerned with cherishing their integrity than with cherishing their intransigence.

De Valera complained that 'the British will now know that if they put the treaty to the country over our heads the country will probably ratify it, and will pay very little heed to our counter-proposals'.[47] But many observers felt that, whatever the people might wish, the Dáil would reject the London compromise. Although they had acquiesced in the London negotiations (during which the cabinet records indicate no demand for or even discussion of republican status) a majority of the deputies remained emotionally or ideologically committed to the idea of an Irish republic. In this way they were unrepresentative of the country at large, and some of the republicans came under intense pressure from angry constituents. James Ryan received numerous resolutions demanding that he should support the treaty, all of them passed either unanimously or by substantial margins, while none of his correspondents sympathized with his opposition to the settlement.[48] His colleague Seán MacEntee admitted that 'so far as any wish was expressed, the unanimous wish of Monaghan was that I should vote for the Treaty'. He was pressed by the two Sinn Féin executives in his constituency to resign his seat

[44] Alec MacCabe, ibid., p. 33 (22 Aug. 1921).

[45] DE, treaty debate, p. 362 (9 Jan. 1922); DE, private sessions, pp. 120, 125, 245 (14, 17 Dec. 1921).

[46] DE, treaty debate, pp. 336–7, 325 (7 Jan. 1922).

[47] De Valera to McGarrity, 27 Dec. 1921, McG, 17,440.

[48] Correspondence, Dec. 1921–Jan. 1922, Ryan MSS, UCDA, P88/68.

because of his anti-treaty views, and he promised to do so at a suitable time, but to the fury of his critics he took no action in this regard until the Dáil was dissolved the following June. Even by the standards of the time, the quarrel was acrimonious. He remarked some months later, 'I did not receive one word to encourage me in the stand I was making, while I was in receipt of countless letters and telegrams urging and ordering me to take the opposite course.'[49]

One anti-treaty deputy resigned his seat to escape from the dilemma of having to choose between his own beliefs and the wishes of his constituents, and many more must have been swayed by the voters' demands. Most people took the view of the *Western People* when it asked of Dáil deputies, 'after all what are they if not the mouthpiece of their constituents? The issues with which we are now faced are too grave to be subordinated to a mistaken sense of delicacy.'[50] Very few shared the sentiments of the club in Arney, Enniskillen, when it wrote to Seán O'Mahony, its anti-treaty deputy, telling him that 'we consider the members of *an Dáil* quite capable of dealing with the Treaty without dictation from the people . . . We selected you to lead us and it is as leader we still regard you . . . dictation to our mind reduces *an Dáil* to the status of a political convention.'[51] Edmund Burke would have been proud of such electors. But even in this instance the messages which O'Mahony received were overwhelmingly in favour of the agreement.

Many observers believed that it was only when the deputies returned home for the Christmas recess, and encountered for the first time the breadth and depth of support for the treaty, that some of them decided to adjust their republican views to the general demand for peace. At long last the people were able to restrain those who spoke and acted in their name. De Valera wrote shortly after Christmas that if the final vote had been taken before the Dáil adjourned, 'it was thought we might have got a majority of one or two against the Treaty'; but the press and the Church were hard at work in its support.[52]

Yet a reverse pattern could also be observed. Public opinion was influenced by the fact that the settlement was opposed by so many Dáil members, including some of the most respected figures in the country. The objections of ministers such as de Valera, Brugha and Stack stimulated dissatisfaction with the treaty's terms on the part of some Sinn Féin supporters whose initial response had been one of welcome or acceptance. The attitude of the *Donegal Vindicator* may be symptomatic of this change. In its first editorial after the treaty was

---

[49] Draft speech, n.d. (May–June 1922), MacEntee MSS, UCDA, P67/60.
[50] *Western People*, 31 Dec. 1921, editorial.
[51] Resolution, 29 Dec. 1921, O'Mahony MSS, NLI, 24,468.
[52] De Valera to McGarrity, 27 Dec. 1921, McG, 17,440.

signed it expressed unhappiness with the oath of fidelity to be taken by Dáil deputies, but reported that

> we thought silence our duty trusting as we do in our leaders. We registered only a little half-hearted regret . . . Now Eamon de Valera has spoken that he cannot counsel acceptance and one may speak the hidden thoughts . . . Eamon de Valera has read aright the nation's mind. Yet will we ever turn down Collins or Griffith? . . . The thing is a puzzle. The men were PLENI-POTENTIARIES.[53]

The *Vindicator* remained puzzled and it continued to waver; a fortnight later it still believed that 'the fact of the five plenipotentiaries having signed it should have been sufficient for Dáil Éireann'. Nonetheless, almost alone among Irish newspapers, it drifted into opposition.

It was clear that the army's reaction would be crucial, and despite de Valera's warning that 'the day any portion of the army does not obey the Government then there is an end of your fight for freedom',[54] many Volunteers both inside and outside the Dáil made it clear that they would not allow their own opinions to be overruled or outvoted. These soldiers had little respect for civilian opinion or authority, and they believed that the people should allow the military to speak on their behalf. Within days of the treaty's signature the staff officers and all brigade commanders of Liam Lynch's 1st Southern Division met in Cork and agreed unanimously that they found its terms unacceptable.[55] This was ominous news for supporters of the agreement, since the 1st Southern had carried out more actions against the British than had any other division in the country. The IRA leader Seamus Robinson pointed out, quite reasonably, that 'if we had no political outlook we would not be soldiers at all', and then went on to demand a military veto on any change in the country's constitution.[56]

Such views were less outrageous in 1922 than they might appear to later generations. The 1916 rebels had not waited for public endorsement before they took the actions which all deputies now supported, and everyone knew that it was military pressure, rather than mass support or political organization, which had driven the British to negotiate with those whom they had denounced as 'gunmen'. IRA men had made sacrifices in fighting for their beloved republic and they would not allow their gains to be frittered away by civilians, however numerous these might be. Why should they be more responsible to the people now than they had been during the past two and a half years?[57]

---

[53] *Donegal Vindicator*, 9 Dec. 1921, editorial.   [54] *DE, private sessions*, p. 134 (14 Dec. 1921).
[55] Liam Lynch and others to Mulcahy, 10 Dec. 1921, RM, P7a/143.
[56] *DE, treaty debate*, p. 290 (6 Jan. 1922).   [57] Kee, *Green flag*, p. 732.

Already during the treaty debate there were threats of violence and fears of civil war. A Galway TD claimed that he had been warned he would be shot if he voted in favour of the settlement.[58] Con Collins, an opponent of the treaty, suggested that 'we Republicans will probably spend the rest of our lives in jail as rebels under the Free State', while Brugha dismissed the arguments of a pro-treaty deputy and declared that the views of 'the men who count' in the constituency, the fighting men, were expressed by the brigade commandants.[59]

The deputies lacked a clear mandate from the people; most of them had been nominated rather than elected to their seats. The Dáil had never been taken seriously by the cabinet, and de Valera showed it little respect. In his letter to Lloyd George on 10 August 1921 he referred to their recent discussions in London, when he had told the prime minister that the Dáil could not accept the British proposals. Now, 'having consulted my colleagues', he confirmed that opinion in writing. However, two weeks later he alluded to what he described as his 'anticipatory judgement'; although the Dáil had not yet convened when de Valera wrote his earlier letter to Lloyd George (on 10 August) he had nonetheless spoken on its behalf. By the time of his second letter it had met and had duly reached the decision which he had already announced in advance: rejection of the latest British offer.[60] Few seem to have been angered or even surprised that the Irish parliament should have been treated in such an offhand manner. One deputy remarked later 'we were sheep in the Dáil. None dare question what was laid before us.'[61] After the treaty was signed some republicans felt that it was unfair and dishonest to give such sudden priority to the decisions of a body which hitherto had been held in low esteem. It was the triumph of constitutional theory over revolutionary practice.

De Valera rejected compromise proposals which had been agreed tentatively by four delegates from each side, and which had then been accepted by Griffith and Collins. (Their main point was that the provisional government would derive its powers from the Dáil rather than from 'the members elected to sit in the House of Commons of Southern Ireland'; this body included the four members from Trinity College and excluded the one Sinn Féin member of the Belfast parliament who did not also hold a seat in the south.)[62]

---

[58] Frank Fahy, *DE, private sessions*, p. 128 (14 Dec. 1921).

[59] *DE, treaty debate*, pp. 318, 329 (7 Jan. 1922).

[60] De Valera to Lloyd George, 10, 24 Aug. 1921, *Dáil Éireann. Official correspondence relating to the peace negotiations*, pp. 10, 13.   [61] De Róiste, diary, 21 Feb. 1922, CAI, U271/A/43.

[62] *DE, private sessions*, pp. 273–83 (6 Jan. 1922); T. Ryle Dwyer, *De Valera's darkest hour: in search of national independence, 1919–1932* (Dublin and Cork, 1982) p. 90; Michael Hayes, 'Dáil Éireann and the Irish Civil War', *Studies*, 58, 229 (1969), pp. 5–7.

Finally the Dáil voted on 7 January, and supporters of the treaty won by the narrow margin of sixty-four votes to fifty-seven. All six women deputies voted against the settlement, probably at least in part because some of them saw themselves as 'representative' figures, as substitutes for martyred male relatives. (Similarly, at a lower level, all the men who worked in the Dáil land settlement commission supported the treaty, and all the women opposed it.[63]) The young were inclined to be more radical than their elders, and the irreconcilable republicans tended to include those who belonged to the gentry, who were foreign-born or reared, or who were of foreign descent.[64] Otherwise it is hard to distinguish voting patterns. The thirty TDs who had been interned in Frongoch in 1916 split evenly on the question.[65] The second Dáil was no more radical than its predecessor; of those deputies who had also belonged to the first Dáil, thirty-four voted for the settlement and twenty-eight against, while of those newly elected in May 1921, thirty voted in favour and twenty-nine against. The difference between the two categories was relatively slight; 55 per cent of the old members supported the treaty as opposed to 51 per cent of the new. Since so many anti-treaty deputies were rejected by their electorates at the first opportunity which arose, there was no more than a tenuous relationship between their own beliefs and those of their constituents.

After his defeat on the question of the treaty de Valera ran for re-election as president, was narrowly defeated, and went into opposition. He was succeeded by Griffith. Count Plunkett had no time for such constitutional niceties, and wrote that

> as it was out of the power of traitors to affect the existing rights of the Republic and of its Government, the powers of the dáil remain vested in the elected persons who have been faithful to these institutions.
>
> Because of these facts, we who voted against the Treaty should exercise our powers and meet as the dáil. [66]

De Valera would later adopt such a policy, but the time for following Plunkett's advice had not yet come.

Divisions

Collins, as chairman of the new provisional government, soon began to take over the powers which had been exercised by Dublin Castle. Griffith and his Dáil

---

[63] Gaughan, *Austin Stack*, p. 138.   [64] Rumpf and Hepburn, *Nationalism and socialism*, p. 34.
[65] O'Mahony, *Frongoch*, pp. 220–1.   [66] Plunkett to de Valera, n.d. [? Jan. 1922], EdeV.

cabinet were content to see power slide gradually towards the new body.[67] Some people imagined that the provisional government would be no more than a means of liaising between the British and Irish cabinets;[68] this did not happen, and instead the Dáil government served as a link between Collins's administration and the republicans. It faded away gradually, and the records of its cabinet meetings ended in April.[69] An opponent later described the continuing existence of the second Dáil as the master-stroke of pro-treaty policy, since it served as a matador's cloak or as a façade behind which the provisional government could consolidate its position.[70]

The treaty not only split the Dáil in two, but it also brought an abrupt end to the unity of the Sinn Féin party which had been achieved in the months before the October 1917 convention. In the course of the debates de Valera claimed that when he returned from Lewes Jail he found that Griffith and Brugha differed as fundamentally then as they did now in 1922, while Collins agreed that 'it was not to-day or yesterday it started'.[71] Divisions emerged which had been buried or had lain dormant during the previous four years.

Yet in the course of waging war against Britain the heat of conflict had welded different elements together, and in many instances the new fractures between moderates and extremists were along somewhat different lines from those of earlier years; the two *blocs* remained more or less intact, but some individuals had changed sides. Collins, for instance, had been prominent among the radicals, but he was above all a pragmatist and his awareness of military realities led him to support an imperfect agreement. On the other hand, de Valera's reputation since 1917 had been that of a moderate, a politician rather than a soldier, and many people were astonished by his new rigidity.[72] The attitudes of some other Sinn Féiners provoked surprise and even scorn; Bishop Fogarty remarked that 'Fr. O'Flanagan is a die-hard – well that is fine for the man with the white flag of 1920.'[73]

Most party members joined in the general celebrations which followed the London agreement. In the active Naas club, for example, only 2 members out of more than 150 opposed the settlement, and this consensus was reinforced a few weeks later when there were 3 dissentients in an attendance of 400.[74] Day after

---

[67] See Joe Lee, 'The challenge of a Collins biography', in Doherty and Keogh, *Michael Collins*, pp. 34–5.   [68] E.g., de Róiste, diary, 12 Jan. 1922, CAI, U271/A/42.

[69] Cabinet minutes, 28 Apr. 1922, NAI, DE, 1/4.   [70] O'Donoghue, *No other law*, p. 202.

[71] *DE, treaty debate*, pp. 272 (6 Jan.), 370 (9 Jan. 1922).

[72] On the attitudes of leading Sinn Féiners towards the treaty, see Jeffrey Prager, *Building democracy in Ireland: political order and cultural integration in a newly independent nation* (Cambridge, 1986), pp. 50–66.   [73] Fogarty to James O'Mara, 9 Apr. 1922, JO'M, 21,550(3).

[74] Club minutes, 30 Dec. 1921, 18 Jan. 1922, NLI, MS 13,561(5).

day, a sympathetic press continued to publish impressive lists of county councils, constituency executives and party branches which welcomed the agreement, in contrast to an insignificant total of opponents. On 5 January the *Irish Independent* claimed that only two Sinn Féin branches had opposed the treaty, and that the balance of support in elected and other bodies was 334 to 10.[75] Initially many such votes were unanimously in favour of the treaty, and almost all others were overwhelming in their support. The reservations expressed by the Fermanagh executives, which represented a total of twenty-three clubs, were understandable in the light of their county's exclusion from the new Free State. Nonetheless, they concluded magnanimously that 'despite the great hardship which the treaty would impose on the nationalists of Fermanagh and Tyrone, it gave a reasonable measure of independence to the twenty-six counties', and that under existing conditions there was no alternative to ratification. This resolution of qualified support was passed by thirty-four votes to eight.[76] The next day the *Freeman's Journal* noted thirty-one Sinn Féin constituency executives in favour and not one against.[77]

The distress and rage of East Cavan were characteristic of the country at large. Eighty party delegates protested unanimously at the ruling which prevented two of their deputies, Griffith and Milroy, from representing their views by voting for the treaty; since both men had been elected for two constituencies, each would be entitled to vote only once. The clubs demanded, in vain, that the county councils representing such 'disfranchised' constituencies should be entitled to send replacement deputies who could support the agreement, and Cavan County Council tried to appoint two new pro-treaty deputies.[78]

The party's support for the agreement was reinforced by the virtually unqualified welcome with which it was received by the press, both at local and at national level. The *Tipperary Star* felt privileged

> to vision with joyful minds and hearts the familiar, age-old figure of the weeping young Maid of Erin, now head erect, marching out from the limbo of thirty generations into the sunlight of Peace Triumphant . . . The rosy Treaty is not without a thorn, but the thorns are so few and small and so ready to decay and disappear with the passing years that little account may be taken of them.[79]

Others could not see the buds for the thorns.

The Church threw its massive weight behind the settlement, and Cardinal

---

[75] *II*, 5 Jan. 1922.   [76] *Derry People*, 7 Jan. 1922.   [77] *FJ*, 6 Jan. 1922.

[78] *II*, 2, 3 Jan. 1922; County council resolution, 31 Dec. 1921, NAI, DE, 4/5/18.

[79] *Tipperary Star*, 10 Dec. 1921, editorial.

Logue warned of the terrible calamity which would befall if the treaty were to be rejected on account of 'mere verbal quibbles'.[80] With relatively few exceptions the wealthy rallied behind an agreement which they hoped would guarantee peace. The prospect of jobs in the new administration was used to win support, and some months later Mary MacSwiney complained that 'week after week Collins' men are trying to seduce the army loyal to the Republic by offers of good salaries and other good things'.[81]

The Sinn Féin party never voted formally on the treaty, but on 12 January it came close to doing so, even if in a partial and indirect manner. A new standing committee was elected by the *ard-chomhairle* (a body consisting of representatives from each of the constituency executives, as well as of the officer board and co-optees). In the circumstances it was almost inevitable that delegates tended to vote for or against candidates on the grounds of their attitudes towards the treaty. The result of the election was a triumph for the moderates, who won eleven posts as opposed to a mere three gained by the republicans. In terms of votes cast for those candidates who were elected, supporters of the treaty received a total of 458 and their opponents 110.[82] Erskine Childers's diary records bleakly 'we were heavily defeated'.[83] Perhaps as a foretaste of the general election results some months later, female candidates performed particularly badly and gained only two of the last three places. Darrell Figgis (anathema to most radicals, and disliked even by some moderates) topped the poll, while among the defeated republicans were Robert Barton, Erskine Childers, Kathleen Clarke, Mary MacSwiney, Countess Markievicz, Margaret Pearse and Hanna Sheehy-Skeffington.[84]

All opponents of the treaty were soon labelled 'republicans', even though some of them (most notably de Valera) had neither hoped nor attempted to achieve a republic during the negotiations with Britain.

The republican reaction

Positions hardened as the debate continued in the Dáil, throughout the country, and in the ranks of the army. De Valera described his compromise proposal, Document No. 2, as 'quite orthodox' since (even though it was modelled on the Anglo-Irish Treaty) it was supported by republicans such as Brugha, Stack and

---

[80] *FJ*, 3 Jan. 1922.

[81] Garvin, *Nationalist revolutionaries*, p. 144; MacSwiney to McGarrity, 29 Apr. 1922, McG, 17,654(3).   [82] *II*, 13 Jan. 1922, article headed 'Sinn Féin to divide'.

[83] Childers, diary, 12 Jan. 1922, TCDL, MS 7815.

[84] Jennie Wyse Power to Nancy Wyse Power, 15 Jan. 1922, RM, P7/D/7.

9.2 Republican propaganda

Mary MacSwiney.[85] But many in the IRA regarded it with contempt, and ten weeks later the inflexible Rory O'Connor declared that he had not even read it.[86] After the Dáil had voted in favour of the settlement, by a margin so narrow as to reveal how unrepresentative it was of Irish nationalists in general, divisions which had already emerged in the army began to become public knowledge. Many of the units which had been most active in the war against Britain were far less inclined to accept a compromise than was the civilian population, and prominent officers demanded that the IRA should come under the supreme control of an executive appointed by an army convention.[87] The government vacillated, first acquiescing in the demand for such a convention and then, when elections resulted in an anti-treaty majority, withdrawing its sanction and banning the assembly. Liam Lynch forgot or abandoned his earlier view that the minority in the Dáil and the army must act on the decision of the majority.[88]

[85] De Valera to McGarrity, n.d. [Christmas 1921], EdeV.   [86] *II*, 23 Mar. 1922.

[87] Rory O'Connor and others to Mulcahy, 11 Jan. 1922, RM, P7/B/191.

[88] Lynch to Div. I/O and Adj., 11 Dec. 1921, IRB correspondence, UCDA, P21/1.

Within days of the Dáil vote the IRB split over the treaty. Lynch led the opposition to Collins, who was president of the supreme council. Like the Volunteers' GHQ, the council supported the treaty, but in each case no orders were given and individual members were allowed make up their own minds. The republican convictions of both bodies were too powerful to alter.[89] A Cumann na mBan convention repudiated the treaty by the overwhelming margin of 419 votes to 63, and declared that members who supported it would be guilty of treason. As a conciliatory gesture, however, it was suggested that moderates should be asked to resign rather than be driven out.[90] Mary MacSwiney subsequently purged the ranks of Cumann na mBan in Cork, and in one extreme case, the Shandon branch, all but four members were expelled.[91]

Even in the Sinn Féin party there were signs of a change, and in some instances earlier support for the agreement was modified or reversed. Most branches had voted on the treaty during the weeks after its signature, but now they were required to pronounce on the issue once more. The *ard-chomhairle* of 12 January (at which the pro-treaty elements had scored such a decisive victory) summoned a special *ard-fheis* to discuss the settlement, and every club and constituency executive was obliged to choose representatives who would attend this convention. Many of these elections were contested fiercely, and supporters of the treaty claimed frequently that unfair tactics were being used by the republicans. Pro-treaty members of the standing committee proposed that anyone chosen as a result of intimidation should be disqualified.[92]

In South Mayo there were protests that some delegates at an executive meeting represented dormant branches, and that other districts had not been circularized.[93] In the northern half of the county the meeting took place in the IRA brigade headquarters, and the result of the vote was predictably republican.[94] Liam de Róiste claimed that in one Cork club Volunteers were brought in to outvote or overawe members who were suspected of favouring the Free State, while in another, only those members who had joined since the truce were summoned to the meeting which chose delegates to the *ard-fheis*.[95] In North Kildare the three republican TDs attended the discussion (although not the subsequent

---

[89] Supreme council, 'The organisation and the new political situation in Ireland', 12 Jan. 1922, McCullough MSS, UCDA, P120/8; O'Beirne-Ranelagh, 'The Irish Republican Brotherhood', in Boyce, *Revolution in Ireland*, p. 152.

[90] Circular, 14 Feb. 1922, MacS, P48a/38(6); *Republic of Ireland*, 14 Feb. 1922.

[91] Brian S. Murphy, 'Politics and ideology: Mary MacSwiney and Irish republicanism, 1872–1942' (Ph.D. dissertation, University College, Cork, 1994), pp. 101–3.   [92] SCM, 13 Feb. 1922.

[93] *Mayo News*, 11 Feb. 1922.   [94] *Western People*, 4 Feb. 1922.

[95] De Róiste, diary, 22, 28 Jan. 1922, CAI, U271/A/42.

vote) and the meeting decided by a margin of two to one to choose an anti-treaty delegate; thereby it reversed its unanimous support for the agreement some weeks earlier. Subsequently the officer board pointed out that the gathering had been illegal, as some of those present had not been authorized by their clubs. No decision was reached and the change seems not to have been repudiated.[96] In Glengarriff (Co. Cork), after the club voted in favour of the treaty by twenty-one to five, its representative to the *ard-fheis* announced that 'as a soldier of the Irish Republic' he would oppose the settlement.[97] Committed party members took advantage of every opportunity to increase their voting strength; for example in Carnew (Co. Wicklow), after the club had voted against the treaty by 71 votes to 50, the secretary pointed out that with a membership of 210 it was entitled to send 4 delegates to the *ard-fheis* and that it would pay the extra £2 needed to exercise this right.[98]

Lobbying within the party was no longer as one-sided as it had been in December. In West Wicklow, for example, the president of the constituency executive circularized clubs exhorting them that 'we have worked hard for the establishment and maintenance of the Republic . . . Do not be blinded by the words "Free State", the so-called "Free State" simply makes Ireland part of the British Empire.'[99] Government supporters observed this change in public opinion. Collins wrote gloomily to his fiancée that, according to the newspapers, 'the Sinn Féin clubs are going strongly Republican', and she replied (naïvely or sarcastically?) 'yes, the Sinn Féin clubs are amusing'.[100] But, like the Church, the national and provincial press maintained its overwhelming support for the treaty.

When the standing committee instructed branches that they should choose delegates to the forthcoming *ard-fheis*, its circular informed them that the main purpose of the meeting would be to interpret the Sinn Féin constitution in the light of the treaty. Representatives would also have to decide the organization's policy in view of a possible election. A copy of the constitution was enclosed with each letter, thereby reminding (or informing) members that two of its three preambles and one of its articles contained references to the 'republic'. Club presidents of republican views or legalistic temperament could use the wording of the resolution to tilt any decision against the treaty. The republican

---

[96] *Kildare Observer*, 7, 28 Jan., 4 Feb. 1922.   [97] *II*, 3 Jan. 1922.

[98] John Byrne to Déogréine Barton, 27 Jan. 1922, RB, 8786(2).

[99] Déogréine Barton, circular, 20 Jan. 1922, *ibid*.

[100] Collins to Kitty Kiernan, 29 Jan., Kiernan to Collins, received 1 Feb. 1922, cited in León Ó Broin and Cian Ó hÉigeartaigh (eds.), *In great haste: the letters of Michael Collins and Kitty Kiernan* (2nd edn, Dublin, 1996), pp. 111, 113.

constitution could be changed only by a two-thirds majority at an *ard-fheis*, and this gave de Valera a considerable advantage over his opponents. On the other hand, thanks to an amendment which he himself had proposed the previous October, the party gave its undivided allegiance to the Dáil, which had already endorsed the agreement.

The struggle for the party's body, mind and soul continued at other levels and in other venues. At the *ard-chomhairle* meeting in January 1922, after a new standing committee had been elected, de Valera opened a debate on the treaty by declaring that they might as well recognize there were now two sides within the movement: those who, back in 1917, had stood for the republic, and those who did not care very much about forms of government. These strands had now parted, and they could not work together electorally without hampering each other. His preference was that they 'should definitely and cleanly divide and know exactly where they stood'. He and his opponent Seán McGarry agreed that if Sinn Féin was a political organization (and McGarry claimed it was nothing else) it could not remain neutral and sit on the fence. Seán MacEntee suggested that the party should split at once, and that the standing committee should implement the inevitable division. In the end it was agreed to do nothing until a specially summoned *ard-fheis* would decide the matter.[101] This was the last time that an *ard-chomhairle* ever met, and ironically its members were reassured that during the five months' interval since they had last convened the number of the party's affiliated branches had risen from 89 to 1,485, and that its financial position was sound. Never had it been more popular or fashionable to be a Sinn Féiner than in the months before the party's final disintegration.

At a meeting of the standing committee in late January Collins and Figgis proposed that only party members who had enrolled before 31 December 1921 could vote for *ard-fheis* delegates; clearly they suspected that their opponents would try to pack the assembly. Stack opposed this suggestion, but it was approved by nine votes to three. The following week saw an even more revealing disagreement, when treatyites overcame republican opposition to holding the vote by secret ballot.[102] Long afterwards when O'Keeffe was asked whether one side did not trust the other at this time he replied 'you could not walk across the street without being distrusted'.[103]

Both sides shared an assumption that Sinn Féin would fall apart, and already before the February *ard-fheis* they had established two rival 'sub-parties', pro- and anti-treaty. The republicans were the first off the mark. As early as 3 January they launched a new paper, *The Republic of Ireland*, which soon expanded from

---

[101] *II*, 13 Jan. 1922.   [102] SCM, 23, 31 Jan. 1922.
[103] O'Keeffe, evidence, 30 Apr. 1948, SFFC, 2B/82/118(42), p. 32.

four to eight pages. Its contributors rallied anti-treaty Sinn Féiners and Volunteers, directing them to ensure that selection meetings for the *ard-fheis* delegates were 'properly convened' and that republicans were duly chosen. They established their own 'Republic of Ireland' offices in Dame Street, and within days of the vote on the treaty Childers referred to a 'party meeting' of republicans at which their organization was consolidated.[104] Opponents of the treaty were directed to convene meetings of Sinn Féin branches, and they were told that invitations should not be confined to party members; 'all other active Republicans who can be relied on to work should be summoned to attend this meeting, especially members of the I.R.A. and Cumann na mBan'.[105] Party gatherings were to be swamped by outsiders.

In Cork city (and possibly elsewhere as well) the republicans took steps to ensure that they would benefit from any revision of the electoral register. The 'Republican Party' sent instructions to Volunteer company captains listing various tasks which they should carry out as a matter of urgency; in particular, the names of anti-treaty voters were to be entered on lists and provided to rate-collectors by the deadline of 3 February. The captains were urged to submit the names of all republican men aged above eighteen and women aged above twenty-six, but that these supporters should be described as being aged over twenty-one and thirty respectively. In other words, they were supplied with written directives to 'pack' the electoral register with names of people not legally qualified to vote. Recipients were warned that 'the following instructions must not be discussed, except among reliable Republicans, so that the supporters of the Free State Party will not know of our actions'.[106]

Collins faced other problems from Volunteers in his home county. On the same day that this circular was drafted, a pro-treaty Sinn Féiner from Clonakilty wrote to him

> I can prove that the I.R.A. are using the authority of their officers to compel the members to do against their will what they would not otherwise do . . . Responsible and highly placed officers of the I.R.A. have informed me that they will not permit their fathers etc. to vote in the coming election . . . a more or less successful effort has been made to rig all the Clubs in South Cork.

Collins replied fatalistically that such measures were adopted elsewhere in the country and that he had little hope of persuading his opponents to change their

---

[104] Childers, diary, 11 Jan. 1922, TCDL, MS 7815.

[105] Seán T. O'Kelly and Harry Boland, *Poblacht na hÉireann* (circular), 14 Feb. 1922, RB, 8786(3).

[106] Sean Moore to company captains, 27 Jan. 1922, Siobhán Lankford MSS, CAI, U169/B/8.

tactics.[107] The republican soldiers continued to show themselves skilled in the tricks of the politicians whom they professed to despise. Their scorn and their success may have fed off one another; the more they disparaged political activity, the more they broke the rules of the game, and the more they prospered. As the head of a government which saw itself as being responsible to the people, Collins was now the victim of the extremism and the indifference towards public opinion which he had done so much to foster in the course of the previous few years. His chickens were coming home to roost.

As well as attempting to pack Sinn Féin meetings and distort the existing electoral register, the republicans also tried to delay the poll by calling for a new register which would give votes to women on the same terms as men. Even if this proposal were to be rebuffed it would serve to delegitimize in advance the electorate's support for the treaty.[108] The government duly rejected the idea. It argued that in 1918 and 1921 Sinn Féin had been happy to use imperfect voting arrangements, and that while the principle was admirable and would be implemented at the first opportunity, in the circumstances the demand amounted to an attempt to postpone the election. Griffith pointed out that his newspapers had advocated equal voting rights between the sexes when no other journals had done so, and at a time when Count Plunkett hung out flags to receive the king of England. (Plunkett retorted, 'I did not pull down the Irish flag.')[109] Three months later the promise was honoured, and the new Free State constitution extended the franchise to women on the same terms as men.

By the end of January republicans were able to claim that twenty-four constituency executives and fifty-three branches nominated anti-treaty delegates to the *ard-fheis* – a dramatic change from the pattern of only weeks before, when long lists of clubs supporting the agreement were matched by virtually no opponents.[110] As had been the case of votes which were taken in the immediate aftermath of the treaty, the records indicate that some decisions were made on personal grounds and that people were described voting in favour of de Valera or of Griffith and Collins. The new anti-treaty party opened its campaign with a large demonstration in O'Connell Street in Dublin on 12 February. One unsympathetic observer noted that 'Dev. looked dreadfully badly, fanatical almost', and wondered could he live long.[111] Brugha heightened tension by warning that there would be trouble if the government did not keep its hands off the army.[112]

---

[107] James O'Crowley to Collins, 27 Jan., Collins to O'Crowley, 31 Jan. 1922, NAI, DE, 2/486.

[108] Garvin, *1922*, p. 124.   [109] *DE, 1921–22*, p. 202 (2 Mar. 1922).

[110] *Republic of Ireland*, 31 Jan. 1922.

[111] Celia Shaw, diary, 11 Feb. 1922, NLI, MS 23,409. De Valera lived for another fifty-three years.

[112] *II*, 13 Feb. 1922.

The provisional government decided to wait until after the *ard-fheis* before organizing meetings at which ministers would speak,[113] but it was only biding its time and in private its followers were already active. An urgent request resulted in James O'Mara providing at once a loan of £2,000 made out to Griffith and Collins – money which was used for their election campaign.[114] Duplicated letters summoned pro-treaty TDs to a special meeting to be held in advance of the *ard-fheis* and warned that a large number of candidates and organizers would be needed for the election campaign.[115] While visiting Dublin Liam de Róiste became involved accidentally in one of a series of meetings between leaders of the 'pro-treaty party'.[116]

The February ard-fheis

Over 3,000 delegates were present when the *ard-fheis* finally convened in the Mansion House on 21 February. It was a male-dominated gathering and less than a hundred women were present, although there was a generous supply of priests. This was probably because many clubs were represented by their presidents, a position which was often held by members of the clergy; but in some cases priests may have been chosen because they would be better able to resist republican pressures than would pro-treaty laymen. It was widely expected that the vote would be close, whatever the result.

There was an early test of strength when de Valera expressed his reservations about voting by ballot and the treatyites defended the standing committee's decision. Three sets of differently coloured voting papers had been prepared and booths had been provided, while no provision had been made for open voting.[117] Stack urged the delegates to overrule the committee, and he argued that they should vote openly because 'no man must shirk his responsibilities at such a time'. To decide whether there should be a secret ballot or a show of hands, a vote was taken on the question – by a show of hands. (The party's rules laid down clearly that all elections should be held by ballot, but they did not specify how other votes should be conducted.) After hands had been raised three times it was announced that the result was a victory for the republicans.

---

[113] PG minutes, 10 Feb. 1922, NAI, G1/1.

[114] Griffith to O'Mara, 19 Jan. 1922; Dan McCarthy and Seán Milroy, receipt, 19 Jan. 1922; McCarthy to O'Mara, 28 Apr. 1922, JO'M, 21,550(3).

[115] Dan McCarthy, circular, 15 Feb. 1922, RM, P7/A/70.

[116] De Róiste, diary, 11 Feb. 1922, CAI, U271/A/42.

[117] O'Keeffe, evidence, 30 Apr. 1948, SFFC, 2B/82/118(41), p. 21.

Some of those present queried this decision, but Collins accepted it and conceded that supporters of the treaty had been out-voted.[118] Erskine Childers's diary recorded 'Republican majority evidently present. Free Staters very mild', and his colleague Kathleen Lynn believed that 'we would have had crushing majority if vote taken'.[119]

A few months later Ernest Blythe claimed that the meeting had been packed against the treaty.[120] Long afterwards an observer claimed that there had been a large but scattered pro-treaty majority, while the republican minority was concentrated in the centre of the hall.[121] But the vote against a secret ballot made it clear that the Sinn Féin party could not be rallied behind the provisional government. The *ard-fheis* did not follow the pattern already established by the Dáil, and de Valera was not deposed as president of the party in the same way as he had already been replaced as president of the Dáil and of the Irish republic. He remained leader of the Sinn Féin party (or rather, of *a* Sinn Féin party) for the next four years.

Despite Kevin O'Shiel's plea that voting should take place without speeches, de Valera spoke for thirty-eight minutes and Griffith for twenty-two. De Valera repeated the argument he had already put forward at the *ard-chomhairle* six weeks earlier: if it proved necessary the party should split into its component parts, and it was much better to have two armies working for Ireland, with a possibility of their reinforcing each other, than to have one army divided against itself and powerless. The precedent of the anti-conscription campaign was preferable to what he described as a false unity which would result in stagnation. He announced that, because there was a Free State majority on the Sinn Féin standing committee, the republicans would organize independently of that body. He urged delegates to change the constitution rather than to belie it, but pointed out that a two-thirds majority would be needed to do so.[122]

The Dáil had modified its commitment to a republic by a simple majority vote, but the party (although bound by its allegiance to the Dáil) could not change its mind so easily. De Valera pointed out that 'if Dáil Éireann had such a solid rule the Ard-Fheis would not have to be there to decide on this question at all'. Unsurprisingly he wished that the Dáil, like Sinn Féin, could not take decisions affecting Ireland's relations with other powers other than by a two-thirds

---

[118] *II*, 22 Feb. 1922.

[119] Childers, diary, 21 Feb. 1922, TCDL, MS 7815; Lynn, diary, 22 Feb. 1922, cited in Gaughan, *Austin Stack*, p. 192. Lynn's diary was not available for consultation in the Royal College of Physicians when this book went to press.   [120] *Free State*, 20 May 1922.

[121] George Lyons, evidence, 2 June 1948, SFFC, 2B/82/118(47), p. B20.

[122] *II*, 22 Feb. 1922; *Republic of Ireland*, 28 Feb. 1922.

majority.[123] In October 1921, when Sinn Féin amended its constitution and proclaimed its allegiance to the Dáil, no-one foresaw the complications which might
arise if the Dáil voted for a measure which would be seen as incompatible with
the party's republican constitution of 1917, and if the measure would then fail
to win the two-thirds majority which was necessary to change the constitution.

Collins defended the treaty in his speech at the *ard-fheis*, arguing that
'England cannot be more powerful here when she is gone than she was before
she went', but he realized the probability of defeat and therefore urged the convention to avoid or postpone a decision. In the words of one admiring opponent, he shifted the main issue in the debate from that of the republic to that of
a party split, and when he argued against a division

> a strong murmur of approval came from thousands of delegates. Obviously
> he had struck the right note, and he was quick to see it. His case for no divi-
> sion was a poor case, but he used the word 'unity' often enough to change
> the whole spirit of the Assembly. The Republic had disappeared as an issue.
> 'No split' became the supreme object of the Organisation.

Collins also alarmed the republicans by threats of an early election. Then 'priest
after priest spoke – all except one who was sorely interrupted – in favour of unity
and threatened the direst penalties if there were division . . . The vigour had
gone out of the Ard Fheis.'[124] One of these priests, a member of the standing
committee, put Sinn Féiners in their place by telling them that he did not care
twopence about any political party, but he did care for the army 'which was
Ireland's sole hope'.

In the course of a long debate delegates warned against following the precedent of the Parnell split. The bitterness of the treaty debates re-emerged, and
Brugha was forced to withdraw his suggestion that Collins had been installed in
his position by the British government. (On the government side Griffith, too,
was sharp-tongued and was prone to make personal attacks on his opponents.
De Valera and Collins were more restrained.) When a republican delegate from
Laois referred to the Black and Tans, Páidín O'Keeffe, his Corkman's sense of
superiority heightened by his county's recent war record, retorted that 'you
didn't fire a shot down there'.

A consensus emerged on postponing both the general election and the split
in the Sinn Féin party. De Valera was particularly anxious that a new Dáil should
not be chosen for at least three months, and not until the Free State constitution had been published. The republicans needed time to organize and seek

---

[123] *II*, 22 Feb. 1922.

[124] Proinnsias Ó Gallchobhair [Frank Gallagher], *Republic of Ireland*, 28 Feb. 1922.

support, and he wanted the electorate to be confronted with questions other than the treaty, an issue on which he and his followers would be condemned to defeat. The *Freeman's Journal* account of the convention referred sarcastically to a group of delegates at a democratic gathering shouting 'no election! no election!'[125] To many contemporaries and to later generations 'it was ironic that those most critical of the delegates for failing to consult the cabinet were themselves so reluctant to consult the people'.[126]

On the second day of the *ard-fheis* the delegates waited patiently for about two hours while de Valera, Griffith, Collins and Stack conferred privately. (In early 1922 the leaders spent much time closeted together; according to Collins he and de Valera had met for four and a half hours on the day preceding the *ard-fheis*.[127]) Speeches were replaced by songs, which ranged from 'The Felons of our Land' to 'Whack Fol de Diddle', but by the time the leaders returned a delegate had taken the stage to declaim Pearse's speech at the grave of O'Donovan Rossa.[128] The meeting then ratified an agreement whereby, 'to avoid a division of the Sinn Féin Organization and avert the danger to the country of an immediate election', and to allow the constitution to be submitted to the voters, the *ard-fheis* would be adjourned for three months. No election would be held during this period, or until the constitution had been presented to the people. (Only weeks earlier Collins had assured British ministers that the provisional government 'were going to the Electorate on the Treaty and not on the Constitution'.[129] Circumstances did not allow him the luxury of consistency.) In the meantime the (pro-treaty) standing committee would be superseded by the officer board, which was evenly balanced between the two sides. It was also agreed that any of the officers unable to attend a meeting could be replaced by substitutes. Technically this replacement of the standing committee by the officer board was unconstitutional, since it did not feature on the agenda of the special *ard-fheis* which had been summoned to deal with a different issue.[130] But no-one noticed or mentioned this at the time.

A republican observer remarked that the *ard-fheis* had been 'stampeded into a desire for at least a temporary unity which overbore every other consideration'. Final votes and unpleasant decisions had been avoided.[131] However, Collins showed impressive skill in averting what had seemed to be the likeliest outcome of the convention: that the Sinn Féin party would repudiate the provisional

---

[125] *FJ*, 22 Feb. 1922.   [126] Lee, *Ireland 1912–1985*, p. 54.

[127] Collins to Kitty Kiernan, 21 Feb. 1922, Ó Broin and Ó hÉigeartaigh, *In great haste*, p. 131.

[128] *FJ*, 23 Feb. 1922.   [129] Conference minutes, 6 Feb. 1922, Cab. 43/6, 22/N/60(4), p. 49.

[130] George Murnaghan, 30 Apr. 1948, SFFC, 2B/82/118(42), pp. 5–6.

[131] *Republic of Ireland*, 28 Feb. 1922.

government, the majority of the Dáil, and the opinion of the country; and that under de Valera's leadership it would reaffirm its belief in the republic. Such a development would have weakened Collins's position in the area where he was strongest, that of civilian support, and it would have reinforced the extremist elements in the army. He also gained a reprieve in matters concerning the party's funds. It had been agreed that he would propose a resolution transferring Sinn Féin's assets to de Valera, but – whether by design or by a highly improbable oversight – he did not do so.

The army split

The divisions in the Sinn Féin party might have appeared menacing, but the real threat to peace and stability came from within the army. Richard Mulcahy, the new minister for defence, played for time, postponed final decisions, and hoped to win over opponents. His tactics were similar to those of Collins. But the formation of a regular army loyal to the Free State excluded and alienated the republicans. In February, fighting almost broke out in Limerick as both sides struggled for possession of the barracks which had been evacuated by the British. The cracks in the IRA widened further on 26 March when republicans defied the Dáil government's prohibition by holding a long-postponed army convention. Only one-third of the possible total of delegates actually attended the meeting in the Mansion House, and almost a quarter of those present came from Lynch's 1st Southern Division.[132] Opposition to the treaty was strongest among the units which had been most active in the war against the British.

The delegates took a new oath which no longer recognized Dáil Éireann as the government of the republic, and they established a separate executive which claimed to represent 80 per cent of the army.[133] This new body would be independent of the Dáil and of the pro-treaty governments headed by Collins and Griffith. It was also independent of 'political' anti-treaty leaders such as de Valera and Brugha; neither was elected, even though de Valera had been president of the Volunteers since 1917. *An tÓglách* denounced the republicans' move as an act of military despotism.[134]

In the course of a press conference which was held in the offices of de Valera's party, Cumann na Poblachta, Rory O'Connor made it clear that radical republicans in the IRA did not recognize any Irish government, and that they had no interest in democratic procedures. 'In effect, the holding of the convention

---

[132] Garvin, *1922*, p. 125; Hopkinson, *Green against green*, p. 67.   [133] *II*, 5 Apr. 1922.

[134] *An tÓglách*, 31 Mar. 1922.

means that we repudiate the Dáil. If a government goes wrong it must take the consequences.' They gave their allegiance only to their own idea of a republic, and when O'Connor was asked if the army would establish a military dictatorship he answered nonchalantly 'you can take it that way if you like'.

In their readiness to enforce their view of what was right, no matter what the majority of the public might decide, he and his colleagues saw themselves as undertaking a responsibility no greater than that which had been assumed by the Easter rebels.[135] That earlier defiance of Irish opinion had already become a model for others, and many of the soldiers shared O'Connor's indifference to the people's wishes. C. S. Andrews remarked later that he had seen nothing wrong with an IRA dictatorship and had merely resented the breakdown in military discipline; but gradually it became clear to him that the army leaders did not envisage establishing such a military dictatorship, and that they also lacked any alternative policy.[136] Their fault was that they were not sufficiently anti-democratic.

De Valera did little to prevent this drift towards militarism which, even if it weakened his own position within the republican movement, nonetheless posed an even greater threat to his enemies in the provisional government. Months later, in the course of the civil war, he remarked that 'Rory O'Connor's unfortunate repudiation of the Dáil, which I was so foolish as to defend even to a straining of my own views in order to avoid the appearance of a split, is now the greatest barrier that we have.'[137] At the time, however, he was so concerned to undermine Collins that he seems to have given little thought to how his remarks might help tilt Ireland towards war, or might even create problems for himself in his own future dealings with recalcitrant soldiers. Yet because he kept his distance from the republican IRA during the early months of 1922, and because he made no effort to assume its leadership, the extremists were able to push him aside and ignore him.[138] He alienated both militants and moderates.

On 14 April O'Connor led a group of armed republicans who seized the Four Courts and other buildings in the centre of Dublin. They announced that no elections would be held 'on the issue at present before the country while the threat of war with England exists', and a few days later Mary MacSwiney declared that 'one thing is certain, the Army of the Republic will not tolerate the subversion of the Republic'.[139] The soldiers would not allow civilians to decide Ireland's future. The disputes in early 1922, and the civil war which formed their

[135] *II*, 23 Mar. 1922.   [136] Andrews, *Dublin made me*, p. 218.

[137] De Valera to Charles Murphy, 13 Sept. 1922, RM, P7a/162, p. 15.

[138] Curran, *Birth of the Irish Free State*, p. 175.

[139] *II*, 27 Apr. 1922; MacSwiney to McGarrity, 29 Apr. 1922, McG, 17,654(3).

climax, were between those who believed that the morally superior should rule regardless of majority preferences, and others who believed in majority rule.[140]

But the actions of the army radicals were not merely a consequence of their belief in the abstract republic. In demanding that they should be governed by their own military executive, rather than by unsympathetic politicians, they also wanted to throw off the constraints which had been imposed on them through their recent involvement with the Sinn Féin party and the Dáil. Control by a civilian cabinet was a distasteful prospect. In many cases such views were complicated by the intrusion of local loyalties, ambitions and rivalries; by 'the elevation of territorial jealousy into high-minded principle'.[141] Between January and April 1922 such attitudes and actions broke the links between the military and political wings of the Sinn Féin movement, and they also ended the theoretical subordination of the army to the Dáil.

De Valera continued to support the anti-treaty IRA. After the seizure of the Four Courts he issued a proclamation to the young men and women of Ireland declaring that the goal was at last in sight and exhorting them 'Ireland is yours for the taking. Take it.'[142] But by now the soldiers needed no such encouragement from politicians, however respectable and influential they might be.[143]

It was against this background of problems with the army that the provisional government continued its efforts to administer the country. It also struggled to draft a constitution which would be acceptable both to the British cabinet and to Irish republicans. Violence became more widespread, and on several occasions it seemed as if the rival factions in the army would engage in outright hostilities. In the six months which ended with the bombardment of the Four Courts on 28 June, more people were killed than in the comparable period of 1919, the first phase of the Anglo-Irish War. The death toll was, however, only a fraction of that caused by sectarian violence in Northern Ireland during the first half of 1922, the victims of which were preponderantly Catholic. The Ulster example was followed in the south, although on a very much smaller scale, and in the course of a few days fourteen Protestants were murdered by the republican IRA in Co. Cork.[144] In some parts of the country, particularly in Leitrim and Sligo, Sinn Féin clubs continued the pattern already established during the months before the truce; their members joined with IRA units in defying central authority and in trying to seize control of local government.[145]

---

[140] Tom Garvin, '"Dev and Mick": the 1922 split as psychological event', in Doherty and Keogh, *Michael Collins*, p. 153.   [141] Fitzpatrick, *Politics and Irish life*, p. 231.

[142] *FJ*, 17 Apr. 1922; *Republic of Ireland*, 20 Apr. 1922.

[143] On de Valera's attempts to win extremist support in early 1922, see Coogan, *de Valera*, pp. 309–14.   [144] Hart, *I.R.A. and its enemies*, pp. 115, 283.   [145] See above, p. 301.

9.3 A British view of Collins's dilemma in 1922

The spring campaign

The Sinn Féin party provided an accurate reflection of the country at large as its component parts continued to drift away from each other. At best the new executive body, the officer board, consisted of an unhappy coalition; at worst, it was a conference between envoys of two separate and mutually hostile factions. In early March the quorum was dropped to three. Frequently, more than half of the members were too busy or too uninterested to attend, and they were represented by proxies. In the light of Sinn Féin's habitual lack of concern with Ulster, they devoted what could be regarded as a disproportionate amount of time to the problems of Northern Ireland. They might not be able to achieve any practical results, but here, in contrast to their quarrels over the treaty, there was at least the chance that they might succeed in agreeing among themselves – even if with no-one else. Yet, at one meeting in April, when the officer board was presented with rival resolutions concerning Northern policy, its three pro-treaty votes cancelled out those of three republicans. As a result no decision was reached.[146]

The humble duties allotted to the party were illustrated by the comment that, as a result of the *ard-fheis* agreement, Sinn Féin 'provides a common ground on which the united strength of all parties may be concentrated for the relief of the people of the North East Counties'.[147] The pro-treaty *Free State* remarked that the party was a lifeless organization, and that if it continued in its present form it might as well be regarded as an archaeological relic; the *Derry People* asked 'where is Sinn Féin now?' and concluded that it seemed to have passed away, unwept, unhonoured and unsung; and it was reported that in Meath and Louth clubs continued to function on 'a non-party basis'.[148] Sinn Féin drifted, aimless and powerless. Many of its leaders in Northern Ireland were arrested and interned, but virtually no-one in the south paid any attention.[149]

The February *ard-fheis* concealed the cracks within the party and maintained at least its nominal unity, but the divisions continued to widen. One symptom of the new realities was the pattern whereby deputies from the rival factions 'paired' with one another for Dáil votes. Both sides sent delegations to raise funds in the United States, and the pleasures of the voyage were enhanced when the two groups crossed the Atlantic on the same ship. The two 'real' parties, pro- and anti-treaty, consolidated their positions.

A treaty election committee met regularly from March onwards, and its

---

[146] Officer board minutes, 25 Apr. 1922, NAI, 2B/82/116(12).   [147] *FJ*, 24 Mar. 1922.

[148] *Free State*, 20 May 1922; *Derry People*, 20 May 1922; *Meath Chronicle*, 25 Mar. 1922.

[149] Phoenix, *Northern nationalism*, p. 223; de Róiste, diary, 23 May 1922, CAI, U271/A/44.

minutes convey an impression of brisk efficiency. Each constituency was expected to create an executive and appoint a director of elections; eventually parish committees would be formed.[150] This committee was supported by business interests, most of its financial backing came from Dublin rather than from the provinces, and by August its income totalled £34,500.[151] The money which had been borrowed earlier from James O'Mara was repaid. Its newspaper claimed a circulation of 23,000 copies, and the committee also envisaged an election bulletin which would contain 'inspiriting news and general hints' and would be modelled on the house journals issued by large business firms.[152] Its backing by the country's 'establishment' was illustrated by an initial contribution of £510 which was sent by the Hotel, Restaurant and Catering Association of Ireland; this included £50 contributions from Jammet's Restaurant and from hotels such as the Shelbourne, Gresham and Hibernian.[153] Although Richard Beamish the brewer ran as an independent candidate for the Dáil, he nonetheless inquired revealingly whether £500 would be regarded as an adequate contribution to the funds of pro-treaty Sinn Féin.[154]

The provisional government decided that the machinery employed in the previous year's elections should be used once more,[155] and it chose Dan McCarthy as its director of elections. He had not only been prominent in the campaigns of the united Sinn Féin party in 1917–18 and 1921, but he had even canvassed for Dolan in Leitrim as long ago as 1907–8. Priests were circularized, invited to make subscriptions, and asked for their help in organizing collections or in co-operating with pro-treaty workers. The propaganda sub-committee recommended that a Griffith-style article on 'how Bulgaria gained complete separation' should be issued in leaflet form. (Publication was postponed.)[156] Sometimes its approach was aloof and gentlemanly, almost disdainful of the base and grubby nature of politics; one advertisement called upon readers to subscribe generously, 'as a national duty', to a fund supporting the campaign of pro-treaty candidates, and these were endorsed with the tepid message that they 'will have our approval'.[157] It anticipated some of the failings of its successors in Cumann na nGaedheal.

The republicans were equally busy. They formed a new party, Cumann na

---

[150] 'Saorstát publicity and election committee' circular, 6 Mar. 1922, RM, P7/A/70.

[151] Pro-treaty committee minutes, 4, 13 Apr., 10 Aug. 1922, FG, pp. 6, 16, 75.

[152] *Ibid.*, 8 May, 11 Apr. 1922, pp. 36, 9.

[153] 'First list of subscriptions to treaty fund', n.d. (Apr. 1922), DELG, 38/1.

[154] De Róiste, diary, 2 June 1922, CAI, U271/A/44.   [155] PG minutes, 3 Mar. 1922, NAI, G1/1.

[156] Pro-treaty committee minutes, 2 May 1922, FG, p. 30.

[157] *Nationalist and Leinster Times*, 29 Apr. 1922.

Poblachta, with a president (de Valera, of course), an officer board, standing committee, trustees, provincial representatives and director of elections. Its structure imitated and duplicated that of Sinn Féin.[158] The republican IRA was not short of money, which it acquired by the simple expedient of raiding banks, and Austin Stack claimed later that the Four Courts garrison lent about £14,000 to help fund the election campaign.[159] The new party's objectives foreshadowed several of those of Fianna Fáil in later years. The first points in its programme were: to uphold, strengthen and gain international recognition of the Irish republic; to preserve the unity of the nation and its national territory; to revive the Irish language; and (as far as practicable) to achieve economic self-sufficiency.[160]

During the election campaign it devoted its attention to the iniquities of the treaty, and remarkably few attempts were made to exploit social grievances. Stack told an audience in Macroom that there would be time enough for various class interests to secure representation when they had finished driving the English out of Ireland.[161] The united Sinn Féin party's deliberate neglect of a social policy was continued faithfully by its republican wing after the split, and nothing could have been further from the truth than a unionist's belief that 'the Republican idealists who followed de Valera were but the unconscious tools of the tyrants of Moscow'.[162] However, the question of partition, an aspect of the treaty which had been virtually ignored in the Dáil debates, now began to feature belatedly in the speeches of some republicans. The enduring myth that Ireland had been partitioned by the Anglo-Irish Treaty, rather than by the earlier Government of Ireland Act, had its origins in the election campaign of early 1922.

In the Dáil and elsewhere, each wing of the old Sinn Féin party tried to score points off the other. For example, the republicans displayed a reforming zeal in demanding that public houses be closed on St Patrick's Day (Brugha: 'surely to goodness everyone can do without intoxicating liquors for one day'), while the government urged tolerance (Griffith: 'if you let out people for a holiday, they ought not to be debarred from getting refreshments').[163] It seemed as if the two sides sought new areas of disagreement.

---

[158] *Republican Party. Officers and standing committee*, n.d., Childers MSS, NLI, 15,444(2).

[159] Comhairle na dteachtaí, minutes, 8 Aug. 1924, Gaughan, *Austin Stack*, pp. 338, 341. Seán Moylan boasted that he had robbed nineteen post offices in the Kanturk area of north Cork (*DE, 1921–22*, p. 340 (28 Apr. 1922)).   [160] *Republic of Ireland*, 22 Mar. 1922.

[161] *FJ*, 12 June 1922.

[162] W. Alison Phillips, *The revolution in Ireland, 1906–1923* (London, 1923), p. 262.

[163] *DE, 1921–22*, pp. 222–3 (2 Mar. 1922).

Week after week, the campaign continued. De Valera's earlier plea that the people should 'not depart from the "definite constitutional way of resolving our political differences" was abandoned as soon as that way failed to resolve the difference in his favour'.[164] It was true, as a republican remarked long afterwards, that 'things were done and events precipitated that he would not have initiated or approved, but which he could not, in the circumstances then prevailing, have easily repudiated or condemned'.[165] His actions during these months must be seen in the context of his diminishing influence.[166]

Nonetheless, some of de Valera's statements were at best incautious and at worst were wildly irresponsible. He told the Dáil that 'only that it is a sovereign assembly I would be the very first to ask the Army to sweep you and the like of you out',[167] and shortly afterwards he issued a series of threats or warnings which received widespread publicity. In Dungarvan he declared that 'it was only by civil war after this that they could get their independence. England had been manoeuvring them into this position, so as to put the bodies of their fellow-countrymen between them and their independence.' The next day he told an audience in Thurles that

> if they accepted the Treaty, and if the Volunteers of the future tried to complete the work the Volunteers of the last four years had been attempting, they would have to complete it, not over the bodies of foreign soldiers, but over the dead bodies of their own countrymen.
>
> They would have to wade through Irish blood, through the blood of the soldiers of the Irish Government, and through, perhaps, the blood of some of the members of the Government in order to get Irish freedom.

In Killarney he was equally blunt: in order to achieve freedom the republicans 'will have to march over the dead bodies of their own brothers . . . the people had never a right to do wrong'.[168] As a pro-treaty journal put it some months later, de Valera believed that an Irish army ought to intimidate Irish citizens in order that British threats might not intimidate them.[169] Yet on other occasions he was less willing to speak out, and when it seemed as if civil war might erupt in Limerick he 'regarded the situation as far too grave to make any statement about it'.[170] He did, however, make private representations to Mulcahy, urging a peaceful settlement;[171] his intransigence was for public consumption, while his moderation and his efforts to avoid civil war were concealed from view. In

---

[164] Townshend, *Political violence in Ireland*, p. 364.   [165] Joseph Connolly, *Memoirs*, p. 238.

[166] Hopkinson, *Green against green*, pp. 70–1.   [167] *DE, 1921–22*, p. 157 (1 Mar. 1922).

[168] *II*, 17, 18, 20 Mar. 1922.   [169] *Separatist*, 24 June 1922.   [170] *FJ*, 10 Mar. 1922.

[171] Valiulis, *Portrait of a revolutionary*, p. 131.

his election speeches during the early months of 1922 de Valera reverted to his attitude of the years before his release from jail in 1917: a military minority had the right to lead or even to dominate the civilian masses. He had depoliticized himself. From the wings John Dillon described these speeches as a 'distinct incitement to Civil War and assassination of Treaty Men, Griffith, Collins and Co.'[172]

De Valera's public views were shared by Brugha, who told a meeting in Navan that the army was bound by its oath to the republic and that it was justified in taking upon itself, temporarily, the functions of government.[173] (Decades later, the trade unionist William O'Brien reminisced about a conference in April 1922, at which Collins and Griffith represented the pro-treaty faction. According to his account Collins asked Brugha 'I suppose we are two of the Ministers whose blood is to be waded through?', and received the reply 'Yes, you are two.'[174]) Throughout the country local warlords were unwilling to relinquish the control which they exercised over their territories, and the republican Seán Moylan warned the Dáil that 'during the war, my word went in North Cork ... my word goes there yet'.[175] Markievicz was more flamboyant, asking whether the Irish people were prepared to sell their nation for a little bit of prosperity, and finding a colourful Biblical analogy with the treaty; the will of the people could go wrong, she informed one audience, and 'it was the will of the people that condemned Our Lord Jesus Christ, when they called out "Crucify Him! Crucify Him!"'[176] (It was perhaps with such vehemence in mind that Stephen O'Mara Jr had written to Harry Boland concerning a republican meeting in Limerick, 'bring no women with you as speakers'.[177])

On the other side, Collins denounced his opponents with characteristic vigour:

> after dropping the Republic while the British were still here, they shout bravely for it now from the safe foothold provided for them by means of the Treaty ... How long must the children remain hungry while you argue whether 'common citizenship', a British King, a Governor-General, has or has not the power still to prevent us from feeding and clothing them? Isn't it time to stop Nero's fiddling?[178]

In a similar mood Seán Milroy mocked those 'whose bravery has grown in proportion as danger disappeared ... They are singing The Soldier's Song ... but

---

[172] Dillon, diary note, 20 Mar. 1922, JD, 6852.   [173] *Meath Chronicle*, 15 Apr. 1922.
[174] O'Brien, *Forth the banners go*, p. 220.   [175] *DE, 1921–22*, p. 340 (28 Apr. 1922).
[176] *Western People*, 1 Apr. 1922.   [177] O'Mara to Boland, 15 Feb. 1922, EdeV.
[178] *FJ*, 6 Mar. 1922.

you never acted a soldier's part.'[179] Griffith displayed his usual optimism in economic matters when he promised that the 150,000 unemployed would have jobs within six months of an Irish government taking office.[180]

Each side ransacked the other's past and defended its own. Collins's 1918 election address was cited by his opponents, so he instigated a search for it; when finally tracked down it revealed, reassuringly, that while he had then referred to 'Sovereign Independence', the 'Independent Nation', 'our National Right to Rule ourselves' and the demand for 'supreme, absolute and final control of all this country', he had never mentioned the fatal word 'republic'.[181] (Similarly, his 1921 address to the electors of Armagh, apart from allusions to 'Republican candidates' and 'Republican nominees', referred to unity, sovereignty and freedom, but not the republic.[182]) The *Republic of Ireland* examined Griffith's writings for potentially embarrassing material, such as his remark in *The resurrection of Hungary* that 'it is a vain thing to lead a nation to the gates of freedom and then tell it to sit contentedly before them'.[183] The pro-treaty *Free State* in return offered a list of fifty proclamations by de Valera, including his statement that he regarded his oath to the republic 'merely as a pledge to the Irish People to do the best for them in any circumstances that may arise'.[184]

The debate rarely reached such levels of sophistication. Violence and intimidation became a natural and obvious, although one-sided, feature of the campaign. In virtually all cases, if not all, the victims were supporters of the treaty, and newspapers were a favourite target. Republicans resented their treatment by a hostile press, which perhaps reached its nadir in the *Western News*. This paper, which had earlier sought subscriptions in support of its 'Irish Free State Propaganda', denounced de Valera as a 'damned Spaniard,' and after the outbreak of the civil war it expressed indifference as to whether he should be shot on sight or reserved for a cage in the Dublin zoo.[185] (Pressure from government supporters could afford to be more subtle, and the *Donegal Vindicator* complained of warnings that a newspaper championing the republic would not have the support of moneyed people.[186]) The radicals' response often took a physical form; the Clonmel *Nationalist* was attacked and its machinery dismantled when the paper refused to print messages from the local republican commander; the *Sligo Champion*'s type was broken up to prevent it from reporting a welcome which Griffith had received; and Dublin newspapers were destroyed in Cork by

---

[179] *Evening Star*, 27 Mar. 1922.   [180] *FJ*, 13 Mar. 1922.

[181] 'Michael Collins, election address', NAI, DE, 2/318.   [182] *Irish Bulletin*, 20 May 1921.

[183] *Republic of Ireland*, 7 Feb. 1922.   [184] *Free State*, 6 May 1922.

[185] *Western News*, 31 Dec. 1921, 14 Jan., 8 July 1922.

[186] *Donegal Vindicator*, 5 May 1922, editorial.

republicans who believed that they contained 'falsehoods', and that the army's internal affairs should not be discussed in the press.[187] The provisional government's election committee wondered whether, as a result of the frequent attacks made on newspapers by opponents of the treaty, the national press submitted its copy to republican headquarters and to the Four Courts garrison for censorship in advance of publication.[188]

Meetings were attacked and disrupted. In Charleville (Co. Cork) a pro-treaty gathering was dispersed by two gunmen who began by firing into the air and then gradually lowered their aim.[189] Military pressure could also take a less direct form, as in Belmullet (Co. Mayo) where republicans addressed a large crowd in the presence of 200 Volunteers.[190] Railtrack was torn up and roads were blocked by trees to prevent Collins from speaking in Castlebar (Co. Mayo).[191] Griffith defied the local commander who prohibited him from addressing a meeting in Sligo town, even though the republicans seized the post office, occupied the main hotels and street corner buildings, fortified their positions with sandbags, cut wires and fired over the heads of the crowds. Several people were injured, but – characteristically – Griffith persevered with his speech.[192] One republican displayed style and imagination in disrupting a pro-treaty meeting in Dungarvan; while the speakers were gathered on top of a lorry he took control of the steering wheel and drove them out of town.[193]

Some opponents of the treaty were diligent in attending their leaders' speeches; the day-book of the provisional government's police force, which took over from the RIC in Drogheda, refers to the republicans commandeering cars in the neighbourhood so that they could travel to a meeting addressed by de Valera in Dundalk.[194] C. S. Andrews confessed later that the republicans seized food from markets or butchers, and had no scruples in requisitioning cars at random; 'in general we treated the population with little consideration'.[195] There was a steady drift back towards violence, and one pro-treaty newspaper remarked that Dublin was already back to the mood of the Black and Tan regime with the noise of arms-fire at night and the streets full of 'insolent lorries'.[196]

By the beginning of April, Collins feared that 'the civil war which they have been threatening is now close at hand', while Liam de Róiste felt that it had

---

[187] *FJ*, 20 Jan. 1922; *Sligo Champion*, 29 Apr. 1922; de Róiste, diary, 18 Feb. 1922, CAI, U271/A/42.

[188] Pro-treaty committee minutes, 19 Apr. 1922, FG, p. 20.

[189] *Enniscorthy Guardian*, 25 Mar. 1922.   [190] *Western People*, 25 Mar. 1922.

[191] *Sligo Champion*, 8 Apr. 1922.   [192] *Leitrim Advertiser*, 20 Apr. 1922.

[193] De Róiste, diary, 28 Mar. 1922, CAI, U271/A/43.

[194] Republican police, day-book, 2 Apr. 1922, Old Drogheda society, Millmount Museum, Drogheda.   [195] Andrews, *Dublin made me*, pp. 220–1.   [196] *Separatist*, 6 May 1922.

already begun.[197] A month later the republican David Kent agreed with him, and the *Kilkenny Journal* despaired to the point of believing that 'it would be just as good to have the country in ruins at once than crumbling and wasting away'.[198] The civilian population tried to avoid occasions which might provoke violence. When the county council demanded that no open air election meetings should be held in Roscommon, it declared that the people already knew the arguments on both sides and that neither party 'can hope to achieve any results from public meetings except by intimidation'.[199] The French consul in Dublin wondered how a stable administration could ever be constructed in the midst of such disorder and confusion.[200] The Labour Party called a one-day national strike against militarism. But the drift towards war continued.

---

[197] Collins to McGarrity, 5 Apr. 1922, McG, 17,436; de Róiste, diary, 5 Apr. 1922, CAI, U271/A/43.

[198] Kent, *DE, 1921–22*, p. 361 (3 May 1922); *Kilkenny Journal*, 20 May 1922, editorial.

[199] *Roscommon Messenger*, 1 Apr. 1922.

[200] Alfred Blanche to Raymond Poincaré, 20 Apr. 1922, Ministère des Affaires Étrangères, Paris; Europe, 1918–1929, Irlande, II, p. 35.

10

THE PACT ELECTION AND THE CIVIL WAR, 1922–1923

Many people feared that the gap between radicals and the moderates could no longer be bridged, but optimists could nonetheless take hope as each lurch towards war was matched by a corresponding move to ensure peace. Negotiations took place between the two sides and several compromise proposals were made, including the idea of holding a plebiscite on the question of the treaty. All of these were rejected by the republicans.[1] On 1 May a group of ten senior army officers, five from each camp, recognized 'the fact – admitted by all sides – that the majority of the people of Ireland are willing to accept the Treaty' and suggested that an agreed election should be held.[2] Fighting reached such a level that a few days later the two sides agreed to a 'truce', provoking the *Leader* to comment that 'we had already drifted into civil armed strife, and the fact of establishing a Truce formally attests that fact'.[3]

A peace committee was established by the Dáil, and its members held a total of sixteen meetings. They discussed the possibility of presenting a joint 'national panel' to the electorate, and while pro-treaty delegates suggested that the ratio between the two sides should be 5:3 the republicans insisted on a proportion of 6:4.[4] Childers referred in his diary to a meeting of the republican party at which he had argued that the 'only way of *really* holding Rep. position in agreed election is to have *same personnel* returned. Next best to have *strength of existing parties* returned. Any reduction hopeless.'[5] The people's wishes in the matter counted for little or nothing. A draft by Harry Boland began provocatively 'we are agreed: – (1) That no issue is being determined by the election', and it proposed that each party should be represented roughly in proportion to its existing strength in the Dáil. The pro-treaty deputies objected 'that Sinn Féin

---

[1] Cabinet minutes, 26 Apr. 1922, NAI, DE, 1/4; Curran, *Birth of the Irish Free State*, p. 185.

[2] *II*, 2 May 1922.

[3] Eoin O'Duffy and Liam Lynch, memo, 4 May 1922, RM, P7/B/191; *Leader*, 13 May 1922, p. 293.

[4] The difference was minor: one ratio would give republicans 37.5 per cent of the seats, the other 40 per cent.   [5] Childers, diary, 16 May 1922, TCDL, MS 7816.

by the Ard-Fheis agreement was a neutral Body . . . That the two parties had under the agreement set up their own electoral machinery and were in perfectly orderly ways doing ordinary routine election work, selecting candidates, propaganda, etc.'[6] No settlement was reached. Finally, not long before the adjourned *ard-fheis* was due to reconvene, de Valera and Collins held a series of meetings which resulted in a 'pact'.

By now Sinn Féin had become little more than the symbol of a feeble will to unity, but the two men decided that – at least in theory – the party should be restored to its former prominence. Under their scheme the divisive spectre of the treaty would be dispelled, and the discredited second Dáil would be given a new lease of life.

The Collins–de Valera pact

The agreement laid down that the rival pro- and anti-treaty factions of Sinn Féin would reunite, and that they would run a joint panel of candidates in which their existing strength in the Dáil would be maintained; thereby it conceded to the republicans the main point which Boland had demanded. In effect Collins simply abandoned the position which had been defended by his colleagues during the recent negotiations. He accepted the most extreme of his opponents' demands: maintenance of their existing share of the seats (47 per cent at the time of the vote on the treaty) rather than an allocation of merely 40 per cent. It was agreed that candidates would be nominated through each of the new party executives, pro- and anti-treaty, and they would then be ratified by Sinn Féin. The Sinn Féin party's function would be no more than that of a rubber stamp, but at least its name, still sacred to many, could be appropriated by both sections.

The crucial clause in the pact was that which allowed other, 'third parties' to run candidates against the joint Sinn Féin panel; there would be no repetition of the 1921 pattern in which every constituency in the south had been uncontested. Recognition of the rights of non-Sinn Féin parties was not a concession extracted from de Valera by a democratic-minded Collins; a few days earlier representatives of both sides had agreed on this point.[7] Article six of the pact read

> after the Election the Executive shall consist of the President, elected as formerly, the Minister of Defence, representing the Army, and nine other

---

[6] *DE, 1921–22*, p. 410 (17 May 1922).   [7] *Ibid.*, pp. 411, 414 (17 May 1922).

> Ministers, five from the majority Party and four from the minority, each
> Party to choose its own nominees. The allocation will be in the hands of
> the President.[8]

So, by a remarkable conjuring trick, the treaty split was to disappear not only
for the duration of the election campaign, but also in its aftermath.

Many on the government side regarded the pact as an undemocratic conspiracy against the electorate; they believed that in the circumstances of 1922 the
treaty was the dominant question on which the people should pronounce. The
attorney general warned that a coalition of the sort envisaged by the pact would
be impossible, since every member of the provisional government would be
obliged to accept the treaty in writing.[9] Griffith was outraged, and as the details
were announced in the Dáil one observer commented on his frown and his dark
mood.[10] (Shortly afterwards, however, in the more congenial surroundings of
The Bailey pub, he conceded that while the agreement was not ideal it was good
enough under the circumstances. Collins, also present, was recorded as being in
high spirits.[11])

The deal was widely criticized. One provincial paper believed that 'a sorrier
Pact it would be difficult to conceive. It treats the public as both children and
fools'; another attacked it for muzzling the electorate, and suggested that in
areas where Labour fielded candidates the electors would be able to punish 'the
patriots who have talked for six months and done nothing but driven the nation
ever more rapidly along the road to chaos and ruin'.[12] The extremist pro-treaty
Separatist went further and, under the heading 'Sack the Lot!', it dismissed Sinn
Féin as being no more than the skeleton of a political machine; the second Dáil
consisted, with very few exceptions, of members selected at caucus meetings
precisely because they lacked political judgement.[13] According to the decision
reached at the February *ard-fheis,* the officer board was responsible for the day-
to-day running of the party, but its pro-treaty members showed little sympathy
for the pact. Three of them objected to the proposal that 'joint canvassing and
public meetings should be arranged in each Constituency'.[14] The British
government was dismayed, Churchill telling his cabinet colleagues that 'it was
an arrangement full of disaster', and warning that its full implementation would
violate the treaty and might necessitate strong measures 'such as the resumption of powers or occupation of Southern areas'.[15]

---

[8] *Ibid.,* p. 479 (20 May 1922).   [9] Hugh Kennedy to Collins, 20 May 1922, RM, P7a/145.
[10] *Republic of Ireland,* 25 May 1922.   [11] De Róiste, diary, 20 May 1922, CAI, U271/A/44.
[12] *Kilkenny Journal,* 27 May 1922, editorial; *Sligo Champion,* 27 May 1922, editorial.
[13] *Separatist,* 27 May 1922.   [14] Officer board minutes, 1 June 1922, NAI, 2B/82/116(12).
[15] Cabinet conclusions, 30 May 1922, Cab.23/30, C.30(22)3.

Most republicans welcomed the pact, and apparently with good reason: it seemed to guarantee them far more seats than a strongly pro-treaty public would give them in a fairly contested election. Childers remarked that his colleagues seemed pleased, and that they regarded the agreement as a humiliation for Griffith and for his 'war party' (those who favoured drastic measures to establish the government's authority). Shrewder than the others, he doubted this.[16] Boland expressed his unease about Collins's intentions, but he believed that the army was the republicans' safeguard; later he reported that 'for the moment, everything is harmonious!!!'[17] But Collins took the view that without such a compromise agreement republican violence would have prevented the elections from taking place. Within days he seemed to have been vindicated, and it was reported that electoral registers seized by opponents of the treaty had been returned.[18]

The Collins–de Valera pact was approved unanimously by the Dáil, and it was then endorsed by the Sinn Féin *ard-fheis* which reconvened after its three-month adjournment 'like an apparition from the past'.[19] The rival election committees began meeting to ratify their candidates. They were also obliged to reject some who had already been chosen: those who had been selected at a time when both sides anticipated that they would contest every seat, and before the recent pact confined each party's numbers to its existing strength. The end result was that the outgoing candidate was endorsed in almost every case. It appeared that, at least as far as 'Sinn Féin' was concerned, the third Dáil would be no more than a continuation of the second.

A few replacements were necessary. Richard Corish, a prominent Labour figure in Wexford, had been elected as a Sinn Féin candidate in May 1921 and had subsequently supported the treaty; now he resigned to run for the Labour Party. Seán MacEntee finally stood down in Monaghan, but this did not satisfy his critics, who wanted him to be replaced by a treatyite rather than by a fellow-republican (as was required by the pact). In protest, the president, two vice-presidents, treasurer and director of elections of the South Monaghan executive all resigned their offices and supported the pro-treaty independent against the republican 'panel' candidate.[20]

Dan Breen, one of the flamboyant heroes of the Anglo-Irish War, was courted by both sides, and his name was the only one to feature on both panel

---

[16] Childers, diary, 20 May 1922, TCDL, MS 7816.

[17] Boland to McGarrity, 30 May, 9 June 1922, McG, 17,424(2).

[18] PG minutes, 25 May 1922, NAI, G1/2.   [19] *Free State*, 20 May 1922.

[20] *Plain People*, 11 June 1922. On Monaghan, see Michael Gallagher, 'The pact general election of 1922', *IHS*, 21, 84 (1979), pp. 407, 412.

lists; he was to take the place of Francis Drohan, the scrupulous deputy who had resigned his seat rather than vote against the treaty and his constituents' wishes. The treatyites secured the honour of paying Breen's nomination expenses, but this proved to have been a dubious achievement when he took up arms against them a month later. During the campaign it was reported that Breen had 'invited' independent candidates to withdraw.[21]

On 1 June the two rival headquarters completed their lists, consulted together, and sent the joint panel of candidates to the officer board of Sinn Féin which duly 'considered' and ratified it. This action, granting a formal seal of approval to the decisions of the two sub-parties, was Sinn Féin's only significant involvement in the election campaign. In earlier negotiations representatives of both sides had been able to agree that candidates would be nominated by 'the present Parties' and that neither the standing committee nor the constituency organization would have the power of veto.[22] Apart from speeches which the party leaders made with varying degrees of conviction, all important activities by Sinn Féiners were carried out on behalf of either the pro- or anti-treaty factions. The party had no platform, it *was* a platform used or stood upon by others.

Many years later, in the course of the Sinn Féin funds case in 1948, the party secretary Páidín O'Keeffe was asked by counsel about the state of Sinn Féin headquarters in Harcourt Street after the Collins–de Valera pact. The dialogue went as follows:

> Q. Was anything being done in the office?
> A. It was a graveyard. It was dead. That was my honest opinion.
> Q. You went in occasionally?
> A. I went in to say a prayer for the dead.

The judge then asked about ghosts, and was told that the office messenger still lived in the building.[23]

For Collins the function of the pact was to diminish violence and to allow for a calm and peaceful election. He was determined to achieve these objectives, even if the means of doing so involved obscuring the principal issue before the country, the treaty, and even if in some areas (those constituencies where no-one opposed the panel candidates) electors were also deprived of the right to vote. Ultimately his gamble paid off, and enough third party candidates were nominated, ensuring enough contested elections, to enable most of the people to make a meaningful choice.

---

[21] *Separatist*, 10 June 1922.   [22] *DE, 1921–22*, pp. 411, 413 (17 May 1922).
[23] O'Keeffe, evidence, 30 Apr. 1948, SFFC, 2B/82/118(42), p. 16.

Any contest was unwelcome for opponents of the treaty, but a pact under which they would retain their existing seats without challenge seemed to pose no threat. As the weaker and less popular wing of Sinn Féin they were convinced (rightly, as things turned out) that the more 'outsiders' or 'third parties' contested seats, the poorer would be their own chances; even if in an indirect manner, the electorate might be able to pronounce its verdict on the treaty.[24] They would be the chief victims of an open election.

The summer campaign

Despite the republicans' wishes and efforts, the two Sinn Féin factions did not have the field to themselves. The Labour Party, farmers' groups and independents also chose candidates, and since every one of them supported the treaty their intervention could only strengthen Collins and weaken de Valera. (One Labour deputy, Patrick Gaffney of Carlow, later refused to take the oath of fidelity to the king and withdrew from the third Dáil.) The PR system made it easier for them to defy their anti-treaty critics, because in constituencies which had more than one non-Sinn Féin candidate the republicans' anger tended to be diffused. Nonetheless many of them faced a grim ordeal during the interval between the announcement of the pact on 20 May and the deadline for nominations seventeen days later.

Third party candidates became targets of attack, and one propaganda sheet denounced them as a 'combination of traitors, domestic foes and enemy aliens', as 'enemies of the Northern victims of the Anglo-Orange blood lust'.[25] The Republican New Ireland warned that if independents intervened in the elections the worst form of chaos would result; 'any candidates who go forward on sectional interests must be regarded as acting in a thoroughly anti-national manner'. A fortnight later the paper claimed that uncontested elections provided the best augury of how the people felt about the pact, and that 'to butt into this election and to oust the members put up by the two sides of the National movement is simply to interfere with the plan of campaign conceived by the National leaders'.[26] Even some opponents of the treaty might have been embarrassed by the content and tone of such articles.

Many third party candidates came under pressure to stand down 'in the national interest'. The most colourful incident was an assault on Darrell Figgis, who was a prominent national figure, a friend of Arthur Griffith, and deputy

---

[24] See, for example, MacEntee's accurate forecast, *DE, 1921–22*, p. 435 (17 May 1922).

[25] *Plain People*, 4, 11 June 1922.   [26] *New Ireland*, 3, 17 June 1922.

chairman of the committee which drafted the Free State constitution. Until recently he had been an erratic member of Sinn Féin, disliked by many in the party but still popular enough to head the poll in the recent *ard-chomhairle* elections. Since then he had become an independent candidate, and he incited other groups (the Labour Party, farmers and businessmen) to challenge panel candidates in the election. Republicans were indignant when pro-treaty Sinn Féiners seemed reluctant to disown him. Shortly before the election, on the night of 12 June, he was accosted in his flat by three men each of whom was armed with a pair of scissors. They carried out what they claimed were their instructions: to 'mutilate' him by cutting off his beard.[27] (Collins's fiancée had expected that something might happen to Figgis and concluded 'he was lucky it was only his beard'.[28])

Republicans in Tipperary threatened that they would not permit elections to be held, and the provisional government authorized Dan Breen to prevent any interference.[29] This was a remarkable act of faith. Shots were fired at Denis Gorey, who represented the farmers in Carlow–Kilkenny.[30] The most serious such incident was the attack on Godfrey Greene, a farmers' candidate in Waterford – East-Tipperary. After being besieged in his house for hours by a group of armed men he was wounded, captured and abducted.[31] He later withdrew from the election. Despite this setback, other third party candidates in the constituency persevered in their campaigns and they won three of its five seats.

It was alleged that different tactics were used in North-West Mayo. On the night before nominations were due to be lodged with the returning officer, the farmers' candidate was visited by two armed men who urged him to withdraw. The republicans were undeterred by his refusal, and, according to one account, the next morning they kidnapped the supporter who had possession of the candidate's nomination papers and detained him until the deadline for submitting them had passed.[32] (The details of this story provoked some scepticism.) The Kerry Farmers' Union decided by a margin of forty votes to sixteen that it would run three candidates, but some of its members met again a few days later and voted by fourteen votes to ten that, 'in the interest of National unity', they would not contest the election after all.[33] In Clare, third party candidates were lobbied outside the Ennis courthouse as the deadline for nominations approached, minute by minute. Patrick Hogan, who had been chosen to contest the seat for Labour, informed the crowd that,

[27] *FJ*, 13 June 1922.

[28] Kiernan to Collins, 13 June 1922, Ó Broin and Ó hÉigeartaigh, *In great haste*, p. 189.

[29] PG minutes, 12 June 1922, NAI, G1/2.   [30] *Kilkenny Journal*, 10 June 1922.

[31] *FJ*, 13 June 1922; *Munster Express*, 17 June 1922; Gorey, *DE, official report*, 1, col. 26 (9 Sept. 1922).

[32] *Mayo News*, 10 June 1922.   [33] *Limerick Leader*, 7 June 1922.

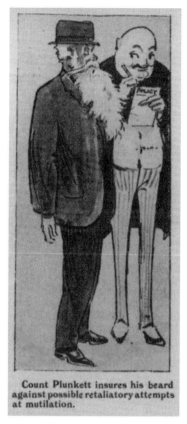

Count Plunkett insures his beard against possible retaliatory attempts at mutilation.

10.1 'Count Plunkett insures his beard'

the Secretary of the Irish Labour Party sent me a wire in which he stated:
'Candidature sanctioned. Best wishes for success.' What can I do?
'Act on your own and withdraw', said a voice. 'Be either a man or a mouse'. . .
'Considering the position', continued Mr Hogan, 'I think –'
'Withdraw first', urged Mr McNamara, 'and make the speech afterwards'.
'All right', said Mr Hogan. 'Drag out my name'.

Accompanied by the two farmers and the independent he abandoned the fight. The farmers later explained they had withdrawn because they believed that a free election would be impossible.[34]

---

[34] *Clare Champion*, 10, 17 June 1922.

In commenting on the state of Ireland *Dublin Opinion* resorted to the spirit of Lewis Carroll's *The Walrus and the Carpenter*:

> We weep for you, the leader said, we deeply sympathize;
> You've got to vote the way *we* want – the man who doesn't – DIES!
> *We* are the Irish Race, and you must see but through our eyes.
> Oh! Citizens, the Army said, Yours is a pleasant lot
> Lift up your head, the Treaty's dead! – but answer came there not
> And this was scarcely odd, because – we'd every one been shot.[35]

The Labour Party's involvement in the election tended to provoke less bitterness than that of farmers and independents; unlike them it inspired no class resentment, and its candidates could not so easily be branded as agents of British rule or influence. Some Volunteers felt that Labour members lacked the basic credentials for election to the Dáil, and a republican complained of one candidate that he had 'never met him in prison, nor in an ambush'.[36] The *Republic of Ireland* placed the party in a different category from the other 'independents', but nonetheless appealed to its past tradition of abstention, and to what was described as its 'habit and instinct of understanding the true needs of the nation'.[37] Labour's energy and efficiency provoked comparisons with Sinn Féin's campaign in 1918, and were contrasted with the complacency shown by its mutually hostile successor parties in 1922. The smugness and even cynicism of some 'Sinn Féin' propaganda was illustrated by one leaflet which supported the pact: 'Rally Round the Panel, Boys . . . Steady! All's well! Don't swop horses crossing the stream.'[38]

After the candidates had been nominated the campaign was generally so calm and orderly that many observers commented on its dullness. Intimidation, which had been such a prominent feature of the period before the nomination deadline, tended to fade away. But there was one part of the country in which controversy and violence persisted until polling day. In Sligo–East-Mayo, as elsewhere, pro- and anti-treaty factions had been prepared initially to contest every seat in the constituency. There, as elsewhere, some newly chosen candidates were expected to step down when the Collins–de Valera pact limited each wing of Sinn Féin to the number of seats which it held already. But there, in contrast to the pattern in all other constituencies except one, two pro-treaty Sinn Féin candidates – who should have withdrawn under the terms of the pact – decided to run as independents. They were attacked with exceptional bitterness.

Naturally, government supporters did not share the republicans' indignation

---

[35] *Dublin Opinion*, June 1922, p. 61.   [36] Gallagher, 'Pact general election', p. 411.
[37] *Republic of Ireland*, 15 June 1922, editorial.   [38] Pamphlet, June 1922, NLI, ILB.300.P5(57).

and dismay when third parties made use of the pact to contest the election. They knew that non-Sinn Féiners would tend to take votes from their opponents rather than from themselves, and that, whatever risk might be run by individual pro-treaty candidates, their cause as a whole could only prosper if the third parties performed well. The provisional government's election committee acquiesced in the pact (as was shown by its repudiation of the independent candidates in Sligo–East-Mayo), but it decided to ignore instructions from Sinn Féin concerning united action with the republicans on behalf of panel candidates. Instead it would 'carry on as a pro-Treaty Election Executive working for the Panel candidates'.[39] Its new separate identity would not be blurred or subsumed. Later it insisted that it would act only as a pro-treaty committee, and that all joint activities would have to be carried out under the auspices of Sinn Féin.[40]

After Figgis had proposed that the republicans should be challenged by third party candidates, more than two weeks elapsed before the pro-treaty newspaper committee decided to discontinue his employment.[41] It is symptomatic of Sinn Féin's disintegration that he could remain a member of its *ard-chomhairle*, while also running for the Dáil as an independent candidate in opposition to the party's 'panel'. On the other side, Childers experienced 'great difficulty in conforming to [the] peace atmosphere' but he refrained from printing some controversial articles in his newspaper.[42]

The two factions' different degrees of commitment to the pact were illustrated by a joint meeting in Sligo which was to have been addressed by Count Plunkett and by all five candidates. Only the republicans attended. Plunkett revealed the poverty of the 'Sinn Féin' campaign when he asked his audience to support the panel candidates 'not because they claimed to be particularly virtuous or because they had done good work in the past, but because the common interests of both sides demanded that there should be common action'.[43]

Two weeks after the pact had been ratified by the Sinn Féin *ard-fheis*, and one week before the elections were due to take place, the *Republic of Ireland* complained about foot-dragging on the part of the treatyites. There were justified suspicions that one section of Collins's party was actually encouraging other, 'non-panel' candidates to go forward. P. S. O'Hegarty's *Separatist* argued, with typical acerbity, that people who had made such a mess of things as members of the second Dáil had done did not deserve another chance; 'if peace conditions are to be stabilised, both war parties must go'. It dismissed the pact as 'a

[39] Pro-treaty committee minutes, 1 June 1922, FG, p. 52.   [40] *Ibid.*, 8 June 1922, p. 55.

[41] *Ibid.*, 12 June 1922, p. 58.   [42] Childers, diary, 23 May 1922, TCDL, MS 7816.

[43] *Sligo Champion*, 17 June 1922.

10.2a The pact: an Irish view

most scandalous and infamous document, a document which prostitutes patriotism to the base uses of Party . . . and which identifies Ireland with the political machine which Sinn Féin has come to be'.[44]

Throughout the country both factions retained their own election agents,
and in spite of urgent pleas for co-operation between members of the panel separate meetings were held in some districts. Republicans complained that they
had asked their 'partners' to issue joint daily appeals for support of panel candidates, but that this proposal had been rejected; Sinn Féin party members had
even canvassed against republicans. They protested that in election week the
treatyites issued propaganda for their section of Sinn Féin rather than for the
whole panel.[45] According to Liam de Róiste, 'so unpopular are the anti-Treaty
candidates here in Cork that if the pro-Treaty Sinn Féin candidates appear on
one platform with them, it will mean a loss of votes: a probable gain, however,
for "independents"'.[46]

Collins repudiated an advertisement, inserted in the press by Cumann na
Poblachta, which claimed that peace would not be secured by voting for 'a Dáil
of warring sections and interests'; the suggestion that third parties were national

[44] *Separatist*, 3, 10 June 1922.   [45] *New Ireland*, 24 June 1922; *Plain People*, 18 June 1922.
[46] De Róiste, diary, 10 June 1922, CAI, U271/A/44.

A SON OF LIBERTY.

Messrs. Collins and de Valera (together). "YOU BELONG TO THE GREATEST AND MOST INTELLIGENT NATION ON EARTH, AND YOU ARE THEREFORE ENTITLED TO CHOOSE YOUR OWN REPRESENTATIVE——"

Southern Irish Elector. "THANK YOU SO MUCH!"

Messrs. Collins and de Valera. "——WHOM WE HAVE ALREADY SELECTED FOR YOU."

10.2b The pact: a British view

enemies was contrary to his agreement with de Valera.[47] Two days later he himself perpetrated the most flagrant violation of the pact. In a speech in Cork, he remarked that, since there were no republicans with him on the platform, he could say what he wished: people should vote for the candidates whom they thought best. De Róiste, who was present in the audience, remarked that although this advice was resented deeply by Cork republicans they 'have little to say, as they were discovered distributing anti-Treaty "literature" of an offensive kind, along with Panel election directions'.[48] The speech was made in time to receive press coverage, and his remarks were publicized in the two days before polling took place. The daily newspapers drew their readers' attention to Collins's advice to vote for 'the Men you think best' and to his uncritical attitude towards non-Sinn Féin candidates. John Dillon remarked a few days later that Collins had played a rather crooked game and that, so far, it had proved successful.[49]

Another grievance felt by the republicans, another example of what they regarded as sharp practice, was the publication of the new Free State constitution only on polling day and not – as had been agreed months earlier – in time for it to become an issue in the election. Despite heroic efforts Collins failed in his efforts to smuggle a disguised republic into the constitution; he was unable to advance beyond the gains which had been secured during the treaty negotiations the previous December.[50] In the course of acrimonious negotiations in London, Churchill had warned him that he would find the British to be as tenacious on essential points as were de Valera and Rory O'Connor.[51] Article 17 of the constitution incorporated the oath of fidelity to the king which had already been included in article 4 of the treaty; as O'Higgins admitted some months afterwards, even though real power lay in the hands of the people, the constitution contained 'the trappings, the insignia, the fiction and the symbols of monarchical institutions'.[52] This was a further blow to prospects for reunifying the movement – but it was superfluous, since by this stage such prospects had virtually disappeared.

The government's supporters cheated. The pact was of value to them only in so far as it permitted an election to take place; without such an agreement the republicans could have (and probably would have) disrupted the campaign,

---

[47] *Free State*, 17 June 1922.   [48] De Róiste, diary, 15 June 1922, CAI, U271/A/44.

[49] Dillon, diary, 20 June 1922, JD, 6852.

[50] See Curran, *Birth of the Irish Free State*, pp. 204–17; D. H. Akenson and J. F. Fallin, 'The Irish Civil War and the drafting of the Free State constitution', *Éire-Ireland*, 5, 4 (1970), pp. 57–63.

[51] Conference minutes, 26 May 1922, Cab.43/6, 22/N/60(7), p. 89.

[52] *DE, official report*, 1, col. 478 (20 Sept. 1922).

making it useless as a test of public opinion. Once it was certain that an election would be held the treatyites tended to lose interest in the pact, and many of them felt free to evade or even repudiate its terms. However the republicans' own campaign of intimidation weakened their complaints about unfair behaviour.

The people's vote

Polling took place on Bloomsday, 16 June. Whether through lack of opportunity or through fear, third party candidates did not stand in seven of the twenty-eight constituencies, and a total of thirty-four 'Sinn Féin panel' deputies (seventeen on each side) were returned unopposed. Trinity College elected, once again, its four independent unionists. In the other twenty constituencies, ninety seats were contested by forty-eight treatyites, forty-one republicans, eighteen Labour representatives, twelve farmers, seventeen independents, and Dan Breen, who was in a category of his own, cherished by both the two main factions. As well as the thirty-four who were unopposed, eighty-three sitting deputies ran for re-election.

With only minor exceptions, the balloting and counting of votes were carried out in a businesslike and uncontroversial manner; an absence of 'the vigorous methods of older days' was noted.[53] Returning officers trained their staffs in the subtleties of PR, and in Cork four trial counts took place before polling day.[54] There was some disturbance in the National University constituency when republicans seized the ballot papers and inspected them after the count had been completed. As always, there were complaints of personation. In Cork it was reported that a young man, appropriately dressed for the purpose, swore that he was a woman whose name was on the electoral register and exercised her vote.[55] It was claimed that in Sligo–East-Mayo ballot papers were burned, personation officers acting for the two independent candidates were kidnapped, unionists were warned to stay at home as they had done in 1918, and when farmers turned up at the polling stations in the evening they found that their votes had been cast for them while they worked in the fields.[56] It was hardly surprising that neither of the independents was elected. Nowhere else was there a comparable volume of complaint, and it may be significant that this was the

---

[53] *Cork Examiner*, 17 June 1922.

[54] S. Ua Muimhneacháin to Local Government Department, 14 June 1922, DELG, 6/44.

[55] De Róiste, diary, 17 June 1922, CAI, U271/A/44.

[56] *II*, 17 June 1922; *Sligo Champion*, 24 June 1922.

only constituency in the country where republicans won a majority of first preference votes.

A few months later, it was remarked that the old hands, familiar with the
techniques of personation, were green with envy at the facility with which the
task was performed in 1922; skilled craftsmen had been replaced by machines.
Ernest Blythe claimed that in one area where 100 per cent of the electorate had
voted, every paper in the ballot box gave the first preference to the same candidate – showing the 'peculiar unanimity of the people in that district dead and
alive'.[57]

Despite such signs of continuity with traditional Irish voting habits, the election results were nonetheless spectacular. In theory they marked a clear victory
for the Sinn Féin panel, which had started the campaign with a bonus of thirty-
four seats already in its pocket, and then secured a further sixty of the ninety
which were contested. In practice no-one outside the republican party, and not
even all those within it, thought along these lines; in whole or in part everyone
calculated the results in terms of votes for or against the treaty. From this point
of view they marked an even more decisive victory for the provisional government and its adherents than might have been anticipated.

Under the terms of the pact both wings of Sinn Féin fielded as many candidates as they already held seats; as a result, they could only lose. The treatyites
suffered modest reverses, being deprived of seven of their forty-eight contested
seats. By contrast the republicans lost twenty-two out of forty-one. (In this cal-
culation Dan Breen, being claimed by both sides, is ascribed to neither.) All the
remaining thirty were won by third party supporters of the treaty, whether
Labour, farmers or independents. Non-Sinn Féiners won just under 40 per cent
of the vote, and over 78 per cent went to the combined 'non-republicans'.

Griffith and Collins topped the poll in their constituencies, and other prominent pro-treaty figures such as Cosgrave and O'Higgins, while coming second,
were nonetheless elected on the first count. Two of the government's seven
defeats were of new candidates who had not yet sat in the Dáil, while all its losses
were to other supporters of the treaty rather than to republicans. The single
prominent member of pro-treaty Sinn Féin to lose his seat was the outspoken
Páidín O'Keeffe. (This may have been the result of fraud; in the course of an
overnight interval during the count, republicans guarding the ballot-boxes were
alleged to have re-assigned some of Collins's first preference votes to one of his
opponents.[58]) Otherwise the government's only embarrassing failure was its
inability to gain a seat in Co. Wexford, where the pro-treaty deputy Richard

---

[57] William O'Brien and Ernest Blythe, DE, official report, 1, cols. 1,845–7 (20 Oct. 1922).
[58] Cork Examiner, 23 June 1922; de Róiste, diary, 22–24 June 1922, CAI, U271/A/44.

Table 10.1 *Percentage of votes in contested seats, 1922, by constituency*

	Government	Republican	'Third party'
Carlow–Kilkenny	31.2	14.3	54.4
Cavan	76.6	–	23.3
Cork city	37.5	19.1	43.3
Cork E/NE	–	49.5	50.5
Cork M/N/S/W/SE	45.7	23.0	31.2
Dublin mid	14.7	19.5	65.8
Dublin NW	81.2	–	18.7
Dublin S	37.6	20.0	42.4
Dublin Co.	35.5	9.3	55.1
Galway	54.5	32.2	13.2
Kildare–Wicklow	26.5	19.0	54.4
Laois–Offaly	53.5	–	46.5
Longford–Westmeath	50.1	17.5	32.4
Louth–Meath	45.9	15.7	38.3
Monaghan	57.5	24.6	17.9
National University	44.8	25.1	30.0
Sligo–E. Mayo	29.5	56.4	14.0
Tipperary M/N/S	32.5	40.2	27.3
Waterford–Tipperary[59]	19.9	20.6	50.2
Wexford	7.2	26.9	65.8

Source: Brian M. Walker (ed.), *Parliamentary election results in Ireland, 1918–92*
(Dublin, 1992), pp. 104–8.

Corish was re-elected under his new (or original) Labour colours. The government had at least the consolation that four of the five Wexford seats were won by supporters of the treaty.

In other areas of the country their performance was remarkable. Only one of the five TDs in Kildare–Wicklow had supported the treaty, and he received more first preference votes than the four republicans combined. The result in Cavan was a triumph of party discipline. Griffith was accompanied by two old colleagues from the days of the pre-rising Sinn Féin party, Walter Cole and Seán Milroy. On the first count the single 'outside' candidate, the farmer P. F. Baxter, received ten times more first preference votes than Milroy. But Griffith's surplus divided 5 per cent for Baxter, 25 per cent for Cole and 70 per cent for Milroy. Cole was then elected, and his surplus divided 5 per cent for Baxter and 95 per cent for Milroy. In this way Milroy, who had secured a mere 565 first preferences out of a total of 24,000 votes on the first count, defeated Baxter by 15 votes on

---

[59] Dan Breen won 9.2 per cent of the vote.

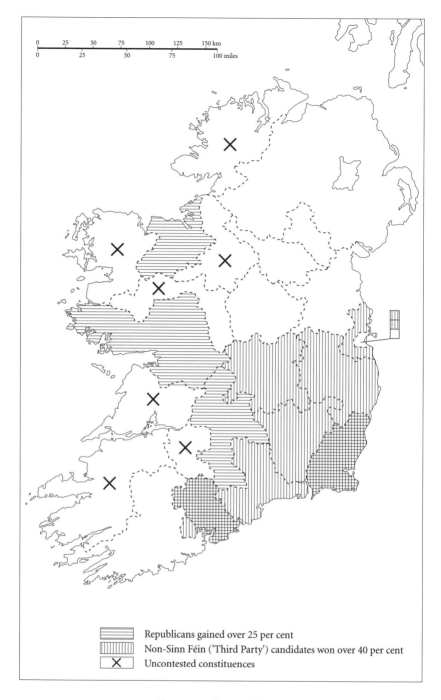

Figure 10.1 The 1922 election

the third. There were no suggestions of fraud, and Baxter commented afterwards on the good order which had characterized the election.[60] Cavan was the only constituency contested by the farmers in which they failed to win at least one seat.

Such loyalty in transfer votes was not always displayed towards the treatyites' panel 'allies'. In neighbouring Monaghan, where resentment at MacEntee's behaviour still lingered even though he was not a candidate, pro-treaty Sinn Féiners passed on nearly twice as many of their second preference votes to the independent candidate as to the republican. In the National University an inspection of the stolen papers revealed that graduates who had voted for pro-treaty Sinn Féin also preferred independents to republicans in assigning their lower-preference votes.[61] It was clear that very many electors were loyal to the treaty and not to the Sinn Féin panel. On the other hand, there was a general tendency for those who voted 'Sinn Féin' to support the panel; over 70 per cent of electors on both sides gave transfer votes to the other wing of the old party when there was no candidate available from their own.[62]

For the first time, many electors could vote for a party whose main concern was with the interests of the poor, rather than of the abstract 'nation', and Labour's success was perhaps the most striking of the whole election. Until now its record had been uninspiring; it had withdrawn in 1918, did so again in 1921, and nearly stood aside in 1922. Only the unexpected delay in calling the election made it possible for the party to fight the election at all. It nominated twenty-two candidates, but four of these withdrew after republicans had urged them not to stand. The pressure was particularly blatant in Clare, where Labour could almost certainly have won a seat. Yet seventeen of its eighteen candidates were elected, and the eighteenth was defeated on the last count by only thirteen votes, the narrowest margin of the election. (No opponent of the treaty ran in this constituency, but Labour supporters claimed nonetheless that republican poll-workers had stolen blocks of ballot papers; if so, this altruistic loyalty to the pact must command a certain respect. More plausible is the claim that policemen in mufti were transported around the constituency to vote in favour of the government deputies, one of whom was the commissioner of the new police force.)[63] Labour could have gained more seats if had been prepared to take risks. It ran one candidate each in Laois–Offaly and Louth–Meath, and since both of them achieved more than double the quota they could almost certainly have

[60] *Anglo-Celt*, 24 June 1922.   [61] *New Ireland*, 24 June 1922; O'Malley, *Singing flame*, p. 80.

[62] Gallagher, 'Pact general election', pp. 418–9.

[63] Arthur Mitchell, *Labour in Irish politics, 1890–1930* (Dublin, 1974), p. 161; William Davin, *DE, official report*, 1, col. 101 (11 Sept. 1922).

pulled in colleagues on their coat-tails. In Dublin city and county the three Labour candidates secured more first preference votes than the six republicans: they gained 18,147 votes to 15,754.

Labour performed best in areas such as Wexford and Kildare–Wicklow, where farm labourers were most numerous. To an extent, however, its high poll reflected public antipathy towards the Sinn Féin movement and the feuding which now characterized it; the electorate seized the chance provided by the pact to vote for someone (perhaps in some cases, for anyone) other than a member of Sinn Féin. In sixteen of the twenty contested constituencies 'Sinn Féin' lost one seat or more. In three constituencies Labour fielded the only opposition to panel candidates, and in two of these it scored its highest vote. The third was North-West Dublin, the only seat which it contested and failed to win, and where (apart from any irregularities which might have taken place) the party was unfortunate in being opposed by a solid *bloc* of four treatyite opponents. As a result it was faced with an unusually loyal pattern of transfers, and it was unable, as elsewhere, to profit at the expense of republicans from the electorate's pro-treaty mood.

The farmers did reasonably well, particularly in view of the republicans' attacks on them, and they won seven of the twelve seats they contested. This was a marginally higher proportion than that of anti-treaty Sinn Féin. The independents experienced mixed fortunes, winning only six seats out of seventeen, but gaining 65 per cent of the first preferences in Mid-Dublin. Second only to Collins, Darrell Figgis scored the highest vote in the whole country.[64] Alone, he secured virtually as many first preference votes as all the six republican candidates in Dublin city and county. (The figures were 15,087 and 15,754.) The attack on him may have ensured a sympathy vote; a beardless Samson, he helped pull down the republicans in the capital. Another independent returned in Dublin was Alfie Byrne, who had sat as a Nationalist MP in Westminster from 1915 until his relatively narrow defeat three years later, and who would retain his Dáil seat as an independent (and a famous Dublin 'character') from 1922 until his death in 1956.

The republicans were the victims of the election. Over half their candidates were defeated, and none of them headed the poll – as treatyites did in twelve constituencies, Labour in five, independents in two and a farmer in one. If, once more but perhaps somewhat unfairly, the votes for Dan Breen are ignored (on the grounds that he was supported by both Sinn Féin factions) the republicans won fewer first preference votes than Labour – even though they fielded more than twice as many candidates. Several of their leading figures lost their seats.

---

[64] Both men represented constituencies with exceptionally large electorates.

10.3 Cartoon images of de Valera, Griffith, Collins, Figgis and Cosgrave

Erskine Childers, who had been subjected to attacks by Griffith and much of the pro-treaty press, scored the second-lowest vote in the whole election. Liam Mellows, a leading member of the republican garrison in the Four Courts, was rejected by Co. Galway, placed last out of eight candidates in a seven-seat constituency. He was the only TD to be defeated west of the Shannon.

Four of the five republican women who ran for election were defeated, and only Mary MacSwiney retained her seat on the last count. None of the other parties ran female candidates. Kathleen Clarke complained later that her fellow-republican club members did not canvass for her, but 'they worked for the men'.[65] For most people (specifically for most men) the revolution was over, and politics could become once more a male preserve.

Other prominent republicans performed adequately, but no more. Brugha was elected on the fourth count in Waterford–East-Tipperary, where government and Labour candidates had been elected on the first. In Kildare–Wicklow Robert Barton (who as a matter of honour had voted in the Dáil for the treaty which he had signed, before transferring immediately to the republican camp)

---

[65] Kathleen Clarke, evidence, 6 May 1948, SFFC, 2B/82/118(43), p. 27.

was the last of five candidates to be elected; but he had reason to be grateful, as his three fellow republicans lost their seats. In the Dublin city and county constituencies, with a total of eighteen deputies, only Seán T. O'Kelly was elected for Mid-Dublin, and he was also the last to be returned. All his five colleagues were defeated. The capital was denounced by one paper for 'returning political twisters, gombeen men and Unionists at the top of the poll, while you threw out the mother of P. H. Pearse'.[66] In Dublin city the pro-treaty parties won 72,000 first preference votes, the republicans 11,000.

Perhaps the republicans' greatest humiliation was reserved for East–North-East Cork, the only constituency in the country, whether contested or not, in which there were no government candidates. All the incumbent TDs were republicans, but although they gained nearly half of the first preference votes, a farmer and an independent took two of their three seats. The farmer topped the poll. The independent (the only one to be elected outside Dublin) had been a pro-treaty Sinn Féin candidate until deprived of the party label by the Collins–de Valera pact. Like his two colleagues in Sligo–East-Mayo he ignored this agreement, but he fared much better than they did. Many of the 5,000 electors in the constituency who voted for him probably thereby also voted for Collins and the treaty in the least indirect way available to them.[67] In Cork city, treatyites, Labour and independents each won more first preference votes than the republicans (although the independents failed to be elected). If there was some satisfaction for the republicans in Munster, where they equalled pro-treaty Sinn Féin's total of seven seats, this was dimmed by Labour's winning eight. There was even less comfort in Leinster where every single constituency was contested and twelve of the seventeen republican candidates were defeated.

A 'national record' was of little help when the electorate showed scant appreciation of the achievements and sacrifices of 1916 or 1919–21. Symbolic figures such as Patrick Pearse's mother and Tom Clarke's widow, heroes of the Easter Rising like Markievicz and of the Anglo-Irish War like Seamus Robinson, all were defeated. Even Dan Breen, the only candidate in the election to feature on both panels, was rejected by the voters of Waterford – East-Tipperary. (The harassed farmers must have felt satisfied that it was their transfers which deprived him of a seat.) In some respects it seemed as if the Irish electors had not merely turned their backs on the War of Independence and wished to put its memories behind them; many of them also showed that they had had enough of the Easter Rising. Long before this, 'the terrible beauty was beginning to lose her good looks'.[68] The people wished to be saved from their saviours; 'they had

---

[66] *Plain People*, 25 June 1922.   [67] See Gallagher, 'Pact general election', p. 417.

[68] Sean O'Casey, *Inishfallen, fare thee well* (London, 1949), p. 114.

not known what they were letting themselves in for when they voted Sinn Fein, and they were only too happy to let themselves out again'.[69] When the electors were given their first serious opportunity to reject the party which had dominated Irish public life for the past five years, many of them did so with enthusiasm. But a considerable proportion of those who voted against the panel or against the republic must have been former (and unconverted) Redmondites who were now able to strike back at their long-triumphant enemy.

The election results were a litany of disaster for the republicans, but perhaps one consolation for them was that things could have been even worse. While all prominent supporters of the treaty had to fight for re-election, republican leaders such as de Valera, Boland, Stack and Plunkett were returned unopposed. If every constituency had been fought, it is likely that the republicans' percentage of the votes cast would have been higher; uncontested areas such as Kerry, Clare and South Mayo had a radical tradition, and they would later support anti-treaty candidates in the 1923 election. But even if this had happened, at least some among the seventeen republicans who were elected unchallenged would almost certainly have been rejected by the voters.

De Valera was probably lucky that he faced no opposition. There is little reason to think that he would have lost his seat, but equally no reason to believe that he would have triumphed as he had done in 1917 and would do again in 1923. (Before polling day, de Róiste was certain that if de Valera, Stack and others had been opposed they would be defeated.[70] This was probably wishful thinking.) De Valera did not have solid backing within the Sinn Féin party in his county. The executive in his own (pre-PR) constituency of East Clare supported the treaty on two separate occasions. The first of these votes (by seventeen votes to nine) was in the immediate aftermath of its signature, and the executive reaffirmed its views a month later, by the substantial margin of twenty-seven votes to eight, at a time when some Sinn Féiners in other districts were already changing their minds.[71] The West Clare executive and the county council had also voted for the treaty by substantial margins.[72] Clare would have had to flout the pattern of every constituency in which polling took place if de Valera were to have avoided embarrassment.

While the pact had made possible the republicans' defeat by allowing the election to be held in the first place, it had also limited their slaughter by allowing a third of them to be returned unopposed. Even more basic to their (partial) survival was the influence of PR. Had the British government not imposed the

---

[69] Conor Cruise O'Brien, *Passion and cunning and other essays* (London, 1988), p. 223.

[70] De Róiste, diary, 6 June 1922, CAI, U271/A/44.   [71] *Clare Champion*, 7 Jan., 4 Feb. 1922.

[72] *Ibid.*, 24 Dec. 1921; *Limerick Leader*, 2 Jan. 1922; *II*, 5 Jan. 1922.

new voting system in 1920-1, and had the 1922 elections been fought by the old 'first past the post' method, the republicans would have been annihilated as thoroughly as the Parliamentary Party had been in 1918. John Dillon, while welcoming the result, must have envied the electoral good fortune of anti-treaty Sinn Féin.

Both before and after the election many republicans insisted that the treaty was not an issue, and they pointed out that the voters had been asked to decide for or against candidates representing the Sinn Féin panel; the contest was described more light-heartedly as one between Panellites and anti-Panellites.[73] However this was a minority view. There was an overwhelming tendency to regard the result as a vote either for or against the treaty, and to see the third party candidates as allies of the government. The voting patterns tend to bear this out, and electors who gave their first preferences to the third parties showed a clear tendency to pass on their lower preferences to pro-treaty Sinn Féiners rather than to republicans. The test can be made with any degree of accuracy only in the case of surplus votes left over after a candidate had been elected on the first ballot.

In the seven constituencies where third party candidates were elected on the first count, and where their surplus votes could have benefited either pro- or anti-treaty Sinn Féin, the ratio of these preferences was almost 2:1 in favour of those who supported the treaty.[74] Third party voters were clearly more divided on the question than were their candidates, who were unanimously pro-treaty; nonetheless the general pattern of their transfers was another blow for the republicans. Lower transfers are less revealing because of the random element involved in the selection of ballot papers to be redistributed, but they also tend to confirm this pattern.

It is difficult to draw detailed conclusions from the results. Much depended on chance circumstances, such as the allegiances of sitting Sinn Féin deputies or the number of third party candidates in a constituency. In much of the west of Ireland the old tradition of unchallenged elections was maintained. Broken only by Galway, where elections were fought in 1918 and 1922, a solid geographical block consisting of South Mayo, Clare, West Limerick, Limerick city and Kerry were all uncontested in the three general elections of 1918, 1921 and 1922.

Nonetheless one pattern emerges clearly: in seven constituencies in the east and south-east of the country, in an arc which stretched from Dublin almost as far as Cork city, over half the electors gave their first preference votes to non-

---

[73] *Leader*, 17 June 1922, p. 416.

[74] The constituencies were Carlow–Kilkenny, Cork City, Cork North-West, Co. Dublin, Mid-Dublin, Louth–Meath and Wexford.

Sinn Féin candidates. And with one exception (Meath), the eight counties which had the highest percentage of people engaged on farms of over 100 acres (40 hectares) matched the seven counties which comprised or included these constituencies where third parties performed best. However, since the votes were divided into support for farmers, independents and Labour candidates they did not form a solid *bloc*. Conversely, the panel candidates won their greatest share of the vote in areas dominated by small farms.[75] In the only two Connacht constituencies where elections were held, the republicans' first preference vote was 2 per cent ahead of that won by pro-treaty Sinn Féin. Even when the third parties are taken into account, a remarkably low 56 per cent of the Connacht electorate voted for the treaty. The west remained more radical than other parts of the country.

Reactions to the election results were predictable. Labour supporters were jubilant, pro-treaty Sinn Féiners were relieved, while the republicans were angry and disillusioned. *New Ireland* complained that Collins had played a confidence trick on de Valera, and quoted a description of him as a triple traitor: he had violated his oath to the Dáil in signing the treaty, to Lloyd George in concluding the pact, and to the pact in deference to Lloyd George.[76] As one defeated candidate to another, Art O'Connor wrote to Childers

> the Election is over thank God and in a way we did better than I expected tho' I would have been better satisfied if it were fought on the straight issue; possibly we might not have got so many votes but at least we could have worked with greater heart and smote our enemies. Next time, however, if there be a next time, I hope we shall have more of the mailed fist.[77]

The traditional links between voting and violence would be maintained.

From some quarters there were claims that the result marked a victory for the panel, and that under the pact a coalition government must be formed. Other opponents of the treaty realized that the monarchist clauses of the Free State constitution rendered any such agreement impossible. De Valera remarked sadly some time later, 'I regard the Pact, tho' apparently a victory, as really a defeat for the Republic', while *The Republic of Ireland* admitted that the Republicans had been childishly sanguine.[78]

One republican's assessment was impressive in its blunt honesty. Writing under the pseudonym 'Fiach', the author conceded that the great majority of the voters in nationalist Ireland had definitely renounced the republican ideal

---

[75] *Census of population, 1926. General report*, p. 28.   [76] *New Ireland*, 1 July 1922.

[77] O'Connor to Childers, 24 June 1922, Childers MSS, NLI, 15,444(2).

[78] De Valera to McGarrity, 10 Sept. 1922, McG, 17,440; *Republic of Ireland*, 29 June 1922, editorial.

which they had appeared to accept between 1916 and 1921. The treaty *had* been an issue; all the independent candidates had made it one, and so had the electorate. There were many mitigating circumstances, but these did not undo 'the grave indictment which the returns seem to launch against the courage and constancy and gratitude of the Irish people'.[79]

Collins's desperate efforts succeeded in bringing him the time he had sought. He was unable to use this breathing space to vindicate his argument that the treaty would be compatible with Irish republicanism, and he had failed to write the king out of the Free State constitution, but at least he could prove that the great mass of the Irish people supported the treaty and the peace which it was expected to provide. He claimed that,

> the election was *declared* to be one in which the Treaty issue was not being decided. The people have chosen to *declare* otherwise. The Government made the Pact with the Anti-Treaty party, believing that only by doing so could an election be held at all. That Pact appeared to muzzle the electorate. The electorate have not allowed the pact to muzzle them.[80]

His wing of the old Sinn Féin party did not have an overall majority among the newly elected deputies, but the treaty would attract far greater support in the third Dáil than it had done in the second. His government would also enjoy a degree of legitimacy which it had been unable to claim until its policies had been endorsed by the electorate.

By what might seem a strange constitutional anomaly, the second Dáil did not dissolve itself when it decreed that elections should be held to choose its successor. It decided instead to reconvene for two final sessions on 30 June and 1 July, immediately before the first meeting of the new parliament.[81] In his diary de Róiste asked himself which members would meet in Dublin, 'is it the present personnel or the new personnel? It all seems haphazard, unmethodical, illogical.'[82] But in some respects this pattern followed the precedent established (at de Valera's suggestion) by the first Dáil a year earlier. At that time Sinn Féin might reasonably have feared that if the Irish parliament ceased to exist while the war with Britain was still in progress, and that if the May 1921 elections were subsequently cancelled by the British government, there would be no means available to re-create an independent Irish legislature. It was decided that the first Dáil would remain in existence until its successor had convened, and that it would then dissolve automatically.[83] Apart from habit and inertia there seems

[79] *Republic of Ireland*, 29 June 1922.   [80] Collins, memo, n.d., RM, P7/B/28, p. 63.

[81] Collins, *DE, 1921–22*, p. 507 (8 June 1922).

[82] De Róiste, diary, 8 June 1922, CAI, U/271/A/44.

[83] De Valera, *DE, 1919–21*, p. 291 (10 May 1921).

to have been no obvious reason for continuing this practice in 1922. In themselves these are probably a sufficient explanation.

Civil war

The changing of the guard, the formal transfer of authority from one parliament to another, was due to take place two weeks after the election; the outgoing second Dáil would hold formal meetings, and its successor would then convene. But political questions were overtaken by the outbreak of heavy fighting on 28 June, when government troops bombarded the republican garrison in the Four Courts. Because of the civil war the summoning of the new third Dáil was postponed repeatedly, and its predecessor never met again in full session. This enabled republican fundamentalists to argue that the second Dáil, chosen in May 1921, remained the only legitimate Irish parliament. They felt free to repudiate all its successors, beginning with that which had already been elected in June 1922, and over the next few decades this belief would lead them into many bizarre and recondite constitutional arguments.[84]

The attack on the Four Courts was the final and decisive stage in a pattern of events which had been leading towards civil war for several months. When the army convention met on 26 March, flouting the prohibition by Griffith's Dáil government, it withdrew the republican forces' allegiance from political and civilian authority. Thereby it ended the subordination of the army to the Dáil which had existed, at least in theory, since Brugha's resolution in August 1919. This military defiance of civilian authority provided an ironic parallel with the Curragh Incident in March 1914, and to the willingness of British officers to resign their commissions rather than put the government's orders into effect.[85] Time after time in the course of the Irish revolution radical nationalists had followed the example provided by Ulster unionists and elements within the British army.

The breach between political leaders and republican soldiers was followed by a long series of provocations on the part of the anti-treaty forces. Collins's provisional government was too weak and too anxious for a peaceful compromise to respond as any normal, established administration would have done in such circumstances; for months, despite complaints by hard-line colleagues such as Griffith, he tolerated challenges to his authority. He remained almost obsessively anxious to avoid bloodshed, despite widespread unease at the continuing indulgence which he showed towards former comrades-in-arms; he believed,

---

[84] For some of these arguments, see below, pp. 436–8, 444–7, 454, 458.

[85] See Edwards, *Eamon de Valera*, p. 98.

'in his desperate, ruthless and sentimental way, that the movement could be kept together because of friendship and trust'.[86] The London *Daily Mail* compared him to Kerensky, and the British commander-in-chief in Ireland reported to London that 'until Collins was prepared to kill somebody things would not be put right'.[87]

By the end of June, however, the treaty had been endorsed massively by the electorate; British pressure for action against the republicans mounted after two IRA men assassinated the unionist Sir Henry Wilson in London (possibly on Collins's orders); and the challenges by members of the Four Courts garrison climaxed in their kidnapping of J. J. O'Connell, the provisional government's deputy chief of staff. These republican extremists repudiated their own leaders, claiming that they were too moderate, and the government had at least some grounds for believing that they planned to launch an attack on the remaining British forces, thereby re-opening the Anglo-Irish War.[88] Collins's patience came to an end at last, the Four Courts were attacked, and the civil war began in earnest.

De Valera promptly supported the besieged garrison and described its members as the best and bravest of the nation; anti-treaty solidarity must be preserved at all costs.[89] He provided the rebels with the prestige associated with his former office of president of the republic, as well as the support of a block of anti-treaty TDs. His actions (and also his earlier inaction) had helped transform the conflict from one in which a government tried to suppress dissent by military groups into a struggle between two armies representing two different traditions.[90] But he intensified rather than created the differences between moderates and radicals, and some republicans would have opposed any conceivable settlement. Tom Barry, for example, longed for combat.[91] There would have been at least some conflict and bloodshed, no matter what de Valera did, and the reasons which led people to join one side or another were often whimsical and illogical. One participant explained long afterwards, 'it all depended on which crowd you got into'.[92]

In military terms, almost all the skill and energy were displayed by the pro-treaty forces rather than by their opponents. The republicans were divided and,

---

[86] Garvin, *1922*, p. 156.

[87] PG minutes, 7 Apr. 1922, NAI, G1/2; Conference minutes, 23 May 1922, Cab.43/1, 22/N/148/1.

[88] See Mulcahy, *DE, official report*, 1, cols. 172–3 (12 Sept. 1922); Hopkinson, *Green against green*, pp. 115–7.

[89] Martin Mansergh, 'The freedom to achieve freedom', in Doherty and Keogh, *Michael Collins*, p. 179.   [90] See Lawlor, *Britain and Ireland*, p. 196.   [91] Hart, *I.R.A. and its enemies*, p. 113.

[92] Sean Harling, in Griffith and O'Grady, *Curious journey*, p. 285.

fatally, their strategy and tactics were defensive. Even in their Four Courts stronghold they failed to make use of the ten weeks which they had at their disposal, and their preparations to resist attack remained quite inadequate. Within days Dublin was in the hands of the government troops, although at a heavy cost: 65 people were killed, 280 were wounded, and further damage was done to the city. The half of O'Connell Street which had survived the Easter Rising was now destroyed.

Some republicans stored petrol and paraffin in the Four Courts, determined to burn or blow up the buildings rather than obey any orders to hand them over. In an act of vandalism pre-eminent amongst so many other comparable atrocities, the Public Record Office (which formed part of the Four Courts defensive positions) was turned into a munitions factory and was mined by its defenders; as a result it was destroyed in an explosion when the building caught fire.[93] Independent Ireland's opportunities for understanding the country's past were impoverished as fragments of irreplaceable documents floated over the city.

The conflict soon spread beyond Dublin, and for six weeks the war consisted of an attack by government forces on their enemies' strongholds, particularly in the 'Munster Republic'. Collins received financial and material assistance from the British, and his army swelled rapidly. He first secured effective control over the midlands and the west, and then attacked the anti-treaty positions in the south. Waterford and Limerick both fell on 21 July. His forces enjoyed the advantage of public support; the republicans were disliked and resented in those areas which they controlled, as the British had been before them. Later one of their number reminisced about how 'in Fermoy, Mallow, and other towns, the people looked at us sullenly, as if we had belonged to a hostile invading army'.[94] De Valera admitted that if the anti-treaty soldiers persisted in their destructive tactics 'the people will begin to treat us as bandits'.[95] In a similar mood the republicans' adjutant general felt obliged to warn that officers should 'constantly keep in mind the fact that we *do* want the people with us, and that they deserve to be treated properly by us. Our behaviour towards them should and will be guided if we remember that we are real soldiers not of the Black and Tan type.'[96] The parallel was ominous.

Many opponents of the treaty continued to think in terms of abstract images rather than of living people, and some of their propaganda illustrated the religious terminology, the detachment from the real world, which had for so long

---

[93] Hopkinson, *Green against green*, p. 122; O'Malley, *Singing flame*, pp. 71, 78, 103–14.

[94] Brennan, *Allegiance*, p. 352.   [95] Curran, *Birth of the Irish Free State*, p. 245.

[96] Conn Moloney to Liam Deasy, 15 July 1922, Captured documents collection, IMA, lot 3(1)(e).

been a feature of the separatist movement. Perhaps the most remarkable is 'the Passion of the Republic':

> the shattered House of Justice is a symbol of the Republican's Ideal. That symbol exhibits all the stigmata of a profound passion. A reproach to men, defiled with ordure, numbered among thieves . . . it was expedient that one man should die for the people.
>
> Cathal Brugha is dead. They have rolled to the stone, setting guards, and declare she [the republic] is dead. Our answer is: no passion but has a resurrection. Our appeal is: to posterity.[97]

Such fervour was no substitute for military strength or skill.

The government forces continued their advance, seizing Cork city in an amphibious assault on 10 August. By the next day, every town in Ireland was in the government's hands, although some would later be regained by anti-treaty forces for brief periods. Only then did the savage phase of the civil war begin, as the republicans resorted to guerrilla tactics, launching a series of attacks on individuals and on property, and waging a campaign of destruction. They did their best to wreck the country's economy. From his prison cell Rory O'Connor preached further devastation, urging his colleagues who were still at liberty that they should burn down the provisional government's ministries and other buildings, and to 'try and make govt impossible by every means'.[98] Liam de Róiste illustrated the widespread exasperation felt by government supporters in his complaint that the republicans believed 'we may all go down in the shipwreck; it matters not to them as long as they can demonstrate that Collins and Griffith cannot control and steer the ship'.[99]

The republicans goaded their enemies into what were often brutal reprisals, confident that these would provoke another change in public opinion similar to those which had already taken place in 1916 and 1919. But their own atrocities made the public indifferent to Free State ruthlessness, and the mass of the population maintained its support for the treaty.[100] The republicans' continuing unpopularity was illustrated by a directive issued by Liam Lynch: 'the civilian population of this area if still acting in this hostile manner must be dealt with sternly'.[101]

The sordid and vicious struggle dragged on until May 1923, and in terms of damage to buildings, roads, bridges and the general infrastructure of the state,

---

[97] 'Handbills for heretics. No. 5. The passion of the republic', Fianna Fáil archives, FF/15.

[98] O'Connor to O'Malley, 12 Sept. 1922, EO'M, P17a/62.

[99] De Róiste, diary, 3 Aug. 1922, CAI, U271/A/45.   [100] Garvin, *1922*, p. 103.

[101] Lynch to Ernie O'Malley, 4 Sept. 1922, RM, P 7a/81, p. 42.

10.4 Free state propaganda

the civil war was far more destructive than the Anglo-Irish War had been. The material losses have been valued at £30 million, and financing the war cost about another £17 million.[102] Estimates of the death toll vary, from a maximum of between 4,000 and 5,000, through a figure of under 4,000 and a remarkably

---

[102] Hopkinson, *Green against green*, pp. 272–3.

precise 927, to a minimum of 600 or 700.[103] A likely total would probably be between 1,500 and 2,000 – more than were killed in the recent war against the British.

As soon as heavy fighting broke out on a serious scale at the end of June all sides lost interest in political and parliamentary matters. The formal dissolution of the outgoing Dáil and the inauguration of its successor were both postponed. The second Dáil never reconvened, while the 'parliament to which the provisional government was responsible' was not summoned until 9 September, and it met then only as the result of frequent demands and complaints by Labour and other opposition TDs. The government preferred to wage war (as it had preferred to conduct all its other activities) without the distraction of parliamentary criticism or control. Months earlier Kevin O'Higgins had described its position as 'vague, undefined and anomalous', and declared that, as a member of its cabinet, he was not responsible to the Dáil but to the parliament of 'Southern Ireland'.[104] This autocratic and (in the literal sense of the word) irresponsible attitude persisted for more than six months.

When the third Dáil finally met almost all the republicans abstained, implementing against an Irish legislature the tactics which Griffith had always wished to use against attendance in the House of Commons. One of the new Dáil's first acts was to sever another link with Westminster. The only republican present was Laurence Ginnell, who had been an MP until 1917. Then he had been suspended and removed by the sergeant-at-arms;[105] now he was expelled for disruptive behaviour. He was consistent.

Once the war began in Dublin, Collins, O'Higgins and other leading government figures left their cabinet posts to take up army appointments, although Collins continued to direct government affairs from behind the scenes. Gavan Duffy reported to Mulcahy his impression that all those who mattered had gone to the Ministry of Defence, leaving only a feeble residue in Government Buildings.[106] All efforts were concentrated on ending the conflict. The Sinn Féin party secretary, Páidín O'Keeffe, was appointed deputy governor of Mountjoy Jail, where he had in his care several former republican Dáil colleagues as well as a member of his own office staff. His superior, the governor, was Diarmuid O'Hegarty, who had been seconded from his post as secretary to the cabinet. As

---

[103] Fanning, *Independent Ireland*, p. 39; Eoin Neeson, *The civil war, 1922–23* (Dublin, 1989), p. 256; S. J. Connolly (ed.), *The Oxford companion to Irish history* (Oxford, 1998), p. 265; John A. Murphy, *Ireland in the twentieth century* (Dublin, 1975), p. 58.

[104] *DE, 1921–22*, p. 125 (28 Feb. 1922). The Southern Irish parliament had held only one meeting.

[105] *Hansard*, 96, cols. 1,455–7 (26 July 1917).

[106] Gavan Duffy to Mulcahy, 29 Aug. 1922, RM, P7/B/100.

well as illustrating the continuing subordination of the party to the state, the appointment of such figures to the post of jailers reveals the provisional government's shortage of men whom it could trust in the opening stages of the civil war.

Cathal Brugha and Harry Boland were killed, one fighting against the government forces and the other attempting to escape from them. Griffith died, aged only fifty-one, but ill and depressed and already a figure belonging to a bygone age. Even though his aims had been achieved beyond all reasonable expectation, in his final weeks he sensed that much of his lifetime's work and his hopes for the future were being destroyed by what he saw as the fanaticism of a younger generation. Then ten days later, on 22 August, Collins was killed in an ambush which Lynch described as 'a most successful operation'.[107] One republican obituary caught some of his qualities, and (although phrased in a naturally partisan manner) illustrated the paradox of his career:

> his buoyant energy, his organising powers, immense industry, and acute and subtle intelligence, his personal charm, gift of oratory and power of commanding implicit devotion in those who served him – all these qualities, together with great personal ambition, he flung without stint into the Republican cause for five years and then, with just the same volcanic energy, skill and resourcefulness into the cause of a Treaty annihilating the Republic.[108]

Collins was the most remarkable figure produced by the Irish revolution, and in the last months of his life his military, administrative and conspiratorial skills were reinforced by a new aptitude for political manoeuvre. His successor was W. T. Cosgrave, the most politically experienced of the pro-treaty Sinn Féin leaders, who united the offices of president of the Dáil and chairman of the provisional government. On the republican side, Erskine Childers, Liam Mellows, Rory O'Connor and at least seventy-four other prisoners were executed.[109] In the midst of these crises and tragedies the second Sinn Féin party died, quietly and almost unnoticed.

Closing time

Throughout the second half of 1922 there were virtually no references to the party at local level, either in the press or elsewhere; a meeting of the North

---

[107] Lynch to Deasy, 28 Aug. 1922, RM, P7/B/90, p. 56.

[108] *Poblacht na hÉireann, Southern edition*, 25 Aug. 1922.

[109] Seventy-seven is the usual total of the executions, though some calculations yield a higher figure.

Meath executive in mid-August is notable for its rarity.[110] On 26 July, a month after the outbreak of the civil war, the Sinn Féin headquarters in Harcourt Street was closed down by Jennie Wyse Power, one of the party's two honorary treasurers. Her reasons were brisk and simple: there was no work to be done, and she did not wish to waste money.[111] Boland and Stack, the two (republican) honorary secretaries, protested at this action, and Stack described it as being 'equivalent to suspending the Sinn Féin Organisation'.[112] He had not realized the messenger was the only staff member left in the building, but his involvement with the party had been limited and such ignorance was hardly surprising.[113] Long afterwards O'Keeffe claimed that he went to the party headquarters with an army lorry and removed valuable documents.[114] The secretary of the St Stephen's Green constituency executive wrote to Harcourt Street seeking directions for Sinn Féin clubs in matters such as funds and affiliation fees, and a copy of his letter bears a pencilled note, 'no use paying affn. fees at the present moment'.[115]

In the immediate aftermath of the treaty the standing committee had decided to vest the party's funds and property in de Valera as trustee, and in October 1922 he wrote to the (pro-treaty) treasurers asking them to implement this decision. At the same time he provided an assurance that the assets would be used for the benefit of the Sinn Féin organization.[116] The treasurers did not reply directly, but instead they summoned a meeting of the standing committee which could authorize them to pay off the party's debts.[117] The republican members of the committee were confused by this move and they sought de Valera's guidance. They pointed out to him that in February the standing committee had been replaced by the officer board, and that when the *ard-fheis* reconvened in May he had announced that the board would retain control of the party until after the election. (No meetings of the board had been held since 1 June.) One of the queries they put to him was, 'what purpose is served by remaining in Sinn Féin Organisation other than cash considerations.'[118]

De Valera was in hiding from the forces of the provisional government, and, fortunately for historians, he communicated with his colleagues in writing. He

[110] *Meath Chronicle*, 19 Aug. 1922.   [111] Joe Clarke to Boland, 27 July 1922, NAI, 2B/82/116(11).

[112] Boland to Wyse Power, 27 July 1922, Stack to Joe Clarke, 29 July 1922, NAI, D/T, S12110B.

[113] Stack to Wyse Power, 18 Aug. 1922, *ibid.*

[114] O'Keeffe, evidence, 30 Apr. 1948, SFFC, 2B/82/118(42), p. 26.

[115] Thomas Darcy to Stack, 6 Sept. 1922, NAI, 2B/82/116(4).

[116] De Valera to Eamonn Duggan, 11 Oct. 1922, NAI, D/T, S12,110B.

[117] Wyse Power and Duggan to Kathleen Lynn, 20 Oct. 1922, NAI, 2B/82/116(4).

[118] Minutes, meeting of republican members, standing committee, 25 Oct. 1922, *ibid.*

replied that Sinn Féin was 'an existing organisation with a constitution exactly suited to Republican purposes and policy'. He believed that the pro-treaty elements were anxious to let the party die, and that, despite their majorities in the standing committee and the *ard-chomhairle*, only financial considerations prevented them from killing it outright. The party's funds and property should be transferred to him. He suggested that republican committees could be formed throughout the country and that their members could be instructed to enter Sinn Féin clubs. They could exert their influence within these clubs, while also being prepared to work separately for anti-treaty candidates in an election.[119]

The next day the two sides confronted each other in 6 Harcourt Street, and the republican members insisted that the officer board should act in place of the full committee. But they were in a minority, they wavered, and one defeatist admitted that they would be satisfied if their opinions were registered in the minutes. The decisive question was whether the officer board should carry on the work of the organization until an *ard-chomhairle* had been summoned, and on this point they were out-voted by eight votes to five. The meeting then continued as one of the standing committee. Agreement was reached on paying off various debts, and the pro-treaty majority endorsed Wyse Power's recent action in refusing to sign cheques to cover the salaries of the office staff. No further expenditure was to be incurred without the standing committee's authority.[120] The minutes were written and signed before those present dispersed, and the committee never met again. (As a postscript, in February 1924 the two treasurers lodged Sinn Féin funds totalling £8,610 with the chancery division of the High Court – an action which would provoke controversy for a further quarter-century.)

De Valera was furious when he learned what had happened, and he wrote that only an *ard-fheis* could put an end to the party; 'to contrive the death of the Organization is deliberate treachery'.[121] Kathleen Lynn, the republican vice-president of the old, united party, who had chaired the final meeting of the standing committee, protested that since the pro-treaty members were in a majority they could do what they liked. She felt little regret at this, and she continued, 'personally I have always thought Sinn Féin unlucky, it held us together only to let us down at the critical moment . . . any real good republicans won't touch it and the Free Staters are determined to kill it'. De Valera reacted forcibly to her letter, praising Sinn Féin's 'glorious record' and reiterating that republicans should have no interest in killing the party.[122]

[119] De Valera to Eamonn Donnelly, 25 Oct. 1922, *ibid.*

[120] Minutes, Sinn Féin standing committee, 26 Oct. 1922, NAI, 2B/82/116(12).

[121] De Valera to Lynn, 28 Oct. 1922, NAI, D/T, S12110B.

[122] Lynn to de Valera, 30 Oct., de Valera to Lynn, 31 Oct. 1922, *ibid.*

Shortly afterwards the republican members convened a meeting of the officer board, and the first item on its agenda was the question of 'Re-opening of Offices'. But Wyse Power and Duggan, her colleague reappeared like avenging angels and announced that their only reason for attending was to reject the board's authority. They made it clear that they would neither hand over any funds nor recognize de Valera as trustee. Having declared that only the standing committee could convene a party *ard-chomhairle*, and that such a move was out of the question because of the condition of the country, they stalked out.[123] It was obvious that pro-treaty elements of Sinn Féin were determined to block any republican moves to take over the remnants of the party.

Cumann na nGaedheal

De Valera was quite right in his belief that his opponents had no interest in retaining or reviving Sinn Féin. Many of them saw the party as tainted by his continuing occupation of the presidency, by its republican constitution which would be difficult to amend, and by distasteful memories of the 'pact' election during which they had been harnessed with their enemies under the banner of Sinn Féin. In denouncing the republicans' actions one treaty supporter remarked that 'men who have been staunch and true all their lives are sick of republicanism, sick even of the name Sinn Féin'.[124] New treatyite structures had grown up in the course of the year, partly within the Sinn Féin organization but to a greater extent independently of it, and these soon began to acquire a life of their own.

The pro-treaty general election committee continued to function on a diminished scale after polling day on 16 June. Griffith believed it was 'absolutely necessary' that the newspaper *An Saorstát/The Free State* should continue after the election, and although he encountered some reluctance (it was noted that 'the paper can hardly ever obtain enough reading matter to make a decent issue') his arguments were accepted in the end. On 29 August all its members agreed 'that the Treaty issue was still paramount and that the Committees should carry on as a pro-Treaty Party'.[125] This intention was to be conveyed to all appropriate TDs. At a special meeting on 7 September Ernest Blythe formally proposed the establishment of a new 'National Party', and after this had been approved unanimously a search for convenient premises was begun.[126]

---

[123] P. J. Little to Austin Stack, 6 Nov. 1922, NAI, 2B/82/116(4).

[124] De Róiste, diary, 28 July 1922, CAI, U271/A/45.

[125] Minutes, pro-treaty committee, 19 June, 29 Aug. 1922, FG, pp. 61, 79.

[126] *Ibid.*, 7 Sept. 1922, p. 87.

In the course of a subsequent discussion Dan McCarthy, the director of elections, proposed that the new party should control the government. This was a more radical break with the past than his colleagues were prepared to accept, and (predictably in the light of recent experience) the reality proved to be very different. The general mood was that they should establish 'a Political Organisation rather than a Party'.[127] The election committee's propaganda department had already come under the control of the Provisional Government, and it was finally absorbed by Desmond FitzGerald's Publicity Department.[128] As had been the case between 1919 and 1921, the government and its bureaucracy would not tolerate excessive signs of independence by the political party.

A month later, on 10 October, a circular from the 'Treaty Election Rooms' referred to suggestions that a new party should be launched. (It was significant that while seven possible names were mentioned, 'Sinn Féin' was not among them.[129]) Mulcahy tried to squash the idea. He believed that the government should continue working out its programme, but that the political atmosphere was unsuitable for activities such as forming a new party, defining its objectives or choosing its name. The only immediate need, he argued, was a machinery which would be revealed as the time for elections approached.[130]

Despite this cool response the organizers persevered, a preliminary conference was held, and on 7 December a meeting took place attended by forty TDs and about sixty others. There was strong opposition to the proposal that 'the Sinn Féin organisation should be captured and kept'. Blythe argued that Sinn Féin had done its work; henceforth the Free State government would implement the party's programme, and a reiteration of ideals was unnecessary when they had in their hands the legislative power to realize their aims. Wyse Power and Milroy warned of the insuperable internal difficulties which would be involved in trying to perpetuate Sinn Féin. In the end there was a large majority in favour of establishing a new political party, the name *Cumann na nGaedheal* was chosen (defeating *An Cumann Náisiúnta* by nineteen votes to sixteen), and from the very beginning the new party adopted the tone which it would maintain. At least for the present there would be no attempt at publicity, and it would have no organizers, but delegates should 'get in touch with the reliable elements in

[127] *Ibid.*, 3 Oct. 1922, p. 95.

[128] FitzGerald to secretary, propaganda committee, 27 July 1922, FG, p. 72.

[129] Brighid Ní Cathain, circular, 10 Oct. 1922, RM, P7/B/325. The names were: An Cumann Náisiunta, People's League, Cumann na nGaedheal, Cumann Sonais na hÉireann, Cumann an tSaorstáit, Páirtí Náisiúnta and United Irishmen.

[130] Mulcahy to Dan McCarthy, 12 Oct. 1922, RM, P7/B/325.

each constituency'.[131] It was to be a modest, respectable, supportive body. Two months later, in February 1923, the final decision was taken to launch the new party throughout the country, but already its TDs had been directed to establish branches in every town and parish.[132]

Cumann na nGaedheal saw itself less as the successor of the pre-treaty Sinn Féin party than of the pro-treaty faction in the split which had divided the movement. One piece of evidence reveals this attitude with particular clarity. It was hardly as a result of mere economy, of the desire to save a few shillings, that Cumann na nGaedheal chose to record its meetings in the same bound volume which had already been used for writing the minutes of the treaty election committee in 1922. Separated only by a missing page, one record flows into the other, and the use of the same book can be seen as a symbol (perhaps unconscious) of continuity and succession.[133]

A few supporters of the treaty protested at the use of Sinn Féin's name by the republicans, and one accused de Valera and his followers of trying 'to confuse the people by donning borrowed plumes'.[134] Most were content to leave the old party behind and move on to a new phase. At least some of Cumann na nGaedheal's attempts to maintain continuity with the past were for merely tactical reasons. One such example was the plan to pay the arrears in rent owed by a moribund Sinn Féin club on the grounds that it was 'important for the organization of the Pro-Treaty party to have a meeting place at its disposal', and that it would be practically impossible to acquire new quarters in the vicinity if the old premises were to be abandoned.[135] There was no sentimental attachment to past glories.

The republican party

On the anti-treaty side de Valera envisaged a far more thorough exercise in taking over the husk of the old Sinn Féin. By autumn 1922 he had become increasingly anxious to re-establish a political base of some sort; without one he was in a weak position *vis-à-vis* the army leaders.

Soon he had an extra need for taking an initiative. He was embarrassed when

---

[131] Minutes, preliminary conference, Cumann na nGaedheal, 7 Dec. 1922, FG, p. 290; 'General election committee' (circular, 21 Dec. 1922), RM, P7/B/325.

[132] James Dolan, circular, 15 Feb. 1923, RM, P7/B/325; Cumann na nGaedheal provisional council minutes, 2 Feb. 1923, FG, p. 302.   [133] Minute book, UCDA, P39/Min/1.

[134] George A. Lyons, *II*, 22 June 1923.

[135] Liam Adderley to Mulcahy, 18 Oct. 1922, RM, P7/B/324.

a memorandum which Liam Mellows had smuggled out of prison was published by the government's publicity department. In it Mellows urged that a provisional republican government should be set up at once; he referred to a scheme by the IRA executive to confiscate and distribute demesnes and ranches; he pointed out that those with a 'stake in the country' had never supported the republic; and he concluded dramatically:

> where is the Government of the Republic? It must be found. Republicans must be provided with a rallying centre and the movement with a focussing point. The unemployment question is acute. Starvation is facing thousands of people. The official Labour movement has deserted the people for the fleshpots of Empire. The F. S. Govt's attitude towards striking postal workers makes clear what its attitude towards workers generally will be. The situation created by all these must be utilised for the Republic.

The government managed to brand the document both as a communistic programme and as a dishonest, cynical gesture. Its damning commentary pointed out that Mellows never claimed that he or his colleagues had been adherents of state socialism, and it warned that 'votes are to be purchased in advance by ruining the "stake-in-the-country" people to provide a bribe for "the men of no property"'.[136] The republicans' conversion to social radicalism was portrayed as an opportunistic ploy to win approval for their purely nationalistic goals. (Mellows's past record would seem to reinforce this interpretation, and in the treaty debates he had expressed concern only about issues such as the oath and the crown.) However sincere or cynical Mellows might have been, de Valera cannot have welcomed the publication of such radical views. He had no wish to see the emergence of a new republican political party whose policies or rhetoric would further alienate the dominant conservative elements in Irish society.

But his immediate problems lay with the republican military commanders. The chief of staff, Liam Lynch, seems to have remained confident of ultimate military success, despite plentiful and accumulating evidence to the contrary. He assumed that the Irish public would change its views and support the radical minority, as it had already done after the 1916 Rising and again after the resumption of hostilities in 1919. All that was needed was perseverance. Just as some of the more moderate republicans did not appreciate that the treaty actually gave them the substance of what they wanted, and that they had won the war against the British, now some of the extremists failed to understand that they had lost the war against the provisional government.

---

[136] *II*, 22 Sept. 1922.

Lynch was a soldier by instinct and temperament; he was a man who, while 'he could have been a great priest . . . did not possess that flexibility of character which would have made him a successful politician'.[137] He was an elitist who ignored the masses, and he described the people as 'merely sheep to be driven anywhere at will'.[138] He remained wary of those who might pander to public opinion, and in the early phase of the war he rejected firmly any idea of forming a republican government. In particular he insisted that only the army executive should consider any peace proposals; this was not the function of politicians who, he suspected, did not share the soldiers' zeal. He remarked that 'the Army has its mind made up to total separation from England; I do not think this also can be said of [the] Party'.[139] Other radicals shared his suspicion of politicians, and from prison Rory O'Connor warned, 'for God's sake beware of the compromising mind of the diplomat'.[140]

A republican writing from Westport revealed the personalized loyalties of many of those involved in the civil war, as well as the IRA's distrust of civilian leaders:

> personally I care a damned sight more at this present moment for Michael Kilroy than for the Irish Republic.
>
> I have no use for the politicians Derrig, Ruttledge and Co. up there in Dublin. Using the fighting men as pawns in a political game and staking Ireland's future in a gambler's throw for their own bid for power.
>
> Is there any hope of peace from your side. I mean from the plain soldiers. De Valera and the wild women are hopeless.[141]

Two months later a press statement by de Valera provoked an angry response from one of the republican soldiers: 'dirty trick, simply for propaganda . . . Wish he were doing some of the fighting.'[142] De Valera might appear intransigent to supporters of the treaty, but to sea-green incorruptible republicans his views were suspiciously moderate. He appreciated that

> the fundamental question is 'the Treaty or not the Treaty' – and we are in a minority on that . . . For Republicans the choice is, therefore, between a heart-breaking surrender of what they have repeatedly proved was dearer to them than life and the repudiation of what they recognise to be the basis of all order in government and the keystone of democracy – majority rule.

---

[137] O'Donoghue, *No other law*, p. 17.   [138] Garvin, *1922*, p. 43.

[139] Lynch to O'Malley, 7, 17 Sept. 1922, RM, P7a/81.

[140] O'Connor to O'Malley, 12 Sept. 1922, EO'M, P17a/62.

[141] John O'Dowd to [?] P. J. McDonnell, 4 Jan. 1923, RM, P7/B/90.

[142] Florence O'Donoghue, diary, 28 Feb. 1923, FO'D, 31,186.

> Is it any wonder that there is, so to speak, a civil war going on in the minds of most of us. [143]

Such complexity and ambivalence were beyond the imaginations of most IRA leaders.

De Valera complained that 'the present position is that *we* have all the public responsibility, and no voice and no authority', and he realized that the republican politicians could not 'get from the Army that unconditional allegiance without which our Government would be a farce'. Partly for this reason, even though it would be constitutionally correct for the party 'acting as legitimate Dáil' to take control of the anti-treaty cause, he rejected the idea and demanded that the army should accept public responsibility. (He also deplored his own earlier folly in supporting Rory O'Connor's repudiation of the Dáil; already his past was catching up with him.)[144] The army executive should call on republican TDs to set up a government, having already agreed in advance the personnel and the broad outlines of policy. De Valera himself had drafted a 'suitable proclamation'.[145]

He was prepared to make peace on the basis of Document No. 2, and he did not 'not want the young fellows who are fighting for the Republic to think otherwise'.[146] He remained devoted to his own idea of external association, even though it was acceptable to no-one else on either side. This obsession paralleled that displayed by Griffith when he had clung for years to his increasingly futile belief in a dual monarchy. De Valera's scheme was forward-looking and even prophetic, while Griffith's had gazed backwards; nonetheless, external association was as inappropriate to the circumstances of 1922 as rosy images of Grattan's Parliament or the Habsburg empire had been in earlier years. The main difference between the two political programmes was that while Griffith's vision was harmless, de Valera's was not. His commitment to his own formula reinforced his rejection of the treaty, and thereby it widened and deepened the divisions which led to civil war. His scheme helped alienate him from the pragmatists who should have been his natural allies, while the radicals viewed it with scorn. In early 1923 Lynch claimed that, in general, the army did not understand such documents; peace could be arranged without referring to them.[147] De Valera, 'the most subtle Irish political intelligence of his generation', was left at the mercy of those whom he regarded as political illiterates.[148]

---

[143] De Valera to McGarrity, 10 Sept. 1922, McG, 17,440.

[144] De Valera to Charles Murphy, 12, 13 Sept. 1922, RM, P7a/162, pp. 13–15.

[145] De Valera, memo to chief of staff and executive, n.d., McG, 17,440.

[146] De Valera to McGarrity, 12 Oct. 1922, McG, *ibid.*

[147] Longford and O'Neill, *Eamon de Valera*, p. 215.   [148] Lee, *Ireland 1912–1985*, p. 150.

At least some members of the republican IRA were anxious for a 'political front' which would function as an auxiliary of the army; Ernie O'Malley remarked that 'there is a war on, and the services of the Political party should be at our disposal'.[149] Eventually, on 17 October 1922, the army executive called on de Valera to form a government and empowered it to make peace, 'provided such arrangement does not bring the country in to the British Empire. Final decision on this question to be submitted for ratification to the Executive.'[150] Shortly afterwards, some of the republican deputies who were still at liberty met in secret and invited him to resume the presidency and to nominate a cabinet. As usual, however, they played only a supporting role; he was duly proclaimed president 'in the name of the army', whose members saw themselves as 'the final custodians of the Republic'.[151] Opponents of the treaty now had a civilian as well as a military leadership, even if one was the creature of the other.

De Valera repudiated the new Dáil, which had finally convened the previous month, although in the days of his pact with Collins he had taken part in the election which created it. Instead, he maintained the continuing legitimacy of its predecessor. Despite his readiness to accept a compromise settlement (provided, of course, that he could dictate its terms), his official communiqué of 5 November 1922 declared that 'the principles which Republicans are defending are by their nature irreducible and not open to compromise. Victory for the Republic, or utter defeat and extermination, are now the alternatives.'[152] He was still boxed in by the extremists, and he remained the political leader of a movement which had little time for politics or politicians.[153] He held no military rank and at times the soldiers treated him with scant respect; as he pointed out towards the end of the war, 'the old contempt for civil or semi-civil work apparently persists'.[154] His treatyite enemies sneered that he was 'unwanted now even by those whom his vanity forced into the field against their countrymen'.[155]

The new republican 'government' was partly controlled by the military, and this strengthened de Valera's determination to establish a political organization which would give him a position of genuine authority. He was already head of a party, the now-moribund Sinn Féin, and he was anxious to realize the potential which this position offered him. One of his prime objectives was to fill the

[149] O'Malley to Deasy, 9 Sept. 1922, Captured documents collection, IMA, lot 3(1)(c).

[150] Executive meeting minutes, 17 Oct. 1922, FO'D, 31,258.

[151] *Republic of Ireland*, 26, 28 Oct. 1922.

[152] De Valera, communiqué, *Daily Bulletin*, 33, 6 Nov. 1922, RM, P7a/158.

[153] Coogan, *De Valera*, p. 327.

[154] De Valera to M. P. Colivet, 13 Mar. 1923, Longford and O'Neill, *Eamon de Valera*, p. 207.

[155] *Free State*, 21 Oct. 1922, editorial.

vacuum which supporters of the treaty had created so gratuitously; to take over the old party's name, its image, and as much of its structure and property as possible. The simplest means of doing this would be by summoning and controlling a Sinn Féin *ard-fheis*, and already two months earlier Stack had written that this would be worth a hundred Dáil meetings.[156] But Jennie Wyse Power had effectively prevented the republicans from using the officer board to convene such an assembly. There remained an alternative, since the constitution laid down that an *ard-fheis* could be summoned by a petition from 200 branches. Accordingly, a circular was sent to opponents of the treaty urging them to organize republican groups within surviving clubs and to take them over, if necessary by building up republican strength within branches which had pro-treaty majorities.

He still feared what his opponents might do, since 'if Sinn Féin is reorganised in its old form and the others have a majority, as they are likely to have, they would be able to select their candidates, etc., etc. in case of an election and we would have no organisation at all'. But the more obvious it was that republicans were involved in reviving and organizing clubs, the more likely it would be that suspicious treatyites would stay away from them.[157] This optimism was soon vindicated, and within a few days his colleague P. J. Ruttledge was able to express confidence that the Free State government intended to abandon Sinn Féin.[158]

On New Year's Day 1923, de Valera and Stack issued a circular in which they referred to the closing down of the party headquarters, and announced that these would soon reopen (under republican management). With unconvincing bravado they repeated de Valera's rash claim of the previous April, that 'Ireland is really ours for the taking' – yet another incautious remark which his enemies would later use against him.[159] But even de Valera could not bring himself to treat the party with any generosity. He remarked to Ruttledge that 'the political organisation ought to be self-supporting, once it is started, and it should be called upon also to pay back to the [republican] Government the money which is now being spent in getting it going again'.[160] Old habits died hard.

These efforts were complicated by the final flicker at local level of the old, united Sinn Féin party: an attempt by nineteen Dublin clubs to summon a special *ard-fheis* which would attempt to end the war. Those who were involved in the scheme appealed to all Sinn Féin constituency executives for help in

[156] Stack to Charles Murphy, 17 Aug. 1922, McKenna Napoli MSS, NLI, 22,620.

[157] De Valera to Stack, 6 Jan. 1923, NAI, D/T, S1297.

[158] Ruttledge to Donnelly, 12 Jan. 1923, NAI, 1094/2/1.

[159] De Valera and Stack, circular, 1 Jan. 1923, NAI, 1094/1/10a.

[160] De Valera to Ruttledge, 5 Jan. 1923, NAI, 1094/2/1.

reconvening the adjourned *ard-fheis* of February/May 1922 and in using it as a means of trying to restoring peace.[161] This worthy Sinn Féin peace committee made no impact whatever on the course of the civil war, and it soon faded away. A far more significant obstacle facing de Valera and his supporters was the harassment which republican Sinn Féin experienced at the hands of the Free State forces. On one occasion the raiders were led by Páidín O'Keeffe himself.[162]

De Valera also had to overcome the obstacle posed by the dislike which some of his followers felt for the name 'Sinn Féin'; in this they agreed fully with their enemies in Cumann na nGaedheal. Plunkett told him that the Sinn Féin organization was dead and that it was 'held in contempt pretty generally'.[163] The old distaste for politics, characteristic of the Volunteers, was continued in different ways by both the pro- and the anti-treaty factions of Sinn Féin. At times it seemed as if de Valera was the only prominent politician in the country who wished to retain the identity and title of the former party. He conceded in one letter that 'the name "Sinn Féin" is, I know, distasteful to many, particularly to some of the old I.R.A. men', but went on to enthuse about its connotations of

> self-recognition, self-reliance, always acting as if Ireland was without ques-
> tion a sovereign independent State and the people of Ireland the exclusive
> source of all authority, and the complete ignoring of any right claimed by
> England to interfere in our affairs . . . This is what the words Sinn Féin mean
> to me.[164]

He still encountered resistance, and his organizing committee recommended founding a body which would be called the 'Irish Republican Political Organisation'. But he would not compromise, and he informed his colleagues that if any of them could not be associated with the take-over of Sinn Féin along the lines which he proposed, they should leave. He concluded with his credo: 'to me, Sinn Féin meant the nation organised. I never regarded it as a mere political machine.'[165] It is clear that several of his colleagues *did* regard it in exactly this manner, and the next day he was informed that they supported unanimously (but provisionally) the English-language name of 'the Irish Independence League'.[166] Although their opposition continued for some time, de Valera had his way in the end and the name 'Sinn Féin' was retained by the new party. He was also conscious of the need for speed, and he was alarmed by

---

[161] Dublin Sinn Féin peace committee, circular, 13 Jan. 1923, RB, 8786(4).

[162] *Republic of Ireland*, 5 Feb. 1923.   [163] Plunkett to de Valera, 20 Jan. 1923, EdeV.

[164] De Valera to Fr Thomas Burbage, May 1923, NAI, D/T, S1297.

[165] De Valera to organizing committee, 31 May 1923, *ibid.*

[166] Eoin Ó Caoimh to de Valera, 1 June 1923, NAI, 1094/8/11.

the emergence of different groups representing farmers, labour and other interests, all of which were opposed to the Cosgrave government:

> if they succeed in organising themselves to any considerable extent it will be nearly impossible to unite them again for a purely national purpose.
>
> It is vital, therefore, that the reorganisation of Sinn Féin as *the* national organisation should be pushed forward with all speed.[167]

All attempts to restructure Irish political life along 'normal' Western lines, and to ease it away from its concentration on nationalist issues, on symbols, on questions of Anglo-Irish relations; all these must be blocked at once. They *were* blocked, and the treaty remained the main symbolic issue of contention in Irish public life for decades to come. The rival successors of the second Sinn Féin party would dominate the politics of independent Ireland.

---

[167] De Valera to A. L., 16 May 1923, NAI, 1094/8/1.

Epilogue:
after the Civil War

11

IRISH REPUBLICANS:
FUNDAMENTALISTS AND COMPROMISERS

The election of June 1922 confirmed what all sides had known for the previous six months: a large majority of the Irish people favoured the treaty. Most of those electors who had never sympathized with Sinn Féin probably supported the 'third party' candidates, who gained 39.7 per cent of the first preference votes. (This group also included disillusioned separatists who were dismayed by the drift towards civil war.) It is correspondingly likely that the bulk of those who voted for Sinn Féin candidates were former members or supporters of the party. The 'panel' vote split 64.4 to 35.6 per cent in favour of the treaty. Collins's faction thus had a strong claim to be the principal heir of the old united Sinn Féin. His successors disowned the party's name, but they could still assert rights of inheritance. Whether they liked it or not (and some did not), 'treatyites' were prominent among the descendants of the Easter rebels and the post-rising Sinn Féin.

The new government ruled in a more rational and modern way than the British had done, and it began implementing traditional separatist, Sinn Féin policies – as in its encouragement and imposition of the Irish language. Over the next few years Cumann na nGaedheal was able to convince most of the Free State's population that in some respects (although certainly not in others) a revolution *had* occurred. Even though mistakes were made and opportunities were lost, they were made and lost by an Irish and not by a British government. For this reason, some of its sins were forgiven.

Its greatest triumph, the consolidation of Irish democracy, was illustrated by the army mutiny of 1924. This incident involved a military ultimatum to the government and disputes between rival elements within the national army, between the IRB and the 'IRA Organization'; it was dismissed blithely by O'Higgins as 'a faction fight between two letters of the alphabet'.[1] The mutiny was a confused affair in which what did not happen was more important than

---

[1] *DE, official report*, 7, col. 3,156 (26 June 1924), cited in Terence de Vere White, *Kevin O'Higgins* (London, 1948), p. 163.

what did. Richard Mulcahy, the minister for defence, supported by three senior generals, used controversial measures to overcome dissent within the army. He was then forced to resign, and the generals were dismissed. Despite this harsh treatment, they did not exploit their military positions to overawe, let alone overthrow, their former colleagues.[2] Independence had been achieved largely by military means, and so had democratic, majority rule during the civil war, but civilians would dominate the new Free State.

Cosgrave's government faced daunting challenges. The widespread disruption caused by the civil war was compounded by an economic depression, and independence was followed by years of hardship rather than by years of plenty. The twenty-six-county Free State was not the resurrected Ireland envisaged by Pearse and Griffith; as Bulmer Hobson remarked long afterwards, 'the Phoenix of our youth has fluttered to earth such a miserable old hen'.[3] The difficulties and disillusionments which accompanied independence gave hope to Cumann na nGaedheal's critics, and in 1925 Mary MacSwiney believed there was

> no doubt that if the Free State had been an economical success and had made the people prosperous, it would be all the more difficult to bring the country back to a sense of its national duty, but the people are worse off today than they have been for many years; they are sick of the Free State and in a very short time they will express their dissatisfaction.[4]

The scale of destruction in 1922–3, and the resulting debts which burdened the new state, forced or enticed the government into those parsimonious measures for which it became notorious. The republicans were responsible for this destruction, and then they used its cost to win votes from a forgetful or opportunistic electorate.[5] Yet despite these grave problems which confronted the new Free State, its opponents could not shake its solidity.

De Valera had ensured that he would retain the name and the symbolic power of Sinn Féin, even though he represented only a minority of those who belonged to the old party. It had died in the course of 1922, but successors bearing its title and representing some of its ideals survived throughout the rest of the century. Their history forms no more than a postscript to that of the second Sinn Féin party, but a brief study of their unhappy careers illustrates aspects of Irish nationalism in general and of republicanism in particular. This final chapter will examine one of the legacies of the Sinn Féin movement which

---

[2] See Valiulis, *Portrait of a revolutionary*, pp. 215–16.

[3] Hobson to Denis McCullough, 5 May 1953, McCullough MSS, UCDA, P120/17.

[4] MacSwiney to Fr Maher, 27 Oct. 1925, cited in Murphy, 'Politics and ideology', p. 253.

[5] Garvin, *1922*, p. 164.

MIDNIGHT ASSASSINS
RAID ON
MRS ℰᴀⱮⱷη ᴆℯ Vᴀ⌊ℯRᴀ.

11.1 Republican propaganda: 'Midnight assassins raid on Mrs De Valera', watercolour by Countess Markievicz

flourished after the Easter Rising – the fortunes and misfortunes of those who clung to its name.

The third Sinn Féin

The circumstances were unpromising when republicans made their first efforts to revive and to take over the old Sinn Féin party in January 1923. The civil war was then in its grimmest phase, and thirty-four of the seventy-seven executions which were carried out by the Free State authorities took place during that month. The government tried to cripple its new rival, and opponents of the treaty were harassed in ways which seemed familiar to those among them who had been active against the British between 1918 and 1921; their leading figures were jailed or forced to go on the run, offices were raided, files were seized, supporters were attacked and meetings were disrupted. They had to wait until the fighting stopped before they could make serious efforts to create a political party. Not until May 1923 did the republican IRA lay down its arms, hoping in vain for a suitable occasion to renew the conflict. (From 1922–3 onwards the name 'IRA', hallowed by its association with the war against the British, was confined to a small group of extremists who were unrepresentative of most Irish nationalists.)

De Valera had long been impatient to resume his political activities, and by now even some of the more militant republicans were prepared to follow his lead. They appreciated that further armed resistance to the Free State was futile, and they hoped that they could follow the example of those Easter rebels who, *faute de mieux*, had transferred their energies so successfully to the electoral battlefield in 1917. P. J. Ruttledge, the republican IRA's adjutant-general, announced that it was the duty of every soldier to join and organize Sinn Féin clubs.[6] A public meeting to re-establish the party was held in the Mansion House on 11 June, but only sixteen branches were represented and less than 150 people attended. This *ad hoc* gathering elected a new organizing committee whose immediate task was to prepare for the forthcoming general election.

De Valera believed that one reason why republicans should take over the old Sinn Féin party was that they had been faithful to the 1917 constitution and did not need to change it.[7] Yet this new, third Sinn Féin violated the constitution by ignoring the officer board and its (pro-treaty) standing committee, and thereby it broke the continuity between the post-rising and the post-civil war-parties.[8] At the time, however, such quibbles would have seemed unimportant or irrelevant.

The republicans made the crucial decision to abstain from the Free State legislature in Leinster House; they viewed the second Dáil elected in May 1921 as the country's only legitimate parliament, and dismissed its successor as a mere imposter. They remained loyal to the body which had voted in favour of the hated treaty. (Also, as O'Higgins reminded them, they chose to ignore the awkward facts that de Valera had been rejected by their revered second Dáil when he ran for re-election as president, and that many of his principal colleagues were subsequently repudiated by the electorate.[9]) Some radicals were

---

[6] Ruttledge to commanding officers, 28 May 1923, NAI, D/T 1297.

[7] De Valera to Ruttledge, 15 Jan. 1923, NAI, 1094/2/1.

[8] Kingsmill Moore, judgment, 26 Oct. 1948, SFFC, 2B/82/117(32), pp. 41, 45.

[9] *DE, official report*, 2, cols. 69–70 (8 Dec. 1922).

predictably dubious about becoming embroiled yet again in the tedious business of politics, but the IRA gave its blessing to anti-treaty candidates.

The party had numerous obstacles to overcome. Many of its leaders and 10,000 of its supporters were in jail or in internment camps, and according to Sinn Féin's reorganizing committee sixty-four of its eighty-five candidates were unable to address the electors for one reason or another.[10] But it possessed dedicated party workers who were determined to avenge their defeat in the civil war, and an inept government also provided them with the sort of publicity for which any political party would be grateful. De Valera announced that, although he was in hiding and was liable to detention, he would address an election meeting in Ennis on 15 August. He was arrested in the course of his speech and was escorted from the platform by Free State troops amidst gunfire and confusion – enabling republicans to portray him plausibly as the victim of a repressive and undemocratic administration.

Sinn Féin performed much better than most observers had expected. The party was the political wing of an army which had recently waged a disastrous civil war in defiance of the majority of the people. Nonetheless it gained a respectable 27.4 per cent of the vote; this was 6 per cent more than the republican wing of Sinn Féin had secured a year earlier, in June 1922. Forty-four Sinn Féin candidates were returned, while two months earlier de Valera's minimum target had been a mere twenty.[11] Republicans won four of the seven seats in Kerry, where atrocities carried out by the Free State army had alienated most of the population, and they headed the poll in four constituencies. Much of the increased vote for Sinn Féin can be explained by the fact that every seat was contested – for the first time ever in an Irish general election (although Northern Ireland continued to follow traditional patterns for decades to come). The party secured a high percentage of the votes in those western counties where the candidates had been returned unopposed in 1922.[12]

This encouraging result concealed underlying weaknesses. Like its predecessor between 1917 and 1922, the new Sinn Féin party was a coalition of different elements, and while it no longer included any non-republicans it remained an uneasy combination of extremists and (relative) moderates, of ideologues and politicians, of fundamentalists and realists. The treaty and the civil war had brought together people of different habits and assumptions, and when peace was restored the divisions between them became steadily more apparent. The

---

[10] Peter Pyne, 'The new Irish state and the decline of the republican Sinn Féin party, 1923–1926', *Éire-Ireland*, 11, 3 (1976), p. 38.

[11] Thomas P. O'Neill, 'In search of a political path: Irish republicanism, 1922 to 1927', in G. A. Hayes-McCoy (ed.), *Historical Studies*, X (Galway, 1976), p. 152.　　[12] See above, p. 408.

third Sinn Féin experienced on a smaller scale and at a slower pace the same sort of problems which had destroyed the second.

De Valera realized that he and his followers were faced with

> not an obviously alien administration, but what appears on the surface to be a home administration set up by, and apparently willing to be deposed by, a majority vote of the people governed . . . the F. S. people have got behind the shield of popular approval and we must get inside it before we can hope to make any real progress.[13]

He sought to wriggle off the dilemma on which he had impaled himself: his dependence on the support of impractical extremists whose commitment to an abstentionist policy would alienate them from the electorate and ensure that they could never win power. They would become politically extinct, reduced to a position comparable to that of the French monarchists.[14] He argued that the party should organize not merely dedicated republicans but also what he called 'Nationalist' or 'Independence' opinion; 'if we do not do it, the other side will and the loss will be immense'. He saw its position as being similar to that of the separatists in late 1916 and early 1917.[15]

But for almost a year de Valera's imprisonment deprived Sinn Féin of its most moderate and sensible voice, and many of his colleagues saw no need to re-think old policies in the light of new circumstances. They failed to appreciate that while abstention from parliament had been a relatively successful tactic between 1917 and 1921, when it was employed against what was perceived to be an alien British government, it was likely to have only a limited appeal to an electorate which was now faced with a native Irish administration. The voters wanted their representatives to act on their behalf as 'constituency ombudsmen'.[16]

A number of republican deputies decided that they would try to enter the new Dáil in Leinster House without taking the oath of fidelity to the king (which by now was widely called the 'oath of allegiance'), but their plan was thwarted when the clerk of the Dáil announced in advance that no TDs would be admitted until they had signed the oath. The opposition 'cabinet' then reiterated its established policy, and abstention soon became a habit as well as a principle. Some republicans were afflicted by self-doubt and seemed unconvinced by their own arguments; at a meeting of their own rival (second) 'Dáil' in January 1924, Countess Markievicz declared that to pose as the government of the republic

---

[13] De Valera to Plunkett, 12 July 1923, EdeV.   [14] O'Neill, 'In search of a political path', p. 162.

[15] De Valera to organizing committee, 31 May 1923, NAI, 1094/1/11.

[16] Peter Pyne, 'The third Sinn Fein party: 1923–1926', *Economic and Social Review*, 1, 2 (1969–70), p. 252. See above, p. 250.

was no more than pretence and play-acting; 'the people have turned us down'. Count Plunkett had less respect for the people's opinions, and he retorted that the question of the majority did not arise, that the republicans' 'government' existed independently of the majority.[17]

The party made substantial progress during its first year. A network of clubs spread throughout the country, and their total increased from 16 in June 1923 to 729 in November.[18] At least on paper, the new Sinn Féin could bear comparison with the old. But in other respects it was passive, and its newpaper complained of the party's laziness and mental dullness, its readiness to wait for something to turn up, and its reliance on the Free State's blunders.[19] Sinn Féin was soon enmeshed in financial problems, with the result that staff members were dismissed, activities were curtailed, and a decision was taken to borrow money. It was haunted by unpaid bills in many parts of the country, and by early 1925 almost every constituency executive was burdened with debts.[20] The republicans were unable to establish a daily paper.

Above all, Sinn Féin failed to develop the electoral momentum which it displayed briefly in 1923. In the course of subsequent by-elections the party contested twenty-three seats and won only four. Its record in local elections was equally unimpressive, and its performance in Northern Ireland was even worse. When it decided to contest the United Kingdom general election in October 1924 the two sitting Devlinite MPs for Fermanagh–Tyrone stood aside in an effort to avoid splitting the nationalist ranks, but the non-unionist vote crashed from 87,671 to 13,497. Despite determined electioneering, all the Sinn Féin candidates were defeated. There was a similar result in the elections for the Belfast parliament seven months later; the party's total of seats fell from six to two, while the Nationalists' rose from six to ten. The pattern of the 1918 elections was confirmed, and henceforth the minority community in Northern Ireland preferred moderate candidates to extremists. Sinn Féin's membership declined in parallel with its electoral failures in both parts of the island, and by March 1925 the number of affiliated branches throughout the country had fallen to 357.[21]

All these developments made political activity seem less attractive to the IRA. In October 1922 the army executive had been prepared, as de Valera later told the republican second Dáil, to 'give allegiance to this government when it was

---

[17] Murphy, *Patrick Pearse*, pp. 142–3.

[18] Secretary's report, *ard-chomhairle*, 27 Nov. 1923, NAI, 2B/82/116(16), p. 15.

[19] Pyne, 'Third Sinn Fein', p. 250.

[20] Standing committee minutes, 8 Aug. 1924, NAI, 2B/82/117(22); hon. secretaries to constituency executives, 8 May 1925, NAI, 2B/82/116(18), p. 62.

[21] Honorary secretaries' report, 19 Mar. 1925, NAI, 2B/82/116(18).

set up, the personnel having been approved in advance';[22] in effect, the army then restored its own nominal subjection to civilian control which its convention had repudiated the previous March, in the aftermath of the treaty. Only when they faced military defeat at the hands of the pro-treaty forces were the soldiers prepared to share responsibility with politicians. The republican IRA was demoralized for some time after the civil war, and it faced enough problems of its own without having to worry about political matters as well. But the military leaders were unimpressed by the achievements of the 'second Dáil' and the third Sinn Féin party, and they wished to preserve the army from any dissensions within these bodies over the question of the abstention policy.[23] In November 1925 the decision which it had taken three years earlier was revoked in its turn.

The IRA, 'tiring of the tedium of politics, abandoned . . . yet again the pretence of deriving its authority from the Irish people, and vested all authority once more in the army council'.[24] One reason given for this action was that the 'government' had developed into 'a mere political party'.[25] There were to be no more lapses such as that which took place during the civil war, and from this time onwards the IRA leaders would always act in the belief that they were responsible to themselves alone. In this respect they followed in the footsteps of the pre-rising IRB whose supreme council had also regarded itself as the government of the 'Irish republic'.

De Valera's departure

These failures made de Valera all the more determined to escape from the impasse into which his own policies had led him. The defection of the IRA removed one of his many problems, and he no longer needed to fear military interference with his plans. He continued his efforts to evade the deadening embrace of those fundamentalists who rejected all flexibility or compromise, but until outside events provided a catalyst his wary colleagues blocked his attempts to break free.

Many Irish nationalists were enraged and ashamed by the failure of the boundary commission which had been established by the treaty, and by the decision of the Dublin, London and Belfast governments to leave intact the border between north and south. There was a widespread feeling that the new

---

[22] *Comhairle na dteachtaí*, minutes, 7 Aug. 1924, Gaughan, *Austin Stack*, p. 320.

[23] Pyne, 'Third Sinn Fein', p. 43.   [24] Lee, *Ireland 1912–1985*, p. 151.

[25] *Report of general army convention, 14th and 15th Novr. 1926* [recte 1925], NAI, D/T, S 5880.

settlement discredited both the treaty and its Cumann na nGaedheal supporters. Republicans were frustrated at being unable to join forces effectively with
the other political parties in the Free State, all of which opposed this agreement.
Even Austin Stack revealed an open mind when he asked de Valera whether Sinn
Féin deputies might be able to bring down the government if they dropped their
policy of abstention:

> could we do it? I mean would there be sufficient opposition to enable us to
> turn the scale? Oath and all I would be inclined to favour the idea (tho' my
> mind is not quite made up) if our going in would defeat the proposal.
> Would it not be the end of the Free State? And what better issue than ter-
> ritorial integrity?[26]

In the event Sinn Féin did not seek admission to Leinster House and Cosgrave's
government was able to survive its humiliation. But de Valera was now prepared
to act decisively in abandoning the old rigid policies which had left the republican movement as a mere spectator of great events, adhering to its outmoded
principles and watching in impotent purity while history was made by its
enemies.

In January 1926 he announced that he would enter the Dáil if he could do so
without taking the oath. (Characteristically, he did not inform the Sinn Féin
standing committee that he was about to make such a statement.[27]) At a specially convened party ard-fheis two months later, MacSwiney, O'Flanagan, Stack
and others opposed his suggestion that, once the oath had been removed,
entrance to the Dáil would become an issue of policy rather than of principle.
MacSwiney rightly dismissed as absurd the idea that the Cosgrave government
would give way on the question. O'Flanagan's amendment, declaring that such
a step was incompatible with Sinn Féin principles, was passed by a narrow
margin (of 223 votes to 218) and was then in turn defeated (by 179 votes to 177)
when it was proposed as a substantive motion. The party was divided more
evenly than the Dáil had been four years earlier, when it debated the treaty.[28]
The split was soon formalized, de Valera resigned the presidency which he had
held since the convention of October 1917, and he and his followers left Sinn
Féin. Shortly afterwards he founded his own new party, Fianna Fáil.

De Valera had remained president of Sinn Féin after the treaty split, but he
soon realized that the party was an unsuitable means of regaining power; its
monarchist pedigree antagonized some republican supporters, and its leadership included too many unworldly zealots. By 1926 Sinn Féin had become little

---

[26] Stack to de Valera, 4 Dec. 1925, EdeV.   [27] Murphy, *Patrick Pearse*, p. 156.
[28] *IT*, 11 Mar. 1926.

more than a burden, but by then – in contrast to his position in 1922–3 – he no longer needed it, and if he could not control the party he could safely abandon it. (In similar fashion the pro-treaty majority had felt able to jettison its predecessor during the civil war.) He could at last escape from the extremists into whose clutches he had thrown himself so unwisely in 1922. He left behind (probably with relief) colleagues such as MacSwiney, O'Flanagan, J. J. O'Kelly, Plunkett and Stack, inflexible partners whose commitment had always outweighed their competence and common sense. At this stage of his career it might be said of de Valera, as was said of Bismarck, that his genius lay in tying himself up in knots and then brilliantly escaping from them.[29]

Most of the politically talented republicans followed de Valera into Fianna Fáil, and – as subsequent events proved – so did most of the republican voters. From the beginning the new party showed an energy and efficiency which the third Sinn Féin had lacked. It was dissatisfied with simply upholding principles, it was concerned with achieving power, and it soon launched a campaign to win over uncommitted voters along with staunch republicans. New branches were formed and new members were recruited. The secretary of the 'fourth', rump Sinn Féin party commented ruefully that 'the other people are most active. It is surprising that they were not able to show any energy or activity during the past year or two.'[30] The party made only a feeble response while officers and thousands of individual members defected to its rival.[31]

De Valera remained determined to block the emergence of class alignments and to perpetuate Irish political divisions along their old nationalistic patterns. He believed it was vital

> that the Free State be shaken at the *next* General Election, for if an opportunity be given it to consolidate itself further as an institution, if the present Free State members are replaced by Farmers and Labourers and other class interests, the national interest as a whole will be submerged in the clashing of the rival economic groups.[32]

Nonetheless, he would not repeat the mistakes of the third Sinn Féin, and his programme provided a synthesis of constitutional and social demands. Unlike his more austere rivals he appreciated that his republican policy could expect to win the support of no more than a section of the population, and he was prepared to appeal to voters' self-interest as well as to their idealism, to their wallets as well as to their hearts. Fianna Fáil concerned itself with material issues such

---

[29] A. J. P. Taylor, *Bismarck* (London, 1955), p. 73.

[30] Daithi Ó Donnchadha to Mary MacSwiney, 28 Apr. 1926, MacS, P48a/42(28).

[31] Gaughan, *Austin Stack*, p. 253.   [32] De Valera to McGarrity, 13 Mar. 1926, McG, 17,441.

as Irish farmers' payment of annuities to the British government, and it urged the protection of vulnerable industries against foreign competition. It would be a populist party. Although its leading members had supported the army against the majority of the people during the civil war, Fianna Fáil soon began to display greater political skill than its pro-treaty opponents. With good reason it prided itself on its realism.

On the periphery

The Sinn Féin party never recovered from the defection of de Valera and his politically minded colleagues. A mere 200 delegates attended its *ard-fheis* later in the year, and the party's condition was so desperate that it would have been forced to vacate its headquarters soon afterwards if Austin Stack, supported by one of the remaining branches, had not provided £10 to pay the rent for at least another month.[33] Its plight was comparable to that of Griffith's party before the rising.

Mary MacSwiney wanted Sinn Féin to abstain from the general election of June 1927, arguing that it could not hope to secure a majority because of the split within the anti-treaty ranks, but Plunkett believed that to cease contesting elections would 'sacrifice one of the very few means of showing that our movement is alive'.[34] A mere fifteen candidates were nominated, and only five of these were elected. Fianna Fáil's leadership, vigour and more attractive programme enabled it to inherit the bulk of the anti-treaty vote, and it won forty-four seats.

Shortly afterwards Kevin O'Higgins was assassinated by republican extremists. When the Sinn Féin standing committee met a day later Stack proposed that the party should deplore the murder, but none of the other nine members who were present seconded his resolution;[35] they were not prepared to condemn violence against such a formidable opponent. By contrast, the government's response was drastic. A new bill would oblige all parliamentary candidates to promise in advance that they would take their seats if elected. Voters would be denied the right to choose abstentionist candidates; de Valera would be forced to swallow his pride and his words, along with the oath of fidelity to the king; and Ireland would at last become a normal democracy with all its main political elements represented in parliament. From Cosgrave's point of view his measure would have the additional benefit of making de Valera appear

---

[33] Standing committee minutes, 11 Dec. 1926, NAI, 2B/82/117(26), p. 10.

[34] Murphy, 'Politics and ideology', p. 288; Plunkett to MacSwiney, 10 Sept. 1926, MacS, P48a/42(44).   [35] Standing committee minutes, 11 July 1927, NAI, 2B/82/117(26), p. 31.

inconsistent and hypocritical, and the new Fianna Fáil party might even fall apart. (Shortly before his death O'Higgins himself had expected a split of this sort.[36]) One incidental consequence of the government's measure was that an abstentionist party such as Sinn Féin could no longer contest elections.

Fianna Fáil deputies entered the Dáil after taking the oath – which de Valera now felt able to dismiss as 'an empty formula'. Many people wished that he had been equally perceptive five years earlier. As the government had hoped, this change of policy further discredited him in many people's eyes, but it did him no damage in terms of electoral support. His decision was vindicated when new elections were held in September 1927 and Fianna Fáil made further advances – even though Cumann na nGaedheal also improved its position, and was able to remain in office for another term. Sinn Féin remained aloof from the contest, but the new legislation was not the only reason for this inaction; its financial problems ruled out any new expenditure.[37] With the exception of its involvement in two by-election campaigns in 1936, another thirty years would elapse before it again ran candidates for the Dáil.

After 1927 independent Ireland evolved into what was effectively a two-party system. Cumann na nGaedheal and Fianna Fáil battled for supremacy, and few outsiders took any interest in the activities of a minor group which was committed to abstaining from the national parliament. Because its principles forbade it to contest Free State elections, the fourth Sinn Féin party was deprived of the need to behave responsibly or to seek public support. It retreated into a republican ghetto where its members were free to act in a self-righteous, self-indulgent and self-destructive manner, and throughout the following decades it became little more than a society of ageing and quarrelsome idealists.

As in so many other small political factions which were committed to hopeless causes, feuds and purges over minor matters of principle helped to while away the idle years. Art O'Connor, de Valera's successor as president of the 'second Dáil', was forced to resign because he had been called to the bar and would therefore be obliged to recognize the Free State. (His critic Mary MacSwiney admitted with touching naïveté that she knew he had studied law, 'but somehow it never occurred to me that he meant to practice'.) Other colleagues engaged in suspect activities; for example, Plunkett recognized the enemy government by paying his taxes, possessing a car licence, and applying for a Free State passport. For family reasons even MacSwiney herself acquired a passport, but this did not engender any greater understanding towards others; she resigned from Sinn Féin in disgust when Fr O'Flanagan was re-elected pres-

---

[36] White, *Kevin O'Higgins*, p. 236.

[37] Standing committe minutes, 28 Aug. 1927, NAI, 2B/82/117(26), p. 37.

THE HEN THAT TOOK **5** YEARS TO LAY AN **EGG**

and then it was empty

11.2 Cumann na nGaedheal propaganda

ident in 1934. His crime was to have become a servant of the Free State by editing a series of schoolbooks. (He did so because he was destitute.[38]) Not long afterwards he was expelled from the party over another trivial issue: his participation in a radio broadcast commemorating the first Dáil.

One long-serving member of the standing committee, Laurence Raul, pointed out that neither Sinn Féin nor the Catholic Church had anything new to offer, since both institutions were founded on truth.[39] Life was exacting but uncomplicated. Sinn Féin had long ago ceased to think or act politically, and to an extent the party and the uncompromising republican members of the second Dáil saw themselves as the guardians of a sacred flame, keeping it alight in the hope that it might guide a later and luckier generation. They represented some

---

[38] Murphy, 'Politics and ideology', pp. 257–8, 312, 350–5.
[39] Carroll, *They have fooled you again*, p. 204.

of the attitudes which had characterized the IRB in the years before it was revitalized by Tom Clarke and Bulmer Hobson; in their own eyes, at least, the wheel had come full circle. They may not have been tolerant or skilful or imaginative, but at least they were consistent. Their attitude is summed up by a passage in J. J. O'Kelly's presidential address to the party in 1928:

> the most obvious results of the Fianna Fáil apostasy have been the inevitable drift and shelving of principles that everywhere follow political compromise . . . The movement prospered while it was kept on a plane too exalted for the corrupt to thrive in . . . we have no prospects to offer but the old unrequited service to a deathless cause.[40]

The party became ever more irrelevant to the concerns of both its friends and its enemies. In reaction to a series of IRA attacks Cosgrave's government banned the IRA itself, Cumann na mBan and ten other groups, but Sinn Féin was considered to be harmless and was left in peace. This insult was reminiscent of the Parliamentary Party's exemption from arrest in May 1918. The party's financial problems worsened. Total expenditure between July 1933 and September 1934 amounted to £463, while only a decade earlier the sum of £2,400 had been spent on one by-election alone.[41] In so far as the third and fourth Sinn Féin parties were a continuation of the second, 'a great national movement had become a political curiosity'.[42]

The position of the republican 'Dáil' of 1921 was even more precarious. The 1926 split resulted in a mass defection, and over the years its numbers dwindled even further. Since by definition the 'deputies' could not be replaced, they worried about what would happen when they died out. By 1938 their membership had fallen to seven. The IRA chief of staff had a simple answer to this problem: the republican government had been established at the request of the army in October 1922, and it should have ceased its activities when the soldiers withdrew their allegiance three years later.[43]

Ultimately the second Dáil followed this grim logic, and in December 1938 it handed over all its powers to the IRA. Its members hoped innocently that the army might renew its allegiance some day. One reason why the republican Dáil

---

[40] Speech, 28 Nov. 1928, HC:DD, II, p. 129. O'Kelly was also addicted to anti-Semitic rant; he believed, for example, that 'in the designs of Anti-Christ [Britain] is to-day the prey of rival groups of unscrupulous Jews'. (J. J. O'Kelly, The Sinn Fein outlook (? Dublin, n.d. [1930/31]), p. 15). Purists can be bigots.

[41] Statement of account, 1934, HC:DD, II, p. 165; Comhairle na dteachtaí, minutes, 8 Aug. 1924, Gaughan, Austin Stack, p. 340.   [42] Rumpf and Hepburn, Nationalism and socialism, p. 89.

[43] Maurice Twomey, conference minutes, 12 Nov. 1931, HC:DD, III, p. 84.

acquiesced in this military takeover was that the new chief of staff, Sean Russell, had shown it the courtesy of asking it to do so; the request that it should transfer its authority comprised a sort of moral recognition on the part of the IRA which had been denied it until then.[44] In theory it retained the right to rescind this decision and resume all its abandoned powers, and this possibility existed until Tom Maguire, the last survivor of the republican second Dáil, died in 1993.[45] It (or he) never did so.

Sinn Féin was not informed in advance that the 'Dáil' would transfer its authority.[46] Yet in theory the parliament and government to which the party pledged allegiance consisted henceforth of the army council of the IRA; its own bizarre constitutionalism placed it at the mercy of a group which despised constitutional politics and majority rule. This abdication in favour of the army was symbolic, and it brought to a natural conclusion the elitist, militarist and anti-democratic (or, perhaps, supra-democratic) tendencies in Irish republicanism.

For many years the IRA had gone its own way, and its repudiation of civilian control in 1925 was followed by an increasingly bloody campaign against the Free State. Ultimately its murders provoked Cosgrave's government into a series of repressive and unpopular measures which in turn assisted Fianna Fáil's electoral victory in 1932. But the IRA's violence was directed almost entirely at other, rival Irish nationalists, and its aim was to perpetuate the Irish Civil War rather than to resume the Anglo-Irish War. For decades the British and the Ulster unionists were immune from anything more than sporadic and half-hearted attacks.

Once he had come to power, and no longer needed the IRA to undermine his Cumann na nGaedheal opponents, de Valera began a skilful campaign to buy off the radicals. He released prisoners, suspended (but did not repeal) the Cosgrave government's Public Safety Act, gave pensions to republicans who had fought in the civil war, and created an army volunteer reserve which might deflect recruits from the IRA. His constitutional changes were equally important. He abolished the oath of fidelity ('allegiance'), degraded the office of the governor-general (who represented the king), and suspended the annuity payments to the British government which were a consequence of the land acts. This confrontational style won him widespread support.

His achievements also proved that Collins had been right and he himself had been wrong in their disagreement over the treaty. Even more than his Cumann na nGaedheal predecessors in office had done, de Valera proved that the treaty *did* give the Free State the freedom to achieve freedom. In the long run he was

---

[44] J. Bowyer Bell, *The secret army: the IRA* (3rd edn, London, 1997), p. 154.   [45] *IT*, 7 July 1993.
[46] Standing committee minutes, 16 Dec. 1938, NAI, 2B/82/117(27), p. 525.

the principal beneficiary of the settlement which he had opposed so fiercely. But many in the IRA were understandably confused by the subtlety and caution which he displayed after he had returned to office. Oliver St John Gogarty displayed greater insight when he wrote to de Valera refusing, 'to assist you in playing Hamlet when your Republicans are howling for Macbeth'.[47]

The IRA was weakened in 1934 when left-wing elements formed their own organization, the Republican Congress, but within a few months it in turn divided into rival factions.

All this time the Fianna Fáil government was able to consolidate its power and its democratic credentials by exploiting the battles between two rival paramilitary groups. Many in the IRA were determined to exact revenge on their pro-treaty enemies, and in the fascistic words of one republican activist, 'while we have fists, hands and boots to use, and guns if necessary, we will not allow free speech to traitors'.[48] Such attitudes provoked a matching response, and supporters of Cumann na nGaedheal formed a body which ultimately took the name of Blueshirts and indulged in fascist-style marches with raised-arm salutes. Yet despite their unpleasant imagery and actions the Blueshirts were basically defensive and harmless; they were less violent than the republican extremists, and – with one exception – they never killed anyone. They were frightened, blustering bullies, and they were easily subdued. Once de Valera had moved against them he was able to act with greater confidence against their rival, and he banned the IRA after its murders had provoked widespread public disgust. The Blueshirts acted as a catalyst in the complex relationship between de Valera's government and the other threat to Irish democracy: those republican gunmen who believed that Ireland was represented by themselves alone, and not by its people or its government.

Throughout the 1930s there were tensions and quarrels between the political and military wings of Irish republicanism, and some of the more radical soldiers would have preferred to abolish the party altogether. One political leader complained that for years the army council 'had been disparaging Sinn Féin up and down the country'.[49] The IRA was even prepared to engage in politics independently of Sinn Féin, and for a while in 1936 it formed its own subordinate party, Cumann Poblachta na hÉireann. This development further weakened

---

[47] Gogarty to de Valera, 15 Apr. 1935, NAI, D/T, S6405C, cited in Adrian Keane, 'Who fears to speak of Easter Week? Reflections on the commemoration of the rising, 1924–1991' (MA dissertation, University College, Dublin, 1996), p. 7.

[48] Sean Cronin, *Frank Ryan: the search for the republic* (Dublin, 1980), p. 45.

[49] Brian O'Higgins to Mary MacSwiney, 13 June 1935, cited in Charlotte H. Fallon, *Soul of fire: a biography of Mary MacSwiney* (Cork and Dublin, 1986), p. 172.

Sinn Féin, some of whose clubs collapsed; for example, the Mallow branch had consisted of IRA men, and it was wound up after they defected to join the new body.[50] Sinn Féin leaders might insist on the party's separate identity, but in practice it was little more than the political manifestation of the army.

In 1936 Sinn Féin modified or abandoned one of its basic principles and it assisted Cumann Poblachta na hÉireann in fighting two by-elections. The results were disastrous, the republican candidates secured a mere 3.6 per cent of the total poll, and the Galway election was notable only as the occasion of Count Plunkett's last campaign. It was at this low point in its fortunes that Sinn Féin chose Margaret Buckley as its president, and thereby became the first party in Ireland to be led by a woman. Things had changed since, less than ten years earlier, its then president had proposed that Sinn Féin should be run exclusively by men, just as Cumann na mBan was run by women.[51] Yet even though the soldiers lost interest in politics once more, and Sinn Féin was left free to pursue its lonely path, the army council banned party members from joining the IRA.[52]

The military takeover of the 'second Dáil' in 1938 did not represent another lurch back towards constitutionalism. On the contrary, the IRA promptly declared war on the United Kingdom, and in January 1939 it began a bombing campaign in England. This move created consternation at the time, but perhaps its most remarkable aspect was that it had been delayed for so long. Ever since 1922 the IRA had sought to revive the passions aroused by the treaty, and its efforts had been directed overwhelmingly against targets in independent Ireland. It seemed at times to have forgotten about the 'hereditary enemy', and all its plans for a major offensive in the North had come to nothing.

De Valera acted forcefully to ensure that Irish neutrality would not be endangered by republican attacks on one of the major European powers. The IRA was driven underground, and in the course of the Second World War its members were arrested, executed and allowed to die on hunger strike. De Valera had long ago outgrown the days when he was prepared to humour and indulge an army acting independently of his government. Once more Sinn Féin was no more than a minor element in official thinking, but it too suffered from the relative rigours of Ireland's wartime 'emergency'. Some of its meetings were banned, and when its thirtieth *ard-fheis* took place in November 1939 the censor directed that newspapers should ignore the proceedings. For many years the party had lain low, but by now it was almost supine. It was forced to make a virtue of its unpopularity, and in 1940 its president declared proudly that

---

[50] Sean Roche to Liam Gilmore, 27 July 1936, *HC:DD*, III, p. 121.

[51] J. J. O'Kelly to MacSwiney, n.d. (*c.* Nov. 1927), cited in Murphy, 'Politics and ideology', p. 309.

[52] Standing committee minutes, 27 May, 10 June 1938, 6 Jan. 1939, NAI, 2B/82/117(27).

'minorities are nearly always right; it was a very small minority that stood at the foot of the Cross, and a very large majority indeed that shouted "Give us Barabbas"'.[53]

In one respect, however, circumstances forced the party to take an initiative, rather than engage in its preferred activity of simply bearing witness to the truth. In 1924 the treasurers of the second Sinn Féin had placed the party's funds in the care of the High Court, and over the decades the capital had doubled and then tripled in value. It posed a strong temptation to impoverished bodies like the third and fourth Sinn Féin parties, but their principles forbade any action which would involve recognition of the Irish state. Despite much discussion and frustration they refrained from pursuing their claim to these assets. Eventually, however, when faced with government measures to dispose of the fund, Sinn Féin relaxed its principles and took legal action to secure the money. This compromise with reality provoked predictable outrage, and some members resigned in disgust.

Six years passed before the case was concluded – and the party lost its claim to be the direct successor of the pre-civil war Sinn Féin. Not only did it fail to secure the windfall which would have transformed its fortunes (financial if not political), but it was damaged further by having to pay a proportion of its costs. These fell on a small number of faithful believers; the party's joint secretary admitted that the memberhip numbered only about a hundred, and he added 'they are just getting old, you know'.[54] By the 1940s Sinn Féin's decline seemed to be terminal.

The lure of politics

Like Jarndyce and Jarndyce in *Bleak House* the Sinn Féin funds case seemed to drag on for ever, and by the time it reached its conclusion Irish public life was transformed. After sixteen years in power de Valera had called an early general election which resulted in his unexpected defeat. His action was provoked by the reappearance of that traditional Irish phenomenon: a reformed gunman who cast aside the certainties of youth to dally on the primrose paths of politics.

Seán MacBride was a radical republican who had been briefly chief of staff of the IRA in 1936. Even then he had aroused suspicions among his more intransigent colleagues by his readiness to venture beyond their own narrow

---

[53] Margaret Buckley, speech, 17 Nov. 1940, *HC:DD*, II, p. 195.
[54] Diarmuid O'Leary, evidence, 7 May 1948, SFFC, 2B/82/118(44), p. 41.

horizons. He was prominent in forming the radical Saor Éire in 1931, and five years later he seems to have supported the short-lived Cumann Poblachta na hÉireann. (Subsequently he denied this.)[55] During the Second World War he established a reputation at the bar by his skilful defence of republican prisoners, and in its aftermath he formed a new party, Clann na Poblachta. Since its aim was to win power in Dublin it was committed to taking seats in Leinster House – thereby ensuring that the IRA would expel any of its own members who joined the Clann.

MacBride followed where first Collins and then de Valera had led, and his party was dismissed as being no more than 'treaty party number three'.[56] But it caught the electorate's imagination, and its flashy image contrasted with that of the older parties in the Dáil and (to an even greater extent) with the drab and dowdy appearance of abstentionist Sinn Féin. It won several by-elections. De Valera attempted to catch it off guard by dissolving the Dáil earlier than expected, but the Clann contested every constituency in the 1948 election, it won ten seats, and MacBride entered the new coalition cabinet as minister for external affairs. In one of the more improbable alliances in Irish political history a former commander of the (post-independence) IRA joined forces with Cumann na nGaedheal's successor, Fine Gael, to share power at de Valera's expense.

It was this government which finally renamed the former Free State 'the Republic of Ireland' and which thereby completed the process of discarding or transcending the treaty. The change in the state's title did not prevent the continuing use of the term 'republican' to describe those radical nationalists who supported military measures against Britain and the Ulster unionists, but for most people constitutional methods seemed to have been vindicated once again. MacBride's sheen was soon tarnished, however, and within a few years this first coalition government was brought down in 1951 by quarrels which centred on him and his party colleague in the cabinet, Noel Browne. Clann na Poblachta soon disappeared as a significant force in public life.

The Sinn Féin party experienced no such dramatic swings of fortune. Its achievement was simply to survive, and in 1949 the new republican newspaper *The United Irishman* remarked that 'for years Sinn Féin has been content to pursue its way quietly and unobtrusively, relying on the small band of loyal stalwarts who have kept the organisation going, in good times and in bad'.[57] Only fifty delegates attended its *ard-fheis*.[58] But in the same year the IRA army

---

[55] Anthony J. Jordan, *Seán MacBride: a biography* (Dublin, 1993), pp. 51, 67; Uinseann MacEoin, *Survivors* (Dublin, 1980), p. 123.   [56] Bell, *Secret army*, p. 244.
[57] *United Irishman*, Dec. 1949.   [58] *IT*, 14 Nov. 1949.

convention forswore further action in the south and finally began to turn its attention north of the border – thus ending thirty wasted years during which it had devoted most of its efforts to challenging governments in Dublin. This move was unpopular with many activists who would have preferred to continue attacking their traditional targets.[59]

The IRA also decided to infiltrate and control Sinn Féin, and its members were directed to enlist in the party. There was a sudden infusion of new blood as they did so, the old guard was supplanted, and in 1950 Margaret Buckley was replaced as president by the IRA activist Padraig MacLogan.[60] The party's (relative) independence of the military wing was brought to an end with remarkable ease and speed. For the next few decades it was little more than the civilian face of the republican army, a mask or a mouthpiece for a soldier with a gun.

Sinn Féin acted as an auxiliary to the IRA in its disastrous border campaign of 1956–62. For a short while it had a nation-wide impact; it contested elections and won seats in both Irish parliaments, although its members abstained from these 'partitionist' institutions. But these gains were transient, and public support faded away long before the IRA abandoned its half-hearted efforts against the northern state. This electoral collapse doubtless reinforced the faith of those who believed that the public should not be consulted about matters which concerned soldiers alone.

By the mid-1960s such traditionalists had to face a new challenge from within the ranks of the movement. Many young members of the IRA began to feel the same sort of frustration which in earlier years had propelled de Valera and MacBride into parliamentary politics. They shared the widespread socialist ideals of the decade, they drifted away from the fundamentalist aspects of Irish republicanism, and they behaved 'like a small, conventional, left-wing political party'.[61] Events in Northern Ireland during the 1960s appeared to vindicate the tastes of the new generation. Even the Unionist Party seemed susceptible to the spirit of the times, and Terence O'Neill portrayed a relatively liberal image, which contrasted with that of earlier, more parochial prime ministers. Naïve enthusiasts began to hope that the system could be reformed in a peaceful and piecemeal manner. Some members of the nationalist community abandoned their dreams of unity with the Republic, attempting instead to modernize and reform the society in which they lived. But rival forces breathed life into traditional, entrenched, sectarian attitudes of precisely the sort which liberal and Marxist idealists found so reactionary and embarrassing. The rest of

---

[59] Tim Pat Coogan, *The IRA* (4th edn, London, 1995), p. 256.
[60] *United Irishman*, Dec. 1950; Coogan, *IRA*, pp. 257–8.
[61] Patrick Bishop and Eamonn Mallie, *The Provisional IRA* (London, 1987), p. 36.

the world might experiment with new ideas, but in Northern Ireland the future belonged to the past.

Events in the late 1960s seemed to parallel or to have been modelled on those before 1916. Many Ulster unionists were horrified at the prospect of democratic reforms which would benefit the nationalist community, even (or particularly) when these were demanded by a London government. They cherished traditional practices such as discrimination and gerrymandering. Those who were loudest in proclaiming their British citizenship were also the most indignant in denying the benefits of 'British' principles and values to their fellow citizens. They were determined that Northern Ireland should remain, by the standards of many critical outsiders, a political slum, the Sicily of the United Kingdom; in O'Neill's more moderate words they were prepared to be 'regarded by the rest of Britain as a political outcast'.[62]

Ian Paisley was the most prominent among those who appealed to the atavistic fears and hatreds of many unionists, and from 1964 onwards he inspired a series of riots and disturbances. Some of those who followed his lead or shared his views were prepared to use force in their efforts to prevent reform; they precipitated a new phase of conflict, and in so doing they revived the moribund forces of Irish republicanism. Following the pattern of the decade between 1913 and 1923, unionists watched in horror as their example was followed by radical nationalists. The initiative was theirs, nonetheless. The first person to die in a bomb attack, the first policeman to be killed, the first civilians to be shot dead, were all victims of extreme unionists.[63] Nationalist violence came later.

Members of the Catholic minority engaged in protest marches to reinforce their demands for equal citizenship. The peaceful nature of these demonstrations was undermined by the attacks of unionist opponents – and also by the actions of a radical minority among the protesters who sought confrontation with their opponents. This group hoped to bring about the destruction of the state, no matter what the consequences might be.[64] The result was a series of battles, which climaxed in August 1969 when streets in Belfast were burned out, thousands fled from their homes, and the British army was sent to restore order. Northern Ireland spiralled downwards into a new round of sectarian hatred. The IRA was caught off-guard by the scale of the violence, and it could not even perform its self-imposed task of defending the nationalist community; it was forced to watch as Catholics welcomed 'enemy' British soldiers as their saviours.

---

[62] Terence O'Neill, *The autobiography of Terence O'Neill* (London, 1972), p. 149.

[63] Jonathan Bardon, *A history of Ulster* (Belfast, 1992), pp. 635, 674.

[64] Eamonn McCann, *War and an Irish town* (3rd edn, London 1993), pp. 91, 99; Paul Arthur, *The People's Democracy, 1968–1973* (Belfast, 1974), p. 41.

Critics could contrast its leaders' inability to exploit these new circumstances with the readiness of Clarke's and Hobson's IRB to seize on Carson's initiative nearly sixty years before.

The movement soon split in two. When the IRA's army council decided that all republican candidates should recognize any parliament to which they were elected, whether in Dublin, Belfast or London, a minority of the members spurned this heresy. One true believer, Ruairí Ó Brádaigh, asked scornfully, 'why not accept the bloody Treaty in the beginning and be done with it?'[65] For such faithful republicans the question of abstention was moral, almost theological; two generations of republicans had made sacrifices, and some had died, in the struggle to defend the legitimacy of the second Dáil against the treaty settlement.[66] The dead hand of the past pointed towards a bloody future. In a similar fashion the proposal was endorsed by most of the delegates at the Sinn Féin *ard-fheis* shortly afterwards, but here too it encountered vehement opposition and it could not secure the two-thirds majority necessary to change the party's constitution. The reformers dismissed their critics with benign condescension, confident that theirs was the path of progress and that history was on their side. They were wrong.

The ballot paper and the armalite

In December 1969, IRA traditionalists broke away from a leadership which they believed had abandoned the struggle for national unity in its pursuit of non-sectarian, working-class solidarity. There was a limit beyond which these purists could not be seduced into whoring after strange Marxist gods. They established a new body which became known as the Provisional IRA, and it was soon accompanied by a political auxiliary – (Provisional) Sinn Féin. If the post-civil-war Sinn Féin is seen as having ended with the split of 1926, this was the fifth party in succession to adopt or maintain the title which Griffith had popularized in the early years of the century.[67] This IRA was the foremost among many groups whose combined actions would devastate Northern Ireland, but it was accompanied by other republican groups, by loyalist paramilitaries and by the crown forces. These rival armies fed off one another.

The following decades were the bloodiest phase in Irish history since the rebellions of 1798, and between the early 1970s and the mid-1990s 3,170 people were

---

[65] Bishop and Mallie, *Provisional IRA*, p. 103

[66] Henry Patterson, *The politics of illusion: a political history of the IRA* (London, 1997), p. 141.

[67] The relevant dates are 1905–17, 1917–22, 1923–6 and 1926–70.

killed in political and sectarian conflict. The events of these years are the subject of a vast literature. The following pages of this book are not intended to provide a balanced coverage (still less, a comprehensive coverage) of the Northern Irish 'troubles'; the aim is rather to select a few events and patterns which illustrate elements of continuity and discontinuity between the fifth and earlier Sinn Féins.

The republicans launched a war of attrition against the crown forces, and they carried out sectarian attacks on the unionist population. They abandoned the aims of the 1960s, of creating a more just and equal Northern Ireland, and in their own eyes 'what had started as a campaign for civil rights was developing into the age-old struggle for national rights'.[68] The IRA believed that it had resumed the war where it had been interrupted half a century earlier, with the truce of July 1921. Its members were determined to defeat and humiliate the British; they would force the Ulster unionists into a united Ireland; and by so doing they would also bring to an end the despised institutions of the Republic. Their ultimate objective remained an abstraction, a geographical image which existed independently of the island's unfortunate inhabitants.

The IRA encouraged and exploited the growing alienation of the nationalist population from the British troops; this was not a difficult task, as the soldiers were often insensitive and partisan in their behaviour. The unionists, too, played into the republicans' hands, and they consolidated the nationalist minority's alienation from the Northern Irish state. In August 1971 'one-sided' internment was introduced; loyalist paramilitaries were ignored, and the list of 452 people to be detained included only opponents of partition.[69] It seemed that the Unionist Party and government were irreformable. The Bloody Sunday massacre of unarmed civilians by the British army in January 1972 horrified all nationalists, as well as many others; following the pattern of 1916, the British manufactured Irish republicans.

Like Paisley and other extreme unionists, the IRA equated compromise with surrender. Its military strategy had little use for politics or politicians. Provisional Sinn Féin functioned as a small protest organization or a support group, and its ability to organize was hindered by arrests, harassment and imprisonment. It did little more than sell newspapers and raffle tickets.[70]

In the early years of the troubles almost all southerners sympathized with nationalist victims of unionist attacks. But it became ever more apparent that the republican paramilitaries were responsible for most of the killing and destruction, and the IRA was soon widely detested. At last, southern public

---

[68] Gerry Adams, *The politics of Irish freedom* (Dingle, 1986), p. 17.

[69] Bardon, *History of Ulster*, p. 682.

[70] Adams, *Politics of Irish Freedom*, p. 70; Adams, cited in Bishop and Mallie, *Provisional IRA*, p. 363.

opinion began to question the bland, blithe assumption that reunification could be accomplished easily. Many people began to wonder whether the Republic's institutions could digest a million hostile unionists; the North and its problems were regarded with growing resentment, fear and shame.[71] This attitude was illustrated by an independent deputy in the course of a Dáil debate. He saw a proposed change to the constitution as 'kow-towing to the Orange thugs of Belfast', and he asked 'who is crazy enough to believe that we should be influenced by that crowd of thugs? . . . God grant that we will never see the day when that "shower" of thugs do come in here'.[72] His views might have been expressed with an exceptional coarseness and honesty, but they were shared to an extent which would have been unthinkable only a few years earlier.

The system of devolved government in Northern Ireland was abolished in 1972, destroyed not only by the attacks of its enemies, but also (and more importantly) by the unionists' own folly. The alliance between the British state and Northern Irish Protestants was brought to an end.[73] But the IRA and its political wing won little credit for this victory, and most of the Catholic population maintained their support for constitutional politics. The Nationalist party in the north collapsed in 1969, as it had done in the rest of the country half a century earlier, but its heir was the new Social Democratic and Labour Party (SDLP), and not the IRA or Sinn Féin.

Moderate unionist and nationalist politicians joined forces in 1973–4 to form a power-sharing executive. This coalition was intended to consolidate and expand the narrow 'middle ground' in Northern Ireland, and to isolate the violent extremists on both sides. It was soon repudiated by a majority of the unionist electors, and it was brought down when a loyalist general strike was reinforced by a campaign of intimidation. The republican minority among northern nationalists dreaded any reconciliation between the two communities and, like its unionist counterpart, it rejoiced in the failure of this attempt at a compromise settlement.

The IRA continued to dominate the republican movement. The army council met before every Sinn Féin annual conference, and in effect it directed the party's activities.[74] When the IRA chief of staff, Seamus Twomey, was arrested in 1977, he was in possession of a directive which included the follow-

---

[71] See Joseph Ruane and Jennifer Todd, *The dynamics of conflict in Northern Ireland: power, conflict and emancipation* (Cambridge, 1996), p. 253.

[72] Joseph Lenehan, *DE, official report*, 263, col. 444 (2 Nov. 1972), cited in J. Bowyer Bell, *The Irish troubles: a generation of violence, 1967–1992* (Dublin, 1993), p. 353.

[73] Ruane and Todd, *Dynamics of conflict*, p. 131.

[74] Brendan O'Brien, *The long war: the IRA and Sinn Féin, 1985 to today* (Dublin, 1993), p. 122.

ing points: 'Sinn Féin should come under Army organisers at all levels . . . Sinn Féin should be radicalised (under Army direction) . . . Sinn Féin should be re-educated.'[75] Sinn Féin should do what it was told.

But as the years of death and destruction brought unification no closer, some republicans began to reconsider their strategy and to wonder whether their cause might be advanced by political as well as by military means. This process was accelerated by the 1981 hunger strikes, in the course of which ten republican prisoners died. These deaths aroused the imagination and even the sympathy of many people who, until then, had rejected the IRA's aims or methods; the Provisionals could now be associated with martyrdom as well as with murder. The hunger strikes were

> the blood-stained bond linking the failures of the past to the failures of the present . . . They were atonement for the mutilations, the meaningless maimings, the innumerable futile brutalities, and the hundreds of violent and misdirected deaths sanctioned in the name of holy nationalism . . . they allowed the IRA to re-establish itself in the heroic mould.[76]

The republicans won a momentous propaganda victory when the first of these hunger-strikers was elected to Westminster in a fortuitously timed by-election, and soon afterwards two of his colleagues were elected to the Dáil. A prominent Sinn Féin member advocated that republicans should take power in Ireland (and not merely in the North) with a ballot-paper in one hand and an armalite rifle in the other. Both 'partitioned states' were to disappear, although the Republic was a less immediate target than the British or the unionists; both the Belfast and Dublin systems 'would have to go into the melting pot'.[77] Yet the ballot-box was a dangerous weapon, since on so many occasions in the past the morale of at least some soldiers had been eroded when the voters rejected them.

This increase in support for the movement encouraged the faction, led by Gerry Adams, which wanted to develop Sinn Féin as a powerful force in both parts of Ireland. The party believed that it was no longer a sect and had become a mass movement.[78] To a limited extent it succeeded in creeping out from under the army's shadow, but the soldiers remained the dominant partner in the relationship. This was appropriate, since many republicans believed that only by bombing and killing could they draw attention to themselves and continue to be a significant element in the public life of the island. But it was also proper in

---

[75] Tim Pat Coogan, *The troubles: Ireland's ordeal 1966–1995 and the search for peace* (London, 1995), p. 208.   [76] Padraig O'Malley, *The uncivil wars: Ireland today* (London, 1983), pp. 267, 269.

[77] *Ibid.*, p. 285; Seán MacStiofáin, *Revolutionary in Ireland* (Farnborough, 1974), p. 209.

[78] Paul Arthur and Keith Jeffery, *Northern Ireland since 1968* (2nd edn, London, 1996) p. 59.

constitutional terms; according to their theory, ever since the 'second Dáil' had surrendered its powers in 1938 the army council was the legitimate government of the country. (It seemed not to matter that in 1969–70, as with the formation of the third Sinn Féin in 1923, institutional continuity with earlier bodies had been broken.) IRA members were informed

> that war is morally justified and that the Army is the direct representative of the 1918 Dáil Éireann Parliament, and that as such they are the legal and lawful government of the Irish Republic, which has the moral right to pass laws for, and to claim jurisdiction over . . . all of its people regardless of creed and loyalty.[79]

As always, the people and their governments counted for little or nothing. Finally, in 1983, the southern leadership of Sinn Féin was replaced by a new, northern group, and Adams was elected president of the party.

Some IRA members were suspicious of these new developments and they felt that politics were receiving too much attention, that the military campaign was being wound down.[80] Nonetheless, the republicans continued to drift towards a 'two-handed' policy, clutching both guns and ballot papers. At the Sinn Féin ard-fheis in 1985 a majority, but not the necessary two-thirds majority, voted in favour of the party's taking any Dáil seats which it might win. A year later the IRA held its first convention since 1969. (This was summoned to pronounce on the same question as its predecessor: Sinn Féin's policy of abstention.) Heedless of the party's inhibitions, the army endorsed the new policy, and Sinn Féin tamely followed this example soon afterwards. Finally it recognized the Dáil in Leinster House, at least to the extent of being willing to allow party members to join its ranks.[81] The only surviving member of the 1921 second Dáil was horrified by this apostasy.

For many decades republicanism had been crippled by what could be described as 'Griffith's revenge'. Griffith's abstentionist ideas had failed before the outbreak of the First World War, and after 1916 they were revived and applied under circumstances which he had never envisaged. After his death his party's name was taken over by extremist republicans who represented a form of nationalism alien to him. They also took over his abstentionist principles which they implemented in the new and unsuitable circumstances of a functioning Irish democracy. Griffith's tactic, which was annexed to further a cause which he would have deplored, helped marginalize the forces of extreme nationalism and thereby strengthened the compromising moderates who fol-

---

[79] Coogan, *Troubles*, p. 208; O'Brien, *Long war*, p. 289.   [80] Bell, *Irish troubles*, p. 701.

[81] Agnès Maillot, *IRA: les républicains irlandais* (Caen, 1996), pp. 208, 252.

lowed the spirit and not the letter of his law. His enemies were poisoned by drinking from his chalice.[82]

Traditionalists were unable to accept this break with a pattern which had been sanctified both by time and by failure. Following the precedent of 1970 they created a new Republican Sinn Féin party, but they did not try to form a rival IRA, and they made few inroads on the strength of Adams's Sinn Féin. It in turn made little impact on the politics of the Republic, where it was seen as a 'northern' party; it did not win a seat in the Dáil for another eleven years, and in the next four general elections its share of the vote ranged from 1.2 to 2.5 per cent. Even though the party's willingness to take its seats in the Dáil was a symbolic turning-point, it made no difference in practice.

Throughout the late 1980s and the early 1990s, as the bombings, the shootings and the killings continued, and as loyalist terror groups killed more people than the IRA, Sinn Féin retained the support of between 30 per cent and 40 per cent of the nationalist community in the North. Its core following was among the young working class and unemployed; it appealed in particular to those who believed that the party and the IRA were 'standing up for second-class Catholics'.[83] But it remained a minority of the northern minority, and it was reinforced by no more than a tiny appendage of southern supporters.

From the late 1980s onwards John Hume, the SDLP leader, sought to convince Sinn Féin that the Ulster unionists, rather than the British government, represented the main obstacle to a united Ireland. He argued that attempts to coerce them would fail.[84] Sinn Féin, and behind it the Provisional IRA, were to be inveigled into the political process. Secret talks took place with the British, and in Dublin the Reynolds government abandoned a policy which had been followed by all previous administrations since the early 1930s, since de Valera's first years in power when he had appeased and then outmanoeuvred the IRA. Reynolds tried to domesticate the republicans; as he described his own tactics, 'we're slowly putting the squeeze on them, pulling them in, boxing them in, cutting off their lines of retreat'.[85] Building on Hume's initiative he and his

---

[82] It has been argued that when members of republican Sinn Féin denounced Griffith they did so basing their attacks on arguments which they borrowed from him (Maume, 'Ancient constitution', p. 123).

[83] Ruane and Todd, *Dynamics of conflict*, p. 73; Fionnuala O'Connor, *In search of a state: Catholics in Northern Ireland* (Belfast, 1993), p. 131.

[84] Paul Bew, Peter Gibbon and Henry Patterson, *Northern Ireland, 1921–1996; political forces and social classes* (London, 1996), p. 223.

[85] Seán Duignan, *One spin on the merry-go-round* (Dublin, 1995), p. 140.

successors worked hard to persuade Sinn Féin that it in turn should persuade the IRA to abandon violence and join the political system.

The republican movement came under intense pressure from Dublin, from increasingly flexible and imaginative London governments, from Washington, and from the powerful Irish-American lobby. By 1994 the peace initiative had taken over from the armed struggle as the central purpose of the movement, and Sinn Féin tried (however implausibly) to be recognized as a conventional political party.[86] At the same time a series of negotiations and agreements between Dublin and London resulted in guarded and conditional invitations to Sinn Féin to enter into negotiations concerning the future of Northern Ireland.

Hitherto, the republicans' political weight had been a reflection of their terror campaign, and the more people they killed the more formidable they seemed to be. Many within their ranks were wary at the prospect of a cease-fire, and they would have agreed with the words of one observer: 'Britain is likely to take the cynical view that republicans in unarmed struggle are like birds without wings.'[87] There was understandable unhappiness at the idea of Sinn Féin becoming a 'normal', respectable political party (and it was an idea which also provoked both distaste and distrust among many who were opposed to the IRA's campaign of terror). On the other hand, there was also a widespread appreciation by many republicans that, although a life of combat was satisfying and fulfilling for some of its participants, and although the IRA could continue bombing and killing indefinitely, its long struggle had brought it no closer to its objective of a united Ireland.

Sinn Féin's support increased as it appeared to be a semi-independent party, rather than a mere front for the IRA, and within a few years its share of the vote in Northern Ireland almost doubled. It became responsible to large numbers of people – voters in their tens of thousands – rather than merely to the army council of the IRA. In these respects it took the path of the second Sinn Féin, rather than of its hermetic successors who had languished for decades on the margins of Irish public life.

Cease-fires and discussions followed. Ultimately Sinn Féin joined in lengthy negotiations which resulted in agreement on a new attempt to bring peace to Northern Ireland. To the disgust of die-hards inside and outside the ranks of the paramilitaries it decided – at long last – to recognize that Irish unity could not come about without the consent of a majority in the North. It also accepted the reality of partition, and retreated further from its policy of abstention, when its

---

[86] Bell, *Secret army*, pp. 650–1.

[87] Coogan, *Troubles*, p. 376; Andrew MacIntyre in *Fortnight*, cited in Bew, Gibbon and Patterson, *Northern Ireland, 1921–1996*, p. 231.

ard-fheis decided by 331 votes to 19 that Sinn Féin candidates should take any seats which they won in elections for the new Northern Irish assembly. Here, for once, it was in tune with Irish opinion; in separate referenda the agreement was endorsed by 85.5 per cent of the Irish electorate (71 per cent in Northern Ireland, and 94 per cent in the Republic). And here again, in its belated readiness to compromise, to postpone the achievement of its objectives, the fifth Sinn Féin party followed the example of the second.

Continuities and contrasts

The various Sinn Féins after 1923 could claim descent from the republican movement of the late nineteenth and early twentieth centuries. (So too, of course, could other, fully democratic parties.) Their fates (which varied) also illustrated the anomalous nature of the second Sinn Féin party which flourished between the Easter Rising and the civil war. Despite a historically understandable distrust of British aims and methods, most Irish nationalists have almost always been surprisingly moderate. They supported extreme measures only under grave provocation, or at times when other, preferred methods were barred to them. To their own contemporaries the republican conspirators usually seemed absurd and even pathetic optimists, unrepresentative of the people for whom they claimed to speak and out of tune with the realities of their times. They might have belonged to the world of Conrad's *Secret agent*.

In the years after 1913, suddenly and almost miraculously, circumstances provided them with an ideal set of opportunities, and these were exploited through a combination of careful planning and good fortune. The Irish revolution, of which Sinn Féin was the political expression, was an accident or an aberration. Yet not only did Irish republicans stage an unpopular rebellion, but they manipulated its emotive aftermath with considerable skill. They formed a highly effective coalition with more moderate and politically minded colleagues, and they managed to win widespread support for at least some of their objectives. They radicalized Irish nationalism, and in the process they became part of a mass movement. Many of them (although not all) were also converted to democratic processes and habits; they politicized themselves. They encountered and sometimes even repelled attempts at domination by colleagues who placed all their faith in guns and bullets.

This post-rising synthesis flourished, and it had a profound long-term influence. Sinn Féin's role in the Irish revolution ensured that when Lloyd George was driven to negotiate in 1921, Irish nationalists were represented by politicians and administrators, as well as by soldiers. Most of their leaders believed in and practised democracy, they felt responsible to a parliament of sorts, and they were anxious to maintain public support.

The unnatural coalition formed in 1917 splintered when it was confronted with the reality of substantial British concessions. Having achieved far more than they had thought possible only a few years earlier, the great mass of Sinn Féin supporters welcomed a compromise settlement; for them the phoenix had already emerged from the ashes, and the country's resurrection was already apparent. They expressed their opinions clearly at the first available opportunity, on 16 June 1922, when they voted for moderation, peace and normality. During the civil war most of the people supported or accepted drastic measures against those radical soldiers who despised their wishes, and then they reverted promptly and almost gratefully to their everyday lives and their ingrained democratic habits. They escaped from the idealists.

In this way they shared the experience of most people in most countries at most times, before, during and after periods of violent upheaval. Yet in some quarters the Irish people have been criticized for this failure in revolutionary stamina; they have been condemned for tolerating or perpetrating a 'counter-revolution' which braked or reined in the most extreme republicans.[88] Others might describe this 'counter-revolution' as an assertion of the people's will, a triumph of democracy.

From the standpoint of some radicals the island suffered from an inadequate burden of grievances, and the people were too easily satisfied. But Ireland before 1921 was not a conventionally oppressed colonial society, and nor (despite the unionist bigotry and discrimination which it experienced) was the nationalist community in Northern Ireland after partition. Even the discontented had limited ambitions, and for many of them the republican cure was often worse than the British or the unionist disease. Despite intermittent upsurges of excitement and indignation, particularly in the decade after 1913 and the years after 1968, most nationalists remained ploddingly, selfishly moderate.

On the other hand, the strong and deep tradition of resistance to British rule and influence, and the passionate commitment to an Irish republic or a united Ireland, were ideals which endured for decades. Their proponents were undeterred by hopeless failure in the past or by miserable prospects in the future; they were undeterred in the late twentieth century by widespread revulsion at the vicious and sectarian manner in which demands for Irish unity were often expressed. The people had supported a revolution once, and that was miracle

---

[88] For example, the president of a later Sinn Féin wrote that his party had taken a step towards reversing the effects of the counter-revolution which followed the Easter Rising (Adams, *Politics of Irish freedom*, p. 160).

enough, yet generation after generation many republicans waited with characteristic patience for an encore. Later Sinn Féin parties provided refuge for optimistic and inflexible militants. But even if popular support was welcome it was not seen as being necessary, and many republicans were able to take literally the title of Pearse's poem, *Mise Éire*, 'I am Ireland'.

After communist forces had suppressed the East Berlin workers' revolt in 1953, Bertolt Brecht made a modest proposal:

> it was said that the people
> Had lost the government's confidence ...
> In that case, would it
> Not be simpler if the government dissolved the people
> And elected another?[89]

Many Irish republicans would have understood and shared these sentiments; they were quite prepared to dissolve or ignore an unworthy, ungrateful people and to appoint another, which would be made in their own image. The 'nation', embodied in a few noble spirits, could survive without the masses; it had done so in the past and would continue to do so in the future. The pattern of 1917–22, when republican radicals and the democratic mass of the population had formed a powerful alliance, was the result of improbable circumstances which did not recur.

Nonetheless, several features link the revolutionary decade with its background and its aftermath: the folly of British governments, officials and soldiers; the intransigence of Ulster unionists who, on two widely separated occasions, helped precipitate sustained outbursts of nationalist rebellion; the seductive charms of peace and normality; the tensions between soldiers and politicians; and the detached, at times even cynical attitudes of moderate nationalists – whether Sinn Féiners or (after 1922) Dublin governments – who had their own interests and responsibilities to protect. Violence and the threat of violence have often extracted reforms which democrats have used to advance their own objectives and reinforce their own positions. Such moderates have often been ready to avail of bloodshed, to benefit from it as well as (sincerely) to disown it. They have frequently been as opportunistic in their attitudes towards the militarists as the militarists have been towards them. The relationship has often, indeed normally, been one of mutual dislike and mutual exploitation.

New patterns also emerged. Just as the question of Irish unionism became confined to north-east Ulster in the course of the nineteenth and early twentieth centuries, so Irish republicanism became virtually confined to a section of the

---

[89] John Fuegi, *The life and lies of Bertolt Brecht* (London, 1994), p. 549.

nationalist minority in Northern Ireland. Ironically this was a group which was all but ignored by the republican leaders until the 1950s, and which did not assume leadership of the movement until the 1980s. Its southern supporters were sometimes articulate, normally vociferous and almost always unrepresentative.

The circumstances of the early years of the century seemed to have been repeated in their broad outlines in the late 1960s and early 1970s, and the unionist backlash against reforms radicalized the browbeaten Northern Irish nationalists. But the obstacles faced by the revolutionaries of the Provisional IRA and its Sinn Féin auxiliary were far greater than those which had been overcome by their predecessors after 1916. At best they could appeal to a minority within the political entity in which they lived, and they failed to receive any significant support or even respect from the citizens of the Republic. There, apart from a few conspirators, revolutionary fervour was confined to rhetoric and reminiscence.

Uncompromising republicans could express views similar to those of de Valera when, in the course of a famous speech in 1929, he remarked of the fourth Sinn Féin party that 'those who continued on in that organisation which we have left can claim exactly the same continuity that we claimed up to 1925'.[90] Only a stalwart few resisted the temptations of ordinary life and the prospect of power. Collins led the way, abandoning or (more probably) concealing the extreme republican views which he had flaunted before his conversion to majority rule. De Valera followed, and after his defection further layers of the onion peeled off one by one; MacBride and Clann na Poblachta; the Marxist IRA of the 1960s; and even the (Provisional) fifth Sinn Féin party, when it jettisoned its policy of abstention from Leinster House and at last, sixty-five years later than the British government, recognized the reality of an independent Irish state.

That independent state was the result of a military and political revolution, of a campaign that was waged by a minority of radicals and was supported, dubiously but decisively, by most Irish nationalists. At times during these years the Sinn Féin party was overshadowed by the army, and its efforts were often disparaged. Nonetheless, its achievements were formidable. It destroyed the home rule movement and it mobilized public opinion behind the demand for full independence; it also enabled the Irish electorate to raise its voice, and to influence, endorse or even repudiate those leaders who spoke on its behalf.

Unlike some other separatist leaders, Griffith had almost always believed in majority rule. During the embattled last months of his life he and Collins failed in their efforts to establish a civilian Irish government by peaceful means, and

---

[90] DE, *official report*, 28, col. 1,400 (14 Mar. 1929).

they could not even mobilize Sinn Féin to represent the people against the army. But, on balance, Griffith could be proud of the party which, in his passionate, pugnacious and pedestrian manner, he had nurtured for so many years. It faltered in early 1922, yet it was the principal means whereby Ireland's constitutional tradition was transmitted through years of turbulence, and it played an important role in ensuring that governments in independent Ireland would be responsible to the people. Sinn Féin was the democratic face of the Irish revolution.

SELECT BIBLIOGRAPHY

PRIMARY SOURCES

In the case of several different categories of primary sources, particularly manuscripts and contemporary printed documents, only those which were of particular importance are mentioned here. Numerous items (especially pamphlets) which have been consulted, but which have been cited only once or not at all, have not been included in these lists. Unless otherwise indicated, all pamphlets can be found in the National Library of Ireland.

The boundaries between the different categories listed below are often fluid, and at times the choice of section has been almost arbitrary.

Manuscripts

ARMAGH

Diocesan Archives
Cardinal Michael Logue
Bishop Patrick O'Donnell of Raphoe

BELFAST

Public Record Office
Charlotte Despard
Cahir Healy
Henry Moloney

Cork

Cork Archives Institute
Liam de Róiste, diary
Seamus Fitzgerald
Siobhán Lankford
Terence MacSwiney

Cork Public Museum
Tomás MacCurtain
Terence MacSwiney

Dublin

Diocesan Archives
Archbishop Edward Byrne
Monsignor Michael Curran
Archbishop William Walsh

Fianna Fáil Archives
Independence movement and Sinn Féin, 1915–28
Foundation of party and early years, 1926–28

Military Archives
Captured documents collection
Michael Collins

National Archives
Robert Barton
Eamon de Valera, captured correspondence
George Gavan Duffy

National Library
Robert Barton
Joseph Brennan
Erskine Childers
Michael Collins – Austin Stack correspondence
Michael Curran, memoir
Liam de Róiste diary, 1917–18 (in Florence O'Donoghue MSS)
Fr Patrick Doyle
Viscount French, diary
Frank Gallagher
George Gavan Duffy

Bulmer Hobson
Kate Kelly
Kilmnacanogue Sinn Féin club minutes
Shane Leslie
Joe McGarrity
Kathleen McKenna Napoli
Maurice Moore
Michael Noyk
Art O'Brien
J. F. X. O'Brien
William O'Brien, MP
William O'Brien (trade unionist)
J. J. O'Connell
Florence O'Donoghue
Seán T. O'Kelly
Seán Ó Lúing
Seán O'Mahony
James O'Mara
Kevin O'Shiel, letter-book
Parliamentary Party minute-book, 1910–18
Count Plunkett
Précis of captured documents
John Redmond
Celia Shaw, diary
Hanna Sheehy-Skeffington
List of Sinn Féin officers
Sinn Féin standing committee minutes, 1918–22
Lily Williams

Trinity College, Dublin, Library
Erskine Childers
John Dillon
Thomas Dillon
Elsie Mahaffy

University College, Dublin, Archives Department
Ernest Blythe
J. R. Clark, diary
Eamon de Valera
Fine Gael minutes
Desmond FitzGerald

Michael Hayes
Sighle Humphries
IRB correspondence
Denis McCullough
Seán MacEntee
Sean MacEoin
Eoin MacNeill
Mary MacSwiney
Terence MacSwiney
Richard Mulcahy
Ernie O'Malley
James Ryan
Sinn Féin minutes, 1912–13, 1919–22
Maurice Twomey

LONDON

House of Lords Record Office
Andrew Bonar Law
David Lloyd George

Public Record Office
John Anderson
Viscount Midleton
Mark Sturgis, diary

OXFORD

Bodleian Library
H. H. Asquith
Augustine Birrell
H. A. L. Fisher, diary
Baron Merrivale (Henry Duke)
Baron Strathcarron (Ian Macpherson)

Government records

NATIONAL ARCHIVES, DUBLIN

Chief Secretary's Office, registered files
Dáil Éireann, cabinet minutes, DE 1/1–4

Dáil Éireann, *oifig an rúnaí* (general secretariat), DE 2
Department of Local Government files, DELG
Department of the Taoiseach [D/T], S files
Proceedings of first and second Dáil and related documents, DE 4
Provisional Government, cabinet minutes, G1
Records of the Dáil Éireann courts (winding up) commission, DE 9–15
Sinn Féin funds case, 2B.82.116–18

PUBLIC RECORD OFFICE, LONDON

Cabinet conclusions, Cab. 23
Cabinet memoranda, Cab. 24
Cabinet committees, Cab. 27
Cabinet papers, Cab. 37
Cabinet letters, Cab. 41
Conferences on Ireland, 1921–22, Cab. 43
Dublin Castle records, CO.903
Nationalist organisations, CO.904/20
Sinn Fein movement, CO.904/23
RIC county inspectors' reports, 1916–21, CO.904/99–116
Intelligence officers' reports, CO.904/157/1
Field general courts martial, civilians, WO.71

MINISTÈRE DES AFFAIRES ÉTRANGÈRES, PARIS

Europe, 1918–1929, Irlande, I & II (microfilm)

Official Publications

DUBLIN

*A brief survey of the work done by the Agricultural Department from April 1919 to August
    1921* (Dublin, 1921)
The constructive work of Dáil Éireann (Dublin, 1921)
Dáil debates
*Dáil Éireann. Official correspondence relating to the peace negotiations, June–September
    1921* (Dublin, 1921)
*High Court of Justice, 1942: Documents discovered by plaintiffs and briefed to counsel on
    behalf of defendant Charles Stewart Wyse Power* (Dublin, 1944)

Irish Bulletin
Census of population, 1926. General report (Dublin, 1934)

LONDON

Census of Ireland, 1911. General report, with tables and appendix (London, 1913)
Correspondence relating to the proposals of his majesty's government for an Irish settlement (London, 1921), Cmd. 1502
Documents relative to the Sinn Fein movement (London, 1921), Cmd. 1108
Hansard
The Irish Convention. Confidential report to his majesty the king by the chairman (London, 1918)
Report on the proceedings of the Irish Convention (London, 1918), Cd. 9019
Royal commission on the rebellion in Ireland. Report of commission (London, 1916), Cd. 8279
Royal commission on the rebellion in Ireland. Minutes of evidence and appendix of documents (London, 1916), Cd. 8311

Contemporaneous published writings

Birmingham, George A., *An Irishman looks at his world* (London, 1919)
Brayden, W. H., *Republican courts in Ireland* (Chicago, 1920)
Briollay, Sylvain, *Ireland in rebellion* (Dublin, 1922)
Byron, Lesley, *Opportunist Sinn Feiners* (London, n.d. [?1921])
Chesterton, G. K., *Irish impressions* (London, 1919)
Collins, Michael, *The path to freedom* (Dublin, 1922)
De Blácam, A., *Towards the republic* (Dublin, 1918)
　　What Sinn Féin stands for (Dublin, 1921)
De Valera, Eamon, *Ireland's case against conscription* (Dublin, 1918)
Ewart, Wilfrid, *Travels in Ireland, 1921* (London, 1922)
Ginnell, Laurence, *The Irish republic. Why?* (New York, 1919)
Goblet, Y. M., *L'Irlande dans la crise universelle (1914–1920)* (2nd edn, Paris, 1921)
Griffith, Arthur, *The resurrection of Hungary: a parallel for Ireland* (Dublin, 1904)
　　When the government publishes sedition (Dublin, n.d. [?1915])
Hackett, Francis, *Ireland: A study in nationalism* (3rd edn, New York, 1919)
Hobson, Bulmer, *The creed of the republic* (Belfast, 1907)
　　Defensive warfare: a handbook for Irish nationalists (Belfast, 1909)
Horgan, J. J. (ed.), *The complete grammar of anarchy, by members of the war cabinet and their friends* (Dublin, 1918)

I.O. [C. J. C. Street], *The administration of Ireland, 1920* (London, 1921)

Johnson, Thomas, *A handbook for rebels* (Dublin, 1918)

Lynd, Robert, *The ethics of Sinn Féin* (Limerick, 1912)

MacDonagh, Thomas, *Literature in Ireland* (Dublin, 1916)

MacNamara, Brinsley, *The clanking of chains* (Dublin, 1920)

MacNeill, Eoin, *Daniel O'Connell and Sinn Féin* (Dublin, 1915)

MacSwiney, Terence, *Principles of freedom* (Dublin, 1921)

Moran, D. P., *The philosophy of Irish Ireland* (Dublin, 1905)

O'Shiel, Kevin, *The rise of the Irish Nation League* (n.d. [1916])

    The 'Sinn Féin 'policy (Dublin, 1907)

Pim, Herbert Moore, *Three letters for unionists only!* (Dublin, n.d. [?1917])

Proportional Representation Society of Ireland, *Sligo's P.R. lead!* (Dublin, 1919)

Ryan, W. P., *The pope's green island* (London, 1912)

Stephens, James, *The insurrection in Dublin* (Dublin, 1916)

Street, C. J. C., *Ireland in 1921* (London, 1922)

Other printed primary sources

Buckland, Patrick (ed.), *Irish unionism, 1885–1923: a documentary history* (Belfast, 1973)

Carroll, F. M. (ed.), *The American commission on Irish independence, 1919: the diary, correspondence and report* (Dublin, 1985)

Cronin, Sean, *The McGarrity papers* (Tralee, 1972)

Edwards, Owen Dudley, and Ransom, Bernard (eds.), *James Connolly: selected political writings* (London, 1973)

Gaughan, J. Anthony (ed.), 'Comhairle na dteachtaí, 7–8 Aug. 1924', in Gaughan, J. Anthony, *Austin Stack: portrait of a separatist* (Dublin, 1979), pp. 319–74

McCartan, Patrick, 'Extracts from the papers of the late Dr. Patrick McCartan', *Clogher Record*, 5, 2 (1965)

MacGiolla Choille, Breandán (ed.), *Intelligence notes, 1913–16* (Dublin, 1966)

MacLochlainn, Piaras F. (ed.), *Last words: letters and statements of the leaders executed after the rising at Easter 1916* (Dublin, 1971)

McHugh, Roger (ed.), *Dublin 1916: an illustrated anthology* (London, 1966)

Martin F. X. (ed.), 'Eoin MacNeill on the 1916 Rising', *IHS*, 12, 47 (1961)

    (ed.), 'The McCartan documents, 1916', *Clogher Record*, 6, 1 (1966)

Middlemas, Keith (ed.), Thomas Jones, *Whitehall diary*, I, III (Oxford, 1969, 1971)

Moody, T. W., and Ó Broin, Leon (eds.), 'The I.R.B. supreme council, 1868–78: select documents', *IHS*, 19, 75 (1975)

Moynihan, Maurice (ed.), *Speeches and statements by Eamon de Valera, 1917–1973* (Dublin, 1980)

O'Brien, William, and Ryan, Desmond (eds.), *Devoy's post bag, 1871–1928* (Dublin, 1948)

Ó Broin, León, and Ó hÉigeartaigh, Cian (eds.), *In great haste: the letters of Michael Collins and Kitty Kiernan* (2nd edn, Dublin, 1996)

Ó Buachalla, Seamus (ed.), *The letters of P. H. Pearse* (Gerrards Cross, 1980)

Ó Deirg, Íosold (ed.), "'Oh! Lord the unrest of soul": the jail journal of Michael Collins', *Studia Hibernica*, 28 (1994)

Pearse, Pádraic H, *Political writings and speeches* (Dublin, n.d.)

Ryan, Desmond (ed.), *Socialism and nationalism: a selection from the writings of James Connolly* (Dublin, 1948)

Stewart, A. T. Q. (ed.), *Michael Collins: the secret file* (Belfast, 1997)

Warwick-Haller, Adrian and Sally (eds.), *Letters from Dublin, Easter 1916: Alfred Fannin's diary of the rising* (Dublin, 1995)

Ward, Margaret (ed.), *In their own voice: women and Irish nationalism* (Dublin, 1995)

Wilson, Trevor (ed.), *The political diaries of C. P. Scott, 1911–1928* (London, 1970)

Newspapers and periodicals

Anglo-Celt

Armagh Guardian

Belfast News-Letter

Catholic Bulletin

An Claidheamh Soluis

Clare Champion

Connachtman

Connaught Telegraph

Contemporary Review

Cork Constitution

Cork County Eagle

Cork Examiner

Derry People

Donegal Democrat

Donegal Vindicator

Dublin Opinion

Dungannon Democrat

Enniscorthy Guardian

Factionist

Freeman's Journal

Free State [An Saorstát]

Irish Freedom
Irish Fun
Irish Independent
Irishman
Irish Nation
Irish News
Irish Statesman
Irish Times
Irish Volunteer
Kerryman
Kilkenny Journal
Leader
Leinster Leader
Leitrim Advertiser
Limerick Leader
Mayoman
Mayo News
Meath Chronicle
Nationalist and Leinster Times
Nationality
New Ireland
An tÓglách
Plain People
Poblacht na hÉireann, Southern Edition
Republic of Ireland [Poblacht na hÉireann]
Representation: the Journal of the Proportional Representation Society
Roscommon Herald
Roscommon Journal
Roscommon Messenger
Round Table
An Saorstát
Saturday Record
Scissors and Paste
Separatist
Sinn Féin
Sligo Champion
Spark
Studies
Times
Tyrone Constitution

United Irishman
Western People

SECONDARY SOURCES

Guides, bibliographies and works of reference

Boylan, Henry (ed.), *A dictionary of Irish biography* (3rd edn, Dublin, 1998)

Carty, James, *A bibliography of Irish history, 1912–21* (Dublin, 1936)

Connolly, S. J. (ed.), *The Oxford companion to Irish history* (Oxford, 1998)

Cullen, Clara, and Henchy, Monica (compilers), *Writings on Irish history* (Dublin, 1986–)

The dictionary of national biography: the concise dictionary, part II, 1901–1950 (Oxford, 1961)

Dod's parliamentary companion, 1916 (London, 1916)

Duffy, Seán (ed.), *Atlas of Irish history* (Dublin, 1997)

Edwards, Ruth Dudley, *An atlas of Irish history* (2nd edn, London, 1981)

Flynn, W. J., *Free State parliamentary companion for 1932* (Dublin and Cork, 1932)

Hayes, Richard (ed.), *Manuscript sources for the history of Irish civilisation* (Boston, 1965; *Supplement*, Boston 1979)

Helferty, Seamus, and Refaussé, Raymond, *Directory of Irish archives* (2nd edn, Dublin, 1993)

Holland, Ailsa C., and Helferty, Seamus, *Guide to the Archives Department, University College, Dublin* (Dublin, 1985)

Irish Times, The Sinn Féin rebellion handbook (Dublin, 1917)

Lee, Joseph (ed.), *Irish historiography 1970–79* (Cork, 1981)

Moody, T. W. (ed.), *Irish historiography, 1936–70* (Dublin, 1971)

Moody, T. W., Martin, F. X., and Byrne, F. J. (eds.), *A chronology of Irish history to 1976: a companion to Irish history, part I* (Oxford, 1982)

    Maps, genealogies, lists: a companion to Irish history, part II (Oxford, 1984)

O'Farrell, Padraic, *Who's who in the Irish War of Independence and Civil War, 1916–1923* (Dublin, 1997)

Public Record Office, *The records of the cabinet office to 1922* (London, 1966)

Thom's Irish who's who (Dublin and London, 1923)

Vaughan, W. E., and Fitzpatrick, A. J. (eds.), *Irish historical statistics: population, 1821–1971* (Dublin, 1978)

Walker, B. W. (ed.), *Parliamentary election results in Ireland, 1801–1922* (Dublin, 1978)

    Parliamentary election results in Ireland, 1918–92 (Dublin, 1992)

Books, articles and dissertations

Adams, Gerry, *The politics of Irish freedom* (Dingle, 1986)

Akenson, D. H., and Fallin, J. H., 'The Irish Civil War and the drafting of the Free State constitution', *Éire-Ireland*, 5, 1, 2, and 4 (1970)

Alter, Peter, *Die irische Nationalbewegung zwischen Parlament und Revolution: der konstitutionelle Nationalismus in Irland, 1880–1918* (Munich and Vienna, 1971)

    'Symbols of Irish nationalism', *Studia Hibernica*, 14 (1974)

Anderson, Benedict, *Imagined communities: reflections on the origins and spread of nationalism* (2nd edn, London, 1991)

Andrews, C. S., *Dublin made me* (Dublin and Cork, 1979)

    Man of no property (Dublin and Cork, 1982)

Archer, J. R., 'Necessary ambiguity: nationalism and myth in Ireland', *Éire-Ireland*, 19, 2 (1984)

Arthur, Paul, *The People's Democracy, 1968–1973* (Belfast, 1974)

Arthur, Paul, and Jeffery, Keith, *Northern Ireland since 1968* (2nd edn, London, 1996)

Augusteijn, Joost, *From public defiance to guerrilla warfare: the experience of ordinary Volunteers in the Irish War of Independence, 1916–1921* (Dublin, 1996)

Bardon, Jonathan, *A history of Ulster* (Belfast, 1992)

Barry, Tom, *Guerrilla days in Ireland* (Dublin, 1949)

Béaslaí, Piaras, *Michael Collins and the making of a new Ireland* (Dublin, 1926)

Bell, J. Bowyer, *The Irish troubles: a generation of violence, 1967–1992* (Dublin, 1993)

    The secret army: the IRA (3rd edn, London, 1997)

Bew, Paul, *Conflict and conciliation in Ireland, 1890–1910: Parnellites and radical agrarians* (Oxford, 1987)

    Ideology and the Irish question: Ulster unionism and Irish nationalism 1912–1916 (Oxford, 1994)

    John Redmond (Dublin, 1996)

Bew, Paul, Gibbon, Peter, and Patterson, Henry, *Northern Ireland, 1921–1996: political forces and social classes* (London, 1996)

Birrell, Augustine, *Things past redress* (London, 1937)

Bishop, Patrick, and Mallie, Eamonn, *The Provisional IRA* (London, 1987)

Blake, Robert, *The unknown prime minister: the life and times of Andrew Bonar Law* (London, 1954)

Bowman, John, *De Valera and the Ulster question, 1917–1973* (Oxford, 1982)

Boyce, D. G., *Englishmen and Irish troubles: British public opinion and the making of Irish policy, 1918–22* (London, 1972)

    Nineteenth-century Ireland: the search for stability (Dublin, 1990)

    Nationalism in Ireland (3rd edn, London, 1995)

    'How to settle the Irish question: Lloyd George and Ireland 1916–21', in Taylor, A. J. P.

(ed.), *Lloyd George: twelve essays* (London, 1971)

Boyce, D. G. (ed.), *The revolution in Ireland, 1879–1923* (Dublin, 1988)

Boyce, D. G., and Hazelhurst, Cameron, 'The unknown chief secretary: H. E. Duke and Ireland, 1916–18', *IHS*, 20, 79 (1977)

Boyce, D. G., and O'Day, Alan (eds.), *The making of modern Irish history: revisionism and the revisionist controversy* (London, 1996)

Boyle, Andrew, *The riddle of Erskine Childers* (London, 1977)

Boyle, John W., 'Irish labor and the Rising', *Éire-Ireland*, 2, 3 (1967)

Bradshaw, Brendan, 'Nationalism and historical scholarship in modern Ireland', *IHS*, 26, 104 (1989)

Brady, Ciaran (ed.), *Interpreting Irish history: the debate on historical revisionism* (Dublin, 1994)

Breatnach, Labhrás, *An Pluincéadach* (Dublin, 1971)

Breen, Dan, *My fight for Irish freedom* (Dublin, 1924)

Brennan, Michael, *The war in Clare, 1911–1921: personal memoirs of the Irish War of Independence* (Dublin, 1980)

Brennan, Robert, *Allegiance* (Dublin, 1950)

Brennan-Whitmore, W. J., *With the Irish in Frongoch* (Dublin, 1917)

   Dublin burning: the Easter Rising from behind the barricades (Dublin, 1996)

British and Irish Communist Organisation, *Aspects of nationalism* (Belfast, 1972)

Brown, Terence, *Ireland: a social and cultural history, 1922–79* (London, 1981)

Buckland, Patrick, *Irish unionism 1: the Anglo-Irish and the new Ireland, 1885 to 1922* (Dublin, 1972)

   Irish Unionism, 2: Ulster unionism and the origins of Northern Ireland, 1886 to 1922 (Dublin, 1973)

   The factory of grievances: devolved government in Northern Ireland, 1921–39 (Dublin, 1979)

   James Craig (Dublin, 1980)

   A history of Northern Ireland (Dublin, 1981)

Budge, Ian, and O'Leary, Cornelius, *Belfast: approach to crisis: a study of Belfast politics, 1613–1970* (London, 1973)

Cahill, Liam, *Forgotten revolution: Limerick soviet 1919: a threat to British power in Ireland* (Dublin, 1990)

Callan, Patrick, 'Recruiting for the British Army in Ireland during the First World War', *Irish Sword*, 17, 66 (1987)

Callanan, Frank, *T. M. Healy* (Cork, 1996)

Campbell, Colm, *Emergency law in Ireland, 1918–1925* (Oxford, 1994)

Carroll, Denis, *They have fooled you again: Michael O'Flanagan (1876–1942), priest, republican, social critic* (Dublin, 1993)

Carroll, Francis M., *American opinion and the Irish question, 1910–23* (Dublin, 1978)

'"All standards of human conduct": the American commission on conditions in Ireland, 1920–21', *Éire-Ireland*, 16, 4 (1981)

Casey, James, 'Republican courts in Ireland, 1919–22', *Irish Jurist*, 5 (1970)

'The genesis of the Dáil courts', *Irish Jurist*, 9 (1974)

Chauvin, Guy, 'The Parliamentary Party and the revolutionary movement in Ireland, 1912–1918' (Ph.D. dissertation, Trinity College, Dublin, 1976)

Chevasse, Moirin, *Terence MacSwiney* (Dublin, 1961)

Clarke, Kathleen, *Revolutionary woman: Kathleen Clarke, 1878–1972: an autobiography* (ed. Litton, Helen), (Dublin 1991)

Clarke, Thomas J., *Glimpses of an Irish felon's prison life* (Dublin and London, 1922)

Coakley, John, 'Typical case or deviant? Nationalism in Ireland in a European perspective', in Hill, Myrtle, and Barber, Sarah (eds.), *Aspects of Irish studies* (Belfast, 1990)

Coldrey, Barry M., *Faith and fatherland: the Christian Brothers and the development of Irish nationalism, 1838–1921* (Dublin, 1988)

Coleman, Marie, 'County Longford, 1910–1923: a regional study of the Irish revolution' (Ph.D. dissertation, University College, Dublin, 1998)

Colum, Padraic, *Arthur Griffith* (Dublin, 1959)

'Darrell Figgis: a portrait', *Dublin Magazine*, 14, 2 (1939)

Colvin, Ian, *The life of Lord Carson*, II and III (London, 1934, 1936)

Combs, James E., 'The language of nationalist ideology: a content-analysis of Irish nationalist publications, 1906–14' (MA dissertation, Houston, 1969)

Conlon, Lil, *Cumann na mBan and the women of Ireland* (Kilkenny, 1969)

Connolly, Joseph, *Memoirs of Senator Joseph Connolly (1885–1961). A founder of modern Ireland* (ed. Gaughan, J. Anthony), (Dublin, 1996)

Coogan, Oliver, *Politics and war in Meath, 1913–23* (Dublin, 1983)

Coogan, Tim Pat, *Michael Collins: a biography* (London, 1990)

De Valera: long fellow, long shadow (London, 1993)

The IRA (4th edn, London, 1995)

The troubles: Ireland's ordeal 1966–1995 and the search for peace (London, 1995)

Costello, Francis J., *Enduring the most: the life and death of Terence MacSwiney* (Dingle, 1995)

'The republican courts and the decline of British rule in Ireland, 1919–1921', *Éire-Ireland*, 25, 2 (1990)

Cronin, Sean, *Frank Ryan: the search for the republic* (Dublin, 1980)

Irish nationalism: a history of its roots and ideology (Dublin, 1980)

Cullen Owens, Rosemary, *Smashing times: a history of the Irish women's suffrage movement, 1889–1922* (Dublin, 1984)

Curran, Joseph M., *The birth of the Irish Free State, 1921–1923* (Alabama, 1980)

Daly, Mary E., *Social and economic history of Ireland since 1800* (Dublin, 1981)

The buffer state: the historical roots of the Department of the Environment (Dublin, 1997)

Dangerfield, George, *The damnable question: a study in Anglo-Irish relations* (London, 1977)

Davis, Richard, *Arthur Griffith and non-violent Sinn Féin* (Dublin, 1974)

'The advocacy of passive resistance in Ireland, 1916–1922', *Anglo-Irish Studies*, 3 (1977)

'Ulster Protestants and the Sinn Féin press, 1914–22', *Éire-Ireland*, 15, 4 (1980)

Deane, Seamus, *Celtic revivals: essays in modern Irish literature, 1880–1980* (London, 1985)

Deasy, Liam, *Towards Ireland free: the West Cork brigade in the War of Independence, 1917–1921* (Cork and Dublin, 1973)

De Paor, Liam, *On the Easter proclamation and other declarations* (Dublin, 1997)

Desmond, Shaw, *The drama of Sinn Féin* (London, 1923)

Devlin, Bernadette, *The price of my soul* (London, 1969)

Devoy, John, *Recollections of an Irish rebel* (New York, 1929)

Dillon, Thomas, 'Birth of the new Sinn Féin and the ard fheis, 1917', *Capuchin Annual*, 1967

Doherty, Gabriel, and Keogh, Dermot (eds.), *Michael Collins and the making of the Irish state* (Cork, 1998)

Dolan, Anne, '"Fumbling in the greasy till": *Dublin Opinion* and the Irish bourgeoisie, 1922–23' (MA dissertation, University College, Dublin, 1996)

Dooher, John, 'Tyrone nationalism and the border question, 1910–25' (M.Phil. dissertation, University of Ulster, 1986)

Dooley, Thomas P., 'Politics, bands and marketing: army recruiting in Waterford city, 1914–15', *Irish Sword*, 18, 72 (1991)

Dublin's fighting story, 1913–1921: told by the men who made it (Tralee, 1949)

Duggan, John P., *A history of the Irish army* (Dublin, 1991)

Duignan, Seán, *One spin on the merry-go-round* (Dublin, 1995)

Dunleavy, Janet, and Gareth, W., *Douglas Hyde: a maker of modern Ireland* (Berkeley, 1991)

Dunne, Tom, 'New histories: beyond "revisionism"', *Irish Review*, 12 (1992)

Duverger, Maurice, *Political parties* (London, 1954)

Dwyer, T. Ryle, *Michael Collins and the treaty: his differences with de Valera* (Cork and Dublin, 1981)

De Valera's darkest hour: in search of national independence, 1919–1932 (Cork and Dublin, 1982)

Edwards, Owen Dudley, *Eamon de Valera* (Cardiff, 1987)

Edwards, Owen Dudley, Evans, Gwynfor, Rhys, Ioan, and MacDiarmaid, Hugh, *Celtic nationalism* (London, 1968)

Edwards, Owen Dudley, and Pyle, Fergus (eds.), *1916: the Easter Rising* (London, 1968)

Edwards, Ruth Dudley, *Patrick Pearse: the triumph of failure* (London, 1977)

James Connolly (Dublin, 1981)

English, Richard, *Radicals and the republic: socialist republicanism in the Irish Free State 1925–1937* (Oxford, 1994)

Fallon, Charlotte H., *Soul of fire: a biography of Mary MacSwiney* (Cork and Dublin, 1986)

Fanning, Ronan, *The Irish Department of Finance, 1922–58* (Dublin, 1978)

Independent Ireland (Dublin, 1983)

'The great enchantment: uses and abuses of modern Irish history', in Dooge, James (ed.), *Ireland in the contemporary world: essays in honour of Garret FitzGerald* (Dublin, 1986)

'The meaning of revisionism', *Irish Review*, 4 (1988)

Farrell, Brian, *The founding of Dáil Éireann: parliament and nation-building* (Dublin, 1971)

'Legislation of a "revolutionary" assembly: Dáil decrees, 1919–1922', *Irish Jurist*, 10 (1975)

Farrell, Brian (ed.), *The creation of the Dáil* (Dublin, 1994)

Farrell, Michael, *Northern Ireland: the Orange state* (London, 1975)

Arming the Protestants: the formation of the Ulster special constabulary and the Royal Ulster Constabulary, 1920–27 (London and Dingle, 1983)

Farry, Michael, *Sligo 1914–1921: a chronicle of conflict* (Trim, 1992)

Fennell, Desmond, *The revision of Irish nationalism* (Dublin, 1989)

Figgis, Darrell, *A chronicle of jails* (Dublin, 1917)

A second chronicle of jails (Dublin, 1919)

Recollections of the Irish war (London, 1927)

FitzGerald, Desmond, *Memoirs of Desmond FitzGerald, 1913–1916* (London, 1968)

FitzGerald, Garret, *All in a life: an autobiography* (Dublin, 1991)

Fitz-Gerald, William (ed.), *The voice of Ireland* (Dublin and London, n.d. [1924])

Fitzpatrick, David, *Politics and Irish life, 1913–21: provincial experience of war and revolution* (Dublin, 1977)

The two Irelands, 1912–1939 (Oxford, 1998)

'Strikes in Ireland, 1914–21', *Saothar*, 6 (1980)

'The geography of Irish nationalism', in Philpin, C. E. (ed.), *Nationalism and popular protest in Ireland* (Cambridge, 1987)

'The logic of collective sacrifice: Ireland and the British army, 1914–1918', *Historical Journal*, 38, 4 (1995)

'Militarism in Ireland, 1900–1922' in Bartlett, Thomas, and Jeffery, Keith (eds.), *A military history of Ireland* (Cambridge, 1996)

Fitzpatrick, David (ed.), *Ireland and the First World War* (Dublin, 1988)

Revolution? Ireland, 1917–1923 (Dublin, 1990)

Forester, Margery, *Michael Collins: the lost leader* (London, 1971)

Foster, R. F., *Modern Ireland, 1600–1972* (Harmondsworth, 1988)

    Paddy and Mr Punch: connections in Irish and English history (Harmondsworth, 1993)

    W. B. Yeats: A life. I: the apprentice mage, 1865–1914 (Oxford, 1997)

    'We are all revisionists now', *Irish Review*, 1 (1986)

Fraser, T. G., *Partition in Ireland, India and Palestine: theory and practice* (London, 1984)

Fussell, Paul, *The Great War and modern memory* (New York and London, 1975)

Gallagher, Michael, 'Socialism and the nationalist tradition in Ireland, 1798–1918', *Éire-Ireland*, 12, 2 (1977)

    'The pact general election of 1922', *IHS*, 21, 84 (1979)

Garvin, Tom, *The evolution of Irish nationalist politics* (Dublin, 1981)

    Nationalist revolutionaries in Ireland, 1858–1928 (Oxford, 1987)

    1922: the birth of Irish democracy (Dublin, 1996)

    'Priests and patriots: Irish separatism and the fear of the modern', *IHS*, 25, 97 (1986)

    'The politics of language and literature in pre-independence Ireland', *Irish Political Studies*, 2 (1987)

    'Unenthusiastic democrats: the emergence of Irish democracy', in Hill, Ronald J., and Marsh, Michael (eds.), *Modern Irish democracy: essays in honour of Basil Chubb* (Dublin, 1993)

Gaughan, J. Anthony, *Memoirs of Constable Jeremiah Mee, RIC* (Dublin, 1975)

    Austin Stack: portrait of a separatist (Dublin, 1977)

    Thomas Johnson, 1872–1963: first leader of the Labour Party in Dáil Éireann (Dublin, 1980)

    A political odyssey: Thomas O'Donnell, M.P. for West Kerry 1900–1918 (Dublin, 1983)

Gearty, Conor, *Terror* (London, 1991)

Gellner, Ernest, *Nations and nationalism* (Oxford, 1983)

Glandon, Virginia E., *Arthur Griffith and the advanced-nationalist press, Ireland, 1900–1922* (New York, 1985)

    'John Dillon's reflections on Irish and general politics', *Éire-Ireland*, 9, 3 (1974)

Golding, G. M., *George Gavan Duffy, 1882–1951: a legal biography* (Dublin, 1982)

Goldring, Maurice, *Pleasant the scholar's life: Irish intellectuals and the construction of the nation state* (London, 1993)

Good, James, *Ulster and Ireland* (Dublin, 1919)

Good, Joe, *Enchanted by dreams: the journal of a revolutionary* (Dingle, 1996)

Greaves, C. Desmond, *Liam Mellows and the Irish revolution* (London, 1971)

    The Irish Transport and General Workers' Union: the formative years, 1909–1923 (Dublin, 1982)

Griffith, Kenneth, and O'Grady, Timothy E., *Curious journey: an oral history of Ireland's unfinished revolution* (Dublin, 1982)

Grote, Georg, 'The Gaelic League, 1983–1993: torn between politics and culture' (MA dissertation, Münster, 1993)

Gwynn, Denis, *John Redmond* (London, 1932)

   The Irish Free State, 1922–27 (London, 1928)

Gwynn, Stephen, *John Redmond's last years* (London, 1919)

Hachey, Thomas E., *Britain and Irish separatism: from the Fenians to the Free State, 1867/1922* (Chicago, 1977)

Hachey, Thomas E., and McCaffrey, Lawrence J. (eds.), *Perspectives on Irish nationalism* (Lexington, 1989)

Hannon, Charles, 'The Irish Volunteers and the concept of military service and defence, 1913–1924' (Ph.D. dissertation, University College, Dublin, 1989)

Harkness, David, *Northern Ireland since 1920* (Dublin, 1983)

Harris, Mary, *The Catholic Church and the foundation of the Northern Irish state* (Cork, 1993)

Hart, Peter, *The I.R.A. and its enemies: violence and community in Cork, 1916–1923* (Oxford, 1998)

   'Michael Collins and the assassination of Sir Henry Wilson', *IHS*, 28, 110 (1992)

   'The Protestant experience of revolution in southern Ireland', in English, Richard, and Walker, Graham (eds.), *Unionism in modern Ireland: new perspectives on politics and culture* (London, 1996)

   'The geography of revolution in Ireland, 1917–1923', *Past and Present*, 155 (1997)

Haverty, Anne, *Constance Markievicz: an independent life* (London, 1988)

Haydon, Anthony P., *Sir Matthew Nathan: British colonial governor and civil servant* (St Lucia, Queensland, 1976)

Hayes, Michael, 'Dáil Éireann and the Irish Civil War', *Studies*, 58, 229 (1969)

Healy, T. M., *Letters and leaders of my day* (London, n.d. [1928])

Henry, Robert Mitchell, *The evolution of Sinn Féin* (Dublin, 1920)

Hobsbawm, Eric, *Nations and nationalism since 1870: programme, myth, reality* (Cambridge, 1990)

Hobsbawm, Eric, and Ranger, Terence (eds.), *The invention of tradition* (Cambridge, 1983)

Hobson, Bulmer, *A short history of the Irish Volunteers* (Dublin, 1918)

   Ireland yesterday and tomorrow (Tralee, 1968)

Hogan, David [Gallagher, Frank], *The four glorious years* (Dublin, 1953)

Holt, Edgar, *Protest in arms: the Irish troubles, 1916–1923* (London, 1960)

Hopkinson, Michael, *Green against green: the Irish Civil War* (Dublin, 1988)

Hoppen, K. Theodore, *Ireland since 1800: conflict and conformity* (London, 1989)

Horgan, John J., *From Parnell to Pearse: some recollections and reflections* (Dublin, 1948)

Hutchinson, John, *The dynamics of cultural nationalism: the Gaelic revival and the creation of the Irish nation state* (London, 1987)

Inglis, Brian, *Roger Casement* (London, 1973)

Inoue, Keiko, 'Sinn Féin and Dáil propaganda, 1919–1921' (M.Phil. dissertation, UCD, 1995)

Jackson, Alvin, *Sir Edward Carson* (Dublin, 1993)

Jenkins, Roy, *Asquith* (London, 1964)

Jordan, Anthony J., *Seán MacBride: a biography* (Dublin, 1993)

Keane, Adrian, 'Who fears to speak of Easter Week? Reflections on the commemoration of the rising, 1924–1991' (MA dissertation, University College, Dublin, 1996)

Kedourie, Elie, *Nationalism* (2nd edn, London, 1961)

Kee, Robert, *The green flag: a history of Irish nationalism* (London, 1972)

Kemmy, James, 'The Limerick soviet', *Saothar*, 2 (1976)

Kendle, John, *Walter Long, Ireland, and the union, 1905–1920* (Dun Laoghaire, 1992)

Kennedy, Dennis, *The widening gulf: northern attitudes to the independent Irish state, 1919–49* (Belfast, 1988)

Kennedy, Liam, *Colonialism, religion and nationalism in Ireland* (Belfast, 1996)

Keogh, Dermot, *The Vatican, the bishops and Irish politics, 1919–39* (Cambridge, 1986)

Twentieth-century Ireland: nation and state (Dublin, 1994)

Kiberd, Declan, *Inventing Ireland: the literature of the modern nation* (London, 1995)

Kingston, W. F., 'The genesis of Sinn Fein' (MA dissertation, University College Dublin, 1949)

Kostick, Conor, *Revolution in Ireland: popular militancy 1917 to 1923* (London, 1996)

Kotsonouris, Mary, *Retreat from revolution: the Dáil courts, 1920–24* (Dublin, 1994)

Laffan, Michael, *The partition of Ireland, 1911–1925* (Dublin, 1983)

'Violence and terror in twentieth century Ireland: IRB and IRA', in Mommsen, Wolfgang J., and Hirschfeld, Gerhard (eds.), *Social protest, violence and terror in nineteenth and twentieth century Europe* (London, 1982)

'"Labour must wait": Ireland's conservative revolution', in Corish, Patrick J. (ed.), *Radicals, rebels and establishments* (Belfast, 1985)

'John Redmond', in Brady, Ciaran (ed.), *Worsted in the game: losers in Irish history* (Dublin, 1989)

'Insular attitudes: the revisionists and their critics', in Ní Dhonnchadha, Máirín, and Dorgan, Theo (eds.), *Revising the rising* (Dublin, 1991)

'The sacred memory: religion, revisionism and the Easter Rising', in Devlin, Judith, and Fanning, Ronan (eds.), *Religion and rebellion* (Dublin, 1997)

Lankford, Siobhán, *The hope and the sadness: personal recollections of troubled times in Ireland* (Cork, 1980)

Laqueur, Walter, *Terrorism* (London, 1977)

Lavelle, Patricia, *James O'Mara: a staunch Sinn-Feiner, 1873–1948* (Dublin, 1961)

Lawlor, Sheila, *Britain and Ireland 1914–23* (Dublin, 1983)

'Ireland from truce to treaty: war or peace? July to October 1921', *IHS*, 22, 85 (1980)

Lee, J. J., *The modernisation of Irish society, 1848–1918* (Dublin, 1973)

    Ireland 1912–1985: politics and society (Cambridge, 1989)

Levenson, Samuel, *James Connolly* (London, 1973)

Limerick's fighting story, 1916–21: told by the men who made it (Tralee, 1948)

Loftus, Richard J., 'The poets of the Easter Rising', *Éire-Ireland*, 2, 3 (1967)

Longford, Earl of, and O'Neill, Thomas P., *Eamon de Valera* (London, 1970)

Luddy, Maria, *Hanna Sheehy Skeffington* (Dublin, 1995)

Lynch, Diarmuid, *The I.R.B. and the 1916 insurrection* (Cork, 1957)

Lyons, F. S. L., *The Irish Parliamentary Party, 1890–1910* (London, 1951)

    John Dillon: a biography (London, 1968)

    Ireland since the famine (London, 1971)

    Culture and anarchy in Ireland, 1890–1939 (Oxford, 1979)

    'From war to civil war in Ireland: three essays on the treaty debate', in Farrell, Brian (ed.), *The Irish parliamentary tradition* (Dublin, 1973)

Lyons, J. B., *The enigma of Tom Kettle: Irish patriot, essayist, poet, British soldier, 1880–1916* (Dublin, 1983)

MacCaba, Alasdair, 'Cradling a revolution', *An tÓglach*, Christmas 1962, p. 7.

McCann, Eamonn, *War and an Irish town* (3rd edn, London, 1993)

Macardle, Dorothy, *The Irish republic* (London, 1937)

McCartney, Donal, 'The political use of history in the work of Arthur Griffith', *Journal of Contemporary History*, 8, 1 (1973)

    'De Valera's mission to the United States' in Cosgrove, Art, and McCartney, Donal (eds.), *Studies in Irish history presented to R. Dudley Edwards* (Dublin, 1979)

McColgan, John, *British policy and the Irish administration, 1920–22* (London, 1983)

McCracken, J. L., *Representative government in Ireland: Dáil Éireann, 1919–48* (Oxford, 1958)

MacCurtain, Margaret, 'Women, the vote and the revolution', in MacCurtain, Margaret, and Ó Corráin, Donncha (eds.), *Women in Irish society: the historical dimension* (Dublin, 1978)

MacDonagh, Donagh, 'Ballads of 1916', *The Bell*, 2, 1 (1941)

MacDonagh, Oliver, *Ireland: the union and its aftermath* (London, 1977)

    States of mind: a study of Anglo-Irish conflict, 1780–1980 (London, 1983)

McDowell, R. B., *The Irish administration, 1801–1914* (London, 1964)

    The Irish Convention, 1917–18 (London, 1970)

MacEoin, Uinseann, *Survivors* (Dublin, 1980)

    The I.R.A. in the twilight years, 1923–1948 (Dublin, 1997)

MacEntee, Seán, *Episode at Easter* (Dublin, 1966)

McKillen, Beth, 'Irish feminism and nationalist separatism, 1914–23', *Éire-Ireland*, 17, 3 and 4 (1982)

MacLysaght, Edward, *Changing times: Ireland since 1898* (Gerrards Cross, 1978)

McMahon, Deirdre, "'A worthy monument to a great man": Piaras Béaslaí's life of Michael Collins', *Bullán*, 2, 2 (1996)

McNally, Maura, 'The 1918 East Cavan by-election' (MA dissertation, University College, Dublin, 1978)

MacStiofáin, Seán, *Revolutionary in Ireland* (Farnborough, 1974)

Maguire, Conor A., 'The republican courts', *Capuchin Annual*, 1969

Maher, Jim, *The flying column – West Kilkenny, 1916–21* (Dublin, 1987)

Maillot, Agnès, *IRA: les républicains irlandais* (Caen, 1996)

Mandle, W. F., *The Gaelic Athletic Association and Irish nationalist politics, 1884–1924* (Dublin, 1987)

Mansergh, Nicholas, *The Irish Free State: its government and politics* (London, 1934)

   Northern Ireland: a study in devolution (London, 1936)

   The Irish question, 1840–1921 (3rd edn, London, 1975)

   The prelude to partition: concepts and aims in Ireland and India (Cambridge, 1978)

   The unresolved question: the Anglo-Irish settlement and its undoing, 1921–72 (New Haven and London, 1991)

   'The Government of Ireland Act, 1920: its origins and purposes. The working of the "official" mind', in Barry, J. G. (ed.), *Historical Studies, IX* (Belfast 1974)

Martin, F. X., '1916 – myth, fact and mystery', *Studia Hibernica*, 7 (1967)

   'The 1916 Rising – a coup d'etat or a "bloody protest"?', *Studia Hibernica*, 8 (1968)

Martin, F. X., (ed.), *The Irish Volunteers, 1913–1915: recollections and documents* (Dublin, 1963)

   Leaders and men of the Easter Rising: Dublin 1916 (London, 1967)

Martin, F. X., and Byrne, F. J. (eds.), *The scholar revolutionary: Eoin MacNeill, 1867–1945* (Shannon, 1973)

Maume, Patrick, *'Life that is exile': Daniel Corkery and the search for Irish Ireland* (Belfast, 1993)

   D. P. Moran (Dublin, 1995)

   'The ancient constitution: Arthur Griffith and his intellectual legacy to Sinn Féin', *Irish Political Studies*, 10 (1995)

Maye, Brian, *Arthur Griffith* (Dublin, 1997)

Miller, David, *Church, state and nation in Ireland, 1898–1921* (Dublin, 1973)

Mitchell, Arthur, *Labour in Irish politics, 1890–1930* (Dublin, 1974)

   Revolutionary government in Ireland: Dáil Éireann, 1919–22 (Dublin, 1995)

Moran, Seán Farrell, *Patrick Pearse and the politics of redemption: the mind of the Easter Rising, 1916* (Washington, DC, 1994)

Mulcahy, Richard, 'The Irish Volunteer convention, 27 October 1917', *Capuchin Annual*, 1967

Murphy, Brian P., *Patrick Pearse and the lost republican ideal* (Dublin, 1991)

Murphy, Brian S., 'Politics and ideology: Mary MacSwiney and Irish republicanism, 1872–1942' (Ph.D. dissertation, University College, Cork, 1994)

Murphy, Cliona, *The women's suffrage movement and Irish society in the early twentieth century* (Hemel Hempstead, 1989)

Murphy, Cormac, 'Revolution and radicalism in County Dublin, 1913–21', in Hill, Myrtle, and Barber, Sarah (eds.), *Aspects of Irish studies* (Belfast, 1990)

Murphy, John A., *Ireland in the twentieth century* (Dublin, 1975)

Murray, Peter, 'Citizenship, colonialism and self-determination: Dublin in the United Kingdom, 1885–1918' (Ph.D. dissertation, Trinity College, Dublin, 1987)

Neeson, Eoin, *The civil war, 1922–23* (Dublin, 1989)

Neligan, David, *The spy in the castle* (London, 1968)

Newsinger, John, 'I bring not peace but a sword: the religious motif in the Irish War of Independence', *Journal of Contemporary History,* 13, 3, (1978)

Nowlan, Kevin B. (ed.), *The making of 1916* (Dublin, 1969)

O'Beirne-Ranelagh, John, 'The IRB from the treaty to 1924', *IHS,* 20, 77 (1976)

O'Brien, Brendan, *The long war: the IRA and Sinn Féin, 1985 to today* (Dublin, 1993)

O'Brien, Conor Cruise, *Parnell and his party 1880–90* (Oxford, 1957)

    States of Ireland (London, 1972)

    Herod: reflections on political violence (London, 1978)

    Passion and cunning and other essays (London, 1988)

    Ancestral voices: religion and nationalism in Ireland (Dublin, 1994)

O'Brien, Conor Cruise, (ed.), *The shaping of modern Ireland* (London, 1960)

O'Brien, Gerard, 'The record of the first Dáil debates', *IHS,* 28, 111 (1993)

O'Brien, Joseph V., *William O'Brien and the course of Irish politics* (Berkeley and Los Angeles, 1976)

O'Brien, William, *Forth the banners go: reminiscences of William O'Brien as told to Edward MacLysaght* (Dublin, 1969)

Ó Broin, Leon, *The chief secretary: Augustine Birrell in Ireland* (London, 1969)

    Dublin Castle and the 1916 Rising (2nd edn, London, 1970)

    Revolutionary underground: the story of the Irish Republican Brotherhood, 1858–1924 (Dublin, 1976)

    No man's man: a biographical memoir of Joseph Brennan, civil servant and first governor of the Central Bank (Dublin, 1982)

    Protestant nationalists in revolutionary Ireland: the Stopford connection (Dublin, 1985)

    Just like yesterday . . . an autobiography (Dublin, 1986)

    W. E. Wylie and the Irish revolution, 1916–1921 (Dublin, 1989)

O'Callaghan, Micheál, *'For Ireland and freedom': Roscommon's contribution to the fight for independence* (Boyle, 1964)

O'Carroll, J. F., and Murphy, John A. (eds.), *De Valera and his times* (Cork, 1983)

O'Casey, Sean, *Drums under the windows* (London, 1945)

    Inishfallen fare thee well (London, 1949)

Ó Ceallaigh, Séamus, *Gleanings from Ulster history* (2nd edn, Draperstown, 1994), appendix, 'Dr. Séamus Ó Ceallaigh's story'

Ó Ceallaigh [O'Kelly], Seán T., 'Arthur Griffith', *Capuchin Annual* (1966)

O'Connor, Emmet, *Syndicalism in Ireland, 1917 – 1923* (Cork, 1988)

    A labour history of Ireland, 1824 – 1960 (Dublin, 1992)

O'Connor, Fionnuala, *In search of a state: Catholics in Northern Ireland* (Belfast, 1993)

O'Connor, Frank, *The big fellow* (London, 1961)

    An only child (London, 1958)

O'Donnell, Peadar, *The gates flew open* (London, 1932)

O'Donoghue, Florence, *No other law (the story of Liam Lynch and the Irish Republican Army, 1916–1923)* (Dublin, 1954)

    Tomás MacCurtain (Tralee, 1958)

O'Donovan, Donal, *Kevin Barry and his time* (Dublin, 1989)

Ó Duibhir, Ciarán, *Sinn Féin: the first election, 1908* (Manorhamilton, 1993)

O'Faolain, Sean, *Vive moi! An autobiography* (2nd edn, London, 1993)

O'Farrell, Padraic, *The blacksmith of Ballinalee: Seán MacEoin* (Mullingar, 1993)

O'Farrell, Patrick, *Ireland's English question* (London, 1971)

    England and Ireland since 1800 (Oxford, 1975)

Ó Fearáil, Padraig, *The story of Conradh na Gaeilge. A history of the Gaelic League* (Dublin, 1975)

Ó Fiaich, Tomás, 'The Irish bishops and the conscription issue 1918', *Capuchin Annual*, 1968

O'Flanagan, Neil, 'Dublin city in an age of war and revolution, 1914–24' (MA dissertation, University College, Dublin, 1988)

O'Halloran, Clare, *Partition and the limits of Irish nationalism: an ideology under stress* (Dublin, 1987)

O'Halpin, Eunan, *The decline of the union: British government in Ireland, 1892–1920* (Dublin, 1987)

    'British intelligence in Ireland, 1914–1921', in Andrew, Christopher, and Dilks, David (eds.), *The missing dimension: governments and intelligence communities in the twentieth century* (London, 1984)

O'Hegarty, P. S., *The victory of Sinn Fein* (Dublin, 1924)

    A history of Ireland under the union, 1801–1922 (London, 1952)

O'Kelly, J. J. [Sceilg], *Stepping-stones* (Dublin, n.d. [1939/40])

O'Leary, Cornelius, *Irish elections, 1918–77: parties, voters and proportional representation* (Dublin, 1979)

Ó Lúing, Seán, *Art Ó Gríofa* (Dublin, 1953)

    I die in a good cause: a study of Thomas Ashe, idealist and revolutionary (Tralee, 1970)

O'Mahony, Sean, *Frongoch: university of revolution* (Dublin, 1987)

O'Malley, Ernie, *On another man's wound* (London, 1936)

　　The singing flame (Dublin, 1978)

O'Malley, Padraig, *The uncivil wars: Ireland today* (Belfast, 1983)

O'Neill, Marie, *From Parnell to de Valera: a biography of Jennie Wyse Power, 1858–1941* (Dublin, 1991)

O'Neill, Terence, *The autobiography of Terence O'Neill* (London, 1972)

O'Neill, Thomas P., 'In search of a political path: Irish republicanism, 1922 to 1927', in Hayes-McCoy, G. A. (ed.), *Historical Studies, X* (Galway, 1976)

O'Rahilly, Aodogán, *Winding the clock: O'Rahilly and the 1916 Rising,* (Dublin, 1991)

Osborough, Niall, 'Law in Ireland 1916–26', *Northern Ireland Legal Quarterly,* 23, 1 (1972)

O'Shiel, Kevin, 'Memoirs of my lifetime', *Irish Times,* November 1966

Ó Snodaigh, Padraig, *Comhghuaillithe na réabhlóide, 1913–1916* (Dublin, 1966)

O'Sullivan, Donal, *The Irish Free State and its senate* (London, 1940)

Ó Tuama, Seán (ed.), *The Gaelic League idea* (Cork, 1972)

Pakenham, Frank (Lord Longford), *Peace by ordeal* (London, 1935)

Patterson, Henry, *Class conflict and sectarianism: the Protestant working class and the Belfast labour movement, 1868–1920* (Belfast, 1980)

　　The politics of illusion: a political history of the IRA (London, 1997)

Paul-Dubois, Louis, *The Irish struggle and its results* (London, 1934)

'Periscope', 'The last days of Dublin Castle', *Blackwood's Magazine,* August 1922

Phillips, W. Alison, *The revolution in Ireland, 1906–1923* (London, 1923)

Phoenix, Eamon, *Northern nationalism: nationalist politics, partition and the Catholic minority in Northern Ireland, 1890–1940* (Belfast, 1994)

Prager, Jeffrey, *Building democracy in Ireland: political order and cultural integration in a newly independent nation* (New York, 1986)

Pyne, Peter, 'The third Sinn Féin party: 1923–1926', *Economic and Social Review,* 1, 1 and 2 (1969–70)

　　'The new Irish state and the decline of the republican Sinn Féin party, 1923–1926', *Éire-Ireland,* 11, 3 (1976)

Rafter, Kevin, *The Clann: the story of Clann na Poblachta* (Cork and Dublin, 1996)

Regan, John M., 'The politics of reaction: the dynamics of treatyite government and policy, 1922–33', *IHS,* 30, 120 (1997)

Ring, Jim, *Erskine Childers* (London, 1996)

Robbins, Frank, *Under the starry plough: recollections of the Irish Citizen Army* (Dublin, 1977)

Rockett, Kevin, Gibbons, Luke, and Hill, John, *Cinema and Ireland* (London, 1988)

Ruane, Joseph, and Todd, Jennifer, *The dynamics of conflict in Northern Ireland: power, conflict and emancipation* (Cambridge, 1996)

Rumpf, E., and Hepburn, A. C., *Nationalism and socialism in twentieth-century Ireland* (Liverpool, 1977)

Ryan, Desmond, *Remembering Sion: a chronicle of storm and quiet* (London, 1934)

   Sean Treacy and the 3rd. Tipperary brigade (Tralee, 1945)

   The rising: the complete story of Easter Week (4th edn, Dublin, 1966)

Ryan, Meda, *The real chief: the story of Liam Lynch* (Cork and Dublin, 1986)

Savage, David, 'The attempted home rule settlement of 1916', *Éire-Ireland*, 2, 3 (1967)

Shannon, Catherine B., *Arthur J. Balfour and Ireland, 1874–1922* (Washington, 1988)

Shaw, Francis, 'The canon of Irish history: a challenge', *Studies*, 61, 242 (1972)

Sinnott, Richard, *Irish voters decide: voting behaviour in elections and referendums since 1918* (Manchester, 1995)

Skinner, Liam C., *Politicians by accident* (Dublin, 1946)

Smith, Anthony D. S., *Nationalism in the twentieth century* (Oxford, 1979)

Staunton, Martin, 'The Royal Munster Fusiliers in the Great War, 1914–19' (MA dissertation, University College, Dublin, 1986)

Stewart, A. T. Q., *The Ulster crisis* (London 1967)

   Edward Carson (Dublin, 1981)

Stubbs, John O., 'The Unionists and Ireland, 1914–18', *Historical Journal*, 33, 4 (1990)

Taylor, A. J. P., *English history, 1914–1945* (Oxford, 1965)

Taylor, Rex, *Michael Collins* (London, 1958)

Téry, Simone, *En Irlande: de la guerre d'indépendance à la guerre civile (1914–1923)* (Paris, 1923)

Thompson, William Irwin, *The imagination of an insurrection: Dublin, Easter 1916* (New York, 1967)

Tierney, Michael, *Eoin MacNeill: scholar and man of action, 1867–1945* (Oxford, 1980)

Townshend, Charles, *The British campaign in Ireland, 1919–1921* (Oxford, 1975)

   Political violence in Ireland: government and resistance since 1848 (Oxford, 1983)

   'The Irish Republican Army and the development of guerrilla warfare, 1916–1921', *English Historical Review*, 94, 371 (1979)

   'The Irish railway strike of 1920; industrial action and civil resistance in the struggle for independence', *IHS*, 21, 83 (1979)

   'The suppression of the Easter Rising', *Bullán*, 1, 1 (1994)

Travers, Pauric, *Settlements and divisions: Ireland 1870–1922* (Dublin, 1988)

   Eamon de Valera (Dublin, 1994)

   'The priest in politics: the case of conscription' in MacDonagh, Oliver, Mandle, W. F., and Travers, Pauric (eds.), *Irish culture and nationalism, 1750–1950* (Dublin, 1983)

Tudor, Henry, *Political myth* (London, 1972)

Tynan, Katharine, *The years of the shadow* (London, 1919)

Ua Ceallaigh, Seán ['Sceilg'/O'Kelly, J. J.], *Cathal Brugha* (Dublin, 1942)

Valiulis, Maryann Gialanella, *Portrait of a revolutionary: General Richard Mulcahy and the founding of the Irish Free State* (Dublin, 1992)

Van Voris, Jacqueline, *Constance de Markievicz: in the cause of Ireland* (Amherst, 1967)

Vaughan, W. E. (ed.), *A new history of Ireland, VI. Ireland under the Union, II, 1870–1921* (Oxford, 1996)

Walker, Brian, *Dancing to history's tune: history, myth and politics in Ireland* (Belfast, 1996)

'The Irish electorate, 1868–1915', *IHS*, 18, 71 (1973)

Walsh, J. J., *Recollections of a rebel* (Tralee, 1944)

Walsh, Louis J., *'On my keeping' and in theirs* (Dublin, 1921)

Ward, Alan J., *Ireland and Anglo-American relations, 1899–1921* (London, 1969)

The Easter Rising: revolution and Irish nationalism (Arlington Heights, 1980)

The Irish constitutional tradition: responsible government and modern Ireland, 1782–1992 (Dublin, 1994)

'Lloyd George and the 1918 conscription crisis', *Historical Journal*, 17, 1 (1974)

Ward, Margaret, *Unmanageable revolutionaries: women and Irish nationalism* (London, 1983)

Maud Gonne: A Life (London, 1990)

Wells, Warre B., and Marlowe, N., *A history of the Irish rebellion of 1916* (Dublin, 1916)

Wheeler-Bennett, John W., *John Anderson, Viscount Waverley* (London, 1962)

White, Terence de Vere, *Kevin O'Higgins* (London, 1948)

Whyte, J. H., *Church and state in modern Ireland, 1923–1979* (Dublin, 1980)

Understanding Northern Ireland (Oxford, 1990)

Williams, Martin, 'Ancient mythology and revolutionary ideology in Ireland, 1878–1916', *Historical Journal*, 26, 2 (1983)

Williams, T. D. (ed.), *The Irish struggle, 1916–1926* (London, 1966)

Secret societies in Ireland (Dublin, 1973)

Winter, Ormonde, *Winter's tale: an autobiography* (London, 1955)

Wohl, Robert, *The generation of 1914* (London, 1980)

Younger, Calton, *Ireland's Civil War* (London, 1968)

Arthur Griffith (Dublin, 1981)

Interviews

At an earlier stage in the author's career, when his interests were more narrowly focused on one aspect or phase of this book (see above, Preface), he interviewed the following:

Máire Comerford; Eamon de Valera; Thomas Dillon; Michael Hayes; Seán MacEntee; Edward MacLysaght; Richard Mulcahy; Liam Ó Briain; Páidín O'Keeffe

Index

abstention, from Dáil, 416, 436, 438, 441, 458, 464

abstention, from Westminster, policy of, 18–19, 74, 87, 416, 438, 458
discussion of, 205, 207
implemented by Parliamentary Party, 1918, 135
Labour and, 158
Plunkett's adoption of, 85, 88
unease at, 250

abstention policy, abandonment of by Sinn Féin, 1998, 460–1

abstract images, 215, 217, 252, 455, 463

Adams, Gerry, 457, 458

agrarian unrest, 78, 188, 273, 301, 310, 314–15
republican courts and, 315–16, 317

All-For-Ireland League, 63, 122, 125, 164, 188
and West Cork by-election, 73–5

Ancient Order of Hibernians (AOH), 59, 123, 183, 206

Andrews, C. S.,
on abstract images, 217
IRA dictatorship, acquiescence in, 375
politicians, contempt for, 280
on republicans, arrogance of, 1922, 384

Anglo-Irish War, 1919–21, 266, 271–98, 310, 331, 341, 348–9

Anglophobia, 35, 75, 137, 214, 351

anti-conscription fund, 139–41, 336

anti-conscription pledge, 139–40

anti-Semitism, 55, 232–3, 294, 446n

arbitration courts, 170, 310–17

ard-chomhairle (Sinn Féin governing body), 146, 173–4, 231, 343–4, 395
in 1919: 175–6, 287, 307
in party structure, 172
question of summoning, 1922, 419, 420
and social conflict, 1919, 254, 258
and treaty, 363, 365, 367, 371

ard-fheis (Sinn Féin party convention), 172, 175
1919: 175, 195–6, 285, 305, 307, 308, 324
1921: 175, 203, 344–5
disappearance of, 1919–21, 287
in party structure, 171–2, 173–4

ard-fheis, February/May 1922, 175, 239, 370–4, 378, 418
adjourned, 373
Collins's speech at, 372
de Valera's speech at, 371–2
elections for, 365–6, 367, 369
opposition to secret ballot at, 370
reconvened, 389
republican majority at, 370–1
women and, 204, 370

army convention, 1922, 374, 411

army mutiny, 1924, 433

army split, 1922, 364, 374

Ashe, Thomas, 262, 264
and Collins, 87
death of, 200, 262–3, 269
and East Clare by-election, 108
and South Longford by-election, 97–8

Asquith, H. H., 37, 298
  and Easter Rising, aftermath of, 50, 52, 54
  and home rule negotiations, 1916, 56–8
Aud, the, 38–9
Auxiliaries, 292, 332

Balfour, A. J., 58
Barry, Kevin, 221, 278
Barry, Tom, 298, 412
Barton, Déogréine, 204, 366
Barton, Robert, 163, 220, 349, 363, 405–6
Bates, Dawson, 339–40
Baxter, P. F., 401–3
Beamish, Richard, 379
Béaslaí, Piaras, 161, 251, 338
Belfast boycott, 231–2, 288, 318
Birrell, Augustine, 16, 40, 49
Black and Tans, 292, 332, 339, 372, 384, 413
Bloody Sunday, 1920, 289, 294
  1972: 455
Bloom, Leopold, 3, 17
Blueshirts, 448
Blythe, Ernest, 193, 353, 371, 400
  on English language, 235
  on Ireland and its people, 218
  on moderate nationalists, 243
  new party, 1922, proposes, 420
  in Reading Jail, 65
  on self-sacrifice, 216
  Sinn Féin, hostility to, 1922, 421
  on Sinn Féin and violence, 1913, 33
  on social policy, republicans' need for
    (1913), 255
  on superiority of soldiers, 196
Boer War, 12, 35
Boland, Harry, 382, 389, 407
  and *ard-fheis*, 1919, 195–6
  death of, 417
  and general election, 1918, 154, 155, 158
  and 'German plot', 144
  honorary secretary, Sinn Féin, 145, 418
  and Labour Party, 1918, 158
  and proportional representation, 327
  vote on treaty, hostility to, 386

Bonar Law, Andrew, 7, 8, 157, 227
  on banning Sinn Féin, 1919, 284
  and conscription, 142, 145, 150
boundary commission, 351, 355, 440–1
Brecht, Bertolt, 463
Breen, Dan, 390, 399, 400
  chosen by both panels, general election,
    1922, 389–90
  defeated, 1922, 406
  on Irish Volunteers and Sinn Féin, 280
  provisional government, trusted by, 392
  on the republic, 244
  and Soloheadbeg, 275
Brennan, Patrick, 111, 153
Brennan, Robert, 155, 158
British policy
  conscription, 130, 132–3, 140, 142, 149–50
  counter-attack, 1920, 292
  'German plot' arrests, 142–5
  home rule negotiations, 1916, 56–8, 60
  partition, 1921, 333
  repressive measures, 1917–18, 269–70;
    1919–20, 271, 284–5, 292
  reprisals, 273–4, 276, 295–6, 297
  treaty negotiations, 246–7, 347, 350–1,
    353
Brodrick, Albinia, 192–3
Browne, Noel, 451
Brugha, Cathal, 268, 278, 300, 305, 349, 380,
    405
  on army's independence of government, 369
  on army's right to rule, 382
  and British cabinet, planned assassination
    of, 138
  character of, 138
  on Collins, 372
  on consulting the people, 271
  death of, 417
  de Valera on, 348
  and fighting men, supremacy of, 1922, 359
  forced collections, prohibits, 299
  and 'German plot', 144, 146
  on government authority, 303
  and IRB, 282

and Irish Nation League, 86
and Irish Volunteer revival, 267
and Mansion House committee, 93
moderates, suspicious of, 86
and oath of allegiance to Dáil and republic,
    245, 282, 356, 411
and Parliamentary Party, cooperation with,
    1918, 138
and party structure, 173
and republicanism, 118, 245
and Sinn Féin constitution, 118
and Sinn Féin, unification of, 105
and treaty negotiations, 348
Buckingham Palace conference, 1914, 58
Buckley [Ua Buachalla], Donal, 337
Buckley, Margaret, 449, 452
Burbage, Fr Tom, 55
Butler, Mary, 21
Butt, Isaac, 5, 23, 75, 122
by-elections
    East Cavan (1918), 146–9
    East Clare (1917), 108–12
    East Tyrone (1918), 126–8
    Fermanagh-South Tyrone (1981), 457
    Galway (1936), 80, 449
    Kilkenny city (1917), 112–13
    King's Co. (1918), 146–7
    North Derry (1919), 309
    North Leitrim (1907–8), 25–9, 379
    North Roscommon (1917), 77–85
    South Armagh (1918), 122–5
    South Longford (1917), 96–103, 193
    South Mayo (1900), 27, 29
    Waterford city (1918), 125–6
    West Cork (1916), 73–5
    in 1917, significance of, 96, 113–16, 187
Byrne, Alfie, 404
Byrne, Joseph, 132

Campbell, James, 55, 58
Carney, Winifrid, 154
Carroll, Lewis, 394
Carson, Edward, 7, 9, 32, 51, 62, 133, 145,
    284

example of, 8, 13, 139, 454
Casement, Roger, 37, 39, 193
    and Howth gun-running, 15
    execution of, 49, 55–6
    and Ulster Volunteers, 226
'Castle document', 38–9
Catholic Bulletin, 55, 81, 263
Catholic Church
    and conscription crisis, 138–42, 147
    hierarchy, and conscription, 139, 141; and
        general election, 1918, 160–1
    and home rule negotiations, 1916, 59
    priests, 91, 149, 198–200, 370
    and Sinn Féin, 198–201
Ceannt, Áine, 202, 300
Ceannt, Eamonn, 33, 43, 235
Censorship, 259–60, 300
Chesterton, G. K., 136
Childers, Erskine, 363, 368, 395
    and Collins–de Valera pact, 389
    defeated, 1922, 405
    on de Valera's extremism, 1922, 353
    execution of, 417
    and Howth gun-running, 15
    on Ulster, 229–30
    vote on treaty, hostility to, 386
Christian Brothers, 193
Churchill, Winston, 271, 388, 398
Cinemas, 264
Citizen Army, 44, 157
civil war, 1922–3, 218, 434, 435
    cost of, 414–15
    course of, 411–17
    drift towards, 303, 374, 376, 386
    fatalities in, 415–16
    fears of, 359, 384–5
Clancy, J. J., 337
Clancy, Peadar, 108
Clann na Poblachta, 451, 464
Clarke, Kathleen, 119, 363
    defeated, 1922, 405, 406
    and term 'Sinn Féin', 69
    and Volunteer Dependants' Fund,
        67

Clarke, Tom, 9, 268
  and Easter Rising, 36, 39, 40, 46
  execution of, 49
  forecast by, 75
  and IRB, 12–13, 34, 446, 454
class conflict, fear of, 252, 258, 259, 310
Cleary, Thomas Stanislaus, 20
Cohalan, Daniel (bishop of Cork), 139, 141
Cole, Walter, 194, 322, 401
Collins, Con, 359
Collins, Michael, 198, 267, 270, 451, 464–5
  acting president, Dáil, 1920, 290
  and ard-fheis, 1919, 195–6
  and Ashe, Thomas, 87–8, 98
  British government's Northern policy, 1921,
    misjudgement of, 334
  chairman, provisional government, 360
  character of, 98, 417
  civil war, efforts of to avoid, 411–12
  on conscription, 133
  and conscription crisis, 136
  death of, 417
  on dogs and poteen, possibility of licensing,
    330
  in Frongoch, 65
  fundraising by, 319
  and general election, 1918, 154, 161, 280,
    383
  and general election, 1921, 334, 336
  and general election, 1922, 382–3, 396–8,
    390, 410
  and 'German plot', 144, 146
  on Griffith, 1917, 87–8
  and home rule negotiations, 1916, 61
  intelligence network of, 37, 144
  on Irish Volunteers and violence, 283–4
  and jobbery, 321
  legends concerning, 278
  and local elections, 1920, 325
  Macready, admired by, 278
  and Mansion House convention, 91
  and moderates in Sinn Féin, suspicion of,
    86, 176, 281

  and North Roscommon by-election, 83, 194
  and October convention, 1917, 120, 195
  and Paris peace conference, suspicion of,
    251
  and Parliamentary Party, suspicion of
    cooperation with, 138
  and party structure, 1917, 173
  political skill of, 1922, 373–4
  president, supreme council, IRB, 282
  and released internees, 66
  and republican police, 317–18
  and republicanism, 98–9, 118, 242, 383
  on Sinn Féin and Dáil government, 320
  Sinn Féin, 1919, dismissive of, 305
  and Sinn Féin, distrust of, 86,
  and Sinn Féin executive, 106
  and South Longford by-election, 96, 98,
    101
  and the squad, 275
  standing committee, excluded from, 1919,
    174, 280, 283
  and treaty, 351, 355
  Volunteer Dependants' Fund, secretary of,
    67, 68
  and Ulster, 228, 334
  and Ulster seats, 1918, 161
  and treaty, 350, 351, 355, 361
Collins–de Valera pact, 1922, 387–9, 390, 394,
    407, 420, 426
  Collins's violation of, 398
  de Valera on, 409
  Dillon on, 398
  Griffith on, 388
  opposition to, 388
  republicans' reactions to, 389
  result of, 390–1
  Sinn Féin, role under, 387, 390
Connolly, James, 157, 214, 252
  execution of, 49, 50
  and Griffith, 17
  on Griffith's Sinn Féin, 254–5
  and Irish Neutrality League, 1914, 129
  on public opinion, 36

conscription
  and Catholic Church, 138–42, 147
  fear of, 128–30, 149–50, 151
  Irish Parliamentary Party and, 134–5
  Irish Volunteers and, 135–6
  Sinn Féin and, 136–8, 140
conscription crisis, 133–49, 270
conscription, into Irish Volunteers, 1921, 302
Conservative Party, 11, 133
  and Ulster unionists, 7–8, 13, 51, 225, 230,
    333, 341
constitution, Free State, 373, 376, 398, 409,
  410
Corish, Richard, 301, 389, 400–1
Cork city, burning of, 296
Corkery, Daniel, 261
Cosgrave, W. T., 278, 320, 400, 441
  chairman, provisional government, 417
  elected, Kilkenny city, 113
  and Fianna Fáil, entry into Dáil of, 443–4
  in Lewes Jail, 65
  militancy, record of, 87
  on Sinn Féin, 1921, 289
countermanding order, 1916, 36, 39, 108
Coyne, Bernard (bishop of Elphin), 79
Craig, James, 13, 339
Cumann na mBan, 70, 104, 121, 284, 446, 449
  banned, 1919, 276, 285
  and Easter Rising, 44
  and Irish Volunteers, 201, 203
  and general election, 1918, 154, 164
  purged by Mary MacSwiney, Cork, 365
  and Sinn Féin, 203
  and treaty, 365
  and women's rights, 201
Cumann na nGaedheal (1900–7), 21, 25
Cumann na nGaedheal (1923–33), 421–2, 444,
  447, 451
  discredited, by failure of boundary
    commission, 441
  record in office, 433–4
Cumann na Poblachta (1922), 367–8, 369,
  379–80, 396–8, 444, 447

aims of, 380
funding of, 380
Cumann Poblachta na hÉireann, 448–9, 451
Curragh Incident, 1914, 7, 411
curfew, 286

Dáil, first (1919–21)
  and agrarian unrest, 315–16, 317
  bureaucracy, 300, 302, 306–7, 318, 321, 342
  cabinet, 282, 300, 309, 319, 323, 359
  and corruption, fear of, 321
  courts, 313–18, 343
  democratic programme of, 259
  dissolution of, 410
  finances, 319–20
  first meeting of, 266, 304–5
  and Irish language, use of, 238
  loan, 319–20
  meetings of, 322
  members of, 191, 192, 194
  ministries, 322
  power in, concentration of, 321
  recognition of state of war, 282–3
  and Sinn Féin, 180, 305, 308–9, 318–19,
    320–1, 342
  suppressed, 285
  and Volunteers, 282
Dáil, second (1921–2)
  and army, 376
  and cabinet, 349–50, 359
  dissolution of, 410–11, 416
  election of, 339–41
  members of, 192, 194, 338, 341
  peace committee of, 1922, 386
  women in, 202
'Dáil, second' (republican) (1921–38), 411,
  426
  transfers authority to IRA, 1938, 446–7,
    458
Dáil, third (1922–3)
  convened, 416, 426
  election of, 399–410
  postponed, 411, 416

Dáil, Local Government Department, 300,
    302–3
    achievements of, 331–2
Daly, P. T., 25, 159
Davis, Thomas, 221
Davitt, Michael, 18, 98
Davitt, Michael, Jr, 79
Deák, Ferenc, 19, 242
democratic programme, 259
de Róiste, Liam, 24, 32, 105, 116, 261, 370
    and second Dáil, dissolution of, 410
    and general election, 1918, 153, 154
    and general election, 1921, 338, 339
    and general election, 1922, 396, 398, 407
    on Government of Ireland Bill, 333
    lunatic asylum, hides in, 296
    on republicans, 1922, 414
    on treaty, 353
    and Volunteers, 196, 281, 365
Derrig, Tomás, 300, 424
De Valera, Eamon, 9, 10, 86, 198, 398, 400,
    452, 464
    on Anglo-Irish War, 1921, 295
    and army, 1921, 349
    arrested, 1923, 437
    autocratic conduct of, 175
    Bismarckian escapology of, 442
    on British rule, 224
    character of, 112
    on class conflict, 258
    and Collins, 349
    and compromise proposals, 1922, 359
    and conscription crisis, 139
    Dáil, contempt of for, 1922, 359, 381
    on Dáil and Sinn Féin, 305–6
    Dáil president, defeated as, 360
    and East Clare by-election, 108–12
    in Easter Rising, 46
    and electoral activity, 96–7
    and external association, 347, 425
    and Four Courts garrison, 412
    on Free State government, 438
    and general election, 1921, 334–6, 338

and general election, 1922, 381–2, 383, 407
    and government authority, 303
    on Griffith's writings, 261
    and Irish language, 234, 237, 238–9
    irresponsible statements by, 1922, 376,
        381–2
    on labour, 254
    in Lewes Jail, 65; release from, 107
    Lincoln Jail, escape from, 278
    MacNeill, defence of, 1917, 119
    and Mansion House conference, 1918, 137
    and Mellows, Liam, 1922, 423
    and militarism, 1922, 375
    on 'national question', primacy of, 428–9,
        442
    oath of fidelity, takes, 444; abolishes, 447
    and O'Connor, Rory, 375, 425
    and party structure, 173
    poetic tribute to, 112
    political base, need for, 1922, 422, 426–7
    politics, suspicion of, 1917, 97
    in power, after 1932, 447–9
    president, Dáil, 245
    president, Irish Republic, 245, 282, 347–8
    president, Irish Volunteers, 268
    president, second Sinn Féin, 117, 170
    and priests, 110, 199
    provocative speeches by, 1917, 110, 113, 248
    and public opinion, 1922, 356
    religious terminology of, 216
    and republican IRA, 1922, 375, 376, 412,
        425, 426
    on republican tactics, 1922, 413
    and republicanism, 118, 119, 229–30,
        241–2, 243, 346–7
    on republicans' dilemma, 1922, 424–5
    represses IRA, 448, 449
    secret ballot, reservations concerning, 1922,
        370
    and Sinn Féin, 1921, 335
    on Sinn Féin and Dáil government, 320–1
    Sinn Féin executive, coopted to, 1917, 194
    and Sinn Féin, 1922, 418–19, 427–9

and third Sinn Féin, continuity with second, 464

third Sinn Féin, resigns from, 1926, 441–2

skill of, in conscription crisis, 139

and South Armagh election (1918), 124

and South Longford by-election, 96–7

and treaty, 353, 356, 447–8

on Ulster, 227, 229–30, 334

and Ulster in treaty negotiations, 232

in United States, 263, 285, 319, 334

on violence, 1917, 248

Devine, Thomas, 80, 84

Devlin, Joe, 257, 327

and constitutional methods, failure of, 135

and East Clare election, 109

and East Tyrone by-election, 127

and general election 1918, 156, 164, 165, 166

and general election, 1921, 141, 334, 336

and home rule negotiations, 1916, 57, 59

and Mansion House conference, 1918, 137

and partition, 334

and South Armagh by-election, 124

and South Longford by-election, 99

and Ulster Nationalists, 166

and Waterford city by-election, 126

on working class, 255

Dillon, John, 6, 62

and conscription, 134, 135, 151

on de Valera, speeches of, 1922, 382

and East Cavan by-election, 146–9

and East Clare by-election, 109

and Easter Rising, 39

and Easter Rising, aftermath of, 49–50, 51, 52, 54, 56

electoral misfortune of, compared with republicans in 1922, 408

and general election, 1918, 156, 157, 160, 162–3, 165

and general election, 1921, 339

and 'German plot', 144

Griffith, loathing of, 147

home rule and conscription, rejects link between, 135

and home rule negotiations, 1916, 57, 59, 60

leader, Irish Parliamentary Party, 125

and Mansion House conference, 1918, 137

and North Roscommon by-election, 84–5

on pact, Collins's violation of, 1922, 398

and party disorganization, 157, 166, 168

pessimism of, 125

and public opinion, 75, 99

and Sinn Féin defeats, 1918, 128

and Sinn Féin resources, 1918, 179

and South Armagh by-election, 124

and South Longford by-election, 99–100

on violence, efficacy of, 274

Dillon, Thomas, 87, 91

Dockrell, Maurice, 165

Document No. 2, 363–4, 425

Dolan, C. J., 25–9, 165

Dolan, James, 165

dominion status, 298, 350

Donegal Vindicator, on treaty, 357–8

Donnelly, Eamonn, 340

Donnelly, Patrick, 123, 124

Dooley, Brighid, 337

Drohan, Francis, 357, 390

Duke, Henry, 68, 130, 132

Dungannon clubs, 21–4, 66

East Cavan by-election, 146–9

East Cavan and treaty, 362

East Clare by-election, 108–12, 130, 199

conscription as issue in, 130

East Tyrone by-election, 126–8

Easter Rising

preparations for, 34–40

course of, 43–6

public reaction to, 47–8

Edward VII, 21

elitism, 214, 218–19, 232, 449–50

and indifference to mass opinion, 235, 243, 249, 424, 458

of soldiers towards civilians, 196, 198, 277, 298–9, 358

emigration, 188–90, 314

enlistment, of Irishmen in British army, 9, 36, 44, 130, 189

Etchingham, Seán, 301, 355

executions
    Barry, Kevin, 278
    Casement, Roger, 49, 55–6
    Easter rebels, 49, 75
    Republicans, in civil war, 417, 435

external association, 347, 425

Fallon, Thomas, 157

famine, the, 220

farm labourers, decline of, 257–8

farmers, in general election, 1922, 391, 392, 393, 404, 406

Farrell, Gerald, 157

Farrell, J. P., 99, 101

fatalities
    in British campaign, 1920–1, 295
    in civil war, 415–16
    in Dublin, 1922, 413
    in Easter Rising, 46
    in Ireland, 1918–21, 295
    among Irish soldiers in First World War, 295
    in Northern Ireland, 1970s–1990s, 454–5

female suffrage, 126, 151, 203, 253

Fianna Fáil, 441–2, 443, 444, 446, 447, 448

Figgis, Darrell, 65, 101, 193, 196, 312, 363
    and ard-fheis, 1919, 195–6
    and general election, 1922, 391–2, 395, 404
    and 'German plot', 144
    on Griffith, 89
    and Howth gun-running, 15
    and October convention, 1917, 120
    and Sinn Féin catechism, 216

film, 264

Fine Gael, 451

First World War, 34, 248, 295
    impact of on Ireland, 35–6, 310
    impact of on Waterford city, 125

Fisher, Warren, 292–4

FitzGerald, Desmond, 46, 47, 65, 421
    and Irish language, 240

flying columns, 275

Fogarty, Michael (bishop of Killaloe), 124, 200, 224,
    on Fr O'Flanagan, 361

Four Courts,
    attack on, 411–13
    seizure by republicans, 375

France, Anatole, 52

Freeman's Journal, 52, 147, 160, 264, 285, 362

French, Viscount
    attempted assassination of, 275, 294
    and conscription, 150
    and Easter Rising, aftermath of, 50
    and 'German plot', 143, 144
    contradictory policies of, 276
    urges repression, 284
    viceroy, 143

Frongoch, prisoner-of-war camp, 64–6, 360
    release of internees from, 66, 75, 248, 267

Gaelic Athletic Association (GAA), 11, 94, 151,
    and 'flapper' meetings, 203
    and Sinn Féin, 68, 193, 206

Gaelic League, 9–10, 11, 21, 32, 234, 236
    banned, 276, 285
    and Sinn Féin, 68, 193, 206, 238

Gaeltacht, 10, 154, 237–8

Gaffney, Patrick, 391

Galway by-election, 80, 449

Galway county councillors, peace move of, 289–90

Gavan Duffy, George, 31, 52, 92, 103, 159
    and peace conference, 180
    on provisional government, 416

general election, 1918
    British repression in, 155
    campaign, 162–4
    Irish Parliamentary Party and, 154, 156–7, 162–3, 166–8
    Labour and, 157–9
    personation in, 164
    results of, 164–8
    Sinn Féin candidates in, 153–4

Sinn Féin expenditure on, 179

Sinn Féin manifesto, 155, 246

Sinn Féin preparations for, 152–5

and Ulster, 160–1, 165–6

women in, 154

general election, 1921

campaign, 339–40

cost to Sinn Féin, 341

preparations for, 334

results of, 340

Sinn Féin candidates in, 338, 339, 341

Sinn Féin manifesto, 335

general election, 1922

campaign, 381–4, 391–8

choice of candidates, 389, 391

Collins and, 369, 382, 410

de Valera and, 369, 381–2, 407

'ingratitude' of electors, 406–7, 409–10

intimidation in, 391–4, 399

farmers in, 391, 392, 393, 404, 406

Figgis, Darrell and, 391–2, 395, 404

Griffith and, 383, 384

pro-treaty Sinn Féin in, 382–4, 398, 400–3,
    409, 410

Labour Party in, 394, 403–4, 406, 409

O'Connor, Art, on, 409

O'Hegarty, P. S., on, 395–6

orderly nature of, 394

personation in, 399–400, 403

proportional representation, impact of, 391,
    407–8

republicans in, 381–2, 392–4, 404–10

results of, 400–10, 433, 462

Sinn Féin propaganda in, 394, 395

uncontested seats in, 399

violence in, 376, 383, 391–4, 399–400

women in, 405

general election, 1923, 437

general elections, 1927, 443–4

General Post Office, Dublin (GPO), 43–4, 45,
    46

George V, 341–2

'German plot' arrests, 143–6, 149, 182

Gibbons, Mother Columba, 200–1

Ginnell, Laurence, 63

expulsions of, 416

and North Roscommon by-election, 81, 83

and South Armagh by-election, 123

and term 'Sinn Féin', 69

Gladstone, William, 18, 298

Gogarty, Oliver St John, 261, 448

Gonne, Maud, 21

Good, James, 262

Gorey, Denis, 392

Government of Ireland ('Partition') Act, 1920,
    232, 250, 333

Grattan's Parliament, 17, 21, 220, 242, 425

reservations concerning, 19, 33, 87

Green, Alice Stopford, 15

Greene, Godfrey, 392

Greenwich mean time, 62

Greenwood, Hamar, 277, 291, 293–4, 296

Griffith, Arthur, 3, 9, 14, 152, 194, 380, 400

abstention, policy of, 18–19, 458

acerbity of, 147, 262, 372

acting president, Sinn Féin, 1919–20, 285,
    306

activities of, 1917, 181–2

anti-Semitism of, 233n

arrest of, 1916, 53

arrest of, 1918, 144, 147

arrest of, 1920, 277, 290

on capitalism, 253

character of, 16–17

on civilian authority, 284

and conscription, 129–30

on Dáil and Sinn Féin, 306

on Davis and treaty, 221

death of, 417

defiance of IRA, 1922, 384

and de Valera, 116–17

and dual monarchy, 17–19, 96, 425

and East Cavan by-election, 146–9

and East Clare by-election, 110

economic policy of, 19, 255–6, 257

and female suffrage, 201

Griffith, Arthur (*cont.*)
  on foreign countries, 223, 262, 263
  and general election, 1922, 383, 384
  and home rule negotiations, 1916, 61
  on Hungary, 3, 18, 223
  and Irish Nation League, 71–2
  and Irish Neutrality League, 1914, 129
  and lock-out, 1913, 253
  and Mansion House committee, 93
  and Mansion House conference, 137
  and Mansion House convention, 91–3
  militant record of, 195
  urges moderation, 245
  and National Council, 23
  and nationalism, 223
  and North Leitrim by-election, 25–9
  and North Roscommon by-election, 81, 177
  and oaths to king, 1922, 356
  and October convention, 1917, 119, 120, 195
  and Parliamentary Party, 19, 147, 262
  and Pim, Herbert Moore, 1916, 71, 72
  and *Playboy of the Western World*, 16–17
  and Plunkett, 89, 116
  president, Dáil, 360
  on pro-treaty publicity, 1922, 420
  in Reading Jail, 1916, 64
  and separatism, 19
  on Sinn Féin membership, 185
  Sinn Féin presidency, resigns, 1917, 117
  on socialism, 253
  on soul of Ireland, 217
  and South Armagh by-election, 125
  and South Longford by-election, 96, 101
  and treaty, 351, 356
  and Ulster, 226
  vice-president, Sinn Féin, 117
  and violence, 1919–21, 248
  on Westminster, 135
  writings of, 261–3
Griffith, Maud, 83, 93, 101, 114, 144
Gwynn, Stephen, 283

Hardinge Commission, 55
Healy, Frank, 73–4
Healy, T. M., 20, 56
  and Clare, 108, 112
  former colleagues, hatred of, 137–8
  and Mansion House conference, 137
  and Sinn Féin after 'German plot' arrests, 146
  on violence, efficacy of, 274, 298
  and West Cork by-election, 74
Hoare, Joseph (bishop of Ardagh and Clonmacnoise), 48
Hobson, Bulmer, 13–14, 31, 446, 454
  on British errors after Rising, 49
  and Dungannon clubs, 21, 24
  and Easter Rising, 38–9, 46
  on independent Ireland, 434
  on National Council, 24
  and North Leitrim by-election, 27
  on public opinion, 30, 36
Hogan, Patrick, 392–3
Home Rule Act, 1914, 8, 323, 332
home rule negotiations, 1916, 56–62, 75
Home Rule Party, *see* Irish Parliamentary Party
Howth gun-running, 15, 33
Hume, John, 459
Humphries, Dick, 45
'Hungarian Policy', 18, 27, 71, 242
Hungarian rising, 1956, 51
hunger strikes, 1981, 457
Hyde, Douglas, 10, 32
  on Irish language, 234

internment, 1971, 455
IRA, *see* Irish Republican Army (1922–), Irish Volunteers
IRB, *see* Irish Republican Brotherhood
Irish Bulletin, 154, 265, 295, 296, 316
  on Sinn Féin and Dáil, 321
  on Ulster, 228
Irish Citizen Army, 44
Irish Convention, 106–7, 134, 230, 251–2

Irish Freedom, 14–15
  on Irish language and Ulster, 233
  on labour, 253–4
  on republicanism, 241
  on Ulster, 226, 228, 233
  on Ulster unionists, 226, 228–9
Irish Independent, 59, 76, 260, 263–4, 362
'Irish-Ireland', 9
Irish-Ireland League, 62
Irish language, 233–40, 276, 351, 433
  as barrier, 235, 237
  classes, 205, 237
  and compulsion, 9–10, 237, 239
  decline of, 9, 234
  de Valera's use of, 237, 238–9
  in general election, 1918, 154
  love of, 234
  as means of advancement, 9–10, 236
  use of in Sinn Féin, 237–40
Irishman, 70, 76, 86, 105, 160, 260
  on English language, 235
  religious terminology of, 216
Irish Nation, 194, 281
Irish Nation League, 62–4, 75, 80, 161,
    170
  and abstention policy, 85, 88, 115
  merges with Sinn Féin, 106
  and North Roscommon by-election, 81–2,
    85
  and partition, 225
  and Pim's Sinn Féin, 1916, 71–2
  and Plunkett, 86, 88–9
Irish Neutrality League, 129
Irish Parliamentary Party, 5, 15, 32
  apparent irrelevance of, 1918, 151
  by-election defeats, 1917, 115–16
  and conscription, 134–5
  demoralization of, 1907–9, 1912–13: 32–3;
    1916: 61–2; 1918: 156
  and East Cavan by-election, 146–8
  and East Clare election, 109
  and East Tyrone by-election, 126–8
  and Easter Rising, aftermath of, 52

  and general election, 1918, 154, 156–7,
    162–3, 164, 166–8
  and 'German plot', 144
  and home rule negotiations, 1916, 56–61,
    156
  and Kilkenny city by-election, 113
  manifesto, 1918 election, 157
  membership of, 8
  nature of, 5–6
  and North Roscommon by-election, 83–5
  and South Armagh by-election, 122–5
  and South Longford by-election, 99–103
  support for, until after Rising, 205
  and Ulster, 1918, 165–6
  and Waterford city by-election, 125–6
  and West Cork by-election, 73–4
  Westminster, departure from, 1918, 135
  Westminster, return to, 1918, 156
Irish-American lobby, 460
Irish Republican Army (1919–21), *see* Irish
    Volunteers
Irish Republican Army (IRA) (1922–), 436,
    464
  bank raids by, 380
  banned, 446, 448, 449
  bombing campaign of, 1939, 449
  campaign of, 1956–62, 452
  campaign of, 1970s–1990s, 454–7, 459–60
  and Cumann Poblachta na hÉireann, 448–9
  and politics, 1922–5, 439–40
  politics, suspicion of, 460
  repudiates politics and civilian control,
    1925, 440, 447
  and Sinn Féin, 1980s, 1990s, 458, 460
  Sinn Féin, relationship with, 1930s, 448–9
  split, 1969, 454
  takes over Sinn Féin, 1949–50, 452
  transfer of powers to, by 'second Dáil', 1938,
    446–7, 458
  unprepared, 1969, 453
  widely detested, 455
Irish Republican Brotherhood (IRB), 11–13,
    14–15, 21, 31, 159, 195–6, 267, 446

Irish Republican Brotherhood (IRB) (*cont.*)
  accepts civilian authority, 282
  1873 constitution of, 34
  and Easter Rising, 34
  and Irish Volunteers, 34, 267
  and labour, 253–4
  military council of, 34
  and republicanism, 241
  revival of, 1917, 68
  on Sinn Féin party, 1912, failure of, 31
  split, 1922, 365
Irish Statesman, 246, 316
Irish Times, 100, 140, 292
Irish Volunteer, 35
Irish Volunteers, 10, 33, 70, 284
  arrogance of, 1921, 298–9
  banned 1919, 276, 285
  and civilian authority, 358
  and conscription crisis, 135–6, 270
  convention, 1917, 267
  and Cumann na mBan, 201
  and Dáil, 282, 376
  democratic structure of, 194
  and East Clare by-election, 110–11
  and Easter Rising, 44
  elitism of, 196, 277, 298–9, 300, 374–5
  expansion of, 1921, 302
  formation of, 13–15
  and IRA, use of term, 245
  and IRB, 14, 34
  and North Roscommon by-election, 81
  overshadow Sinn Féin, 1918, 146
  and Plunkett, 103
  policing activities of, 280, 314–15, 318
  and politics, 103, 107, 115, 163–4, 174, 196,
    277, 297
  reorganization of, 1916–17, 75, 77, 267–8
  and republicanism, 245
  and Sinn Féin, 193–8, 244, 281–2, 297, 300,
    325, 376
  'Sinn Féin', dislike of term by, 68–9
  split, 1914, 15
  and treaty, 355, 358–9, 364, 374
  and West Cork by-election, 74

Johnson, Thomas, 137, 158, 259, 286, 296
Jesuits, 193
Jones, Thomas, 132
Joyce, James, 4, 17

Keating, Geoffrey, 223
Kelly, Denis (bishop of Ross), 48
Kelly, Tom, 30, 93, 155, 158, 194
  on 'gunmen' in Dáil, 154–5
  on Sinn Féin's poverty, 1915, 70
Kent, David, 153, 385
Kent, William, 153
Keynes, J. M., 218, 350
Kilkenny city by-election, 112–13, 213
Kilmichael, 294
King's Co. vacancy, 1918, 146–7
Kingsmill Moore, T. C., on treaty, 353–4
Kitchener, Earl, 37
Knocklong, 271–2, 275

Labour movement
  Easter Rising, divided by, 157
  and Limerick soviet, 272–3
  opposition to conscription, 135
  political divisions within, 157–9
Labour Party, 319, 389
  demands convening of third Dáil, 416
  and democratic programme, 1919, 259
  and general election, 1918, 157–9
  and general election, 1921, 338–9
  and general election, 1922, 388, 391, 394,
    403–4, 406, 409
  general election programme of, 1918, 159
  and general strike against militarism, 1922,
    385
  and local elections, 1920, 327, 328, 329
Land League, 14, 110, 189, 312
Land War, 5
Lansdowne, marquess of, 60, 62, 130
Larkin, Jim, 69, 253, 254
Larne gun-running, 124, 226
Leader, The, 223–4, 236, 386
Leitrim, unruliness of, 1921–2, 301,
    376

Leitrim Guardian, 27, 29
Lenehan, Joseph, 456
Lewes Jail, Irish prisoners in, 65, 96–8, 106–7, 248, 252
Liberal Party, 5, 7, 11, 133
Liberty League, 92, 103–6, 117, 170
Limerick soviet, 272–3, 319
List, Friedrich, 19, 223, 256
Lloyd George, David, 151, 227, 332, 341, 359, 461
  on British forces, indiscipline of, 297
  and Catholic Church, in conscription crisis, 141
  and conscription, 130, 132
  on de Valera and Collins, 347
  and Easter Rising, aftermath of, 52–3, 56
  and Frongoch internees, release of, 77
  and 'German plot' arrests, 142–5
  on Griffith, arrest of, 277
  and home rule, 1918, 157
  and home rule negotiations, 1916, 56–8
  and Irish Convention, 106, 251
  Keynes on, 350
  and Lewes prisoners, release of, 106
  and O'Flanagan, 1920, 290–1
  and republicanism, 230, 347
  and treaty negotiations, 247, 346–7, 349–50
local elections, 1920, 323–9
  candidates, selection of, 325
  franchise, 326
  Labour Party and, 327, 328, 329
  personation in, 329
  rural elections, June, 328–9
  Sinn Féin campaign, 328
  Sinn Féin programme, 326
  Ulster, results in, 327, 329
  urban elections, January, 326–7
local government, disruption of, 330–1
Logue, Cardinal Michael, 340
  and home rule negotiations, 1916, 59
  and general election, 1918, 161, 165, 336
  protests against travel restrictions, 286
  and republics, 124

  and South Armagh by-election, 124
  and treaty, 362–3
Long, Walter, 7,
  chairs cabinet committee on Ireland, 332–3
  and Catholic hierarchy in conscription crisis, 141
  and conscription, 132, 133, 150
  and Dáil courts, 316–17
  and 'German plot' arrests, 143
  and home rule negotiations, 1916, 60, 62
  Irish republicanism, understanding of, 285
  on the squad, 275
Longford Leader, 68, 98, 102
Ludendorff offensive, 132, 151
Lynch, Diarmuid, 153
Lynch, Finian, 95
Lynch, Liam, 298, 425
  character of, 424
  chief of staff, republican IRA, 423
  on Collins, death of, 417
  distrust of the people, 424
  and military discipline, 303
  optimism of, in civil war, 423
  on public hostility, 414
  and treaty, 358, 364, 365
Lynch, Patrick, 109, 130
Lynd, Robert, 218, 225–6, 228
Lynn, Kathleen, 193, 202, 371, 419

MacBride, John, 12, 27, 224, 267
MacBride, Joseph, 199
MacBride, Seán, 450–1, 452, 464
McCartan, Patrick, 31, 90, 101, 226, 241
  and South Armagh by-election, 123–5
McCarthy, Dan, 155, 182, 208, 379, 421
McCullough, Denis, 12–13, 34
MacCurtain, Tomás, 192, 195
  on Volunteers and Sinn Féin, 281
MacDermott, Seán, 34, 38, 49, 50, 268
  on Larkin and socialism, 254
MacDonagh, Joseph, 289
MacDonagh, Thomas, 38, 235
MacEntee, Seán, 336, 367
  on Dáil and army, 279

MacEntee, Seán (*cont.*)
  on Dáil and Sinn Féin, 306
  and Easter Rising, 45–6
  and general election, 1921, 338, 340
  on partition, 232
  and public opinion, 1922, 356–7
  resigns seat, 1922, 389, 403
  and South Armagh by-election, 124
McGarrity, Joe, 23, 25
McGarry, Seán, 367
McGilligan, Patrick, 309
McGrath, Joe, 154, 322
McGuinness, Frank, 96, 99, 193
McGuinness, Joe, 101, 102, 193
  chosen as candidate, South Longford, 96–8
MacHugh, Charles (bishop of Derry), 59, 63,
  160
McKenna, Patrick, 99, 100, 102
MacLogan, Padraig, 452
MacLysaght, Edward, 252, 257
McNabb, Russell, 127–8
MacNamara, Brinsley, 101
MacNeill, Eoin, 10–11, 13, 194, 212, 268
  arrested, 1916, 53
  on Belfast republicans, 229
  and conscription crisis, 140
  on conditions for a rising, 38
  and countermanding order, 36, 39
  Gaelic League and Irish Volunteers,
    inspiration of, 10
  and Irish language, 234
  in Lewes Jail, 65
  and October convention, 1917, 119, 195
  and 'Sinn Féin', 69
  and Sinn Féin Rathmines branch, 181
MacNeill, Swift, 156
Macpherson, Ian, 269, 284
Macready, Nevil, 278, 292, 343, 412
  on Griffith's policy, implementation of, 330
MacRory, Joseph (bishop of Down and
  Connor), 59
MacSwiney, Mary, 363, 441–2, 444
  on army, 375
    on the dead, 221
    on Easter Rising, aftermath of, 64
    elected, 1922, 405
    on Free State government, problems of,
      434
    and general election, 1918, 244
    and general election, June 1927, 443
    on Griffith and treaty, 351
    O'Flanagan, disgust for, 1934, 444–5
    the people, suspicious of, 348
    on treaty negotiations, 347, 356
    and Volunteers and Liberty League, 104
MacSwiney, Terence, 31, 221
    death of, 279, 308
    on Irish language, 235
    and mid-Cork executive, Sinn Féin, 288
    Easter Week, embarrassment concerning,
      267, 279
Maguire, Tom, 447, 458
Mahon, Bryan, 142–3
Mansion House committee, 1917, 93, 105, 170,
  252
Mansion House conference, 1918, 137, 139,
  140, 141
Mansion House (Plunkett) convention, 1917,
  90–3, 94, 103, 117, 170
Markievicz, Countess Constance, 40, 50, 193,
  201, 268, 363, 382
    arrested, 1920, 322
    elected, 1918, 154
    and general election, 1922, 382, 406
    minister for labour, 202, 322
    and October convention, 119, 120, 198
    and republican 'government', 1924,
      scepticism concerning, 438–9
    and Sinn Féin executive, 106
    and treaty, 355, 356
martial law, 56, 292
Martyn, Edward, 72
Maxwell, John, 8, 46, 49–51
    and conscription, 129
    and O'Dwyer, Bishop, 51, 200
    and public opinion, 53, 54, 57, 61

Meehan, Francis, 156–7
Mellows, Liam
  death of, 417
  defeated, 1922, 405
  radical programme of, 423
Midleton, Viscount, 133
Milroy, Seán, 87, 118, 119, 212, 226, 290, 308
  arrested, 155
  and East Cavan by-election, 146
  and East Tyrone by-election, 127
  and general election, 1922, 362, 382–3,
    401–3
  and Mansion House convention, 92–3
  on Volunteers, aloofness of, 300
Mitchel, John, 98, 220
Molony, Helena, 119, 154
monarchism, Irish, 19–20, 117, 243
monarchism, British, 246
Moore, Maurice, 52, 53, 84–5
Moran, D. P., 223–4
Moylan, Seán, 279, 382
Mulcahy, Richard, 278
  and army mutiny, 434
  and civilian authority, 283
  and general election, 1918, 154
  and 'German plot', 146
  on IRA indiscipline, 298
  minister for defence, 374
  reluctance of to form new party, 1922, 421
  tactics in 1922, 374
'Munster Republic', 413
Murnaghan, George, 161, 337
Murphy, John, 67
Murphy, William Martin, 263
Murray, T. C., 261

Nathan, Matthew, 37, 44
Nation League, see Irish Nation League
National Aid Society, 67–8
National Council, 21–5, 26
National Relief Fund, 67
National University of Ireland, constituency
  of, 399, 403

National Volunteers (Redmondite), 15, 52, 62,
  129
Nationalists, see Irish Parliamentary Party
Nationality, 86, 100, 105, 136, 209, 260
  circulation of, 33
  contents of, 263
  financial contributions, acknowledgments
    of, 177
  and Irish language lessons, 237
  and monarchy, 242
  and peace conference, 251
  on Sinn Féin, 1917, 94, 121
  suppression of, 264
  on weapons, 248
Naval Intelligence, British, and Easter Rising,
  36–7
New Ireland, 64, 76, 89, 391, 409
Nicholls, George, 222
North Derry by-election, 309
North King Street, killings in, 1916, 55
North Leitrim by-election, 25–9, 177, 379
North Roscommon by-election, 64, 76, 78,
  80–5, 123
  significance of, 82, 96, 115
Northern Irish nationalists
  discrimination against, 462
  moderation of, 439, 456
  protests by, 453

oath of allegiance, to Dáil and republic, 245,
  246, 282, 356, 411
oath of fidelity ('allegiance') to king, 351, 354,
  398, 438, 441
  abolition of, 447
  taken by de Valera, 444
Ó Brádaigh, Ruairí, 454
O'Brien, William, MP, 63
  de Valera, underestimation of, 138
  former colleagues, hatred of, 137
  and Mansion House conference, 137
  and West Cork by-election, 73–4
O'Brien, William (trade union leader), 244
  on Brugha, 1922, 382

O'Brien, William (trade union leader) (*cont.*)
  and general election, 1918, 159
  and Mansion House committee, 93, 137,
    157–8
  and Mansion House conference, 137
  and North Roscommon by-election, 83, 137
  and separatists, cooperation between, 1917,
    85–6
O'Brien, William Smith, 98
O'Callaghan-Westropp, George, 111
O'Casey, Sean, 126
Ó Conaire, Padraic, 111
O'Connell, Daniel, 29, 123, 135, 205, 280, 284
  provides model, 18, 312
O'Connell, J. J., 222, 412
O'Connor, Art, 315–16, 317, 444
  on general election, 1922, 409
O'Connor, F. J., 89–90, 121
O'Connor, Frank, 234
O'Connor, James (attorney general), 133
O'Connor, Rory, 106, 398
  and Collins, 98
  compromise, warns against, 424
  death of, 417
  democracy, indifference to, 374–5
  destruction, urges, 414
  Document No. 2, rejects, 364
  Four Courts, seizure of, 375
  and Plunkett, 87, 91
O'Connor, T. P., 52–3, 59
October convention, 1917, 118–21, 193, 243,
  279
O'Doherty, Seumas, 81, 85–6
O'Donnell, Patrick (bishop of Raphoe), 59,
  63–4, 200
O'Donoghue, Florence, 240, 299
O'Donovan Rossa, Jeremiah, 78, 98
O'Duffy, Eoin, 299–300
O'Dwyer, Edward (bishop of Limerick), 51,
  124, 200
O'Flanagan, Fr Michael, 302, 361, 401, 442
  Church authorities, difficulties with, 79,
    149, 200

and East Cavan by-election, 149
and general election, 1918, 153, 155, 162
and general election, 1921, 339
and 'German plot', 145
home rule settlement, 1916, support of,
  78–9, 87, 228
and land distribution, 83
and Mansion House committee, 93
and Mansion House convention, 92–3
and North Roscommon by-election, 78, 81,
  83, 85
and October convention, 1917, 120
O'Kelly, and Plunkett, alliance with, 87
and party structure, 173
peace initiative, 1920, 290–1, 336
peacemaking role, 1917, 99
Sinn Féin, expelled from, 445–6
on Sinn Féin, nature of, 214
and Sinn Féin split, 1926, 441
Sinn Féin, vice-president of, 117, 145
terrorist acts, warns against, 294
women candidates, dubious about, 202
An tÓglách, 150, 270, 279
  on army convention, 1922, 374
  on emigration, 190
  on military arrogance, 299
  on violence, 277
O'Hegarty, Diarmuid, 308, 320, 338, 416–17
  on Ulster, 226–7
O'Hegarty, P. S., 23, 25–6, 31
  on Belfast boycott, 231–2
  and general election, 1922, 395–6
  war, hopes for, 1904, 12
O'Higgins, Brian, 153, 311
O'Higgins, Kevin, 400, 444
  on army mutiny, 433
  death of, 443
  on Free State constitution, 398
  on provisional government, 416
  on republicans, rejection of, 436
  on sacrifice, equality of, 330
  Sinn Féin, warns, 1921, 301–2
  on treaty, 355

on Ulster, 227
O'Keeffe, Páidín, 332, 335, 343, 372
  defeated, 1922, 400
  on distrust, 1922, 367
  and general election, 1918, 154
  and general election, 1921, 336, 340
  in hiding, 1919, 285
  as jailer, 416–17
  militancy, record of, 87
  and O'Flanagan, 290
  party general secretary, 195
  republicans, raids, 418, 428
  temper and vocabulary of, 337
  on Ulster, 229
  on vengeance, 224
O'Kelly, James, 77–8, 80
O'Kelly, J. J. ('Scelilg'), 238, 239, 442
  anti-Semitism of, 446n
  and Catholic Bulletin, 81, 263
  and Fianna Fáil, 446
  and general election, 1918, 154, 165
  and North Roscommon by-election, 81
  O'Flanagan and Plunkett, alliance with, 87
  Plunkett, criticism of, 1917, 90
  and separatists, cooperation between, 1917,
    85–6
  and South Longford by-election, 96
O'Kelly, Seán T., 31, 90, 155, 244
  elected, 1922, 406
  and Paris peace conference, 251
Old Ireland, 231–2
O'Leary, Daniel, 73–4, 79–80
O'Leary, John, 12
O'Mahony, Seán, 357
O'Malley, Ernie,
  on consulting the people, 271
  as legendary figure, 278
  on politicians, role of, 426
  on soldiers and civilians, 280, 281–2
O'Mara, James, 30, 93, 177, 370
O'Mara, Stephen, 93, 194
O'Mara, Stephen, Jr, 382
O'Neill, Charles, 122

O'Neill, Laurence (lord mayor of Dublin), 137,
  336
O'Neill, Terence, 452, 453
O'Rahilly, Michael ('the O'Rahilly'), 13, 30, 33
O'Shiel, Kevin, 63, 148–9, 194, 305, 371
  and 'inducement', 316
O'Sullivan, Gearóid, 95

Paisley, Ian, 453, 455
'panel', the, 387, 396, 400, 403, 408, 409, 433
Paris Commune, 1871, 51
Parliamentary Party, see Irish Parliamentary
  Party
Parnell, Charles Stewart, 5, 18–19, 75, 123,
  220–1
  as model or warning, 74, 110, 254, 279
partition, 232, 250, 333–4
  myth concerning, 380
peace conference, 180, 207, 247, 250–1
peace negotiations, 1922, 386
Pearse, Margaret, 363, 406
Pearse, Patrick, 9, 10, 32, 205, 221, 463
  and Easter Rising, 38, 40, 45–7
  on emigrants, 190
  execution of, 49
  and Gaelic League, 235
  on Ireland, 219, 223
  and monarchy, 241
  on Parnell, 254
  on population growth, 256
  religious imagery of, 215–16
  on Synge, 17n
  on violence, 247
Peasant, The, 23
personation, 111, 162, 164, 329, 399–400, 403
Phillips, John, 96
Pim, Herbert Moore, 77
  character of, 70–1
  and Irish Nation League, 71
  and Mansion House convention, 92
  and Sinn Féin party, 1916, 71–2, 75
  and Ulster unionists, 226, 229
  and Waterford city by-election, 126

plenipotentiary status, of Irish treaty
negotiatiors, 349–50
Plunkett, Count George Noble, 115, 268, 407,
442, 444
anti-Semitism of, 232–3
and Dáil, 360
and the dead, 221
early career of, 79–80
and Galway by-election, 80, 449
and general election, 1922, 395
Irish Nation League, dislike of, 71, 88, 91
and landless men, 311
and Liberty League, 91–2, 103–6
majority of the people, scorn of for, 439
and Mansion House committee, 93
and Mansion House convention, 90–3
and North Roscommon by-election, 79, 84
O'Flanagan and O'Kelly, alliance with, 87
on O'Flanagan, future of, 302
and separatists, cooperation between, 1917,
85–6
on Sinn Féin, contempt for, 1923, 428
Sinn Féin, defeated in election for vice-
presidency of, 117
on Sinn Féin, inactivity of, 1919, 310
Sinn Féin', use of term by, 69
and treaty negotiations, opposition to, 348
quarrelsomeness of, 86
on Volunteers and Sinn Féin, 281
Plunkett, Countess, 93
Plunkett, Joseph, 40, 44, 79
politics, suspicion of, 81, 308, 424
by Collins, 281
by de Valera, 97
by Irish Republican Army, 455, 460
by Irish Volunteers, 103, 174, 196, 279, 300,
325
by MacNeill, 15
by Sinn Féin factions, 1922, 428
power-sharing executive, 1974, 456
PR, see proportional representation
Prisoners' Aid Society, 75, 177
propaganda, Sinn Féin, 200, 248, 259–65, 288,
318, 326

in East Cavan, 147–9
in East Clare, 110
Dáil ministry, taken over by, 309
in general election, 1918, 155, 163
in general election, 1922, 394, 395
in late 1916, 72, 75
in North Roscommon, 83–4
on peace conference, 250–1
in South Longford, 100–1
proportional representation (PR)
in general election, 1921, 202, 333, 335–6
in general election, 1922, 391, 399, 407–8
in local elections, 1920, 323–5, 327
Proportional Representation Society, 324,
326
Provisional Government, 1922
and Dáil government, 360–1
preparations for election, 370, 379
problems of, 376
weakness of, 411
Public Record Office, destruction of, 413

radicalization, of Irish nationalists, 8, 274, 276,
285–6, 297
railway strike, 1920, 286
Raul, Laurence, 445
Redmond, John, 6, 15, 32, 38, 232
and conscription, 129
death of, 125
demoralization of, 1916, 62
and enlistment, 9, 96, 129
and Easter Rising, aftermath of, 50
Frongoch internees, advice concerning, 77
and home rule negotiations, 1916, 57–62
and Irish Convention, 252
and North Roscommon by-election, 84–5
and West Cork by-election, 73
Redmond, Captain William,
and general election, 1921, 339
retains seat, 1918, 164
and Waterford city by-election, 125–6
Redmond, Major Willie, 107
Redmondites, see Irish Parliamentary Party
religious imagery, 53, 215, 216, 413–14

Renunciation Act, 1783, 17, 26
Repeal League, 62
Representation of the People Act, 1918, 126, 151, 207
reprisals, British, 295–6, 297
reprisals, Irish, in civil war, 414, 437
Republic, The, 23, 26
Republic of Ireland, The, 367–8, 394, 395
'republican', use of term, 451
Republican Congress, 448
Republican Sinn Féin, 1986, 459
republicanism, 4, 214, 241–7, 303, 346–8, 426
  Collins and, 98–9
  in general election, 1918, 163
  in 1917, 87, 117
  sacred texts of, 246
  silence on, 1921, 246, 346–7, 356
republicans
  and moderates in Sinn Féin, 1917, 110
  and Plunkett, 1917, 87
  and Sinn Féin constitution, 118–19
republicans (1922), 363
  and electoral register, 368
  and general election, 1922, 404–7
  political skills of, 1922, 369
Reynolds, Albert, 459
Resurrection of Hungary, 4, 26, 27, 118, 205, 383
  contents of, 3, 17–18
  Macready on, 330
RIC, *see* Royal Irish Constabulary
Robinson, Seamus, 337, 406
  on army and politics, 358
Royal Dublin Society, 79
Royal Irish Constabulary (RIC), 6, 32
  besieged, 275–6
  and conscription, fear of, 129, 134
  on conscription, opposition to, 140, 142
  despair of, 1921, 342
  and Easter Rising, aftermath of, 54
  and Easter Rising, reactions to, 48
  and general election, 1921, 337, 339
  Irish Parliamentary Party, information on, 8

ostracization of, 291, 312–13
retreat of, 269, 291–2, 313
on separatism, 1916–17, 70
on Sinn Féin, after truce, 342
Sinn Féin, information on, 178, 184–5
Russell, George ('AE'), 134, 246
Russell, Sean, 447
Ruttledge, P. J., 424, 427, 436
Ryan, James, 69, 301
  and public opinion, 1922, 356
Ryan, Michael J., 217
Ryan, W. P., 23

sectarian attacks, 231, 294–5, 376, 453, 455, 462
separation women, 126, 127
Separatist, The, 388, 395–6
Shaw, George Bernard, 277
Sheehy-Skeffington, Francis, 55–6
Sheehy-Skeffington, Hanna, 202, 203, 344, 363
  and 1918 election, 154
Shipsey, Michael, 73–4
Shortt, Edward, 145, 150, 276
Sinn Féin, 25, 27, 29, 30, 33
Sinn Féin funds case, 170, 353, 419, 450
Sinn Féin League (1907), 25
Sinn Féin party (first, 1905–17)
  decline of, 30–3, 70
  on female suffrage, 202, 253
  fortunes of, 23–5, 30–3
  in late 1916, 70–2
  name, appropriation of to Volunteers and Easter Rising, 33, 69–70
  and North Leitrim by-election, 25–9
  origins of, 21, 26
  and proportional representation, 324
Sinn Féin party (second, 1917–22); *see also* under *ard-chomhairle*, *ard-fheis*, standing committee
  after truce, 1921, 342–5
  age structure of, 184, 188, 191, 193, 197–8
  and agrarian unrest, 316–17
  banned, 1919, 276, 285
  Britain, image of, 224

Sinn Féin party (second, 1917–22) (*cont.*)
    class composition of, 188–92
    and class conflict, avoidance of, 252, 258
    clubs, activities of, 205–11
    and Collins–de Valera pact, 387, 390
    and conscription crisis, 136–8, 140
    constituency executives (*comhairlí
        ceanntair*), 170, 171, 181, 208, 211, 344
    constitution, 1917, 119, 169, 170, 183, 246,
        420, 427, 436
    constitution amended, 1919, 173–4,
    constitution amended, 1921, 345, 372
    contraction of, 1919, 309
    courts, 206, 310–14
    and Dáil, 180, 308, 321, 342
    and Dáil cabinet, 309, 318–19, 320–1, 342
    and Dáil Local Government Department,
        332
    decline of, 1919, 307–10
    democratic structure of, 206
    Department of Agriculture, 176
    de Valera and, late 1922, 426–7
    disruption of, 1919–21, 175, 183
    driven underground, 1919–21, 284–5,
        288–9
    and East Cavan by-election, 146, 148–9
    and East Clare by-election, 108–12
    and East Tyrone by-election, 126–8
    economic programme of, 256–7
    executive, 1917, 175
    expenditure, 1917, 113, 119, 178
    finances, 177–80, 319
    Fund, 1917, 177
    funds, 1922, 374, 418, 420
    and general election, 1918, 152–68
    and general election, 1921, 334–41
    and general election, 1922, 390, 396
    and 'German plot', 143, 182
    headquarters, 95, 180–3, 196, 288, 336, 390,
        418
    inactivity of, late 1922, 417–18
    inclusive nature of, 181
    indebtedness of, 1919, 179

Irish language, policy towards, 236–7
Irish language, use of, 237–40
Irish Parliamentary Party, continuity with,
    252
Irish Parliamentary Party, cooperation with,
    1918, 137–8
and Irish Volunteers, 193–8, 244, 281–2,
    297, 325, 376
and Labour, 1918, 158
and labour unrest, wariness of, 1919, 273
manifesto, general election, 1918, 155
manifesto, general election, 1921, 335
and Mansion House convention, 94
membership, 183–93
Nationalists, cooperation with, general
    election, 1921, 334–6
and North Roscommon by-election, 81, 83
officer board, 172–3, 228, 373, 378, 436
and the past, 220–3
peace committee of, 1923, 427–8
presidency, 117, 174
rejection of, by treaty supporters, 421–2
religion, of members, 192–3
reorganization of, in 1921, 343–4
republicans' dislike of, 1922–3, 419–21, 428,
    441
and republicanism, 119, 241–6, 347–8, 420
revival of, 1917, 94–6
sobriety of members, 212–13
social policy, absence of, 253–5
and South Armagh by-election, 122–5
and South Longford by-election, 100–2
spread of, 1917, 94, 104, 181, 205
structures, 119, 170–3, 211
suppression of, 288
and treaty, 361–3, 365–8, 369
and Ulster, 160–1, 333–4, 336, 339–41, 378
and Ulster unionists, 225–32
and violence, 249
and Waterford city by-election, 126
and women, 202–4
Sinn Féin party, third (1923–6)
    de Valera and, 434–6, 441–2

formation of, 427–8, 436

fortunes of, 439

and general election, 1923, 437

harassment of, 436

in Northern Ireland, 439

split, 1926, 441–2

weaknesses of, 437, 439

Sinn Féin party, fourth (1926–70)

collapse of support for, 1926, 443

condition of, in 1940s, 450, 451

IRA, relationship with, 1930s, 448–9

IRA, takeover by, 1949–50, 452

irrelevance of, 1930s, 446

O'Flanagan, expulsion of from, 445

self-indulgence of, 444

split, 1970, 454

Sinn Féin party, fifth (1970–), 464

abstention policy, abandonment of, 458, 460–1, 464

auxiliary to IRA, 455, 456, 457

formation of, 454

northern leadership of, 464

support for, 459, 460

Sinn Féin Review, 264

Sligo local elections, 1919, 323–4

Smyth, Thomas, 156

Social, Democratic and Labour Party (SDLP), 456, 459

Soloheadbeg, 266, 271, 272, 275

Somerville, Edith, 214

Somme, battle of, 59–60

South Armagh by-election, 100, 122–5

election fund, 178

Sinn Féin extravagance in, 123

South Longford by-election, 96–103

opposition to contest, 96–8

election fund, 100, 177

South Mayo by-election, 27, 29

soviets, 272–3, 301, 312, 319

Spark, The, 43, 129

squad, the, 275

Stack, Austin, 95, 278, 344, 407, 442

abstention policy, flexibility on, 441

Cumann na Poblachta, on funding of, 380

director of elections, 1921, 335

on local government economies, 330

and O'Higgins, assassination of, 443

and Parliamentary Party, 161

role in 1916, shame concerning, 267

secret ballot, opposition to, 1922, 367, 370

on Sinn Féin courts, 314

and Sinn Féin, late 1922, 418

and third Sinn Féin, formation of, 427

and treaty negotiations, 348

war, pines for, 349

wartime losses, indifferent to, 1921, 287

standing committee, Sinn Féin, 178, 182, 210, 231, 239

ambitions of, 182, 304

cabinet ministers excluded from, 174, 280, 283

and conscription crisis, 138, 143–4

disruption of, 1920–1, 287, 336

and East Cavan by-election, 146

final meeting of, 418–19

functions of, 172, 176

and Labour, 1918, 158

new members of, 1918, 175–6

officer board, superseded by, 373

and South Armagh by-election, 125

and Ulster seats, 1918, 161

women and, 202

Stephens, James, 47, 52, 69, 247–8, 255

Studies, 55

Sturgis, Mark, 283, 294, 296, 353

Sweeney, Joseph, 45

Sweetman, Dom Francis, 153

Sweetman, John, 72, 74, 153

Sweetman, Roger, 153, 163

on IRA and violence, 249, 289, 338

Synge, John Millington, 16–17

Tipperary Star, on treaty, 362

Tone, Wolfe, 35, 215, 230

Transport Union, 159

Treacy, Seán, 271

treaty
  ard-chomhairle and, 367
  army and, 351–3, 358
  cabinet and, 354
  Collins and, 351, 355
  de Valera and, 353, 356
  terms of, 350–1
treaty debates, 354–60
  Ulster and, 232, 355
treaty election committee, 378–9, 420
  continuity with Cumann na nGaedheal, 422
  finances of, 379
  in general election, 1922, 395
treaty negotiations, 346–50
  republic and, 246, 347, 351, 354, 356
  Ulster, as tactic in, 232
Trinity College, Dublin, constituency of, 164,
  339, 359, 399
Tully, Jasper, 80, 84
Twomey, Seamus, 456–7

Ulster Unionists, 33, 125, 127, 459, 463
  and Conservative Party, 7–8, 13, 51, 225,
    230, 333, 341
  and home rule negotiations, 1916, 60
  and general election, 1918, 165, 166, 168
  and general election, 1921, 339–40
  and local elections, 1920, 327, 329
  and nationalists, 230
  in 1960s, 452–3
  in 1970s, 456
  opinion in Republic on, 1970s, 456
  and partition, 333
  and proportional representation, 1921, 333
  Sinn Féin and, 224–32
Ulster Volunteers, 7, 13–14, 51, 66, 226, 298
Ulysses, 4, 17
Union of Motor Drivers, 286
Unionists, southern, 60, 74, 165, 230, 294–5,
  331, 376
United Irish League (UIL), 101, 152, 206
  in Clare, 108

decline of, 8
and home rule negotiations, 1916, 58, 59
inactivity of, 1916–18, 61
meetings in North Roscommon, 1916, 80
United Irishman, 3
University College, Cork, 286
University College, Dublin, 54, 91, 278
University College, Galway, 191

violence, electoral, 29, 102, 123, 126, 162
  in general election, 1922, 383–4, 392, 394,
    399–400, 409
Volunteer Dependants' Fund, 66–8
Volunteers, *see* Irish Volunteers

Walsh, J. J., 257
Walsh, William (archbishop of Dublin), 90,
  124
  and conscription crisis, 139
  and South Longford by-election, 102, 124,
    200
War of Independence, *see* Anglo-Irish War
Waterford city by-election, 125–6
Wells, H. G., 43
West Cork by-election, 73–5
Wimborne, Viscount (viceroy), 39
Wilson, Henry, 412
women
  Easter rebels and, 201
  and the franchise, 126, 151, 369
  in general election, 1922, 405
  in local elections, 1920, 327
  in public life, 154, 202, 449
  in Sinn Féin, 201–4
  and treaty, 360
Wyndham Act, 3
Wyse Power, Jennie, 201, 202, 239, 421
  closes Sinn Féin offices, 418, 419
  and standing committee, 1922, 419–20, 427

Yeats, William Butler, 17, 56, 261
Young, Samuel, 146